Universal Semantic Communication

Brendan Juba

Universal Semantic
Communication

Dr. Brendan Juba
School of Engineering and Applied Sciences
Harvard University
Cambridge, MA
USA

Computer Science and Artificial Intelligence
    Laboratory (CSAIL)
Massachusetts Institute of Technology
Cambridge, MA
USA
bjuba@alum.mit.edu

ISBN 978-3-642-44079-3   ISBN 978-3-642-23297-8 (eBook)
DOI 10.1007/978-3-642-23297-8
Springer Heidelberg Dordrecht London New York

ACM Classification (1998): F.0, E.4

Printed on acid-free paper

Springer is part of Springer Science+Business Media (www.springer.com)

Foreword by Oded Goldreich

The thesis on which this book is based is quite unusual in its contents. It initiates and formulates a totally new research direction and provides initial results about this direction. Specifically, it puts forward a general theory of goal-oriented communication, where the focus is not on the raw data being communicated but rather on the goal being achieved by the communication.

Before continuing let me make a personal comment. Having been involved in the research presented here, I may be suspected as being biased with respect to its value. My view, however, is to the opposite: I view my involvement in the late stages of this research as strong evidence of my fascination with this new direction and my admiration of its significance.

With this preliminary remark in place, let me turn back to the work itself, which I consider to be work of a fundamental nature. The essence of this work is a novel mathematical theory that attempts to capture a key aspect in communication – its meaning. Following a dominant approach in twentieth century philosophy, this work associates the meaning of communication with the goal achieved by it, and *provides a mathematical framework for discussing all these natural notions*. This framework is based on a general definition of the notion of a goal (i.e., a goal of communication), and leads to a problem that is "complementary" to the problem of reliable communication (considered by Shannon in establishing Information Theory). Specifically, the new theory refers to parties that do not, a priori, agree on a communications protocol (i.e., on a language), and aims at providing strategies for overcoming this initial misunderstanding (between the parties) towards achieving a given goal.

On top of the intellectual interest in definitions and results regarding general concepts such as the "meaning of communication" and goal-oriented collaborations, I wish to highlight the *potential relevance of the theory of goal-oriented communication to computer practice*. In a variety of settings, users are trying to obtain various services from designated servers (e.g., printers, web-servers, etc), while not necessarily having full understanding of the functionality of the servers. The users may be humans or computers, and the same applies to the servers. Either way, in many cases, the user does not know the server well, and consequently each party may send messages that the other party does not understand or, possibly worse, misunderstands. Of course, I am not saying that the solutions provided so far can be implemented in practice, but I do think that they should be thought of as feasibility results and as first steps in a study of conditions under which initial lack of understanding can be overcome, and where the "expense" of overcoming the lack of understanding can be quantified.

One key ingredient in the design of strategies for overcoming initial mis-understanding (between parties) towards achieving a given goal, is the identi-fication of a main concept, called sensing, that captures the parties' ability to check whether progress is made towards achieving the goal. The work shows that if sensing is available, then the gap between a priori mutual understand-ing and lack of it can be bridged. For example, if providing the parties with an adequate interpreter allows them each to achieve their (possibly different) goals, then they can achieve their goals also without such an interpreter (al-though they may misunderstand each other and err at the beginning). Or, if each server (in a predetermined class of servers) can help some user (who understands the server) achieve its goal, then there exists a (so-called uni-versal) user strategy that achieves the goal no matter with which server it communicates.

While the work presents initial feasibility results, it does not neglect to introduce complexity measures that quantify the quality of various solutions. In some (central) cases, seemingly wasteful solutions are shown to be the best possible, which indicates that the search for better solution should focus on identifying natural special cases and providing more efficient solutions for these cases. Initial attempts in this direction are also presented here.

Needless to say, to clarify all the foregoing, one needs to provide rigorous definitions, theorems, and proofs, while linking these formal ingredients to the informal motivation outlined above. This, and more, is indeed the content of this work.

Preface

Abstract

Is meaningful communication possible between two intelligent parties who share no common language or background? We propose that this problem can be rigorously addressed by explicitly focusing on the goals of the communication. We propose a theoretical framework in which we can address when and to what extent such semantic communication is possible.

Our starting point is a mathematical definition of a generic *goal for communication*, that is pursued by *agents* of bounded computational complexity. We then model a "lack of common language or background" by considering a *class* of potential partners for communication; in general, this formalism is rich enough to handle varying degrees of common language and backgrounds, but the complete lack of knowledge is modeled by simply considering the class of all partners with which *some* agent of similar power could achieve our goal. In this formalism, we will find that for many goals (but not *all*), communication without any common language or background *is* possible. We call the strategies for achieving goals without relying on such background *universal protocols*.

The main intermediate notions introduced by our theory are formal notions of feedback that we call *sensing*. We show that in many natural settings of interest, sensing captures the essence of whether or not reliable universal protocols can be constructed: we find that across settings, sensing is almost always sufficient, usually necessary, and generally a useful design principle for the construction of universal protocols. We support this last point by developing a number of examples of protocols for specific goals. Notably, we show that *universal delegation of computation* from a space-efficient client to a general-purpose server is possible, and we show how a variant of TCP can allow end-users on a packet network to *automatically* adapt to small changes in the packet format (e.g., changes in IP).

The latter example above alludes to our main motivation for considering such problems, which is to develop techniques for modeling and constructing computer systems that do not require that their components strictly adhere to protocols: said differently, we hope to be able to design components that function properly with a sufficiently wide range of other components to permit a rich space of "backwards-compatible" designs for those components. We expect that in the long run, this paradigm will lead to *simpler* systems because "backwards compatibility" is no longer such a severe constraint, and we expect it to lead to more *robust* systems, partially because the components should be simpler, and partially because such components are inherently robust to deviations from any fixed protocol.

Unfortunately, we find that the techniques for communication under the *complete* absence of any common background suffer from overhead that is too severe for such practical purposes, so we consider two natural approaches for introducing some assumed common background between components while retaining some nontrivial amount of flexibility. The first approach supposes that the designer of a component has some "belief" about what protocols would be "natural" to use to interact with other components; we show that, given sensing and some sufficient "agreement" between the beliefs of the designers of two components, the components can be made universal with some relatively modest overhead. The second approach supposes that the protocols are taken from some restricted class of functions, and we will see that for *certain* classes of functions and *simple* goals, efficient universal protocols can again be constructed from sensing.

Actually, we show more: the special case of our model described in the second approach above corresponds *precisely* to the well-known model of *mistake-bounded on-line learning* first studied by Bārzdiņš and Freivalds, and later considered in more depth by Littlestone. This connection provides a reasonably complete picture of the conditions under which we can apply the second approach. Furthermore, it also seems that the first approach is closely related to the problem of *designing good user interfaces* in Human-Computer Interaction. We conclude by briefly sketching the connection, and suggest that further development of this connection may be a potentially fruitful direction for future work.

About this book

This book contains a revised edition of my Ph.D. dissertation, completed under the supervision of Madhu Sudan, and submitted to the Department of Electrical Engineering and Computer Science at MIT on August 30, 2010. As is typical for such works, portions of its contents have appeared (or will appear) in papers published elsewhere. The list of these other publications to date, along with the changes to the text since the submitted version, appears in the Bibliographic notes section below.

Organization

Although the Introduction is certainly a good place to start, a reader who wishes to "jump in" may start with Chapter 2 followed by Chapter 6, in which the technical core of the work is developed, for "finite" and "infinite" goals, respectively. (The latter is more general, but also more technically involved.) Chapters 2–5 only address finite goals, while Chapters 6–9 are primarily focused on infinite goals.

Variations on this main theory are considered in Chapters 5 and 7. Chapter 5 refines the notions of Chapter 2 to address other kinds of resource limitations, such as limitations on the available memory or number of random bits available. Chapter 7 considers some other relaxations of the basic models, such as allowing our algorithms to sometimes fail at finite goals, or granting users the ability to initiate small "exploratory" goals, which respectively may broaden the kinds of goals that can be achieved, or improve the efficiency of solutions.

Potential applications (i.e., example goals) are the focus of Chapters 3 and 9, but also appear along the way in Chapters 5 and 6, and Chapters 4 and 8 concern ways to improve the efficiency of the schemes presented here.

Prerequisites

The main requirement for understanding the work presented here is some basic familiarity with the theory of algorithms and/or computational complexity at the undergraduate level, for example, as covered by Sipser's textbook [141]. Some knowledge of calculus or algebra at an undergraduate level is also essential for some of the proofs.

While it would not have been reasonable to include a review of the above background, I have included some appendices covering any material that is useful or essential that a reader with this background may not have encountered (or may have forgotten), specifically a review of the basic notions and results from probability in Appendix A, and an introduction to interactive proofs in Appendix B. Some material on game theory that may well be completely unfamiliar to such a reader, which is used on occasion (in Chapters 4 and 9), is presented in Appendix C.

Bibliographic notes

The main differences between this revised edition and the original version submitted to MIT (beyond the inclusion of the aforementioned Appendices) occur primarily in Chapters 5 and 9. Specifically, in Section 5.5.2, the original version achieved universal delegation of computation by logspace devices using a rather involved construction of public-coin logspace interactive proof systems for P-complete problems due to Goldwasser, Kalai, and Rothblum [73], together with a generic result (based on the work of Condon and Ladner [49]) that showed that any such proof system for P-complete problems would be necessarily logspace-competitive. This has all been replaced by a relatively simple, direct construction of a (private-coin) logspace-competitive proof system (Theorem 5.27). On the other hand, the bounds claimed in Chapter 9 were simplified by the use of a cleaner analysis (as presented by Cesa-Bianchi and Lugosi [43]) of the algorithm Exp3.P.1 for the nonstochastic bandit problem than that originally presented by Auer et al. [10]. A complete presentation of this improved analysis appears in Appendix C. A few additional remarks on the schemes presented in Chapter 9 – specifically, viewing the schemes from a protocol-level (i.e., specification level) perspective, pointing out connections to IPsec, and remarking on the scope of their applicability – are also included in this version, in response to feedback I've received.

The foundations of the work presented here are based on one previously published work with Madhu Sudan [83], and a couple of technical reports with Madhu Sudan [84] and Oded Goldreich and Madhu Sudan [70]. More specifically, the introductory chapter closely follows the paper with Madhu Sudan [83], while the technical report with Madhu Sudan [84] contains an *early* version of Chapters 3 and 5 (and thus implicitly also Chapter 2). Chapter 6, on the other hand, is a modified version of the technical report with Oded Goldreich and Madhu Sudan [70], and the second half of Chapter 7 is also adapted from the same report. (Likewise, the initial section of Chapter 8 appeared in the aforementioned technical report.) More generally, the present form of Chapter 2 (in contrast to the version described in the technical report with Madhu Sudan [84]) and thus also the present formulation of this work benefitted immensely from the input from Oded Goldreich.

Following submission of the thesis, some of the work presented here appeared in conference papers: specifically there is a paper with Madhu Sudan [85] based on the main contents of Chapter 4, and a paper describing the work with Santosh Vempala [86] comprising the core of Chapter 8, as well as Section 4.4 (in Chapter 4).

The rest of the work in this book was previously unpublished. I have tried to note throughout when the work was particularly indebted to the contributions of others. In general though, *unless otherwise noted, the work presented in this book is joint work with Madhu Sudan.*

Acknowledgements

It seems fitting to start with my parents.

Over the years at MIT, I've slowly come to realize that a graduate student couldn't wish for better parents. You see, my parents both entered doctoral programs, so they knew what the allure was, and what challenges lay ahead; at the same time, moreover, my parents both *dropped out* of graduate school with master's degrees, so there was no sense of pressure or unrealistic expectations. Finally, they demonstrated that even if things didn't work out for me at MIT, it would still be possible to lead a rich, fulfilling life. It took me a long time to realize how uncommon that was.

On the subject of support, I also want to thank my wife, Angelina. As I write these acknowledgements, she's sitting next to me, plugging away at the research for her own thesis. The writing process over the last year or so has been a grueling, all-consuming, long, hard slog, but she's endured it about as well as anyone could. Her companionship and the sense of solidarity with it has prevented the writing process from turning isolating and lonely. Moreover, she's acted as my test audience more times than could reasonably be expected of anyone, and some of the material here has benefitted substantially from her careful feedback.

I'm also deeply indebted to my officemates, especially those that were here during the early days of this work (and long "middle years" of graduate school) – Swastik Kopparty, Paul Valiant, Guy Rothblum, and Ben Rossman, and later Jing Chen – for the feedback, sanity checks, and numerous helpful conversations they provided while the work presented here was taking form. Similarly, I'd like to thank the rest of my groupmates over the years, Sergey Yekhanin, Victor Chen, Elena Grigorescu, Shubhangi Saraf, Tali Kaufman, and Jakob Nordström for conversations, feedback, and support of various kinds. Thanks to Jacob Scott for keeping the pressure on me to go to the gym regularly back in the early days. (Seriously.)

I want to thank Lenore Blum for suggesting that I should try a REU— prior to that, I hadn't realized that the kind of problem-solving that I liked was called "research." I also want to thank Steven Rudich for his course 15-251, "Great Theoretical Ideas in Computer Science" (and also for his course on computational complexity, as a result of which, I no longer have any fear of hard problems). I grew immeasurably as a result of my involvement in 15-251, both as a student and as a TA.

Moreover, I'd also like to thank Steven Rudich for several interesting conversations about "alien communication," i.e., the subject of this work. I had influential conversations about this work with a number of other people, including Eran Tromer, Leslie Valiant, Leslie Kaelbling, Adam Kalai, and Bob Berwick. Eran and Adam have been enthusiastic about the work, and provided numerous helpful insights – Adam specifically helped to inspire the model of Chapter 4, and Eran more generally – while the conversations with Professors Valiant and Kaelbling helped point the way towards the connection to on-line learning in Chapter 8. Bob Berwick directed me to the relevant background in Philosophy of Language. I had some *particularly* helpful conversations with Santosh Vempala, and several of the results here are joint work with Santosh, as indicated. Likewise, I want to thank David Sontag and Dan Roy for their continued enthusiastic interest in the work, and their suggestion of the connection to PAC-Bayes that inspired Chapter 4. Finally I want to thank Ryan Williams for several conversations, for his continued interest and support in this work, and (perhaps most of all) for his willingness to read some of our early drafts.

I'd like to thank my committee members, Mike Sipser and Silvio Micali. Mike had two particularly rare qualities: first, he took the time to read the write-ups that I sent to him, and second, he was almost always available. Silvio, on the other hand, has given me substantial, highly relevant advice over the years, on this work, and more generally. Also, although relative to him I'm a mere novice at the art of a good definition, I owe much of what I know to some of the early courses I had with him.

Now, I wish to acknowledge the influence that Oded Goldreich has had throughout this work. To put it briefly, anywhere the formalism is clear and the terminology suggestive, it is due to Oded, and anywhere the work seems hasty and awkward, it is the result of my own attempt to fill in.[1] Chapter 6 closely follows a technical report on which Oded was the principal author [70], and the present version of the framework in Chapter 2 (and by extension, Chapter 5, as well as the rest of the thesis!) was in turn deeply influenced by the choices made by Oded in reformulating and extending my earlier work with Madhu (from [84]) to the infinite execution setting. I want to thank Oded, first for his vote of confidence in our work, and subsequently for his untiring efforts to make it comprehensible. A theoretical framework such as the one proposed here would be no good to anyone if no one could make sense of it!

I'd also like to acknowledge the influence Manuel Blum has had, both on the direction of this project, and on me as a researcher. It's fair to say that the two years I worked with Manuel at Carnegie Mellon shaped my taste and identity as a researcher, and probably the main reason I was originally interested in the questions considered in this work was that I was looking for another way to make progress on some of the questions that Manuel had raised while I was working with him. I've had the pleasure of conversations with Manuel about this work several times since, and they've all proved immensely helpful. Manuel also continues to be perhaps *the* most amazingly supportive person I have ever met, and I can't thank him enough.

Finally, it's an honor to acknowledge the influence, direction, support, and contributions of my advisor, Madhu Sudan. After working with Manuel, I was looking for another significant but colorful, wide open problem to work on, and so when Madhu suggested working on "the problem of establishing a common language," during my first year, I was hooked. I'm extremely grateful for his willingness to work closely with me on these problems, as well as for his support, advice, and encouragement over the long years since. So long, Madhu! And, thanks for all the sushi.

Brendan Juba

Cambridge, Massachusetts
August, 2010

---

[1]The reader may confuse this for modesty, but a simple comparison of Chapter 2 with the original technical report [84] should clear up any lingering doubts.

The work presented here was supported by an Akamai Presidential Fellowship, an NSF Graduate Research Fellowship, and NSF grants CCR-0514915 and CCF-0726525; the preparation of this book was supported by NSF grant CCF-0939370. The publication of this Springer edition was made possible by the cooperation and efforts of Ronan Nugent of Springer.

Contents

Chapter 1

Introduction

Consider the following fantastic scenario: an extraterrestrial named "Alice" contacts an earthling named "Bob" via radio waves. Suppose further that Bob has set up a transmitter, so that he can respond to Alice's message. In a strict sense, Alice and Bob now have the capability to *exchange information*— but can they ever hope to have a *meaningful* conversation?

1.1   Technical motivation

The philosophical substance of this question is self-evident: how does information carry semantic content, and in particular, does this require some common background or language to be "hard-wired" into the (genetic) code of the participants? Thus, it is unsurprising that philosophers have considered such issues, and we will examine this context in Section 1.4.1. What is less obvious is that there are equally compelling technical motivations for studying the semantics of communication, especially communication without a common background.

Most of these motivations arise in the context of computer networks, especially out of the technical challenges posed by the internet. The development of the modern protocols underlying the internet was guided by the following "robustness principle" due to Postel et al. [150]: "be liberal in what you accept, and conservative in what you send." Our work focuses on the first clause of this fundamental principle; the theoretical question is, how liberal can a fixed protocol be? Naturally, we expect that a rigorous treatment of this problem will lead to simpler, more robust protocols for the following reason. It has been observed that these protocols are subject to constant revision and evolution, as deficiencies in the scalability, security, etc. of the protocols are revealed over time. Modifying the protocols, however, clearly either involves updating all of the relevant deployed software or designing the updated protocol to be backwards-compatible with the old protocol. In practice, the first

B. Juba, *Universal Semantic Communication*,
DOI 10.1007/978-3-642-23297-8_1,
© Springer-Verlag Berlin Heidelberg 2011

option demands an extensive coordinated effort by many individuals and the second option leads to a less elegant design; neither option is ideal. Our hope is that the use of a sufficiently liberal protocol would broaden the class of "backwards-compatible" protocols to include suitable designs, thus allowing us to avoid both of the drawbacks described when modifying the protocols at a given point.

Similar considerations also apply in the context of peripherals—consider the process of attaching a new printer to an old computer. Ideally, we would like for the computer to have the capability to print documents using the printer "out of the box," but of course this does not always hold in practice. Instead, we often find that we need to install a new driver for the printer obtained from some third party, either provided on the disk, downloaded from the internet, or written from scratch with considerable effort. As with the internet protocols, it is not reasonable to expect that a single fixed protocol that remains static over time should be employed by all pairs of devices – certainly, at a minimum, over time the data we transmit tends to become richer, as when a monitor with higher resolution and color depth is attached – and this says nothing of what should be done when fundamentally new kinds of devices are attached to the computer. In this context, our question is, for how broad a class of devices can a single driver successfully operate? If this class is sufficiently broad, then we might hope to be able to install a driver that does not need to be updated by a third party when we attach new hardware.

Along these lines, a more abstract and less pressing (but no less intriguing) issue arises in the semantics of data. As we demand richer kinds of data, file formats change—e.g., the documents produced by a modern office productivity suite now include a plethora of auxiliary information, including at least formatting, fonts, etc., leading to a format that vastly differs from the old ASCII text format. There are a number of competing, incompatible formats, and the task of reading these documents either involves using different software for the different formats, or using a reader that is compatible with these numerous formats. We might hope, in this context, that it is possible to store the data in such a way that the contents of the file can outlive the particulars of the data format that they are stored in, that a new reader does not need to know explicitly about the particular (archaic or idiosyncratic) format of the file in order to recover its contents. In this way, we would hope that the semantics of the file could be made less dependent on its syntactic formatting, and thus this problem is the most closely related to the "classic" problem of making the contents of a message independent of the language used to express it.

More radically, Lanier [94] has suggested adopting a "protocol-free" approach to the architecture of computer systems. He observes that the fundamental assumption in protocol-oriented architectures, that the components in a computer system strictly adhere to the stated protocols, leads to catastrophic failure modes when the components do not actually adhere to these protocols—failure modes that are an everyday experience, since strict adherence is almost impossible to achieve in any system of even moderate complexity. Moreover, along the lines of our discussion above, he notes that the requirement that components adhere to given protocols results in the mandatory adoption of old design decisions in the construction of new systems, and similarly, the mandatory adoption of old ideas and architectures—a process he calls "sedimentation." As an example, he notes that the "file" architecture for information storage was a debatable design decision that has since become "a fact of life, as fundamental as a photon" (in his words). Lanier's hope is that an alternative to the protocol-oriented approach will yield a more effective means of engineering large, complex systems—a task that we can barely achieve with any competency today.

Although our work is most concretely motivated by the first of these contexts, all four are questions about to what extent the semantics of communication can be decoupled from the syntactic form of the communication, and we believe that our results will be relevant to all four. In particular, contrary to Shannon's assertion that the semantics of a message are "irrelevant to the engineering problem" in the opening lines of his seminal paper [135], we hope to demonstrate that the semantics of the communication are of fundamental importance to the engineering problems of communication in modern applications.

Moreover, since the entire problem in each case is how a fixed design for a communications system can cope with the task of operating with other systems whose designs and purposes were *unanticipated* at the time of the original system's design, *we believe that a theoretical evaluation of the quality of communications systems is inherently necessary.* That is, since in every case the issue is whether or not the system can cope with circumstances that were not anticipated until after the design was fixed, an *empirical evaluation,* in which the communications system is tested in operation with existing systems, inherently fails to address the key property that we desire in our systems—since indeed, the designs of the existing systems used in the evaluation were (or at least, could easily have been) anticipated at the time of the system's release, assuming that the system's evaluation occurs before its release, of course! By contrast, a theoretical evaluation can guarantee that a design can operate successfully with an entire *class* of potential other systems. Although the classes of systems we consider is always limited, in many cases we view these limitations on the systems as inherent—as we may consider the class of polynomial-time bounded systems to encompass all "reasonable" systems that we will ever encounter, as a consequence of the strong Church-Turing thesis, for example. In any case, even when the class under consideration is not the result of considering some inherent limitations, it at least provides some basis for evaluating and comparing the flexibility and robustness of proposals for the designs of communications systems.

1.2   Limits of our scope, or: what this book is not about

Put succinctly, our work concerns *communication*, not *languages*. In particular, the kinds of communication considered in Section 1.1, although they may be structured as TCP/IP packets or in some other arbitrary way, should fall under our domain. To take a natural example, the "dance" employed by honeybees to convey the location of sources of pollen to other bees fits our criteria for "communication," even though it seems unlikely that the bee can be said to have a "theory of mind" or any such thing. Indeed, taking a page from Shannon we can say that it is irrelevant to the general problem of communication whether or not the bee, a computer, or even an extraterrestrial ascribes intentions to others or builds models of objects in its surrounding environment. Indeed, we expect that in some cases such assumptions will *aid* communication, but in accordance with our primary motivation as outlined in Section 1.1, and in accordance with positions held by various modern philosophers – see Section 1.4.1 and the overview in Section 2.1 for more – what counts for us in the first case is what communication *does*, not how it has been realized in various natural systems.

Thus, in contrast to the scope of the fields of Linguistics, Semiotics, or Cognitive Science, we are not interested in the structure of human languages for their own sake; in particular, we do not assume a priori that the communication must be structured as a grammar with terms—as a "language," as generally construed. Nor are we concerned with categorizing the various concepts employed by the human mind and asking if other communicators share this conceptual scheme. If such structure should arise from general considerations in our model, so be it, and so much the better for these other fields, but we do not regard these structures as fundamental.

1.3   History and prior work

In this book, we must consider as prior work the contributions of two vastly different traditions—first, the empirical tradition of approaches to the *problem* of communication with extraterrestrial intelligence (CETI), and second, the formal tradition of the *solution* of a computational theory of semantic communication. Due to the vast differences between these traditions, we will survey them separately. Likewise, we will separately attempt to give the philosophical context for our contributions in Section 1.4.1, and we will mention in passing some similarities to approaches in other communities in the final section, which surveys the contributions of our work and contrasts them with the prior approaches.

1.3.1 Prior work on CETI

In spite of the fantastic nature of the question of whether or not communication with an extraterrestrial is possible, it has been seriously considered in the past. The most notable early attempt, unique in its depth and scope, is the language LINCOS proposed by Freudenthal [60]. In LINCOS, semantic concepts are gradually introduced by means of examples, building on one another, until a rich enough language has been constructed to express the desired message. Freudenthal claims that it is possible to send messages discussing mathematics, physics, and even simple stories, provided that the recipient is sufficiently "humanlike." Although LINCOS sounds like a positive answer to our question, a closer inspection reveals a host of unresolved difficulties. On the one hand, it is unclear under what conditions a recipient should be considered "humanlike," and on the other, it is not even clear that a message written in LINCOS would be understood by a human recipient who did not have the assistance of Freudenthal's suggestive notation, or who did not know the language's purpose a priori. Similar attempts based on pictographs, like the messages famously included on the Voyager space probes or sent from the Arecibo radio telescope in 1974 [9], are further described by McConnell [111]. The basic problem with all of these schemes is that there is no reason to believe that they will succeed: these schemes lack formal foundations, and thus there is no way to demonstrate that they achieve their intended purpose.

The problem of communication with extraterrestrials was discussed seriously at a pair of conferences held in 1964 and 1971 [145, 129]. These conferences were nearly dominated by radio astronomers, following the earlier proposal by Cocconi and Morrison [47] that radio waves would be ideal for such communication, and the physics of detection and communication took center stage—Cocconi and Morrison themselves had been content with the problem of recognizing a signal of "artificial" origin from an extraterrestrial civilization. Still, the semantic communication problem was mentioned in passing at both conferences. In the 1971 conference, the overall tone was considerably less optimistic, especially towards LINCOS, and there seemed to be no clear consensus among the participants as to whether or not communication should be possible. Notably, Minsky expressed optimism that communication should be possible, and sketched an argument for a message in the form of a program, a proposal that is arguably similar to Fitz's extension to LINCOS, CosmicOS [59].

Although the same caveats concerning LINCOS still apply to Minsky's suggestion, it is particularly notable that years later Minsky also sketched an argument for the validity of such approaches [113]. The essence of Minsky's argument is that it should be possible to send a message in which the correct interpretation is distinguished by being less contrived (complicated) than the alternatives. Although this is an appealing suggestion, unfortunately it is not clear how to formally achieve this effect. The immediate problem one faces when attempting to pursue this approach is that it is still unclear how to model the recipient's "interpreting" of the message.

1.3.2 Formal theories of communication problems

The oldest and most fundamental study of communication problems is the theory of information due to Shannon [135]. Many of the basic concepts we require to begin discussion of the problems that follow – e.g., the architecture of a communication channel, the measure of information in bits and sufficiency of the binary channel, etc. – were laid out in Shannon's original paper. Indeed, discussion of the problems in this book would be entirely premature if not for Shannon's work. On the other hand, as noted in the introduction, Shannon boldly dismissed the semantic aspects of communication as "irrelevant," and focused exclusively on the problem of maximizing the rate of information transmission between a fixed source and receiver. This assumption was valid in the application envisioned by Shannon, in which the algorithms for encoding and decoding a message are designed as a fixed pair, but fails to hold in modern applications in which the devices at different ends of the channel were designed and implemented at different times by different parties, as described in Section 1.1.

Similar assumptions are present in the more recent theory of communication complexity due to Yao [161]. Yao's setting is distinguished from Shannon's in that the parties at both ends of the communications channel have private information, and both parties know that they are communicating for the purposes of computing some shared function f, which takes the private information from both as input. As in Shannon's theory, the protocols are designed as a fixed pair, and the aim is to minimize the total amount of information exchanged in computing f. The introduction of the shared function f associates some semantics with the information exchanged, and in this sense our approach is similar, but as previously stated, our major task is to eliminate the assumption that the protocols are designed as a fixed pair.

This end is partially achieved by the theory of interactive proofs of Goldwasser, Micali, and Rackoff [74], and in many cases our work draws on and extends technical results in this area. The setting of interactive proofs again involves two parties exchanging information over a communications channel, but unlike in earlier work, the parties are given *conflicting* aims: one party is designated a prover and the other a verifier, which are of course respectively analogous to the source and receiver in Shannon's setting. The verifier possesses an input string x, and for some fixed property R, wishes to know whether or not x has the property R. As in Yao's setting, both parties are aware of R (and also x) but now, in contrast to all previous settings, the verifier is computationally limited. Moreover, the prover has some sort of computational advantage – either computational power or simply the result of some infeasible computation – and the prover wishes to convince the verifier that x has property R, regardless of whether or not this is so. In particular, the verifier's algorithm must be robust against *all* possible prover strategies when x does not satisfy R. Although in our setting Alice is not trying to mislead Bob – he simply does not understand her – this kind of "robustness" against a vast collection of possible behaviors is what we desire, and for this reason, the theory of interactive proofs turns out to be particularly pertinent. Likewise, we also demand that Bob's protocol only utilizes limited computational resources, and in some cases this motivates our communication problems too. The major difference between the setting of interactive proofs and our setting is that, in some sense, the prover "knows" the protocol used by the verifier, and this allows the prover to convince the verifier when x has the property R—in practice, a satisfactory prover protocol for this case is still designed with the verifier protocol as a fixed pair, as was done in Shannon's setting and Yao's setting, which we wish to avoid, as previously discussed.

1.3.3 Similar work in other areas

It turns out that work that is technically and/or conceptually similar has appeared previously in a variety of other areas—most notably, Jaron Lanier's "Phenotropics" [94] (alluded to in Section 1.1) and Stuart Russell and Devika Subramanian's "Asymptotic Bounded Optimal Agents" [127]. A proper discussion and comparison of the similarities and differences between these works and the work presented here will require us to describe our approach in more detail, though. Thus, we defer the discussion until after giving an overview of our work in the next section.

1.4 Overview of our contributions

We now turn to outlining our work and highlighting its contributions. Our main contribution is an approach to study semantic communication by explicitly formulating goals for the communication. Moreover, as a consequence of our generic mathematical definition of a goal, we are able to formally study semantic communication *in general* by considering the class of all possible goals for communication. We propose that, when studying the semantics of communication without a common language, one should have in mind an explicit, precisely formulated *verifiable goal* for the communication. In short, possession of such explicit goals is necessary and sufficient for the design of protocols that reliably achieve them. Thus, this observation about generic goals also will permit us to describe when, and to what extent, semantic communication is possible between two parties.

In the rest of this section, we will describe our approach and contributions in more detail; in particular, we will give a more detailed outline of the present document in Section 1.4.3. Moreover, in this section, we will attempt to clarify our contributions in the context of the numerous disciplines and areas that turn out to have considered related subjects, including Philosophy (next, in Section 1.4.1) and (theoretical approaches to) Artificial Intelligence. We will also attempt to clarify our technical contributions in the context of other results and areas of Theoretical Computer Science that feature various kinds of similarities and relationships to our work. Of course, in the latter cases, the distinction tends to be technical, and so the latter discussion is postponed until Section 1.4.4, following the aforementioned overview of our work, and a moderately detailed technical example illustrating our approach and contributions in the context of the goal of solving computational problems, in Section 1.4.2.

1.4.1   Philosophical context

If the reader is only interested in designing and building systems, he or she does not need to accept our claim that our results address *all* semantic communication, but the fact that our results seem to be sufficient to cover all such cases are the grounds on which we feel justified in making such claims. The idea that communication must be considered as means to an end and thus that the semantics of communication should be identified with its usage was first championed by Dewey in 1925 [53], and later brought to the forefront of philosophy by Wittgenstein [156, 157] in his "language games," as he argued that most, if not all of the seemingly deep questions that had been studied in philosophy had arisen as a result of a basic misunderstanding of the workings of language—that, outside of being used to some end, our words – and hence questions about them – are quite meaningless. Moreover, the fact that this conclusion seems to have been reached independently many times over[1] reassures us that it is a reasonable characterization. "Goals" in our sense then arise naturally when we distinguish between successful and unsuccessful usage of a language; we say that a "goal is achieved" when language is used successfully to some end.

So we see that the idea that the semantics of communication must be understood in terms of the goals of communication has been implicitly present in the language-focused inquiry of modern philosophy for quite some time, but more recently Gauker [62] explicitly invoked goals for communication for the purposes of resolving some questions about contexts and the semantics of reference in the philosophy of language. Thus, we believe that our identification of "semantic communication" with "goal-oriented communication" is not only plausible, but entirely reasonable, since various aspects of natural languages do not seem to make sense unless viewed through the lens of goals.

With respect to this context, then, our main contribution is two-fold:

1. We supply a mathematically precise framework for formal goals

---

[1]cf. Dewey's footnote at the end of Chapter 5 of *Experience and Nature* [53]; indeed, Madhu Sudan and I also reached this conclusion before we were acquainted with the philosophical literature, although I don't think that our ignorance of the past 80 years of work in philosophy should be celebrated by calling it "independent!"

2. We introduce computational and quantitative aspects to this study of goal-oriented language usage

where we especially stress the "goal-oriented" aspect in the second point above—it is certainly true that linguists, led by Chomsky [44, 45], have considered computational aspects of languages, but these treatments did not focus centrally on the ends that language serves to achieve. Gold [66, 65], on the other hand, was originally motivated by the question of the computational feasibility of language learning, and considers some computational aspects of language, and we will contrast our work with Gold's at the end of this section. We opt to postpone our discussion of the relationship of our work to that of Gold and others since the differences in our approach are best illustrated by means of an example, which we provide next.

1.4.2 An example: computational goals

We illustrate our approach with our first example of a universal communications protocol from prior work [83]. We will formalize a computational goal for communication and state feasibility and infeasibility results for universal communication in this setting. More specifically, we define a notion of a "helpful" Alice, and the goal of a "universal" Bob. We show that there is a universal Bob that can decide PSPACE complete problems when interacting with any sufficiently powerful and helpful Alice. We also prove a matching negative result showing that Bob cannot decide problems outside of PSPACE, provided the "language" of Alice is sufficiently unknown. Again crucial to this step is formalizing the concept of the language being unknown. We will return to this setting in Chapter 3, where we show how this goal fits into the formal framework introduced in Chapter 2 and how the theorems about generic goals in our framework yield the theorems we claim here as corollaries.

Basic notation

As this section is intended to serve as an illustration, we will adopt simplified notation, borrowed from the classical setting of interactive proofs, for use in this section only. We start by setting up our basic notation for interactive computation. We assume that Alice and Bob exchange messages by writing finite length strings from a binary alphabet on common tapes; we assume that there are two tapes, one which only Alice can write to and only Bob can read, and one which only Alice can read and only Bob can write to. We assume that the interaction proceeds in rounds, and they are well synchronized[2], i.e., they only write after the other has finished reading, and they know when the other has finished writing. Thus a history **m** of the interaction consists of

---

[2]This and similar syntactic assumptions may already be questioned in the general setting of "intergalactic communication." Indeed these simplify our task, however they do not trivialize the problem and we are optimistic that these can be removed at a later stage.

a sequence of pairs of strings $\mathbf{m} = \langle (m_1^{A \to B}, m_1^{B \to A}), \ldots, (m_k^{A \to B}, m_k^{B \to A}) \rangle$ where $(m_i^{A \to B}, m_i^{B \to A}) \in \{0,1\}^* \times \{0,1\}^*$. The messages $m_i^{A \to B}$ are written by Alice, and $m_i^{B \to A}$ by Bob. Each player may toss random coins and have some private inputs. For example, the $k + 1$th message written by Alice is a function of the k messages from Bob in the history thus far, as well as Alice's randomness and private inputs. We describe her response by the function $A(\mathbf{m})$. (We remark that we don't highlight her randomness and private inputs, since these will be irrelevant to Bob.) Similarly Bob's messages are also (probabilistic) functions of the history and any private inputs he may have. Bob's message on private input x and history $\mathbf{m}$ is denoted $B(x; \mathbf{m})$. Once again this function may depend on the history of random coins tossed by Bob but we will suppress this aspect in our notation.

Conditioned on a history $\mathbf{m}$, Alice's responses in the future may be viewed as a new incarnation of Alice. We use $A_{\mathbf{m}}$ to denote her future responses and thus $A_{\mathbf{m}}(\mathbf{m}') = A(\mathbf{m} \circ \mathbf{m}')$ where $\mathbf{m} \circ \mathbf{m}'$ denotes the concatenation of the histories $\mathbf{m}$ and $\mathbf{m}'$.

At the end of an interaction with Alice, Bob will output a Boolean verdict. $(A, B(x))$ will denote the random variable produced by Bob's output following the interaction between Alice and Bob, where Bob has private input x. We will abuse notation in a natural way to let a decision problem (set) Π also denote a Boolean function: $\Pi(x) = 1$ if $x \in \Pi$ and $\Pi(x) = 0$ otherwise.

Definition 1.1. We say that *Alice helps Bob decide a problem* Π if for every $x \in \{0,1\}^*$, it is the case that $\Pr\left[(A, B(x)) = \Pi(x)\right] \geq 2/3$.

Main definitions and results in the computational setting

Our general approach is to consider the situation where Bob interacts with some member of a large class $\mathcal{A}$ of Alices, but does not know which specific member of the class he is interacting with. Essentially, we would like Bob to be successful in deciding the problem Π for every member of the class $\mathcal{A}$. (Sometimes we may also wish to consider what Bob does when Alice does not belong to $\mathcal{A}$.) In order to make this viable, the class $\mathcal{A}$ should only include Alices that are powerful (enough to decide Π), and helpful. While the former is easy to formalize, the latter notion is somewhat subtle. One aspect we'd like to capture here is that her ability to decide Π should be based on her "external characteristics," namely on her input/output response, but this is still insufficient. For instance suppose that for each round i, Alice has chosen a random bit b_i (known only to her) and then answers any question y with the bit $\Pi(y) \oplus b_i$. In this setting her input/output response at time i represents her ability to decide Π – someone who knew some b_i would be able to easily obtain $\Pi(y)$ for any y – but this is clearly not detectable by (poor) Bob. This introduces an additional element that "helpfulness" must capture, namely Alice's behavior as a function of the history of messages thus far.

In the following definition we attempt to formalize the notion of a powerful and helpful Alice by setting minimal restrictions on Alice. Roughly, we insist that Alice be able to help *some* Bob′ decide Π, conditioned on *any* prior history. The requirement that Alice should be able to help some Bob′ decide Π is necessary if we would like to design a specific Bob to decide Π by interacting with Alice. Moreover, observe that if no such Bob′ exists, no matter what is said to Alice and no matter in what language, Alice provides no assistance, so the difficulty is surely not merely one of "lack of a common language." The requirement that this should happen independent of any history does restrict Alice somewhat, but we argue that it is a simple way to overcome issues such as the time-varying Alice described above, and therefore a reasonable "universal" principle.

Definition 1.2 (Π-Helpful Alice). We say that Alice is Π-*helpful* if there exists a probabilistic algorithm Bob and a polynomial p, such that for every prior history $\mathbf{m}$, the incarnation of Alice conditioned on the history, $A_{\mathbf{m}}$, helps Bob decide Π in $p(n)$ steps (independent of $\mathbf{m}$).

We remark that this Alice is *not* assumed to be an oracle; her responses may depend on $\mathbf{m}$ in general,[3] and this is essential for our approach to claim any relevance. We only require that *Bob is successful independent of* $\mathbf{m}$.

We now formalize Bob's goal in this computational setting.

Definition 1.3 (Π-Universal). We say that Bob is a universal decider for a decision problem Π, or Π-universal, if for any Π-Helpful Alice, Alice helps Bob decide Π and there exists a polynomial p such that for every instance $x \in \{0,1\}^*$ Bob runs in expected time $p(|x|)$.

The main theorem in this setting is the following result, which gives a universal Bob for problems in PSPACE.

Theorem 1.4. *For every PSPACE complete problem Π, there is a Bob that is Π-universal.*

This result uses the power of interactive proofs and in particular the fact that PSPACE has short interactive proofs [103, 134]. Effectively Bob attempts to get from Alice, not only the answer to a question of the form "Is $x \in \Pi$?", but also an interactive proof of this answer. The full treatment appears in Chapter 3.

Next we will rule out the possibility of obtaining a Π-Universal Bob for Π ∉ PSPACE. We prove this by showing that for every probabilistic polynomial time bounded Bob, there exists a Π-helpful Alice such that the decision problem (promise problem to be more precise) that Alice helps Bob decide is contained in PSPACE.

Theorem 1.5. *Let Π be a decision problem that is not in PSPACE. Then for every probabilistic algorithm B, there exists a Π-helpful A such that B fails to decide Π with the help of A.*

---

[3]Hence, in particular, checkability of Π will be insufficient; such issues are considered in more detail in Section 3.3.3.

Perhaps a more distressing consequence of the level of generality we seek is that the running time of the universal Bob constructed in Theorem 1.4 is exponentially long in the description length of the shortest asymptotically optimal protocol for interpreting Alice (in Bob's encoding). Notice that with a trusted third party, Bob would have had only a polynomial dependence on the encoding of this protocol. The next theorem asserts that this is necessary.

For simplicity, we will present this result in terms of the "password closure" of a helpful Alice:

Definition 1.6. Given any Alice A, the *password closure of A*, denoted $\mathcal{PW}(A)$, is the following class of Alices: for each $x \in \{0,1\}^*$, $\mathcal{PW}(A)$ contains the password-protected Alice with password x, A^x, described as follows. A^x sends only empty messages to Bob until she first receives the message x in round i, whereupon she responds with A applied to the suffix of the history following round i.

Notice that the password closure of a Π-helpful Alice A contains only Π-helpful Alices (in particular, that help various other Bobs with the same asymptotic running time); therefore, an exponential lower bound for the running time of a Π-universal Bob on this subclass is also a meaningful lower bound for the overhead of the Π-universal Bob in general.

Theorem 1.7. *Let Π be a* PSPACE-*complete decision problem, and let A be a Π-helpful Alice. Then, unless* PSPACE = BPP, *if a probabilistic algorithm Bob decides instances of Π using the help of any Alice in $\mathcal{PW}(A)$ with passwords of length ℓ in time $t_\ell(n) = O(n^k)$, Bob must run for $\Omega(2^{|x|})$ rounds with A^x.*

Note that in a family of helpful password-protected Alices, whenever Alice expects a password of length ℓ, since Alice is a black-box to Bob, Bob cannot try every password in a number of rounds that is subexponential in ℓ, and thus must output a verdict without Alice's help. Moreover, this Alice helps a protocol of description length $\ell + O(1)$, so the construction in Theorem 1.4 is qualitatively optimal for password-protected families. We will return to this theorem and its proof when we consider issues with the efficiency of our protocols in Chapter 4.

1.4.3 Overview

Returning to the general setting, we first lay out a framework for discussing communication problems in a system of interacting agents. Our model agents are straightforward extensions of the interactive Turing machines introduced in interactive proofs [74] and fit the definition of agents used by the artificial intelligence community (cf. the textbook of Russell and Norvig [126]). We give generic mathematical definitions of a goal for communication, (e.g., solving a computational problem as outlined in Section 1.4.2) that is pursued by an agent in our model system.

Models of goals for communication

In slightly more detail, we introduce our framework in three stages. We first consider a special case of goals that are to be achieved within a (polynomial) time bound in Chapter 2, and introduce all of our main terminology in that simplified context; we then refine our model to address more general classes of resource-bounded agents in Chapter 5. Finally, in Chapter 6, we broaden the kinds of goals of communication we consider to include goals in which the agent wishes to keep communicating successfully over time, i.e., in which the agent never "completes" its job, where success at the goal is equated with the agent "mastering" its task, so that it only makes a reasonable number of mistakes.

Universal communication for verifiable goals

In each of these chapters, we develop notions of feedback that we call *"sensing,"* that the agent may or may not be able to obtain with respect to a given goal, in hopes of evaluating its progress towards achieving that goal. We then support our proposal that one should pursue universal communication by first precisely formulating an explicit *verifiable goal for communication* with theorems about the capabilities of these agents—specifically, we show that if sensing is possible with a *class* of partners, then an agent can achieve its goal with *any* given partner in that class, as illustrated for a computational goal in Theorem 1.4.

Indeed, the theorems are sufficiently general to permit the agent to succeed, even if the class contains *every* partner with which communication is *feasible* (i.e., given only that the partner is *"helpful,"* in the terminology of Section 1.4.2)—so then, given sensing, we can design agents that overcome any "language barrier" and achieve their goals. We refer to the aforementioned setting, in which communication with a given partner is merely assumed to be feasible for *some* (other) agent, as the *universal setting*, and the agents that succeed in the universal setting employ *universal communication*, as suggested by the title of the present work.

Extent and limits of the verifiability of goals

Moreover, conversely, in the case of goals that are (reliably) achieved in bounded time (as considered in Chapters 2 and 5), we see that communication with any class of partners requires sensing to be possible with that class of partners, and in this sense we will find that verifiability is (often) necessary for universal communication. We will also see that sensing must be possible in a "weak" sense in the broader case of the goals we consider in Chapter 6. The stronger kinds of feedback will be observed to lead to limits to the kinds of goals that can be achieved, along the lines of Theorem 1.5 in Section 1.4.2; the basic theorems are again proved in Chapters 2, 5, and 6, and the respective applications appear in Chapters 3, 5, and 6. We will see that the aforementioned "weak" kind of verifiability is *not* bound by these limits in Chapter 7. We will note that analogues of this weak verifiability correspond to an agent that may make some errors, and we will see that such agents (that are allowed to fail sometimes) can achieve much harder goals, albeit in a weaker sense.

Nevertheless, we also show how verifiable goals can be formulated for a variety of natural goals for communication in Chapter 3, in support of our claim that most natural semantic communication can be modeled as communication in pursuit of verifiable goals. Our treatment of computational goals (from Section 1.4.2) in particular is refined further in Chapter 5, to show that general polynomial-time computation is a verifiable goal for weak (logarithmic space bounded) devices—and so, in a somewhat realistic sense, universal delegation of computation by these weak devices is possible. Also, returning to our motivation outlined in Section 1.1, we will address a more sophisticated example goal in Chapter 9: we will construct a protocol for end-users on a packet network that automatically adapts to (sufficiently small) changes in the network's packet format.

On the overhead of universal communication

Now, the drawback of our techniques is that in general, our universal protocols incur some substantial overhead, especially in the running time, as illustrated by Theorem 1.7 for computational goals. Again, Theorem 1.7 shows that *in general*, this overhead is *unavoidable*, (and in particular, this means that the universal setting described above suffers from such overhead, so universality comes at some cost) but it does not rule out the existence of (broad) special cases that do not suffer such prohibitively large overhead. Thus, we will develop two approaches to reducing this overhead by considering different kinds of special cases.

The first approach, described in Chapter 4, is designed for the model developed in Chapter 2. In this approach, we suppose that both parties have some "belief" about what constitutes a "natural" communication strategy. We then show that *if these beliefs are similar* and both parties are attempting to communicate effectively with respect to their own beliefs, then the overhead is small. Actually, more generally, we can give a quantitative relationship between the overhead and the difference in beliefs (of course, given that these terms are all formalized in an appropriate way); we can also show that, for communication with low overhead to be possible, there must also exist some common "belief" with respect to which the indistinguishable members of a class of potential partners are all communicating effectively.

The second approach, described in Chapter 8, is designed for the model of goals developed in Chapter 6. In this approach, the agent only wishes to communicate as well as some simple agent—or, equivalently, assumes that some extremely simple rule suffices to communicate successfully. In this context, then, we can show that methods exist to determine from sensing what the rule must be, while making relatively few mistakes. Such methods actually turn out to be precisely *learning algorithms* for a well-known model of learning (we will comment on this relationship in more detail in the next section). Thus, prior work gives a pretty clear picture of what is possible and what is not, given the strong notion of sensing we developed in Chapter 6. Unfortunately, these methods turn out to only exist for *extremely* simple kinds of rules. Still, we note that some *stronger* kinds of feedback would allow richer kinds of rules to be learned, and we hope that this will be a fruitful direction for future work.

1.4.4 Contributions of this book in the context of its relationship to other work

We now attempt to clarify our contributions in the context of other existing areas of work in Computer Science.

Phenotropics

As noted in Section 1.1, Lanier [94, 95] has suggested searching for alternatives to protocol-oriented architectures. Furthermore, like us, he also notes that Shannon's information theory is an inadequate framework for developing such an alternative that does not take the context or "significance" of bits into account.

In his essay, Lanier proposed one alternative approach, that he calls "*statistical surface binding*" or (in other subsequent writings, cf. [95]) "*phenotropics.*" His suggestion is that software might instead be based on "measurement" of other components and then using "signal processing" and "pattern classification" techniques. His approach suggests developing "an operating system whose components recognize, interpret, and even predict each other," [94] and he aims to "build large computers using pattern classification as the most fundamental binding principle, where the different modules of the computer are essentially looking at each other and recognizing states in each other, rather than adhering to codes in order to perfectly match up with each other." [95]

Lanier's exposition of his alternative architecture has been criticized for being rather vague (cf. the published responses to [95]).[4] Lanier stresses that his approach to developing such an alternative is ultimately purely empirical, though—essentially, if and when he succeeds at building a complex system based on such an alternative design philosophy, then his success will be proof of the quality of his principle.

Of course, part of the difficulty Lanier faces in conveying his ideas is that, again, the existing conceptual frameworks are inadequate to even describe

---

[4]Indeed, as far as we have found, the above description of the computer systems Lanier aspires to build contain about as much detail as Lanier has committed himself to anywhere in describing his alternative approach.

the problem that his approach is attempting to avoid, which is to say that the necessary groundwork for him to be able to clearly state the problem did not even exist. We view our development of suitable conceptual foundations for the discussion of these problems as our main contribution. We believe that they are sufficient to enable clear and precise discussion of the problems Lanier is attempting to solve, and to evaluate his proposals.

Another benefit of the possession of such a conceptual framework is that it enables one to begin to understand what inherent limits exist. For example, Lanier asks,

> Who's to say that a computer is present? To a Martian, wouldn't a Macintosh look like a lava lamp? It's a thing that puts out heat and makes funny patterns, but without some cultural context, how do you even know it's a computer? If you say that a brain and a computer are in the same ontological category, who is recognizing either of them? Some people argue that computers display certain kinds of order and predictability (because of their protocol-centricity) and could therefore be detected. But the techniques for doing this wouldn't work on a human brain, because it doesn't operate by relying on protocols. So how could they work on an arbitrary or alien computer? [95]

He never really comes back to explicitly answer this question, but he eventually seems to suggest that what distinguishes a "computer" (or "consciousness") is the "information bandwidth"—that the predictability he alludes to above is a consequence of it only interacting with its external environment in a limited way. We take a very different approach, but we obtain something like a precise answer to his question in Section 5.5.2: roughly, in analogy to the example developed in Section 1.4.2, we show that a sufficiently powerful general purpose computer *can* be recognized *without* cultural context, since a weak device can "offload" computational work to the more powerful computer without knowledge of the powerful computer's interface.

Another related major difference in Lanier's work is that his proposed approach to capturing the semantics of communication is in terms of "legacies," in the sense of assumptions and/or design decisions that have become embedded in the workings of computer systems [94]—actually, more boldly, he suggests that "semantics" should be *defined* in terms of how information is interpreted as a consequence of these legacy assumptions. Of course, the "semantics" of communication in our sense are *not* formalized this way, and we feel that goals capture what is significant about the systems we wish to design. Nevertheless, this is more of a question of terminology, of which definition we wish to grace with the label "semantics" (i.e., a question of "philosophy") than a real conceptual distinction in the work. Arguably, we can capture "legacies" in our framework by restricting the class of partners, or by introducing a prior distribution over the class of protocols (as proposed in Chapter 4), and this turns out to be important in ensuring that certain goals may be feasibly achieved by a single flexible communications system with a large class of other systems (cf. Chapters 3, 4, 8, and 9).

The Semantic Web and semantic interoperability

Put briefly, the objective of the Semantic Web [25] is to enable data and services on the World-Wide Web to be processed automatically by artificial agents. Thus, the ultimate objectives and criteria for success are related to our motivation and criteria for success—in particular, the ultimate purpose and meaning of "semantics" in both cases is that it enables agents to accomplish the various precisely defined goals that we may desire. In particular, when data and services may be shared among systems in service of such goals, we may say that the systems are *semantically interoperable*, and both the Semantic Web project and the present work concern semantic interoperability. Beyond this common subject of study, though, the two bodies of work are completely orthogonal.

In the first place, the Semantic Web project demands that semantic interoperability will be possible (to some specified degree of functionality) as its fundamental objective, and then the project seeks to provide sufficient support to make this objective possible. For example, the basic technique to integrate semantics with data on the web is to assume that a tag in some standard language (e.g., RDF) has been attached to the data, describing *what* the data signifies [25]. Specifically and crucially, the project requires the establishment of *standards* for the integration of semantics; in particular, the project assumes that a community (in which semantic interoperability is to be supported) possesses a shared, standard *ontology*, encoding the relationships among kinds of data [25, 133].

The existence of a shared, standard ontology and data format side-steps the core of the questions we seek to address, which concern whether and how one can cope with the very *absence* of standards. Of course, if we could show that standards were unnecessary in a sufficiently strong sense – e.g., as essentially promised by LINCOS [60], as discussed in Section 1.3.1 – then this would have direct implications for potential architectures for the Semantic Web—it would obviate the need for *standard* data formats, ontologies, and so forth, and permit universal semantic interoperability. Unfortunately, as again discussed in Section 1.3.1, Freudenthal's expectations for LINCOS seem overly optimistic.

So then, in contrast to the Semantic Web project, the subject of our work demands that we model the breakdown of standards as our first objective, and then we ask what is possible under such circumstances. While we can show that universal interoperability – specifically, universal access to services – *is* possible in some cases, as shown for example by Theorem 1.4, we don't guarantee (or even necessarily anticipate) that the degree of richness of interoperability demanded by the Semantic Web project will be feasible in our settings. Indeed, continuing along the lines of Section 1.4.2, we see that in the complete absence of standards, some goals become impossible to achieve (cf. Theorem 1.5), while communication in general may quickly become prohibitively expensive (cf. Theorem 1.7).

Still, there is potential for our work to be informed by work on the Semantic Web and vice-versa; we ultimately are motivated more by a desire to find schemes that are feasible, and thus we are led to consider not just situations where there is no common background, but rather contexts where common backgrounds (i.e., standards) exist to various degrees. In Chapter 4, in particular, we consider such a setting and show how the performance of agents can be made to degrade (somewhat) gracefully with a particular measure of common context. Obtaining interoperability across ontologies is a particularly challenging problem for the Semantic Web [133] (and to our knowledge, it is not handled to any moderate degree of scale), and we might hope that techniques such as those considered in Chapter 4 could one day capture and address such problems, although this is well beyond what we accomplish here. Conversely, the Semantic Web may provide a good example of a setting in which a nontrivial level of semantic interoperability is achieved, and moreover, the design choices made in the Semantic Web might help direct the development of a more general theory, for example by suggesting what may be necessary for rich semantic interoperability.

Gold's approach to Linguistics and Learning in the Limit

Gold's original motivation for introducing his well-known model of "learning in the limit" [66] was studying the learnability of languages; in particular, Gold mentions that "nontrivial models of the usages of language," which are to comprise a second stage of his program of study, are constructed in a lesser-known manuscript [65]. Taken together, these two works bear conceptual and technical similarities to the current work that we now discuss.

Superficially, the difference between our theory of goal-oriented communication and Gold's approach to Linguistic theory outlined in the technical report [65] is that Gold is essentially interested in natural languages, whereas as described in Section 1.2, our interests are strictly more general. On a second look, however, there are some significant similarities in the approach: the main conceptual similarity between our theory of communication and Gold's linguistic theory is that he characterizes a natural language in terms of a "suitability relation," indicating whether or not an utterance represents an appropriate use of the language in a given situation. Thus, Gold's suitability relations play a role roughly analogous to our referees (in the definition of a goal) together with one of our environment-server systems. Put this way, it is clear that on the one hand, there is a strong similarity in the model of what constitutes correct communication (cf. our discussion in Section 1.4.3); on the other hand, it is also clear that the difference in our model is that Gold does not decouple the speaker's goal from the language used to achieve the goal, and so his model is not suitable for capturing *universal* communicators. Still, one of his basic requirements for a "Linguistic theory" is that in the theory, the natural languages should be among the *learnable* languages in some appropriate model, which in Gold's case led to the proposal of the learning in the limit model [66].

Gold's learning model [66], meanwhile, features some technical similarities to our work. In particular, Gold's central technique in the learning in the limit model is learning by enumeration, which we also employ in our basic results (in Chapters 2, 5, 6, and 7), and his criteria for successful learning is similar to our basic criteria for successful communication in our model of goals in infinite executions (specifically, "compact" goals) as presented in Chapter 6. One major difference is that we are not strictly interested in learning the same kinds of predicates presented either in Gold's work or, as far as we can tell, those considered in the vast subsequent body of work on the learning in the limit (or inductive inference) model, at least as surveyed by Angluin and Smith [6]: we stress that our model of goals of communication (and our environments) are richer than those usually considered by those studying learning in the limit, cf. the examples of Chapter 3 and especially Chapter 9, and so the learning in the limit model may be captured as a special case (e.g., as illustrated in Example 6.45 or as presented in Chapter 8). We hope that the relationship between our work and these models is clarified in Chapter 8, where we show that *"generic"* constructions of universal protocols from our main notion of sensing for a class of *very simple* goals correspond to mistake-bounded learning algorithms somewhat like those considered by Gold.

Gold's approach to Artificial Intelligence

Gold also had further results in Artificial Intelligence that have some technical similarities to our work [64, 67]—indeed, as our model agents conform to the definition of agents used by the artificial intelligence community (again, as described by Russell and Norvig [126]), it turns out that our work bears the closest similarity to some later work in AI, which we will describe and contrast our results against in the next section.

In the case of Gold's work [67], he introduced "universal goal-seeking agents" for certain restricted classes of goals—specifically, optimizing the total reward obtained by an agent in a deterministic finite-state environment. He shows that for any finite-state agent, there is an environment of one more state for which the finite state agent fails badly, and for any finite collection of finite state agents, there is an environment of polynomially related size in which all of the agents do badly. By contrast, he shows that there is a primitive recursive agent that does achieve optimal reward in *all* finite-state environments. There are two substantial differences between Gold's approach in this work and our work. The first difference is that we fix part of the environment and only demand that our agents succeed with all *reasonable* variations of the other part, i.e., for which success is possible by some agent of similar complexity. The second difference is that Gold only considers two extreme classes of agents: finite-state agents and primitive recursive agents. By contrast, in our opinion, all of the *interesting* classes of agents (and all of the classes we consider) are of some intermediate complexity, such as polynomial time agents.

We note that Gold, in his thesis [64], noted these same limitations. Specifically, he remarked that the aforementioned result on finite-state agents had led him to believe that *truly universal* AI is *impossible*. He suggested instead that perhaps agents exist for "special classes" of goals, which is essentially the framework of the present work. He also noted that the recursion-theoretic results don't address the questions of whether or not inference is feasible *in practice*, and suggested measuring, e.g., the computation time and memory requirements of the agents, which is also the approach taken presently. Still, Gold's work didn't follow up on these suggestions in much depth. The most he says about the time to learn in the limit (a result also appearing in [66]) is that whenever his method makes mistakes on a target function at a later round than another method, then there's some other function (i.e., the hypothesis of his method at that point, specifically) which his method identifies sooner than the competing method. Of course, in his defense, computational complexity was just then being born, and at the time, much less was known about the subject than is known today.

Artificial Intelligence: Bounded Optimality

In summary, broadly, our approach is to prove theorems about the capabilities of computational agents of limited complexity—namely, we wish to design an agent that succeeds at a goal of communication whenever *some* bounded agent is able to do so. As such, in a sense, our universal protocols could be broadly considered as examples of *bounded-optimal* agents, in the sense of Russell and Wefald [128], who advocated framing AI as the study of "bounded-optimality." In particular, our framework of goals and agents (and some of our basic results) are strikingly similar to those in the theory of bounded-optimal agents introduced by Russell and Subramanian [127].[5]

Russell and Subramanian describe "task environments" corresponding roughly to our goals and environments, except that instead of our time-independent notion of success or failure in "achieving goals," they obtain a real-valued payoff given by a time-dependent "utility function," where the agent then aims to maximize its payoff; and "bounded optimal agents" that obtain utilities in the task environment as high as any agent from a bounded class. Of particular interest to us are their description of "universal asymptotic bounded optimal agents," which achieve utilities as high as any compu-

---

[5]Again, although I would hesitate to call it "independent," Madhu Sudan and I were embarrassingly unaware of the contributions of Russell and Subramanian when we started, in spite of the fact that the first publication of their work predates ours by nearly fifteen years.

tationally limited agent while using resources that are greater by at most a constant factor than the resources used by the corresponding limited agent. Russell and Subramanian show that these agents can be constructed under some conditions, but only for utility functions that decrease to zero over time (i.e., so the decaying utility forces the agent to act quickly). More generally, this is in line with the conceptual framework promoted by Russell and Wefald—they constrain their search by supposing that deliberation by an agent comes at a cost in utility, and so there is an optimal "sweet spot" that an efficient agent could hope to approach in practice.

By contrast, as a consequence of our focus on modeling *communication* rather than real-time actions, we consider the case where the (potential) utility is not dropping over time, but we still desire that the agent's computation time is limited by some reasonable (polynomial) bound. We then show that such a computationally limited agent can be programmed to efficiently achieve a goal (by communicating with some other party) *if and only if* the agent can compute feedback on whether or not its goal has been achieved. Another consequence of this difference in focus is that we construe the interaction differently – as proceeding in coarser "rounds" – which simplifies our model.

Hutter's Universal AI

The aforementioned constructions of optimal agents are also reminiscent of some results by Hutter [81]. There are a few differences: the first one is that Hutter's results are proved in a control-theoretic (reinforcement learning style) setting, in which the environment provides the agent with the value of its payoff at each moment in time. Now, we stress that although our restricting our attention to "goals" is significant, this is unsurprisingly not novel to our work – goals in such a framework were explicitly considered under different motivations by Wooldridge [160], for example – and in general goals and utilities are equivalent, as one may always give a goal of the form, "achieve utility u." Rather, the significance of goals and the major novelty of our work lies in our ability to prove *limitations* on the capabilities of the bounded agent by showing that it fails to achieve its goal – results that are vital to any theoretical study – and the corresponding results stated in terms of utilities are somewhat less natural. For example, crucially, we can show that in our setting the agent must compute its own "payoff," i.e., whether or not its goal has been achieved, in contrast to Hutter's setting.

Still, one may view our generic constructions of universal protocols from sensing as being constructions of universal agents from reinforcement (and we do take such a view explicitly in Chapter 8); the more subtle difference here is that Hutter's construction achieves a superior constant factor in its running time, but relies on a notion of "provable equivalence" that we would not expect to be available in general, as in general, the agent has no way of knowing what environment it is operating in. To be more precise, our *partners* are black boxes to the agent *in general*, and there is no use in attempting to prove theorems about their behavior. Of course, one can take the maneuver of considering a restricted class of partners that one *can* reason about, and an analogue of Hutter's work could be carried out in such a setting, in hopes of obtaining better performance without sacrificing too much flexibility (although unfortunately, Hutter's construction only succeeds at converting an infeasibly large *multiplicative* constant overhead to an infeasibly large *additive* constant overhead). Again, in Chapter 8, we consider some such restricted classes, and find that existing techniques would permit us to design agents that would even be *feasible in practice*, but only with some severely restricted (but nevertheless nontrivial) classes of partners.

Computational learning theory

Broadly speaking, although the notions of computational learning theory played essentially *no* role in the development of the basic framework and theorems, we have found that learning theory is extremely relevant to addressing the questions of how the overhead experienced by universal protocols may be reduced. In particular, the central result of Chapter 8 mentioned above actually shows that when we consider communications protocols for goals in infinite executions (i.e., "goals to maintain") and focus on the number of failures as a measure of quality as introduced in Chapter 6, then the problem of constructing universal protocols from sensing that is viable with restricted kinds of user strategies is *precisely* the same problem as considered in the on-line learning model first introduced by Bārzdiņš and Frievalds [19] and subsequently investigated in depth by Littlestone [101]. Thus, the aforementioned "existing techniques" that allow us to design agents that are computationally feasible in practice are actually techniques for the design of efficient on-line learning algorithms. The relationship of this mistake-bounded on-line learning model to other models of learning is fairly well understood, and we are able to obtain a reasonably complete picture of what is possible and what is not from "basic sensing" in a somewhat limited special class of goals.

Learning theory, and in particular PAC-Bayesian analyses, as first introduced by Shawe-Taylor and Williamson [136] and McAllester [110], also serve as a source of inspiration for another approach to designing computationally feasible protocols in Chapter 4. In this case, unlike in Chapter 8, the setting is actually very different and the existing work does not seem to be so technically useful to us. Nevertheless, we found the approach taken by PAC-Bayesian analyses to be highly relevant at a conceptual level.

Program checking

Another, more substantial result of our focus on communication is that we can obtain further results that stress the point that the verifiability of the goal is of the utmost significance: in the absence of common language or background, we can show that the verifiability requirements are particularly strong, as strong as required in the setting of interactive proofs. In some sense, this also supports the extended form of the robustness principle which in practice guided the development of the protocols underlying the internet [36]—the philosophy that one should assume that the network is filled with malicious entities, and design to handle the worst possible case, even if a malicious human could never be so devious.

Thus, for example, the explicit design of a universal communications protocol for a computational goal described in Section 1.4.2 resembles the program checkers of Blum and Kannan [33]. It uses interactive proof systems for PSPACE-complete sets [103, 134] to verify a particular instance x of a particular problem in PSPACE Π using an unreliable "interpretation" of Alice's (the server's) statements as being about a sequence of other instances of PSPACE-complete problems, which are used to efficiently construct a proof about $\Pi(x)$.

We consider the question of the relationship of our universal protocols to program checkers in some depth in Section 3.3.3. It turns out that the proper characterization of computational problems with universal protocols in terms of interactive proofs, given in Theorem 3.12, is quite similar to Blum and Kannan's characterization of the problems with program checkers in terms of interactive proofs—in particular, as we note in Corollary 3.13, these characterizations show that whenever a problem has a universal protocol, it also has a program checker. Thus, essentially all of our examples of problems with universal protocols from Section 1.4.2 and Section 3.3.4 are familiar examples of problems with program checkers. Of course, we know that the converse is unlikely to hold, as we discuss in Section 3.3.3.

Moreover, we give a variety of examples of goals in Chapter 3 and Chapter 9 that are *not* computational goals, but for which we can design universal protocols. Indeed, in our motivating examples from Section 1.1, the reader should note that "solving computational problems" only encompassed rather little of what we wish for our protocols to achieve for us, and when our goal is something other than solving a computational problem, it doesn't really make sense to talk about our objectives in terms of "program checking." In some sense, our work can be viewed as the generalization of program checking to other tasks achieved by computer systems.

Levin's universal search algorithms

Our basic constructions of universal protocols, as presented in Proposition 2.27 (and in Theorem 5.23 for other classes of agents) are completed by efficiently enumerating all possible "interpretations," so that whenever a suitable protocol for interpreting the server exists, the protocol is able to efficiently achieve the goal and obtain feedback indicating that the goal is achieved. This argument extends a similar argument by Levin [97] which gave an optimal universal search procedure for total functions in NP. Moreover, the corresponding class of problems for which our *interactive* universal protocols can be constructed has an arguably nicer characterization, given in Theorem 3.12, as the class of function problems that have "competitive interactive proof systems," originally introduced by Bellare and Goldwasser [21] for rather different reasons.

This construction is sufficiently generic that it encompasses all verifiable goals in a straightforward way, which demonstrates that verifiable goals are sufficient for universal communication. Of course, Levin's work was only concerned with solving computational problems, whereas as we noted in the context of program checking above, our constructions address goals of communication that may have rather little to do with computation, so in a sense our work generalizes Levin's technique as well.

Actually, in a sense, we can see that our work, and in particular our focus on *communication* makes *essential* use of the "universal" aspect of Levin's universal search technique. In the case of Levin's algorithm, we know that the universal algorithm is *asymptotically* optimal, but we know that it necessarily incurs a steep overhead over the running time of any other fixed algorithm that it chooses to run. Thus, unless the optimal running times are achieved by an infinite sequence of algorithms (which is possible), Levin's algorithm is virtually guaranteed to be actually *slower* than an algorithm that only runs the few relevant algorithms from the enumeration. In such a case, this observation raises the question of why one should use Levin's algorithm at all, instead of one of these other algorithms. Of course, the answer is that if one knew an "explicit" optimal algorithm for the problem one *wouldn't* run Levin's algorithm. The virtue of Levin's technique is that it is always available, regardless of whether or not we understand how to design good algorithms for a problem, and when one (merely) uses the technique to solve computational problems, this feature of the technique is underutilized. By contrast, it is essential for the purposes of a flexible communications protocol that we exhibit a single, fixed protocol that can communicate with as broad a class of partners as possible, and moreover, it is likewise inherent to the problem in this case that we have no prior knowledge or understanding of what kind of protocol to use. We thus believe that the technique is more naturally suited to our generalized setting than it was to Levin's original setting.

Moreover, as a consequence of our focus on communication, we can also unconditionally show (in Chapter 4) that in many cases, such enumeration strategies are essentially optimal, in contrast to Levin's setting, where the best possible results are based on assumptions such as P $\neq$ NP, as obtained by Trevisan [146]. Again, to our knowledge, no such limitation results are known in the asymptotic bounded optimal agent framework of Russell and Subramanian, an omission which we can also attribute to our restricting our focus to goals, rather than general time-dependent real-valued utilities. Since the optimality of enumerations is unfortunate, we also consider some variants on our main definitions. We explore characterizations of when goals can be achieved more efficiently in Chapters 4 and 8, in hopes of demonstrating that some goals can be achieved with a broad if not entirely unrestricted class of partners, without paying the enormous overhead incurred by the enumerations used in Levin's technique.

Chapter 2

Theory of finite goal-oriented communication

This chapter describes a formal theory of semantic communication in terms of "goals" for communication. In this chapter, we focus exclusively on *finite goals,* where an agent wishes to reach some desired state of being, in contrast to *infinite goals* where an agent wishes to maintain some desirable state over time, which we will introduce in Chapter 6. We will describe our model for communicating agents and state our main definitions; in particular, we will introduce the "basic universal setting" for finite goals, in which we aim to design an agent for a finite goal that achieves the goal of communication with a partner in polynomial time whenever some other polynomial time agent could communicate with that partner. We then prove some basic results about this model—in particular, theorems characterizing when universal communication is possible with a given class of partners.

Subsequent chapters will depart from this basic model in a variety of ways. For example, in Chapters 4 and 7, we will depart from this setting by respectively employing a more restricted setting to obtain a more efficient protocol or weakening the reliability requirements to obtain more powerful protocols. On the other hand, in Chapter 5, we will show that the theorems introduced in this chapter hold for classes of users with differing computational resources

The theory and results developed in this chapter first appeared in an early form in a technical report [84] extending previously published work [83] with Madhu Sudan; the vastly cleaner version of the framework presented here is derived from a later technical report with Oded Goldreich and Madhu Sudan [70], and generally owes its present clarity and simplicity to Oded Goldreich.

B. Juba, *Universal Semantic Communication,*
DOI 10.1007/978-3-642-23297-8_2,
© Springer-Verlag Berlin Heidelberg 2011

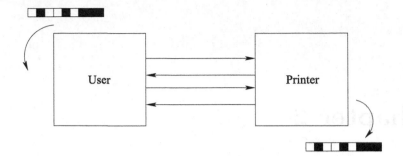

Figure 2.1: A user communicating with a printer

2.1 An informal overview of the theory

We begin by attempting to motivate the development of the basic notions in our theory from its foundations in modern philosophy. We will informally illustrate the considerations that lead to the specific choices we make in the formal development in Section 2.2, and we will give an overview of some of our main results – two from Section 2.3 and one from Chapter 4 – at the same intuitive, informal level.

2.1.1 Goals: a formal explication of meaning

Communication is a means to an end, and the "meaning" of a message is no more and no less than the conditions under which it is used. This view of meaning and language was proposed simultaneously by various authors in the 1920s, and was brought to prominence through Wittgenstein's "language games" [156, 157]. Following Wittgenstein, we can clarify what we mean by using a simple language game as an example; we have chosen one that, while simple enough to have stood among the original examples, we hope is also sufficiently familiar to impart our motivations for studying "semantic communication."

Consider the everyday case where we, situated at a PC, communicate with a printer (say, via a printer cable for simplicity). The players in this game are ourselves at the PC, which we will refer to together as the "user," and the "printer." At some point, the user has in mind a sequence of white and black dots that he or she would like printed on a page, and after our printer driver exchanges some signals with the printer – suppose it sends the message "010010111" across the cable – the printer produces a sheet of paper with our desired sequence of dots (see Figure 2.1 for a schematic). In our scenario, the message "010010111" has *meaning*: upon hearing it, the printer produces some particular sequence of white and black dots. The philosophical claim is that *there is no more to meaning in general*, nothing deeper happening in any act of communication.

More generally, the user's printer driver communicates successfully when the printer produces the same sequence of dots on its sheet of paper as we had envisioned (composed in our word processor, etc.). In particular, we could distinguish between cases in general where the printer produces the pattern we had in mind and cases where, as a result of using the wrong driver for example, the printer produces some other, garbage output. We take this distinction of cases where communication succeeds and cases where it fails as fundamental, and we say that the goal of communication is to enact successful communication. Thus, the goal of communication for the user is that the printer should produce the pattern of dots envisioned by the user.

From an engineering standpoint, this is well enough, since such goals are all we ever aim to facilitate with a particular implementation. Perhaps this talk about meaning even seems a little irrelevant—we recall that Shannon [135] explicitly disregarded everything occurring beyond the sender and receiver at the two ends of the communications channel. The philosophical claim is only relevant in that it asserts that by studying goals of communication in general, we cover *all possible* scenarios for communication, and we will never find occasion to consider any requirements more demanding than the correct usage of messages in our solutions to any communication problem.[1]

We will insist on baking these wider aspects of goals of communication in to our models since, unlike Shannon, we will attempt to confront the problems that arise when the sender and receiver have not agreed on a communication protocol in advance. For example, we might imagine that the cable serves as a binary channel, and that one printer, P_0 interprets a '0' as a white dot to be printed, and a '1' as a black dot, while another printer, P_1 interprets a '1' as a white dot and a '0' as a black dot. Such choices of encoding are arbitrary, after all, and ideally we would like for the user to be able to succeed at his or her goal regardless of whether the cable is attached to P_0 or P_1. One might hope that, like Shannon, we could dispense with talk about "meaning" and simply have the user figure out the printer's encoding.

Unfortunately, it turns out that without a protocol having been fixed *a priori*, the situation is more severe in some subtle ways, and this naïve approach is generally doomed to failure. Leaving the printers aside for a minute, suppose that Alice and Bob speak different natural languages and wish to have a discussion via some binary channel. We would expect that a third party who knows both languages could give finite encoding rules to Alice and Bob to facilitate this discussion, and we might be tempted to ask that a "universal protocol" translate Alice's statements into the same statements in Bob's language that the third party would have selected and vice-versa. In the absence of the third party, this is unreasonable to expect, though: Quine [121]

---

[1] Wittgenstein's claim was actually stronger than this, asserting that *human language* is described by no more and no less than a collection of similar but ultimately distinct language games. We won't need this stronger claim, since we only consider communications systems, in which case it is somewhat evident that the "language games" for different tasks may vary.

has suggested that mutually incompatible interpretations of a language may be entirely consistent with observation, and hence indistinguishable from "correct."

We can observe an example of Quine's "indeterminacy" in the setting where Alice and Bob are restricted to using the binary channel for communication: suppose that Alice and Bob were given encoding rules that were identical to those that a third party would have given them, except that some symmetric sets of words have been exchanged—say, Alice thinks "left" means "right," "clockwise" means "counter-clockwise," etc. (If we wished to be more formal, we could consider objects such as graphs with nontrivial automorphisms, as done in Example 2.20.) Unless they were given some additional means to tell that these basic concepts have been switched, observe that they would still have a conversation that is entirely sensible to each of them, and yet Bob would be interpreting Alice incorrectly. Thus, if we are to have any hope of constructing universal protocols at all, we must work with the broader model and be prepared to accept interactions that are indistinguishable from successes as "successes" as well.

Even the simple example of the two printers P_0 and P_1 immediately raises some important issues, since as we have set things up so far, this task may be *impossible*. We have in mind some dot we want printed first, perhaps a white dot, and if we send a '0' first, this is incorrect for P_1, whereas if we send a '1' first, this is incorrect for P_0. The obvious fix is that we should allow ourselves to print some "test pages" first, which amounts to relaxing our notion of "successful communication" in our language game. For simplicity, we will say that the user's goal is achieved if the desired pattern of dots appears as the suffix of the printer's output. A user who accomplishes this with both P_0 and P_1 is said to be universal with respect to the class $\{P_0, P_1\}$ and the relaxed goal of printing (henceforth G_{print}), or $\{P_0, P_1\}$-universal for G_{print}.

More broadly, we will only attempt to address goals of communication that are "forgiving" in the sense that for every state of the other players (e.g., the printers) it is still possible to achieve the goal, and we will likewise require our universal users to achieve the goal regardless of the initial states of the other players. Notice that this restriction to forgiving goals rules out some thornier scenarios that actually arise in the real world: for example, the printer might have some special string that allows us to "update" the firmware, which, if used incorrectly, could prevent the printer from either printing new pages or responding to new firmware updates. Ultimately, we would like to guarantee that this kind of catastrophic failure is extremely unlikely to happen, but addressing these issues is not our aim for the time being, and we will simply rule such issues out of bounds.

2.1.2 Sensing functions

From the definition of the relaxed goal of printing G_{print}, an approach to designing a $\{P_0, P_1\}$-universal user for G_{print} springs immediately to mind: send a '0' to the printer; if a white dot is produced, we know we are connected to P_0, otherwise we know we are connected to P_1, and either way we can print accordingly. It seems almost too obvious to mention, but this is fine just so long as we are permitted to watch the dots leaving the printer.

If we cannot see the printer's output – perhaps it is in another room – then again, our goal is impossible: this time, supposing that the final dot should be white, again sending a '0' last is incorrect for P_1, and sending a '1' last is incorrect for P_0. Although we might be tempted to try to relax the goal further here – perhaps just require our desired pattern to appear as a substring – this snag only hints at a deeper problem.

Leaving the printer P_1 aside for a minute, we will describe a class of "password-protected printers," or more generally the password closure of a player which we will denote $\mathcal{PW}$, which will have further importance later: for a fixed player P, for each binary string (password) σ, $\mathcal{PW}(P)$ contains the player P^σ that ignores messages unless they are prefixed by σ, and otherwise drops σ and responds to the suffix as P would. So for example, $\mathcal{PW}(P_0)$ contains the printer P_0^{1101} that ignores messages that do not start with "1101" and upon receiving "1101010010111" prints the same pattern that P_0 would print upon receiving "010010111."

Without any feedback from the printer, a $\mathcal{PW}(P_0)$-universal user for G_{print} (or even a further relaxed printing goal) can never stop trying—otherwise, the user will only have tried a finite number of passwords, whereas there are infinitely many distinct passwords, and thus certainly some corresponding printers which would have simply ignored every message sent by the user before he or she gave up. Needless to say, this is undesirable behavior either way: we would like to be able to succeed at our goal and move on to do something else.

We would be in good shape if only we could obtain a signal that our pattern had been printed successfully. More generally, what we are after is a binary-valued sensing function V for our goal that the user can reasonably compute from his or her goal and history of messages (exchanged with the other players or their broader environment). By "reasonably compute," we mean that V can be computed in probabilistic polynomial time (in terms of some reasonable parameter associated with the goal, such as the length of the pattern to be printed), and we will say that the sensing function is safe with a player P if whenever it produces a '1' during an interaction with P, the user can "halt" (i.e., stop sending messages) and the goal will be achieved.

A safe sensing function specifies a *sufficient* condition for achieving the goal, but not a *necessary* one—as stated, it may be that the goal is achieved and we do not know about it. In particular, the function that always evaluates to '0' is quite safe, but also quite useless. Similarly, any safe sensing function

for our earlier notion of printing – i.e., one that only outputs '1' if the output
of the printer is *precisely* the pattern we have in mind – is also safe for the
weaker goal G_{print}, but as we noted, the strong goal is impossible to achieve
universally with $\{P_0, P_1\}$.

The guarantee we are after turns out to be similar to the kind of "forgiving" conditions we demanded earlier when we relaxed the strong printing
goal to G_{print}—we want a sensing function which, no matter the state of the
other players, can still be made to produce a '1' by further interactions. In
particular, we wish to constrain the kind of behavior required of us to behavior which we could be realistically expected to exhibit, that is to say, behavior
that can be generated by probabilistic polynomial time computation. To be
more precise, we now say that the sensing function V is viable with some
fixed player if there is some probabilistic polynomial time computable user
behavior such that for any state of the other player, the interaction of the
user behavior with the other player leads to a point where V outputs '1' with
high probability. The notion of a safe and viable sensing function leads us
directly to our first theorem, which reassures us that we are on the right
track:

Theorem (Theorem 2.25, informal statement) *For any class of play-
ers $\mathcal{P}\ell$ and goal G, there is a probabilistic polynomial time $\mathcal{P}\ell$-universal user
for G if and only if there is a sensing function for G which is safe and viable
with every member of $\mathcal{P}\ell$.*

The proof is simple: taking a probabilistic polynomial time $\mathcal{P}\ell$-universal
user for G, we observe that the function that checks to see if the user would
halt is a safe and viable sensing function. On the other hand, given such
a sensing function, there is a standard trick (due to Levin [97]) by which
we dovetail all (probabilistic) user behaviors, so that each runs with only a
constant factor slowdown. We are guaranteed that V will output a '1' by
viability, and if we halt when this happens, safety guarantees that we have
succeeded at the goal G. Moreover, because we only have a constant factor
slowdown, viability guarantees that we run in probabilistic polynomial time
when communicating with each fixed player in $\mathcal{P}\ell$. Thus, safe and viable
sensing functions are precisely the functions that tell universal users when
they should halt.

2.1.3 Capabilities and limits of universal users

Readers who are familiar with Levin's enumeration technique will recall that
the "constant factor overhead" it incurs in the running time is actually exponential in the length of the corresponding program. For even moderately
large programs, this "constant factor" may be enormous. By contrast, we
expect that any reasonable design of a universal user for the two printers
$\{P_0, P_1\}$ will not require this kind of overhead. We are left to wonder if

the enumeration technique is merely a crutch, whether or not the kind of overhead it exhibits is really essential in general.

For a sufficiently broad class of players, the overhead turns out to be essential. This is easiest to see by considering the password closure of some player; there are 2^ℓ passwords of length ℓ, so a user who sends fewer than 2^ℓ messages cannot expect a response from every member of the password closure who uses a password of length ℓ. Thus:

Theorem (Theorem 4.3, informal statement) *A $\mathcal{PW}(P)$-universal user for a goal G that requires another player to act must send $\Omega(2^\ell)$ messages to P^σ for some σ of each length ℓ.*

Since the passwords of length ℓ can be "hard coded" into programs at the cost of ℓ additional bits, this is the same qualitative relationship between program lengths and running times as shown by Levin's enumeration technique. So, the generic users constructed by this proof technique come at some substantial "cost" in their running time. We may well wonder what this high price buys us.

The price in running time turns out to buy us a remarkable kind of robustness, which we describe presently. Fix a goal of communication G, and consider the class $\mathcal{P}_G$ of G-helpful players P for whom there is some corresponding probabilistic polynomial time user U_P such that, no matter the state of the player P, U_P succeeds at G with P. A $\mathcal{P}_G$-universal user for a goal G then *succeeds at G whenever it is feasible for some user to reliably do so.* In particular, the class of G-helpful players encompasses players who we can think of as speaking in some foreign or alien language, so a universal user for this class would serve as a universal communicator. Of course, since passwords can be built in to user behaviors, $\mathcal{P}_G$ contains all of the password-protected versions of its players, and therefore we cannot expect such a powerful user to be too efficient.

The class of G-helpful players also contains wilder differences in behavior than mere password protection—since a sufficiently long password can map messages outside of any finite domain, *every possible* behavior on a finite set of finite histories is exhibited by some player in $\mathcal{P}_G$. This observation leads to the following important requirement on universal users' sensing functions:

Theorem (Theorem 2.37, informal statement) *If a sensing function is safe for every player in $\mathcal{P}_G$, then the sensing function must be safe for all players, even malicious and unhelpful ones.*

The proof of this theorem is somewhat subtle, and would demand more precision than we have been employing so far. We will need the definitions from Section 2.2, and the full proof will appear in Section 2.3. The main idea, though, is that when a malicious player is able to trick a user into halting prematurely, there is a finite subset of the histories in which the user is fooled that occur with an arbitrarily small loss in probability. Thus, the representative of the finite malicious behavior in $\mathcal{P}_G$ would also trick the user into halting prematurely; turning this around, if the user doesn't halt prematurely with such players, then the user also must not halt prematurely with malicious players.

A corollary of this theorem (together with our first theorem) is that the existence of a $\mathcal{P}_G$-universal user for G is equivalent to the existence of a sensing function for G that is viable for $\mathcal{P}_G$ and always safe. So for example, the results described in Section 1.4.2 follow from our characterization by well-known facts and techniques—as we will demonstrate in Section 3.3. Thus, the characterization helps shed light on the capabilities and limits of "universal communication" in ways we will illustrate in Chapter 3.

2.2 Model of communication and goals

We begin by describing the basic model of communicating *agents* and their *goals* in a broader *environment*. We will distinguish between two kinds of agents in our language games: agents that represent ourselves, that we call *users*, and other agents that we interact with, who we call *servers*. We will then describe *universal* protocols that a user can employ to reliably achieve these goals, and minimal *helpfulness* conditions on servers which permit goals to be reliably attained with that server. In the basic "universal setting," we aim to construct a universal protocol that reliably succeeds under these minimal conditions, like the protocol described in our prior work [83]. Our model (if one removes the servers) and basic universal protocols respectively turn out to be very similar to the model of agents and "Asymptotic Bounded Optimal Agents" introduced by Russell and Subramanian [127], so our work could be thought of as a study of communication in a variant of their model, and we will take care to point out where the models diverge.

2.2.1 Agents: users, servers, and their environment

In familiar terminology from the Theory of Computation, we consider an interaction between several parties, (at least) the environment, and two agents, a user and a server, that proceeds in rounds. We will assert that, on each round, all parties are in one of countably many states,[2] and that the parties share communication channels, which likewise carry a finite sequence of symbols – elements of $\{0,1\}^*$ – and hence the overall system is in one of countably many states.[3] We will denote this countable state space of the system by Ω. Thus, Ω is a product of the following sets: for each ith party

---

[2]This is without loss of generality—the environment's state could be a history of the entire interaction up to the present round.

[3]We note that the restriction that a channel only carry finitely many distinguishable symbols in one unit of time seems to be an unstated conclusion of Shannon's model. In particular even if a channel is capable of carrying an arbitrary real number in $[-1,1]$, but introduces Gaussian error, the capacity of the channel reduces to a finite amount.

in the interaction, there is an internal state space $\Omega^{(i)}$, and for each pair of parties (i, j), there is a communications channel carrying a message from i to j with state space $\Omega^{(i,j)}$. We denote the index of the user by u, the environment by e, and the server (when there is precisely one) by s.

The actions of all three parties will be dictated by a local function, the party's respective strategy:

Definition 2.1 (Strategies). The *strategy* of the ith party in a system is a function $P_i : \Omega^{(i)} \times \left(\times_{j \neq i} \Omega^{(j,i)} \right) \to \Omega^{(i)} \times \left(\times_{j \neq i} \Omega^{(i,j)} \right)$ representing the party's actions in the current round: P_i takes as input the party's state and incoming messages at the beginning of the round, and computes the party's new state and outgoing messages for the following round.

Although the parties' strategies only operate on the specified "local" components of the global state, for convenience we may abuse notation by writing a strategy as a function mapping Ω to itself.

The communication channels corresponding to $\Omega^{(e,u)}$ and $\Omega^{(e,s)}$ model the agents' senses, whereas $\Omega^{(u,e)}$ and $\Omega^{(s,e)}$ model the agents' actions in the environment. This model naturally fits the same basic outline of agents described elsewhere (e.g., in the AI textbook of Russell and Norvig [126] and references described there). The channels joining the user and the server, on the other hand, are intended to model communication between the agents. Although less standard, this feature of the model is undoubtedly also employed elsewhere (e.g., in the study of multi-agent systems).

Likewise, in the following section, we will introduce a notion of *goals* for these agents, that resembles definitions appearing elsewhere—roughly, the agent's goal will be to have some effect on the environment. One difference in our work is that the goals, rather than the agents, come to play the central role in our study. In particular, a crucial difference between our setting and some settings considered elsewhere (e.g., the universal agents of Hutter [81]) is that we do not assume that "utilities" are computed for us by the environment—in our setting, in general it will be up to the agent to decide whether or not it is satisfied.

2.2.2 Goals of communication

Our objective is to study communication in general, particularly communication when the details of a protocol have not been fixed in advance. To determine when such robust communication is possible and particularly when it is impossible, we first need a formalization of communication problems in general, which we provide next, in terms of "goals." As described in Section 2.1, the goal of communication will specify a subset of states in which communication was used successfully.

We find it cleanest to formally describe a goal of communication in terms of the formal states of the environment. This is so because it will permit us to freely vary the agents involved and the language they speak without worrying about how these variations affect the goal—in particular, such a formal model decouples the requirements on a user from its implementation, giving us the freedom to implement the same user strategy in a variety of ways.[4] Thus, goals will be formally represented by a *pair* of the environment's strategy (thus describing the semantics of its states) together with a subset of "successful" states which we define using a "referee" predicate:[5]

Definition 2.2 (Finite referees and successful states). A *finite referee* is a function from a state of the environment to a Boolean value, $R : \Omega^{(e)} \to \{0, 1\}$. We say that $\{\sigma \in \Omega^{(e)} : R(\sigma) = 1\}$ is the set where communication is *successful*.

We specify that the referee is "finite" in contrast to the "infinite" goals that we will introduce in Chapter 6, where rather than aiming to reach a successful state, the user wishes to remain in a successful state during an infinite execution. When it is understood from context, we will drop the specification that the referee is "finite" or "infinite."

In particular now, and in contrast to the infinite goals we will consider later, we will only concern ourselves with settings where a user wishes to spend only a finite amount of time in pursuit of a goal. This certainly models the aims of common "client software" and other typical applications of PCs, such as the printing example described in Section 2.1, as well as the "sub-goals" that an agent studied in AI might wish to pursue.[6] We model this by giving the user a distinguished "halting state" that signifies the end of the execution:

Definition 2.3 (Halting). The *halting state* σ_F is a distinguished member of $\Omega^{(u)}$. When the user's strategy outputs σ_F, we say that the user *halts*.

As with standard Turing machines, we can think of entering the halting state in our model as "returning from a function call," and correspondingly, a desirable "post condition" for a user strategy is that the user halts in a successful state.

Definition 2.4 (Achieving goals). We say that the user *achieves* the goal specified by a referee R and an environment with states $\Omega^{(e)}$ if the user halts and communication was successful: that is, when $\sigma^{(u)} = \sigma_F$ and $R(\sigma^{(e)}) = 1$.

---

[4] Russell and Subramanian [127] describe at length similar motivations for modeling their agents as abstract functions as they introduce their model.

[5] As such, our goals are directly analogous to the "task environments" of Russell and Subramanian [127], except that instead of their time-dependent real-valued utilities, we use a Boolean-valued referee. We prefer not to cast our model in terms of utilities since agents' limitations are more naturally stated in terms of goals.

[6] Although these goals are formally similar to the "episodic" task environments of Russell and Subramanian [127], we conceive of them differently—namely, Russell and Subramanian envision that each round corresponds to a constant number of steps of the execution and the episode is ended when the agent selects a single action, whereas we consider a longer execution in which each round corresponds to some polynomial number of steps and the agent may take many actions before electing to terminate the execution.

We reiterate that the goal is given by the pair of the environment's strategy and the referee. In a deterministic environment, there is only one set of reachable successful states, and hence, although there may be many ways of achieving the goal, in a sense there is only one aim for the user. Although most goals are not of this form, we can give at least one interesting example of such a goal.

Example 2.5 (Turing test). We recall Turing's famous test [149], which we can model in simplified form as follows. We consider two classes of "servers," computers and humans, which we denote as S_1 and S_2, containing agents that are assumed to report their respective class affiliations to the environment. We assume that in each round, the environment records the message "i" reported by the server as a member of S_i, and the environment stores the last message sent from the user in its internal state (i.e., so $\sigma^{(e)}$ is a pair, $(\sigma^{(u,e)}, i)$). If the user's last message to the environment is "i" where $S \in S_i$, then $R(\sigma^{(e)}) = 1$. Otherwise, $R(\sigma^{(e)}) = 0$.

To describe most interesting goals in our model, we need to consider richer kinds of environments, which we will introduce next.

Non-deterministic and probabilistic environment strategies

It is evident that, in our model as described thus far, a deterministic environment cannot even capture the goal achieved by the *printer driver* in the story described in Section 2.1. The difficulty is that for the printer driver, success in printing the various "patterns the user has in mind" should correspond to disjoint sets of states of the environment, whereas with a deterministic environment, the referee predicate specifies only one such set. We can capture the goal of printing and much more by instead considering a *class* of environments, which we capture with non-deterministic strategies:

Definition 2.6 (Non-deterministic strategies). A *non-deterministic strategy* is a set of strategies; an *actual strategy* is a member of this set.

For simplicity, we will generally assume that the environment's strategy is formally non-deterministic (since this is almost always the case), preferring to consider even deterministic environments as being given by a singleton set of strategies. Operationally, we will think of the environment as non-deterministically (i.e., adversarially) choosing an actual strategy from its non-deterministic strategy. The significance of this from the user's perspective is that the user's strategy needs to achieve the goal with every actual strategy that the environment could choose from its set of strategies.

The various actual strategies of the environment are direct analogues of the "input" in classical computation, whereas the user's strategies are analogues of the various functions one might try to compute. To continue this analogy, and enable the quantitative study of the user's strategies, we associate a size parameter with the environment:

Definition 2.7 (Size parameter). For a given non-deterministic environment strategy $\mathcal{E}$, the *size parameter* is a function $n : \mathcal{E} \to \mathbb{N}$ taking the environment's actual strategy $E \in \mathcal{E}$ to its size $n = n(E)$.

The size parameter is used to determine, for example, the running time of a program implementing the user's strategy. It is the generalization of the "input lengths" from classical computational complexity theory to our model.

The basic use of non-deterministic strategies is best illustrated by demonstrating how it captures our printing goal (i.e., the goal achieved by a printer driver):

Example 2.8 (Printing). The goal of printing G_{print} is given by a non-deterministic environment $\mathcal{E}$ such that for each string to be printed, $x \in \{0,1\}^*$, there corresponds an environment $E_x \in \mathcal{E}$ which on each round stores the last message sent by the server together with x in its state, and forwards that message together with x to the user. $R(\sigma^{(\mathsf{e})}) = 1$ if x is the server's last message, and R evaluates to 0 otherwise. The size parameter, $n(E_x)$, is the length of x.

The formalism of non-deterministic strategies can capture much more than simply specifying the "user's input." Although the environment's state space is countable, we expressly avoided specifying that the environment's actual strategy has a finite description; indeed, we permit this strategy to be given by an arbitrary function, and we permit the non-deterministic strategy to contain uncountably many actual strategies. In particular, if we define the environment's actual strategies so that the environment's state contains an index that is updated on each round, then since the environment never repeats states, this non-deterministic choice of actual strategy makes the infinitely many "non-deterministic choices" that may occur during execution. This use of non-determinism models changes to the environment by events that are independent of the interaction between the user and server; changes that only depend on the current state of the environment, and that are otherwise entirely arbitrary.

The reason we choose to formalize non-determinism as the environment making an "up-front" choice is that it will enable us to sanely introduce randomness to the model, by allowing the actual strategies to be randomized functions. Indeed, the advantage of this approach (as opposed to allowing the environment to make non-deterministic choices "on-line") is that it will allow us to talk sensibly about the probabilities of events concerning the execution of the actual strategy. We first formally specify the definition of probabilistic strategies:

Definition 2.9 (Probabilistic strategies). A *probabilistic strategy* of the ith party in a system is a random process P_i representing the party's actions in the current round: for each state of the ith party and each sequence of incoming messages at the beginning of the round P_i associates a distribution over the ith party's states and outgoing messages for the following round. That is, for each element of $\Omega^{(i)} \times \left(\times_{j \neq i} \Omega^{(j,i)} \right)$, P_i associates a distribution over $\Omega^{(i)} \times \left(\times_{j \neq i} \Omega^{(i,j)} \right)$.

As indicated by the definition, in general, we allow all parties to use probabilistic strategies; since probabilistic strategies can easily capture deterministic strategies by using a strategy P_i for which each outcome in its distribution's support occurs with probability 1, we will in fact formally assume that *all* parties in the interaction use a probabilistic strategy as we proceed. Thus, our formal definition of a finite goal of communication is as follows:

Definition 2.10 (Goals). A *finite goal of communication* is given by a pair, consisting of the environment's non-deterministic probabilistic strategy and a finite referee.

We remind the reader that the referee determines its verdict by examining the state of the environment, where the meaning of these states (in the sense discussed in Section 2.1) is determined by the environment's strategy. In particular, since the environment can maintain the entire history of the interaction as reported by the agents in its state, we can set up a goal of communication in which the referee computes an arbitrary function of these interpretations of the interaction together with the rest of the environment's state.

Once the environment's non-deterministic choice of an actual probabilistic strategy is fixed, the resulting system under consideration is a (stationary) discrete time Markov process with countable state space Ω, stopped when the user halts:[7]

Definition 2.11 (Executions). An *execution* of a system consisting of m probabilistic strategies $P_1, \ldots, P_m$ is an Ω-valued discrete time stochastic process $\{X_t\}_{t=1}^{\tau}$ such that $\tau \in \mathbb{N} \cup \{\infty\}$ is the random index of the first round in which the user halts and for each $i \in [m]$ and each $t < \tau$, $(X_{t+1}^{(i)}, (X_{t+1}^{(i,j)})_{j \neq i}) \leftarrow P_i(X_t^{(i)}, (X_t^{(j,i)})_{j \neq i})$ An execution *starting from global state* $\sigma_1 \in \Omega$ is defined similarly, except we fix X_1 to σ_1.

For a fixed system, we can thus speak freely of "the probability that the user achieves the goal" in an execution, since this is simply $\Pr[R(X_\tau^{(\mathbf{e})}) = 1]$ in familiar terminology.

2.2.3 Universal users

Now that we possess a formal model of a generic finite communication problem, we return to our original motivation, an investigation of the extent to

---

[7]The sequence of σ-algebras associated with each round is defined in the obvious way, and it is easy to verify that the "first time the user halts" is a stopping time due to our Markovian setup.

which communication can be made independent of the details of any particular protocol. To this end, we will begin to explicitly consider the role played by other entities in the interaction—entities which, in hopes of emphasizing the applications of our model to computer networks, we will refer to as "*servers.*" Roughly, we wish to design user protocols that achieve a fixed goal with an arbitrary member of a large *class* of servers; such a user is said to be "universal" for the class of servers, and in this way, the user protocol is able to communicate effectively in spite of variations in the server protocols. Presently, we turn to refining this notion of a desirable universal user protocol.

Our first refinement is motivated by our observation in Section 2.1 that in order to have any hope of universality, we must restrict our attention to goals that are "forgiving" of an initial failure of the user protocol to communicate adequately with the server. Since we would like to describe such goals without reference to a particular user protocol, the cleanest and simplest definition of such a forgiving goal is stated as a guarantee that no matter what state the execution has entered, a good user protocol can still communicate successfully—so any prior failed attempts at communication are then "forgiven" by the referee. (We will refine this definition to refer only to states of the execution that can be *feasibly* reached in Chapter 4, which will substantially broaden the applicability of our notions.) Such a user protocol that communicates successfully from any state that the execution could have entered could surely be said to be "robust," motivating the following definition:

Definition 2.12 (Robustly achieving goals). A pair of user strategy U and server strategy S are said to *robustly achieve the goal* $G = (\mathcal{E}, R)$ *with probability* p if for every $E \in \mathcal{E}$ and every state σ in which the user strategy is started from its initial state, the probability that the user achieves the goal in the execution of (E, U, S) started from σ is at least p.

Naturally, a goal that is robustly achieved by some pair of user and server turns out to be forgiving of initial failures by the user to communicate:

Proposition 2.13 (Robust achievement overcomes initial miscommunication). *Let* U' *be a user strategy that, except in an event of probability zero, begins executing according to user strategy* U_0 *from its initial state after some finite number of rounds. Let* S *be any server and* $G = (\mathcal{E}, R)$ *be a goal. Then if* (U_0, S) *robustly achieves the goal* G *with probability* p, *then so does* (U', S).

Proof Let $\tau_0 \in \mathbb{N} \cup \{\infty\}$ be the random index of the first round in which U' begins executing U_0 from its initial state. Recalling the definition of robust achievement, we know that U_0 achieves the goal in the execution (E, U_0, S) started from state σ_{τ_0} with probability p; that is, when U_0 halts, R is satisfied with probability p. Since this execution is identical to the suffix of the execution (E, U', S) starting from round τ_0, when U' halts, the distribution over the states of E is identical in both executions. Thus, U' achieves the goal with probability p as well. ■

With this refined notion of achieving goals in hand, we turn to providing a definition of a user protocol that operates with a large class of servers. Given that our attention is restricted to goals that may be robustly achieved, it is natural and desirable to ask for a user protocol that itself *robustly* achieves the goal; this way, we do without an assumption that we "know" that the environment (and server) start in some predetermined initial state. With this caveat in mind, the definition is natural.

Definition 2.14 (Universal users). We say that a user strategy U is $(\mathcal{S}, p)$-*universal for a goal* G if for every $S \in \mathcal{S}$, (U, S) robustly achieves G with probability p. If for every $S \in \mathcal{S}$ there is a negligible function $\epsilon : \mathbb{N} \to [0, 1]$ such that U is $(\mathcal{S}, 1 - \epsilon(n(E)))$-universal for G, then we simply say that U is $\mathcal{S}$-*universal for* G.

Although we are primarily interested in these robust universal users, we will find a few occasions where robust achievement is out of the question (or an open question) but we can show that a weaker kind of universal user exists, one that is sensitive to the initial state.

Definition 2.15 (Weakly universal user). Suppose that $\mathcal{S}^*$ is a set of pairs (S, σ) where S is a server strategy and σ is a global state. We then say that a user strategy U is *weakly* $(\mathcal{S}^*, p)$-*universal for a goal* $G = (\mathcal{E}, R)$ if for every $E \in \mathcal{E}$ and $(S, \sigma) \in \mathcal{S}^*$, (U, S) achieves G with probability p in the execution (E, U, S) started from global state σ.

Time-bounded user strategies

We now further refine our notion of a desirable user protocol by focusing on the model of computation implementing the protocols. We motivate these considerations by observing that *in practice,* we would only be interested in protocols that are efficiently computable, which we naturally associate with "polynomial time computable." Of course, to make sense of this notion, we rely on a given parameterization of the *size* of the environment, as described in Definition 2.7. Thus:

Definition 2.16 (Time-bounded user strategies). Fix a universal interactive Turing machine ϕ, and a non-deterministic environment strategy $\mathcal{E}$ with size parameter n. For a function $t : \mathbb{N} \to \mathbb{N}$, we say that a user strategy U is *time-t bounded* if there is a program on ϕ such that for every server strategy S and every state of $E \in \mathcal{E}$ in the execution with S and E, ϕ computes U until it halts and runs for no more than $t(n)$ steps. When U is time-t bounded for a polynomial t, we say that U is a *polynomial time protocol.*

From a *purely formal* perspective, there is nothing special about polynomial time, and thus we consider other classes of protocols explicitly in

Chapter 5, but surely the case of polynomial time protocols is the most intuitive and the one of greatest natural interest. Since fixing the class of algorithms will also lead to a simplification in the notation and presentation more generally, *henceforth we restrict our attention to polynomial time protocols.*

Once we have bounded the computational resources available to the user, it becomes interesting to consider the goal of solving computational problems (posed by the environment). Indeed, this is the goal considered in Section 1.4.2. We now show how this goal is formalized in the present terminology.

Example 2.17 (Computation). Fix a computational problem Π. The goal of solving Π, G_Π, is given by a non-deterministic environment $\mathcal{E}$ such that, for each instance x of Π, there corresponds an environment $E_x \in \mathcal{E}$ which on each round sends x to the user and stores the last message sent by the user together with x in its state. $R(\sigma^{(e)}) = 1$ if the user's last message is $\Pi(x)$.[8] The size parameter $n(E_x)$, is simply the length of x.

For a problem Π that can be solved in polynomial time, we remark that G_Π can be achieved robustly without the server's assistance. This stands in contrast to the goal of printing from Example 2.8, which inherently depends on the server's assistance.

2.2.4   Helpful servers

We close this section with a description of an important class of server strategies, one that is maximal in a sense that we will describe shortly. Recall that our aim was to study protocols for communication when the details of a protocol have not been fixed in advance, and that we captured such protocols in Definition 2.14: these protocols robustly achieve a fixed goal with an arbitrary member of some (large) class of servers. It is natural to consider, in conjunction with such a definition, the *largest possible* class of servers. In this case, one constraint on such servers that would immediately follow from the existence of a universal user is that some user strategy exists that robustly achieves the goal. We call such servers, which permit *some* user strategy to robustly achieve the goal, "helpful" servers.

Definition 2.18 (Helpful servers). We say that a server strategy S is *p-helpful* for a goal G if there exists a polynomial time user protocol U such that (U, S) robustly achieves the goal with probability p. We denote the class of p-helpful servers for a goal G by $\mathcal{S}_{G,p}$. If S is $1 - \epsilon(n(E))$-helpful for a goal G and some negligible function $\epsilon : \mathbb{N} \to [0,1]$, then we simply say that S is *helpful for G*, and we denote the class of such servers by $\mathcal{S}_G$.

---

[8]We take Π to be a promise function problem, so not every string x counts as an instance, but for those that do, we assume $\Pi(x)$ is a nonempty set. So, if no satisfactory pair (x,y) exists, then we assume that some special string $\perp$ indicating this is in $\Pi(x)$.

In particular, a polynomial time $(\mathcal{S}_{G,p}, p)$-universal protocol for G robustly achieves G with probability p with any server for which some (unknown) other polynomial time protocol robustly achieves G with probability p. This is rather like the notion of (asymptotic) bounded optimality used by Russell and Subramanian [127]: the protocol achieves G essentially as well as any other bounded protocol. We call the problem of achieving a goal with respect to the class of all helpful servers for the goal the basic "universal setting," and in Section 1.4.2, we asserted that a nontrivial goal (i.e., computation) can be achieved in the basic universal setting. In the present chapter, we will primarily examine generic goals in general settings. We will, however, give one result about the basic setting in this chapter and another one in Chapter 4, which motivate looking beyond it.

2.3   Sensing and universality

Not every goal can be reliably achieved. Consider the following goal:

Example 2.19 (Guessing coins). The environment's non-deterministic strategy is given by $\mathcal{E} = \{E_n\}$, where E_n tosses n fair coins and stores them, along with the user's last message in its state, and provides no other feedback. The referee declares success if the user's last message equals the coin tosses. Notice, since the coin tosses are independent of the user's strategy, no user strategy succeeds in E_n with probability greater than 2^{-n}.

Of course, goals such as the one described in Example 2.19 are immediately ruled out if we restrict our attention to goals with *helpful* servers. One might even hope that we could achieve any goal whenever a helpful server exists for that goal. Unfortunately, it turns out that the situation is more severe in some subtle ways for a user who wishes to communicate with the members of a broad class $\mathcal{S}$: goals which the user could hope to achieve "in principle" with the aid of a trusted third party (since the server is helpful) may turn out to be unattainable "in practice" due to the user misunderstanding the server.

We can observe an example of this by recalling our informal example when Alice and Bob speak different natural languages and are restricted to using the binary channel for communication. In this example, Alice spoke one of two languages that were identical except that the words for "left" and "right," "clockwise" and "counter-clockwise," etc. were switched. Since Alice and Bob are restricted to using the binary channel, unless they possess some prior shared knowledge of some physical objects or they are given some other means to fix an orientation, Bob has no way of distinguishing the two languages. In particular, if Bob's goal is to determine whether Alice has in mind "left" or "right," this is an example of a goal which cannot be achieved reliably with a collection of helpful Alices. For the sake of completeness, we also give an abstract, formal example that some readers may find more compelling:

Example 2.20 (Identifying a vertex). Fix a graph with a nontrivial automorphism π and vertex set V. In the environment's non-deterministic strategy $\mathcal{E} = \{E_v\}_{v \in V}$, on each round, E_v sends v to the server, and stores v with the user's last message in its state. The referee declares success if the user's last message is "v."

Suppose that the class of helpful servers contains S_ι and S_π, which are identical, except that S_π applies π to the environment's message (the corresponding user needs only to apply π^{-1} to its last message). Since S_ι with $E_{\pi(v)}$ is indistinguishable from S_π with E_v, regardless of whether the user sends v or $\pi(v)$, the user is wrong with one pair, and hence this is an example of a goal which cannot be achieved reliably with a collection of helpful servers.

Example 2.20 is not so strange if we keep in mind that the channel connecting the server with the environment may model an entirely different kind of communications channel from the channel connecting the user and the server. For example, it may model some communication internal to the server or it may be the encoding of some kind of video input to the server, whereas the user-server channel may be across the internet. Since $\pi(v)$ is just as good a representation of the vertex v as "the identity," there is no reason to expect that the server should use one or the other, and these kinds of issues fall entirely within our intended scope.

We claim that the difficulty in Examples 2.19 and 2.20 is that the environment and server provide the user with no means to tell whether or not communication is succeeding. In the remainder of this section, we introduce "sensing functions" that capture such "means to tell whether or not communication is succeeding," and prove that (at least for finite goals) the feedback from sensing is precisely what is required for the construction of universal protocols.

2.3.1   Sensing: safety and viability

Roughly, a sensing function for a goal is some locally computable function that allows the user to effectively guess the referee's verdict. Intuitively, a "locally computable function" is one that the user can compute from the "user's view" of the execution: a history of its states and messages exchanged with other parties in the execution. This is not quite sufficient for many nontrivial examples of sensing, though, because whenever sensing relies on a probabilistic test, we require that the user's messages were drawn from an appropriate distribution; the soundness of the test may not hold if the distribution is skewed. A simple, natural, and sufficient means to address this issue is to provide the sensing function with the outcomes of the (fair) coin tosses used during the execution of the user protocol. We will elect not to provide the sensing function with the user's states in the execution since these may be meaningless without a description of the user protocol (and when a user protocol is fixed, the sensing function can just as well recover the states from the coins and messages). Thus, we have the following definition of the user's view.

Definition 2.21 (User's view). The *user's view* of an execution is given by the list of the user's incoming and outgoing messages and coin tosses on each round of the execution.

Now, a sensing function takes the user's view of the execution to a Boolean verdict, which we take as a prediction of the referee's verdict. A good sensing function should satisfy two complementary properties that we call "safety" and "viability." Roughly, a safe sensing function guesses conservatively— when it predicts that the referee is satisfied, then the referee is actually satisfied with high probability. A viable sensing function, on the other hand, is effectively nontrivial, in the sense that some feasible user strategy can lead the sensing function to guess that the referee is satisfied. Note that a sensing function must satisfy both safety and viability to be meaningful: a sensing function that predicts that the referee is never satisfied is trivially safe but unviable, whereas a sensing function that predicts that the referee is always satisfied is trivially viable but unsafe. We need both properties for the sensing function to be of any use.

Definition 2.22 (Sensing, safety, and viability). A *sensing function* is a Boolean function of the user's view of the execution.

- We say that the sensing function is *p-safe* for a goal $G = (\mathcal{E}, R)$ with a server S if for any $t \in \mathbb{N}$, user strategy (as a probabilistic strategy in which the underlying sample space is given by coin tosses), and $E \in \mathcal{E}$, the probability that $R(X_t) = 1$ conditioned on the sensing function outputting 1 when run on the user's view up to round t is at least p. If there exists some negligible function $\epsilon : \mathbb{N} \to [0, 1]$ such that the sensing function is $1 - \epsilon(n(E))$-safe for G with S, then we say that the sensing function is *safe* for G with S.

- We say that the sensing function is (t, p)-*viable* for a goal G with a server S if there exists a user strategy U_S such that with probability at least p, when started from any state of the server and environment, U_S runs for t steps in expectation and the sensing function outputs 1 on the user's view of the execution (E, U_S, S). If there exists some negligible function $\mu : \mathbb{N} \to [0, 1]$ such that the sensing function is $(t, 1 - \mu(n(E)))$-viable for G with S, then we say that the sensing function is t-viable for G with S.

(When G or S is understood from context, we may drop the mention of them.)

To illustrate sensing, we describe a sensing function for our printing goal.

Example 2.23 (Sensing for printing). Recall the definition of our printing goal G_{print} given in Example 2.8: the environment chooses a string x that it sends to the user, along with the last message printed by the server on each round, and the referee is satisfied whenever these strings are the same. Thus, since both of these strings are present in the user's view, the function that checks that they are equal is 1-safe with *every* server strategy. Furthermore, if the server S is p-helpful for G_{print} with a user protocol running in time t, then this sensing function is (t, p)-viable for G_{print} and S.

A nontrivial example of sensing is given by a sensing function for the goal of solving problems in PSPACE, considered in Section 1.4.2. It turns out that this construction, when combined with Theorem 2.35 (a strengthened variant of Theorem 2.25 below), immediately yields Theorem 1.4, the "positive" claim from Section 1.4.2.

Example 2.24 (Sensing for computation). Recall the goal of solving a computational problem Π, described in Example 2.17. A nontrivial safe sensing function computable in polynomial time can be constructed for $\Pi \in$ PSPACE. Let (P_Π, V_Π) be a public-coin interactive proof system with perfect completeness, soundness error ϵ, and a binary prover (as essentially given by Shamir [103, 134]) for the set of pairs $(x, \Pi(x))$, which is clearly in PSPACE whenever Π is. Then V simulates V_Π by providing it the user's coin tosses from each round,[9] and providing it a specially marked subsequence of the messages from the user to the environment as the messages from the prover; V only outputs 1 if the user's last message is y such that in the preceding rounds, V_Π would accept on input (x, y). Since V_Π is a public-coin proof system with soundness error ϵ, V is $(1 - \epsilon)$-safe for G_Π and all server strategies.

If Π is additionally PSPACE-complete then it turns out that V is also $(1 - \mu'_S, t_S)$-viable for G_Π with any $1 - \mu_S$-helpful server for some polynomial t_S and negligible functions μ_S and μ'_S. To see this, observe that given the polynomial time user U_0 such that (U_0, S) achieves G_Π with probability $1 - \mu_S$, we can construct a user strategy U^* that first uses U_0 with S to obtain $\Pi(x)$, subsequently stores the entire history of coin tosses, and uses this history together with $(x, \Pi(x))$ to compute the polynomial time reduction from the optimal prover's next message to an instance of Π, which it solves by again using U_0 with S. Since (P_Π, V_Π) has perfect completeness, the optimal prover's messages satisfy V_Π, and hence V. Since U^* invokes U_0 at most a polynomial number of times and μ_S is negligible, the simulation satisfies V with probability $1 - \mu'_S$ for some other negligible function μ'_S. Finally, since U^* also runs in some polynomial time t_S with S, V is $(t_S, 1 - \mu'_S)$-viable for G with S as claimed.

Both of these examples of sensing functions have the desirable property that they are viable with all servers that are helpful for their respective goals. We will see in the next section that this means that they yield universal users

---

[9]V considers V_Π to reject if insufficiently many coins are provided on any round.

for the basic universal setting, i.e., they achieve the goal in polynomial time whenever it is possible for some polynomial time user to do so.

2.3.2   Sensing is necessary and sufficient for finite goals

We now show that the feedback from a suitable sensing function is precisely what is required to successfully communicate with a broad class of servers. We prove the following theorem:

Theorem 2.25 (Sensing is equivalent to universality). *Let any goal G and any class of servers $\mathcal{S}$ be given along with polynomials $t_S : \mathbb{N} \to \mathbb{N}$ for every $S \in \mathcal{S}$. Then there exists a sensing function that is safe and $O(t_S)$-viable for G with every $S \in \mathcal{S}$ if and only if there is an expected $O(t_S)$-time bounded $\mathcal{S}$-universal user for G.*

More precisely, we prove Theorem 2.25 in two parts. We show first that given a universal user for a class of servers, we can construct a sensing function with essentially no loss in parameters, so in this sense, if it is possible to communicate with the class of servers, then sensing is (at least implicitly) available with that class of servers. We then show how to construct a universal user for the class of servers given a sensing function for that class of servers. Actually, the proof of Proposition 2.26 (and to a lesser extent, Proposition 2.27 below) is essentially immediate given the observation that *sensing functions are precisely the functions that tell a universal user when to halt.* Since this turns out to be a useful observation in its own right, we include it in the conclusion of the first proposition.

Proposition 2.26 (Sensing is necessary for universality). *Let U be a universal user strategy for a goal G and a class of servers $\mathcal{S}$ be given along with functions $t_S : \mathbb{N} \to \mathbb{N}$, and $\mu_S, \epsilon_S : \mathbb{N} \to [0,1]$ for every $S \in \mathcal{S}$ such that in the execution (E, U, S) U halts with probability $1 - \epsilon_S(n)$, and conditioned on it halting, runs in $t_S(n)$ steps in expectation and with probability $1 - \mu_S(n)$ achieves the goal. Then the function V of the user's view that outputs 1 iff the user sent the same messages as U on each round and on the final round U would halt, is a sensing function that is $1 - \mu_S$-safe for G with respect to every $S \in \mathcal{S}$, and $(t_S, 1 - \epsilon_S)$-viable for G with respect to every $S \in \mathcal{S}$. Furthermore, V is computable in time t_S whenever U runs in time t_S.*

Proof   Given a universal user strategy U for a goal G and class of servers $\mathcal{S}$ that halts with probability $1 - \epsilon_S$ and conditioned on halting, achieves G with probability $1 - \mu_S$, let V be the function described in the statement of the proposition. Notice that V is computable in time $t_S(n)$ given that U runs in time $t_S(n)$.

Let any $E \in \mathcal{E}$ and $S \in \mathcal{S}$ be given, and consider the execution (E, U, S). Observe that when U halts, by construction V outputs 1, which occurs with probability $1 - \epsilon_S(n)$ by assumption, and U runs for $t_S(n)$ steps in expectation by assumption. Therefore, V is $(t_S(n), 1 - \epsilon_S(n))$-viable for G with respect to every $S \in \mathcal{S}$. Similarly, consider any $E \in \mathcal{E}$, $S \in \mathcal{S}$, and user strategy U^*, and suppose that V outputs 1 in some round t of the execution (E, U^*, S). If (U^*, S) failed to achieve the goal in round t with probability greater than μ_S, notice that since U would have produced the same interaction as U^* on the corresponding views, in particular, there would exist a set of coin tosses and messages occurring with probability greater than μ_S on which (U, S) would also have failed to achieve the goal. Therefore (U^*, S) can only fail with probability μ_S when V outputs 1, i.e., V is $1 - \mu_S$-safe for G with every $S \in \mathcal{S}$. ∎

Proposition 2.27 (sensing is sufficient for universality). *For a class of servers $\mathcal{S}$, let functions $t_S : \mathbb{N} \to \mathbb{N}$, $\epsilon_S : \mathbb{N} \to [0, 1/3]$, and $\mu_S : \mathbb{N} \to [0, 1]$ for each $S \in \mathcal{S}$, and a goal G be given, and suppose there exists a sensing function V for G that is $1 - \mu_S(n)$-safe with every $S \in \mathcal{S}$, $(t_S(n), 1 - \epsilon_S(n))$-viable with every $S \in \mathcal{S}$, and expected $t_S(n)$-time computable with every $S \in \mathcal{S}$. Then there is an expected $O(t_S(n))$-time bounded $(\mathcal{S}, 1 - O(t_S(n) \cdot \mu_S(n)))$-universal protocol for G.*

Proof Our argument borrows heavily from a classic result due to Levin [97].

Construction. Given a sensing function V, we enumerate protocols in stages, where in stage i we enumerate protocols of length up to $i - 2 \log i$: on each protocol of length ℓ, we spend up to $t = \frac{2^i}{\ell^2 2^\ell}$ steps simulating the protocol until it halts, and then running V on the resulting view. When V outputs 1, we halt.

Analysis. When executing with a server $S \in \mathcal{S}$, since V is given to be $(t_S(n), 1 - \epsilon_S(n))$-viable for G with S, there is some expected t_S-time bounded user strategy U_S of length ℓ_S that, for any state of the execution, satisfies V with probability $1 - \epsilon_S(n) \geq 2/3$. Since V is furthermore assumed to be expected $t_S(n)$-time computable, when $t > 32 t_S(n)$ (in stage i^*), we run U_S until it halts in the first $16 t_S(n)$ steps with probability at least $15/16$ and then see V output 1 in the next $16 t_S(n)$ steps with probability at least $\frac{2}{3} - \frac{1}{16}$. Thus, we run U_S r additional times with probability at most $\left(\frac{11}{24}\right)^r$.

Notice that if we run r additional stages, we spend an additional

$$\sum_{i=i^*}^{i^*+r} \sum_{\ell \leq i - 2 \log i} 2^\ell \frac{2^i}{\ell^2 2^\ell} \leq \sum_{\ell \leq \ell_s + r} \sum_{i=i^*}^{i^*+r} \frac{2^i}{\ell^2} \leq O(2^{i^*+r})$$

steps, which occurs with probability at most $\left(\frac{11}{24}\right)^r$. Thus, the overall expected running time is at most $O(\sum_{r=1}^{\infty} 2^{i^*} 2^r (11/24)^r) = O(2^{i^*})$ where $2^{i^*} = 2^{\ell_s + 2 \log \ell_s + 1} t_S(n)$, so this is $O(t_S(n))$.

By the assumed safety of V, each time we run V, it outputs 1 when the referee is not satisfied with probability at most $\mu_S(n)$. By a union bound, since we run V at most $O(t_S(n))$ times in expectation, this occurs with probability at most $O(t_S(n)\mu_S(n))$. Since, from any state of the execution, we halt with probability 1 and never halt unless V outputs 1, we only fail to achieve the goal when V outputs 1 and the referee is unsatisfied. Thus, since $S \in \mathcal{S}$ and the starting state was arbitrary, our protocol robustly achieves the goal with every $S \in \mathcal{S}$ with probability $1 - O(t_S(n) \cdot \mu_S(n))$, as needed. ∎

Thus, the search for universal user protocols for a finite goal can be cast as the search for safe and viable sensing functions for that goal. In many cases, the problem of constructing sensing functions is either simpler and more natural or can be addressed with existing techniques in a relatively straightforward way, as demonstrated by Examples 2.23 and 2.24, respectively. In the basic universal setting, we will see how this characterization can also be used to demonstrate limitations on universal users.

2.3.3 Extensions and variants of sensing: alternative constructions

In a sense, Theorem 2.25, on the equivalence of sensing functions and universal users in finite goals, is the central result of the present chapter. The notions of "sensing function" and "universal user" employed in that result, while natural enough and perhaps the simplest definitions, are surely not the *only* reasonable definitions one might state. In the present section, we will explore some main variants of these definitions that turn out to be useful in the construction of universal users in some situations. In particular, we will first consider some useful ways in which the kind of sensing functions required by Proposition 2.27 can be weakened while still obtaining the same conclusion—briefly, we can design sensing for a related goal featuring any number of "private outputs" and we can assume that the source code of the user protocol is given as input to the sensing function. We will then consider stronger variants of the definitions of sensing and universal users featuring "controllable safety," that is, where the safety of the sensing function and correspondingly, the probability that the universal user achieves the goal can be efficiently controlled to be bounded by some a priori known quantity, independent of the server. Such control over the error can be obtained in many natural situations, notably when the algorithm employed by the sensing function permits its success probability to be amplified by standard techniques, and this variant in particular will allow us to easily obtain the results claimed in Section 1.4.2.

Using some relaxed sensing functions

We first discuss some ways in which Proposition 2.27 can be strengthened, constructing a universal user from a relaxed notion of sensing that will be convenient to use in Chapter 3 when we provide more examples of universal users for a variety of goals. Essentially, in Corollary 2.30 below, we will observe that the technique used to prove Proposition 2.27 is strong enough to obtain a universal user even when the sensing function requires "private outputs" that are taken to be ignored by the environment, and even when the sensing function depends on the code of the user strategy.

We begin by describing "private outputs" in more detail. As motivation, recall that, as we noticed in the construction of our sensing function for computation (in Example 2.24), it was useful for the user to send some messages to the environment that did not directly help achieve the goal. It turns out to be convenient in the design of sensing functions generally to further assume that the user's messages to the environment and the environment's states are structured as a tuple, in which some components of the user's current message are only stored in special components of the environment's state for a single round and then discarded. We will refer to these components as the user's *private outputs*, since the states of the execution are otherwise unaffected by these parts of the message. Formally:

Definition 2.28 (Private outputs). Suppose that the states of the environment and messages of the user are products of $k + 1$ components, i.e., of the form $\Omega_0^{(e)} \times \Omega_1^{(e)} \times \cdots \times \Omega_k^{(e)}$ and $\Omega_0^{(u,e)} \times \Omega_1^{(u,e)} \times \cdots \times \Omega_k^{(u,e)}$ respectively, such that every actual strategy E of the environment is given by $k + 1$ independent functions $E_0, \ldots, E_k$ such that components $1, \ldots, k$ of E only depend on the respective components of the user message, and component 0 is independent of these components of the user message. Then we say that components $1, \ldots, k$ of the user's message are *private outputs*.

In general, we allow the private outputs to affect the state of the environment for a single round, and thus influence the referee. In the design of sensing functions, however, it will be useful to assume the existence of additional private outputs that are not only discarded, but moreover also known to be ignored by the referee. We will show how to handle this assumption in Corollary 2.30, below.

Our second relaxation is to consider sensing functions that are assumed to have access to the program for the user strategy in addition to the user's view. We refer to such sensing functions as *grey-box* sensing functions (and, when we wish to make the distinction clear, we will refer to the sensing functions of Definition 2.22 as *black-box* sensing functions). Except for this additional input, the following definition is essentially identical to Definition 2.22.

Definition 2.29 (Grey-box sensing). Fix a reference universal interactive Turing machine ϕ. A *grey-box sensing function* is a Boolean function of a program U for ϕ and the user's view of an execution in which the user employs U as its strategy.

- We say that the grey-box sensing function is *p-safe* for a goal $G = (\mathcal{E}, R)$ with a server S if for any round $t \in \mathbb{N}$, program U for ϕ, and $E \in \mathcal{E}$, whenever the sensing function outputs 1 in an execution with S in round t, the referee also outputs 1 in round t with probability at least p. If there exists some negligible function $\epsilon : \mathbb{N} \to [0,1]$ such that the grey-box sensing function is $1 - \epsilon(n(E))$-safe for G with S, then we say that the grey-box sensing function is *safe* for G with S.

- We say that the grey-box sensing function is (t, p)-*viable* for a goal G with a server S if there exists a program U_S for ϕ such that with probability at least p, when started from any state of the server and environment, U_S runs for at most t steps in expectation and the grey-box sensing function outputs 1 on U_S and the user's view of the execution (E, U_S, S). If there exists some negligible function $\mu : \mathbb{N} \to [0,1]$ such that the grey-box sensing function is $(t, 1 - \mu(n(E)))$-viable for G with S, then we say that the grey-box sensing function is t-viable for G with S.

It is easy to see that a grey-box version of a black-box sensing function can be obtained by merely ignoring the code of the user strategy. Furthermore, grey-box sensing functions can equivalently be thought of as a (uniform) family of sensing functions, one for each user strategy.

We now turn to the statement and proof of Corollary 2.30.

Corollary 2.30 (Grey-box sensing functions with private outputs are sufficient for universality). *Let $G = (\mathcal{E}, R)$ be a finite goal, and let G' be a version of G with any number of additional private outputs that are ignored by the referee. For a class of servers $\mathcal{S}$, let functions $t_S : \mathbb{N} \to \mathbb{N}$, $\epsilon_S : \mathbb{N} \to [0, 1/3]$, and $\mu_S : \mathbb{N} \to [0,1]$ for each $S \in \mathcal{S}$ be given, and suppose there exists a grey-box sensing function V for G', that uses an efficient reference universal interactive Turing machine ϕ, is $1 - \mu_S(n)$-safe with every $S \in \mathcal{S}$, $(t_S(n), 1 - \epsilon_S(n))$-viable with every $S \in \mathcal{S}$, and expected $t_S(n)$-time computable with every $S \in \mathcal{S}$. Then there is an expected $O(t_S(n))$-time bounded $(\mathcal{S}, 1 - O(t_S(n) \cdot \mu_S(n)))$-universal protocol for G.*

Proof Consider the following modification of the construction used in the proof of Proposition 2.27:

Given a grey-box sensing function V, we enumerate protocols on ϕ in stages, where in stage i we enumerate protocols of length up to $i - 2 \log i$: on each protocol of length ℓ, we spend up to $t = \frac{2^i}{\ell^2 2^\ell}$ steps simulating the protocol until it halts, only forwarding to the environment the components of the user's messages that exist in G. If the current protocol halts within t steps, we then run V on the current protocol and resulting simulated view, including the extra components of the user's messages in G'. When V outputs 1, we halt.

Since the referee in G' is assumed to ignore the components of the user's message not present in G, the referee in G is satisfied on the projection of an execution (E, U, S) of G' iff the referee in G' would also be satisfied with the corresponding execution. Thus, the safety and viability of V with G' are sufficient for the analysis w.r.t. G, and the rest of the proof is identical to that of Proposition 2.27. ∎

Thus, Corollary 2.30 places a handful of additional tools at our disposal for the design of universal users. We will see how these ease matters in Chapter 3. Of course, we stress that as a consequence of Proposition 2.26, strictly speaking we never *needed* either the extra power of grey-box sensing or additional private outputs for sensing—and in fact, these features actually provide no extra power. These features are merely a matter of convenience.

Controlling the probability of errors

We now turn to consider stronger variants of both sensing and universal users that will turn out to be equivalent, yielding an incomparable variant of Theorem 2.25 that will be extremely useful when it is available to us. It will not always be available due to the following somewhat obvious yet counterintuitive point about goals (when viewed as a generalization of computational problems): *one cannot always amplify correctness.*

Example 2.31 (Safety cannot always be amplified). Consider the following goal: on each round, the environment flips a (private) fair coin to decide whether or not the referee is satisfied. If the referee is satisfied, the environment sends '1' to the user; otherwise, the environment sends '0' to the user with probability $1 - \epsilon$ and '1' with probability ϵ. The function that reports this message from the environment is a $\frac{1}{1+\epsilon}$-safe sensing function for this goal (and $(O(1), 1)$-viable). It is not hard to see that no sensing function (and no universal user) can do better since the environment's choice of "false positives" versus "positives" is independent of the user.

Still, in many situations, particularly situations of natural interest, sensing is possible by means of probabilistic tests where the correctness of the test can be amplified by the usual means, e.g., repeating the test many times and taking a majority vote. We capture such sensing functions with the following definition.

Definition 2.32 (Sensing with controllable safety). We say that a sensing function has *controllable safety* for a goal G with a server S if it takes a rational number (in binary) as an additional input, and on input ϵ it is $(1 - \epsilon)$-safe for G with S. We will abuse notation and let $|\epsilon|$ denote the *length* (in binary) of this input.

When appropriate, we will describe the running time of the sensing function explicitly, but generally we will consider it "efficient" if it runs in time polynomial in the length of ϵ in bits, as well as the size parameter $n(E)$.

When such sensing functions are available, we can correct for one of the main deficiencies of the universal users constructed by Proposition 2.27, the dependence on the (unknown) server in their success probabilities. In fact, the existence of such stronger sensing functions turns out to be (again) equivalent to the design of stronger universal user protocols, where the probability of failure can likewise be controlled to fall below any desired tolerance level, as is the case for probabilistic polynomial time algorithms. Before we prove this, we give a formal definition of such protocols, and a natural example of a class of algorithms captured by them.

Definition 2.33 (Universal users with controllable error). We say that a user strategy is $\mathcal{S}$-*universal with controllable error for a goal* G if for every $S \in \mathcal{S}$ and rational $\epsilon > 0$, U takes as auxiliary input ϵ given in binary, and $(U(\epsilon), S)$ robustly achieves G with probability $1 - \epsilon$.

Again, we will explicitly comment on the running time of these universal users when appropriate, but we expect "efficiency" to mean a running time that is polynomial with respect to the length of ϵ in bits and the size parameter.

We briefly digress to show how we can capture Valiant's PAC-learning model [152] as a goal for communication in which the class of servers corresponds to the class of concepts. The usual (ϵ, δ) definition of a PAC-learning algorithm will correspond to a user with controllable error for this goal, and we will furthermore note that in this setting, sensing with controllable safety is always available.

Example 2.34 (PAC-learning). We can define the goal of (improper, distribution-free) PAC-learning by a class of environments $\mathcal{E} = \{E_{D,n,\epsilon}\}$, parameterized by $n \in \mathbb{N}$, $\epsilon \in \mathbb{Q}$, and a distribution D over $\{0,1\}^n$, and a referee that, in $E_{D,n,\epsilon}$ interprets the messages from the user and server as representations of circuits computing functions $C_U, C_S : \{0,1\}^n \to \{0,1\}$, and is satisfied iff $\Pr_{x \in D}[C_U(x) = C_S(x)] \geq 1 - \epsilon$. On each round, $E_{D,n,\epsilon}$ sends x sampled from D to both the user and the server, and sends ϵ to the user.

Naturally, a concept class $\mathcal{C}$ corresponds to a class of servers $\mathcal{S}(\mathcal{C})$ in the following way: for each function $C \in \mathcal{C}$, there is a server S_C in $\mathcal{S}(\mathcal{C})$ that responds to a message $x \in \{0,1\}^n$ from the environment by sending $C(x)$ to the user, and sending a circuit computing C on $\{0,1\}^n$ to the environment.

Thus, a user with controllable error who achieves this goal with every server in $\mathcal{S}(\mathcal{C})$ in $m + 1$ rounds outputs a circuit after receiving m samples such that the circuit is $1 - \epsilon$ close to $C \in \mathcal{C}$ on inputs of length n under the distribution D with probability at least $1 - \delta$, for every n, ϵ, and D specified by the environment and every input to the user δ, as needed for PAC-learning (with sample complexity m). In particular, if the user runs in time polynomial in n, $1/\epsilon$, and $\log 1/\delta$, then we capture precisely the usual notion of efficient PAC-learning.

Moreover, in this setting, we have a generic sensing function with controllable safety: $V(\delta)$ outputs 1 iff the circuit proposed by the user disagrees with at most $\epsilon m - \sqrt{\frac{m}{2} \log \frac{1}{\delta}}$ of the m samples. Then, Hoeffding's inequality tells us that if V accepts, then with probability at least $1 - \delta$, the proposed circuit agrees with C with probability at least $1 - \epsilon$ under D. It should be immediately clear that the sensing function is viable with any class of servers corresponding to a PAC-learnable concept class.

We are now ready to prove a variant of Theorem 2.25, showing an equivalence of sensing functions and universal users in this alternative, "controllable error" setting:

Theorem 2.35 (Sensing functions with controllable safety are equivalent to universal users with controllable error). *Let any goal G and any class of servers $\mathcal{S}$ be given, along with a polynomial $t_S : \mathbb{N} \times \mathbb{N} \to \mathbb{N}$ and function $\delta_S : \mathbb{N} \times \mathbb{Q} \to [0, 1/3]$ for every $S \in \mathcal{S}$. Then there exists a sensing function with controllable safety, running in expected time $\tilde{O}(t_S(n, |\epsilon|))$, and $(\tilde{O}(t_S(n, |\epsilon|)), 1 - \delta_S(n, \epsilon))$-viable for G with every $S \in \mathcal{S}$ iff there is an expected $\tilde{O}(t_S(n, |\epsilon|))$-time bounded $\mathcal{S}$-universal user with controllable error for G. Furthermore, given a universal user with controllable error, the sensing function we obtain indicates whether or not the user would halt on a given view with input ϵ.*

Proof The reverse direction is essentially immediate: for each fixed ϵ, we have a $(\mathcal{S}, 1 - \epsilon)$-universal user and we can apply Proposition 2.26 to find that the function described in the furthermore claim is a sensing function with controllable safety. Thus, all that remains to show is that we can obtain a universal user with controllable error from a sensing function with controllable safety. To do so, we will need to revisit the construction of a universal user from Proposition 2.27 in some detail.

Construction. We again enumerate protocols in stages $i = 1, 2, \ldots$, where in each ith stage we enumerate protocols of length up to $i - 2 \log i$. On each protocol of length ℓ, we spend up to $t = \frac{2^i}{\ell^2 2^\ell}$ steps running the protocol until it halts and then (if the protocol halted) running our sensing function with safety parameter $\varepsilon = \epsilon 2^{-(i+2\ell+1)}$. If the sensing function accepts, then we halt, and otherwise we continue.

Analysis. Fix any $S \in \mathcal{S}$. Since the sensing function is $(\tilde{O}(t_S(n, |\varepsilon|)), 1 - \delta_S(n, |\varepsilon|))$-viable, some expected $\tilde{O}(t_S(n, |\varepsilon|))$-time bounded user strategy U_S of length ℓ_S satisfies V on any safety parameter ε with probability $1 - \delta_S \geq 2/3$ from any state of the execution. Likewise, V is $\tilde{O}(t_S(n, |\varepsilon|))$-time computable, and so for some constants C, k, and C', if

$$t = \frac{2^i}{\ell_S^2 2^{\ell_S}} > C t_S(n, |\varepsilon|) \log^k t_S(n, |\varepsilon|) \geq C' t_S(n, |\epsilon| + i) \log^k t_S(n, |\epsilon| + i)$$

then U_S runs to completion and V outputs 1 with probability at least $13/24$. Observe that since t_S is a polynomial, this inequality is satisfied for some sufficiently large value of i, i^*. In particular, if t_S has maximum degree D in its second argument,

$$i^* \geq \log(C't_S(n, |\epsilon|) \log^k t_S(n, |\epsilon|)) + (D+1) \log \log(C't_S(n, |\epsilon|) \log^k t_S(n, |\epsilon|))$$

suffices, and when we run r additional stages, we spend $O(2^{i^*+r})$ steps total, which occurs with probability at most $(11/24)^r$. Therefore, we find that the total expected running time of our universal user is at most

$$O\left(\sum_{r=1}^{\infty} 2^{i^*} 2^r (11/24)^r\right) = O(2^{i^*}).$$

Now, we see that using the minimum value for i^*, the expected running time is

$$O(t_S(n, |\epsilon|) \log^{D+k+1} t_S(n, |\epsilon|)) = \tilde{O}(t_S(n, |\epsilon|))$$

as claimed.

Now, note that in phase i, by our controlled safety guarantee, for each protocol of length ℓ, we only risk halting without success with probability $\epsilon 2^{-(i+2\ell+1)}$. Thus, by a union bound, our total probability of halting without success is given by

$$\sum_{i=1}^{\infty} \sum_{\ell \leq i-2\log i} 2^{\ell} \epsilon 2^{-(i+2\ell+1)} \leq \epsilon \sum_{i=1}^{\infty} 2^{-i} \sum_{\ell=1}^{\infty} 2^{-\ell} = \epsilon$$

as needed for a universal user with controllable error. ∎

So, for example, since we noted in Example 2.34 that there is a sensing function that is safe and viable for every class of servers corresponding to a PAC-learnable concept class, the universal learning algorithm of Goldreich and Ron [72] can be obtained (up to logarithmic factors) as a corollary of Theorem 2.35.

Before we move on, we note that just as the argument used in Proposition 2.27 was strong enough to provide the same quality of universal user from a grey-box sensing function which required additional private outputs (Corollary 2.30), the argument in Theorem 2.35 also yields a universal user with controllable error from a grey-box sensing function which requires additional private outputs, so long as it also features controllable safety.

Corollary 2.36 (Grey-box sensing functions with private outputs and controllable safety are sufficient for universal users with controllable error). *Let G be a finite goal and let G' be a version of G with any number of additional private outputs that are ignored by the referee. For a class of servers $\mathcal{S}$, let functions $t_S : \mathbb{N} \times \mathbb{N} \to \mathbb{N}$ and $\delta_S : \mathbb{N} \times \mathbb{Q} \to [0, 1/3]$ for each $S \in \mathcal{S}$ be given and suppose there exists a grey-box sensing function V for G' with controllable error, that uses an efficient reference universal interactive Turing machine ϕ,* *is $(t_S(n, |\epsilon|), 1 - \delta_S(n, \epsilon))$-viable with every $S \in \mathcal{S}$, and expected $t_S(n, |\epsilon|)$-time computable with every $S \in \mathcal{S}$. Then there is an expected $\tilde{O}(t_S(n, |\epsilon|))$-time bounded $\mathcal{S}$-universal protocol for G with controllable error.*

The proof is no more than a concatenation of the arguments of Corollary 2.30 and Theorem 2.35.

2.3.4 Safety requirements in the basic universal setting

We now present one of two limitation results that motivate considering classes of servers other than the class of all helpful servers for a goal (the other result is postponed until Chapter 4). We show that whenever a sensing function is safe with all servers that are helpful for a given goal (i.e., in the basic universal setting) then the sensing function is actually safe with *all* server strategies, even malicious and unhelpful ones. This explains why our only examples of sensing functions that are safe (and viable) for all helpful servers for a goal (e.g., given in Examples 2.23 and 2.24 so far; more examples are given in Chapter 3) are actually safe with all servers.

In particular, this result implies that the sensing functions we obtain from Proposition 2.26 for universal users in the basic universal setting are also actually safe with all servers. It is easiest to see why we consider this to be a limitation of the basic universal setting by considering computational goals: the result says that computational goals with universal users can only exist for problems with interactive proof systems. Thus, Theorem 1.5 from Section 1.4.2, stating that we can only hope to give universal users for computational goals corresponding to problems in PSPACE, follows from the special case of this result for computational goals. The present result says, furthermore, that any goal that can be achieved in the basic universal setting for finite executions has a cryptographic-strength test of its achievement. Therefore, when a goal permits no such test, we must either leave the basic universal setting and consider a smaller class of servers, or else we must switch to the infinite executions setting and find a means to achieve the goal without sensing (we prove an analogous theorem for sensing in infinite executions in Chapter 6).

Theorem 2.37 (Safety with all helpful servers implies safety with all servers). *Let G be a goal and suppose that V is a sensing function that is p-safe for G with respect to every $S \in \mathcal{S}_{G,p'}$ for some nonempty $\mathcal{S}_{G,p'}$. Then V is also p-safe for G with respect to every server strategy.*

Proof Suppose that V is not p-safe for G with respect to some server strategy S. Then, for some $E \in \mathcal{E}$, some user strategy U, and some initial state σ, there are finite executions (E, U, S) starting from σ occurring with probability $p + \delta > p$ for which V outputs 1 on the user's view, but the referee is not satisfied in the corresponding state of the execution; we will call such an execution a violation of safety.

The total probability of such a violation can be written by summing over triples consisting of round numbers, finite sequences of coin tosses, and lengths of the longest message sent by the user: a triple contributes to the sum the probability of a first violation in the execution occurring at the round number using precisely that sequence of coin tosses in which the user's longest message is the given length. Since every execution with a violation is witnessed by one such triple, the sum equals $p + \delta$; in particular, since this is a countable sum that may be written as a limit, there is some finite subset of these triples for which the sum is at least $p + \delta/2 > p$. Let M be the maximum length of the longest user message over this set of triples.

Let $S' \in \mathcal{S}_{G,p'}$ be given, and consider the following server strategy $\tilde{s}$: $\tilde{s}$ has states corresponding to states of S and states of S'. It behaves identically to S until it receives a message from the user consisting of 0^{M+1}, whereupon it enters some state of S' and behaves identically to S'.

We first argue that $\tilde{s} \in \mathcal{S}_{G,p'}$. Given a polynomial time user protocol U' such that (U', S') robustly achieves G with probability p', let $\tilde{u}$ be the user strategy that first sends 0^{M+1} to the server, and then follows U', and notice that $\tilde{u}$ is also a polynomial time user protocol. Let any state of the environment be given. Now, if $\tilde{s}$ starts in any state of S, $\tilde{u}$ sends 0^{M+1} in the first round, so $\tilde{s}$ enters a state of S' and the execution $(E, \tilde{u}, \tilde{s})$ starting from the second round is identical to an execution of (E, U', S'). Thus, since (U', S') robustly achieves G with probability p', $(\tilde{u}, \tilde{s})$ achieve G in these executions with probability p'. If, on the other hand, $\tilde{s}$ starts in any state of S', again, the execution $(E, \tilde{u}, \tilde{s})$ starting from the second round is identical to an execution of (E, U', S'), so $(\tilde{u}, \tilde{s})$ also achieves G in these executions with probability p', and we see $(\tilde{u}, \tilde{s})$ robustly achieves the goal with probability p'. Therefore, $\tilde{s} \in \mathcal{S}_{G,p'}$.

We claim that despite this, executions of $(E, U, \tilde{s})$ violate safety with probability at least $p + \delta/2 > p$. To see this, notice that in executions where $\tilde{s}$ starts in the state $\sigma^{(s)}$ of S, $(E, U, \tilde{s})$ is identical to (E, U, S) started from σ until U sends a message of length greater than M. M was chosen so that our finite set of triples describes an event of (E, U, S) occurring with probability at least $p + \delta/2$ in which U never sends a message of length greater than M and a violation of safety occurs; the corresponding executions of $(E, U, \tilde{s})$ are also violations of safety since the user's view and the distribution over states of the environment are identical. Therefore, V is not p-safe with $\tilde{s} \in \mathcal{S}_{G,p'}$. ∎

We remark further that Theorem 2.37 also holds in the controlled error setting, since we can apply the theorem to the sensing function for each fixed value of the safety parameter ϵ. Thus, we find analogously:

Corollary 2.38 (Controllable safety with all helpful servers implies controllable safety with all servers). *Let G be a goal and suppose that V is a sensing function with controlled safety for G with respect to every $S \in \mathcal{S}_{G,p}$ for some* *nonempty* $\mathcal{S}_{G,p}$. *Then* V *is also a sensing function with controlled safety for* G *with respect to every server strategy.*

Chapter 3

Verifiable goals for communication

We saw in Chapter 2 that our sensing functions are sufficient to capture all finite goals for which we can design protocols, but we only gave two examples of such sensing functions: Example 2.23, a sensing function for the goal of printing described in Example 2.8; and Example 2.24, a sensing function for the goal of computation, first described in Section 1.4.2 and then formally revisited in Example 2.17. It is not immediately clear how many more *interesting* goals actually have universal protocols! Fortunately, we can show that many goals can be captured by safe and viable sensing functions, and hence have universal protocols—in fact, we believe that most (if not all) reasonable goals for communication can be captured in this way. We will support this claim by developing a variety of examples of goals, and demonstrating how we can provide sensing for each of the goals. These examples are adapted from an early technical report [84].

3.1 Notation and definitions

Our first two examples – the goal of printing and the goal of computation – suggest a dichotomy in the kinds of goals we have for communication. Namely, the former goal cannot be achieved without the aid of a server, whereas the latter goal does not require the aid of a server in general. Motivated by this observation, we introduce a simple taxonomy of goals for communication to guide our discussion.

Control-oriented goals

The first family of goals captures goals like the printing goal that depend on the aid of a server. The server in particular can only influence the states of

B. Juba, *Universal Semantic Communication,*
DOI 10.1007/978-3-642-23297-8_3,
© Springer-Verlag Berlin Heidelberg 2011

the environment – and hence, the achievement of the goal – via the messages it sends to the environment, these are goals that might require the server to *do* something. We call these goals *control-oriented*, since they rely on the ability of the user to control (or at least influence) the server's actions.

Definition 3.1 (Control-oriented goal). We say that a goal $G = (\mathcal{E}, R)$ is *control-oriented* if for some $E \in \mathcal{E}$, $R(\sigma^{(e)})$ is not independent of the server's messages. We say that G is *purely control-oriented* if for each $E \in \mathcal{E}$, R is determined by the history of the server's messages.

Complementing the definition of control-oriented goals, we will also formally define a "nontrivial" subclass of (control-oriented) goals for which the user explicitly needs a server's assistance to have any hope of achieving the goal. We model a server providing "no assistance" by a strategy that sends only an empty message to all other parties.

Definition 3.2 (Nontrivial goal). Let T denote a *trivial server* that sends empty messages on all rounds. A goal $G = (\mathcal{E}, R)$ is considered *nontrivial* if for every polynomial time user protocol U, there is a $E \in \mathcal{E}$ such that R never outputs 1 in the execution (E, U, T).

We will also revisit this notion in Chapter 4 when we describe password-protected servers.

Intellectual goals

The other families in our taxonomy will take some more care to describe. Turning to the goal of computation, the aspect that we wish to capture is that the user *doesn't* need to "do anything"—that is, the only important part of the states of the environment are the messages from the user, and even then, achievement of the goal only depends upon the user sending a single "right" message, so a sufficiently (computationally) powerful user strategy could always succeed at such goals in a single round. We will refer to these goals as *intellectual goals*.

The reason intellectual goals are more challenging to describe is that unlike control-oriented goals, we need to be mindful of how the environment treats the messages from the user. We might want to say, for example, that while the user *can* influence the environment, it *doesn't need to*. An informal example of how this might happen is if our model environment also allows the user to search Google for answers to its computational problems, or allows the user to request a different instance of the problem if the initially provided instance is too hard. A sufficiently powerful user might be able to solve the problems without using these extra features, but less powerful users might find it beneficial to interact with the environment in other ways. We would still like to say that such a goal is an intellectual goal.

We note that the modeling of the environment in our goal is entirely under our control, and whether or not a goal is considered to be an "intellectual goal" will depend on how it has been (or "can be") modeled. To be more specific, we recall the definition of *private outputs* (given in Definition 2.28): roughly, we assume that the environment's states and user's messages to the environment are both structured as tuples in which some components of the user's message only affect the corresponding components of the environment's state, and moreover that the effect only lasts for a single round. Note that, in contrast to the application of private outputs in Corollary 2.30 where the private outputs are known to be ignored by the referee, we took care to ensure that in general the referee's verdict was permitted to depend on the contents of the private outputs on each round.

With this definition of private outputs in hand, we are ready to define intellectual goals:

Definition 3.3 (Intellectual goal). We say that a goal $G = (\mathcal{E}, R)$ is an *intellectual goal* if for some $E \in \mathcal{E}$, R depends on the user's private outputs. It is *purely intellectual* if for every $E \in \mathcal{E}$, the verdict of R is determined by private output components of the user's message.

We remark that *no* purely intellectual goal that can be achieved in a polynomial number of rounds can be nontrivial (in the sense of Definition 3.2), since a user that sends random messages succeeds at any such goal with positive probability in polynomial time. We would still like to have a definition to capture intellectual goals for which the server's assistance is essential to success. We can achieve this by introducing a parameterized notion of nontriviality.

Definition 3.4 (Parameterized nontriviality). We say that a goal $G = (\mathcal{E}, R)$ is $(t(n), \epsilon(n))$-*nontrivial* if no user running in time $t(n)$ can satisfy R with the trivial server and every $E \in \mathcal{E}$ with probability greater than $\epsilon(n)$.

The parameterized notion of nontriviality will be useful partially in assessing the scope of limitations on universal users' running times (in Chapter 4), but also as a "sanity check" on the definition of some intellectual goals in the present chapter.

We note that in contrast to the goals of printing and computation, the goal of the Turing test examiner in Example 2.5 is neither purely intellectual, since it depends on the server reporting its affiliation, nor purely control-oriented, since it depends on the user's verdict. We can take the user's verdict to be a private output, though, so it is *both* an intellectual goal and a control-oriented goal.

3.2 Control-oriented goals

We start by considering some of the simplest and most natural goals for communication, goals that may be purely or impurely control oriented. Recall that these are goals for which success is influenced by the server's actions on the environment. Starting with these goals is natural for two reasons. First, we hope that these goals give a sense that many practical aspects of communication are captured by our theory. Second, these goals allow us to start with some examples of goals and sensing that are particularly simple from a technical standpoint, and so they serve as a good warm-up for the gradually more complex examples that follow later in this chapter.

We have already seen one such motivating example of a control-oriented goal—the goal of *printing*, introduced in Example 2.8. Actually, we have also seen that it is easy to construct a sensing function (with perfect soundness) for this printing goal in Example 2.23, and thus by Proposition 2.27, we know that there exists a universal user for printing which, in particular, *never* halts without succeeding. We will revisit printing, and give a generic class of goals, capturing many natural (purely) control-oriented goals for which the design of sensing functions is likewise immediate—*transparent* goals, in which the environment's state is visible to the user, and the referee's predicate is easy to compute.

We will then consider one more example of goals that may not be purely control-oriented, but are surely not computational goals, and are likewise naturally included in this setting: goals of *searching*, e.g., in a file system, a physical environment, or the web. We can consider this goal from either of two perspectives, the "client" or the "search engine," and while these are essentially the same goal (swapping which entity is labeled the "user" and which is the "server" in our model), both perspectives are instructive to consider.

3.2.1   Transparent goals

A *transparent* goal is one in which deciding whether or not the goal is achieved on the current round is easy for the user essentially by definition. Formally, we mean the following:

Definition 3.5 (Transparent goal)**.** A goal $G = (\mathcal{E}, R)$ is *transparent* if the messages sent to the user by every $E \in \mathcal{E}$ are structured as a tuple in which one component is always the state of E at the current round and R is probabilistic polynomial time computable.

Thus, by running an algorithm for R on E's self-reported state, the user can efficiently decide whether or not the goal is presently achieved.

Proposition 3.6 (Transparent goals have sensing functions)**.** *Let any transparent goal $G = (\mathcal{E}, R)$ be given. Then there is a probabilistic polynomial time computable sensing function with controllable safety for G that, on input ϵ, is $(t(n), 1 - \mu(n) - \epsilon)$-viable for some polynomial $t(n)$ with every $(1 - \mu(n))$-helpful server for G.*

Proof V simply runs the probabilistic polynomial time algorithm for computing R, guaranteed to exist since the goal is transparent, repeating it

$O(\log \frac{1}{\epsilon})$ times and taking a majority to decide if the referee is satisfied. Since it follows by Hoeffding's inequality that this suffices to decide whether or not R is satisfied with probability greater than ϵ, this is a sensing function with controllable safety for G with any server. To see that it is also viable, note that for any given $(1 - \mu(n))$-helpful server for G, there is a user strategy running in some polynomial time $t(n)$ that achieves G with probability $1 - \mu(n)$. When this strategy achieves G, $R(\sigma^{(e)}) = 1$ by definition, so our sensing function is satisfied unless it makes an error; again by Hoeffding's inequality the probability of computing R incorrectly is at most ϵ, so by a union bound, the probability that V is satisfied is at least $1 - \mu(n) - \epsilon$, as claimed. ∎

We are interested in transparent goals because one of the main messages of Chapter 2 is that feedback is essential in the design of users for finite goals, and transparent goals represent one natural way in which such feedback might be obtained. This is especially true in the case of purely control-oriented goals, where the messages from the server to the environment – which, remember, are not assumed to be visible to the user – determine success or failure at the goal. For such goals, when feedback is obtained, it is often because we can "see" the relevant state of the environment as the server works on it. We note that our model of the printing goal in Example 2.8 is an example of such a transparent, purely control-oriented goal, and furthermore that this was a natural property of the goal, even though it did formally depend on how we chose to model printing.

It follows immediately from the existence of good sensing functions with controllable safety for such goals, described in Proposition 3.6, and from the construction of universal users with controllable error from sensing functions in Theorem 2.35 that all transparent goals have efficient universal users with controllable error:

Theorem 3.7 (Transparent goals have efficient universal users with controllable error). *Let G be a transparent goal and let $\mathcal{S}$ be a class of $(1 - \mu(n))$-helpful servers for G for some $\mu : \mathbb{N} \to [0, 1/3)$. Then G has a $\mathcal{S}$-universal user with controllable error for G that runs in expected polynomial time with each $S \in \mathcal{S}$.*

We further remark that if our sensing function can be computed in deterministic polynomial time, we can obtain a sensing function that is perfectly safe (in contrast to the loss in safety in Proposition 3.6), and then we can obtain a universal user from Proposition 2.27 that achieves the goal with probability 1 (this is what we mean by "$(\mathcal{S}, 1)$-universal") and is slightly more efficient.

3.2.2 Searching

We now consider a *class* of goals modeling "search." Roughly, in such goals, the environment models a large space, and the goal is satisfied if the user can locate a suitable "object" (independently specified by the environment) in that space. As such, the environment plays a relatively active role in the satisfaction of the goal.

Definition 3.8 (Search). We say that a goal $G = (\mathcal{E}, R)$ is a *goal of search* if every $E \in \mathcal{E}$ sends a description of a property V_O that is probabilistic polynomial time computable in the size parameter $n(E)$ to one entity – the *client* – and R is satisfied iff the environment receives a message ℓ from the client such that the response of E to ℓ satisfies V_O. If the responses of each $E \in \mathcal{E}$ to the client are according to a fixed function f_E, we say that G is a *goal of search in static environments*.

Our definition only describes goals of search up to a "class" of goals, since we do not specify which party is the client, nor the other party's interface to the environment—variously, the user might be the client and the server might possess an "index" of the space, might control access to locations in the space, or might be able to modify the space's contents to satisfy the user's specification, if the environment is not static. Nevertheless, the goal permits sensing by the client essentially by definition, and thus every such goal has universal users when the user is the client.

Theorem 3.9 (Universal clients with controllable error exist for any goal of search). *Let G be a goal of search in which the user is the client, and let S be a class of $(1 - \mu(n))$-helpful servers for G for some $\mu : \mathbb{N} \to [0, 1/3)$. Then G has an $\mathcal{S}$-universal user with controllable error that runs in expected polynomial time with each $S \in \mathcal{S}$.*

Proof We observe that, by running the provided code for the predicate V_O $O(\log \frac{1}{\epsilon})$ times on the environment's last message and taking a majority vote, we can obtain a sensing function with controllable soundness. Likewise, since the referee is satisfied by definition when the function V_O computes is satisfied, if S is $(1 - \mu(n))$-helpful, (to some $t(n)$-time bounded strategy) we find that the described sensing function is $(t(n), 1 - \mu(n) - \epsilon)$-viable. Thus, we can apply Theorem 2.35 to find that there is an $\mathcal{S}$-universal user for G with controllable error. ∎

Awareness and searching

We remark that there is a close connection between our model of searching (in static environments) here and the model of computational awareness proposed by Devanur and Fortnow [52]. In their model, Alice is an agent with oracle access to an environment and some input context. Alice also possesses an enumeration procedure M, and Devanur and Fortnow define her "unawareness" of a string (w.r.t. M) to be the time it takes for her to print the string using M. The correspondence with our model is simple: Alice plays the role of the client, and her input context contains the property V_O

provided by the environment to the client. If the environment is static, her interaction with the environment is equivalent to that of an oracle machine interacting with its oracle, and the time it takes for the client to succeed at the goal is precisely its unawareness of a location ℓ satisfying V_O. One of the results Devanur and Fortnow state for this model is that by using a universal enumeration M, Alice's unawareness of any object is optimal up to a constant factor, and so in some sense, is (asymptotically) independent of her actual choice of enumeration procedure. Naturally, this corresponds to our construction of a universal user for search, whose running time is optimal up to a constant factor.

There are a few differences, of course, and neither our goals of search completely subsume the model introduced by Devanur and Fortnow, nor vice-versa. A minor difference is that in our model, the environment need not be static. Devanur and Fortnow also implicitly consider such cases, but in their modeling they still consider it to be an oracle, and they do not consider the effects of this statefulness on the "unawareness." A more substantial difference is our emphasis on communication – the introduction of a server playing the role of, e.g., a search engine – that they would have generally modeled as an aspect of the (stateless) environment. In such aspects, our goals of searching are somewhat richer. On the other hand, they consider (un)awareness with respect to all kinds of strings, not merely those "specified" by the input context, nor merely locations in the environment, and along such lines, they likewise do not assume that the input context is necessarily a description of some property V_O. In this sense, their model is more general than our goals of searching.

Search from a search engine's perspective

Note that, in our definition of goals of search, we did not specify which entity should play the role of the client—inspired by a conversation with Manuel Blum [32], we now briefly consider searching when the "server" (in the model of Chapter 2) plays the role of the client for the goal. In this case, the user plays the role of, e.g., a "search engine," and a helpful client provides the search engine with enough information about V_O for the search engine to provide assistance, and then must actually query some appropriate location.[1]

The goal is now arguably more interesting because it is easy to see that mere "helpfulness" in this sense is not sufficient to permit achieving such a goal in a finite execution: the issue is that, while searching is trivially verifiable by the client, it may not be verifiable to other entities. Success at the goal in a finite execution would therefore typically rely on some further assumptions about the class of clients—perhaps we assume that the client

---

[1] An alternative view is that we are trying to design a "very helpful server," and we'll develop a framework that is more appropriate to this perspective in Chapter 4. Although we won't consider the design of such servers in much depth in this work, we will return to the question in some more detail and suggest it as a direction for future work in Section 10.1.3.

notifies the search engine that it is terminating its session, or else we assume, e.g., that the queries are in English and the client visits locations that the server suggests. In the latter case, the problem is strictly a problem of interpreting the client's English queries, and not a problem of overcoming the lack of a common language per se. It is still interesting to note that this latter problem is a fair specification of "the problem solved by Google." The point more generally is that in many natural cases, it may still be interesting to consider S for a rather limited subset of the class of all helpful "servers" for a goal—here, it models the variety of ways an English-speaking Google user might express a query V_O. We will return to this more general point in Section 3.5 and again in Chapter 4 where we explore how restricting the class of servers in natural ways (i.e., making natural assumptions about the server) will allow us to achieve goals that would otherwise be unverifiable and hence impossible, or to achieve goals more efficiently than would otherwise be possible.

Although such assumptions about the class of servers are often reasonable, we also note that the infinite execution model introduced in Chapter 6 – in which the client is given an infinite sequence of queries and hopes to eventually succeed at its searches – is also a reasonable model to consider for this problem, and in that model, feedback (i.e., verifiability) is not strictly necessary. Such a direction may provide avenues for "universal" search engines, and it is not hard to see how to leverage the construction for universal users without feedback we introduce there to obtain a weak version of such a search engine.

3.3   Computational goals

We now consider computational goals, as introduced in Example 2.17. We begin by showing how results from interactive proofs allow us to easily obtain the results claimed in Section 1.4.2 (originally appearing in prior work [83]). Returning to the fantastic scenario sketched there, we suppose that Bob has been contacted by some computationally powerful extraterrestrial Alice, and we ask what Bob can learn by communicating with her. We do not limit Alice's computational power a priori: we imagine that she can solve *any* computational problem, and thus see how Bob's *lack of understanding* places inherent limitations on the communication. Again, we model the lack of understanding by considering a *class* of Alices, defined by the existence of a suitable communications protocol (i.e., "language"), and we ask that Bob's protocol work with *every* member of this class. In this case, since it turns out that verifiability of the goal is necessary and sufficient, the inability of Bob to verify solutions to problems outside PSPACE prevents Bob from using Alice's help to solve such problems, but interactive proofs allow Bob to use Alice's help to solve PSPACE-complete problems, as sketched in Section 1.4.2.

More generally, we characterize the class of function problems for which the corresponding goals have polynomial time bounded universal users in the basic universal setting. We will show that this is *precisely* the class of function problems for which the problem has a "competitive proof system," first introduced in the work of Bellare and Goldwasser [21]. In particular, we mean decision problems for which both the problem and its complement are contained in the class compIP.

Technically, we proceed as follows. We start by recalling the computational goals associated with a class of computational problems, and effectively invoke Theorem 2.25 to cast the existence of universal protocols for these goals in terms of the existence of sensing functions. On the one hand, given competitive proof systems, we will mimic the construction of a sensing function sketched in Example 2.24, note that this sensing function features controllable safety, and then apply Theorem 2.35 to obtain a universal user. (We note that it is essential to use Theorem 2.35 rather than Proposition 2.27 since we want universal users for which the probability of error is independent of the unknown server; these universal users have controllable error immediately since we can always run them several times and take majorities to amplify their correctness.) On the other hand, Theorem 2.37 shows that whenever a universal user exists for a computational problem, then the sensing function we obtain from that user by Proposition 2.26 is a good verifier for an interactive proof system. In particular, the fact that the user is viable with *all* helpful servers implies that this sensing function is satisfied when interacting with an oracle for the problem, which is a competitive prover strategy.

The results claimed in Section 1.4.2 then follow as immediate corollaries since compIP $\subseteq$ PSPACE, every PSPACE-complete problem is in compIP, and PSPACE is closed under complement. We will also examine a variety of other consequences of our characterization: we will see that universal users only exist for functions with program checkers and that under a reasonable complexity-theoretic hypothesis, there exist problems in NP that do not have universal users. We will also consider some representative examples of computational problems other than PSPACE-complete problems that have universal users. Finally, we will close this section with some initial remarks on what our constructions say about communication without a common language.

3.3.1 Main definitions in this setting

For a computational problem Π, we recall the computational goal $G_\Pi = (\{E_x\}_x, R)$, defined in Example 2.17: essentially, in E_x, the user is given x on every round, and the user succeeds in E_x if its last message is an element of $\Pi(x)$. In this case, it is easy to see that the class of Π-helpful Alices described in Section 1.4.2 is *essentially* the class of $(G_\Pi, 2/3)$-helpful servers, $\mathcal{S}_{G_\Pi, 2/3}$:[2] a server S is in $\mathcal{S}_{G_\Pi, 2/3}$ if there exists some user strategy

---

[2]The only difference is that Π-helpfulness only demands that Alice is helpful for all *message histories*, whereas $(G_\Pi, 2/3)$-helpfulness demands that the server is helpful for all

U_S such that (U_S, S) robustly achieves G_Π (outputs $y \in \Pi(x)$ in each E_x) with probability at least 2/3. Similarly, a Π-universal Bob is essentially an expected polynomial time bounded $(S_{G_\Pi, 2/3}, 2/3)$-universal user strategy, that is, it robustly achieves G_Π with every $S \in S_{G_\Pi, 2/3}$ with probability at least 2/3, and runs in expected time $p_S(|x|)$ with S, for some polynomial p_S. For convenience, in the present section we will return to using the terminology "Π-helpful" and "Π-universal," with the understanding that we really mean $(G_\Pi, 2/3)$-helpful servers and $(S_{G_\Pi, 2/3}, 2/3)$-universal users, respectively.

Precisely, we wish to know for which problems Π it is possible to construct a Π-universal user. Since it will turn out to be for a generalization of the decision problems Π such that both Π and its complement have *competitive interactive proof systems*, we recall the relevant definitions next.

Competitive interactive proofs

Competitive interactive proofs were introduced by Bellare and Goldwasser [21] to study the complexity of the prover in an interactive proof system. Roughly, these are interactive proof systems for set membership in which the prover can be efficiently simulated using oracle queries to the set. In particular, the question of the existence of competitive interactive proof systems is a generalization of the decision-versus-search question for NP proof systems— simulating the interaction between the prover and the verifier using an oracle for the set allows one to generate "proofs" of membership in polynomial time, given the ability to decide membership. Precisely, the definition is as follows:

Definition 3.10 (Competitive interactive proof system). Let P be a probabilistic polynomial time interactive oracle Turing machine and let V be a probabilistic polynomial time interactive Turing machine. We say that (P, V) is a *competitive interactive proof system* for a set S if

1. **(Completeness)** For every $x \in S$, the probability that V accepts when interacting with P^S on common input x is at least 2/3.

2. **(Soundness)** For every $x \notin S$ and every interactive Turing machine $\tilde{P}$, the probability that V accepts when interacting with $\tilde{P}$ on common input x is at most 1/3.

We say that P is a *competitive prover strategy*. We let compIP denote the class of decision problems Π with competitive interactive proof systems for membership in Π (viewed as a set), and we let co$-$compIP denote the class of decision problems such that their complements are in compIP. For a general computational problem Π,[3] we say that Π has a competitive proof system if the set $\{(x, y) : x \text{ an instance of } \Pi, \ y \in \Pi(x)\}$ has a competitive interactive proof system.

---

states, including those that cannot be reached by any message history. We trust that the reader will not be too upset at this modest weakening of our ambitions.

[3]Recalling that we are primarily interested in relational promise problems for which every instance x is associated with a nonempty set $\Pi(x)$.

Note that our definition is somewhat overloaded—we can view a decision problem either as a set, or as a relational problem (deciding whether "$\Pi(x) = b$" is true). That is, Π (as a relational computational problem) has a competitive interactive proof system iff the corresponding set $\Pi = \{x : \Pi(x) = \{1\}\}$ is in compIP $\cap$ co$-$compIP. We are forced to make this mildly confusing convention because while the relevant concept for our purposes will be competitive proof systems for (relational) computational problems, the definition of compIP is classical and related to other concepts, so we wish to leave it intact.

For example, since a competitive interactive proof system is, in particular, an interactive proof system, compIP $\subseteq$ IP. The proofs of Theorems 1.4 and 1.5 will rely on a few easy consequences of the constructions used to show IP = PSPACE [103, 134] which we will recall briefly, partially to illustrate competitive interactive proof systems.

Proposition 3.11. *Let* Π *be a PSPACE-complete decision problem. Then there is a competitive interactive proof system for the relational computational problem* Π.

Proof Notice that if $\Pi \in$ PSPACE, the the set of pairs $(x, \Pi(x))$ is also in PSPACE, and thus we let V be the verifier for a proof system for this set, as given by Shamir. Since the soundness conditions are the same as for standard interactive proofs, we know that V is sound, and we only need to show that V has a competitive prover strategy.

We note that, given a partial message history, we can loop over all sequences of coin tosses of V and subsequent messages that the prover could send, to recursively compute an optimal next message in polynomial space. In particular, the problems of deciding whether or not the ith bit of the first optimal prover message is a '1' and deciding whether the message has length i, are in PSPACE.

Thus, since Π is PSPACE-complete, there exist polynomial time reductions of these two problems to Π. In particular P^Π can store the current message history and invoke these reductions repeatedly to read off an optimal next message in polynomial time from queries to Π. In particular, since Shamir's prover succeeds with probability at least $2/3$ for $(x, \Pi(x))$ (it actually succeeds with probability 1), so does P^Π. ∎

We stress that what we have actually argued is that PSPACE-complete problems, when viewed as sets, are contained in compIP $\cap$ co$-$compIP.

3.3.2 Characterization of functions with polynomial time universal protocols

We now present our characterization of functions having polynomial time universal protocols in the basic universal setting as those problems for which competitive proof systems exist. This result is closely related to Theorem 2.25, with competitive proof systems readily providing us with a sensing function (as demonstrated in Example 2.24) and (invoking Theorem 2.37) conversely the universal protocol's sensing function providing us with a competitive proof system for function problems almost immediately.

Thus, in summary, we get a complete characterization for function problems:

Theorem 3.12. *Let* Π *be a promise function problem. There is a* Π-*universal user if and only if* Π *has a competitive proof system.*

Proof

($\Rightarrow$:)   Given a Π-universal user U, we construct a competitive proof system (P, V) for Π as follows. Let P^{Π} respond to any message x with $\Pi(x)$ (obtained from the Π oracle). This is trivially a competitive prover strategy.

Note that P^{Π} is Π-helpful, to the user who simply forwards the instance to P^{Π} and returns its response. Therefore, in the execution of the system (E_x, U, P^{Π}), U runs for $p(n)$ steps in expectation and halts for some polynomial p, and returns $\Pi(x)$ with probability at least $2/3$.

We are now ready to describe the verifier strategy. Let V simulate U interacting with E_x for up to $24p(n)$ steps on three independent runs, and accept iff at least two of the three runs lead U to halt with a final message that matches the claimed value of $\Pi(x)$. It is easily verified that, when interacting with P^{Π}, V accepts $(x, \Pi(x))$ with probability greater than $2/3$, as needed.

To see that V is sound, note that by Proposition 2.26, the function indicating when U halts is a $2/3$-safe sensing function for G_{Π}, which by Theorem 2.37 is also $2/3$-safe with every server strategy. Thus, when interacting with any $\tilde{P}$, U only halts with a wrong answer in any of the three runs with probability at most $1/3$ independently; thus, for a false claim (x, y) U only halts with output y with probability at most $1/3$ on each run, and so we see that V accepts (x, y) with probability less than $1/3$. Thus, (P, V) is a competitive proof system for Π.

($\Leftarrow$:)   Given a competitive proof system for Π, we will construct a viable sensing function for G_{Π} with controlled safety, and then invoke Theorem 2.35 (actually Corollary 2.36) to obtain a universal user with controllable error. Fixing $\epsilon = 1/3$ for this user protocol then gives a Π-universal user.

Construction.   Let (P_{Π}, V_{Π}) be a competitive proof system for Π. Our grey-box sensing function V for G_{Π} with two private outputs and controlled safety is then as follows: V only accepts transcripts from protocols that simulate a fixed syntactic composition of V_Π with some other protocol that simulates a prover (and provides the claim for $\Pi(x)$); the first private output will essentially contain a claimed value for $\Pi(x)$, and the second private output will produce a sequence of messages that will be used as the prover's messages in a simulated run of the proof system. In more detail, the private outputs have an initial bit indicating whether they contain an appropriate message for the simulation, followed by the contents of the message when the first bit indicates that such a valid message is provided. On auxiliary input ϵ, V simulates V_Π $O(\log \frac{1}{\epsilon})$ times on input (x, y) where x is given by the environment on each round and y is given by the first private output on each round; the simulation starts on the first round after y is valid, and V is assumed to output 0 unless the first private output is marked as valid. The simulation proceeds by taking the messages produced on the private output when they are valid to be the messages from the prover, and using the same coin tosses as used by the user's protocol to simulate V_Π. When V_Π would halt instead of sending a next message, V records its verdict and starts a new simulation on the following round. V outputs 1 if and only if, after the last simulated run, V_Π accepted in a majority of runs and the user's last message to the server is y.

Controllable safety. We first note that since V checks that the user's protocol is of the form of some private-coin simulation of (V_Π, P') for some prover protocol P', the soundness of V_Π holds for the user's simulation. Therefore, by Hoeffding's inequality and the soundness of V_Π, an appropriate choice of $O(\log \frac{1}{\epsilon}) = O(|\epsilon|)$ repetitions suffices to guarantee that V is $(1 - \epsilon)$-safe for G_Π with any server.

Viability. We will now show that the sensing function described above is viable with every Π-helpful server. Suppose that S is Π-helpful; then we know that there is some polynomial time user strategy U_S that robustly achieves G_Π with S with probability $2/3$. Thus, suppose that our user strategy simulates interactions between V_Π and P_Π by using U_S to simulate the Π-oracle. More precisely, the strategy P' first uses U_S on x with S to obtain a claim for $\Pi(x)$, and then simulates P_Π until P_Π invokes its Π-oracle on some instance w; P' then switches to simulating U_S in E_w with S until U_S would halt, returning some message z (as its guess for $\Pi(w)$) to E_w. P' repeats this simulation several times (we will specify how many times in the analysis), and if a majority of them agree that $\Pi(w) = z$ for some z, P' then resumes the simulation of P_Π using z as the response from the oracle. We note further that as long as the number of repetitions of the simulation of (V_Π, P') is sufficiently large, if P' faithfully simulates P_Π^Π, then V_Π accepts $(x, \Pi(x))$ with probability at least $5/6$.

Since U_S correctly returns $\Pi(w)$ in any E_w with probability at least $2/3$ regardless of the state of S, and neither E_w nor E_x sends any messages to S, the simulated version of U_S with E_w also returns $\Pi(w)$ with probability at least $2/3$ when interacting with S, even though this simulation is actually carried out with S interacting with E_x. Since both of the strategies in our competitive proof system run in probabilistic polynomial time (relative to the oracle for Π), there is a polynomial upper bound $p(n)$ on the number of oracle calls needed for an instance of size n. Therefore, by Hoeffding's inequality, $O(\log n|\epsilon|)$ repetitions suffice to bring the probability of error per invocation below $O(\frac{1}{|\epsilon|p(n)})$; therefore, since there are $p(n)$ invocations of U_S per simulation and $O(|\epsilon|)$ simulations, by a union bound, we can guarantee that every simulation of the Π-oracle by P' succeeds with probability at least $5/6$. Thus, by another union bound, the probability that either P' fails to accurately simulate P_Π^Π or P_Π^Π fails to convince V_Π is at most $1/3$. Thus, since U_S and the strategies employed in the competitive proof system are all polynomial time computable, the $O(|\epsilon|)$ simulations of (V_Π, P') can also be computed in time $p'(n, |\epsilon|)$ for some polynomial p', and hence V is a $(p'(n, |\epsilon|), 2/3)$-viable sensing function for G_Π with S.

We note that V runs in time comparable to the corresponding user strategy (since both simulate V_Π $O(\log \frac{1}{\epsilon}) = O(|\epsilon|)$ times), and thus by Corollary 2.36, there is an $\tilde{O}(p'(n, |\epsilon|))$-time bounded $S_{G_\Pi, 2/3}$-universal user with controllable error; fixing $\epsilon = 1/3$, this gives a Π-universal user, as desired.

∎

3.3.3   Main consequences of the characterization

Having obtained a characterization of the functions for which efficient universal users can be designed, we now briefly examine some of the major consequences of this characterization. Principally, we show that the results claimed in Section 1.4.2 follow as immediate corollaries from Theorem 3.12. We will also note two other corollaries that follow largely from work by Bellare and Goldwasser on the class compIP.

Our first corollary is the main theorem from Section 1.4.2:

Theorem 1.4 *For every PSPACE complete problem Π, there is a Bob that is Π-universal.*

Proof Proposition 3.11 says that PSPACE-complete problems (as relation problems) have competitive proof systems, so the claim follows immediately from Theorem 3.12. ∎

We next immediately obtain the impossibility result stated in Section 1.4.2:

Theorem 1.5 *Let* Π *be a decision problem that is not in PSPACE. Then for every probabilistic algorithm B, there exists a Π-helpful A such that B fails to decide Π with the help of A.*

Proof Suppose Π is a decision problem with a Π-universal user. The reverse direction of the characterization provided by Theorem 3.12 shows than any such decision problem Π is contained in compIP $\cap$ co−compIP. Since compIP $\subseteq$ IP $=$ PSPACE, the theorem follows. ∎

That is, no matter how powerful or helpful the "extraterrestrial" is, as a result of our potential misunderstanding of the communication, we cannot learn the answers to problems outside of PSPACE, and Theorem 1.4 shows that the hardest problems for which solutions can be communicated without a common language are the PSPACE-complete problems.

A further consequence of our characterization is that all functions with universal users have program checkers, as introduced by Blum and Kannan [33].

Corollary 3.13. *Let Π be a decision problem with a Π-universal user. Then Π has a program checker.*

Proof We recall a result of Bellare and Goldwasser [21], compIP $\subseteq$ fr−IP. Since Blum and Kannan [33] showed that the class of checkable decision problems is precisely fr−IP $\cap$ fr−co−IP $\supseteq$ compIP $\cap$ co−compIP, our claim follows immediately from Theorem 3.12. (Alternatively, it can be verified that our construction of a competitive proof system from a universal user yields an explicit construction of a program checker directly, but we leave the details to the interested reader.) ∎

We stress, however, that the converse is unlikely to hold—a result of Babai, Fortnow and Lund [14] shows that EXP-complete problems have program checkers, but Theorem 1.5 shows that all decision problems with universal protocols are contained in PSPACE, so if all checkable problems also had universal protocols, we would find PSPACE $=$ EXP, which is widely considered unlikely.

We also remark that one more of the results of Bellare and Goldwasser is relevant here: assuming NEE $\not\subseteq$ BPEE (i.e., some problem in nondeterministic doubly-exponential time cannot be decided in bounded-error probabilistic doubly-exponential time), NP $\not\subseteq$ compIP. Together with Theorem 3.12, this yields yet another limitation of universal users:

Corollary 3.14. *If NEE $\not\subseteq$ BPEE, then there exists $\Pi \in$ NP for which Π-universal users do not exist.*

Put more plainly, because (under a reasonable hypothesis) there are decision problems for which constructing proofs is strictly harder than deciding instances, if we interact with a server that is *only* capable of deciding instances of such problems, we can't ensure that we recover the correct verdicts by means of communicating with that server.

3.3.4   Beyond PSPACE-completeness: more examples of universal protocols for computational problems

PSPACE-complete problems are not the only problems with competitive interactive proofs. Some of the nicest classic examples are not most naturally stated as decision problems. For example, it is well known that the work of Lund et al. [103] gives a proof system for a #P-complete problem in which the prover can be simulated with queries to a #P-complete problem—a competitive proof system for a counting (function) problem.

Likewise, Levin's original technique for universal algorithms solving (total) function inversion problems – for a total polynomial time function f, given y, find an x such that $f(x) = y$ – can be used here: we only need to check that the output x satisfies $f(x) = y$. Since the "prover" can be taken to be any inversion oracle for f, this is essentially a competitive proof system for a function problem, and we can design universal protocols for such problems, including integer factorization and discrete logarithms.

Actually, although in general these inversion problems may themselves be general relational problems rather than function problems (i.e., there may be several distinct values of x that map to the same y under f, each of which would count as a solution to the inversion problem) and so the construction of Theorem 3.12 may not apply as stated in cases where the function f to be inverted is not one-to-one, the construction in Theorem 3.12 can easily be modified to cover such cases. The key point here is that verification here is noninteractive – we only need to evaluate $f(x)$ for the value of x suggested by a single interaction with the server – so we can guarantee correctness with high probability for any single claimed solution x. This is of course in contrast to relation problems for which we might have a nontrivial competitive proof system, where amplification of the correctness of our simulated oracle queries cannot be achieved by taking majority votes, since different sessions with the server may well all return distinct values. We note that this multi-valued aspect is also the problem with applying our construction of a proof system from a universal user to relation problems, so for general relation problems, neither direction of our characterization is known to hold.

Our characterization of decision problems having universal users in terms of compIP is useful in providing further examples. Bellare and Goldwasser [21], in considering zero-knowledge aspects of competitive proof systems, noted that both Graph Isomorphism and Graph Non-Isomorphism possess competitive interactive proofs (a result originally due to Goldreich, Micali, and Wigderson [71]); therefore, Graph Isomorphism has a universal protocol.

Finally, Bellare and Goldwasser noted that while Quadratic Non-Residuosity has a well-known competitive interactive proof (it was the first example, due to Goldwasser, Micali, and Rackoff [74]), it is unclear whether or not Quadratic Residuosity has an interactive proof, so it is unclear whether or not Quadratic Residuosity has a universal protocol. On the other hand, it is easy to see that we can construct a universal protocol for a related goal:

Example 3.15 (Modular square roots). Let $G_{SR} = (\{E_{(x,n)}\}_{x \in \mathbb{Z}_n^*}, R)$ be the following goal: on each round, $E_{(x,n)}$ sends (x, n) to the user (and stores this pair in its state). R accepts if either x is a quadratic non-residue and the user's last message is a string corresponding to "non-residue" or x is a quadratic residue and the user's last message is some $y \in \mathbb{Z}_n^*$ such that $y^2 = x$ (mod n).

That is, we can obtain a universal protocol for the modular square root partial function. The relevant sensing function is fairly obvious: it checks that either a square root is given for x in the range of the squaring function modulo n (although this may be multiple-valued, this poses no trouble since our verification has perfect soundness), or that a valid interactive proof of non-residuosity of x modulo n has been given. In this way, we obtain a universal protocol for a problem for which the natural decision version does not seem to have a universal protocol.

3.3.5 Communication in spite of indeterminacy

The protocol claimed in Theorem 1.4 (constructed in the proof of Theorem 3.12) implies that Bob can obtain wisdom from a powerful extraterrestrial Alice for the following simple but easily overlooked reason: Alice can be Π-helpful without knowing which problem Π Bob has in mind! To be Π-helpful for $\Pi \in$ PSPACE, Alice only needs to help some $B^A \in \mathcal{P}$ solve *some* PSPACE-complete problem $\tilde{\Pi}$; then, since Π polynomial time reduces to $\tilde{\Pi}$ via some polynomial time (Cook) reduction F, there is some $B' \in \mathcal{P}$ who simulates F composed with B^A, so Alice is also Π-helpful since Alice helps B' decide Π. In this case, Alice might think the conversation is about some problem $\tilde{\Pi}$, whereas Bob is "really" interested in help solving some entirely different problem Π. We observed in Section 2.3 that such "gaps" between the interpretations possessed by Alice and Bob are essentially unavoidable; the interesting observation here, which could be made repeatedly throughout this chapter, is that these differences of interpretation do not pose any barrier to the pursuit of a goal, and so in spite of what one might naïvely expect, they do not need to be eliminated to enable successful communication.

3.4 Intellectual curiosity

Let us return again to the story from Chapter 1. In Section 3.3, we characterized precisely the class of problems that Bob could solve with a powerful Alice without knowledge of a common language. The solution we presented was only really interesting for problems that Bob cannot solve on his own. Unfortunately, it also turned out that, in order for Bob to learn the answer to, e.g., a PSPACE-complete question from Alice, our solution required that Alice be able to solve *any* problem in PSPACE, which we don't believe to be feasible, even for some advanced extraterrestrial civilization. If we still believe that feasible computation is characterized by polynomial time, it is hard to see what benefit can be obtained from computing functions by interacting with another party who faces the same fundamental computational constraints, and thus even if language were not an issue, a party who still could not compute the desired instances "on demand."

Not all intellectual goals involve computing a hard function on a specific instance, though, and we could imagine that Alice, although constrained by the usual laws of efficient computation during her interactions with Bob, has access to some store of knowledge (e.g., of mathematics or physical laws) that has been generated by inefficient means over the lifetime of her civilization. In particular, we may wish to grant Alice the latitude to suggest a context where she knows something as in the following example.

Suppose Alice wishes to submit results to Bob, who is serving on the program committee for the nth Intergalactic Conference on the Mathematical Foundations of Computer Science. Bob is expecting to obtain from Alice a proof of a "deep" theorem, to be presented at the conference. Informally, but more specifically, Bob is only willing to accept theorems with proofs that no efficient entity lacking prior knowledge would be able to reliably produce.[4] In the interest of fairness to alien civilizations, Bob would like to evaluate Alice's submission regardless of the language she uses.

Our formalization of this will be in terms of computational depth [8], which we describe next. We will minimally wish that the user (program committee member) outputs a theorem ϕ followed by an output containing a proof of ϕ such that any proof of ϕ has t-time bounded depth at least $f(k) = \Theta(\log k)$ conditioned on ϕ, so in this sense the theorem is "hard." We want a little bit more than this, though, so that the produced theorem is a product of Alice's submission, not merely something that Bob imagined on his own, and we will subsequently address these moderately subtle issues in Section 3.4.2.

3.4.1   A primer on computational depth

Intuitively, *computational depth* is meant to capture the amount of useful, non-random information in a string. For example, strings that are efficiently generated from short programs and random strings are not "deep" in our sense, but solved random instances of a hard-on-average computational problem should be "deep." The original definition of *logical depth*, due to Bennett [23], captured this intuition by measuring the shortest running time of a short program producing the string in question. On the other hand, Bennett's definition was difficult to work with, and so we use a new, much simpler notion of depth given by Antunes et al. [8]. In this new definition, we measure this "amount of information" in bits, so in our latter example,

---

[4]Note that we do not necessarily condone this measure of quality, nor do we know of a demonstrably better one. We only wish to provide a reasonable model of an existing process.

we expect the depth to be roughly the number of bits in the solutions (i.e., minus the bits describing the instances), and indeed this is essentially how we define depth below.

As preliminaries, we will need to recall the definitions of *prefix machines* and *Kolmogorov complexity*. Kolmogorov complexity (especially as defined on prefix machines) has many interesting properties that are beyond the scope of this thesis. The interested reader is referred to the textbook by Li and Vitányi [99].

Definition 3.16 (Prefix machine). We say that a Turing machine M with two inputs is a *prefix machine* if, for any two strings x and y such that x is a prefix of y, and any third string z, $M(x, z)$ and $M(y, z)$ do not both halt. If, for every prefix machine M', there exists some string p such that for all x and y $M'(x, y) = M(px, y)$ and M has running time greater than M' by no more than a factor of $O(|p| + |x| + |y|)$ for all such M', p, x, and y, we say that M is an *efficient universal prefix machine*.

So, the strings on which a prefix machine halts form a prefix-free set, and a pair from the set (x, y) can be uniquely recovered from their concatenation, xy, (which may represent, for example, the composition of programs computing functions f and g) which has length $|x| + |y|$. In this sense, the strings are *self-delimiting*, and this property makes prefix machines particularly appealing to use for the definition of Kolmogorov complexity, a measure of program length.

Definition 3.17 (Prefix Kolmogorov Complexity). Fix a reference efficient universal prefix machine U, and let U^t denote the corresponding t-time bounded machine. The *prefix Kolmogorov complexity* (or, simply *Kolmogorov complexity*) of a string x conditioned on a string y, denoted $K(x|y)$, is the length of the shortest string p such that $U(p, y) = x$. The *t-time bounded prefix Kolmogorov complexity* of x conditioned on y, denoted $K^t(x|y)$, is the length of the shortest string p such that $U^t(p, y) = x$.

It is easy to see by counting that at least half of all strings of a given length cannot compress by more than one bit. It is similarly easy to establish a more general quantitative relationship, and the underlying moral is that *random strings have high Kolmogorov complexity*. More generally, strings with high Kolmogorov complexity are essentially as good as random strings to a fixed, "reliable" algorithm ("reliable" in the sense that only a few faulty strings of coin tosses exist) since an algorithm which exhibits different behavior on such a string would readily yield a means to compress it to its index in this small set of faulty strings. (Again, a reader unfamiliar with these notions and unsatisfied with our informal treatment is referred to Li and Vitányi [99].) So, strings of maximal Kolmogorov complexity are essentially random strings, and more generally, the Kolmogorov complexity of a string x is the length of a "random" description of x, or the "amount of randomness" (in bits) contained in x. Since, relative to an efficient, reliable algorithm, this randomness can be "replaced" by tossing fresh coins, we might intuitively hope that the following definition captures the minimal amount of information that is "needed" by an efficient randomized algorithm to reconstruct something computationally equivalent to a given string x:

Definition 3.18 (Computational depth). The *t-time bounded computational depth* of x conditioned on y, denoted $\mathsf{depth}_t(x|y)$ is defined to be $K^t(x|y) - K(x|y)$. The *t-time bounded computational depth* of a set S conditioned on y, denoted $\mathsf{depth}_t(S|y)$, is defined to be $\min_{x \in S}\{\mathsf{depth}_t(x|y)\}$.

We don't know how to show this directly, but work by Antunes et al. [7] has shown that this intuition holds, given the following standard derandomization assumption:

Assumption 3.19 (Good pseudorandom generators). For every polynomial time bound t, there is an efficiently computable function $G_t : \{0,1\}^{s(n)} \to \{0,1\}^n$ such that $s(n) = O(\log n)$ and for all t-time bounded decision procedures A,

$$\left| \Pr_{x \in \{0,1\}^n}[A(x) = 1] - \Pr_{y \in \{0,1\}^{s(n)}}[A(G_t(y)) = 1] \right| < 1/6$$

This assumption is widely assumed to hold, as a consequence of evidence in the work of Impagliazzo and Wigderson [82].

Paraphrased slightly, Antunes et al. [7] prove the following:

Theorem 3.20. *Fix any nonempty set S_x decidable in time $t_S(|x|)$ from an auxiliary input x. There is a randomized algorithm running in time $O(2^{\mathsf{depth}_t(S_x|x)}(t + t_S(|x|)))$ given input x and the algorithm for S_x, that outputs some $y \in S_x$.*

This yields the following immediate corollary, roughly corresponding to our original intuition:

Corollary 3.21. *Under Assumption 3.19, for every fixed polynomials $t(k)$ and $t_S(|x|)$, and every nonempty set S_x decidable in time $t_S(|x|)$ by some algorithm A_x from an auxiliary input x, there exists some $y \in S_x$ that can be recovered in time polynomial in $|x|$ and k from a description of length $|A_x| + O(\mathsf{depth}_{t(k)}(S_x|x) + \log k + \log|x|)$ given input x.*

In particular, if S_x is the set of witnesses for x under some NP-relation R, $|A_x| = O(1)$ so some witness of x has a description of length $O(\mathsf{depth}_{t(k)}(S_x|x) + \log k + \log|x|)$. If additionally $\mathsf{depth}_{t(k)}(S_x|x)$ is $O(\log|x|)$ over all x, then the algorithm claimed in Theorem 3.20 runs in polynomial time with respect to x and k.

On the other hand, Antunes et al. [7] also observe the following:

Proposition 3.22. *Under Assumption 3.19, if there is a polynomial $t(|x|)$ such that there is a randomized algorithm outputting a member of S_x on input* *x in $t(|x|)$ steps, then there is some member $y \in S_x$ that can be recovered in time $t'(|x|)$ for some polynomial t' from a description of length $O(\log|x|)$. In particular, $\mathsf{depth}_{t'(|x|)}(S_x|x) = O(\log|x|)$.*

In summary, we have the following

Proposition 3.23. *Fix an NP-relation R with corresponding decision problem Π_R. Under Assumption 3.19, the following are equivalent:*

1. *The search problem for R can be solved in randomized polynomial time.*

2. *There is a polynomial t such that for all $x \in \Pi_R$ $\mathsf{depth}_{t(|x|)}(R_x|x) = O(\log|x|)$.*

3. *There is a polynomial t such that for every $x \in \Pi_R$, some member of R_x can be recovered in $t(|x|)$ steps from a description of length $O(\log|x|)$.*

The characterization in Proposition 3.23 is simple enough, but it leads to some subtle scenarios which we will now illustrate. Suppose that we have a one-way function, f. Let $R = \{(x,y) : y = f(x)\}$ be our NP-relation, and let $R|_n$ denote $\{(x,y) \in R : |x| = n\}$. We can sample $(x,y) \in R|_n$ easily, so for some polynomial t, $\mathsf{depth}_{t(n)}(R|_n) = O(\log n)$. On the other hand, since f is one-way, for y such that $y = f(x)$ for some x, $\mathsf{depth}_{t(n)}(R_y|y) = \omega(\log n)$ for all polynomials t. In particular, for any pair $x \in R_y$, $\mathsf{depth}_{t(n)}(x|y) = \omega(\log n)$. But notice: for a random $x \in \{0,1\}^n$, $\mathsf{depth}_{t(n)}(x) = O(\log n)$. Thus, it is the *context* of y that makes x deep. It is easy to see how this happens from the definition: given an input y, there is a natural, computationally inefficient coding for x, so $K(x|y)$ cannot be too large.

3.4.2 Formalizing a goal of intellectual curiosity

Now that we have recalled the notion of computational depth and the relevant results, we are ready to formalize the setting described in our story. Recall that Bob wishes to referee Alice's submission to the Intergalactic Conference on the Mathematical Foundations of Computer Science, and he aims to vet submissions for "deep" theorems, and he wishes to do so independent of the language Alice uses.

The rough strategy Bob will employ as a reviewer is a natural one: he will try to prove Alice's result "on the fly," and if he fails he will conclude that the theorem is hard. The subtle point here is that the reviewer is not only evaluating the output, but also translating both the theorem and the proof from an unknown language; we need to somehow separate the knowledge of the proof from the knowledge and effort employed in "understanding" and "translating" it—namely, the product of this process should be based on the submission, and not a theorem that the reviewer produced on his or her own during the translation process.

Formally, for a given selectivity parameter k and polynomial $t_1(k)$, we wish that the proof has $t_1(k)$-time bounded depth at least $f_1(k) = \Omega(\log k)$

conditioned on the theorem, guaranteeing that the theorem is "deep" on its own merits. Furthermore, if the committee member spends t steps discussing the proof with the author, then we wish to only accept theorems with proofs having t-time bounded depth at least $f_2(t) = \Omega(\log t)$, where this dependence on t rules out reviews from reviewers who end up (inadvertently) proving the theorem themselves during the translation process rather than faithfully representing the submission's contents. We will need this quantity to be conditioned on the reviewer's "prior knowledge" and translation strategy to rule out reviews from reviewers who (again, inadvertently) "pollute" the submission with their own insights during translation. Since we know that conditioning can increase or decrease the depth of a string substantially – additional auxiliary inputs can, respectively, either provide context that makes a string deep, or provide immediate access to a string that makes it shallow – the depth conditioned on just the theorem, and the depth conditioned on the translator's knowledge are, in general, quite different, and both of these conditions are necessary.

The goal.   Precisely now, we fix three functions, f_1, t_1, and f_2. The goal G is given by an environment $\mathcal{E} = \{E_k\}$ where E_k sends the user the selectivity parameter k on each round and records the transcript of the interaction with the server as (assumed to be) reported by the user, and a referee R that is only satisfied if the user sends a message ϕ marked as a "theorem," followed by a message marked "proof," containing a proof of ϕ, such that

1. Any proof of ϕ has $t_1(k)$-time bounded depth at least $f_1(k)$ conditioned on ϕ.

2. For some (user) translation strategy U that, on the provided transcript, enters a state $\sigma^{(\mathrm{u})}$ when it produces ϕ, and then produces a proof of ϕ t steps later, the produced ϕ does not have a proof of t-time bounded depth $f_2(t)$ conditioned on ϕ, $\sigma^{(\mathrm{u})}$, and the code for U.

Note that it follows from Proposition 3.22 that assuming pseudorandom generators against polynomial time with logarithmic seeds exist, since we can easily simulate the t step execution of any user strategy U' and the trivial server in t steps, if U' interacting with the trivial server outputs a theorem ϕ and a proof at most t steps later with probability at least ϵ, then the t-time bounded depth of the proof conditioned on ϕ, the code for U', and the state of U' when it outputs ϕ is at most $O(\log t)$. Hence, the goal is (t, ϵ)-nontrivial given an appropriate choice of f_2 (i.e., one that is $\Omega(\log t)$), so the proof (at least) must depend on Alice's submission.

3.4.3 Constructing universal reviewers: sensing functions for goals of intellectual curiosity

We now wish to describe a universal reviewing strategy by giving a sensing function for the goal described above. In light of the second condition (stipulating a lower bound on the depth conditioned on the code for the translator) it should not be surprising that it will be substantially easier to give a grey-box sensing function for this goal than to give a black-box one. Our construction will use an efficient probabilistic algorithm Π such that $\Pi(x; t, d|y)$ either outputs a proof of x or $\bot$, which we interpret as "I don't know." Using Theorem 3.20, we can obtain an algorithm Π that finds polynomial length proofs of x having t-time bounded depth conditioned on y of d with high probability, running in time $O(2^d(t + p(|x|)))$ for some polynomial p (depending on the verification time for proofs of x).

Construction. For the above choice of Π, we define $V(\epsilon)$ to accept if and only if the following holds: the user U' has sent a message ϕ marked "theorem" to the environment while entering a state $\sigma^{(u)}$, followed by another message containing a proof of ϕ marked "proof" t steps later, satisfying the following two conditions in all of $O(\log 1/\epsilon)$ independent trials:

1. $\Pi(\phi; t_1(k), f_1(k)) = \bot$

2. $\Pi(\phi; t, f_2(t)|U', \sigma^{(u)}) = \bot$

Correctness: safety and viability of our sensing function. Note that since our choice of Π finds proofs of theorems with depth $f_1(k)$ conditioned on ϕ or $f_2(t)$ conditioned on ϕ, U', and $\sigma^{(u)}$, with high probability on each run, in $O(\log 1/\epsilon)$ runs, V rejects such theorems with probability $1 - \epsilon$; since we see that the goal is achieved whenever the produced theorem and proof satisfy the depth conditions, V is $(1 - \epsilon)$-safe, and thus has controllable safety. Moreover, whenever Alice is helpful for G, we see that there must be some polynomial time U' that produces theorems and proofs that satisfy both conditions in an execution with Alice; since the runs of Π complete in polynomial time, it follows again from Proposition 3.22 that, assuming that good pseudorandom generators exist, the runs of Π only find theorems of depth $O(f_1(k) + \log t_1(k) + \log p(|\phi|))$ or $O(f_2(t) + \log t + \log p(|\phi|))$ with any reasonable probability. Thus, $V(\epsilon)$ (taking ϵ fixed) is viable with Alices producing theorems deeper than these bounds. We can therefore construct universal reviewers for our conference using Corollary 2.36.

3.5 Tests

So far, we have seen how to design sensing functions (and hence universal protocols) for goals that are classified as purely intellectual or purely physical in our taxonomy; we now consider some goals – tests – that are necessarily both intellectual and physical—*intellectual* because they depend on the user reaching a correct verdict, and *physical* because the correct verdict depends on the server. We begin by recalling the goal of the Turing test examiner, as considered in Example 2.5. There, we had two possible classes of "servers," S_1 and S_2, which corresponded to computers and humans, respectively, and the goal was that we wanted to report to the environment whether we were conversing with a computer or a human—formally, sending the verdict "i" when we are communicating with a member of S_i.

Remarks on formalizations of the Turing test

Before we continue, we make two remarks concerning Turing's original formulation of the test [149]. First, Turing's formulation involved the examiner communicating with one member from each of the classes, and required the examiner to label one a human and one a computer; we could model this by introducing a second "server" as a fourth party in the system, but we hope that the reader will agree that this would be a needless complication at the moment. Second, Turing originally focused on the role of the *computer*, rather than the *examiner* as we do here: in Turing's exposition, the computer was said to pass the Turing test if the examiner would not succeed at this goal better than chance, and the ability to pass the test was taken as *defining* "intelligence." We stress that we only consider the examiner's goal here, and note that some of the weaknesses of Turing's proposal stem from ambiguities concerning the role of the examiner.

In the original exposition, Turing only indicated that the computer should pass the test with a single examiner, although remarks he made subsequently indicated that he felt that the computer should pass with a representative sample of the population playing the role of the examiner [138]. Now, although on the one hand, it is hard to fault the test as a sufficient condition for intelligence if the computer is made to pass with *all* examiners (perhaps with some minor caveats, which we mention in the next section), on the other hand, it isn't clear what the computer passing with one examiner or an examiner randomly selected from the general population says about its ability to pass with all examiners—and hence, whether or not the test, as administrable in practice, is really suitable as a definition of "intelligence." In particular, distinctly *unintelligent* algorithms such as Weizenbaum's Eliza [155] do surprisingly well at fooling the average examiner. Perhaps if we had an optimal strategy for the examiner, then the computer passing against such a strategy would suffice to guarantee that the machine could pass against any other examiner, but of course, we don't have such a strategy.

Tests amenable to formal analysis

Ultimately, we won't attempt to formalize the Turing test any further: due to our inability to further characterize the classes of strategies corresponding to either unintelligent computers or humans, at present we have no provably good means to distinguish the two. Consequently, we have no suggestions for designing sensing functions, let alone strategies for Turing tests.

Before we leave Turing tests behind entirely, we note that a CAPT-CHA [153] is *precisely* a strategy for the examiner when S_1 is the class of currently known time-efficient algorithms, and von Ahn et al. describe a variety of such strategies. Thus, a CAPTCHA *successfully* distinguishes computers from humans in practice. Of course, if we expect AI to be possible, then *in principle* we would only expect to be able to give a strategy for a test that, at best, distinguished some class S_1' of *unintelligent* strategies from the class of human strategies—an "optimal" strategy for the examiner as alluded to above. We note that a CAPTCHA is therefore not a Turing test in the sense that it isn't intended to provide a definition of "intelligence," but rather a test that distinguishes strategies that can't be used for solving a hard AI problem from human strategies. As such, CAPTCHAs provide a useful filter, preventing the automated abuse of a variety of web applications at present. We note that CAPTCHAs have been partially analyzed in a manner similar to a cryptographic protocol: since a strategy for passing the CAPTCHA would solve an open problem in AI, we know that no presently available algorithms can be used to pass the CAPTCHA. On the other hand, since we still have no formal model of human strategies or capabilities, we can't formally show that humans pass the CAPTCHA—we can only note that empirically, they have demonstrated the ability to pass with high probability.

Instead of discussing Turing tests or CAPTCHAs any further, in the rest of this section, we will exhibit a test of *computational ability* (irrespective of whether or not this corresponds to "intelligence") which we *can* analyze, and will illustrate several important issues in the design of such tests. Very roughly, we will describe a strategy allowing an examiner to distinguish a class of servers with limited computational abilities from servers exhibiting powerful computational abilities.

3.5.1   A test of computational ability

Attempt #1.   Suppose we take "limited computational ability" to mean that the server employs a strategy implemented by an algorithm running in time $t(n)$ for some polynomial t, and that we would like to distinguish servers with such limited strategies from servers which use strategies that cannot be implemented within such limits. We immediately encounter our first difficulty: any finite function (on strings of length $n < N$ for some finite bound N) can be hard-coded into a linear-time algorithm via a look-up table, so in a bounded-length test every server is indistinguishable from some linear-time server strategies. The analogue of such "cheating" has been raised as an issue with the Turing test by Block's "Aunt Bertha machine" [28] which, by means of a hard-coded table, would mimic Block's fictional Aunt Bertha in any conversation lasting up to an hour.

The fix for this issue in the Turing test suggested by Shieber [139] was to restrict our attention to algorithms of some bounded program length $k(n)$ that is sufficiently small to prevent answers from being hard-coded, but large enough to permit the use of all "feasibly produced" algorithms. Since the size of the table must grow exponentially with the length of the conversation, moderate length conversations would require an astronomically large table, and we can expect that any machine we'd ever encounter in practice would only have resources falling well within some much more modest bound. We will likewise only attempt to distinguish powerful servers from weak servers running some short program, and starting from some simple initial configuration – clearly otherwise, the corresponding table could be stored in the program's configuration – and thus, we will only attempt to give a *weakly universal* strategy (cf. Definition 2.15). For our purposes, we only will be able to give a "reasonably efficient" test (running in time polynomial in n) for $k(n) = O(\log n)$; the existence of examiner strategies that are more efficient with respect to the program lengths of the limited examinees' strategies is an open question.

Attempt #2.   Thus, minding this first caveat, we would *ideally* like to distinguish servers using a strategy that can be computed in time $t(n)$ by a $k(n)$-bit program from servers using a strategy that cannot be computed in time $t(n)$, but this still demands too much—there will always exist server strategies that cannot be computed in time $t(n)$, but are indistinguishable from some time $t(n)$ strategy on some large set of histories. For example, for any given examiner, there is a server strategy that simulates some time $t(n)$ server unless it receives some long string, longer than the examiner would send at that point in the execution with any reasonable probability. This server strategy is never distinguished from a time $t(n)$ server by the aforementioned examiner (or any examiner sending similarly short messages) with high probability. We stress that the difficulty exposed here is that the hard-to-compute aspects of a server strategy demanding substantial resources may be elusive—in the language of the Turing test, this would be like the case of an intelligent but uncooperative subject who either sees no reason to participate or wishes to fail the test for some reason.

The natural fix for the Turing test in this case is to relax the guarantee: we only guarantee that the test passes a subject who is "trying" to pass. The corresponding fix for our test of computational ability is to restrict the class of powerful server strategies $\mathcal{S}_2$ to those strategies that readily provide evidence of their abilities; roughly, in this case, to strategies that are helpful for some class of sufficiently hard computational problems. Even merely requiring that the server is helpful is not enough—for any fixed examiner, constructions of servers similar to the aforementioned "uncooperative" servers (and similar to the servers constructed in the proof of Theorem 2.37) yield server strategies that are helpful but nevertheless simulate some time $t(n)$ bounded server with the fixed examiner. More precisely, our fix is then to require that the server helps some user programs of length at most $b(n)$ bits solve hard computational problems.

Of course, for this to be a meaningful restriction, the problems that the server helps the user solve must be harder than the user could solve on its own. More to the point in this case, for the restriction to distinguish the powerful servers from the limited servers, the problems must be harder than any that the user could solve with any $k(n)$-bit server program running in time $t(n)$. Thus, supposing that the server helps $b(n)$-bit user programs running in time $t'(n)$, it will suffice to ask that the server is helpful to some such user for simulating any time $t(n) + t'(n)$ computation by a $f(n) = O(b(n) + k(n))$-bit program from a $p(n)$-bit state for some polynomial $p(n)$.

A goal for testing computational ability. We will need to modify the goal of Example 2.5 to accommodate our new parameters t, t', k, b, f, p : $\mathbb{N} \to \mathbb{N}$ (described above). The environment's non-deterministic strategy $\mathcal{E} = \{E_n\}_{n \in \mathbb{N}}$ (where E_n has size n) merely sends n to the user and server and records n along with the current messages from the user and the server.

Essentially, we will assume two classes of servers, $\mathcal{S}_1$ and $\mathcal{S}_2$. We assume that on each round, any member S of $\mathcal{S}_1$ sends a message consisting of $(1, \ell)$ where ℓ is the length of the program running in time $t(n)$ computing the strategy used by S; and, any member S of $\mathcal{S}_2$ sends a message consisting of $(2, \ell(n))$ where $\ell(n)$ is the minimum length of a user program running in $t'(n)$ steps needed for S to be $(G_\Pi, 1)$-helpful for the problem Π of simulating some $f(n)$-bit program from a $p(n)$-bit initial state for our reference universal Turing machine for $t(n) + t'(n)$ steps, and deciding whether it accepts. (Recall that the goal of deciding Π, G_Π, was described in Example 2.17.)

The referee, now, is satisfied in the following three cases:

1. The server's message is $(1, \ell)$ such that $\ell > k(n)$, so the weak server's program is too long.

2. The server's message is $(2, \ell)$ such that $\ell > b(n)$, so the server does not exhibit its power to sufficiently simple user strategies.

3. The user's message is "i" such that the server's message is of the form (i, ℓ), so the server is a member of $\mathcal{S}_i$.

Remarks on the goal's formulation. Several remarks are in order. We begin by noting that the first two cases in the definition of the referee provide the necessary relaxations of our goal to circumvent the problems that felled our first two attempts at formulating a test of computational ability. The consequence of this weakening of our goal is that a user succeeding at the goal either outputs "1," and therefore concludes that "either the server is weak (case 3) or the server does not exhibit its power to simple strategies (case 2)" or outputs "2," and then concludes that "either the server is powerful (case 3) or the server has a very long program (case 1)." We also saw that related relaxations were needed for the Turing test, as presumably with other goals for testing abilities.

This goal also illustrates a more general point about the modeling of goals for tests: note that the server's "truthfulness" with respect to the environment is not at issue. Rather, by design, the classes of servers S_1 and S_2 only contain servers that report their relevant properties – membership in S_i, program lengths, etc. – directly to the environment. In this way, the referee's verdicts can depend on these properties without requiring us to make any messy (and invariably incomplete) general specification of what properties of the server the referee "sees"—in short, the referee sees what the server tells it, which we can supply by design (and corresponding assumption on S) as appropriate to the application at hand.

3.5.2 Examiner strategy for a test of computational ability

We now turn to constructing a "universal" examiner strategy for testing the computational abilities of servers from our two classes: S_1^*, consisting of "weak" servers that

1. Employ strategies that are time $t(n)$ bounded.

2. On each round, send a message $(1, \ell)$ to the environment such that their strategy is computed in time $t(n)$ by a program of length ℓ (that also specifies the program's initial state).

and S_2^*, consisting of "powerful" servers that

1. Employ strategies that are $(G_\Pi, 1)$-helpful to some time $t'(n)$ user strategy for the problem Π of deciding whether or not an $f(n)$-bit program accepts from a given $p(n)$-bit state in time $t(n) + t'(n)$.

2. On each round, send a message $(2, \ell(n))$ to the environment (in response to the environment's message "n") where $\ell(n)$ is the minimum length such that with the server, a user program of length $\ell(n)$ running in time $t'(n)$ decides Π, the problem of deciding whether an $f(n)$-bit program accepts from a $p(n)$-bit state in time $t(n) + t'(n)$.

3. May start from any state.

We will aim to give an examiner strategy running in polynomial time for fixed polynomials $t(n)$ and $t'(n)$, and functions $b(n)$ and $k(n)$ that are $O(\log n)$ (we will specify $f(n) = O(\log n)$ and a polynomial $p(n)$).

Helpfulness is clearly not an issue—every member of $\mathcal{S}_1^* \cup \mathcal{S}_2^*$ is helpful to either the user that sends "1" to the environment, or to the user that sends "2." Thus, moreover, the message of Theorem 2.25 – that the goal ought to be distilled down to distinguishing $\mathcal{S}_1^*$ from $\mathcal{S}_2^*$ – is mere common sense.[5] It is interesting that, despite this, we will find it easier to proceed by designing a protocol directly.

Theorem 3.24. *Let polynomials $t(n)$ and $t'(n)$, and $O(\log n)$ functions $k(n)$ and $b(n)$ be given. Then, for an appropriate choice of reference universal Turing machine, there are functions $f(n)$ and $p(n)$ such that for the corresponding test of computational ability and classes $\mathcal{S}_1^*$ and $\mathcal{S}_2^*$, there is a weakly $(\mathcal{S}_1^* \cup \mathcal{S}_2^*, 1)$-universal strategy for testing computational ability that is computable in polynomial time.*

Proof

Overview.   At a high level, our construction will enumerate all weak (time $t'(n)$ and $b(n)$-length) user strategies, and attempt to diagonalize against all weak user-server pairs—a powerful server will help some weak user to compute the diagonal function, but the weak servers will all be caught, thus allowing us to reliably distinguish the two kinds of servers. Towards this end, we will rely on the ability to simulate the interaction between a time $t'(n)$ user strategy with a program length of $b(n)$ and a time $t(n)$ server strategy with a program length of $k(n)$ via a time $t(n) + t'(n)$ program of length $f(n)$, for an appropriate choice of $f(n) = O(\log n)$ (these will be our only constraints on the choice of f).

Choice of $f(n)$ and universal Turing machine.   If our programs are given by deterministic $O(\log n / \log \log n)$ state controls, for example, then each has an $O(\log n)$-bit description (given by a list of $O(\log \log n)$-bit "next state" transitions), and it is no issue to redirect a transition to one program's "wait for response" state to the other's "resume" state; it is not hard to see that the length of each item in the list increases by at most an additive constant in this combined program, and thus that the length of the combined program is greater than $k(n) + b(n)$ by at most a constant factor—and thus, we can choose $f(n) = O(k(n) + b(n)) = O(\log n)$.

Choice of $p(n)$.   We rely on $k(n)$ and $b(n)$ being $O(\log n)$ so that there are only a polynomial number of weak user-server pairs, thus allowing us to enumerate the entire set of pairs in polynomial time. Assuming that we only run each weak user once for each weak server, and given the polynomial time

---

[5]Technically, Theorem 2.25 does not apply since we will only aim to construct a *weakly universal* protocol, and moreover, it is not clear that a satisfactory analogue of Theorem 2.25 would even hold for weakly universal protocols. Nevertheless, the *"moral"* of the theorem is still common sense here!

bound $t(n)$ on the running time of a weak server in this interaction, there is therefore a polynomial upper bound on the number of bits needed to describe the state of any weak server at any point during our interaction with that server—this will be our choice of $p(n)$.

With these technicalities out of the way, we can describe our scheme in more detail.

Construction.   For each possible $k(n)$-bit server, we will maintain a table indicating what the current state of that server would be; if the responses of the actual server are inconsistent with one of the $k(n)$-bit servers, we will mark that server as "inconsistent" in the table.

For each $b(n)$-bit user strategy, we will loop over the remaining consistent $k(n)$-bit server strategies until we detect a failure of that user strategy in the following sense: given the conjectured current state of a $k(n)$-bit server, we will prepare an instance of the problem, "does the current $b(n)$-bit user strategy reject when interacting with the current $k(n)$-bit server started from its current state?" by swapping the outputs of the user strategy. We will both simulate the interaction of the $b(n)$-bit user and the $k(n)$-bit time $t(n)$ server on that instance, and run our $b(n)$-bit user strategy on that same instance with the server; if the answers disagree, then the $b(n)$-bit strategy is considered to have *failed*, and we move on to the next weak user strategy; otherwise, we will move on to testing the same weak user strategy with the next weak server. Regardless of whether or not the user strategy failed, we update the current states of the servers in our table according to the last interaction.

If, for some $b(n)$-bit user strategy, no failure is detected with any of the remaining $k(n)$-bit server strategies, we return "2" and halt. Otherwise, after all $b(n)$-bit user strategies have failed, we return "1" and halt.

Analysis.   First, note that since there are a polynomial number of weak user strategies and weak server strategies, and each runs in polynomial time, the user strategy described above is performing a polynomial number of polynomial time computable simulations. Therefore, our user strategy runs in polynomial time.

Turning to correctness, we will naturally separately consider the behavior of our strategy when we interact with members of $\mathcal{S}_1^*$ and members of $\mathcal{S}_2^*$. We note first that we are allowed to output either verdict if the server is a member of $\mathcal{S}_1^*$ with a program length greater than $k(n)$, or if the server is a member of $\mathcal{S}_2^*$ which is not helpful for our decision problems of interest to weak users of length at most $b(n)$, so it only remains to show that our strategy works when neither of these conditions hold.

It is particularly easy to show that the strategy works for servers in $\mathcal{S}_2^*$ now. Whenever a server S in $\mathcal{S}_2^*$ is helpful to one of the weak users of length at most $b(n)$, then when we reach that user in the enumeration, S will help it decide every instance of our diagonal problem; therefore, at that point, our strategy will find that $b(n)$ did not fail on any of the instances, and correctly output "2" and halt.

To see that our strategy works for servers S in $\mathcal{S}_1^*$, note that when S is computed by a program of length at most $k(n)$, each $b(n)$-bit user strategy will fail to correctly decide "does the current $b(n)$-bit user strategy reject when interacting with the current $k(n)$-bit server started from its current state?" when we consider S as the current $k(n)$-bit server. Thus, each $b(n)$ will fail by the point it reaches S in the inner loop; since every weak user will therefore fail, we finally (correctly) output "1" and halt. ■

3.5.3 Promises and verifiability

There is a moral to the story of the development of our test for computational ability. Recall that our original ambitions – to distinguish time $t(n)$ bounded server strategies from server strategies requiring more time – had to be scaled back substantially by means of a collection of *"promises"* (i.e., assumptions) concerning the goal and the class of servers. The difficulties we encountered stemmed from the fact that, under a variety of conditions, weak servers could be indistinguishable from strong servers—that is, there were many cases in which success at our goal *could not be verified,* and we were only able to succeed once we eliminated these cases by assumption.

The same observation is likely to be relevant to other goals, given that we know by Theorem 2.25 and its variants that (robust) universal users can only be constructed for verifiable goals; therefore, if a goal is not verifiable, it must be weakened before we can have any hope of designing a universal user for it. Such weakening can take the form of either a relaxed referee, a restricted class of servers, or both—as we saw here.

More broadly, one could envision situations where we could assume various kinds of "commonality" (common knowledge, etc.) between the server and user, and these would be reflected in restrictions on the class of servers that the protocol is designed to work with. The benefits of such restrictions are not merely limited to which goals can be achieved, and in particular, we will see ways in which a user can also exploit such kinds of restrictions to attain greater efficiency in its communication in Chapter 4.

Chapter 4

Conditions for efficiency in finite executions

The theory described in the previous sections engages in some abuse of our notions of "efficiency." Although it is easily seen to be necessary and reasonable that our protocol should use different polynomial running time bounds for each server $S \in \mathcal{S}$, the Levin-style enumerations incur an overhead in the running time that, for the user protocol U_S used to interact with S, is $2^{O(|U_S|)}$ where $|U_S|$ is the length of our program for U_S. Since we expect $|U_S|$ to be of moderate size, $2^{O(|U_S|)}$ is enormous, and it is natural to wonder if there is a better method. In this chapter, we will show that unfortunately, *this cost is unavoidable in general.*

Still, the class of "password-protected" servers used to show the lower bound is intuitively designed *not* to allow easy access; thus, there is reason to hope that a more open server might not force us to pay such a prohibitively large price. To an extent, these hopes are fulfilled: we will show how a different construction of a universal user protocol can take advantage of a natural sense of "commonality" – a notion of "natural user strategies" – when the server is designed to efficiently aid a large collection of such natural user strategies in achieving the goal.

We will also consider another upshot of restricting our attention to such servers: we will be able to relax our various requirements on *all states* of a server to a requirement merely on the *effectively reachable* states. Such a relaxation will substantially broaden the applicability of the theory, to include servers that are allowed to become completely unhelpful so long as this is unlikely to be observed in practice.

Finally, we will describe some joint work with Santosh Vempala [86], in which we consider the consequences of the lack of a suitable common notion of "natural user strategies" across a class of servers. In particular, we will show that when no such common notion exists under which all of the servers

B. Juba, *Universal Semantic Communication,*
DOI 10.1007/978-3-642-23297-8_4,
© Springer-Verlag Berlin Heidelberg 2011

are easy to use, then no common efficient universal algorithm can be designed for that class.

4.1 Running time lower bounds via passwords

We are motivated by the undesirable exponential dependence on the length of the relevant program for a user protocol in the running times of the constructions of universal users given in Proposition 2.27, Theorem 2.35, and the like. We will show that the qualitative behavior of the running time of the generic constructions of universal users in Proposition 2.27, etc. is optimal whenever the class of servers contains "password-protected" servers and the goal requires that the user obtain the server's assistance—nontrivial goals, as specified in Definition 3.2. Since these password-protected servers are "helpful" (to users possessing the passwords), our results demonstrate that the qualitative behavior of the running time of any universal user in the basic universal setting for such nontrivial goals is undesirably large. Although Definition 3.2 does not capture purely intellectual goals (and hence the result we have just described does not suffice to prove Theorem 1.7 concerning computational goals, originally appearing in our first paper [83]) we will also show that the results also carry over to our parameterized notion of nontriviality, given in Definition 3.4, which *does* capture purely intellectual goals.

A different variant of these lower bounds appeared previously in a technical report [84], and we will prove another similar lower bound on the number of errors occurring in an infinite execution in Chapter 8. The technique of deriving lower bounds by considering "passwords" is itself quite natural and hence unsurprisingly not new to this work—we believe it was first discovered by Moore [115].

4.1.1 Lower bound for nontrivial goals

We will first show the lower bound for the original, simpler notion of nontriviality, which is well-suited to physical goals. To begin, recall that in our models of nontrivial goals, we chose to model a server providing "no assistance" as the server employing a strategy that only sent empty messages to all other parties; a nontrivial goal in the sense of Definition 3.2 was then one that could not be achieved with such a server. Along these lines, a "password-protected" server is one that provides no assistance to a user until it receives a message from the user that matches its password.

Definition 4.1 (Password-protected server). For every server strategy S and string $x \in \{0,1\}^*$, the *password-protected version of S using password x*, denoted S^x, is a server strategy which is identical to S except for an extra "waiting for password" state (not used by S), in which it sends empty messages to all other players; it remains in the waiting state until it receives a message from the user containing x, from which it enters an initial state of S.

A user for a large collection of password-protected versions of servers must incur substantial overhead compared to the respective optimal user strategies for each server because whenever the user does not know the password, the user has no choice but to try all possible passwords in the class, which implies a lower bound on the user's running time. We address this claim in two parts. First, we observe that given a user strategy for any server, we can construct user strategies for each password-protected version of that server which are not much less efficient than the original user strategy with the unprotected server.

Proposition 4.2 (Password-protection preserves helpfulness). *Let S be a server strategy and U be a t-time bounded user protocol such that (U, S) robustly achieves a goal with probability p. Then, for every password x of length less than ℓ, there is a $t + \ell$-time bounded user protocol U^x such that for the password protected version of S using password x S^x, (U^x, S^x) also robustly achieves the goal with probability p.*

Proof Given the t-time bounded user protocol U that robustly achieves the goal with S with probability p and the password x of length less than ℓ, the user strategy U^x that sends x to the server and then runs U from its initial state is $t + \ell$-time bounded.

Let an arbitrary initial state of the environment be given. If S^x starts in the waiting state, notice that after the first round, the execution of U^x with S^x is identical to some execution of U with S; therefore, since both executions send the same messages to the environment and (U, S) achieves the goal in an execution started from this state with probability p, so does U^x with S^x. If S^x starts in any other state of S, we again notice that after the first round, the execution of U^x with S^x is identical to some execution of U with S, so again U^x with S^x achieves the goal from this state with probability p since U with S does. Thus, (U^x, S^x) robustly achieves the goal with probability p. ∎

Now that we see that the running time of a good strategy for a fixed password-protected server only depends linearly on the length of the password, we show that the running time of a universal user depends *exponentially* on the lengths of the passwords. The lengths of the descriptions of the optimal user strategies similarly depend only linearly on the lengths of the passwords, so this shows that the exponential dependence on these lengths in the generic construction of universal strategies used in Proposition 2.27 is qualitatively optimal for classes containing all the password-protected versions of a server using passwords of each given length.

Theorem 4.3 (Exponential overhead is necessary for nontrivial goals with password-protected servers). *For a nontrivial goal G and any server that is* *helpful for G, for every user strategy U, integer ℓ and $\delta \in (0,1)$, there is a password x of length ℓ such that U does not achieve G in less than $\delta 2^{\ell}$ rounds with the server using password x with probability at least δ.*

Proof Let any user strategy U be given and let T be a trivial server. Since G is a nontrivial goal, there is some $E \in \mathcal{E}$ such that the referee is never satisfied in the execution (E, U, T). Since the expected total number of times the user sends strings of length ℓ in the first $\delta 2^{\ell} - 1$ rounds is less than $\delta 2^{\ell}$, by a pigeonhole argument, we see that there must be some string x of length ℓ such that the user does not send a message consisting of x in $\delta 2^{\ell} - 1$ rounds with probability at least δ. Therefore, if we consider the execution (E, U, S^x), we see that the first $\delta 2^{\ell} - 1$ rounds of this execution are identical to the execution (E, U, T) with probability at least $1 - \delta$. In particular, since the referee is never satisfied in (E, U, T), the referee is only satisfied in (E, U, S^x) during the first $\delta 2^{\ell} - 1$ rounds with probability at most δ. The theorem follows. ∎

In particular, Proposition 4.2 immediately implies that whenever a p-helpful server for a goal exists, the class of all p-helpful servers for the goal contains all of the password-protected versions of that server, so the lower bound of Theorem 4.3 applies to the basic universal setting for nontrivial goals. That is, if we wish to avoid the exponential overhead incurred by the construction employed in Proposition 2.27, then we must look at classes of servers more restricted than the class of all p-helpful servers for a nontrivial goal.

4.1.2 Extension to parameterized nontriviality

Thus, Theorem 4.3 is already sufficient to motivate searching for new restrictions on the class of servers in some cases. We stress that this effect actually holds *much* more broadly than Theorem 4.3 would strictly suggest. The problem with Theorem 4.3 is that unless the referee is never satisfied with some actual strategy of the environment, a purely intellectual goal cannot be nontrivial in the sense of Definition 3.2. In particular, our exponential lower bound on the overhead of users for computational goals, Theorem 1.7 from Section 1.4.2, *does not* follow from Theorem 4.3.

Recall that we had also introduced a parameterized notion of nontriviality, in Definition 3.4, to capture situations where although the goal may be achievable by a user on its own, the user expects to reduce the time requirements by communicating with a server. We will show how Theorem 4.3 can be adapted to show a lower bound for goals that are nontrivial in this parameterized sense. Thus, we will see that actually, most goals of natural interest require exponential overhead in general.

Theorem 4.4 (Exponential overhead for goals that are nontrivial in the parameterized sense). *If $G = (\mathcal{E}, R)$ is $(t(n), \epsilon(n))$-nontrivial then for every* *user strategy U, (G, p)-helpful server strategy S, integer ℓ and $\delta \in (0,1)$, there is a password x of length ℓ such that U does not simultaneously achieve G in less than $\delta 2^\ell$ rounds and run in time less than $t(n)$ with probability greater than $\delta + \epsilon(n)$ with the server using password x.*

Proof The argument essentially follows the same basic outline as the proof of Theorem 4.3, with a few new technicalities:

Suppose for contradiction that some user strategy U could achieve G in less than $\delta 2^\ell$ rounds and less than $t(n)$ steps with every server using a password x of length ℓ with probability $\delta + \epsilon(n) + \delta_E$ for some $\delta_E > 0$.

Since G is $(t(n), \epsilon(n))$-nontrivial, we can find some $E \in \mathcal{E}$ such that U cannot satisfy R with the trivial server T when it runs in $t(n)$ steps with probability greater than $\epsilon(n)$. Now, by a pigeonhole argument (just as in the proof of Theorem 4.3) there must be a string x of length ℓ such that in the execution (E, U, T), the user does not send a message consisting of x within the first $\delta 2^\ell - 1$ messages with probability at least δ.

Consider the execution (E, U, S^x). Conditioned on U failing to send x to S^x, (U, S^x) sends the same messages to the environment as (U, T); in particular, since this occurs with probability at least $1 - \delta$, and we assumed that U achieved G with S^x in $t(n)$ steps with probability $\delta + \epsilon(n) + \delta_E$, by a union bound, we see that U should also achieve G with T in $t(n)$ steps with probability at least $\epsilon(n) + \delta_E$. Recall, now, that E was chosen so that R was only satisfied with (U, T) when U ran in $t(n)$ steps with probability at most $\epsilon(n)$, a contradiction. Therefore, no such user U can exist. ∎

Theorem 4.4 now yields, in particular, our exponential lower bound on the number of rounds needed to achieve our goal of computation for PSPACE-complete problems as a corollary. The definitions of Π-helpful and "deciding instances of Π" were originally given in Section 1.4.2, and later revisited in Section 3.3.1; to understand the theorem below, it suffices to know that "deciding instances of Π" (as defined in Section 1.4.2) means achieving the goal of computing Π, G_Π as defined in Example 2.17, with probability at least $2/3$.

Theorem 1.7 *Let Π be a PSPACE-complete decision problem, and let A be a Π-helpful Alice. Then, unless PSPACE = BPP, if a probabilistic algorithm Bob decides instances of Π using the help of any Alice in $\mathcal{PW}(A)$ with passwords of length ℓ in time $t_\ell(n) = O(n^k)$, Bob must run for $\Omega(2^{|x|})$ rounds with some A^x.*

Proof Suppose that the goal of deciding Π, G_Π, were not $(p(n), 7/12)$-nontrivial for every polynomial $p(n)$; this would imply that some user interacting with the trivial server could decide Π with probability $7/12$ in polynomial time. Of course, this immediately yields a BPP algorithm for Π, and hence since Π is PSPACE-complete, we would have PSPACE = BPP.

Therefore, unless PSPACE = BPP, G_Π is $(p(n), 7/12)$-nontrivial for every polynomial $p(n)$. Theorem 4.4 now shows that for any user protocol, for every length ℓ, if the user's running time with servers with passwords of length ℓ is bounded by a polynomial $t_\ell(n)$, then there is some password x of length ℓ such that the user cannot achieve G_Π with A^x with probability $2/3$ in fewer than $\frac{1}{12}2^\ell$ rounds. ■

Since, with the one exception of the goal of testing computational ability in Section 3.5 – which was designed for a highly specialized class of servers – all of the goals we have considered so far were either nontrivial in the sense of Definition 3.2 or in the sense of Definition 3.4, we see that enumeration is unfortunately qualitatively optimal for many (perhaps most) natural goals of interest in the basic universal setting. Since this exponential "constant" in the running time of a universal user protocol is extremely undesirable, we need to explore means of restricting the class of servers so that it does not contain, e.g., password-protected servers, but is still broad enough to yield useful protocols.

In particular, recalling Proposition 4.2, these results suggest that, e.g., merely restricting the complexity of the user protocols that the servers help cannot suffice for obtaining a more efficient universal user; intuitively, we need some definition that rules out the degenerative "hiding" behavior of the password-protected servers. Alternatively, one might hope to find a measure of the "degeneracy" of a server and we might then hope to find a protocol for which the efficiency scales appropriately with this quantity. In the next section, we will see one example of how such notions can be made precise, and under some natural conditions, a universal protocol can run more efficiently.

4.2   A Bayesian refinement of helpfulness

In the previous section, we saw that as a consequence of our counting "password-protected" servers as "helpful" servers that our universal users were expected to work with, we had no hope of giving a really efficient user strategy—the number of rounds required under such conditions often grows exponentially in the length of the user protocol needed to successfully communicate with the server (cf. Theorems 4.3 and 4.4). This is a dissatisfying state of affairs since, in applications, one surely never expected a protocol that could quickly break into a password-protected server; we would have been quite happy to use a protocol that was only efficient when the server was not designed to keep us out in the first place. Thus, we desire a refinement of our notion of "helpfulness" to include only easy-to-access servers, and a protocol that can take advantage of such servers, both of which we will develop presently, inspired by "PAC-Bayesian" analyses in learning theory [110, 136].

The suggestion that PAC-Bayes (and/or a Bayesian approach more generally) may be relevant to developing a notion of a more "proactive" helpful server is due to Dan Roy and David Sontag [125]. Some of the notions we develop here were also inspired by conversations with Adam Kalai.

4.2.1 Basic notions: priors and benchmarks

As a starting point, we suppose that there is a *server designer* who is attempting to design an easy-to-access server for some fixed goal G that is known to all parties. Once we have a notion of what kind of server a benign designer might produce, we will be able to ask whether or not we, as users, can generally access such servers and achieve G efficiently with their assistance.

Towards developing a notion of an easy-to-access server, we will first reflect on what goes wrong with password-protected servers. Formally, the reason a long password provides security is that, for a user who does not have the password, accessing the server requires searching through an exponentially large space. Of course, this only holds if the password is properly chosen—if the password does not have enough "randomness," then it may be possible to break it by searching through a smaller space: in practice, for example, by searching through the words in the dictionary. Relative to the dictionary, such weak passwords have short descriptions, and may be considered "easier to guess" or more "natural." Thus, as a first stab at a notion of easy-to-access along these lines, we might wish to say that a server should operate with a user protocol with a short description.

The problem with the "short description" requirement is that there could be a gap between *our* notion of a short description and the server designer's notion. One might be tempted to retort that a basic result in Kolmogorov complexity is that these description lengths should not differ by more than a constant [99], but this is no help at all: for a given password string x, we could consider a programming language for which the instruction "print x" has a very short (e.g., two-bit) code. If the server's designer happens to use such a programming language, then a user with the password x might seem very natural indeed, and we are back where we started. Indeed, in general, there is no bound on how large this "$O(1)$" term might be. Although this is a particularly pathological choice of programming language, it is intuitively clear at least that in practice, some programs are substantially easier to write in one language than another and vice-versa. Thus, it is clear that this first attempt is inadequate, and we will have to give up something here.

Roughly, we will give up on a universal notion of "natural" programs, and allow our performance to degrade with the gap between our notion of which user protocols are "natural" choices, and the server designer's notion of "natural" user protocols. We will formalize "naturalness" in terms of *probability distributions over user protocols*. Or, in *Bayesian* language, we will talk about a *prior belief* over user protocols, in which the probability assigned to a protocol U corresponds roughly to the (assumed) probability that a user drawn from the "general population" will use protocol U. Thus,

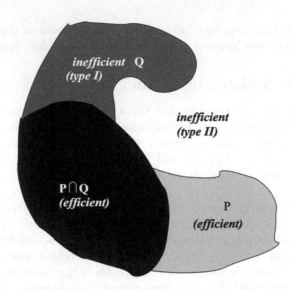

Figure 4.1: An illustration of the two types of inefficiencies; P denotes the set of user protocols given high weight by the prior distribution P, and similarly Q denotes the set of user protocols given high weight by the prior distribution Q.

as a user, we may have a prior distribution P describing our beliefs about which protocols would be "natural" to run – in particular, which protocols we believe the *server designer* to be anticipating – and the server designer may have a *different* prior distribution Q, capturing how likely the designer believes users are to run various strategies.

Now, we suppose that the server designer will attempt to construct a server strategy S that helps as many natural user strategies as possible to achieve a goal G efficiently—which means, in this case, that a protocol drawn from distribution Q achieves G with the designed server S in reasonable time with as high probability as possible. Now, what we hope is that if the user and the server designer mostly agree on which user strategies are natural, then the user, using a universal user strategy designed with the prior distribution P in mind, will also achieve G with S in reasonable time. Thus, as illustrated in Figure 4.1, if the user does not achieve G efficiently with S, we should be able to explain this by saying that either

I. there was a mismatch in the expectations of the user and the server designer, e.g., about what kind of programming language is natural, or

II. the server was not designed to be easily accessed, e.g., it is password-protected.

Closeness of priors

The notion of "closeness" of priors that we will use is the *statistical distance* between distributions P and Q, denoted $\Delta(P, Q)$. Precisely, if $P(x)$ and $Q(x)$ are the probabilities assigned to outcome x by P and Q respectively, $\Delta(P, Q) = \frac{1}{2} \sum_x |P(x) - Q(x)|$. It is useful to note that the statistical distance may be alternatively defined as the advantage given by the best choice of event A in distinguishing P from Q, i.e., $\Delta(P, Q) = \max_A |P(A) - Q(A)|$.

We note that our notion of priors associated with users and server designers is sufficient to capture our preliminary notion of "natural" strategies as those with short descriptions, and that two different programming languages that can be easily translated have a "reasonable" bound on their distances.

Example 4.5 (Uniform distributions). Given a programming language (universal interactive Turing machine ϕ), we can consider a *"uniform distribution"* over programs P_ϕ in which each program of length $\ell \in \mathbb{N}$ has probability $2^{-(\ell + 2\lfloor \log \ell \rfloor + 1)}$. Equivalently, we can consider a corresponding "prefix free" encoding of the program of length ℓ (in the sense of Definition 3.16) by prepending ℓ in binary, itself preceded by a string of zeros of length $\lfloor \log \ell \rfloor$ (note that the high-order bit of ℓ is a 1); P_ϕ then corresponds to a distribution that is sampled by choosing uniform bits until a 1 appears, choosing a length ℓ based as above on the number of 0s it obtained before the first 1, and then choosing ℓ uniform bits to obtain a program for ϕ.

The basic results of Kolmogorov complexity may then be adapted to tell us that the distance between the uniform distributions corresponding to ϕ and ψ is bounded by a constant: we can consider a program $p_{\phi:\psi}(p')$ on ϕ that simulates ψ on a hard-coded program string p' embedded in its code with some modest overhead in its running time; if p' is of length ℓ, then p' need not increase the length of $p_{\phi:\psi}$ by more than ℓ, and hence by the concavity of the logarithm function, $p_{\phi:\psi}(p') + 2\lfloor \log p_{\phi:\psi}(p') \rfloor + 1$ need be no more than $c_{\phi:\psi} + \ell + 2\lfloor \log \ell \rfloor + 1$ for some constant $c_{\phi:\psi}$. Therefore, the strategy corresponding to program p' has weight at least

$$2^{-(c_{\phi:\psi} + \ell + 2\lfloor \log \ell \rfloor + 1)} = 2^{-c_{\phi:\psi}} P_\psi(p')$$

for each such program p'; we therefore see that for every strategy U, (letting U correspond to the event that we sample a program for U of a suitably low running time) $P_\phi(U) \geq 2^{-c_{\phi:\psi}} P_\psi(U)$ and we say P_ϕ *dominates* P_ψ. Of course, we similarly find that $P_\psi(U) \geq 2^{-c_{\psi:\phi}} P_\phi(U)$ for another appropriate constant $c_{\psi:\phi}$. Thus, for any U, $P_\psi(U) - P_\phi(U) \leq (1 - 2^{-c_{\phi:\psi}}) P_\psi(U)$ and $P_\phi(U) - P_\psi(U) \leq (1 - 2^{-c_{\psi:\phi}}) P_\phi(U)$ so we can bound the statistical distance of P_ψ and P_ϕ as $1 - 2^{-\max\{c_{\phi:\psi}, c_{\psi:\phi}\}}$.

Benchmark distributions

It may also be natural for the designer of a server for helping users achieve a goal G to assume that users will only use strategies that will (eventually) achieve G; certainly, our universal users will fit the bill whenever they can be constructed. In this case, the server designer may have a prior Q for which every user strategy in the support of Q will achieve G with any candidate server design, and the designer's sole objective is then to design a server S that minimizes the running time of these users with S. Q is then the *"benchmark"* distribution used by the server designer in evaluating various candidate designs, which motivates the following definition:

Definition 4.6 (Benchmark running time). For a goal G, a server strategy S, and a user protocol U, let $t_{U,S}(n)$ denote the maximum expected running time of U in an execution (E, U, S) over E of sizes at most n. Then, for a distribution over user protocols Q, the *Q-benchmark running time for G with S*, denoted $t_{Q,S}(n)$, is given by the expected value of $t_{U,S}(n)$ when U is sampled from Q.

Now, supposing we have a prior distribution P that is close to the benchmark distribution Q used by the server designer, we would hope to be able to construct a user strategy that achieves G with a server S in time comparable to the Q-benchmark running time for G with S.

4.2.2   Uniform viability

Ultimately, we aim to construct universal users which have more desirable running times when the server designer's prior is close to our prior. Naturally, as in the generic construction of universal users presented in Proposition 2.27, we will rely on the availability of an appropriate kind of *sensing* for the goal. Again, we know that some kind of sensing must be available in order for it to be feasible for us to reliably achieve the goal. The construction of Proposition 2.27, however, worked by searching the space of user protocols for a protocol that satisfied the *viability requirement* of Definition 2.22 with the given server, where it was given that some such user protocol existed, i.e., that the server was viable for our sensing function. Now, in general, there may be a "gap" between user protocols that achieve a goal with a server S, and protocols that witness viability of a sensing function with S, even when the sensing function is viable with all helpful servers; our example of sensing for computational problems in Example 2.24 (and discussed in more detail in Section 3.3) is a concrete example of such an instance, and the user protocol witnessing viability in our generic construction of a viable sensing function from Proposition 2.26 is actually the given universal user protocol. Indeed, satisfying a sensing function may be much more demanding of a user-server pair than merely achieving a goal, and we have seen examples (Example 2.20 and Corollary 3.14) of goals where servers may be helpful but no safe and viable sensing function exists (under a reasonable hypothesis, in the case of Corollary 3.14).

Now, note that our assumption about the server designer is merely that he or she attempts to optimize the running time and fraction of "natural" user protocols achieving the goal G with the designed server. Since our constructions of sensing tend to be relatively ad-hoc and it is unclear what we might even want to constitute "natural" sensing for a goal, in general it would be completely unreasonable to expect that the server designer has designed the server with our particular sensing function in mind. Thus, in order for our assumption about the server designer helping many natural user protocols achieve the goal to lead to a construction of an efficient user protocol, we will modify the viability condition that our sensing function satisfies: we will assume that the viability condition satisfied by our sensing function is *uniform* in the sense that there is an associated generic (black-box) reduction that, given a protocol that achieves G with a server S, uses that protocol as a subroutine to satisfy the sensing function with S. Note that this is an extremely natural paradigm, and essentially *the* natural way to show that a sensing function is viable with the class of all helpful servers— and indeed, all of our example constructions of universal users in the basic universal setting proceeded by constructing such uniformly viable sensing functions.

In order to proceed, we will need to define what we mean by such a "reduction" in an interactive setting. Noting that in the specific case of computation, we wished to invoke the "solution" to our sub-problem many times, we see that in particular we desire a generalization of a Cook reduction to an interactive setting. Thus, we will rely on the following definition of an *interactive oracle protocol:*

Definition 4.7 (Interactive oracle protocols). A *universal interactive oracle Turing machine with interactive oracle strategy O*, ϕ^O, is modeled by a pair of entities $(\phi^{(\cdot)}, O)$, in which $\phi^{(\cdot)}$ is a universal interactive Turing machine which may, at unit cost, start O running from its initial state; while O is running, $\phi^{(\cdot)}$ plays the role of the environment with respect to O, and O interacts with the remaining entities in place of $\phi^{(\cdot)}$. An *interactive oracle protocol U^O* is given by a program $U^{(\cdot)}$ for $\phi^{(\cdot)}$ and an oracle strategy O.

For a given interactive oracle protocol U^O, a non-deterministic environment strategy $\mathcal{E}$ with size parameter n, and a function $t : \mathbb{N} \to \mathbb{N}$, we say that U^O is *time-$t(n)$ bounded* if for every server strategy S and every state of $E \in \mathcal{E}$, in the execution of $\phi^{(\cdot)}$ on the program $U^{(\cdot)}$ with oracle strategy O, $\phi^{(\cdot)}$ runs for no more than $t(n)$ steps before it halts; if $\phi^{(\cdot)}$ on program $U^{(\cdot)}$ never runs for more than $t(n)$ steps on any oracle, then we simply say that $U^{(\cdot)}$ is *time-$t(n)$ bounded.*

Now that we possess the necessary groundwork to precisely describe a generic reduction from satisfying a sensing function with a server S to achieving G with S, we are ready to give the refined notion of viability that we will use.

Definition 4.8 (Uniform viability). We say that a sensing function V is $(p(n), r(n), 1-\delta(n), 1-\epsilon(n))$-*uniformly viable* for a goal G and a class of server

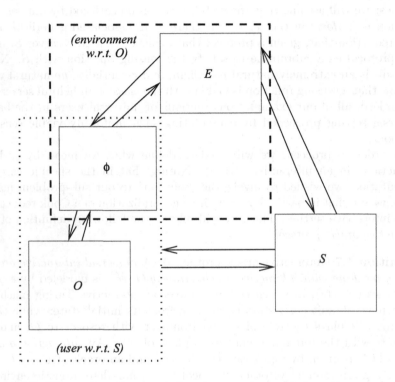

Figure 4.2: The system corresponding to an universal interactive oracle Turing machine $\phi^{(\cdot)}$ with interactive oracle strategy O, executing with an environment's actual strategy E and a server strategy S. S exchanges messages with O while $\phi^{(\cdot)}$ is invoking O, and otherwise exchanges messages with $\phi^{(\cdot)}$.

strategies S if there is some interactive oracle user protocol $U^{(\cdot)}$ running in expected time $p(n)$ such that, given a user strategy U_S that robustly achieves G with S in environments of size up to $r(n)$ with probability $1 - \delta(n)$, V outputs 1 on the user's view with probability at least $1 - \epsilon(n)$ in the execution (E, U^{U_S}, S) from any state of the server and environment.

4.2.3   An efficient universal protocol for close priors

We can now present the main theorem of this section, refining Proposition 2.27 given that we have a safe and *uniformly viable* sensing function, and given that we have a *sampleable* prior distribution P. (Of course, if we could not obtain samples from P, we would not expect it to be particularly useful in designing an algorithm!) The theorem then follows the same paradigm as the family of PAC-Bayesian bounds in learning theory, introduced by McAllester [110] and Shawe-Taylor and Williamson [136]: we obtain a worst-case bound that degrades with the distance between our prior and the distribution used by the server designer. Thus, when our prior closely matches the designer's distribution, our performance roughly matches what the designer would anticipate us to obtain by using protocols sampled from the "natural" distribution; in particular, when the server designer expects that we should be able to run efficiently by using natural protocols, and our notions of natural protocols largely agree, we do achieve the goal efficiently.

Theorem 4.9 (Universal users for servers with a close prior). *For a class of servers $\mathcal{S}$, let functions $\delta_S : \mathbb{N} \to [0,1]$, $t_S : \mathbb{N} \to \mathbb{N}$, $p_S : \mathbb{N} \to \mathbb{N}$, $p_U : \mathbb{N} \to \mathbb{N}$, $r : \mathbb{N} \to \mathbb{N}$, $\mu_S : \mathbb{N} \to [0,1]$, $\nu_S : \mathbb{N} \to [0,1]$ and $\epsilon_S : \mathbb{N} \to [0,1/3]$ and a distribution on user protocols Q_S be given for each $S \in \mathcal{S}$. Let G be a goal with a $(1 - \mu_S(n))$-safe and $(p_U(n), r(n), 1 - \nu_S(n), 1 - \epsilon_S(n))$-uniformly viable sensing function V computable in expected time $p_S(n)$ with $S \in \mathcal{S}$, and such that G is achieved with S in $(t_S \circ r)(n)$ steps with probability $1 - \nu_S(n)$ in environments of size up to $r(n)$ by a $1 - \delta_S(n)$ fraction of user strategies under Q_S. Let P be any efficiently sampleable distribution over protocols. Then, for*

$$T_S(n) = 18\big((t_S \circ r)(n) \cdot p_U(n) + 6p_S(n)\big) \cdot$$
$$\frac{1}{1 - \delta_S(n) - \Delta(P, Q_S)} \log^2 \frac{1}{1 - \delta_S(n) - \Delta(P, Q_S)}$$

there is an expected $T_S(n)$-time bounded $(\mathcal{S}, 1 - \mu_S(n)T_S(n))$-universal protocol for G.

Proof   We use a variant of the protocol used in the proof of Proposition 2.27, in which the enumeration of protocols is replaced by simply sampling repeatedly from our given distribution P.

Construction.   Let $U^{(\cdot)}$ be the interactive oracle user protocol guaranteed to exist by the $(p_U(n), r(n), 1 - \nu_S(n), 1 - \epsilon_S(n))$-uniform viability of our sensing function V. Our protocol is then as follows:

- For $i = 1, 2, \ldots$, repeat the following:

    - For $j = 1, \ldots, i - 2\log i$, and $k = 1, \ldots, 2^j$, repeat the following:

        1. Sample a protocol $\tilde{U}$ from P.
        2. For up to $t = 2^{i-j-2\log j}$ steps, simulate $U^{\tilde{U}}$ and run V on the resulting transcript if $U^{\tilde{U}}$ halts; if V accepts, halt.

Analysis.   Since we assumed that $U^{(\cdot)}$ was as guaranteed by the $(p_U(n), r(n), 1 - \nu_S(n), 1 - \epsilon_S(n))$-uniform viability of V with $S \in \mathcal{S}$, for any user strategy $\tilde{U}$ running in $(t_S \circ r)(n)$ steps that achieves G with S with probability $1 - \nu_S(n)$ in environments of size up to $r(n)$, V outputs 1 on the view generated by $U^{\tilde{U}}$ with probability at least $1 - \epsilon_S(n) \geq 2/3$. If a $1 - \delta'$ fraction of the user strategies under P achieve G with S with probability at least $1 - \nu_S(n)$ in $(t_S \circ r)(n)$ steps in environments of size up to $r(n)$, then if $t > (t_S \circ r)(n)p(n) + 6p_S(n)$, since V runs in expected time p_S and $U^{(\cdot)}$ only runs $\tilde{U}$ with environments of size up to $r(n)$, with probability at least $2/3 - 1/6 = 1/2$, we see V run to completion and output 1 on the view generated by $U^{\tilde{U}}$, given that we successfully sampled such a $\tilde{U}$. We will call these $\tilde{U}$ *good protocols*.

If $i \geq i^* = \log((t_S \circ r)(n)p(n) + 6p_S(n)) - \log(1 - \delta') + 2\log\log \frac{1}{1-\delta'}$, then for $j = 1, \ldots \log\frac{1}{1-\delta'}$, we run each protocol we sample for at least $(t_S \circ r)(n)p(n) + 6p_S(n)$ steps, and there are precisely

$$\sum_{j=1}^{\log \frac{1}{1-\delta'}} 2^j = 2\frac{1}{1-\delta'} - 1$$

such samples in phase i^*; we therefore obtain a good protocol in phase i^* and run it for sufficiently many steps with probability at least $1 - (1-\delta')^{2\frac{1}{1-\delta'}-1} \geq 1 - \frac{1}{(1-\delta')e^2}$, where each time we then succeed and halt with probability at least $1/2$. Moreover, in phase $i^* + k$, there are $2^{k+1}\frac{1}{1-\delta'} - 1$ such samples, and thus if we group our samples into batches of $2\frac{1}{1-\delta'}$, in each of our first $2^k - 1$ batches, we only fail when we either fail to hit a good protocol, or when a good protocol fails, which by a union bound occurs in each group with probability at most $1/2 + 1/e^2$, and thus at most $(1/2 + 1/e^2)^{2^k-1}$ overall. Since the total running time up to phase $i^* + k$ is

$$\sum_{i=1}^{i^*+k} \sum_{j=1}^{i-2\log i} 2^j \frac{2^i}{j^2 2^j} \leq \frac{\pi^2}{3} 2^{i^*+k}$$

our expected running time is at most

$$\frac{\pi^2}{3}2^{i^*}\left(1+\sum_{k=0}^{\infty}2^{k+1}\cdot(1/2+1/e^2)^{2^{k+1}-2}\right)$$

where we can bound the sum by, e.g., for $s = 6$,

$$\frac{1}{1/2+1/e^2}\left(\sum_{k=1}^{s}2^k(1/2+1/e^2)^{2^k-1}+\right.$$

$$\left.\frac{2^{s+1}(1/2+1/e^2)^{2^{s+1}-1}}{1/2-1/e^2}+\frac{(1/2+1/e^2)^{2^{s+1}}}{(1/2-1/e^2)^2}\right) < 4.2$$

which can be verified numerically. Thus, our running time is at most

$$18((t_S\circ r)(n)p_U(n)+6p_S(n))\frac{1}{1-\delta'}\log^2\frac{1}{1-\delta'}$$

We now note that since the probability of sampling a good protocol under Q is at least $1-\delta_S(n)$, $1-\delta' \geq 1-\delta_S(n)-\Delta(P,Q)$; our protocol's running time is therefore at most $T_S(n)$. Moreover, since our sensing function is $(1-\mu_S(n))$-safe with S and our protocol only halts when V outputs 1, where we run the sensing function at most $T_S(n)$ times, by a union bound, our probability of halting when G is not satisfied with S is at most $1-\mu_S(n)T_S(n)$. Thus, our protocol is an expected $T_S(n)$-time bounded $(S, 1-\mu_S(n)T_S(n))$-universal protocol, as claimed. ∎

As a corollary, by Markov's inequality we also show that if the server designer evaluates the server with respect to a benchmark distribution (over user protocols that always achieve G) and our prior is close to the server designer's benchmark distribution, then the running time of our universal protocol is comparable to the benchmark running time.

Corollary 4.10 (Universal users running in time comparable to a server's benchmark time). *Let μ_S, ν_S, ϵ_S, and Q_S be given along with a goal G with a sensing function V satisfying the conditions of Theorem 4.9, and* $\mathrm{supp}(Q_S)$ *containing only user strategies U_S such that (U_S, S) robustly achieves G with probability $1-\nu_S(n)$. Let $t_{S,Q}(n)$ be the Q_S-benchmark running time of users for G with S. Then, for*

$$T_S(n) = 69((t_{S,Q}\circ r)(n)p_U(n)+3p_S(n))\left(\frac{1}{1-\Delta(P,Q_S)}\log\frac{2}{1-\Delta(P,Q_S)}\right)^2$$

there is an expected $T_S(n)$-time bounded $(S, 1-\mu_S(n)T_S(n))$-universal protocol for G.

Proof For each server $S \in \mathcal{S}$, put $\delta_S(n) = \frac{1}{2}(1 - \Delta(P, Q_S))$. Then, Markov's inequality gives that, for a choice of user protocol U according to Q_S, the running time of U with S, $t_{U,S}(n)$, is at most $\frac{2t_{S,Q}(n)}{1 - \Delta(P,Q)}$ with probability at least $1 - \frac{1}{2}(1 - \Delta(P, Q_S)) = 1 - \delta_S(n)$. Applying Theorem 4.9 (using the slightly tighter bound from the proof) with $t_S(n) = \frac{2t_{S,Q}(n)}{1 - \Delta(P, Q_S)}$ now easily yields a protocol with the claimed performance. ∎

We note that distributions induced by the program lengths of a set of good strategies (i.e., conditioning the distributions in Example 4.5 on a set of good strategies), when applied to Corollary 4.10, gives us an overhead in the running time that is at most exponential in the length of the program that translates one language to the other, which is about as much as we could hope to prove in general. We would still hope that the difference in the priors would be less than this in many natural settings.

4.3   Effective conditions for efficient users

There is an additional benefit to restricting our attention to user strategies that are "natural" in some sense, such as having short programs: it will allow us to broaden the applicability of our theory to include servers that are only helpful to these "natural" strategies, by restricting our attention to only those states of the server that can be feasibly reached by natural user strategies.

4.3.1   Servers with a designated class of properly functioning states

Many real-world devices provide the ability to update their internal software. When used properly, this feature allows the inevitable bugs in the software to be patched as they are discovered. Unfortunately, we can see that any device that has this feature is not "helpful" in the sense of Definition 2.18: if we consider a user strategy that "updates" the internal software of the device by replacing it with a program that does nothing, we find that this user reaches a state of the device where it simulates the trivial server, where we noted at the outset of this chapter that the trivial server is generally not helpful.

We might still hope that if the feature that allows a user to update the device's software is password-protected, then we could ignore the fact that the device has this feature—after all, we know that it is generally infeasible to find a long password intentionally, let alone by accident. We might then reasonably expect that as long as it is possible to figure out how to use an idealized, truly helpful version of the device efficiently, we should be able to figure out how to use the real device without discovering that the real version can be "broken" by an unfortunate choice of user program. Essentially, we will ultimately show this by stating a variant of Theorem 4.9 for servers that are unlikely to break with respect to their design distributions.

Thus, the key definition enabling us to state such a theorem captures subsets of server states that are hard for "natural" users to distinguish from the set of all server states. Whereas the set of all server states is trivially "closed" in the sense that no user can causes the server to enter some new state, we say that such a set of states that is merely "hard" for "natural" users to exit is *effectively closed* with respect to the given notion of natural users. In anticipation of future applications, we will actually define "effectively closed" sets of *pairs* of server states and environment states, and obtain the desired notion of effectively closed sets of server states as a special case.

Definition 4.11 (Effectively closed). For a non-deterministic environment strategy $\mathcal{E}$ with size parameter $n : \mathcal{E} \to \mathbb{N}$, a server S, a distribution over user strategies P, $t : \mathbb{N} \to \mathbb{N}$, and $\gamma : \mathbb{N} \to [0, 1]$, we say that the set of server and environment states $\Theta \subseteq \Omega^{(\mathrm{s})} \times \Omega^{(\mathrm{e})}$ is $(t(n), \gamma(n))$-*effectively closed with respect to P* if, for every $(\sigma^{(\mathrm{s})}, \sigma^{(\mathrm{e})}) \in \Theta$ and $t \leq t(n)$, for a user strategy U drawn from P, $(X_t^{(\mathrm{s})}, X_t^{(\mathrm{e})}) \in \Theta$ with probability at least $1 - \gamma(n)$ in the execution (E, U, S) started from $(\sigma^{(\mathrm{e})}, \sigma^{(\mathrm{u})}, \sigma^{(\mathrm{s})})$ for the initial state $\sigma^{(\mathrm{u})}$ specified by U, where the probability is taken over the choice of U from P and the random evolution of the execution.

Similarly, a set of server states Θ_S for a server S is said to be $(t(n), \gamma(n))$-*effectively closed with respect to P in $\mathcal{E}$* if the set $\Theta_S \times \Omega^{(\mathrm{e})}$ is $(t(n), \gamma(n))$-effectively closed with respect to P.

We stress that it was again essential that we invoke some notion of "natural" user strategies like the one provided by prior distributions. Merely considering "time efficient" users, for example, wouldn't capture the effective impossibility of guessing a password, because hard-coded user behavior can include the password; worse, hard-coded behavior can even simulate *any* strategy for any finite number of rounds (much as in the proof of Theorem 2.37), so such a notion would collapse to merely characterizing the *reachable* server states, which is surely not the kind of relaxation we were after. By contrast, we can see that a collection of states can be effectively closed in the presence of password-protected servers:

Example 4.12 (Password-protected servers can have effectively closed states). Fix any distribution over user strategies P and any non-deterministic environment $\mathcal{E}$, and let S be any server strategy. Then, supposing that a user strategy U is drawn from P, the same argument as used to prove Theorem 4.3 shows that for every $\ell \in \mathbb{N}$ and $\delta \in (0, 1)$, there is some password x of length ℓ such that for the password-protected version of S with password x, S^x, the "waiting for password" state is $(\delta 2^\ell, \delta)$-effectively closed with respect to P and $\mathcal{E}$.

Of course, we are not presently interested in servers that are indistinguishable from the (unhelpful) trivial server, but rather servers that are indistinguishable from *helpful* servers. Naturally, this can be formally accomplished by weakening the notion of robust achievement to only quantify over a *subset* of global states. It is then immediate to obtain the desired variant of helpfulness, by substituting this weaker definition for the original definition of robust achievement:

Definition 4.13 (Robust achievement, refined). For a goal $G = (\mathcal{E}, R)$, server strategy S, set of pairs of states of the server and environment Θ, and a user strategy U, we say that the pair (U, S) *robustly achieves the goal G with probability p with respect to* Θ if for every $E \in \mathcal{E}$ and every state σ such that $\sigma^{(u)}$ is the initial state of U and $(\sigma^{(s)}, \sigma^{(e)}) \in \Theta$, the probability that the user achieves the goal in the execution (E, U, S) started from σ is at least p.

Definition 4.14 (Effectively helpful server). We say that a server strategy S with a set of states Θ_S is *p-effectively helpful* for a goal G if there exists a polynomial time user protocol U such that (U, S) robustly achieve the goal with probability p with respect to $\Theta_S \times \Omega^{(e)}$.

Although we don't require it in the definition, it is our intent to consider effective helpfulness with respect to an effectively closed set of server states. Then, for example, a modification of the server in which transitions out of the designated set of states were replaced by "self-loops" would be helpful in the original sense, and our effectively helpful server is indistinguishable from the helpful modification by natural user strategies, in the sense that they produce indistinguishable executions. In this case, we will generally refer to the effectively closed set of states as states where the server is *functioning properly*, and if the server leaves this set of states, then we will say that the server *breaks*.

We could similarly state a definition of a universal user in which the robust achievement requirement was relaxed to robust achievement with respect to the set of states associated with the server (and environment), but in fact, we have already formally stated a variant of universal user strategies that are appropriate to the present setting: recall that, for a set of server-state pairs $\mathcal{S}^*$, a $(\mathcal{S}^*, p)$-*weakly universal user*, as introduced in Definition 2.15, was only guaranteed to achieve G with probability p with a server S when the execution started from some global state σ associated with S in $\mathcal{S}^*$. For the current purposes, it suffices to merely give the convention that the set of pairs of servers and associated functioning states (S, Θ_S) corresponds to the set of server-global state pairs $\mathcal{S}^*$ containing a pair (S, σ) for each σ such that $\sigma^{(u)}$ is the user's initial state and $\sigma^{(s)} \in \Theta_S$. Then it can be checked that an $(\mathcal{S}^*, p)$-weakly universal user is one such that (U, S) robustly achieves G with probability p with respect to $\Theta_S \times \Omega^{(e)}$ for each pair (S, Θ_S), as desired.

4.3.2   Effective refinements of sensing

Towards developing an analogue of Theorem 4.9 for servers that are only effectively helpful, we will need to also develop an appropriately weakened notion of sensing. This is inevitable: safe and viable sensing in the original sense for a server implies, by Theorem 2.25, that the server is helpful in the original sense. At a minimum, it is obvious that we will need to weaken the viability requirement, and we will handle this first. We will also weaken the safety requirement, for the reason that we want to handle, e.g., servers that can be reprogrammed, as discussed at the outset, in which case, if we wished to rely on some special property of the class of servers for safety, this property could fail to hold of a server if it was reprogrammed improperly.

It is not difficult to state an appropriate "basic" weakening of sensing that only demands viability with respect to properly functioning states of the server, analogous to our weakening of helpfulness in Definition 4.14:

Definition 4.15 (Effectively viable sensing function). We say that a sensing function V is (t, p)-*effectively viable* for a goal G with respect to a server S and a set of server states Θ_S if there exists a user strategy U_S such that in any execution (E, U_S, S) for $E \in \mathcal{E}$ started from a state σ such that $\sigma^{(u)}$ is the initial state of U_S and $\sigma^{(s)} \in \Theta_S$, with probability at least p, U_S runs for t steps in expectation and V outputs 1 on the user's view of (E, U_S, S).

Ultimately, though, as discussed in Section 4.2.2, we will require a definition of viability that is more closely related to the notion of effective helpfulness. Hence, paralleling the development of Definition 4.8, we state a uniform variant of Definition 4.15 which guarantees a black-box reduction from obtaining positive indications in the properly functioning states to robustly achieving G in the properly functioning states. Note that if the reduction requires multiple calls to its oracle strategy, then we will need a guarantee that the provided strategy not only achieves the goal, but also does not break the server, so that the same strategy can be invoked more than once.

Definition 4.16 (Uniform effective viability). For a set $\mathcal{S}^*$ of servers S with associated sets of states Θ_S, we say that V is $(p(n), r(n), 1-\delta(n), 1-\gamma(n), 1-\epsilon(n))$-*uniformly effectively viable* for G and $\mathcal{S}^*$ if there is some interactive oracle user protocol $U^{(\cdot)}$ running in expected time $p(n)$ such that, for every server S and associated set of states Θ_S in $\mathcal{S}^*$,

1. Given any user strategy U' that in executions (E, U', S) started from states σ such that $\sigma^{(u)}$ is the initial state of U_S and $\sigma^{(s)} \in \Theta_S$, halts in states σ_τ such that $\sigma_\tau^{(s)} \in \Theta_S$ with probability at least $1 - \gamma(n)$, in an execution $(E, U^{U'}, S)$ started from a state σ_0 such that $\sigma_0^{(u)}$ is the initial state of $U^{U'}$ and $\sigma_0^{(s)} \in \Theta_S$, every tth state of the execution X_t in which $U^{U'}$ is not invoking U' has $X_t^{(s)} \in \Theta_S$ with probability at least $1 - t\gamma(n)$.

2. Given a user strategy U_S that robustly achieves G with S with respect to $\Theta_S \times \Omega^{(e)}$ in environments of size up to $r(n)$ with probability at least $1 - \delta(n)$, V outputs 1 on the user's view with probability $1 - \epsilon(n)$ in

the execution (E, U^{U_S}, S) from any state σ such that $\sigma^{(u)}$ is the initial state of U^{U_S} and $\sigma^{(s)} \in \Theta_S$

We noted in Section 4.2.2 that all of our examples of sensing functions that were viable with respect to the class of all helpful servers for a goal were actually uniformly viable with respect to the class of all helpful servers. It can likewise be easily verified that, moreover, when we instead consider a class of effectively helpful servers with respect to a set of states that are effectively closed with respect to a given prior over user strategies, the very same sensing functions are still safe, but also uniformly effectively viable (potentially with some loss in $\epsilon(n)$ due to the possibility that the server may break during the reduction), since the efficient reductions only interact with the server by running the oracle strategy repeatedly.

We now turn to developing a less demanding refinement of safety of a sensing function, one that will apply to servers that are only hard for "natural" users to distinguish from servers that actually satisfy the safety requirement. To be more precise, we *don't* mean that the servers produce indistinguishable user views, but rather that it is hard for "natural" users to distinguish the server from a safe server by producing an execution in which safety is actually violated. Naturally, much as in the definition of an effectively closed set of states, the desired relaxation may be obtained by replacing the original universal quantification over user strategies for which safety should hold (in Definition 2.22) by a "probabilistic" quantification with respect to the given prior over user strategies.

Definition 4.17 (Effectively safe sensing function). We say that a sensing function V is *p-effectively safe* for a goal $G = (\mathcal{E}, R)$ with respect to a server S with a set of functioning states Θ_S and a distribution over user strategies P if, for any $E \in \mathcal{E}$ and round $t \in \mathbb{N}$, for a user strategy U sampled according to P, when V outputs 1 on the user's view of the first t rounds of the execution (E, U, S) started from the initial state of U and any state of the server from Θ_S, then R outputs 1 in round t with probability at least p.

Of course, as we noted earlier, our existing examples of sensing functions that were safe with respect to the class of all servers did not require a relaxed notion of safety. The only cases where such a notion becomes important is when we need to assume some further property of the servers to achieve the goal, and where we want to consider the possibility that this property could fail to hold with some small probability. Naturally, since our main objective is to study communication in the *absence* of assumptions (or at least, in the presence of minimal assumptions), we have tended to avoid assuming properties of our servers. The only formal examples of such properties that we have considered were that the servers "truthfully" reported the functions they computed in the goal of PAC-learning in Example 2.34, and that the servers "truthfully" reported their afilliations (and length parameters) for the goals of testing, as considered in Section 3.5, although in the latter case we did not explicitly construct a sensing function. We informally considered another case where the assumption of some property would be necessary in Section 3.2.2, when we considered searching from a search engine's perspective. Looking ahead, we will later consider *resettable* servers in Section 7.2.2, and this is another natural example of a property on which we might wish to base safety, that could fail to hold.

4.3.3 A universal user for servers that are easy to use and hard to break

Now that the definitions for the relaxed setting are in place, we can prove the desired analogue of Theorem 4.9, showing that when our prior is close to a server's design distribution, there is a strategy under which the server is not much more likely to break than the design distribution would predict, and moreover, when it does not break, we manage to achieve our goal in time comparable to what the server's design distribution would predict. Thus, for our purposes, it is sufficient to operate with a server that was designed to be easy to use and hard to break, provided that our notion of "natural strategies" is sufficiently close to that used by the server designer.

There is one major caveat in the adaptation: we do not obtain a bound on the expected running time of the universal user. This is inevitable when the server is allowed to break with positive probability, since we know nothing about the server's behavior when it breaks, so the user may not halt in such cases. We chose to simply bound the expected running time conditioned on the server not breaking, but it would also have been possible to provide a tighter description of the distribution of running times (than, e.g., can be recovered by means of Markov's inequality).

Theorem 4.18 (Effectively universal users under close priors). *Given a goal* $G = (\mathcal{E}, R)$, *consider any class of servers with associated sets of functioning states,* $\mathcal{S}^*$ *and associated distributions over user strategies* Q_S *and time bounds* t_S *for each* $(S, \Theta_S) \in \mathcal{S}^*$. *Let functions* $\delta_S, \mu_S, \nu_S, \gamma_S : \mathbb{N} \to [0, 1]$, *and* $\epsilon_S : \mathbb{N} \to [0, 1/3]$ *be given for each* $(S, \Theta_S) \in \mathcal{S}$. *Suppose there is a* $(1 - \mu_S(n))$-*effectively safe and* $(p_U(n), r(n), 1 - \nu_S(n), 1 - \gamma_S(n), 1 - \epsilon_S(n))$-*uniformly effectively viable sensing function* V *for* G *with respect to* S, Θ_S, *and* P *that is furthermore computable in expected time* $p_S(n)$ *for every* $(S, \Theta_S) \in \mathcal{S}^*$; *finally, suppose that for a* $1 - \delta_S(n)$ *fraction of user strategies* U *under* Q_S, (U, S) *robustly achieves the goal with probability* $1 - \nu_S(n)$ *with respect to* Θ_S *in environments of size up to* $r(n)$. *Then, for*

$$T_S(n) = \left((t_S \circ r)(n) \cdot p_U(n) + 6p_S(n) \right) \cdot$$
$$\frac{1}{1 - \delta_S(n) - \Delta(P, Q_S)} \log^2 \frac{1}{1 - \delta_S(n) - \Delta(P, Q_S)}$$

if Θ_S *is* $(C_S T_S(n), \gamma_S(n))$-*effectively closed with respect to* Q_S *in* $\mathcal{E}$ *for* $C_S \geq 1$, *then there is an* $(\mathcal{S}^*, 1 - 2^{-C_S} - 18(\mu_S(n) + \gamma_S(n) + \Delta(P, Q_S))T_S(n))$-

weakly universal user for G, that breaks S with probability at most $18(\gamma_S(n)+$ $\Delta(P, Q_S))T_S(n) + 2^{-C_S}$, and conditioned on S remaining in states in Θ_S, runs in expected time $18T_S(n)$.

Proof We will use the same algorithm as in the proof of Theorem 4.9, and at a high level, our approach will be to first pretend that we are sampling from Q_S instead of P. We then note that when the class of server states Θ_S is effectively closed with respect to our sampling distribution, we obtain a bound on the probability that the modified protocol breaks the server. We then return to the analysis of the real algorithm, and pay a penalty due to the statistical distance between Q_S and P for each sample.

Then, given that the server does not break, we can apply the same analysis as before to bound the probability of failure and running time. Thus, a union bound gives the overall failure probability (by adding in the probability that the server breaks), and we obtain the claimed condition on the running time when the server does not break immediately.

Before beginning, we will note that we can bound the probability that we will break the server while running the oracle strategy guaranteed by uniform effective viability on a user strategy sampled from Q_S in the "obvious" way:

Claim 4.19. *Let $U^{(\cdot)}$ be the interactive oracle user protocol running in expected time $p_U(n)$ guaranteed by the uniform effective viability of V for G and S^*. Then, if Θ_S is $(C_S T_S(n), \gamma_S(n))$-effectively closed with respect to a distribution Q_S over user strategies in $\mathcal{E}$, and we sample a strategy U' from Q_S, the probability that $U^{U'}$ breaks the server within $t \le C_S T_S(n)$ steps when started from its initial state and the server starts in a state in Θ_S is at most $t \cdot \gamma_S(n)$.*

Proof We will divide the execution of $U^{U'}$ into steps where it is invoking U' and steps where it is not; suppose that in the first t steps, $U^{U'}$ invokes U' t_1 times. We now consider the probability that these t_1 independent invocations of U' break the server.

Suppose that when S is started from any state in Θ_S, the probability that a *fixed* U' breaks S in E is at most $\gamma_{U'}(n)$. Then, when we run U' t_1 times independently, we know that given that $t_1\gamma_{U'}(n) < 1$, that $(1 - \gamma_{U'}(n))^{t_1} \le 1 - t_1\gamma_{U'}(n)$, so therefore the probability that U' breaks S in any of the t_1 runs is at most $t_1\gamma_{U'}(n)$. Now, we note that when U' is instead sampled from Q_S, since we run U' for at most $C_S T_S(n)$ steps, the $(C_S T_S(n), \gamma_S(n))$-effective closedness of Θ_S guarantees that $\mathbb{E}_{U'}[\gamma_{U'}(n)] \le \gamma_S(n)$; so, by linearity of expectation, the probability that the U' sampled from Q_S breaks S in any of its t_1 independent runs is also at most $t_1\gamma_S(n)$.

Now, by the definition of uniform effective viability, we also know that when our oracle strategy is not invoking U', it breaks S with probability at most $\gamma_S(n)$ per step; thus, over the first t steps of $U^{U'}$ for U' sampled from Q_S, the total probability that the server breaks is at most $t\gamma_S(n)$, as needed.

∎

Therefore, a union bound together with Claim 4.19 yields that the total probability that our algorithm breaks the server (when sampling from Q_S) in the first t steps is also likewise at most $t\gamma_S(n)$ up to phase $\bar{i} = \log C_S T_S(n) + 1$, since the maximum running time allocated to algorithms in phase i is 2^{i-1} steps. If we can argue that the algorithm only runs for T steps in expectation given that it does not break, then the probability that it breaks can be bounded by the probability that it runs past phase $\bar{i}$ plus $T\gamma_S(n)$. Now, we note that since we sample from Q_S at most T times in expectation, this means that we can bound the probability that the server breaks when we actually sample from P by the probability that we run past phase $\bar{i}$ plus $T(\gamma_S(n) + \Delta(P, Q_S))$.

We now return to the running time analysis of the protocol that actually samples from P, following the analysis in the proof of Theorem 4.9. When the server does not break, we note that the protocols actually sampled from P and run for $(t_S \circ r)(n)$ steps achieve G in environments of size up to $r(n)$ with probability at least $1 - \delta_S(n) - \Delta(P, Q_S)$; therefore, uniform effective viability gives us that such a *good protocol* $\tilde{U}$ when run as the oracle strategy $U^{(\cdot)}$ for $(t_S \circ r)(n)p_U(n)$ steps generates a user view that V accepts with probability $1 - \epsilon_S(n) \geq 2/3$. We also know that V runs in $6p_S(n)$ steps with probability at least $5/6$, so when we schedule $U^{\tilde{U}}$ and V to run for $(t_S \circ r)(n)p_U(n) + 6p_S(n)$ steps, V outputs 1 with probability at least $1/2$.

Therefore, continuing along the lines of the proof of Theorem 4.9, for each phase

$$i^* + k \geq i^*$$
$$= \log((t_S \circ r)(n)p_U(n) + 6p_S(n)) +$$
$$\log \frac{1}{1 - \delta_S(n) + \Delta(P, Q_S)} + 2\log\log \frac{1}{1 - \delta_S(n) + \Delta(P, Q_S)}$$

we obtain $2^k - 1$ groups of $2\frac{1}{1-\delta_S(n)+\Delta(P,Q_S)}$ samples, where when we actually sample from P, each group fails to obtain a positive indication with probability at most $1/2 + 1/e^2$. So, as long as the server has not broken, we only fail to obtain a positive indication in round $i^* + k$ with probability at most $(1/2 + 1/e^2)^{2^k - 1}$, and so by the same calculation as before, the expected time until we obtain a positive indication is at most $18T_S(n)$, given that the server does not break.

Moreover, the probability that we run past phase $\bar{i} = \log C_S + 1 + i^*$ can now be seen to be the probability that we fail to obtain positive indications in rounds $i^*, i^* + 1, \ldots, i^* + \log C_S + 1$, giving us

$$2^{\log C_S + 3} \log \frac{1}{1 - \delta_S(n) - \Delta(P, Q_S)} - (\log C_S + 3)$$

independent runs. We have at least $2C_S$ batches of $2\frac{1}{1-\delta_S(n)-\Delta(P,Q_S)}$ runs, each of which fail to provide a positive indication with probability at most

$(1/2 + 1/e^2)$. Thus, since $(1/2 + 1/e^2)^2 < 1/2$, the probability of us failing to obtain a positive indication before the end of phase $\bar{i}$ is at most 2^{-C_S}. So, the overall probability that the server breaks is at most $2^{-C_S} + 18(\gamma_S(n) + \Delta(P, Q_S))T_S(n)$, as claimed.

Likewise, since our algorithm only actually runs $U^{(\cdot)}$ for algorithms U' sampled from P repeatedly, provided that the server has not broken up to the tth round, we see that effective safety (with respect to P) provides that sensing yields a false positive with probability at most $\mu_S(n)$. It therefore follows that the probability that we halt without success when the server does not break is at most $18T_S(n)\mu_S(n)$; by a union bound, then, we also achieve the goal with probability at least $1 - 2^{-C_S} - 18(\mu_S(n) + \gamma_S(n) + \Delta(P, Q_S))T_S(n)$, so the strategy is weakly universal for $\mathcal{S}^*$ as claimed. ∎

4.4 Lower bounds in the absence of a common prior

Upon reflection, Theorem 4.18 was ultimately a *positive* application of a *negative* result; namely, by showing that it was difficult to accomplish some bad behavior, i.e., "breaking the server," the user could safely accomplish some relatively easy task without needing to be too concerned about the unknown insurmountable dangers that a more powerful user might encounter. Thus, the definitions developed in Section 4.3 – specifically the definition of an effectively closed set of states – were ultimately tools for proving lower bounds. In this section, we turn to examining what kind of lower bounds they can be used to obtain more generally. The results we describe are joint work with Santosh Vempala [86].

4.4.1 A generic lower bound when no common prior exists

Our first lower bound will be a lower bound on the number of algorithms that an *oblivious* schedule (in particular, such as the Levin-style enumerations and the iterative sampling algorithm used in the proof of Theorem 4.9) must use to escape from a bad set of states whenever a class of servers does not allow the existence of a common prior under which escaping the bad set is easy. We will subsequently refine it to handle adaptive algorithms under the assumption that executions with servers in their respective collections of bad states produce indistinguishable user views.

Note that these lower bounds provide additional justification for the introduction of prior distributions—a move which we originally justified by appealing to the "natural appeal" of such notions. That is, suppose that we wish to achieve some goal that cannot be achieved while the execution is in one of our "bad sets" – again, our canonical example of a bad set of states that is hard to escape and generally necessary to escape to achieve a goal is the set of "waiting for password" states in executions with password-protected servers – then, our lower bounds will demonstrate that when the class of servers lacks a suitable common notion of "natural users" under which escaping the bad sets is easy, a universal user cannot be too efficient, and in particular, the best possible running time more generally is roughly that which would be obtained by sampling from the best common distribution. In our intended application of the following theorem, we consider δ to be a relatively large constant (e.g., $\delta = 1/2$) and ϵ is very small (perhaps "exponentially" small in the right context).

Theorem 4.20 (A lower bound when no common prior exists). *Let $G = (\mathcal{E}, R)$ be a goal and S be a class of servers such that for every $E \in \mathcal{E}$ and $S \in \mathcal{S}$ we have designated some set of pairs of states of E and S, $\Theta_{S,E}$. Let $\delta \in [0, 1]$ be given. Now, suppose that there is some $(t, \epsilon) \in \mathbb{N} \times [0, 1]$ such that for every distribution over user strategies from the class $\mathcal{U}$, Q, there is some $E \in \mathcal{E}$ and $S \in \mathcal{S}$ such that $\Theta_{S,E}$ is (t, ϵ)-effectively closed with respect to Q in E. Then, for any sequence of user strategies and running times $(U_1, t_1), (U_2, t_2), \ldots$ such that each $t_i \leq t$, there is some $S \in \mathcal{S}$ and $E \in \mathcal{E}$ such that if in the execution where the user runs U_1 for t_1 steps, U_2 for t_2 steps, and so on, the first step τ for which $(X_\tau^{(s)}, X_\tau^{(e)}) \notin \Theta_{S,E}$ is at most $\sum_{i=1}^{k} t_i$ with probability at least δ, then $k \geq \frac{1}{\epsilon(1 + 1/\delta)}$.*

Proof Consider a zero-sum game between a *"user"* player and a *"server/-environment"* player, in which the strategy sets are $\mathcal{U}$ and $\mathcal{S} \times \mathcal{E}$, respectively, and the payoff of U with (S, E) is given by the maximum probability, over executions starting from initial states from $\Theta_{S,E}$, that the execution exits $\Theta_{S,E}$ in t steps. Note that our assumption on distributions over $\mathcal{U}$ shows that the server/environment player always has a good counter-strategy for any distribution over user strategies. Note also that since t is finite, the user effectively has only finitely many distinct strategies. Thus, given that no good distribution over user strategies exists, Loomis' Corollary [102] (see Appendix C) yields that there is some distribution $\tilde{Q}$ over $\mathcal{S} \times \mathcal{E}$ such that when any user strategy $U_1 \in \mathcal{U}$ is run for $t_1 \leq t$ steps with a server and environment pair (S, E) drawn from $\tilde{Q}$ and started in any state of $\Theta_{S,E}$, the probability that the execution (E, U_1, S) enters a state σ such that $(\sigma^{(s)}, \sigma^{(e)}) \notin \Theta_{S,E}$ is at most ϵ.

We claim that it will follow by induction on k that, given that the execution never entered a state σ such that $(\sigma^{(s)}, \sigma^{(e)}) \notin \Theta_{S,E}$ during the runs of $U_1, \ldots, U_{k-1}$, during the t_k step run of U_k, the probability that the execution enters such a state σ is at most $\frac{\epsilon}{1-k\epsilon}$. Indeed, given that if we ran U_k for $t_k \leq t$ steps given that $U_1, \ldots, U_{k-2}$ had not entered a state $(\sigma_{t^*}^{(s)}, \sigma_{t^*}^{(e)}) \notin \Theta_{S,E}$ for some t^*, U_k would only have entered such a state with probability at most $\frac{\epsilon}{1-(k-1)\epsilon}$. Therefore, conditioning on the event that this also did not happen during the run of U_{k-1} only increases the probability that U_k causes the execution to exit the associated $\Theta_{S,E}$ by a factor of $\frac{1}{1-\epsilon/(1-(k-1)\epsilon)}$, so the probability is still at most

$$\frac{\epsilon}{1-(k-1)\epsilon}\frac{1}{1-\epsilon/(1-(k-1)\epsilon)} = \frac{\epsilon}{1-k\epsilon}$$

as needed.

Therefore, noting that while $k\epsilon < 1$, our bound on the probability of exiting $\Theta_{S,E}$ only grows with each run, we see that a union bound over the first k runs gives a total probability of exiting $\Theta_{S,E}$ in the first k runs of at most $\frac{k\epsilon}{1-k\epsilon}$. In particular, some (S^*, E^*) in the support of $\tilde{Q}$ must give the sequence $(U_1, t_1), \ldots, (U_k, t_k)$ probability at most $\frac{k\epsilon}{1-k\epsilon}$ of exiting $\Theta_{S^*,E}$. Thus, if we exit $\Theta_{S^*,E}$ with probability at least δ by the end of the kth run, we see that this requires $k \geq \frac{1}{\epsilon(1+1/\delta)}$, as needed. ∎

We now extend Theorem 4.20 to cover adaptive algorithms, given that the servers generate indistinguishable views so long as they remain in the bad states. Again, our password-protected servers that say nothing while the execution leaves them in their respective "waiting for password" states are an example of such servers. The key point is that in this case, the algorithm generates a schedule nearly independently of the actual server it faces, permitting us to essentially reduce to the earlier analysis.

Corollary 4.21 (Good algorithms require a common prior when servers are indistinguishable). *Let G, $\mathcal{U}$, $\mathcal{S}$, sets of states $\Theta_{S,E}$ for each $E \in \mathcal{E}$ and each $S \in \mathcal{S}$, and $\delta \in [0,1]$ be given as in Theorem 4.20. Suppose that there is some fixed $E \in \mathcal{E}$ such that for every distribution Q over $\mathcal{U}$, there is some $S \in \mathcal{S}$ such that $\Theta_{S,E}$ is (t,ϵ)-effectively closed with respect to Q in E. Suppose further that for any $U \in \mathcal{U}$ and any pair of servers S_1 and S_2 from $\mathcal{S}$, for any $(\sigma_1^{(s)}, \sigma_1^{(e)}) \in \Theta_{S_1,E}$, there is some $(\sigma_2^{(s)}, \sigma_2^{(e)}) \in \Theta_{S_2,E}$ such that the distribution over user views in the first t steps of the execution (E, U, S_1) started from a state $(\sigma_1^{(e)}, \sigma^{(u)}, \sigma_1^{(s)})$ is γ-statistically close to the user view in the first t steps of the execution (E, U, S_2) started from the state $(\sigma_2^{(e)}, \sigma^{(u)}, \sigma_2^{(s)})$. Then for any algorithm U that on each step either starts running a new strategy from $\mathcal{U}$ from its initial state or continues running the same strategy from $\mathcal{U}$ for up to at most t steps, there is a server $S \in \mathcal{S}$ such that if U reaches a state σ such that $(\sigma^{(s)}, \sigma^{(e)}) \notin \Theta_{S,E}$ with probability at least δ by running up to k strategies from their initial states, then $k \geq \frac{1}{\epsilon(1+1/\delta)+\gamma/\delta}$.*

Proof As in the proof of Theorem 4.20, we set up a zero-sum game with the same payoffs, but we restrict the second player's strategy set to (S, E) for any $S \in \mathcal{S}$ and the given, fixed $E \in \mathcal{E}$. Letting $\tilde{Q}$ be the distribution over the second player's strategies obtained by Loomis' Corollary in the proof of Theorem 4.20, consider the following experiment. For a strategy S sampled from $\tilde{Q}$ and a starting state $(\sigma^{(s)}, \sigma^{(e)}) \in \Theta_{S,E}$, suppose we sample a second strategy S_0 from $\tilde{Q}$ and consider the execution (E, U, S_0), started from the corresponding initial state $(\sigma_0^{(s)}, \sigma_0^{(e)}) \in \Theta_{S_0,E}$. Now, suppose that we analyze the choices of U from (E, U, S_0) in the execution with S and E started from $(\sigma^{(s)}, \sigma^{(e)})$; since S is chosen independent of (E, U, S_0), we find that for each strategy run by U, the same bound on the probability that U causes S and E to exit the set $\Theta_{S,E}$ within $T \leq t$ steps holds as before. The same bound also holds if we first choose the state of S_0, and start S from its corresponding state. We thus obtain the same bound on the probability that S and E exit $\Theta_{S,E}$ after U chooses k strategies.

Now, note that as long as the execution with S and E remains in $\Theta_{S,E}$, since the distribution over user views with S starting from $(\sigma^{(s)}, \sigma^{(e)})$ is γ-close to the distribution over user views with S_0 starting from $(\sigma_0^{(s)}, \sigma_0^{(e)})$ for each strategy run by U, and the choice of U of whether to continue running the same algorithm, or to start running some other $U' \in \mathcal{U}$ at each ith step is a function of (the prefix of) the user's T-step view, the distribution over the choices of U over its run of up to k strategies changes in statistical distance by at most $k\gamma$ in response to the actual S_0 drawn from $\tilde{Q}$ that U is executing with. Therefore, the probability that U chooses some strategy from $\mathcal{U}$ to run that can exit $\Theta_{S_0,E}$ by the Tth step increases by at most $k\gamma$, so if we consider the number of strategies a user must run to exit $\Theta_{S,E}$ (i.e., when S was chosen independently of the view) with probability at least $\delta - k\gamma$, this is a lower bound on the number of strategies for U to exit $\Theta_{S_0,E}$ with probability at least δ when S_0 is sampled from $\tilde{Q}$. We can, as before now, find some $S^* \in \mathcal{S}$ such that the probability that the user exits after running k strategies is no greater than this bound; noting that $k\gamma < k\gamma/(1 - k\epsilon)$, we obtain the claimed bound. ∎

Note that we can also apply Corollary 4.21 to the case where the sets $\Theta_{S,E}$ are chosen to be states of the execution where a given sensing function fails. This will allow us to obtain lower bounds on the performance of any user strategy that uses such a sensing function.

Chapter 5

Computational complexity of goals

In the basic universal setting developed in Chapter 2, we restricted our attention to the class of probabilistic polynomial time bounded agents. This was a natural choice, given our usual association of polynomial time algorithms with the notion of "efficient computation" in accordance with the strong version of the Church-Turing thesis proposed by Cobham [46] and Edmonds [57]. It turns out that our main theorems for goals in finite executions hold for many classes of agents other than the class of polynomial time bounded agents, and so in the present chapter, derived from an early technical report [84], we seek their proper generalizations.

In order to generalize the statements of these theorems, though, we need an abstract definition of a complexity class, which is a highly nontrivial feat, and the traditional abstract approach to complexity, due to Blum [31], is not so convenient for our purposes. We won't seek to give a *definition* of a complexity class in its place, though; rather, we'll specify the properties of the classes we require, similar to Cobham's approach [46], and we will merely note that many natural complexity classes satisfy these properties. In particular, we will see that a closure property for a class of *interactive* functions that is particularly well-suited to our purposes is closure under "parallel composition" in the sense of Hoare [80]. We'll also give abstract generalizations of Levin's efficient enumerations [97] for other complexity classes, and note that many natural complexity classes also have efficient enumerators.

We can then show that analogues of our main theorems hold for generic complexity classes $\mathcal{C}$ satisfying certain properties, primarily closure under parallel composition and efficient enumerability. In particular, we introduce the $\mathcal{C}$-bounded universal setting in which a user attempts to succeed at a goal by communicating with a server using resource bounds in accordance with

B. Juba, *Universal Semantic Communication*,
DOI 10.1007/978-3-642-23297-8_5,

the class $\mathcal{C}$ whenever some other agent from $\mathcal{C}$ could achieve the goal with that server.

In particular, these theorems will hold for computational goals and for the class of polynomial time and logspace bounded users, and we will conclude the chapter by examining which computational problems have polynomial time and logspace bounded universal users (analogous to Section 1.4.2 and Section 3.3). Compellingly, we will find that P-complete problems have such universal users, which demonstrates that "universal delegation" of polynomial time computation is possible for logspace users.

5.1 Generic complexity classes for interactive computation

We begin by revisiting the model of agents and interactive computation introduced in Section 2.2. There, and more broadly in Chapter 2 (as well as Chapters 3–4), we restricted our attention to polynomial time bounded users. The decision to restrict our attention to this familiar class of algorithms allowed us to get on with the development or our basic theory of semantic communication with a minimal amount of hassle, since polynomial time is a familiar, robust model of computation—in particular, the definition of a stateful polynomial time bounded agent we introduced there is equivalent to the definition of a strategy as a polynomial time function from message histories to next messages, as presented in Section 1.4.2 (and the latter is the way interactive algorithms are typically *defined* in "modern" treatments). We now find it necessary to revisit the models we use, in the interest of treating resource-bounded computation more generally, *especially* computation that does not have the full power of polynomial time, since this will be useful for some proposed applications (e.g., to universal delegation of computation). Note, for example, that the two definitions of interactive algorithms described above are *not* equivalent if the user's memory usage is limited. The models we develop here will apply broadly to these classes, as well as pointing to the right notions for capturing efficient users for goals in infinite executions, which we will introduce in Chapter 6.

5.1.1 Model of interactive computation

Recall that our *agents* were each given by a *probabilistic strategy*, assigning a distribution over the outgoing message channels and state space of the agent for each state of the incoming message channels and internal state for that agent. The execution of a system of agents proceeded in *rounds*, in which given a state of the system, each party's strategy induced a distribution over the local states of the system for the next round of the execution, so that jointly, the parties' strategies induced a stationary Markov process on the global states of the system. The agent representing the user was also assumed to have a distinguished *halting* state, and the execution was stopped and the user's performance evaluated once the user entered its halting state.

We won't need to be too deeply concerned with the usual details of the model of computation for the strategies, and for our current purposes the reader should equally well be able to follow the present development when keeping any sufficiently strong model of computation in mind – such as multi-tape Turing machines[1] or RAM machines – provided that we can define memory configurations and time bounds for the machine model in a reasonable way. What we *will* need to consider carefully here are the aspects of the model that are special to interactive computation. Specifically, we will find it convenient to view the usual models of computation as decomposed into a communicating network of *modules*. To be more precise, we view our users as containing the following modules:

1. A deterministic *control* module, having a *control state* – corresponding to either the Turing machine's control state or the registers of a RAM machine – and *memory configuration* – corresponding to the state of the internal working memory of the machine – running some fixed program.

2. An *input* module for each incoming message channel that the control module may read from.

3. An *output* module for each outgoing message channel that the control module may write to.

4. A *random bit generator* module that, on an appropriate signal from the control module, responds with a uniform random bit.

5. A *suspend execution* module that, on an appropriate signal from the control module (e.g., the message "1"), commits to the outgoing messages and waits until the next round of the execution.

6. A *halting* module that, on an appropriate signal (e.g., receiving an incoming message consisting of "1"), triggers the end of the execution.

The space of messages associated with the communication channels joining modules will depend on our model of computation. For example, in the Turing machine model, we may assume that they carry messages from a finite set—in particular, in the case of a Turing machine with two-way access to its input, the transition function of the finite state control is usually assumed to produce a tuple with a head-movement component from the set $\{\leftarrow, \rightarrow\}$ indicating whether it should read the next symbol of the input tape or the previous symbol on the next computation step, and in our model, we assume that these symbols are passed as messages to the input module; the response of the input module should of course be the indicated symbol of the

---

[1]I.e., with Turing machines in the class having *any* given number of tapes—classes of k-tape Turing machines for bounded or fixed k will be too restrictive for us.

input. In the usual model of sublinear time computation, on the other hand, random access to the input is permitted, and in this case the messages to the input module indicate *indices* of the incoming message i.e., of $\log \ell$ bits if the message has length ℓ. The crucial point will be that the size of the internal messages should be sufficiently small that when we consider a class of resource-bounded control modules, we find that the class is closed under parallel composition as described in Section 5.1.3.

Now, there is a natural correspondence between a network of modules and a system of agents as described in Section 2.2, and we will essentially use the same language to describe them. Specifically, we can associate a *strategy* with each module as well as a state capturing the agent's current state along with some additional information, e.g., the Turing machine's head position. We can then talk about executions of the modules, noting that except for the random bit generator, the modules are deterministic. In particular, we will define parallel composition in terms of systems of agents, but our intent is to apply it to modules to construct a strategy for an agent.

5.1.2   Bounded resources and simulation

Now, in the present chapter, we are interested in interactive algorithms that achieve a given goal with a large class of servers $\mathcal{S}$ while satisfying various bounds on their usage of computational resources. The natural and obvious way to do this is to assert that the algorithm should be a member of some class of algorithms $\mathcal{C}$ that never use more of a given resource than a specified amount in any execution of a system with an environment of a given size (e.g., $5n^2$ bits of memory in environments of size n). In some cases, such as if we specify the number of gates in a circuit implementing the algorithm, then this approach makes sense, though we would have to be sure to use the "right" circuit for the given size of the environment. In general, though, we wish to consider the resources used by an algorithm when interacting with an arbitrary member of a class of servers $\mathcal{S}$ for which there is no common a priori bound on the resources required to communicate with the various members. We stress that we wish to be able to invoke the *same* algorithm with *any* member of $\mathcal{S}$ and *any* actual strategy of the environment, knowing only that it will use an "appropriate" amount of resources for the given server and environment strategy. In particular, we would like to handle a wide variety of resource bounds without needing to treat each one individually. Our approach in the current chapter is to require that with each server S, for our fixed user U there exists some appropriately resource-bounded version U_S (i.e., that is a member of our class $\mathcal{C}$) such that then for every $E \in \mathcal{E}$, U behaves like U_S, and U_S uses only an appropriate amount of resources in (E, U_S, S). We need an appropriate notion of "U behaves like U_S" for this to achieve the desired effect, though, which leads us to introduce the following strong notion of *simulation*:

Definition 5.1 (Simulation). We will say that an agent A' *simulates* an agent A in a collection of computation histories if there is a surjective mapping σ from control states of A' to control states of A and a projection π mapping memory configurations of A' to memory configurations of A such that for all histories in the collection, A' simulates A, the mapping ψ from configurations of A' to configurations of A obtained from σ and π is surjective on the set of configurations of A occurring in the history, and if for configurations c_i and c_{i+1} of A' $c_i \rightarrow c_{i+1}$ (on random bit b), then it is either the case that $\psi(c_i) = \psi(c_{i+1})$ or $\psi(c_i) \rightarrow \psi(c_{i+1})$ (on random bit b).

Notice that if A' simulates A, A' takes at least as many steps on each history in the collection, uses at least as much space, and uses at least as many coin tosses. Typical examples of such simulations are the standard "clock" and "ruler" simulations for obtaining time and space bounded versions of arbitrary algorithms whenever the bounding functions are *time* and *space* *constructible*, respectively. For reference, we recall the definition of time and space constructibility below:

Definition 5.2 (Time and space constructibility). We say that a function $t : \mathbb{N} \rightarrow \mathbb{N}$ is *time-constructible* if there is an algorithm that computes $t(n)$ on input n within $t(n)$ steps. We say that a function $s : \mathbb{N} \rightarrow \mathbb{N}$ is *space-constructible* if there is an algorithm that, on input n, computes $s(n)$ using space at most $s(n)$.

So then, for example, a "ruler" simulation for the RAM machine model may be constructed as follows:

Example 5.3 (Space-bounded simulation on a RAM machine). Given any algorithm A and a space-constructible bound $s(n)$ (and given the size n), one construction of a "ruler" simulation of A would first compute $s(n)$ in space $s(n)$, and use this as the initial value of a counter that meters the space usage in the simulation of A. The simulation then only writes to odd-numbered words of memory (i.e., by adding a low-order bit of '1' to every index A would visit in our simulation), and uses the adjacent even-numbered words to place a mark every time A would visit a new address—that is, whenever A would visit an address, we first check the adjacent word to see if a mark is present, and if not, we mark the adjacent word, and decrement the counter before simulating the read or write by A. Thus, when the counter reaches 0, if A tries to visit a new address, we halt the simulation, and so the simulation takes only $O(s(n))$ space overall.

The simulations for other resources (in our models of interest) are even simpler.

Thus, we can introduce resource bounds by introducing a class $\mathcal{C}$ of bounded algorithms and require in each case that the behavior of our agent A when interacting with a server $S \in \mathcal{S}$ should be simulateable by some member $A_S \in \mathcal{C}$—namely, by the "clock" and/or "ruler" simulation of A with the appropriate bounding function(s) for S. Since we use the particularly strong notion of simulation described above, the requirement that A_S simulates A for some A_S taken from a resource-bounded class $\mathcal{C}$ implies a bound on the resources used by A during its execution with S.

Definition 5.4 (($(\mathcal{C}, p)$-bounded protocol). For a class of agents $\mathcal{C}$ and a function $p : \mathbb{N} \to [0, 1]$, we say that an agent A is $(\mathcal{C}, p)$-*bounded* with respect to a system with a non-deterministic environment strategy $\mathcal{E}$ if there exists $A' \in \mathcal{C}$ such that for every $E \in \mathcal{E}$ and every initial state of the system in which A' is started from its initial state and given the size parameter n as auxiliary input, with probability at least $p(n)$ (over the execution), A' simulates A in the execution $(E, A, \ldots)$. If $p \equiv 1$, we simply say A is $\mathcal{C}$-*bounded* with respect to $\mathcal{E}$.

We note that although there are many natural cases – e.g., computational goals – where the size parameter is given by the length of the environment's message, in general the user doesn't necessarily have access to the value of the size parameter during the execution, so the fact that a user strategy U is $\mathcal{C}$-bounded only says that U uses an "appropriate" amount of resources in each system, even though U may have no a priori way of knowing what amount is appropriate. Still, while $(\mathcal{C}, p)$-boundedness captures the aforementioned uniform complexity bounds, we note that it also captures the "trivial" case where the agent A was a member of $\mathcal{C}$ to begin with: we can take the maps σ and π to be the identity map, so A can be said to simulate itself (with $p \equiv 1$) and thus if $A \in \mathcal{C}$, A is $\mathcal{C}$-bounded in the above sense (as it can simply ignore the size parameter), and so we can still use it for nonuniform resource bounds such as circuit size. Although we *won't* be able to construct universal users via enumeration for such classes, the sensing requirements described in Section 5.3 *will* hold for such kinds of resource-bounded agents.

5.1.3   Composition

The constructions underlying our theorems will require us to be able to take an agent with bounded resources, and produce a new agent satisfying a similar resource bound that performs some simple additional tasks. We can obtain such results naturally by *composing* members of the class whenever the class is closed under the appropriate notion of composition. In this section we will introduce our main notion of composition – "parallel" composition – which will play the leading role in the subsequent developments. We will also introduce a less important notion of "sequential" composition, that we will still desire to invoke on occasion. In both cases, most of the usual classes of interactive algorithms will be closed under the respective notions of composition.

Parallel composition

The crucial basic property that we will require of the resource-bounded classes of agents (or rather, of control modules) that we consider in the present chapter is *closure under parallel composition,* in the sense of Hoare [80], which we will now describe in more detail.[2] Suppose we have a system of $k > 2$ agents containing agents with indices a and b. Suppose we choose to take a and b together as a "group"—that is, for any ith player that previously had outgoing channels (i, a) and (i, b) and incoming channels (a, i) and (b, i) joining it to a and b, these channels are relabeled as (distinct) channels joining i to some index c. Then informally, the *parallel composition* of the strategies of indices a and b is the corresponding strategy for c that simulates the two component strategies together. (See Figure 5.1 for a diagram.)

Definition 5.5 (Parallel composition strategy). For agents using strategies A and B, at indices a and b respectively in a system of $k > 2$ agents, suppose that in a corresponding system of $k - 1$ agents, indices a and b are replaced by index c with internal state space

$$\Omega^{(c)} = \Omega^{(a)} \times \Omega^{(a,b)} \times \Omega^{(b,a)} \times \Omega^{(b)}$$

i.e., so that for any states of a and b, and any contents of the channels joining a and b, there is a corresponding internal state of c, $\sigma^{(c)} \in \Omega^{(c)}$. The *parallel composition of A and B,* denoted $A\|B$, is the strategy $(A\|B)(\sigma_0)$ given by associating the distribution $A(\sigma_0^{(a)}, \sigma_0^{(\cdot,a)})$ over the (a) and (a, b) components of $\sigma^{(c)}$ and over the respective $\sigma^{(a,i)}$ components for $i \neq$ b, and similarly for the distribution given by B.

We note that the system $((A\|B), \ldots)$ started from state σ_0 and the system $(A, B, \ldots)$ started from the corresponding state produce identically distributed executions under the appropriate formal maps, and likewise simply produce identical distributions as long as we project away the (c) and (a), (a, b), (b, a), (b) components, respectively, since the other components of the global state are untouched by the aforementioned formal maps.

Parallel composition will be useful to us as a natural way to combine interactive algorithms to obtain new algorithms. The crucial point in the context of this chapter is that for an appropriate model of computation, if the individual strategies A and B use only a limited amount of a resource, then the parallel composition $A\|B$ does not use (much) more than a multiple of the amounts of the resource used by A and B. (We note that we only count the time spent by A or B when they are not halting or suspended.) Precisely:

---

[2]Actually, if one ignores the internal states, our agents are captured reasonably well by Hoare's theory of *communicating sequential processes,* as our executions projected down to the communication channels are distributions over traces for the corresponding *processes* (in Hoare's language). The only awkward aspect is simulating the synchronous round-wise communication among agents.

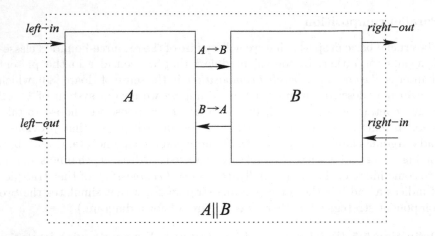

Figure 5.1: The parallel composition of agents A and B exchanging messages with each other on channels $A \to B$ and $B \to A$ yields an agent $A\|B$ that produces executions distributed identically to those produced by a system containing A and B when $A\|B$ communicates over the channels *left-in* and *left-out* previously used by A and the channels *right-in* and *right-out* previously used by B.

Proposition 5.6 (Resources usages remain bounded under parallel composition). *In either the RAM machine or multi-tape Turing machine model of computation, suppose that in every system $(A, B, \ldots)$ of size n in which A and B are run from designated starting states until one of them halts (resp., they both suspend execution), A can be computed in $t_A(n)$ steps, using space $s_A(n)$, and $r_A(n)$ random bits; and B can be computed in $t_B(n)$ steps, using space $s_B(n)$, and $r_B(n)$ random bits. Suppose furthermore that $\Omega^{(a,b)}$ and $\Omega^{(b,a)}$ can each be represented in $m(n)$ symbols in systems of size n. Then $A\|B$ can be computed from the corresponding starting state in $O(t_A(n) + t_B(n))$ steps, using space $6 \max\{s_A(n), s_B(n), m(n)\}$ and $r_A(n) + r_B(n)$ random bits. Moreover, the construction of $A\|B$ also simulates A and B in any execution.*

Sketch of proof In the RAM model, this is accomplished by designating one out of every six consecutive words of memory to a, b, and two buffers for (a, b), and (b, a), respectively; in the multi-tape Turing machine model, this is even easier, since we can simply designate appropriate numbers of tapes for A and B, and introduce new tapes for our two buffers for (a, b) and (b, a), giving these tapes independent read-only and write-only heads.[3] Thus, the state and inputs/outputs of A and B can be accessed freely at unit cost (alternating the use of buffers for the messages, i.e., using one buffer to store

---

[3]Alternatively, we could give each tape one head, and copy from an "input" tape to an "output" tape when we switch control from A to B, at a cost of $m(n)$ additional steps per switch in the time complexity.

odd-numbered messages between A and B and the other one to store the even-numbered ones) and we can simulate the strategies, alternating between them each time one of them suspends execution, and halting when both suspend execution or one of them halts. The common random bit generator is thus also shared naturally since only one strategy is simulated on any given step. Moreover, the control and memory configurations of A and B respectively can be obtained via appropriate maps, so this construction simulates both A and B. ■

The abstract significance of Proposition 5.6 (and the way we will invoke it) is that classes of algorithms defined by bounds on their time, space, and/or randomness complexities that are closed under constant factors (and have appropriately chosen internal communications channels) are closed under parallel composition. Formally,

Definition 5.7 (Parallel composition closed). We say that a class of agents C is *parallel composition closed* if for any pair of agents A and B in C simulating agents A' and B' in a collection of histories, $A\|B$ is also in C, and moreover, there is a parallel composition agent $(A'\|B')$ such that the agent realizing $(A\|B)$ in C simulates $(A'\|B')$ in the same collection of histories.

We insist on the simulation condition, of course, because we may want to use the fact that a particular implementation of $(A\|B)$ is in C to bound the complexity of some other agent—somewhat dryly:

Proposition 5.8. *Let C be a class of agents defined by bounds on the time, space, and/or randomness usage of its members such that the bounding functions are closed under constant factors, and the length of internal messages is less than the space complexity. Then C is parallel composition closed.*

Sketch of proof Suppose A and B simulate A' and B', respectively in some collection of histories, and that A and B are in C. Suppose we construct $(A\|B)$ and $(A'\|B')$ according to the construction of Proposition 5.6; we immediately have that $(A\|B) \in C$, so it only remains to show that $(A\|B)$ simulates $(A'\|B')$ in the given collection of histories. Since the memory configurations of A and B are interleaved in $(A\|B)$ in the same way as in $(A'\|B')$, the interleaving of the respective projections for A and B is still a projection from the memory configuration of $(A\|B)$ recovering the memory configuration of $(A'\|B')$. Likewise, the respective control maps for A and B can be used to obtain a mapping relating the control states of $(A\|B)$ and $(A'\|B')$ since in any segment of the computation, only one of the strategies is being executed, and within this segment, the state of the inactive member remains fixed, while the states of the active member are related between $(A\|B)$ and $(A'\|B')$ via the appropriate map either relating the control states of A and A' or relating B and B'. ■

Of course, in trivial cases where $A' = A$ and $B' = B$ (as would happen for circuits, for example), then in our construction $(A'\|B') = (A\|B)$, and there is even less to say.

Parallel composition versus composition of functions: a technical point

In the interest of pre-empting a potential point of confusion, we note that our notion of parallel composition of agents only generally captures the composition of functions in a limited sense, when the composition can be computed in an on-line fashion. This permits a less sophisticated construction of parallel composition agents than the usual construction for composition of space-bounded functions, which requires re-computing the "inner" function so that we can simulate two-way access to its output by the "outer" function. We couldn't even hope to simulate two-way access to the (buffered) output of an agent in a space-bounded manner in general since that agent may interact with other parts of the system that we would have no control over in the simulation. Thus, we need to buffer the messages sent by A and B to one another on the previous round in the internal state of the agent (and this is why we explicitly restrict the size of messages sent between A and B). It is fortunate that we can, for the most part, make do with this relatively weak kind of composition—since the parallel composition of agents is easier to construct, we expect a wider variety of classes of agents to be closed under parallel composition. The one exception we will encounter in this chapter, where the composition of functions is required, is in the construction of Theorem 5.26 creating users for computational goals from interactive proof systems, which consequently has a substantially reduced domain of applicability. (Indeed, Theorem 5.26 has the most restrictive hypotheses of any of the results in this chapter, and only applies to a relative handful of settings.)

Sequential composition

We will also wish to use Hoare's notion of *sequential composition* [80] on occasion. In our framework, this is an even simpler notion:

Definition 5.9 (Sequential composition). Given strategies A and B with designated initial states for the same agent in a system, the *sequential composition* of A and B, denoted $(A; B)$ is the strategy that runs A from its initial state until it would halt, and then instead of halting, runs B from its initial state.

We say that a class of agents $\mathcal{C}$ is *closed under sequential composition* if for any pair of agents A and B in $\mathcal{C}$, an agent realizing $(A; B)$ is also in $\mathcal{C}$.

In both the RAM machine model and multi-tape Turing machine model, it is fairly evident that any of the usual resource-bounded classes are closed under parallel composition: if A can be computed in time/space/randomness

(t_A, s_A, r_A), and B can be computed in (t_B, s_B, r_B), then without fear we can compute $(A; B)$ in time/space/randomness $(t_A + t_B, s_A + s_B, r_A + r_B)$, and then whenever the bounds provided by Proposition 5.6 suffice to guarantee that $(A\|B)$ is in $\mathcal{C}$ given A and B in $\mathcal{C}$, this bound also guarantees that $(A; B)$ is in $\mathcal{C}$.

5.1.4 Basic agents: the toolkit

We now describe a few basic kinds of agents that we will require in the constructions we use in our proofs. Generally, these agents will have extremely simple implementations as deterministic finite-state transducers so it will be clear that they belong to the class of bounded agents in question, and hence when that class is closed under parallel composition, we will be able to use these basic agents in parallel composition constructions to obtain new agents in the same class. Of course, in each individual case, we still need to verify that such implementations exist.

Logic gates and fanout

We assume that there are agents computing any logic gate of finite fan-in: precisely, for each gate $G : \{0,1\}^k \to \{0,1\}$, there is an agent with k input channels and one output channel such that when the k input channels contain some $(x_1, \ldots, x_k) \in \{0,1\}^k$, that agent writes $G(x_1, \ldots, x_k)$ to its output channel. Likewise, we assume that there is a fan-out agent, that has one input and two outputs, that on any input, writes it to both of its outputs. Note that by parallel composition of a constant number of these agents, we can construct an agent computing any finite-size circuit; if the circuit is acyclic, then on any input, the circuit suspends execution in a finite number of steps and uses no random bits, nor any memory beyond its finite-state control.

Equality test

Building on the above example, we assume that there is an agent implementing the following kind of *on-line equality tester*: the agent has two inputs, which we will label i and j, and one output. From its initial state, the agent outputs 1 until it receives inputs on i and j that are not equal, whereupon the agent outputs 0. Although this may be represented as a cyclic circuit, given that some care would need to be taken to ensure that such a representation produces messages in finite time, we feel it is more natural to note that this may be represented as a simple two-state finite-state transducer.

Fixed padding

For each integer i, we will assume that the following *padding agent* is in our class: the agent has one input channel and one output channel, and it outputs i 0s before copying each subsequent message from its input channel to its output channel. Of course, this agent may be implemented by an $i + 1$-state finite-state transducer.

Copying

We will also need a *copying agent* that "forwards" the contents from an input module to an output module. The complexity of such an agent depends on the model of computation: in the Turing machine model, given end-markers, this can be realized as a two-state transducer whereas in the RAM machine model, it seems to require a counter.

5.2   On the computational complexity of goal-oriented communication

Now that we have refined our model of interactive algorithms, we return to our main concern, understanding how and to what extent communications protocols can be made more robust and flexible. In particular, we now introduce some variants of the basic universal setting introduced in Chapter 2 in which we consider classes of algorithms defined by other resource bounds, including other complexity measures and classes of time complexity bounds other than simply all polynomials.

5.2.1   The complexity of interpreting versus the complexity of learning to communicate

Recall that in the basic universal setting, we had fixed polynomial time bounded algorithms as our class of interest, and we wanted a protocol that ran in polynomial time with each fixed server for which some other protocol could achieve our goal in polynomial time. As a starting point to motivate the development of the current chapter, suppose we wish to take a more refined view of the various roles played by the protocols we have constructed. Our basic architecture, introduced in the construction of Proposition 2.27 and employed in many constructions since, combined an *enumeration* with a *sensing function*, and we succeeded at our goal when we found a *good protocol* in the enumeration. The alternative construction we have seen, described in Theorem 4.9, used sampling instead of enumeration (and a uniform reduction instead of running the protocol directly), but otherwise the architecture was quite similar. For the present discussion, we will call the protocols we seek *interpreters* – that is, we will refer to *the protocols that satisfy the viability condition of our sensing function* with a server as interpreters – and we will identify the roles played by the universal users as

1. Searching for an interpreter.

2. Interpreting the communication with the server.

3. Verifying successful communication.

We previously indicated that we would be happy so long as we had a polynomial time bound for the components carrying out each of these tasks, but we have *already* seen an example where this was *not* so: in the test of computational ability, described in Section 3.5, we demanded that interpretation of the powerful servers was achieved by some very limited protocol, having a short description and time complexity bounded by a *fixed* polynomial, even though we were still happy to have an examiner that ran in polynomial time for an arbitrary polynomial. The requirement on our interpreters allowed us to achieve the third task, distinguishing powerful servers from weak ones. We will see another example in Chapter 9 where limiting the class of interpreters we consider is crucial in allowing us to verify that communication was successful, where moreover, we are motivated primarily by a desire for *correctness* rather than by other measures of computational efficiency. Meanwhile, in Chapter 8, we will see examples where limiting the class of interpreters allows us to achieve the first task much more efficiently, but still by using a protocol much more sophisticated than the interpreters that actually interact with the server for us (as we will see, the interpreters in this case will really necessarily be given by *extremely* simple algorithms). The point is that *in general*, there will be ample reason to draw a distinction between the class of algorithms that communicate for us, and the class of algorithms carrying out the other two tasks—which will consequently dominate the resource consumption of our universal users. That is, in the settings that we will consider in general, there will be *two* classes of agents under consideration, the class of users $\mathcal{U}$ (for which we wish to design a universal user strategy) and the class of interpreters $\mathcal{I}$, where we will naturally need that $\mathcal{I} \subseteq \mathcal{U}$, but $\mathcal{I}$ may frequently be a *strict* subclass of $\mathcal{U}$.

5.2.2 Helpfulness for generic classes of users

Most of the definitions capturing goal-oriented communication made no reference to resource bounds whatsoever, and so they will persist without modification even as we consider other kinds of complexity measures (although we will explicitly bound the complexity of, e.g., our universal users by other measures). The only two exceptions are the definitions that reference the class of algorithms capturing the interpreters, i.e., the definition of a *helpful* server and *viable* sensing, and more broadly the definition of a good sensing function, which was specialized to the class of polynomial time bounded users in a somewhat subtle way. Sensing will need to be essentially reworked for it to generalize properly, and we defer the discussion to the next section. The definition of helpfulness has a much more immediate generalization that we discuss presently. Essentially, we simply replace the mention of the class of polynomial time protocols with an arbitrary class $\mathcal{C}$:

Definition 5.10 $((G, \mathcal{C}, p)$-Helpful). We say that a server S is $(G, \mathcal{C}, p)$-*helpful* for a goal G, a class of agents $\mathcal{C}$, and $p : \mathbb{N} \to [0, 1]$ if there exists $U_S \in \mathcal{C}$ such that (U_S, S) robustly achieve the goal with probability $p(n)$ in environments of size n.

Now, although we have stressed that we permit the class of interpreters to differ from the class for which we aim to construct a universal user in general, there are still some cases – notably, the goal of computation as considered in depth in Section 3.3 – in which the entire purpose of invoking a universal user is to accomplish a goal using less resources, and it is natural to simply desire that interpreting the server's communication does not pose an obstacle by requiring more resources than we wish to allow the universal user. That is, if we want a $\mathcal{C}$-bounded universal user for a goal, then we may naturally desire to construct a universal user for the class of servers that are helpful for the class $\mathcal{C}$—which is, of course, the largest possible class of servers for which we could hope to give a $\mathcal{C}$-*bounded universal user*, much as the class of all helpful servers was the largest class for which we could hope to give a polynomial time universal user in the basic universal setting. To contrast this common set-up with the basic universal setting, we will refer to this as the $\mathcal{C}$-*bounded universal setting*. We feel that the goals of greatest natural interest in $\mathcal{C}$-bounded universal settings are computational goals, and we will revisit these goals at the end of this chapter.

5.3   Sensing modules

We now turn to reworking sensing for classes of users other than polynomial time bounded users. The objective will be to obtain a definition of sensing with generic classes of users for which an analogue of Theorem 2.25 holds, establishing the equivalence of the design of sensing and universal users. Actually, the analogue of Proposition 2.27, constructing universal users from sensing, will only hold when the class is *enumerable* (which, in turn, necessitates a new definition in the abstract approach of the current chapter), whereas an analogue of Proposition 2.26, showing that sensing must be possible with complexity comparable to that of any universal user strategy (whenever universal users can be constructed), holds much more broadly. Thus, we actually defer the presentation of the positive direction of our analogue of Theorem 2.25 until the next section. Nevertheless, the existence of an analogue of this theorem is our litmus test for the suitability of a notion of sensing, and will serve as a guide for our discussion.

5.3.1   Safety and viability for generic classes of agents

We already hinted at the problem with our original definition of sensing for polynomial time bounded users when we were motivating our refined model of interactive computation, but we now spell it out explicitly: our

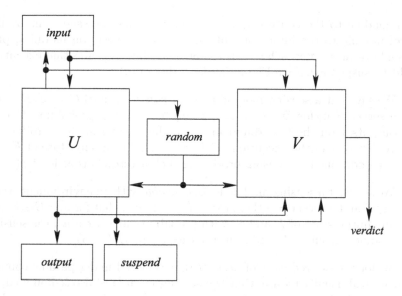

Figure 5.2: When used with a control module U, the sensing module V receives a copy of the messages sent to U by the input module and random bit generator module, and receives a copy of the messages sent by U to the input, output, and suspend execution modules. Each time execution resumes after it is suspended, V issues a verdict, roughly indicating whether it believes the referee is satisfied.

original definition of sensing relied on the equivalence of polynomial time functions of histories and functions computable by polynomial time strategies. Thus, we had the option of introducing sensing either way, and much as in Section 1.4.2 and most modern treatments of interactive computation, we felt it was simpler to introduce sensing as a polynomial time function taking user views to positive or negative indications. The *right* definition though, i.e., the one that generalizes, is one that treats sensing as a separate, stateful *module* in the user that produces verdicts in an on-line fashion from the view of the *control module* (i.e., interacting with the rest of the system via the user's input and output modules).

This amended notion of a sensing *module* now plays essentially the same role that sensing functions played in our earlier treatment. In particular, its verdicts should again satisfy notions of *safety* and *viability*, meaning that positive indications indicate that the goal has actually been achieved with high probability, and that positive indications can be obtained, respectively. These notions will also be generalized to hold for arbitrary classes of agents in a manner similar to our generalization of helpfulness in the previous section.

Definition 5.11 (Sensing module). A *sensing module* is a module that, when given a copy of the messages sent by the input module and random bit generator module to the control module, along with the messages sent by the control module to the input, output, and suspend execution modules, produces a Boolean *verdict* each time the control module indicates that execution should be suspended. (See Figure 5.2 for a diagram.)

- We say that a sensing module is $(\mathcal{C}, p)$-*safe* for a goal $G = (\mathcal{E}, R)$ with a server S if, for any $U \in \mathcal{C}$, and any $E \in \mathcal{E}$, the probability that R outputs 1 on the first round in which the sensing module produces a verdict of 1 in the execution (E, U, S) started from any state of E and S (conditioned on sensing producing such a verdict) is at least $p(n)$.

- We say that a sensing module is $(\mathcal{C}, p)$-*viable* with an environment strategy $\mathcal{E}$ and a server S if there exists $U_S \in \mathcal{C}$ such that for any $E \in \mathcal{E}$ and any initial state of E and S, with probability at least $p(n)$, the sensing module outputs a 1 verdict in the execution (E, U_S, S).

Now, for the desired class of users $\mathcal{U}$ that is closed under parallel composition, we will usually require that the sensing module is also $\mathcal{U}$-bounded, so that the parallel composition of the sensing module and the control module yields another $\mathcal{U}$-bounded agent;[4] on the other hand, we will need the sensing module to satisfy $(\mathcal{I}, p)$-*safety* and $(\mathcal{I}, p)$-*viability* for the class of interpreters $\mathcal{I}$, where we again stress that in general, $\mathcal{I}$ may not be equal to $\mathcal{U}$ for a variety of reasons.

5.3.2   On the necessity of sensing and its safety requirements

Now that we have a suitable notion of sensing for generic classes of agents, it turns out to be easy to obtain generalizations of our theorems from Chapter 2 showing that strong sensing is necessary; as we noted at the outset of this section, we need additional hypotheses such as enumerability to obtain a construction of universal users from sensing, and so we will have more work to do before we can obtain analogues of our positive results. For now, we first prove an analogue of Proposition 2.26 in the $\mathcal{C}$-bounded universal setting.

Proposition 5.12 (Sensing is necessary for universal users in the generic bounded universal setting). *Let $\mathcal{C}$ be a class of agents that halt with probability 1 containing the fanout, on-line comparison, and AND agents, that is closed under parallel composition. Let U be a universal user strategy for a goal G and a class of servers $\mathcal{S}$ such that for each $S \in \mathcal{S}$ there exists $U_S \in \mathcal{C}$ and functions $\epsilon_S, \mu_S : \mathbb{N} \to [0,1]$ such that in the execution (E, U, S), U_S simulates U with probability $1 - \epsilon_S(n)$, and in the executions (E, U_S, S) where U_S simulates U, U_S achieves the goal with probability $1 - \mu_S(n)$. Let V be*

---

[4]Strictly speaking, this *also* assumes that modules computing the fanout, described in Section 5.1.4, are also available in $\mathcal{U}$ and these are also involved in the parallel composition, but this is surely not at issue in most cases of interest.

the agent that computes U on the messages from the input and random bit modules, and outputs the AND of U's halting signal and the result of the on-line comparison of the user's output with the output of U as its verdict. Then V is a $(\mathcal{C}, 1 - \epsilon_S)$-bounded $(\mathcal{C}, 1 - \mu_S)$-safe and $(\mathcal{C}, 1 - \epsilon_S)$-viable sensing module with each $S \in \mathcal{S}$.

Proof Let any server $S \in \mathcal{S}$ be given, and V be the agent described above. Now, for the agent U_S that simulates U in the execution (E, U, S) for each $E \in \mathcal{E}$ with probability $1 - \epsilon_S(n)$, consider the agent V_S obtained by the same construction as V with U_S substituted for U in the parallel composition. Now, since the fanout, on-line comparison, and AND agents are in $\mathcal{C}$ and U_S is the $\mathcal{C}$-bounded agent that simulates U with S, $V_S \in \mathcal{C}$, and moreover V_S simulates V with probability $1 - \epsilon_S(n)$, the same as U_S simulating U, we find that V is $(\mathcal{C}, 1 - \epsilon_S)$-bounded.

Now, let any $E \in \mathcal{E}$, $U' \in \mathcal{C}$, and $S \in \mathcal{S}$ be given, and consider the execution (E, U', S) with the control module of U' attached to V. Note that when V produces a 1 verdict, then U' produced an execution that is identical to the execution that U would have produced (note that the behavior of the *control module* of U' is *deterministic*). Thus, if V output 1 and U' failed to achieve the goal with probability δ, we'd find that in the same execution with U, occurring with probability at least δ, U would also fail. Since U is assumed to achieve the goal with probability at least $1 - \mu_S(n)$, though, we find that $\delta \leq \mu_S(n)$, so V is $(\mathcal{C}, 1 - \mu_S(n))$-safe, as needed.

Likewise, for any $E \in \mathcal{E}$ and $S \in \mathcal{S}$, for the agent $U_S \subset \mathcal{C}$ that simulates U with probability at least $1 - \epsilon_S(n)$, we find that since U_S must halt, and U and U_S produce the same outputs in this case, V produces a 1 verdict on the round in which U_S halts. Thus, V is also $(\mathcal{C}, 1 - \epsilon_S(n))$-viable in $\mathcal{E}$ with S. ∎

Likewise, we can obtain an analogue of Theorem 2.37 for the $\mathcal{C}$-bounded universal setting; Proposition 5.12, together with the following theorem, show that the signal to the halting module of a $\mathcal{C}$-bounded universal user is an unconditionally safe test of a goal's achievement, computable by members of $\mathcal{C}$. In the case of a computational goal, for example, we will see that this is the key step showing that a universal user can be used to obtain a verifier for an interactive proof system.

Theorem 5.13 (Safety with all helpful servers for a generic class of interpreters implies safety with all servers). *Let $\mathcal{C}$ be a class containing the padding agents and closed under parallel composition. For a goal G, suppose that V is a sensing module that is $(\mathcal{C}, p)$-safe for G with every $(G, \mathcal{C}, p')$-helpful server. Then, if a $(G, \mathcal{C}, p')$-helpful server exists, we find that V is also $(\mathcal{C}, p)$-safe for G with every server strategy.*

Proof The argument is very similar to the proof of Theorem 2.37. Consider a sensing module V that is not $(\mathcal{C}, p)$-safe for G with respect to some server

S. Then there must exist $E \in \mathcal{E}$, $U \in \mathcal{C}$, and some initial state σ such that in the execution (E, U, S) started from σ, V outputs a 1 verdict, but R is not satisfied with probability $p + \delta > p$.

Now, we can find some finite set of executions for which the probability that V outputs a 1 verdict but R is not satisfied is at least $p + \delta/2 > p$; in this set of executions, there is some finite maximum length of the messages sent by U up to the first round in which V outputs a 1 verdict, M.

If no $(G, \mathcal{C}, p')$-helpful servers exist, there is nothing to show, so suppose that some helpful server S' exists, along with some $U_S \in \mathcal{C}$ that robustly achieves G with probability p'. Now, consider the server $\tilde{s}$ with states given by a *pair* of a state of S and a state of S'; on each round in which $\tilde{s}$ receives a message of the form $0^{M+1}x$ from the user, $\tilde{s}$ responds as S' would if the user's message were instead x, and updates the component of its state corresponding to a state of S' accordingly. Otherwise, on message y from the user, $\tilde{s}$ responds as S would on its current state for S, and updates the state for S accordingly.

By hypothesis, the padding agent that adds $M + 1$ symbols of padding is also in $\mathcal{C}$, and so since $\mathcal{C}$ is closed under parallel composition, the agent that pads each message from U_S with $M + 1$ symbols is also in $\mathcal{C}$. Now, we note that since this agent with $\tilde{s}$ generates identical executions with every $E \in \mathcal{E}$ from every initial state of the environment and $\tilde{s}$ as U_S would generate with E and S' from some appropriate state of S' (given by a projection of the state of $\tilde{s}$), and thus since U_S robustly achieves the goal with S' with probability p', so does our padded version of U_S with $\tilde{s}$. Thus, $\tilde{s}$ is $(G, \mathcal{C}, p')$-helpful as well.

But we see that in the chosen set of executions, U does not send messages of length longer than M, and so $\tilde{s}$ behaves identically to S in these executions up to the round in which V would output a 1 verdict. Thus, we see that in this set of executions occurring with probability greater than p, V outputs a 1 verdict with $\tilde{s}$ when R is not satisfied, so V is not $(\mathcal{C}, p)$-safe with all $(G, \mathcal{C}, p')$-helpful servers. ∎

5.4   Universal users for enumerable classes

Our main theorem in the basic universal setting was Theorem 2.25 and its variants, establishing that the construction of a universal user was possible whenever the construction of a sensing function was possible, and vice-versa. In the previous section, we developed a notion of sensing for the $\mathcal{C}$-bounded universal setting that we could show is broadly necessary for the construction of $\mathcal{C}$-bounded universal users. The more interesting, positive direction of Theorem 2.25, however, remained out of reach.

Part of the difficulty was that the class $\mathcal{C}$ could have been instantiated as the class of agents with an efficient *nonuniform* implementation, such as the class of agents implementable by polynomial-size circuits, for example. In such a case, the number of possible strategies that a user could employ grows with the environment's size parameter; in particular, it is easy to see that the circuits may have a hard-coded password of size similar to the environment's size parameter. Therefore, along the lines of Section 4.1, we find that a user requires exponential time in the size parameter to communicate with the class of all helpful servers with this class $\mathcal{C}$. Clearly, additional hypotheses are needed for the construction of a universal user.

The hypothesis that we used in Chapter 2, of course, was the *efficient enumerability* of polynomial time algorithms, as first discovered by Levin [97]. While the efficient enumerability of polynomial time algorithms is a surprising fact, given that *even* time-bounded algorithms can be enumerated in a time-efficient way, it is not surprising that most other natural resource-bounded classes of algorithms also have efficient enumerations (with respect to their various resource measures). Thus, in this section, we present a generic definition of efficient enumerability, and show that it, together with a notion of "resettability" that most uniform algorithms are easily seen to possess, suffices to obtain constructions of universal users.

5.4.1 Enumerable complexity classes

The key ingredient in Levin's construction of "universal search algorithms" as well as our construction of time-bounded universal users in Proposition 2.27, was Levin's technique for time-efficient enumeration of time-bounded algorithms. Recall, the technique guaranteed that for every algorithm A there was a constant factor overhead C such that the enumeration scheduled A to run for t steps within Ct steps for every t. In both Levin's algorithms and our user strategies, although the enumeration itself is an infinite schedule, we had a source of feedback (from sensing, in our case) that could stop the enumeration by the time some appropriate algorithm finished running. Thus, if the algorithm A was time-$t(n)$ bounded, then the efficient enumerator was time-$(C \cdot t(n))$ bounded.

Recall that in the present chapter, in Section 5.1.2, we chose to model the resource bounds satisfied by such algorithms by saying that there was a member of some efficient class of algorithms $\mathcal{C}$ that simulated the enumerator in a strong sense (cf. Definition 5.1). Of course, as stressed in Section 5.2.1, we sometimes wish to communicate via interpreters that are weaker than our universal users, since there are cases (such as our tests of computational ability in Section 3.5) that rely on the relative weakness of our interpreters. Thus, in such a case, it's sufficient for the enumerator to have complexity similar to that of the user rather than the interpreters. Thus, we state the definition below for a class of interpreters $\mathcal{I}$ and a class of users $\mathcal{U}$, and allow for the possibility that $\mathcal{I} \subsetneq \mathcal{U}$.

Definition 5.14 (Efficiently enumerable class). We say that a class of agents $\mathcal{I}$ that halt with probability 1 is $\mathcal{U}$-*efficiently enumerable* (or, if $\mathcal{I} = \mathcal{U}$, simply *efficiently enumerable*) if there is some *efficient enumerator* agent U with an additional internal "restarting" output channel such that,

1. Whenever U outputs 1 on its restarting channel in any system $(U, \ldots)$, there is some $I \in \mathcal{I}$ such that U simulates I until the next round in which U outputs a 1 on its restarting channel.

2. For each $I \in \mathcal{I}$ there is some agent $U_I \in \mathcal{U}$ and a pair of random indices $\tau_0 \leq \tau \in \mathbb{N}$ such that in any system $(U, \ldots)$, U outputs 1 on its restarting channel at round τ_0 and outputs 0 during rounds $\tau_0 + 1, \ldots, \tau$, U simulates I starting from round τ_0 until I would halt at round τ, and U_I simulates U up to round τ of the execution.

The "restarting" indications are primarily a technical convenience—in most implementations of efficient enumerators, and certainly in all of the constructions we will see here, they are trivially available. In order to take advantage of these signals, we will need to amend our definition of sensing slightly: it was originally defined in an *unforgiving* way, in that the sensing module is now stateful, and our original definition of viability only guaranteed that a positive verdict would be produced if the sensing module and the user strategy were started simultaneously. Thus, rather like our original refinement of "goals" to "forgiving goals" in Section 2.2.3, we refine the notion of a sensing module to a *resettable* sensing module with a viability condition that is likewise ready to "forgive" an initial miscommunication by the user once it receives a "reset" signal.

Definition 5.15 (Resettable sensing). We say that a sensing module is *resettable* if it has an additional "reset" input channel.

- We say that a resettable sensing module is $(\mathcal{C}, p)$-*safe* for a goal $G = (\mathcal{E}, R)$ with a server S if, given that each time the appropriate "reset" indication (e.g., a "1") is provided on the reset channel the control module simulates some strategy from $\mathcal{C}$ until the next reset indication, the probability that R outputs 1 on the first round in the execution (E, U, S) in which the sensing module outputs 1 is at least $p(n)$ conditioned on the sensing module producing a 1 verdict.

- We say that the resettable sensing module is $(\mathcal{C}, p)$-*viable* in an environment $\mathcal{E}$ with a server S if there exists an agent $U_S \in \mathcal{C}$ such that in an execution S and any $E \in \mathcal{E}$, and any state of S and E at round τ_0, if the "reset" signal is then provided on the reset channel and the user subsequently uses the same strategy as U_S, then with probability at least $p(n)$, there will be some round $\tau > \tau_0$ in which the sensing module outputs a 1 verdict.

Of course, for the classes of enumerable agents $\mathcal{C}$ that we consider, it is usually not an issue to "reset" the state of an agent (or more properly, the state of its modules) since there is usually a space bound that is less than the agent's time bound, so we can obtain a modified version of the agent that, on an appropriate signal, can be made to wipe out its memory and return to its initial control state. More abstractly, the agents satisfy the following:

Definition 5.16 (Resettable agents). We say that a class of agents $\mathcal{C}$ is *resettable* if their control modules have an additional "reset" input channel such that, when the reset channel receives a "1" message, the control module resets to its initial configuration.

We'll also use resettable sensing in our construction of universal users, but we note that when the class of agents is resettable (which, as we've argued above, it usually is for the classes of resource-bounded agents that we would generally consider) then Proposition 5.12 can be amended to produce a *resettable* sensing module as follows:

Corollary 5.17 (Universal users for classes of resettable agents yield resettable sensing). *Let $\mathcal{C}$ be a class of time-bounded resettable agents containing the fan-out, on-line comparison, and AND agents, that is closed under parallel composition. Let U be a universal user strategy for a goal G and a class of servers $\mathcal{S}$ such that for each $S \in \mathcal{S}$ there exists $U_S \in \mathcal{C}$ and functions $\epsilon_S, \mu_S : \mathbb{N} \to [0,1]$ such that in the execution (E, U, S), U_S simulates U with probability $1 - \epsilon_S(n)$, and in the executions (E, U_S, S) where U_S simulates U, U_S achieves the goal with probability $1 - \mu_S(n)$.*

Let V be an agent that computes a fan-out on its reset channel, that computes U on the messages from the input and random bit modules and the reset channel, and outputs the AND of U's halting signal and the result of the on-line comparison of the user's output with the output of U as its verdict, forwarding the second copy of the reset message to the on-line comparison agent. Then, when V is run with a user strategy running for $t(n)$ steps and $S \in \mathcal{S}$, V is a resettable $(\mathcal{C}, 1 - t \cdot \epsilon_S)$-bounded $(\mathcal{C}, 1 - t \cdot \mu_S)$-safe and $(\mathcal{C}, 1 - \epsilon_S)$-viable sensing module.

Proof Note that since U_S simulates U until it halts with probability $1 - \epsilon_S$, whenever U_S is run after a reset message, V is satisfied with probability $1 - \epsilon_S$, as needed for resettable viability. We likewise find that since V was $(\mathcal{C}, 1 - \mu_S)$-safe and $(\mathcal{C}, 1 - \epsilon_S)$-bounded when run from its initial configuration, and it is run from its initial configuration at most $t(n)$ times, a union bound gives the claimed safety and boundedness of V with the given user strategy and S. ∎

Now, the appearance of the agent's running time in the conclusion of Corollary 5.17 is the first observable sign that, unfortunately, the classes of agents that we are considering in this setting are substantially less general. Of course, as we noted at the outset of this section, we were already prepared to accept that the classes of algorithms we would consider for the construction of our universal users would be substantially less general, but the reader may find it unfortunate that we found it necessary to introduce time bounds (specifically) into the discussion. It seems, though, that this is another necessary restriction: consider the following example.

Example 5.18 (Agents that take unbounded time). Consider the following two-state agent: in the first state, as long as it receives a 0 from the server, it remains in the first state; when it receives a 1 from the server, it enters the second state and halts. Now, consider a class of servers S such that for every $t \in \mathbb{N}$, there is a server S_t that sends 0 t times and then sends a 1; in any execution with some $S_t \in S$, the agent enters the second state and halts, and yet whenever we run the agent for T steps, for any server S_t with $t > T$, we do not witness this.

Likewise, for any agent A that robustly achieves some goal with a server S that never sends empty messages, we can construct an agent A' that suspends its transition to a new control state as long as it continues to receive empty messages from the server, and we can construct servers S_t that sends t empty messages before each message S would send. A' now robustly achieves the goal with every S_t, but if the goal is nontrivial, no a priori bound T on the number of steps for which we run algorithms of space complexity and length at most that of A' will suffice.

In particular, we invite the reader to suppose that he or she wishes to construct a (purely) space-efficient enumeration. When should the enumeration move on from the two-state machines to the three-state machines? The point of Example 5.18 is that there *is* no good time, nor any safe signal that we've exhausted the capabilities of, e.g., the two-state machines. In fact, perhaps contrary to our intuition, construction of a (purely) space-bounded efficient enumeration is *harder* than construction of a time-bounded efficient enumeration, despite the fact that space may be re-used! Thus, we only expect to be able to construct efficient enumerations in the context of some time-bound. Of course, in the case of *computational problems*, space-bounded algorithms were implicitly time-bounded by their configuration count. Thus, we wish to reassure the reader that the familiar, *natural* space-bounded algorithms that he or she is familiar with also satisfy some natural class of time bounds as well, and so we aren't conceding much on this point.

Now, we are ready to present some further constructions of efficient enumerations—Levin's original construction [97] (and in particular, our application of it in Proposition 2.27) is easily seen to be satisfactory for essentially all classes of purely time-bounded users. Thus, we will focus on constructions of efficient enumerators that are, for example, time and space bounded, as we do in our first construction below. It is a straightforward extension of Levin's time-efficient enumeration of time-bounded algorithms.

Proposition 5.19 (Efficient enumeration of time and space bounded algorithms). *Let C be the class of agents satisfying some collection of time bounds $\mathcal{T}$ closed under constant factors, and space bounds closed under constant factors such that for a given time bound $t \in \mathcal{T}$ the corresponding space bound* is given by $s = f_s(t) = \Omega(\log t)$ for some monotone, time-t and space constructible function $f_s : \mathbb{N} \to \mathbb{N}$ which satisfies $f_s(C \cdot t) = O(f_s(t))$ for every $C \in \mathbb{N}$. Then $\mathcal{C}$ is efficiently enumerable.

Proof We enumerate algorithms in stages, where in stage i we loop over all algorithms of length $\ell \leq i - 2\log i$. For each algorithm of length ℓ, and $t = 2^{i-\ell-2\log \ell}$ we compute $s = f_s(t)$ (in t steps and space s); we then output a "restarting" indication and simulate the algorithm for up to t steps or until it either halts or tries to use space greater than s. Note that each algorithm our enumerator runs between restarting indications is therefore in $\mathcal{C}$.

Suppose we are interested in some agent $A \in \mathcal{C}$ with an algorithm of length ℓ_A and time bound $t_A(n)$. Note that A is run for $t_A(n)$ steps in phase $i_A(n) = \log t_A(n) + \ell_A + 2\log \ell_A$. Now, up to phase $i_A(n)$, our enumerator runs algorithms for

$$\sum_{i=1}^{i_A} \sum_{\ell \leq i - 2\log i} 2^\ell \frac{2^i}{\ell^2 2^\ell} \leq \sum_{\ell=1}^{\ell_A + 2\log \ell_A} \frac{2^{i_A+1}}{\ell^2} \leq \frac{\pi^2}{3} 2^{\ell_A + 2\log \ell_A} t_A(n)$$

steps. Since we can amortize the time to maintain our loops and counters, and the set of time bounds $\mathcal{T}$ defining $\mathcal{C}$ are closed under constant factors, we see that this time bound is also in $\mathcal{T}$; moreover, for $C_A = (\pi^2/3) 2^{\ell_A + 2\log \ell_A}$, we give the algorithms space at most $f_s(C_A t_A(n)) = O((f_s \circ t_A)(n))$ by assumption, and since our space bounds are all $\Omega(\log t)$, accounting for the space needed to track the phase and maintain the clock, we still use space at most $O((f_s \circ t_A)(n))$. Therefore, since the space bounds are closed under constant factors (and given by monotone functions of t), there is some time bound $t_A' \geq t_A$ such that our enumerator runs in time t_A' and uses space $(f_s \circ t_A')$.

Therefore, for the algorithm U_A that, on auxiliary input n, simulates our enumerator with a clock of $t_A'(n)$ and a "ruler" of $(f_s \circ t_A')(n)$, we see that $U_A \in \mathcal{C}$, and moreover, in any environment of size n, in the phase where U_A simulates A for at least $t_A(n)$ steps, since f_s is monotone, we also give it a space bound of at least $(f_s \circ t_A)(n)$, so U_A simulates A until it halts. ∎

Proposition 5.19 shows in particular that we have efficient enumerators for agents that run in polynomial time and logspace (by taking $f_s(n) = \log n$), and agents that run in time $O(n^k)$ and space $O(n^\epsilon)$ for fixed k and ϵ (by taking $f_s(n) = n^{\epsilon/k}$). In this case, the time or space bound of the enumerator may be somewhat worse than that of the optimal agent—e.g., it is bounded by time/space $(n^k, k\log n)$ for the minimum $k \in \mathbb{N}$ satisfied by the target algorithm. Still, we do obtain a simultaneous bound on both resources, as desired.

Now, note that the construction of a time and space efficient enumerator in Proposition 5.19, like in the original time-efficient enumeration, always uses an "appropriate" amount of time and space without necessarily knowing the size parameter, and therefore without explicitly knowing a priori how much time or space will be appropriate. If one is given the size parameter as input, though (such as in the case of computational goals), we find that it is also possible to use almost arbitrary (independent) sets of bounding functions for the time, space, and randomness. This covers most natural cases, e.g., we could specify that the algorithms use "quasi-polynomial time," "space $O(n^\epsilon)$," and "polylogarithmic randomness," and we would find that the class of algorithms with bounding functions given by such a product set is efficiently enumerable as a consequence of the following construction.

Proposition 5.20 (Efficient enumeration given size parameters). *Let $\mathcal{C}$ be a class of algorithms defined by a product set of enumerable time, space, and randomness bounding functions that are closed under constant factors, such that*

1. *The space bounds are space-constructible*

2. *The time bounds are time-constructible*

3. *For every time bound function t, there are space bound functions that are $\Omega(\log t)$ and computable in time t*

4. *For every randomness bound, there is a time bound that is greater*

Then, if the size parameter n is given as an auxiliary input, $\mathcal{C}$ is efficiently enumerable.

Proof We dovetail the three enumerations with an enumeration of algorithms, and thus obtain an enumeration of 4-tuples $\{(A, t, s, r)_i\}_{i=1}^\infty$. Then, for $i = 1, 2, \ldots$, we output a "resetting" indication and for the tuple $(A, t, s, r)_i$ we run algorithm A for up to $t(n)$ steps or until it either halts, tries to use space greater than $s(n)$, or tries to use more than $r(n)$ random bits. Note that each such algorithm is in $\mathcal{C}$.

Now, for any member A^* of $\mathcal{C}$ running in time $t_A(n)$, space $s_A(n)$, and randomness $r_A(n) \leq t_A(n)$, we know that this tuple appears at some index i^* in the enumeration; we could consider the enumerator U_A that stops after this index, and note that it satisfies the simulation requirement.

To see that $U_A \in \mathcal{C}$, we let $t^*(n)$ be the maximum time bound occurring by index i^*, let $r^*(n)$ be the maximum randomness bound (note $r^*(n) \leq t^*(n)$), and, let $s^*(n)$ be the maximum space bound. Now, since the class of bounding functions are closed under constant factors, $t'(n) = i^* t^*(n)$ is in the collection of time bounds, as is $r'(n) = i^* r^*(n)$. Furthermore, we are given that there is some space bound $s'(n)$ that is $\Omega(\log t^*(n))$ (and therefore also $\Omega(\log r^* n)$) and computable in time $t^*(n)$. Thus, U_A requires total space at most $O(s'(n))$, time at most $O(t^*(n))$, and randomness at most $O(r^*(n))$ for functions t^*, s', and r^* in the collection of bounding functions. Therefore, since the class of bounding functions is also closed under constant factors, $U_A \in \mathcal{C}$. ∎

We will also be able to incorporate the extensions of sensing described in Section 2.3.3; note that the proof of Corollary 2.30 only referred to specific properties of our *enumeration*, which also happen to be satisfied by the enumerators constructed in Proposition 5.19 and Proposition 5.20: we only need to use an appropriate encoding of algorithms, and note that the enumerator has the code of the algorithm available when it is about to simulate the algorithm. Thus, we obtain the desired extensions of our enumerators as a corollary:

Corollary 5.21 (Extended enumerations of time, space, and randomness bounded algorithms). *The constructions of Proposition 5.19 and Proposition 5.20 also yield enumerations of agents with any fixed number of auxiliary inputs and private outputs, and on a resetting indication, output the description of the algorithm that it will simulate until the next resetting indication. The maximum length of any algorithm output by the enumerations for any U_I running in t steps witnessing the C-boundedness of the enumerator for any $I \in C$ are $O(\log t)$ and $O(1)$, respectively.*

5.4.2   Sensing suffices for universal protocols for enumerable user classes

Now that we have a generic notion of efficiently enumerable classes of agents, we have all of the necessary notions to construct universal users in generic settings. In particular, for a suitable analogue of the "negligible" functions for polynomial time in a C-bounded setting, we can obtain the following analogue of Theorem 2.25:

Theorem 5.22 (Constructions of universal users are equivalent to constructions of sensing in bounded settings). *Let C be an efficiently enumerable class of resettable agents that is closed under parallel composition and containing the fan-out, AND, and on-line equality test agents, and let any goal G and any class of servers S be given along with a set of functions $\{\text{negl}\} = \{\epsilon : \mathbb{N} \to [0,1]\}$ such that for every time bound $t(n)$ of an agent in C, and every $\epsilon \in \{\text{negl}\}$, $t \cdot \epsilon \in \{\text{negl}\}$ as well. Then, there is a $(C, 1 - O(\epsilon_S))$-bounded $(S, 1 - O(\epsilon_S))$-universal user for G for some $\epsilon_S \in \{\text{negl}\}$ iff there is a $(C, 1 - O(\epsilon_S))$-bounded resettable sensing module that is $(C, 1 - O(\epsilon_S))$-safe and $(C, 1 - O(\epsilon_S))$-viable for G for some $\epsilon_S \in \{\text{negl}\}$ with every $S \in S$.*

One direction, obtaining sensing from a universal user, is a corollary of Proposition 5.12, noting that the user strategy and equality test used in the construction of sensing in that proposition are members of C and therefore resettable. The other direction follows from Proposition 5.23, described below.

Proposition 5.23 (Universal users for enumerable classes can be constructed from sensing). *For a given class of agents U containing the fan-out agent that* *is closed under parallel composition, consider any $\mathcal{U}$-efficiently enumerable class of agents $\mathcal{I}$. Let any goal G and class of servers $\mathcal{S}$ be given. Suppose that for each $S \in \mathcal{S}$ we have functions $\mu_S, \epsilon_S, \delta_S : \mathbb{N} \to [0,1]$, and a resettable sensing module V that is $(\mathcal{U}, 1 - \delta_S(n))$-bounded with every user in $\mathcal{U}$, $(\mathcal{I}, 1 - \mu_S(n))$-safe, and $(\mathcal{I}, 1 - \epsilon_S(n))$-viable for G with S. Then there is a $(\mathcal{S}, 1 - (\mu_S(n) + \epsilon_S(n)))$-universal user U for G that is $(\mathcal{U}, 1 - (\delta_S(n) + \epsilon_S(n)))$-bounded with every $S \in \mathcal{S}$.*

Proof We give an abstract, generic version of the construction of Proposition 2.27.

Construction. Let U_0 be the efficient enumerator for $\mathcal{I}$. Now, U is the agent obtained by attaching V to the control module of U_0, providing the output on U_0's "restarting" channel as the input to the "reset" input channel of V, and using the verdict of V as the input to the halting module instead of the output of U_0.

U **achieves** G. Let any $S \in \mathcal{S}$ be given, and consider the agent $I_S \in \mathcal{I}$ witnessing the $(\mathcal{I}, 1 - \epsilon_S(n))$-viability of S for V in every $E \in \mathcal{E}$. Now, we know there is some $U_{I_S} \in \mathcal{U}$ such that

1. Between any two "restarting" indications, U_{I_S} simulates some $I \in \mathcal{I}$.

2. At some random index τ_0, U_{I_S} outputs a "restarting" indication and simulates I_S until it halts.

Let U'_S be the parallel composition of U_{I_S} attached to V with the verdict of V supplied to the halting module (i.e., the construction of U with U_0 replaced by U_{I_S}).

   Since I_S is the agent witnessing the resettable viability of S with V, regardless of the state of the execution at index τ_0, U_0 (and therefore also U_{I_S}) provides a "restarting" indication to V at round τ_0, and so V subsequently produces a 1 verdict with probability $1 - \epsilon_S(n)$, at which point U'_S halts by construction; since each I that U_{I_S} simulates up until it simulates I_S is in $\mathcal{I}$, the $(\mathcal{I}, 1 - \mu_S(n))$-safety of V with S for G gives that when V produces a 1 verdict, G is achieved with probability at least $1 - \mu_S(n)$. By a union bound, therefore, U'_S achieves G with probability at least $1 - (\mu_S(n) + \epsilon_S(n))$. Now, because U_{I_S} simulates U_0 until I_S halts, and U'_S is obtained by substituting U_{I_S} for U_0 in the construction of U, we find that when I_S obtains a positive indication, U'_S and U both halt, and thus U'_S simulates U. U then also must achieve G with probability at least $1 - (\mu_S(n) + \epsilon_S(n))$. Thus, U is $(\mathcal{S}, 1 - (\mu_S(n) + \epsilon_S(n)))$-universal for G.

U **is** $\mathcal{U}$-**bounded.** Since V is $(\mathcal{U}, 1 - \delta_S(n))$-bounded, let $V_S \in \mathcal{U}$ be the agent that simulates V with probability $1 - \delta_S(n)$ with S and U_{I_S}. Let U''_S

be the agent obtained by attaching V_S to U_{I_S} and supplying the verdict of V_S to the halting module.

Since $\mathcal{U}$ is closed under parallel composition and contains the fan-out agent, and $U_{I_S} \in \mathcal{U}$, we know that $U_S'' \in \mathcal{U}$ as well. Thus, since V_S simulates V with probability at least $1 - \delta_S(n)$, and U_S'' is obtained from U_S' by substituting V_S for V in the parallel composition, U_S'' simulates U_S' with probability at least $1 - \delta_S(n)$ as well. Likewise, as we saw above, U_S' simulates U in turn whenever V provides a positive indication, which occurs with probability $1 - \epsilon_S(n)$. Therefore, by composing the maps, we find that U_S'' simulates U with probability $1 - (\delta_S(n) + \epsilon_S(n))$, and we have that U is $(\mathcal{U}, 1 - (\delta_S(n) + \epsilon_S(n)))$-bounded with S, as claimed. ∎

It also follows from Corollary 2.30 (as a parallel corollary to Proposition 5.23) that we can construct $\mathcal{U}$-bounded universal users from grey-box sensing for users with auxiliary inputs and private outputs whenever the enumerator is of the appropriate form (e.g., as given by Corollary 5.21). We'll see an application of this in the next section when we apply Proposition 5.23 to construct universal users for computational goals.

5.5 The complexity of universal users for computational problems

The development of sensing and universal users in the previous sections of the present chapter was necessarily rather abstract—the point was to show that our main theorems hold much more broadly than simply for the setting of polynomial time bounded agents considered in Chapter 2. Still, in the absence of any examples of natural interest captured by these definitions, the reader may rightly feel troubled by this pervasive abstractness. We now seek to exhibit an interesting example of a goal in settings captured under the new classes of agents, and not by our earlier polynomial time setting, as evidence that these new settings are interesting.

Our example goals, of course, will be computational problems. These goals are a natural choice for several reasons: first, we recall that in Section 1.4.2 (as in our first paper [83]), computational goals pointed the way to all of our major theorems, and served as a compelling first example; second, computational problems are likely to provide a clear illustration of the benefit achieved by communication, by showing that an agent obtains something that he or she could not produce on his or her own (due to the agent's computational limitations); and third, computational problems seem to provide the *most* natural motivation for considering classes of agents beyond polynomial time.

We will find ourselves rewarded for our choice by analogues of Theorem 3.12 from Section 3.3 for new classes of agents, characterizing the classes of computational problems solvable by universal users in a $\mathcal{C}$-bounded universal setting in terms of "$\mathcal{C}$-competitive interactive proofs," which we will define in this section but seem to be quite natural in their own right. In particular, and perhaps most compelling of all, we will see an application of this characterization to the familiar class of polynomial time and logspace bounded agents: we will see that it is easy to construct a logspace-competitive interactive proof system for a P-complete problem. It then follows as a consequence of our characterization for the polynomial time and logspace bounded setting these agents can engage in *universal delegation of computation*—a polynomial time and logspace agent can "delegate" *any* polynomial time computation to *any* server that is capable of solving such problems, *without knowing anything about how to communicate with the server a priori.*

5.5.1   Competitive interactive proofs for generic classes

Recall that we first considered competitive interactive proofs (Definition 3.10), as introduced by Bellare and Goldwasser [21], in Section 3.3. (P, V) was said to be a competitive interactive proof system for a decision problem Π if P was a probabilistic polynomial time oracle machine such that (P^Π, V) was an interactive proof system for Π. The original motivation of Bellare and Goldwasser was to obtain a generalization of the decision-versus-search question for NP proof systems: simulating the interaction between P and V using an oracle for Π allows one to generate "proofs" in polynomial time given the ability to decide Π, so competitive interactive proof systems give such a generalization. In a similar spirit, we introduce the following modification of their definition to generic classes:

Definition 5.24 (Generic competitive interactive proof system). Let P be an agent with two fixed input channels and two sets of communication channels for other agents, and let V be an agent in $\mathcal{C}$ with three fixed input channels (and size parameter given by the total lengths of the inputs on these channels) and a communication channel for a second agent, that produces a Boolean output when it halts. Then we say that (P, V) is a $\mathcal{C}$-*competitive interactive proof system for a problem* Π if the parallel composition of P and V with the first two fixed input channels shared and a fan-out on the communications channels joining them is also in $\mathcal{C}$, and moreover,

1. **(Completeness)** For every instance x of Π and $\epsilon \in \mathbb{Q}^+$, if P is attached to an oracle for Π, P and V are attached to one another, and both are given x and y for $y \in \Pi(x)$ as their first two inputs, the probability that V accepts when given ϵ as its third input is at least $1 - \epsilon$.

2. **(Soundness)** For every pair (x, y) such that $y \notin \Pi(x)$ and $\epsilon \in \mathbb{Q}^+$, if V is given x, y, and ϵ as its inputs and attached to any other agent, the probability that V accepts is at most ϵ.

We note that we've replaced the fixed constant probabilities for soundness and completeness with probabilities controlled by an auxiliary input ϵ. This implicitly assumes that C is strong enough to allow the error rate to be reduced by sequential repetition, for example. For most classes we consider, bounded by reasonable functions of time, space, and randomness, this is not an issue, but as we will need the ability to amplify the correctness of the proof system and it turns out to be somewhat awkward to carry out the amplification in an abstract setting, we prefer to take it as given that such amplification is available.

This definition has similar virtues to its polynomial time counterpart—if it exists, then one can generate a proof in C, given that one is interacting with an oracle for Π. This is the main observation involved in the following theorem:

Theorem 5.25 (Universal users yield competitive proof systems). *Let C be a class of agents closed under sequential and parallel composition, containing the fan-out, logic, on-line equality, fixed padding, and copying agents. Then, for any function problem Π, if there is a C-bounded universal user for Π with controllable error for the class of all $(G_\Pi, C, 2/3)$-helpful servers, there is a C-competitive interactive proof system for Π with a deterministic prover strategy.*

Proof We suppose we are given a C-bounded universal user $U(\epsilon)$ for Π with controllable error for the class of all $(G_\Pi, C, 2/3)$-helpful servers. In particular, the agent that forwards its input to the server and forwards its response to the environment and halts is in C because the copying agent is and C is closed under sequential composition; note that this agent achieves G_Π with an oracle for Π, which is therefore $(G_\Pi, C, 2/3)$-helpful. We then find that there is some $U' \in C$ that simulates U in its interaction with a server using an oracle for Π as its strategy.

Construction of prover and verifier. Now, our proof system is therefore as follows: the verifier is given by the composition of U' with a test that checks that the output of U' matches the verifier's second input and that U' halts; since the copying, AND, and on-line equality test agents are in C, and C is closed under parallel composition, this verifier is also in C. The prover is given by an agent that ignores its fixed inputs and forwards its incoming messages from the verifier to the oracle, and forwards the oracle's responses back across its communications channel to the verifier; note that this prover is deterministic, as claimed. The parallel composition is in C since we can attach the verifier directly to the communications channel for the oracle and forward a copy of the communication on these channels to an external output.

Completeness. Since in E_x, $U'(\epsilon)$ outputs $\Pi(x)$ and halts with probability at least $1 - \epsilon$ when interacting with an oracle for Π, and the prover behaves identically to the oracle for Π, we find that the verifier accepts on inputs x, $\Pi(x)$, and ϵ when interacting with our prover with probability at least $1 - \epsilon$, as needed.

Soundness. Now, we note that by Proposition 5.12, the function $V(\epsilon)$ that checks to see that $U(\epsilon)$ would have halted is a $(\mathcal{C}, 1 - \epsilon)$-safe sensing function for G_Π with the class of all $(G_\Pi, \mathcal{C}, 2/3)$-helpful servers, and hence by Theorem 5.13, it is actually a $(\mathcal{C}, 1 - \epsilon)$-safe sensing function with the class of *all* servers. Thus, $U(\epsilon)$ only halts when outputting $y \neq \Pi(x)$ with probability at most ϵ, no matter which server it interacts with. Therefore, on inputs x, $y \neq \Pi(x)$, and ϵ, our verifier's test is only satisfied with probability at most ϵ, no matter what strategy the prover uses, as needed. ∎

As Theorem 5.25 only involves our results from Section 5.3.2 establishing the strong sensing requirements of the $\mathcal{C}$-bounded universal settings, it inherits a rather broad scope from those results.[5] By contrast, of course, we recall that the construction of universal users in Section 5.4 required us to assume that $\mathcal{C}$ was efficiently enumerable, so it is no surprise that a converse to Theorem 5.25 will require at least that much. Actually, we will see, such a construction may depend on somewhat more.

All of the trouble arises from the fact that the prover's oracle is considered to be "external" to the prover-verifier system in a competitive interactive proof system—the prover can query the oracle on any instance it can compute, irrespective of the instance's size, written to an external buffer, and the oracle answers in unit time. This is all fine until we set out to introduce a simulation of the oracle by another agent in such a way as to allow the parallel composition of the prover, verifier, and oracle simulations to all lie within the class $\mathcal{C}$. At a minimum, $\mathcal{C}$ then seems to need to be closed under composition of functions in some suitable sense, and its resource bounds need to allow for the oracle to run on any instance computed by the prover within its own resource bounds. These are some specialized requirements, and so we will no longer aim for abstract generality, and simply focus explicitly on classes of uniform time, space, and randomness bounded agents, which are the only classes we presently know how to enumerate efficiently, anyway.

Now, as long as the class is defined by a collection of time and randomness bounds that are closed under composition with the time bounds in the class (i.e., if bounding functions (t_1, r_1) and (t_2, r_2) are in the class, then so is $(t_1 \circ t_2, r_1 \circ t_2)$), and the class is efficiently enumerable, closed under parallel composition, etc., then it is not too hard to see that the construction in the proof of Theorem 3.12 (with the time-bounded enumeration perhaps replaced by the enumeration of Proposition 5.20 if there is a randomness bound) will

---

[5]Though, we expect that in many of the cases where the present theorem applies, it may be vacuous, since for example we don't expect universal users for nontrivial goals to be possible in the setting of nonuniform polynomial size circuits, cf. our discussion at the outset of Section 5.4.

suffice; we leave the details to the interested reader, and focus instead on the case of computation with a (sublinear) space bound. In this case, we will show that it is still possible to obtain a converse by applying all of the usual tricks for composing space-bounded functions.

Theorem 5.26 (Universal users for computation from competitive proof systems for time and space bounded classes). *Let C be a class of time/space/-randomness bounded agents that are efficiently enumerable given a size parameter, that have two auxiliary inputs and a private output, and such that the enumerator provides the algorithm along with each resetting indication, and that when the enumerator runs for at most t steps, the length of this algorithm is at most $O(\log t)$.*

Suppose further that the time bounds of C are $\Omega(\log(1/\epsilon))$; with time bound t, the space bound $\Omega(\log(t/\epsilon))$ is in C; the randomness bounds are either all 0 or else with time bound t, randomness bounds of $\Omega(\log(t/\epsilon))$ are in C; and furthermore, for any two sets of bounds (t_1, s_1, r_1) and (t_2, s_2, r_2) in C, the set of bounds of the form $(\tilde{O}(t_1(t_2 \circ t_1)), O(s_1 + (s_2 \circ t_1)), O(r_1(r_2 \circ t_1)))$ is also contained in C.

Then for any function problem Π such that the range of Π on inputs of length n has length $O(s(n, 1))$ for some space bound s in C, if there is a C-competitive interactive proof system for Π with a deterministic prover, there is a $(C, 1 - \epsilon)$-bounded universal user $U(\epsilon)$ for Π with controllable error for the class of all $(G_\Pi, C, 2/3)$-helpful servers.

In particular, as discussed above, note that the time bounds must be closed under composition; this naturally suggests that the time bound should be polynomial, quasipolynomial (i.e., of the form $2^{\text{poly} \log(n)}$) or "elementary"

(of the form $2^{2^{\cdot^{\cdot}}}$). Of course, since the space and (nonzero) randomness bounds must also be at least logarithmic in the time bound, the corresponding minimal bounds are $\log n$, $\text{poly} \log n$, and "elementary" (where the last case, consequently, is not so interesting). Nevertheless, polynomial time is the class of time bounds of greatest natural interest (and quasipolynomial time is of secondary interest). Since the size parameter is given as input, Proposition 5.20 gives that essentially all natural classes of bounding functions are enumerable in this case, so the composability requirement is the main restriction.

Proof Our objective will be to construct a sensing module from the proof system so that we can invoke Proposition 5.23. We will construct a uniformly viable (cf. Section 4.2.2) grey-box sensing module with private outputs.

Construction of grey-box sensing. We can construct a resettable sensing module as follows. We will assume that the user agent has private input and output channels; note that this class of agents (i.e., with the same resource bounds as C and private outputs) is still enumerable. Let (P, V) be the C-competitive proof system for Π. Our grey-box resettable sensing module

$V'(\epsilon)$ is now given by the following algorithm: we keep a count of the number of times i in which we have received the "reset" signal; on the ith reset, we first check that the user is some appropriate parallel composition of the agent U_V we construct below (i.e., for uniform viability) and some other agent. If so, we provide the composed agent $(U_V \| \cdot)$ with ϵ and i as its auxiliary inputs, and output a 1 iff U_V halts and outputs a 1 on its private output.

The agent $(U_V \| \cdot)(\epsilon, i)$ is now as follows. Since (P, V) is $\mathcal{C}$-competitive, we first consider the agent simulating $(P \| V)$ in $\mathcal{C}$, computing it in time/space/-randomness (t_1, s_1, r_1). We then construct U_V as follows: $U_V(\epsilon, i)$ first computes $\epsilon_i = {}^{\epsilon}/_{4i(i+1)}$, and then simulates $(P \| V(\epsilon_i))$. The parallel composition $(U_V \| U')(\epsilon, i)$ then simulates $(P \| V(\epsilon_i))$ with U' attached to P as its oracle; since this communication is across P's output module, we must recompute the messages of P on the current round of an interaction between V and P to simulate access by U' to P's queries as follows.

Suppose that when P tries to write its first symbol to the output module to its oracle, we make a copy of the state of the parallel composition of P and V; we continue the execution of the parallel composition of P and V until P suspends its execution, and needs a response from its oracle. We then begin running U', recomputing the composition of P and V (supplying 0 to all requests for random bits) to obtain each bit of the query that U' reads. Now, recall that P is a deterministic strategy (and cannot read V's next message until it suspends execution), and so therefore P's query is a deterministic function of its (externally visible) message history up to the current round. Therefore, since the parallel composition produces the same distribution over messages as the individual strategies, the query of P is independent of the random bits generated in the parallel composition, so U' obtains the same bits as P wrote originally. Moreover, since the parallel composition satisfies a time, space, and randomness bound of (t_1, s_1, r_1) (with probability 1), the query of P is computed in time/space/randomness $(t_1, s_1, 0)$, and we note that the query has size at most t_1.

Now, furthermore, $(U_V \| U')(\epsilon, i)$ actually computes the responses of U' by invoking U' $j = O(\log(t_1/\epsilon_i))$ times and taking its "majority response" (when it has one) using the following well-known algorithm (due to Boyer and Moore [35]) for computing the majority element in a data stream:

$(U_V \| U')$ maintains a potential for the "candidate" element, initialized to 0; whenever the count is zero, the algorithm takes the current element in the stream as a new "candidate" element with potential 1. When the algorithm encounters an element in the stream that matches the candidate, it increments the potential, and otherwise it decrements the potential. At the end of the stream, the algorithm outputs the candidate element. It is easy to see that the candidate must be the majority element: suppose that all of the non-majority elements in the stream are identical, and suppose that we take the potential to be "negative" whenever the candidate element is the minority element. Then each time we see the majority element, we increment this modified potential, and every time we see the minority element we decrement it—but, since the potential starts at zero and the majority element appears in over half of the locations, the final potential must be positive, so the majority element is the candidate at the final step.

The private output of $(U_V \| U')(\epsilon, i)$ is now the verdict of $V(\epsilon_i)$ in the simulation of $((P \| U') \| V(\epsilon_i))$ described above.

V' and $(U_V \| \cdot)$ are $\mathcal{C}$-bounded. Suppose V' is run with some agent U' in $\mathcal{C}$ with time/space/randomness (t_2, s_2, r_2). V' itself is deterministic since it merely checks that the current user strategy is of the right form and, if so, watches its output. The time to maintain the counter can be amortized to $O(t)$ time total, and the space for maintaining the counter and checking user strategies need not be larger than $O(\log t_2)$, so V' can be computed in space $O(\log t_2)$ as well. Thus, we see that V' is in $\mathcal{C}$ (i.e., with $\delta_S \equiv 0$ with all servers).

As for U_V, since the counter V' maintains has value at most t_2, and the calculation of ϵ_i for $i \le t_2$ can be done in time $O(\log(1/\epsilon) \log t_2)$, the time to compute ϵ_i during the execution with the agent is $O(t_2 \log(1/\epsilon) \log t_2)$, and it only requires space $O(\log(t_2/\epsilon))$.

Now, to simulate U_V in the parallel composition with U', the data stream algorithm used at most $\log j$ space for the potential and needed to store the output of U', which, as a potential element of Π, is assumed to be within some space bound $s'(n, 1)$ in $\mathcal{C}$. We can amortize the time of maintaining the counter to $O(1)$ steps per operation. So, our simulation of U_V, recomputing P to simulate each bit read by U' likewise takes time/space/randomness $(O(t_2 \cdot t_1 \log(t_1/\epsilon_i)), s_1 + s' + \log \log \frac{t_1}{\epsilon_i} + O(1), r_1)$, and so its total bound is

$$(O(t_2 \cdot t_1 \log(t_1/\epsilon) \log t_2), s_1 + s' + \log \log(t_1/\epsilon) + \log(t_2/\epsilon) + O(1), r_1)$$

which is also in $\mathcal{C}$. Thus, since $U' \in \mathcal{C}$, we find that for this particular simulation, the parallel composition $(U_V \| U')$ is also in $\mathcal{C}$ since $\mathcal{C}$ is closed under parallel composition.

Every helpful server is viable with V' and $(U_V \| \cdot)$. Let any $(G_\Pi, \mathcal{C}, 2/3)$-helpful server S be given; then there is some agent $U_S \in \mathcal{C}$ for which U_S robustly achieves G_Π with S with probability at least $2/3$. Now, although we know that U_S is $\mathcal{C}$-bounded in the system (E_x, U_S, S), we now consider U_S in the system $(E_x, U_V(\epsilon, i), U_S, S)$ (i.e., for which we wish to replace U_V and U_S by $(U_V \| U_S)(\epsilon, i)$), and we wish to show that U_S still satisfies a bound in $\mathcal{C}$, and moreover that V and therefore U_V accepts in the parallel composition. Since $U_S \in \mathcal{C}$, we know that it runs in some appropriate time/space/randomness bound (t_2, s_2, r_2).

Recall that $(U_V \| U_S)(\epsilon, i)$ invokes U_S $j = O(\log(t_1/\epsilon_i))$ times for each query and takes a majority vote using the data stream algorithm described above. Our simulation of U_S then runs in time/space/randomness $(O(j \cdot t_2), s_2 + \log j, j \cdot r_2)$. We noted above that all of the queries of P to U_S

were of size at most t_1; since we took $j = O(\log(t_1/\epsilon_i))$, U_S can therefore be simulated on P's (at most t_1) queries in time/space/randomness

$$(O((t_2 \circ t_1) \cdot t_1 \log \frac{t_1}{\epsilon_i}), (s_2 \circ t_1) + s_1 + \log\log \frac{t_1}{\epsilon_i} + O(1), O((r_2 \circ t_1) \log \frac{t_1}{\epsilon_i}))$$

which is in $\mathcal{C}$ by assumption.

We now argue that this user strategy satisfies V. Note that when U_S is run in E_x with S, since U_S outputs $\Pi(x)$ with probability $2/3$ on each trial, Hoeffding's inequality yields that in j trials it is the majority element with probability $1 - \exp(-18j)$. Therefore, for any t_1, we reduce the error probability to $\epsilon_i/(4t_1)$ by taking $j = O(\log(t_1/\epsilon_i))$, as done above. Note that by a union bound, the probability that the majority vote of j repetitions of U_S does not compute Π correctly during the simulation of P (which makes at most t_1 queries) is at most $\epsilon/4$. Therefore, by the completeness of (P, V), $V(\epsilon_i)$ is satisfied in an interaction with P using U_S with probability at least $1 - \epsilon_i \geq 1 - \epsilon/4$, and hence, since $V'(\epsilon)$ simply checks that $V(\epsilon_i)$ is satisfied in this interaction, by a union bound over the probability that we always compute P's queries correctly and the probability that P convinces V, $V'(\epsilon)$ is $(\mathcal{C}, 1 - \epsilon/2)$-viable in $\mathcal{E}$ with S.

V' **is safe.** We note that by the soundness property of V, on input ϵ_i (on the ith reset) V only accepts $y \neq \Pi(x)$ with probability at most ϵ_i, no matter what user strategy it interacts with; therefore, by a union bound, the probability that it ever produces an accepting verdict on a bad output is at most $\sum_i (\epsilon/4)^1/_{i(i+1)} = \epsilon/4$. Since V' only considers agents that are parallel compositions of V with other agents, we therefore see that $V'(\epsilon)$ is $(\mathcal{C}, 1 - \epsilon/4)$-safe.

Conclusion: obtaining the universal user. We have assume that $\mathcal{C}$ is efficiently enumerable, and we have constructed a sensing module that is bounded, safe, and viable with reset. We can now invoke the same argument used in the proof of Proposition 5.23, additionally incorporating the extensions to private outputs and grey-box sensing from Corollary 2.30; note that we have assumed that the enumerator for $\mathcal{C}$ includes the appropriate auxiliary inputs and private outputs, and that the code of the algorithm is provided as needed for our sensing module. So, we obtain a $(\mathcal{C}, 1-\epsilon)$-bounded universal user $U(\epsilon)$ with error $1 - \epsilon$ for the goal of computing Π with every $(G_\Pi, \mathcal{C}, 2/3)$-helpful server, as claimed. ∎

5.5.2   Computational goals for logspace agents

We will close this chapter with some applications of our generalized results, by investigating the computational capabilities of agents running in polynomial time and logspace. First, we show an application to delegating polynomial time computations to unknown servers by polynomial time and logspace agents, and second, we discuss the challenges in determining how powerful polynomial time and logspace agents can be as was done in Section 3.3 for polynomial time agents.

Logspace agents delegating computation

Section 3.3 demonstrated how any agent who can compute PSPACE can communicate the results to a polynomial time universal agent. This was an example of *delegation of computation*—the polynomial time agent had an instance of a problem in PSPACE in mind, encoded as an instance of a PSPACE-complete problem, and was able to obtain the solution to the instance from the powerful server. If we believe that PSPACE-complete problems cannot be solved by any agent in a reasonable amount of time, though, it is hard to see what practical value the resulting protocol has, if any. In light of this, the more interesting question to ask is if, in a similar way, polynomial time agents can communicate the results of "hard" computations to some weaker universal agent; in this section, we will envision the weaker universal agent "delegating" the problem to the polynomial time agent. For example, we might imagine wishing to use a weak handheld wireless device to solve some hard problem, e.g., solving a linear program, using the aid of some foreign server that happens to be within its range. Our objective here will be to design a protocol for the weak device that allows it to use *any* server which can be accessed by a lightweight communications protocol. (In Section 3.4, by contrast, we considered a *different* variant of this question, showing that polynomial time agents could share knowledge among themselves, as opposed to delegating computation to more powerful agents.)

We will model our weak devices as polynomial time and logspace bounded agents. It turns out that it is then a simple matter to adapt a result of Condon [48] (or, in a sense, proofs of the Cook-Levin theorem) to give a logspace-competitive proof system for arbitrary polynomial time computations with a deterministic prover. Then, since the class of polynomial time and logspace agents is efficiently enumerable (using the enumeration of Proposition 5.19, for example) and satisfies the hypotheses of Theorem 5.26, we obtain a universal user for any P-complete computational problem.

Theorem 5.27 (Logspace-competitive proof system for P). *There is an $\mathcal{L}$-competitive proof system with a deterministic prover strategy for a P-complete decision problem.*

Proof The P-complete problem we consider is "bounded acceptance," i.e., with instances parsed as triples of binary strings (M, x, y). Then we define $\Pi_{BA}(M, x, y) = 1$ iff M is an encoding of a (deterministic) Turing machine and M run on input x reaches an *accept* state within $t = |y|$ steps.

Π_{BA} **is P-complete.** It's immediate that Π_{BA} is P-complete, since on the one hand, the reduction for any $\Pi \in P$ only needs to prepend an encoding of the (constant-size) polynomial time machine M that witnesses $\Pi \in P$, construct the appropriate encoding of x, compute an appropriate (polynomial) time bound $t(|x|)$, and output an encoding of 0^t. For the reader's favorite choice of encoding of triples (e.g., self-delimiting) this is all easily done in logspace. Conversely, for a reasonable choice of encoding of M, the simulation of M on input x for t steps can be done without much effort in time $O(n^2)$ – we move a "clock" and our encoding of M with the head position on the simulator's worktape, so each of the $O(n)$ steps is simulated in time $O(n)$ – so $\Pi_{BA} \in P$.

Proof system for Π_{BA}. The (honest) prover sends the verifier a t-step computation history for M on input x repeated $2t$ times.

The verifier first checks that M is a valid encoding of a Turing machine. The verifier then checks that the first (t-symbol) configuration sent by the prover is correct—x with the tape head in the initial state over the first symbol of x, followed by blank symbols. The verifier also chooses a random index i between 1 and t and stores the symbols sent by the prover at that location and its neighbors; the verifier then checks, in the following configuration, that the prover sends a symbol at index i that correctly follows from the window stored from the previous round. If not, the verifier rejects immediately. Otherwise, the verifier repeats this check for a new random index for each step of the computation. In the final configuration, the verifier also checks that the prover sends an accepting configuration (i.e., containing an accept state of M), and rejects otherwise. Finally, if the verifier has not rejected after repeating these checks $2t$ times (over $2t$ histories). the verifier accepts.

The honest prover is in deterministic logspace using an oracle. First, note that the prover can be implemented in logspace relative to an oracle for Π_{BA} as follows. Consider a polynomial time Turing machine M' that on input $(x, 0^i, 0^j, 0^k)$, outputs 1 iff the kth bit of the jth symbol of the ith configuration of M on input x is a 1 (e.g., M' may be a modified version of the previous simulation of M that runs in time $O(n^2)$). Note that there is a logspace reduction from the problem decided by M' to Π_{BA}. Then the prover uses four counters ℓ, i, j, k, in which ℓ counts the number of histories output so far (up to $2t$), and repeatedly queries its oracle for Π_{BA} on the reduction to Π_{BA} from M' on input $(x, 0^i, 0^j, 0^k)$ to produce the histories it sends to the verifier.

The verifier is in $\mathcal{L}$. The verifier is also easily seen to be in $\mathcal{L}$: beyond the same counters as the prover, the verifier can easily compute the initial configuration in logspace and compare that with the prover's claimed configuration, the verifier can (for a reasonable encoding of M) easily check that the final configuration contains a (single) accept state, and on each round, the verifier can generate and remember a new random index (in $\log t$ bits) and the window around it, deleting the old random index and window at the end of the round. Again, for a reasonable encoding of M, the verifier can also compute the contents of a location from the window containing it from the previous configuration in logspace (by look-up in the transition function, if M's tape head is present).

Completeness. By definition, successive configurations of M on input x, sent by the honest prover, satisfy all of the checks the verifier could make, with the possible exception of the final configuration. But, if M accepts on input x within $t(|x|)$ steps (i.e., $\Pi_{\mathrm{BA}}(M, x, y) = 1$), then the final configuration must be an accept configuration, and so this final check passes, too. Thus, the proof system has perfect completeness.

Soundness. Suppose M does not accept x within t steps. Now, for each history that the prover sends, if the initial configuration is incorrect, or the final configuration is not an accept configuration, the verifier rejects. So, suppose that in each history sent by the prover, the first configuration is correct and the final configuration is an accepting configuration. Then, there must be some first step, in which configuration $i + 1$ does not follow from the ith configuration of M on input x. In particular, there must be some jth symbol in which the $(i + 1)$th configuration differs from the actual $(i + 1)$th configuration M on input x. Now, since the ith configuration sent by the prover is correct by assumption, if the verifier chooses index j for step $i + 1$, it detects the inconsistency. This occurs with probability at least $1/t$ independently for each history sent by the prover.

Therefore, since the prover must send $2t$ histories and (if M does not accept x within t steps) since the verifier catches the prover on each history independently with probability at least $1/t$, the probability that the verifier *does not* reject is at most $(1 - 1/t)^{2t} \leq 1/e^2 \leq 1/3$ as needed. ∎

Thus, the proof system constructed in Theorem 5.27 is precisely as needed for the application of Theorem 5.26. Noting that since the particular P-complete problem Π that is used can be converted into any other P-complete problem Π' by a logspace reduction, if a server is helpful for $G_{\Pi'}$, it is also helpful for G_Π; and likewise, our universal user can first apply the reduction from Π' to Π and then use the construction for G_Π to achieve $G_{\Pi'}$. We therefore obtain:

Theorem 5.28 (Logspace universal users exist for P-complete problems). *Let Π be a P-complete problem under logspace reductions and let $\mathcal{L}$ be the class of polynomial time and logspace bounded agents. Then there is a $(\mathcal{L}, 1 - \epsilon)$-bounded universal user $U(\epsilon)$ with controllable error for G_Π with the class of all $(G_\Pi, \mathcal{L}, 2/3)$-helpful servers.*

We thus see that it is possible to delegate any polynomial time computation to a server that can solve P-complete problems without needing to know a protocol (or even "which" P-complete problem the server was "designed" to solve). Note that, analogous to the proof of Theorem 1.7 (given in Section 4.1), any such G_Π is clearly nontrivial (in an appropriate parameterized sense) unless BPL = P, so something interesting has been achieved.

Classifying the computational capabilities of logspace universal protocols

Of course, one of our objectives in Section 3.3 was not just to construct a universal protocol, but to give a characterization of the class of problems which have polynomial time universal protocols. Correspondingly, we have a characterization of the problems with polynomial time and logspace universal protocols:

Theorem 5.29. *Let $\mathcal{L}$ be the class of polynomial time and logspace agents. A Boolean function problem Π has a $(\mathcal{L}, 1 - \epsilon)$-bounded universal user $U(\epsilon)$ with controllable error for G_Π with the class of all $(G_\Pi, \mathcal{L}, 2/3)$-helpful servers iff there is an $\mathcal{L}$-competitive proof system $(P^\Pi, V(\epsilon))$ for Π in which the prover's strategy is deterministic.*

One direction of Theorem 5.29 follows from Theorem 5.25. The other direction follows from Theorem 5.26 since the class of polynomial time and logspace agents is efficiently enumerable by Proposition 5.19.

Now, along the lines of Section 1.4.2, we might *also* wish to know just how *powerful* the problems that can be solved by logspace universal protocols are. That is, we might again imagine that Bob is communicating with an all-powerful Alice, and we might again wish to know how his lack of understanding limits what he can learn from Alice—with the twist now that Bob is additionally restricted to run in logspace. Formally, this corresponds to finding the class of problems Π that can be reduced to a problem Π' for which there exists a universal protocol in the polynomial time and logspace bounded setting.

In the basic universal setting, we had Theorem 1.4, which showed that PSPACE-complete problems had universal users – thus implying that universal users with sufficiently powerful servers can decide every problem in PSPACE – and Theorem 1.5, which showed that polynomial time users could not decide problems outside PSPACE. Thus, the class of problems that a user can solve with an all-powerful server in the basic universal setting is *precisely* PSPACE.

We obtain a similar limitation result for polynomial time and logspace universal users in Theorem 5.29—since the verifier in an $\mathcal{L}$-competitive proof system is a polynomial time verifier, problems with $\mathcal{L}$-competitive proof systems also fall within IP = PSPACE, and therefore this class is no larger than PSPACE since the reductions can also be computed in PSPACE. This is the best limitation result we know; it is possible that this is tight, but we do not know how to show this.

We saw, in the previous section, that it is possible to construct logspace universal users for all of polynomial time. But, we don't know of an $\mathcal{L}$-*competitive* proof system for any problem outside polynomial time. By contrast, the construction due to Condon [48] alluded to in the previous section converts a polynomial time verifier into a verifier that runs in polynomial time and logspace. So for example, given $\Pi \in$ PSPACE, we would let V_Π be the verifier for an interactive proof for membership in the function relation for Π as before, and Condon's construction then converts V_Π into V'_Π that runs in polynomial time and logspace. The basic idea is that the prover sends the verifier a history for the computation of V_Π while computing with the prover, and the verifier checks a random location in the configurations on each transition (just as done in the proof system of Theorem 5.27). In slightly more detail, in the modified proof system, the logspace verifier chooses the coin tosses for V_Π (sending these to the prover), and the prover maintains the state of V_Π, sending the next configuration of V_Π in each round. In each round, just as in the proof system constructed in Theorem 5.27, the verifier chooses a random location in the configuration, and stores a small window around that location; on the following round, while the prover is sending the next configuration of V_Π, V'_Π checks that the cell at the chosen location (in the middle of the window) was updated in some acceptable way. Since V_Π is a polynomial time verifier, each configuration has polynomial size, and any inconsistencies are detected with $1/\text{poly}(n)$ probability; thus, sequential repetition is again sufficient to guarantee the verifier a probability $2/3$ of catching a cheating prover.

We can, of course, construct a polynomial time and logspace sensing module for this proof system, and construct a polynomial time and logspace user from the sensing module as done in Theorem 5.26. Although the existence of the honest prover guarantees that the class of servers for which the sensing module is *viable* is nonempty, it isn't clear at all whether or not this class is the class of $(G_\Pi, \mathcal{L}, 2/3)$-helpful servers. Theorem 5.29 tells us that the complexity of the prover is the key issue here, and it isn't clear how we could simulate the prover in Condon's proof system without using polynomial space, for example, or whether or not some other suitable proof system exists, and hence it isn't clear whether or not a universal user exists in the $\mathcal{L}$-universal setting for a PSPACE-complete Π. Thus, the capabilities of users in the $\mathcal{L}$-bounded universal setting remains open.

Chapter 6

Theory of goal-oriented communication in infinite executions

Our model of goals in finite executions, as first introduced in Chapter 2, captured many natural goals for communication, as illustrated in Chapter 3. This framework only captured goals that could be modeled as the user trying to reach a certain state of the environment by communicating with the server, though; another kind of goal that is *not* captured by this framework is a goal in which the user tries to maintain effective communication with the server *over time*. As such goals arise naturally in many contexts, we are motivated to introduce a new framework that does capture such goals—in fact, we'll even see at the end of this chapter, in Section 6.4, that this new framework can even capture the finite-execution framework as a special case, and so the new framework will subsume the earlier framework, at the cost of some (moderate) additional technical complexity.

Specifically, the model we introduce defines goals for communication (between a user and a server) as properties of *entire infinite executions* of an environment-user-server system. We adapt all of the key notions from the finite execution setting to appropriate analogues in this new infinite execution setting in Section 6.1; in particular, we develop a somewhat different notion of *sensing* in Section 6.1.4, that is more concerned with *detecting failure* than *predicting success*.

Actually, moreover, our development for infinite executions will feature different levels of quality of sensing, *weak* and *strong* sensing; we will see that this distinction is relevant when we consider the relationship between sensing and universal users for infinite execution goals in Section 6.2: *strong* sensing will allow us to obtain universal users with guarantees on the number of errors they make, but will only exist under circumstances similar to sensing

B. Juba, *Universal Semantic Communication*,
DOI 10.1007/978-3-642-23297-8_6,
© Springer-Verlag Berlin Heidelberg 2011

in the finite execution setting (that is, only when the goal is even verifiable with adversarial "servers"); *weak* sensing, by contrast, will be available more generally, but will not provide bounds on the number of errors (which are highly desirable to have). Still, this distinction can be exploited to achieve goals that cannot support strong sensing, as we will see in Chapter 7. We will see, furthermore, in Section 6.2.3, that some goals in infinite executions do not require feedback at all! Thus, this new setting turns out to be quite different from the finite execution model we studied in previous chapters.

Finally, in Section 6.3, we'll see how the model can incorporate some further features that will be relevant in later chapters. In particular, we'll see how to capture some cases where the *size parameter* varies over time and develop universal users that achieve error bounds in an appropriate size-weighted sense. We'll also see a definition of a class of goals in which the user engages in multiple "sessions" (i.e., multiple sub-goals) concurrently, that in addition to being of natural interest, will be useful to us in Chapter 9.

All of the work described in this chapter is joint work with Oded Goldreich and Madhu Sudan, and is adapted from a technical report [70].

6.1   Goals and sensing for infinite executions

Our objective in this section is to develop a new framework for modeling *communication in infinite executions*. Specifically, the model we introduce defines goals for communication (between a user and a server) as properties of *entire infinite executions* of an environment-user-server system. Of course, the class of all such properties is *much* too general to be of any interest, so in Section 6.1.1, we formulate some key special cases—notably, that of *multi-session* goals, in which each session may correspond to a sub-goal of the variety considered in the finite execution model. We will see in Section 6.1.3 that our earlier notions of achieving goals and helpful servers translate to this new setting by essentially replacing the old definitions with the corresponding new definitions. We will also briefly consider how our measures of the complexity of user strategies should be modified in an infinite execution setting, in Section 6.1.2.

Finally and most significantly, we will develop notions of *sensing* for infinite execution goals in Section 6.1.4. These notions will be central to the rest of this chapter, and moreover (in contrast to the ease with which we adapted helpfulness and robust achievement to infinite executions) will turn out to be quite different from the kind of sensing we worked with in the finite execution model. As we hinted at in the introduction, the difference is that sensing for infinite executions only needs to detect miscommunication *after the fact*. Keeping this in mind, we will actually introduce three kinds of sensing: *weak* sensing, in which we only require that failures are eventually detected, and that viable servers only incur finitely many (detected) errors; *very strong* sensing, in which *all* failures *must* be detected within a specified time bound, and viable servers only trigger failures within a bounded initial period; and, finally, *strong* sensing, in which the error detection is relaxed (from very strong sensing) to allow sensing to "forgive" a few errors, provided that the user strategy can recover from them, and will only incur a bounded number of errors in the long run. Ultimately, the weak and strong versions (and not the very strong version) will be the main subjects of interest in subsequent sections.

6.1.1 Goals in infinite executions

Recall that our model of goals in finite executions only captured the goals that arose in a certain context—that is, goals in which we were happy so long as we could make the environment's state satisfy some desired property (i.e., the property corresponding to a finite execution referee). Another natural kind of "goal" that we could have considered is goals in which we wish to *maintain* some desired property in the environment over time; or, equivalently for our purposes, we could have asked for our agents to keep communicating successfully over time. So, as this kind of goal is *not* naturally captured by the finite execution framework of Chapter 2, we will consider a more general notion of achieving goals, a notion that refers to an infinite execution of the system. Intuitively, this may capture reactive systems whose goal is to repeatedly achieve an infinite sequence of sub-goals (where the individual sub-goals may correspond to the kinds of finite goals considered in Chapter 2) and in particular may capture the desired behavior of servers on a network or operating systems. Thus, we again augment the environment with a referee, which rules whether such an *infinite execution* (actually, the corresponding sequence of the environment's local states) is successful.

Definition 6.1 (Infinite execution referees and successful executions). An *infinite execution referee R* is a function from infinite executions to a Boolean value; that is, $R : \Omega^\omega \to \{0, 1\}$ (or, actually, $R : (\Omega^{(\mathrm{e})})^\omega \to \{0, 1\}$). Indeed, the value of $R(\sigma_1, \sigma_2, \dots)$ only depends on $\sigma_1^{(\mathrm{e})}, \sigma_2^{(\mathrm{e})}, \dots$ (and it may be written as $R(\sigma_1^{(\mathrm{e})}, \sigma_2^{(\mathrm{e})}, \dots)$). We say that the infinite execution $\overline{\sigma} = (\sigma_1, \sigma_2, \dots) \in \Omega^\omega$ is *successful* (w.r.t. R) if $R(\overline{\sigma}) = 1$.

As in finite executions, the combination of the environment's strategy and a referee gives rise to a notion of a goal. Intuitively, the goal is to affect the environment in a way that is deemed successful by the referee. Formally, we have a definition quite similar to Definition 2.10:

Definition 6.2 (Goals in infinite executions). A *goal of communication* for infinite executions is given by a pair, consisting of the environment's non-deterministic probabilistic strategy and an infinite execution referee.

We can illustrate this new setting by presenting a couple of familiar goals from finite executions as goals in infinite executions:

162   *Theory of goal-oriented communication in infinite executions*

Example 6.3 (Predicting the environment's coins). A simple, but impossible to achieve, goal is predicting the environment's coin tosses. This goal may be formulated by considering a (single actual)[1] environment strategy that, at each round, tosses a single coin and sets its local state according to the coin's outcome, and a referee that checks whether (at every round) the message sent by the user to the environment was equal to the environment's state on that round. Since this environment's actual strategy does not communicate any information to the user, no user strategy may succeed with positive probability—since the number of rounds exceeds the logarithm of the reciprocal of any positive number, the user's probability of satisfying the referee goes to zero in the limit.

Note that in this example no server can help the user to achieve its goal (i.e., succeed with positive probability). In contrast, if the environment communicates its state to the server, and the referee checks whether the message sent by the user to the environment (at each round) equals the environment's state two rounds before, then an adequate server may help the user succeed with probability 1.

Example 6.4 (Solving computational problems posed by the environment). For a fixed decision problem Π, consider a non-deterministic environment strategy that in round r generates an arbitrary r-bit string, denoted x_r, and communicates it to the user, and a referee that checks whether, for every $r > 2$, the message sent by the user to the environment at round r equals $\Pi(x_{r-2})$. Indeed, this goal can be achieved by the user if and only if in round $r + 1$ it has computational resources that allow for deciding Π on instances of length r.

Note that also in this example no server can help the user, since the user obtains the "challenge" at round r and needs to answer at round $r+2$ (which does not allow for communicating the challenge to the server and obtaining the server's answer in time). In contrast, if the goal is modified such that the referee checks the user's message in round r against the environment's message in round $r-3$, then communicating with a server that has computing power that exceeds the user's power may be of help. Indeed, in this modified goal, communication between the user and the server allows the user to obtain computational help from the server. By contrast, in the next goal, the server's help is required, regardless of computational resources.

Example 6.5 (Printing). Think of the server as a printer that the user wishes to use in order to print text that is handed to it by the environment. That is, consider a non-deterministic environment strategy that at each round r generates an arbitrary bit $b_r \in \{0, 1\}$ and communicates b_r to the user, and a referee that checks whether, for every $r > 2$, the message sent by the server to the environment at round r equals b_{r-2}.

---

[1]Indeed, in this example, the environment's non-deterministic strategy is a singleton, containing a single actual strategy.

Indeed, the only way that a user can achieve this goal is by transmitting b_r to the server in time $r + 1$, and counting on the server to transmit this bit to the environment in round $r + 2$.

Compact goals

Examples 6.3–6.5 belong to a natural class of goals, which we call *compact*. In compact goals, success can be determined by looking at sufficiently long (but finite) prefixes of the actual execution. Indeed, this condition refers merely to the referee's predicate, and it guarantees that the set of successful executions is measurable with respect to the natural probability measure (see Appendix A). Furthermore, the compactness condition also enables the introduction of the notion of sensing of success (see Section 6.1.4).

By incorporating a record of all (the relevant information regarding) previous states in the current state, it suffices to take a decision based solely on the current state.[2] As in the case of the referee function R, the temporary decision captured by R' is actually a function of the environment's local state (and not of the entire global state).

Definition 6.6 (Compactness). A referee $R : \Omega^\omega \to \{0, 1\}$ is called *compact* if there exists a function $R' : \Omega \to \{0, 1, \perp\}$ (or, actually, $R' : \Omega^{(e)} \to \{0, 1, \perp\}$) such that for every $\overline{\sigma} = (\sigma_1, \sigma_2, \ldots) \in \Omega^\omega$ it holds that $R(\overline{\sigma}) = 1$ if and only if the following two conditions hold

1. *The number of failures is finite:*

   There exists T such that for every $t > T$ it holds that $R'(\sigma_t) \neq 0$ (or, actually, $R'(\sigma_t^{(e)}) \neq 0$).

2. *There are no infinite runs of $\perp$:*

   For every $t > 0$ there exists $t' > t$ such that $R'(\sigma_{t'}) \neq \perp$.

The function R' is called *the temporal decision function.*

Indeed, the special symbol $\perp$ is to be understood as suspending decision regarding the current state. Definition 6.6 asserts that an execution can be deemed successful only if (1) failure occurs at most a finite number of times and (2) decision is not suspended for an infinite number of steps. (A stronger version of (Condition 2 of) Definition 6.6 may require that there exists B such that for every $t > 0$ there exists $t' \in [t + 1, t + B]$ such that $R'(\sigma_{t'}) \neq \perp$.)[3]

---

[2] That is, consider a definition analogous to Definition 6.6, where $R' : \Omega^* \to \{0, 1, \perp\}$ and the conditions refer to $R'(\sigma_1, \sigma_2, \ldots, \sigma_i)$ rather than to $R'(\sigma_i)$. Then, using $(\sigma_1, \sigma_2, \ldots, \sigma_i)$ as the ith state allows us to move to the formalism of Definition 6.6. Furthermore, in typical cases it suffices to include in the ith state only a "digest" of the previous $i - 1$ states.

[3] It is tempting to suggest an even stronger version of Definition 6.6 in which both T and B are absolute constants, rather than quantities determined by the sequence $\overline{\sigma}$; however, such a stronger definition would have violated some of our intuitive desires. For example,

Multi-session goals. Examples 6.3–6.5 actually belong to a natural sub-class of compact goals, which we call *multi-session goals.*[4] Intuitively, these goals consist of an infinitely repeated finite execution goal, where each of the corresponding finite (sub-)executions is referred to as a "session." In other words, these goals consists of an infinite sequence of sub-goals, where each sub-goal is to be achieved in a finite number of rounds, which are called the current session, and the environment's state is (non-deterministically) reset at the beginning of each session (indeed, as in Example 6.4). We further restrict such goals in the following definition, where these restrictions are aimed at capturing the intuitive notion of a multi-session goal.

Definition 6.7 (Multi-session goals). A goal consisting of a non-deterministic environment strategy $\mathcal{E}$ and a referee R is called a *multi-session goal* if the following conditions hold.

1. *The environment's states:* The local states of the environment are partitioned into three non-empty sets consisting of *start-session* states, *end-session* states, and *(intermediate) session* states. Each of these states is a pair consisting of an *index* (an integer representing the index of the session) and a *contents* (representing the state of the actual execution of the session).[5] The initial local state corresponds to the pair $(0, \lambda)$, and belongs to the set of end-session states.

2. *The referee suspends its verdict until reaching an end-session state:* The referee R is compact. Furthermore, the corresponding temporal decision function R' evaluates to $\bot$ if and only if the current state is not an end-session state.

3. *Starting a new session:* When in an end-session state, the environment moves non-deterministically to a start-session state while increasing the index. Furthermore, this move is independent of the actual contents of the current end-session state. That is, for each actual environment strategy $E \in \mathcal{E}$, the value of E is invariant over all possible end-session states that have the same index (i.e., for every two end-session states

---

we wish to focus on "forgiving" goals that are achieved even if the user adapts a good strategy only at an arbitrary late stage of the execution, and so we cannot afford to have T be execution invariant. Also, for an adequate notion of "size" (of the current state), we wish to allow the user to achieve the goal by interacting with a server for a number of rounds that depends on this size parameter (and suspend decision regarding success to the end of such interactions). In fact, we even "forgive" infinite runs of $\bot$s if they result from a permanent increase in the size parameter.

[4]Actually, to fit Examples 6.4 and 6.5 into the following framework we slightly modify them such that the environment generates and sends challenges only at rounds that are a multiple of three. Thus, the ith session consists of rounds $3i, 3i + 1, 3i + 2$. Such an adaptation is also a case of a 3-*round multi-session goal* as introduced in Section 8.2.1.

[5]The states are augmented by an index in order to allow for distinguishing the same contents when it occurs in different sessions. This is important in order to allow different non-deterministic choices in the different sessions (cf. Condition 3).

(i, σ') and (i, σ''), it holds that $E(i, \sigma')^{(e)} = E(i, \sigma'')^{(e)} \in \{i + 1\} \times \Omega$, and similarly for $E(i, \cdot)^{(e, \cdot)}$.

Optional: The environment can also notify the user that a new session is starting, and even whether or not the previous session was completed successfully (i.e., with R' evaluating to 1). Analogous notifications can also be sent to the server.

4. *Execution of the current session:* When in any other state, the environment moves probabilistically while maintaining the index of the state (i.e., for every $E \in \mathcal{E}$ and such state (i, σ'), it holds that $E(i, \sigma') = (i, \cdot)$). Furthermore, the movement is independent of the index as well as of the actual environment strategy; that is, for every $E_1, E_2 \in \mathcal{E}$ and every $i_1, i_2 \in \mathbb{N}$ and $\sigma', \sigma'' \in \Omega$, it holds that $\Pr[E_1(i_1, \sigma') = (i_1, \sigma'')]$ equals $\Pr[E_2(i_2, \sigma') = (i_2, \sigma'')]$.

The execution of a system that corresponds to Definition 6.7 consists of a sequence of sessions, where each session is a sequence of states sharing the same index. Indeed, all the states in the ith such sequence have index i, and correspond to the ith session. The temporal decision function R' determines the success of each session based solely on the state reached at the end of the session (which also includes the session's index), precisely as a finite execution referee would determine success in an execution corresponding to the ith session. Recalling our definition of a referee for a compact goal, now, it follows that the entire execution is successful if and only if all but finitely many sessions are successful. We stress that, except for the index, the environment's local state carries no information about prior sessions. Furthermore, with the exception of the initial move into a start-session state, the environment's actions during the session are oblivious of the session's index. (In contrast to the environment's action, the strategies of the user and server may maintain arbitrary information across sessions, and their actions in the current session may depend on this information.)

Repetitive (multi-session) goals. A special type of multi-session goals consists of the case in which the environment repeats the non-deterministic choices of the first session in all subsequent sessions. We stress that, as in general multi-session goals, the environment's probabilistic choices in each session are independent of the choices made in other sessions.[6]

Definition 6.8 (Repetitive goals). A multi-session goal consisting of a non-deterministic environment strategy $\mathcal{E}$ and a referee R is called *repetitive* if its non-deterministic choice is independent of the index; that is, for every $E \in \mathcal{E}$

---

[6]Indeed, a stronger notion, which we do not consider here, requires that the environment also repeats the probabilistic choices of the first session in all subsequent sessions. We note that this stronger notion cannot be captured in the current formalism.

and every $i \in \mathbb{N}$ and $\sigma' \in \Omega$, it holds that $E(i, \sigma') \equiv E(1, \sigma')$.[7]

Indeed, any multi-session goal using an environment strategy that makes no non-deterministic choices (cf., e.g., Example 6.3) is a repetitive goal. An example of a repetitive goal that does involve non-deterministic choices follows.

Example 6.9 (Repeated guessing with feedback). Consider a non-deterministic environment strategy that generates an integer i and proceeds in sessions. Each session consists of two rounds, where in the first round the user sends a guess to the environment, and in the second round the environment notifies the user whether or not its guess was correct (i.e., whether or not the message sent by the user in the first round equals i). The referee deems a session successful if the user sent the correct message i. Indeed, by recording all previous failed attempts, the user can eventually succeed in a single session, be informed about it, and repeat this success in all subsequent sessions.

Indeed, the feedback provided by the environment is essential for the user's ability to (eventually) succeed in guessing the environment's initial choice. In particular, note that no user strategy can reliably guess the environment's choice correctly in the first $i - 1$ sessions, let alone the first one, so the natural corresponding finite execution goal is unachievable.

Generalized multi-session goals. Our formulation of multi-session goals mandates that the current session must end before any new session can start (see Definition 6.7). A more general formulation, which allows concurrent sessions, is postponed to Section 6.3.2 (cf. Definition 6.53). Note that Examples 6.4 and 6.5 fit this general formulation without any modification (cf. Footnote 4).

6.1.2 The computational complexity of strategies

In contrast to the finite execution setting, it no longer makes sense to talk about, e.g., the "total time" spent by the user in an infinite execution. Since strategies are essentially functions, it is natural to generally define their time complexity as the complexity of the corresponding functions, and this is always a reasonable notion in infinite executions.

In the case of multi-session goals, though, the connection to finite execution goals motivates an arguably more natural notion of time complexity: since each session corresponds to a finite execution, the natural corresponding notion of time complexity is *the total time spent by the user during a session*, i.e., the time complexity of the user strategy in the finite executions sense.

---

[7]We used $X \equiv Y$ to indicate that the random variables X and Y are identically distributed. Note that if σ' is an end-session state, then $E(i, \sigma')$ and $E(1, \sigma')$ are actually fixed strings (and they must be equal).

We caution that this correspondence is not as strong as it first seems, since the termination of a session is under the *environment's* control, whereas the termination of an execution in the finite-execution setting was always under the *user's* control. Thus, we'll explicitly mention when we wish to consider the "per-session" time complexity.

Of course, considerations similar to the above hold for the randomness complexity, and we can consider both "per-round" and "per-session" versions. On the other hand, whenever we consider the *space* complexity of a strategy (as, e.g., we did in Chapter 5 for finite executions), the natural notion refers to the maximum space used by the user during the computation of its strategy across the entire infinite execution, in particular, including the space consumed to store the user's internal state across rounds of the execution. We note that the intuitive notion of an "efficient" user strategy in infinite executions should generally be *both* polynomial time and polynomial space bounded, where the polynomial time bound no longer implies a corresponding polynomial space bound.[8]

As before in the finite execution setting, we define the complexity of a (user) strategy with respect to the specific party (i.e., server) with which it interacts. This convention facilitates reflecting the phenomenon that some servers allow the user to "save time"; that is, the complexity of the user is lower when interacting with such servers. In contrast to the finite execution setting, though, we define complexity with respect to the *size* of the *current state* (rather than with respect to the length of its description or with respect to the environment's strategy, as was the case in finite executions), where *size* is an adequate function of the state that need not equal the length of its description. Nevertheless, typically, the size will be polynomially related to the length, but this relation need not be fixed a priori.

6.1.3   Achieving goals and helpful servers

We have already touched on the notion of achieving a goal in an infinite execution, but now we turn to define it formally, while assuming that the corresponding referee is compact (as per Definition 6.6). As detailed in Appendix A, the compactness assumption implies that the set of successful executions is measurable (with respect to the natural probability measure). The basic definition of achieving a goal is as follows.

Definition 6.10 (Achieving goals in infinite executions). We say that a pair of user-server strategies, (U, S), *achieves the goal* $G = (\mathcal{E}, R)$ if, for every $E \in \mathcal{E}$, a random execution of the system (E, U, S) is successful with probability 1, where success is as in Definition 6.1.

---

[8]In particular, in the absence of the space bound, we may encounter situations where a multitape Turing machine would experience unbounded time overhead over a time-efficient RAM machine—and, unfortunately, we will actually encounter such a situation in Chapter 7.

Recall that by Definition 2.11, our convention is that (unless stated differently) the execution starts at the system's (fixed) initial global state. However, in the sequel we will be interested in what happens when the execution starts in an arbitrary state, which might have been reached before the actual execution started. This reflects the fact that the environment is not initialized each time we (users) wish to achieve some goal, and the same may hold with respect to the servers that we use. Thus, a stronger notion of achievable goals arises.

Definition 6.11 (Robustly achieving goals in infinite executions). We say that a pair of user-server strategies, (U, S), *robustly achieves the goal* $G = (\mathcal{E}, R)$ if for every $E \in \mathcal{E}$ and every global state σ_1 a random execution of the system (E, U, S) starting in state σ_1 is successful with probability 1.

Indeed, this notion of robust achievability is again "forgiving" of an initial portion of the execution that may be carried on by inadequate user and/or server strategies. A more refined definition, which quantifies over a subset of the possible states, is postponed to Section 6.3 (see Definition 6.54). Most importantly, this refined definition allows us to consider the (natural case of the) set of all global states in which the user's local state is reset to some initial value, as we did when considering finite executions. (Indeed, in contrast to resetting the environment, resetting the user seems feasible in many cases, and seems less demanding than resetting the server.)

Proposition 6.12 (Robustness allows ignoring execution prefixes). *Let U_t (resp., S_t) be a user (resp., server) strategy that plays the first t rounds using the user strategy U_0 (resp., server strategy S_0) and plays all subsequent rounds using the user strategy U (resp., server strategy S). Then, if (U, S) robustly achieves the goal $G = (\mathcal{E}, R)$, then so does (U_t, S_t).*

The proof only uses the hypothesis that (E, U, S) is successful when started in a state that may be reached by an execution of E with an arbitrary pair of user and server strategies. Indeed, for all practical purposes, the definition of robust achievability may be confined to such initial states (i.e., in Definition 6.11, we may quantify only over states σ_1 that can be reached in some execution of the system (E_0, U_0, S_0), where $E_0 \in \mathcal{E}$ and (U_0, S_0) is an arbitrary user–server pair).

Proof The proposition follows by considering the execution of the system (E, U, S) starting at the state, denoted σ_1, that is reached after t rounds of the system (E, U_0, S_0). (Indeed, σ_1 may be a distribution over such states.) By combining the robust achievability hypothesis (which refers to the execution of (E, U, S) started at σ_1) and the compactness hypothesis (which allows discarding the first t steps of (E, U_t, S_t)), we conclude that the execution of (E, U_t, S_t) (started at any state σ_1') is successful with probability 1. ∎

Achievable goals. We may say that a goal $G = (\mathcal{E}, R)$ is *achievable* (resp., *robustly achievable*) if there exists a pair of user-server strategies that achieves (resp., robustly achieves) G. Indeed, as hinted before, predicting the environment's coins (i.e., Example 6.3) is an unachievable goal, whereas the goals of Examples 6.4 and 6.5 are (robustly) achievable. Note, however, that the printing goal (i.e., Example 6.5) is achievable by a very simple user–server pair, whereas solving the computational problems posed by the environment (i.e., Example 6.4) is achievable only by a sufficiently powerful user (i.e., one that can decide membership in D). Thus, achievable goals are merely our starting point; indeed, *starting with such a goal G*, we shall ask what should be required of a user–server pair that achieves G and what should be required of a user that can achieve this goal when paired with any server that is taken from a reasonable class.

Helpful servers

Our focus is on the cases in which the user and server need to collaborate in order to achieve the goal. Indeed, in order to collaborate, the user and server may need to communicate, and in such a case they furthermore need to understand one another. The latter requirement is non-trivial when the server may be selected arbitrarily within some class of helpful servers, where just as in the finite execution setting (cf. Definition 2.18), a server is helpful if it can be coupled with some user so that this pair achieves the goal— even in this case, the mere existence of a suitable user strategy U does not suffice because we may not know this strategy. Still, we must start with the assumption that such a user strategy U exists, which leads to the definition of a helpful server.

Fixing an arbitrary (compact) goal $G = (\mathcal{E}, R)$, we say that a server S is *helpful* if there exists a user strategy U such that (U, S) achieves the goal. Just as we did with helpfulness for finite executions, we will strengthen this helpfulness requirement in two ways. Firstly, we will require that (U, S) robustly achieves the goal, rather than merely achieves it. This strengthening reflects our interest in executions that start at an arbitrary state, which might have been reached before the actual execution started (cf. Definition 6.11). Secondly, along the lines of Definition 5.10 in the generic finite execution setting, at times we may require that the user strategy U (for which (U, S) robustly achieves the goal) belongs to some predetermined class of strategies $\mathcal{U}$ (in particular, e.g., the class of polynomial time user strategies, as was the case for our original notion of helpfulness, Definition 2.18).

Definition 6.13 (Helpfulness). A server strategy S is $\mathcal{U}$-*helpful* (w.r.t. the goal G) if there exists a user strategy $U \in \mathcal{U}$ such that (U, S) robustly achieves the goal G.

When $\mathcal{U}$ is not specified, we usually mean that helpfulness holds with respect to the class of all computable user strategies.

6.1.4   Sensing for goals in infinite executions

We recall that "sensing" was an essential concept for goals in finite executions (cf. the results of Section 2.3). The notion of feedback we developed for finite executions, however – i.e., predicting the verdicts of a finite referee – does not immediately translate to anything meaningful in the context of the referees used in goals in infinite executions. Still, we saw that the achievability of the goal of "repeated guessing with feedback" (i.e., Example 6.9) relied on the feedback provided to the user regarding its success in previous sessions. More generally, we will find that an analogue of finite-execution sensing that refers to the temporal decision function of a compact goal instead of a finite-execution referee is very natural. Such a formulation introduces a few new twists, notably that as with the feedback provided by the repeated guessing goal, we no longer need to be so concerned with *predicting* what the referee will decide on the current round so much as eventually determining what the verdicts were in earlier rounds of the execution. In general, such feedback is reasonable to assume in the context of many multi-session goals, and (as we shall see) such feedback can also be helpful to the user in non-repetitive goals.

Intuitively, we shall consider environment strategies that allow the user to sense its progress towards achieving the goal, where this sensing should satisfy adequate safety and viability conditions. Loosely speaking *safety* now means that if the user gets a positive indication (i.e., senses progress) almost all the time, then the goal is actually achieved, whereas *viability* means that when the goal is achieved the user gets positive indication almost all the time. Thus, infinitely many negative indications should occur if and only if the execution fails. (As usual, we will represent a positive indication by the value 1, and a negative indication by 0.)

The aforementioned indication is provided by a separate stateful module, as developed in Section 5.3. That is, as motivated in Section 5.2.1, we view the user's state space as decomposed into a product space $\Omega^{(\mathrm{u})} = \Omega^{(\mathrm{i})} \times \Omega^{(\mathrm{v})} \times \Omega^{(\mathrm{c})}$ where $\Omega^{(\mathrm{i})}$ is the state of the *interpreter* strategy that the user uses to communicate, $\Omega^{(\mathrm{v})}$ is the state of the *sensing* strategy, and $\Omega^{(\mathrm{c})}$ is the state of the *controller* strategy that incorporates the feedback from sensing and modifies the interpreter strategy accordingly. In the present chapter, we won't be so concerned with user strategies consuming sub-linear space as we were in Chapter 5, but properly speaking, we still consider the sensing strategy to be a module "attached" to the interpreter as described in Definition 5.11 (also cf. Figure 5.2), and thus the sensing module "watches" the input/output behavior of the interpreter (and its coin tosses) to determine its verdicts. (The controller likewise obtains the same inputs as the sensing strategy, along with the indication produced by sensing on the current round, and chooses an interpreter strategy for use on each round.)

The sensing strategy is required to be viable and safe. Note that our new notion of viability is again not meaningful without safety, and vice versa; for example, under any reasonable definition, the all-zero function is (trivially) safe, whereas the all-one function is (trivially) viable. Although we will be interested in safety and viability with respect to classes of possible servers, we find it useful to define restricted notions of safety and viability that refer to a fixed server strategy.

Definition 6.14 (Sensing function, weak version). Let $G = (\mathcal{E}, R)$ be a compact[9] goal and S be a server strategy. The predicate $V : \Omega \to \{0, 1\}$ (or rather $V : \Omega^{(v)} \to \{0, 1\}$) is *safe* with respect to (U, S) (and G) if, for every $E \in \mathcal{E}$ and every $\sigma_1 \in \Omega$, letting $\overline{\sigma}$ denote a random execution of the system (E, U, S) starting at state σ_1, with probability 1, it holds that if $R(\overline{\sigma}) = 0$ then for infinitely many t it holds that $V(\sigma_t) = 0$. The predicate V is *viable* with respect to (U, S) if, for every $E \in \mathcal{E}$ and every $\sigma_1 \in \Omega$, with probability 1, it holds that $V(\sigma_t) = 0$ holds for finitely many t.

Indeed, if V is viable and safe with respect to (U, S) (and G), then (U, S) robustly achieves the goal G, because viability implies that a random execution yields finitely many negative indications, whereas safety implies that in such a case the goal is achieved. In particular, if V is safe with respect to (U, S), then, with probability 1, if V evaluates to 0 finitely many times, then the corresponding temporal decision function R' evaluates to 0 finitely many times.

The foregoing reference to the temporal decision function R' suggests stronger (i.e., quantified) notions of sensing. Intuitively, we seek a stronger notion of (safe) sensing in which failure (as per R') is sensed after a bounded number of steps (rather than eventually). Similarly, a stronger notion of viability should guarantee a positive indication after a bounded number of steps (rather than eventually). That is, in both cases, the "grace period" (of bad sensing) is explicitly bounded rather than merely postulated to be finite. This bound will be stated in terms of an adequate notion of "size" (of the current state), denoted $\mathsf{sz}(\sigma)$, thus allowing the grace period to depend on the "complexity" (or rather the "size") of the relevant states. For simplicity, *we assume here that the size of the various states remains invariant throughout the execution*; the general case (in which the size varies) will be dealt with in Section 6.3.1. Anyhow, we assume that the size of the current state is known to the user in the present development.

Our formulation will be further simplified by observing that the quantification over all initial states (which also takes place in Definition 6.14) allows us to focus on grace periods that start at time 1 (rather than considering grace periods that start at time t for any $t \in \mathbb{N}$). These considerations lead to the following definition, which is a straightforward strengthening of Definition 6.14.

---

[9]Actually, the current definition does not refer to the compactness condition (and is applicable also w.r.t. non-compact goals). The compactness condition was added here for consistency with the following definitions, which do refer to it (or rather to the temporal decision function provided by it).

Definition 6.15 (Sensing function, very strong version). Let $G = (\mathcal{E}, R)$, S, U, and V be as in Definition 6.14, and let $\mathbf{sz} : \Omega \to \mathbb{N}$ be the aforementioned size function. We say that V is *very strongly safe* with respect to (U, S) (and G) if there exists a function $B : \mathbb{N} \to \mathbb{N}$ such that, for every $E \in \mathcal{E}$ and every $\sigma_1 \in \Omega$, the following two conditions hold.

1. If $R'(\sigma_1) = 0$, then, with probability at least $2/3$, for some $t \leq B(\mathbf{sz}(\sigma_1))$ it holds that $V(\sigma_t) = 0$, where σ_t denotes the system's state after t rounds.

2. If for every $i \in [B(\mathbf{sz}(\sigma_1))]$ it holds that $R'(\sigma_i) = \bot$, then, with probability at least $2/3$, for some $t \in [B(\mathbf{sz}(\sigma_1)) + 1, 2B(\mathbf{sz}(\sigma_1))]$ it holds that $V(\sigma_t) = 0$, where σ_i, σ_t are as above.

Analogously, V is *strongly viable* with respect to (U, S) if, for every $E \in \mathcal{E}$ and every $\sigma_1 \in \Omega$, with probability at least $2/3$, for every $t \geq B(\mathbf{sz}(\sigma_1))$ it holds that $V(\sigma_t) = 1$. We say that strong viability holds perfectly if the foregoing holds with probability 1 (i.e., for every $E \in \mathcal{E}$ and every $\sigma_1 \in \Omega$, with probability 1, it holds that $V(\sigma_t) = 0$ holds for finitely many t).

We note that satisfying the first safety condition of Definition 6.15 implies that, for every $E \in \mathcal{E}$ and $\sigma_1 \in \Omega$ and every $T > 0$, if $R'(\sigma_T) = 0$ then, with probability at least $2/3$, for some $t \in [T, T + B(\mathbf{sz}(\sigma_T))]$ it holds that $V(\sigma_t) = 0$, where σ_i denotes the system's state after i rounds. Analogous statements apply to the second safety condition and to the viability condition (of Definition 6.15). It follows that very strong safety (resp., viability) as in Definition 6.15 implies weak safety (resp., viability) satisfying Definition 6.14 (because infinitely many sensing failures imply infinitely many disjoint B-long intervals containing sensing failure).[10] All of this will apply also to the following definition (which is a relaxation of Definition 6.15).

In order to motivate the following definition, note that Definition 6.15 requires that failure be detected even if the execution has recovered from it. For example, the first safety condition requires that V senses that $R'(\sigma_1) = 0$ (i.e., $V(\sigma_t) = 0$ for some $t \leq B(\mathbf{sz}(\sigma_1))$) even if $R'(\sigma_i) = 1$ for every $i > 1$. Insisting on detection of an old (initial) failure that is no longer relevant seems

---

[10]The foregoing sketchy justification seems to suffice for the case of strong viability that holds perfectly, but even in such a case a more rigorous argument is preferable. Indeed, suppose that strong viability holds (in the non-perfect sense), and consider the event F that there are infinitely many negative sensing indications. For any execution prefix $\sigma_1, \ldots, \sigma_t$, strong viability implies that the probability that F holds and $\sigma_1, \ldots, \sigma_t$ is observed is at most $1/3$ the probability that $\sigma_1, \ldots, \sigma_t$ is observed. But now, F is a measurable event in the sigma-algebra generated by these prefix events (see Appendix A) and so, writing F in terms of these events, we find that the probability of F occurring is at most $1/3$ the probability of F occurring—that is, F must occur with probability zero, and so weak viability holds. Dealing with the safety conditions is somewhat more complicated. One has to show that the very strong safety condition implies that the probability that a random execution $\overline{\sigma}$ is unsuccessful (i.e., $R(\overline{\sigma}) = 0$) and yet $\{t \in \mathbb{N} : V(\sigma_t) = 0\}$ is finite is zero. Properly, this follows by an application of the Borel-Cantelli Lemma.

unnecessary, and it may make the design of sensing functions (unnecessarily) harder. The following (relaxed w.r.t. Definition 6.15) definition requires detection of an initial failure only in the case that the entire execution has failed. In other words, if the sensing function "believes" that the possible initial failure is no longer relevant, then it is not required to signal an alarm.

Definition 6.16 (Sensing function, strong version). Let $G = (\mathcal{E}, R)$, S, U, and V be as in Definition 6.14. We say that V is *strongly safe* with respect to (U, S) (and G) if there exists a function $B : \mathbb{N} \to \mathbb{N}$ such that, for every $E \in \mathcal{E}$ and every $\sigma_1 \in \Omega$, the following conditions hold.

1. If $R'(\sigma_1) = 0$, then, with probability at least $2/3$, either $R(\overline{\sigma}) = 1$ or for some $t \le B(\mathbf{sz}(\sigma_1))$ it holds that $V(\sigma_t) = 0$, where $\overline{\sigma} = (\sigma_1, \sigma_2, \dots,)$ denotes a random execution of the system (E, U, S).

2. If for every $i \in [B(\mathbf{sz}(\sigma_1))]$ it holds that $R'(\sigma_i) = \perp$, then, with probability at least $2/3$, either $R(\overline{\sigma}) = 1$ or for some $t \in [B(\mathbf{sz}(\sigma_1)) + 1, 2B(\mathbf{sz}(\sigma_1))]$ it holds that $V(\sigma_t) = 0$.

The strong viability condition is exactly as in Definition 6.15.

We mention that the strong sensing version (i.e., as per Definition 6.16) implies the weak one (i.e., as per Definition 6.14).[11] We will refer mainly to the weak and strong versions (i.e., Definitions 6.14 and 6.16, respectively); the very strong version (i.e., Definition 6.15) was presented mainly for clarification.

Safety with respect to classes of servers. Sensing is crucial when the user is not sure about the server with which it interacts. Recall that Section 6.1.3 ended with a declared focus on achievable goals; but this only means that the adequate user U can be sure that *it achieves the goal when it interacts with an adequate server.* But this user may not be aware that the server is actually not the designated one, and in such a case if interaction with this server is not leading to success, then the user may wish to be notified of this failure. For this reason, we will be interested in sensing functions V that satisfy the safety condition with respect to (U, S) for every S in a set of servers $\mathcal{S}$.

Definition 6.17 (Safety w.r.t. classes of servers). For each version of safety, we say that V is *safe with respect to U and the server class $\mathcal{S}$* (and the goal G) if for every $S \in \mathcal{S}$ it holds that V is safe with respect to (U, S) (and G).

Safety and viability with respect to classes of interpreters. Our motivation for considering sensing was that we wanted feedback to distinguish successful strategies from unsuccessful ones; as in the goal of repeated

---

[11] This requires a proof; cf. Footnote 10.

guessing in Example 6.9, we could then search through the space of interpreter strategies to find one that led to success. To support such a search, we therefore would like for our sensing function to be safe with not just a single user strategy, but with the entire *class* of user strategies we intend to search through. Thus:

Definition 6.18 (Safety w.r.t. classes of interpreters and servers). For each version of safety, we say that V is *safe with respect to the interpreter class* $\mathcal{I}$ *and the server class* $\mathcal{S}$ (and the goal G) if for every $I \in \mathcal{I}$ it holds that V is safe with respect to I and the server class $\mathcal{S}$.

On the other hand, in order for such a search to be ultimately successful, we only need to know that *some* user strategy in the class is viable, not that, e.g., some a priori fixed strategy is viable. Thus, for viability, the relevant notion is the following.

Definition 6.19 (Viability w.r.t. classes of interpreters). For each version of viability, we say that V is *viable with respect to the class of interpreters* $\mathcal{I}$ *and* S if there exists some $I \in \mathcal{I}$ such that V is viable with respect to (I, S).

Grey-box sensing and private outputs.   As discussed before for finite-execution sensing in Section 2.3.3, the notions of sensing we consider here can be extended to incorporate additional information from the interpreter or about the interpreter. In *grey-box* sensing, we assume that the description of the interpreter strategy used on the current round is provided as an additional input to the sensing strategy, i.e., as an input from the controller; as we noted in Section 5.4.1, such input is a feature that is easily obtained from most enumeration strategies. Meanwhile, *private outputs* are an orthogonal consideration, in which we consider a class of interpreters which have additional output channels, beyond those that are present in the environment for the goal under consideration, that are only forwarded to the sensing strategy (and not to the environment). Such additional information is usually easily incorporated, as long as the private outputs either do not exceed the user's space bound, can be processed by sensing in an on-line fashion, or can be recomputed (e.g., if the interpreter is deterministic). Again, in the present chapter, we won't be so concerned with the user's space complexity, and so it will be feasible to temporarily store the interpreter's private outputs during the current round.

6.2   On universal users in infinite executions

Now that we have laid out the basic framework of goal-oriented communication in infinite executions, we return to our main subject of interest, the construction of *universal* user strategies for achieving goals with a collection of servers. More specifically, along the lines of Section 2.3 in Chapter 2 for finite executions, we will examine the relationship between the feedback provided by our new notion of sensing for infinite execution goals, and universal users for those goals.

Roughly, we show two things: first, we will show that our weakened notion of feedback for infinite executions, that merely detects failures post-hoc rather than predicting successes, is a suitable kind of feedback for the construction of universal users. We'll actually provide three successively stronger constructions: the first construction, in Section 6.2.1, only requires weak safety (as defined in Definition 6.14), but provides no guarantee on the number of errors besides "finiteness." Since this finite bound actually depends on the unknown server strategy, the guarantee is so weak as to be almost meaningless (cf. computable functions have algorithms that similarly run in "finite time"), and so we are motivated to introduce a refined notion of achieving goals *with a bounded number of errors* in Section 6.2.4, and show that strong safety (with strong viability, along the lines of Definition 6.16) allows us to construct a universal user strategy with only a linear increase in the number of errors (Theorem 6.36). Upon closer inspection, though, we find that the class of user strategies satisfying strong viability, in which the *period* of miscommunication instead of the *number of errors* is bounded, may be more restrictive than we would like—in particular, we can only obtain the latter kind of guarantee in our constructions. Thus, we also introduce a relaxed notion of viability that only counts the number of errors, and finally construct a universal user strategy that can take advantage of this relaxed viability, with a quadratic increase in the number of errors (Theorem 6.41). Depending on circumstances, one of these last two theorems should be a suitable infinite-execution analogue of our constructions of universal users in finite executions (e.g., as first presented in Proposition 2.27), and we'll see a couple of examples – Example 6.44 and Example 6.45 – that illustrate this point.

Along the way, we will also consider the relationship of universal users to sensing in infinite executions; broadly speaking, the second thing we will show is that the connection to sensing is surprisingly weak in the infinite execution setting, as compared to finite executions. We will only present a construction of sensing that provides a converse to our first theorem, providing a weakly safe sensing function in Proposition 6.26, which as noted above, may be so weak as to be almost meaningless; we will also see, in Section 6.2.5, that sensing with *strong* safety in a basic universal setting is bound by the same limitations as sensing in finite executions, namely, as established first in Theorem 2.37, such sensing must be safe with *all* servers. We will find in Section 6.2.3, though, that constructions of universal users in infinite executions are *not* always bound by such limitations, and in fact, in a weak but still meaningful sense, it is *possible* to construct universal users *without* any significant feedback. Thus, although strong sensing is still available in most goals of interest, it isn't strictly necessary for the construction of universal users in the infinite execution setting, and we'll see in Chapter 7 that it is possible to take advantage of this difference.

6.2.1   Universality and sensing in infinite executions

Recall that the basic setting of interest to us is when the user wishes to achieve a goal which requires the user to communicate with a server. When allowed to interact with a known (to us) helpful server, we may achieve the goal (if we use the strategy U that is guaranteed by Definition 6.13). But *what happens when we are allowed to interact with a server that is selected arbitrarily among several helpful servers?* Specifically, suppose that both S_1 and S_2 are $\mathcal{U}$-helpful (in the infinite execution sense, now), does this mean that there exists a user strategy U (let alone in $\mathcal{U}$) such that both (U, S_1) and (U, S_2) achieve the goal? As shown next, similar to our demonstration in Section 2.3 for goals in finite executions, the answer still may be negative.

Example 6.20 (Using one out of two different printers). Continuing Example 6.5, for every $i \in \{0, 1\}$, consider a printer S_i such that, in each round, upon receiving the message b from the user, the printer S_i sends the message $b \oplus i$ to the environment. That is, if at round $r + 1$ the server S_i receives b, then at round $r + 2$ it sends the message $b \oplus i$ to the environment. Note that each of these two server strategies is $\{U_0, U_1\}$-helpful, where U_i is a user strategy that at round $r + 1$ sends $b_r \oplus i$ to the server, where $b_r \in \{0, 1\}$ denotes the message sent by the environment to the user in round r. However, there exists no user strategy U such that both (U, S_0) and (U, S_1) achieve the goal.

Indeed, one may think of U_1 and S_1 as using, for communication between them, a different language than the one used by the environment (i.e., they interpret 0 as 1, and 1 as 0). Thus, the situation is again essentially similar to that considered in Example 2.20 for finite executions: the communication between the various pairs of parties may represent communication in different systems or over vastly different media. As another example suggested by our calling the goal of Example 6.5 "printing," we may suppose that the user obtains email (from the environment), which the user sends to the printer in some adequate format, while the printer produces an image (in the environment). Thus, Example 6.20 can be made more realistic by saying that there exist two text formatting functions, denoted f_0 and f_1 (e.g., Postscript and PDF) such that the following holds: if, at round r, user U_i receives the email text T_r (from the environment), then it sends $f_i(T_r)$ to the server in round $r + 1$, whereas when server S_j receives the message M from the user it prints an image of $f_j^{-1}(M)$ (i.e., it sends the message $f_j^{-1}(M)$ to the environment).

Example 6.21 (Two printers, modified). Continuing Example 6.20, we consider a modified goal in which the environment sends in each round a pair of bits (b, s) such that b is as above (i.e., as in Examples 6.5 and 6.20) and s indicates whether the referee is satisfied with the last message received by the server. In this case, there exists a simple user strategy U such that both (U, S_0) and (U, S_1) achieve the goal. Specifically, U first behaves as U_0, and if it gets an indication (in round 3) that printing failed, then it switches to using U_1.

Indeed, in this case the environment's messages suggest a sensing function that is both safe and viable (w.r.t. the server class $\{S_0, S_1\}$). This sensing function allows the user to recover from failure (by learning with which server it interacts and acting accordingly).

Universal users. The user strategy U of Example 6.21 achieves the corresponding goal when coupled with any server strategy in the class $\mathcal{S} \overset{\text{def}}{=} \{S_0, S_1\}$. Thus, we may say that U is $\mathcal{S}$-universal—it satisfies a definition essentially identical to our definition of "universal users" for finite executions except, of course, that the goal is now a goal in infinite executions, and we use the corresponding notion of robust achievement for goals in infinite executions.

Definition 6.22 (Universality). A user strategy U is $\mathcal{S}$-*universal* (w.r.t. the goal G) if for every server strategy $S \in \mathcal{S}$ it holds that (U, S) robustly achieves the goal G.

Now, as usual, we are primarily motivated by a desire to *construct* universal user strategies. The following theorem provides our first seemingly general construction of an $\mathcal{S}$-universal user. Furthermore, it justifies our introduction of a weaker definition of sensing for infinite executions, establishing that every $S \in \mathcal{S}$ can be used by a user strategy that is viable with respect to S for a sensing function that is safe with respect to $\mathcal{U}$ and the server class $\mathcal{S}$.

Theorem 6.23 (On the existence of universal strategies). *Let $G = (\mathcal{E}, R)$ be a compact goal, $\mathcal{U}$ be a set of user strategies and $\mathcal{S}$ a set of server strategies such that the following two conditions hold.*

1. *There is a sensing strategy with sensing function V such that V is weakly safe with respect to $\mathcal{U}$ and $\mathcal{S}$ (and G) and for every $S \in \mathcal{S}$, V is strongly viable with respect to $\mathcal{U}$ and S. Furthermore, the mapping $U \mapsto B$ is computable,[12] where B is the bounding function guaranteed by the strong viability condition.*

2. *The set $\mathcal{U}$ is enumerable.*

Then, there exists an $\mathcal{S}$-universal user strategy (w.r.t. G). Furthermore, if the (strong) viability condition holds perfectly, and for each $U \in \mathcal{U}$, the

---

[12]We view the bounding function B for strong viability as a function of the user strategy U. Indeed, an alternative formulation of the conditions is obtained by replacing the current mapping and enumeration requirement by requiring that the set of pairs (U, B) such that $U \in \mathcal{U}$ and B is the corresponding strong viability bound for V is enumerable.

composition of U with the sensing strategy and the enumeration is also in $\mathcal{U}$, then, for every $S \in \mathcal{S}$, the complexity of the universal user strategy when interacting with S is upper-bounded by the complexity of some fixed strategy in $\mathcal{U}$ (when interacting with S).

Just as in the finite execution setting, if U is $\mathcal{S}$-universal, then every $S \in \mathcal{S}$ must be $\mathcal{U}$-helpful for any $\mathcal{U}$ that contains U. Thus, *we cannot have $\mathcal{S}$-universal users whenever the server class $\mathcal{S}$ contains unhelpful strategies.* And indeed, Condition 1 (which implies weak sensing as per Definition 6.14)[13] implies that every $S \in \mathcal{S}$ is $\mathcal{U}$-helpful. We will see that Condition 1 is *necessary*, cf. Proposition 6.26. (Although strictly speaking, in this connection, we note that Theorem 6.23 can be extended to employ grey-box sensing and private outputs, along the lines of Corollary 2.30.) Note, though, that only weak safety is required in Condition 1. We mention that there is an intuitive benefit in having strong safety, but this benefit is not reflected by the statement of the theorem. We shall return to this issue in Section 6.2.4.

Proof We construct a user strategy, denoted U, that operates as follows. The strategy U enumerates all $U_i \in \mathcal{U}$, and emulates each strategy U_i as long as it (via V) obtains no proof that U_i (coupled with the unknown server $S \in \mathcal{S}$) fails to achieve the goal. Once such a proof is obtained, U moves on to the next potential user strategy (i.e., U_{i+1}). If this "proof system" is sound, then U will never be stuck with a strategy U_i that (coupled with the unknown server $S \in \mathcal{S}$) does not achieve the goal. On the other hand, the completeness of this "proof system" (i.e., the hypothesis that every $S \in \mathcal{S}$ is $\mathcal{U}$-viable) implies that there exists a U_i that (once reached) will never be abandoned.

Needless to say, the foregoing argument depends on our ability to construct an adequate "proof system" (for evaluating the performance of various $U_i \in \mathcal{U}$). Let B_i be the bounding function guaranteed by the strong viability condition of U_i with V; that is, viability guarantees that (with an adequate S) the sensing function V will indicate success after at most $B_i(\mathbf{sz}(\cdot))$ rounds. Thus, a good strategy is to wait for the system to recover (from potential past failures) for $B_i(\mathbf{sz}(\cdot))$ rounds, and abandon the current U_i whenever V indicates failure after this grace period. A more accurate description follows.

Let us first analyze the case where the (strong) viability condition holds perfectly; that is, with probability 1 (rather than with probability 2/3, as in the main part of Definition 6.15). Suppose that U starts emulating U_i at round t_i, and denote the system's state at this round by σ_{t_i}. Then, *for the first $b_i \leftarrow B_i(\mathbf{sz}(\sigma_{t_i}))$ rounds strategy U just emulates U_i, and in any later round $t > t_i + b_i$ strategy U switches to U_{i+1} if and only if $V(\sigma_t) = 0$.*

Claim 6.24. *Suppose that U_i' is strongly and perfectly viable with respect to (U_i, S), and consider $\overline{\sigma}$, a random execution of (E, U, S). Then, if this execution ever emulates U_i, then it never switches to U_{i+1}.*

---

[13] Again, this requires proof, along the lines sketched in Footnote 10.

Proof Let t_i and b_i be as above. Then, by the strong viability condition, for every $t > t_i + b_i$, it holds that $V(\sigma_t) = 1$. ∎

Claim 6.25. *Suppose that (U, S) does not robustly achieve the goal and consider a random execution of (E, U, S). Then, recalling that each V is (weakly) safe (w.r.t. (U_i, S)), this execution emulates each U_i for a finite number of rounds.*

Combining the foregoing two claims with the hypothesis that for every $S \in \mathcal{S}$ there exists a user strategy $U_i \in \mathcal{U}$ and a sensing function V such that V is strongly viable with respect to (U_i, S), it follows that (U, S) robustly achieves the goal.

Proof Let σ_1 be a global state such that a random execution of the system starting at σ_1 fails with positive probability, and let $\overline{\sigma}$ be such an execution (i.e., $R(\overline{\sigma}) = 0$). Let t_i and b_i be as above. Then, by the (weak) safety of V w.r.t. (any) $S \in \mathcal{S}$ (cf., Definition 6.14), for some $t'' > t_i + b_i$ (actually for infinitely many such ts), it holds that $V(\sigma_{t''}) = 0$, which causes U to switch to emulating U_{i+1}. ∎

The above analysis assumes perfect (strong) viability, which may not hold in general. In order to cope with imperfect viability (i.e., a strong viability condition that holds with probability $2/3$) we need to modify our strategy U. Specifically, we will use a "repeated enumeration" of all machines such that each machine appears infinitely many times in the enumeration. Furthermore, for every i and t there exists an n such that U_i appears t times in the first n steps of the enumeration (e.g., use the enumeration $1, 1, 2, 1, 2, 3, 1, 2, 3, 4, \ldots$). Using a modified version of Claim 6.24 that asserts that if the execution starts emulating U_i then it switches to U_{i+1} with probability at most $1/3$ (equiv., stays with U_i forever), we derive the main claim of the theorem (because after finitely many R'-failures, strategy U returns to emulating U_i).

Regarding the furthermore claim, we note that the complexity of U (when interacting with S) is upper-bounded by the maximum complexity of the composition of each of the strategies $U_1, \ldots, U_i$ with the sensing and enumeration strategies, where i is an index such that (U_i, S) robustly achieves the goal. Note that by the additional hypothesis, these composed strategies $U_1', \ldots, U_i'$ are also contained in $\mathcal{U}$. ∎

On the computational complexity of the universal strategy. Note that Theorem 6.23 asserts that, for every server $S \in \mathcal{S}$, the computational complexity of the universal strategy (when interacting with S) is comparable to the computational complexity of some user strategy in $\mathcal{U}$ (when interacting with S). Thus, if $\mathcal{U}$ denotes the class of user strategies that are implementable in probabilistic polynomial time when interacting with any fixed $S \in \mathcal{S}$ (where the polynomial may depend on S), then the universal strategy resides in $\mathcal{U}$. Indeed, this stands in contrast to standard universality results in complexity theory, where the universal machine does not reside in the class for which it is universal.[14] The reason that the universal strategy of Theorem 6.23 escapes this fate is that its complexity is measured with respect to the server that it interacts with, and so it may afford to spend a different amount of time when emulating each of the corresponding user strategies.

Sensing requirements for universal users in infinite executions

Recall that in the finite execution setting, there was a strong connection between universal users and sensing functions: if U was $\mathcal{S}$-universal, then as we saw in Proposition 2.26 (and Proposition 5.12), we could always obtain a *safe and viable* sensing function with U for $\mathcal{S}$. This yielded a general equivalence between our notions of sensing and universal users, which was rather useful to us, e.g., in identifying the precise power of universal users for computational goals in Sections 3.3 and 5.5. In light of this context, it is natural to wonder if, analogously, we can obtain a sensing function from a universal user for infinite executions. While the answer turns out to be affirmative, we warn the reader in advance that the resulting construction turns out to be rather disappointing.

Proposition 6.26 (Universal strategies have trivial sensing strategies). *If U is $\mathcal{S}$-universal, then there exists a grey-box sensing function V such that V is strongly viable with respect to $(U, \mathcal{S})$ and (weakly) safe with respect to $\mathcal{U}$ and $\mathcal{S}$.*

Indeed, as its title indicates, the sensing strategy provided by the proof of Proposition 6.26 is rather trivial (and is based on the hypothesis that for every $S \in \mathcal{S}$ it holds that (U, S) achieves the goal).[15] Still, Proposition 6.26 may be regarded as meaningful as a *necessary condition for the design of $\mathcal{S}$-universal users*; that is, *we must be able to design a sensing strategy that is both weakly safe and viable for the class of servers $\mathcal{S}$.*

Proof Let V be the function that is identically 1 if the user strategy is U and identically 0 otherwise, and consider any $S \in \mathcal{S}$. Then, viability of V (under any version) holds trivially. The weak version of safety (i.e., Definition 6.14) also holds vacuously for V (w.r.t. (U, S)), because for every $E \in \mathcal{E}$ a random execution of (E, U, S) starting at any state σ_1 is successful with probability 1. ∎

Another interpretation of Proposition 6.26 is that the availability of our weakened notion of sensing doesn't say much at all, in contrast to the notion

---

[14]Note that completeness results avoid this fate by padding the instances.

[15]Interestingly, strong safety does not seem to follow because of the discrepancy between the bounded nature of the strong safety condition and the unbounded nature of the definition of achieving a goal. This discrepancy is eliminated in Section 6.2.4.

of sensing required for finite executions. Or, if we prefer to take an optimistic point of view, this interpretation suggests that universal users in infinite executions may be much easier to construct. The optimistic view turns out to be essentially correct, as we'll see in Chapter 7.

6.2.2 Sensing in the basic universal setting for infinite executions

Recall that we framed the problem of communication in the absence of a common language (in finite executions) as the problem of achieving a fixed goal of communication with the class of all helpful servers for that goal— the existence of a user strategy that achieved the goal with the server's help guaranteed that the only issue was how to communicate effectively with the server. We are likewise interested in considering this "basic universal setting" for goals of communication in infinite executions, by which we of course mean we are interested in designing user strategies that achieve a fixed goal with the class of all servers that are helpful for that goal, where we now mean helpfulness in the infinite execution sense.

Now, Proposition 6.26 and Theorem 6.23 relate universality with sensing. Specifically, Proposition 6.26 asserts that, if U is S-universal, then there is a (grey-box) sensing strategy such that the associated sensing function V is weakly S-safe (and, actually, safe with all user strategies) and every $S \in \mathcal{S}$ is strongly viable with U. On the other hand, Theorem 6.23 (essentially) asserts that, if V is weakly safe for $\mathcal{S}$ and $\mathcal{U}$, and $\mathcal{U}$-viable with every $S \in \mathcal{S}$, then there exists an S-universal user strategy. Indeed, both S-universality and safe and viable sensing with $\mathcal{S}$ become harder to achieve when $\mathcal{S}$ becomes more rich (equiv., are easier to achieve when $\mathcal{S}$ is restricted, of course, as long as it contains only helpful servers), and we note that the class of all helpful servers for a goal is the richest class for which sensing could possibly be feasible, and therefore also the *hardest*.

Therefore, the actual issue in the basic universal setting is again moving from helpfulness to *viability* for some suitable sensing strategy. That is, the actual issue is transforming user strategies that witness the helpfulness of some class of servers $\mathcal{S}$ into user strategies that witness viability with respect to sensing that is safe for the same class of servers $\mathcal{S}$. (Recall that we discussed such issues at length for the finite execution setting in Section 4.2.2.) A simple case when such a transformation is possible (and, in fact, is straightforward) is presented next.

Definition 6.27 (Goals that allow trivial sensing). We say that a compact goal $G = (\mathcal{E}, R)$ *allows trivial sensing* if, at each round, the corresponding temporal decision function R' evaluates to either 0 or 1, and the environment notifies the user of the current R'-value; that is, for every $E \in \mathcal{E}$ and every $\sigma \in \Omega$, it holds that the first bit of $E(\sigma)^{(e,u)}$ equals $R'(\sigma)$.

We note that compact goals that allow $\perp$-runs of a priori bounded length (as in Footnote 3) can be converted to (functionally equivalent) compact goals that allow no $\perp$-values (w.r.t. R').[16]

By letting V output the first bit it receives from the environment (i.e., $V(\sigma)$ equals the first bit of $\sigma^{(\mathrm{e},\mathrm{u})}$), we obtain a sensing strategy that is strongly safe with respect to any pair (U, S) and is strongly viable with respect to any (U, S) that robustly achieves the goal. Thus, we obtain:

Proposition 6.28 (Trivial sensing). *Let $G = (\mathcal{E}, R)$ be a compact goal that allows trivial sensing, and $\mathcal{U}$ be a class of users. If a server strategy S is $\mathcal{U}$-helpful w.r.t. G, then there is a sensing function V such that the strategy S is strongly viable for V w.r.t. $\mathcal{U}$ and, for every class of server strategies $\mathcal{S}$, V is strongly safe with $\mathcal{U}$ and S for G.*

By combining Proposition 6.28 and Theorem 6.23, we obtain

Theorem 6.29 (Trivial sensing implies universality). *Let G and $\mathcal{U}$ be as in Proposition 6.28, and suppose that $\mathcal{U}$ is enumerable and that $\mathcal{S}$ is a class of server strategies that are $\mathcal{U}$-helpful w.r.t. G. Then, there exists an $\mathcal{S}$-universal user strategy (w.r.t. G). Furthermore, for every $S \in \mathcal{S}$, the complexity of the universal user strategy is upper-bounded by the complexity of some fixed strategy in $\mathcal{U}$.*

Proof The sensing function V that arises from Definition 6.27 satisfies Condition 1 of Theorem 6.23 (i.e., V is fixed, $B = 1$, and the viability and safety conditions hold perfectly and in a very strong sense). Condition 2 of Theorem 6.23 holds by the extra hypothesis of the current theorem, which now follows by applying Theorem 6.23. ■

A variant on allowing trivial sensing. One natural case that essentially fits Definition 6.27 is that of a "transparent goal" as considered in Section 3.2.1, which intuitively corresponds to the case that the user sees the entire state of the environment. Formally, a *transparent goal* was defined as an environment that communicates its current state to the user (at the end of each round). Thus, ability to compute the corresponding temporal decision function R' puts us in the situation of a goal that allows trivial sensing. Consequently, analogously to Theorem 6.29 (and Theorem 3.7 for finite executions), we conclude that

---

[16]That is, for R' as in Definition 6.6, we assume here the existence of a function $B :$ $\mathbb{N} \to \mathbb{N}$ such that $R(\overline{\sigma}) = 1$ only if for every $t > 0$ there exists $t' \in [t+1, t + B(\mathbf{sz}(\sigma_1))]$ such that $R'(\sigma_{t'}) \neq \perp$. In such a case, the goal can be modified as follows. The states of the modified environment will consist of pairs $(\sigma^{(\mathrm{e})}, i)$ such that $\sigma^{(\mathrm{e})}$ is the state of the original environment and i indicates the number of successive $\perp$-values (w.r.t. R') that preceded the current state. Thus, the index i is incremented if $R'(\sigma^{(\mathrm{e})}) = \perp$ and is reset to 0 otherwise. The modified temporal decision function evaluates to 1 on input $(\sigma^{(\mathrm{e})}, i)$ if and only if either $R'(\sigma^{(\mathrm{e})}) = 1$ or $i < B(\mathbf{sz}(\sigma))$ and $R'(\sigma^{(\mathrm{e})}) = \perp$.

Theorem 6.30 (Transparent goal implies universality). *Let G be a compact, transparent goal. Suppose that $\mathcal{U}$ is an enumerable class of user strategies and that $\mathcal{S}$ is a class of server strategies that are $\mathcal{U}$-helpful w.r.t. G. Then, there exists an $\mathcal{S}$-universal user strategy (w.r.t. G). Furthermore, for every $S \in \mathcal{S}$, the complexity of the universal user strategy is upper-bounded by the complexity of some fixed strategy in $\mathcal{U}$ and the complexity of the temporal decision function R'.*

Beyond trivial sensing. Going beyond goals that allow trivial sensing, we note that a viable and safe sensing function may arise from the interaction between the user and the server (and without any feedback from the environment). An instructive example of such a case, first discussed back in Section 1.4.2, is reformulated next using the present terminology.

Example 6.31 (Solving computational problems, revised). Continuing Example 6.4, we consider a multi-session goal that refers to a decision problem, D_0. In each session, the environment non-deterministically selects a string and sends it to the user, which interacts with the server for several rounds, while signaling to the environment that the session is still in progress. At some point, the user terminates the session by sending an adequate indication to the environment, along with a bit that is supposed to indicate whether the initial string is in D_0, and the referee just checks whether or not this bit value is correct. Indeed, a simple two-round interaction with a server that decides D_0 yields a user-server pair that achieves this goal, where the user strategy amounts to forwarding messages between the environment and the server. But what happens if a probabilistic polynomial time user can interact with a server that decides D, where D is an arbitrary decision problem that is computationally equivalent to D_0? That is, we say that a server is a D-*solver* if it answers each user message z with a bit indicating whether or not $z \in D$, and we ask whether we can efficiently solve D_0 when interacting with a D-solver for an arbitrary D that is computationally equivalent to D_0.

- Clearly, for every $D \in \mathcal{D}$, any D-solver is $\mathcal{U}$-helpful, where $\mathcal{D}$ denotes the class of decision problems that are computationally equivalent to D_0, and $\mathcal{U}$ denotes the class of probabilistic polynomial time user strategies (strategies that in each session run for a total time that is upper-bounded by a polynomial in the length of the initial message obtained from the environment).[17] Specifically, such a user may employ some polynomial time reduction of D_0 to D.

- More interestingly, as shown implicitly in Section 3.3, if D_0 has a program checker [33], then the program checker provides a sensing strategy that is is safe with $\mathcal{F}$ and $\mathcal{U}$ for G and which is strongly viable for $\mathcal{U}$ with

---

[17]Indeed, our definition of $\mathcal{U}$ restricts both the complexity of the user strategy as a function and the number of rounds in which the user may participate in any session.

the D-solver for every $D \in \mathcal{D}$, where $\mathcal{F}$ is the class of all memoryless strategies[18] and $\mathcal{U}$ is as above.

The argument amounts to constructing an adequate user strategy U for the D-solver that attempts to answer the initial message obtained from the environment by forwarding it to the server; our (grey-box, or equivalently, uniformly viable) sensing strategy verifies the correctness of the answer by ensuring that the user runs the program checker for D_0. Specifically, V checks that U emulates the composition of the program checker with a potential program for D_0 by using the hypothetical D-solver via a reduction (of D_0 to D) that, in particular, maintains no state across invocations (on instances of D_0), and then the verdict of the program checker determines the verdict of V. Note that this V is therefore strongly viable with respect to $\mathcal{U}$ and the D-solver, and safe with respect to $\mathcal{F}$ (and $\mathcal{U}$), where the crucial point is that the strategies in $\mathcal{F}$ are memoryless, and so a reduction interacting with such a strategy is also memoryless. Furthermore, the bound in the strong viability condition is the constant 1, since a solver is correct in each round.

Recall that program checkers exist for PSPACE-complete and EXP-complete problems (cf. [103, 134] and [14], respectively).[19]

By invoking Theorem 6.23, we obtain an $\mathcal{S}$-universal user strategy, where $\mathcal{S}$ denotes the class of all D-solvers for $D \in \mathcal{D}$. Furthermore, for every $S \in \mathcal{S}$, when interacting with S this universal strategy can be implemented in probabilistic polynomial time.

Example 6.31 provides a rather generic class of goals that have $\mathcal{S}$-universal user strategies, where $\mathcal{S}$ is a class of "adequate solvers" (and furthermore these universal strategies are efficient). This class of multi-session goals refers to solving computational problems that have program checkers, and universality holds with respect to the class of servers that solve all computationally equivalent problems. We stress that the environment strategies underlying these goals provide no feedback to the user, which indeed stands in sharp contrast to the goals that allow trivial sensing (of Definition 6.27).

We mention that the class of "adequate solvers" $\mathcal{S}$ considered in Example 6.31 is actually a strict subset of the class of all $\mathcal{U}$-helpful servers, where $\mathcal{U}$ is as in Example 6.31. In the context of Section 3.3, we actually established a stronger result, which can be reformulated as referring to the class of all servers that are helpful in a strong sense that refers to achieving the goal with a bounded number of errors. (Recall that a general helpful server may cause a finite number of sessions to fail, whereas the aforementioned

---

[18]Recall that strategies map pairs consisting of the current local state and the incoming messages to pairs consisting of an updated local state and outgoing messages. In the case of memoryless strategies there is no local state (or, equivalently, the local state is fixed).

[19]See also [15].

solvers do allow achieving the goal without making any errors.) For details, see Section 6.2.4.

6.2.3   Universality without feedback

While Theorem 6.29 and Example 6.31 provide universal users based on sensing functions that rely on feedback either from the environment or from the server (respectively), we note that universality may exist in a meaningful way also without any feedback—below, we identify a class of goals for which this is possible. That universality is possible without feedback is a rather striking fact when considered in the context of Proposition 2.26 on the necessity of sensing for goals in finite executions (and likewise Proposition 5.12 for other classes of users): it shows that *the infinite execution setting is fundamentally different from the finite execution setting.*

Example 6.32 (Multi-session "forgiving" communication goals). For any function $f : \{0,1\}^* \rightarrow \{0,1\}^*$, we consider the multi-session goal in which each session consists of the environment sending a message, denoted x, to the user and expecting to obtain from the server the message $f(x)$. That is, the environment starts each session by non-deterministically selecting some string, x, and sending x to the user, and the session ends when the user notifies the environment so. The session is considered successful if during it, the environment has obtained from the server the message $f(x)$. (Indeed, this notion of success is forgiving in the sense that it only requires that a specific message arrived during the session, and does not require that other messages did not arrive during the same session.) The entire execution is considered successful if at most a finite number of sessions are not successful. Note that this goal is non-trivial (i.e., it cannot be achieved when using a server that does nothing), and yet it can be achieved by some coordinated user-server pairs (e.g., a user that just forwards x to the server coupled with a server that applies f to the message it receives and forwards the result to the environment).

Proposition 6.33 (A universal strategy for Example 6.32). *Let $G = (\mathcal{E}, R)$ be a goal as in Example 6.32, and $\mathcal{U}$ an arbitrary enumerable class of user strategies. Let $\mathcal{S}$ be a class of server strategies such that for every $S \in \mathcal{S}$ there exists $U \in \mathcal{U}$ and an integer n such that in any execution of (U, S), starting at any state, all sessions, with the possible exception of the first n ones, succeed. Then, there exists an $\mathcal{S}$-universal user strategy for G.*

Note that the hypothesis regarding $\mathcal{S}$ is stronger than requiring that every server in $\mathcal{S}$ be $\mathcal{U}$-helpful (which only means that for some $U \in \mathcal{U}$ the pair (U, S) robustly achieves the goal).[20]

---

[20]This only means that for every $S \in \mathcal{S}$ there exists $U \in \mathcal{U}$ such that, in any execution of (U, S) starting at any state, there exists an integer n such that all sessions, with the possible exception of the first n ones, succeed. In the hypothesis of Proposition 6.33, the

Proof For simplicity, we first assume that $n = 0$ (for all $S \in \mathcal{S}$). In this case, the universal strategy, denoted U, will emulate in each session a growing number of possible user strategies, and will notify the environment that the session is completed only after completing all these emulations. We stress that in all these emulations we relay messages between the emulated user and the server, but we communicate with the environment only at the beginning and end of each session. Specifically, in the ith session, U emulates the first i strategies in the enumeration, denoted $U_1, \ldots, U_i$. For every $j = 1, \ldots, i$, we start the emulation of U_j by feeding U_j with the initial message obtained from the environment in the current (i.e., ith) session (as if this is the first session). (Thus, in the ith real session we only emulate the first session of each of the U_js.) When emulating U_j, for $j < i$, we use U_j's notification (to the environment) that the session is over in order to switch to the emulation of the next strategy (i.e., U_{j+1}). When the emulation of U_i is completed (i.e., when U_i notifies the environment that the session is over), we notify the environment that the session is over.

Suppose that U interacts with the server $S \in \mathcal{S}$, and let j denote the index of a user strategy U_j such that (U_j, S) achieves the goal (in the strong sense postulated in the hypothesis). Then, for every $i \geq j$, considering the time $t_{i,j}$ in the ith session in which we start emulating U_j, we note that the subsequent execution with S yields the adequate server message to the environment, regardless of the state in which S was at time $t_{i,j}$. Thus, with the possible exception of the first $j - 1$ sessions, the pair (U, S) will be successful in all sessions, and hence (U, S) robustly achieves the goal.

We now turn to the general case, where n may not be zero (and may depend on $S \in \mathcal{S}$). In this case, we modify our emulation such that in the ith real session we emulate each of the user strategies (i.e., $U_1, \ldots, U_i$) for i sessions (from each U_j's point of view), where we use the message we received in the ith real session as the message sent to U_j in each of the emulated sessions. That is, let x_i denote the message that U receives from the environment at the beginning of the ith real session. Then, for $j = 1, \ldots, i$, the modified strategy U emulates i sessions of the interaction between U_j and the server (but, as in the case $n = 0$, does not notify the environment of the end of the current session before all emulations are completed). Each of these i emulated sessions (in which U_j is used) starts with feeding U_j the message x_i (as if this were the message sent by the environment in the currently emulated session).

For the modified strategy U and every $S \in \mathcal{S}$, with the possible exception of the first $\max(j - 1, n)$ sessions, the pair (U, S) will be successful in all sessions, where j is as before and n is the bound guaranteed for S. ∎

Digest. Proposition 6.33 asserts that there exist universal user strategies for (non-trivial) goals in which no feedback whatsoever is provided to the user.

---

order of quantification is reversed (from "for every execution there exists an n" to "there exists an n that fits all executions").

These goals, however, are very forgiving of failures; that is, they only require that during each session some success occurs, and they do not require that there are no failures during the same session. Hence, we have seen three types of universal users. The first type exist for goals that allow trivial sensing (as in Definition 6.27), the second type rely on sensing through interaction with the server (as in Example 6.31), and the third type exists for multi-session goals that allow failures in each session (see Proposition 6.33).

6.2.4 Quantification of errors and delays

In this section we present two refined versions of Theorem 6.23. The first one is merely a quantified version of the original, where the quantification is on the number of errors, which relies on the quality of the sensing functions in use. The second version introduces a more flexible universal user, which uses a relaxed notion of viability in which only the total number of negative indications (rather than the length of the time interval in which they occur) is bounded.

A quantified version (bounding the number of errors)

As stated in Section 6.2.1, the universal user strategy asserted in Theorem 6.23 does not benefit from the potential *strong safety* of sensing functions. The intuitive benefit in such sensing functions is that they may allow the universal strategy to switch earlier from a bad user strategy, thus incurring fewer errors. Indeed, this calls for a more refined measure of achieving goals, presented next.

Definition 6.34 (Achieving goals (Definition 6.10), refined). Let $G = (\mathcal{E}, R)$ be a compact goal and $R' : \Omega \rightarrow \{0, 1, \bot\}$ be as in Definition 6.6. For $B : \mathbb{N} \rightarrow \mathbb{N}$, we say that a pair of user-server strategies, (U, S), *achieves the goal G with B errors* if, for every $E \in \mathcal{E}$, a random execution $\overline{\sigma} = (\sigma_1, \sigma_2, \ldots)$ of the system (E, U, S) satisfies the following two conditions:

1. The expected cardinality of $\{t \in \mathbb{N} : R'(\sigma_t) = 0\}$ is at most $b \overset{\text{def}}{=} B(\mathbf{sz}(\sigma_1))$.

2. The expected cardinality of $\{t \in \mathbb{N} : (\forall t' \in [t, t+b]) \, R'(\sigma_{t'}) = \bot\}$ is at most b.

When B is understood from the context, we say that the execution $\overline{\sigma}$ contains an *error in round t* if either $R'(\sigma_t) = 0$ or for every $t' \in [t, t + B(\mathbf{sz}(\sigma_1))]$ it holds that $R'(\sigma_{t'}) = \bot$. If $\overline{\sigma}$ contains at most $B(\mathbf{sz}(\sigma_1))$ errors, then we write $R_B(\overline{\sigma}) = 1$.

Note that Definition 6.34 strengthens Definition 6.10, which (combined with Definition 6.6) only requires conditions analogous to the above where B may depend on the execution $(\sigma_1, \sigma_2, \ldots)$. Intuitively, whereas Definition 6.10

only requires that the number of errors in a random execution be finite, Definition 6.34 requires a bound on the number of errors such that this bound holds uniformly over all executions (as a function of the size of the initial state). A similar modification should be applied to the definition of robustly achieving a goal. Lastly, we refine the definition of strong sensing functions (i.e., Definition 6.16), by replacing all references to R by references to R_B (and specifying the relevant bound B in the terminology). (We also seize the opportunity to replace the fixed error-probability bound of $1/3$ by a general bound, denoted ϵ.)

Definition 6.35 (Strong sensing (Definition 6.16), refined). Let $G = (\mathcal{E}, R)$, S, U and V be as in Definition 6.16. For $B : \mathbb{N} \to \mathbb{N}$ and $\epsilon : \mathbb{N} \to [0, 1/3]$, we say that V is (B, ϵ)-*strongly safe* with respect to (U, S) (and G) if, for every $E \in \mathcal{E}$ and every $\sigma_1 \in \Omega$, the following conditions hold.

1. If $R'(\sigma_1) = 0$, then, with probability at least $1 - \epsilon(\mathbf{sz}(\sigma_1))$, either $R_B(\overline{\sigma}) = 1$ or for some $t \leq B(\mathbf{sz}(\sigma_1))$ it holds that $V(\sigma_t) = 0$, where $\overline{\sigma} = (\sigma_1, \sigma_2, \dots,)$ denotes a random execution of the system (E, U, S).

2. If for every $i \in [B(\mathbf{sz}(\sigma_1))]$ it holds that $R'(\sigma_i) = \perp$, then, with probability at least $1 - \epsilon(\mathbf{sz}(\sigma_1))$, either $R_B(\overline{\sigma}) = 1$ or for some $t \in [B(\mathbf{sz}(\sigma_1)) + 1, 2B(\mathbf{sz}(\sigma_1))]$ it holds that $V(\sigma_t) = 0$, where here the probability refers to the execution suffix $(\sigma_{t+1}, \sigma_{t+2}, \dots,)$.

Analogously, V is (B, ϵ)-*strongly viable* with respect to (U, S) if, for every $E \in \mathcal{E}$ and every $\sigma_1 \in \Omega$, with probability at least $1 - \epsilon(\mathbf{sz}(\sigma_1))$, for every $t \geq B(\mathbf{sz}(\sigma_1))$ it holds that $V(\sigma_t) = 1$. We say that strong viability (resp., safety) holds *perfectly* if $\epsilon \equiv 0$ holds in the viability (resp., safety) condition, and in such a case we say that V is B-*strongly viable* (resp., B-*strongly safe*).

Note that the existence of a B-strongly safe and viable sensing function w.r.t. (U, S) (as in Definition 6.34) implies that (U, S) robustly achieves the goal with $2B$ errors (as in Definition 6.35). Intuitively, B errors result from the delay of the viability condition, and another B from the safety condition (i.e., the allowance to fail sensing if $R_B = 1$). If the sensing function is only $(B, 1/3)$-strongly safe and viable, then (U, S) robustly achieves the goal with $O(B)$ errors.

We comment that the foregoing definitions are simplified versions of more appropriate definitions that we only sketch here. For starters, note that the bounding function B is used in Definition 6.34 in three different roles, which may be separated: (1) bounding the expected number of errors of Type 1 (in Item 1), (2) bounding the expected number of errors of Type 2 (in Item 2), and (3) determining the length of $\perp$-runs that is considered an error of Type 3. Thus, R_B should be replaced by R_{B_1, B_2, B_3}, where B_1, B_2, B_3 are the three separated bounding functions. In Definition 6.35, the bounding function B is used in six different roles: three roles are explicit in the two items analogous to the roles in Definition 6.34 and three are implicit in the use of R_B (which should be replaced by R_{B_1,B_2,B_3}). Separating all these bounding functions is conceptually right, since the various quantities are fundamentally different. Still we refrained from doing so for the sake of simplicity.[21]

With the foregoing definitions in place, we are ready to present a refined version of Theorem 6.23. The universal strategy postulated next achieves the goal with a bounded number of errors, where the bound depends on the bounds provided for the strong sensing functions.

Theorem 6.36 (Universal strategies (Theorem 6.23), revisited). *Let* $G = (\mathcal{E}, R)$ *be a compact goal,* $\mathcal{U}$ *be an* enumerable *set of user strategies,* $\mathcal{S}$ *be a set of server strategies, and* $\epsilon : \mathbb{N} \to [0, 1/3]$ *such that the following two conditions hold:*

1. *There exists a sensing strategy* V *such that for every* $U \in \mathcal{U}$, *there is an associated bounding function* B *such that* V *is* (B, ϵ)-*strongly safe with* U *and* $\mathcal{S}$ *for* G, *and for every* $S \in \mathcal{S}$ *there exists a user strategy* $U \in \mathcal{U}$ *such that for the bounding function* B *associated with* U, V *is* (B, ϵ)-*strongly viable with respect to* (U, S). *Furthermore, the mapping* $U \mapsto B$ *is computable.*

   Let $\mathcal{B}$ *denote the set of bounds that appear in the image of this mapping; that is,* $\mathcal{B} = \{B_i : i \in \mathbb{N}\}$, *where* B_i *is the bound associated with the* ith *user strategy in* $\mathcal{U}$.

2. *One of the following two conditions hold.*

   (a) *The (strong) viability condition holds perfectly (i.e.,* $\epsilon \equiv 0$).

   (b) *For every* i, *it holds that* $B_{i+1} < B_i/2\epsilon$.

Then, there exists an $\mathcal{S}$-*universal user strategy* U *such that for every* $S \in \mathcal{S}$ *there exists* $B \in \mathcal{B}$ *such that* (U, S) *robustly achieves the goal* G *with* $O(B)$ *errors, where the constant in the* O-*notation depends on* S. *Furthermore, if the (strong) viability condition holds perfectly and the composition of any* $U \in \mathcal{U}$ *with the sensing and enumeration strategies is also contained in* $\mathcal{U}$, *then, for every* $S \in \mathcal{S}$, *the complexity of* U *is upper-bounded by the complexity of some fixed strategy in* $\mathcal{U}$.

Proof Following the proof of Theorem 6.23, we first consider the case in which *both* the (strong) viability and safety conditions hold perfectly; that is, $\epsilon \equiv 0$ in (both the viability and safety conditions of) Definition 6.35. Recall that the universal user strategy U enumerates all $U_i \in \mathcal{U}$, and consider the corresponding bounding function B_i, where V is B_i-strongly safe (w.r.t. U_i and $\mathcal{S}$). Specifically, suppose that U starts emulating U_i at round t_i, and denote the system's state at this round by σ_{t_i}. Then, *for the first* $b_i \leftarrow$

---

[21]Likewise, it is conceptually correct to replace R_B (and actually also R) in Definition 6.35 (resp., Definition 6.16) by a stricter condition that requires no errors at all after time B. Again, this was avoided only for the sake of simplicity.

$B_i(\mathbf{sz}(\sigma_{t_i}))$ rounds, strategy U just emulates U_i, and in any later round $t >$ $t_i + b_i$ strategy U switches to U_{i+1} if and only if $V(\sigma_t) = 0$.

Note that Claims 6.24 and 6.25 remain valid, since we maintained the construction of U. However, we seek a stronger version of Claim 6.25. Let us first state the analogue of Claim 6.24.

Claim 6.37. *Suppose that V is B_i-strongly viable and safe with respect to (U_i, S), and consider a random execution of (E, U, S). Then, if this execution ever emulates U_i, then it never switches to U_{i+1}. Furthermore, in this case, for t_i and b_i as above, it holds that the number of errors (w.r.t. the bound b_i) occurring after round t_i is at most $2b_i$.*

The furthermore part follows by observing that B_i-strong viability implies that for every $t \geq t_i + b_i$ it holds that $V(\sigma_t) = 1$, whereas B_i-strong safety implies that the number of errors (w.r.t. the bound b_i) occurring after round $t_i + b_i$ is at most b_i (because otherwise R_{B_i} evaluates to 0, and so $V(\sigma_t) = 0$ must hold for some $t > t' > t_i + b_i$, where t' is some time in which such a fault actually occurs).

Claim 6.38. *Let $i \geq 1$ and suppose that (U, S) does not robustly achieve the goal with $4\sum_{j \in [i]} B_j$ errors. Consider a random execution of (E, U, S), and, for $j \in \{i, i+1\}$, let t_j denote the round in which U started emulating U_j. Then, recalling that for each j, V is B_j-strongly safe (w.r.t. (U_j, S)), the expected number of errors (w.r.t. the bound B_i) that occur between round t_i and round t_{i+1} is at most $4b_i$ where $b_i \overset{\text{def}}{=} B_i(\mathbf{sz}(\sigma_1))$. In particular,*

1. *The expected cardinality of $\{t \in [t_i, t_{i+1}] : R'(\sigma_t) = 0\}$ is at most $4b_i$.*

2. *The expected cardinality of $\{t \in [t_i, t_{i+1}] : (\forall t' \in [t, t+b_i]) R'(\sigma_{t'}) = \bot\}$ is at most $4b_i$.*

Combining the foregoing two claims with the hypothesis that there is a sensing strategy V such that for every $S \in \mathcal{S}$ there exists a user strategy $U_i \in \mathcal{U}$ such that V is B_i-strongly viable and safe with respect to (U_i, S), it follows that (U_i, S) robustly achieves the goal with B errors, where $B(s) = 2B_i(s) + 4\sum_{j \in [i-1]} B_j(s)$. Note that indeed $B(s) = O(B_j(s))$ for some $j \leq i$, where the constant in the O-notation depends on i (and hence on S).

Proof We proceed by induction on i (using a vacuous base case of $i = 0$). Let σ_1 be a global state such that the expected number of errors produced by a random execution of the system starting at σ_1 exceeds $b = 4\sum_{j \in [i]} B_j(\mathbf{sz}(\sigma_1))$ (i.e., either $|\{t \in \mathbb{N} : R'(\sigma_t) = 0\}| > b$ or $|\{t \in \mathbb{N} : (\forall t' \in [t, t+b]) R'(\sigma_{t'}) = \bot\}| > b$). By the induction hypothesis, the expected number of errors that occur before round t_i is at most $4\sum_{j \in [i-1]} B_j(\mathbf{sz}(\sigma_1))$, and some errors (w.r.t. the bound b_i) occur after round $t_i + b_i$, where $b_i = B_i(\mathbf{sz}(\sigma_1))$. That is, there exists $t > t_i + b_i$ such that either $R'(\sigma_t) = 0$ or for every $t' \in [t, t+b_i]$ it holds that $R'(\sigma_{t'}) = \bot$. In the first case the first

(B_i-strong) safety condition (w.r.t. $S \in \mathcal{S}$) implies that for some $t'' \in [t, t+b_i]$ it holds that $V(\sigma_{t''}) = 0$, whereas in the second case the second (B_i-strong) safety condition implies that for some $t'' \in [t' + 1, t' + b_i] \subset [t + 1, t + 2b_i]$ it holds that $V(\sigma_{t''}) = 0$. In both cases, the fact that $V(\sigma_{t''}) = 0$ (for $t'' > t_i + b_i$) causes U to switch to emulating U_{i+1} at round $t'' + 1$ (if not before). Hence, if $t > t_i + b_i$ is set to the first round that contains an error (following round $t_i + b_i$), then the number of errors (w.r.t. the bound b_i) during the emulation of U_i is at most $b_i + (t'' - t) \leq 3b_i$. The claim follows. ∎

The foregoing analysis also applies when the (strong) safety condition holds only with probability $1 - \epsilon$, where $\epsilon = \epsilon(\mathbf{sz}(\sigma_1))$, because there are many opportunities to switch from U_i, and each one is taken with probability at least $1 - \epsilon$. More precisely, except for the first $b_i + 4\sum_{j \in [i-1]} B_j(\mathbf{sz}(\sigma_1))$ errors, each error yields an opportunity to switch from U_i soon, and each such opportunity is accounted for by at most $2b_i$ errors. Thus, in addition to the $3b_i$ errors that occur when we have perfectly strong safety, we may incur $j \cdot 2b_i$ additional errors with probability at most ϵ^j, which gives an expected number of additional errors that is upper-bounded by $\sum_{j \in \mathbb{N}} \epsilon^j \cdot 2b_i j < 2b_i$. Hence, Claim 6.38 holds also in the general case, when replacing $4\sum_{j \in [i]} B_j$ by $6\sum_{j \in [i]} B_j$.

In contrast, in order to cope with imperfect (strong) viability (i.e., a strong viability condition that holds with probability $1 - \epsilon$), we need to modify our strategy U. We use the same modification (i.e., "repeated enumeration") as at the end of the proof of Theorem 6.23. Since each additional repetition occurs with probability at most ϵ, the expected number of failures will remain bounded. Specifically, if U_i is repeated $r \geq 1$ additional times, then the expected number of errors is at most $\sum_{j \in [i+r]} 6B_j$, and so the expected number of errors is bounded by $\sum_{r \geq 0} \epsilon^r \cdot \sum_{j \in [i+r]} 6B_j$. Using the hypothesis $B_{j+1} < (2\epsilon)^{-1} \cdot B_j$, which implies $B_{i+r} < (2\epsilon)^{-r} \cdot B_i$, we upper-bound this sum by $12\sum_{j \in [i]} B_j$, and the main claim follows.

Regarding the furthermore claim, we note that the complexity of U is upper bounded by the maximum complexity of the composed strategies $U'_1, \ldots, U'_i$, where i is an index such that (U_i, S) robustly achieves the goal, and each U'_j is obtained by composing U_j with the strategies for sensing and enumeration. Indeed, by the extra hypothesis, each U'_j is also a member of $\mathcal{U}$, as needed. ∎

Theorem 6.36 versus Theorem 6.23. Indeed, Theorem 6.36 utilizes strongly safe sensing functions, whereas Theorem 6.23 only utilizes weakly safe sensing functions, but the conclusion of Theorem 6.36 is much more appealing: Theorem 6.36 provides an absolute (in terms of state size) upper bound on the number of errors incurred by the universal strategy, whereas

Theorem 6.23 only asserts that each infinite execution of the universal strategy incurs finitely many errors. We stress that a user strategy that incurs (significantly) fewer errors should be preferred to one that incurs more errors. This is demonstrated next.

Example 6.39 (Goals with delayed feedback). Consider a goal G and classes of users and servers as in Theorem 6.36, and suppose that B is a class of moderately growing functions (e.g., constant functions or polynomials). Suppose that, for some huge function $\Delta : \mathbb{N} \to \mathbb{N}$ (e.g., an exponential function), for every execution $\bar{\sigma}$ and every $t \in \mathbb{N}$, the user can obtain $R'(\sigma_t)$ at round $t + \Delta(\mathbf{sz}(\sigma_t))$. This implies a very simple universal strategy via a simple adaptation of the principles underlying the proof of Theorem 6.29, but this strategy may incur $\Theta(\Delta)$ errors. In contrast, recall that the universal strategy provided by Theorem 6.36 incurs $O(B)$ errors, for some $B \in \mathcal{B}$.

Refined helpfulness. The refined (or rather quantified) notion of achieving a goal suggests a natural refinement of the notion of helpful servers. This refinement is actually a restriction of the class of helpful servers, obtained by upper-bounding the number of errors caused by the server (when helping an adequate user). That is, for any bounding function $B : \mathbb{N} \to \mathbb{N}$, we may consider servers S that are not only $\mathcal{U}$-helpful but can rather be coupled with some $U \in \mathcal{U}$ such that (U, S) robustly achieves the goal with B errors. We say that such servers are $\mathcal{U}$-*helpful with B errors.*

Using relaxed viability

The notion of helpfulness with an explicitly bounded number of errors is not compatible with our current notion of bounded viability (cf. Definition 6.35). The point is that B-strong viability allows failure indications to occur only till time B, whereas helpfulness with B errors refers to the total number of errors. Wishing to utilize such helpful servers, we relax the notion of strong viability accordingly.

Definition 6.40 (A relaxed notion of strong viability). Let $G = (\mathcal{E}, R)$, S, U and V be as in Definition 6.16. For $B : \mathbb{N} \to \mathbb{N}$ and $\epsilon : \mathbb{N} \to [0, 1/3]$, we say that V is (B, ϵ)-*viable* with respect to (U, S) (and G) if, for every $E \in \mathcal{E}$ and every $\sigma_1 \in \Omega$, with probability at least $1 - \epsilon(\mathbf{sz}(\sigma_1))$, the cardinality of $\{t \in \mathbb{N} : V(\sigma_t) = 0\}$ is at most $B(\mathbf{sz}(\sigma_1))$. If $\epsilon \equiv 0$, the we say that V is B-*viable.*

Indeed, while helpfulness with B errors refers to the expected number of errors, the notion of $(B, \cdot)$-viability refers to the probability that the number of failure indications exceeds B. Needless to say, the latter bound is easily related to an upper bound on the expected number of failures.

Theorem 6.41 (Theorem 6.36, revisited). *Let $G = (\mathcal{E}, R)$, $\mathcal{U}$, $\mathcal{S}$, V, ϵ and $\mathcal{B}$ be as in Theorem 6.36, except that the sensing function V is (B_i, ϵ)-viable* with U_i (as per Definition 6.40) rather than (B_i, ϵ)-strongly viable (as per the viability condition in Definition 6.35). Then, there exists an $\mathcal{S}$-universal user strategy U such that for every $S \in \mathcal{S}$ there exists $B \in \mathcal{B}$ such that (U, S) robustly achieves the goal G with $O(B^2)$ errors, where the constant in the O-notation depends on S. Furthermore, if B-viability holds (i.e., the sensing function V is $(B_i, 0)$-viable with some U_i) and the composition of any $U \in \mathcal{U}$ with the sensing and enumeration strategies also resides in $\mathcal{U}$, then, for every $S \in \mathcal{S}$, the complexity of U is upper-bounded by the complexity of some fixed strategy in $\mathcal{U}$.

Sketch of proof Following the proof of Theorem 6.36, we first consider the case in which *both* the viability and safety conditions hold perfectly (i.e., $\epsilon \equiv 0$, both in the viability condition of Definition 6.40 and in the safety condition of Definition 6.35). We modify the universal user strategy U used in the proofs of Theorems 6.23 and 6.36 such that it switches to the next strategy after seeing sufficiently many failure indications (rather than when seeing a failure indication after sufficiently many rounds). Specifically, suppose that U starts emulating U_i at round t_i, and denote the system's state at this round by σ_{t_i}. Then, *strategy U emulates U_i until it encounters more than $b_i \leftarrow B_i(\mathsf{sz}(\sigma_{t_i}))$ rounds $t > t_i$ such that $V(\sigma_t) = 0$ holds, and switches to U_{i+1} once it encounters the $(b_i + 1)$th such round.*

We shall show that Claims 6.37 and 6.38 remain essentially valid, subject to some quantitative modifications. Specifically, Claim 6.37 is modified as follows.

Claim 6.42. *Suppose that V is B_i-viable and B_i-strongly safe with respect to (U_i, S), and consider a random execution of (E, U, S). Then, if this execution ever emulates U_i, then it never switches to U_{i+1}. Furthermore, in this case, for t_i and b_i as above, it holds that the number of errors (w.r.t. the bound b_i) occurring after round t_i is at most $b_i + b_i^2$.*

The furthermore part follows by observing that B_i-viability implies that $|\{t > t_i : V(\sigma_t) = 0\}| \leq b_i$, whereas B_i-strong safety implies that if more than b_i errors occur after round $t' > t_i$, then $V(\sigma_{t''}) = 0$ must hold for some $t'' \in [t', t'+b_i]$ (since in this case R_{B_i} evaluates to 0). Thus, if errors appear at rounds $t_1', \ldots, t_m' > t_i$ such that $t_1' < t_2' < \cdots < t_m'$, then failure indications must occur in rounds $t_1'', t_2'', \ldots, t_{m-b_i}'' > t_i$ such that $t_j'' \in [t_j', t_j' + b_i]$ (for every $j \in [m - b_i]$). Since at most b_i of these intervals may intersect at any index, it follows that $(m - b_i)/b_i \leq b_i$. Thus, Claim 6.42 follows. As for Claim 6.38, it is modified as follows.

Claim 6.43. *Let $i \geq 1$ and suppose that (U, S) does not robustly achieve the goal with $3\sum_{j \in [i]} B_j^2$ errors. Consider a random execution of (E, U, S), and, for $j \in \{i, i+1\}$, let t_j denote the round in which U started emulating U_j. Then, recalling that V is B_j-strongly safe (w.r.t. (U_j, S)), the expected number of errors (w.r.t. the bound B_i) that occur between round t_i and round t_{i+1} is at most $3B_i^2(\mathsf{sz}(\sigma_1))$.*

Combining Claims 6.42 and 6.43 with the hypothesis that for every $S \in \mathcal{S}$ there exists a user strategy $U_i \in \mathcal{U}$ such that V is B_i-viable and B_i-strongly safe with respect to (U_i, S), it follows that (U_i, S) robustly achieves the goal with B errors, where $B(s) = 2B_i^2(s) + 3\sum_{j \in [i-1]} B_j^2(s)$. Note that indeed $B(s) = O(B_j^2(s))$ for some $j \leq i$, where the constant in the O-notation depends on i (and hence on S).

Sketch of proof Following the proof of Claim 6.38, we proceed by induction on i. Let σ_1 be a global state such that the expected number of errors produced by a random execution of the system starting at σ_1 exceeds $3\sum_{j \in [i]} B_j^2(\mathsf{sz}(\sigma_1))$. By the induction hypothesis, the expected number of errors that occur before round t_i is at most $3\sum_{j \in [i-1]} B_j^2(\mathsf{sz}(\sigma_1))$, and so at least $3b_i^2$ errors occur after round t_i, where $b_i = B_i(\mathsf{sz}(\sigma_1))$. The first $(b_i + 1)b_i$ errors must (by B_i-strong safety) cause more than b_i failure indications (i.e., rounds $t > t_i$ such that $V(\sigma_t) = 0$), which causes U to switch to emulating U_{i+1} as soon as $b_i + 1$ such indications are encountered, which occurs at most another b_i rounds after the last detected error (again by B_i-strong safety). Hence, the number of errors (w.r.t. the bound b_i) during the emulation of U_i is at most $3b_i^2$, and the claim follows. ∎

As in the proof of Theorem 6.36, we need to extend the analysis to the general case in which $\epsilon \leq 1/3$ (rather than $\epsilon = 0$). The extension is analogous to the original one, where here each repetition causes an overhead of $O(B^2)$ (rather than $O(B)$) errors. ∎

On the use of different bounding functions for safety and viability. For simplicity, we assumed that the bounding functions for safety and viability with the ith user strategy were the same function B_i, and the conclusion of Theorem 6.41 gave a bound of $O(B^2)$ errors for some bounding function $B \in \mathcal{B}$. Now, it may be useful for applications to note that if we had separate bounding functions for safety and viability – suppose the bounding function for safety associated with the ith user is B_i^s, and the bounding function for viability is B_i^v – and if the algorithm were modified to switch after encountering more than B_i^v failure indications, then the argument in the proof of Theorem 6.41 would give $O(B^s \cdot B^v)$ errors for some pair of bounding functions (B^s, B^v). The reason is, of course, that in the proof of Claim 6.42, at most B_i^s intervals (of length B_i^s) may now intersect in the same index, and thus the number of errors incurred by a good strategy is at most $B_i^s(B_i^v + 1)$. Likewise, in the proof of Claim 6.43, $\Omega(B_i^s \cdot B_i^v)$ failures while the algorithm is running U_i are enough to ensure that at least $B_i^v + 1$ failure indications occur, and so we switch to U_{i+1}.

Example 6.44 (Solving computational problems, revised again). We consider the same goal as in Example 6.31, but here we consider the possibility of achieving this goal when interacting with an arbitrary server that is $\mathcal{U}$-helpful with a polynomially bounded number of errors (rather than interacting with an arbitrary D-solver). Recall that we consider the multi-session goal of solving instances (selected non-deterministically by the environment) of a decision problem, D_0, and $\mathcal{U}$ denotes the class of probabilistic polynomial time user strategies. This is a multi-session version of the goal studied in Section 3.3, and the solution can be nicely cast in the current framework. Specifically:

- As shown in Section 3.3, if both D_0 and its complement have competitive interactive proof systems, then for some polynomial B, there exists a sensing function that is B-viable and $(B, 1/3)$-strongly safe with respect to the class of $\mathcal{U}$-helpful with B errors servers.[22]

  The proof of the foregoing claim is essentially identical to the positive direction of Theorem 3.12: the user invokes the interactive proof system while playing the role of the verifier, and uses the helpful server in order to implement the designated prover strategy.

  Recall that adequate interactive proof systems exists for PSPACE-complete problems and some problems in SZK that are believed not to be in P (cf. [103, 134] and [71], respectively).[23]

- By invoking Theorem 6.41 we obtain an $\mathcal{S}$-universal user strategy, where $\mathcal{S}$ denotes the class of all $\mathcal{U}$-helpful servers. Furthermore, for every $S \in \mathcal{S}$, when interacting with S this universal strategy can be implemented in probabilistic polynomial time.

We also note that as in Chapter 5, analogous reasoning can be applied to other classes of user strategies, such as polynomial time and logspace strategies.

Another illustration of the difference in error bounds may be obtained by considering the kinds of learning algorithms that the various settings capture. Recall that we showed in Example 2.34 that in the finite-execution setting, users with controllable error naturally captured Valiant's PAC-learning model [152]. In contrast to the finite-execution setting now, and as a prelude to Chapter 8, we show that the setting of Theorem 6.36 naturally captures a well-known model of *on-line learning* as considered by Bārzdiņš and Frievalds [19] and Littlestone [101]; we will return to this model in more depth in Section 8.2.3.

---

[22]In fact, strong safety holds with respect to all possible servers. This fact follows from the unconditional soundness of the interactive proof system (i.e., soundness holds no matter which strategy is used for the cheating prover).

[23]Recall that we need interactive proof systems in which the designated prover strategy is relatively efficient in the sense that it can be implemented by a probabilistic polynomial time oracle machine with access to the problem itself. We reviewed some known constructions of such proof systems in Sections 3.3.1 and 3.3.4.

Example 6.45 (Mistake-bounded on-line learning). Suppose we fix a space of functions $f : X \to Y$. The goal of mistake-bounded on-line learning is a multi-session goal given by a non-deterministic environment strategy in which the environment non-deterministically selects an infinite sequence of elements of X, $\mathcal{E} = \{E_{\bar{x}} : \bar{x} = \{x_i \in X\}_{i=1}^{\infty}\}$, such that each ith session lasts a single round, and consists of $E_{\bar{x}}$ sending x_i to both the user and server. The referee's temporal decision function R' is satisfied iff the server receives a message consisting of "1" from the server.

Now, each concept class $\mathcal{C} \subseteq \{f : X \to Y\}$ corresponds naturally to a class of servers $\mathcal{S}(\mathcal{C})$ in the following way: for each $f \in \mathcal{C}$, there is a server $S_f \in \mathcal{S}(\mathcal{C})$ such that in each round, the server stores the message $x \in X$ it received from the environment until the next round; the server then sends "1" to the user and environment if the user sent a message $y \in Y$ on that round such that $y = f(x)$ for the previous message x that the server received from the environment, and sends "0" to the user and environment otherwise.

Thus, the messages from the server indicate whether or not the user successfully predicted $f(x)$, and the user incurs an error precisely when $f(x)$ is predicted incorrectly. We note that 1-strongly safe and 1-strongly viable sensing with respect to $\mathcal{U}$ and S_f is trivially available for this goal whenever f can be computed by members of $\mathcal{U}$, and so if $\mathcal{C}$ can be computed by members of $\mathcal{U}$, Theorem 6.36 applies to give a universal on-line learning algorithm that achieves a mistake bound of $O(i)$ for the ith function in the class, since the viability condition holds perfectly, and the bounding functions for safety and viability are both 1.

By contrast, we note that Theorem 6.23 (and more generally, use of the weak definitions of safety or viability introduced in Definition 6.14) would only be guaranteed to produce a user strategy that makes *finitely many* mistakes, with no a priori bound on how large this "finite number" should be (in particular, it could depend on the environment's non-deterministic choices).

Still, the conclusion obtained in Example 6.45 is itself somewhat suboptimal: it is still closer in spirit to older definitions of "learnability in the limit" or "inductive inference," [66, 29]. By contrast, we would like to say that whenever $\mathcal{C}$ is efficiently learnable in m mistakes, then our universal algorithm makes $f(m)$ mistakes for some moderately growing function f, so that the performance of the universal learning algorithm matches (as well as possible) the performance of the optimal learning algorithm for the unknown class $\mathcal{C}$. Theorem 6.36 doesn't allow for such conclusions, though, because the failures of a good on-line learning algorithm may be spread out over time, perhaps well past the initial "grace period." But we see now that these mistake-optimal learning algorithms actually satisfy the *relaxed* viability conditions, so we will be able to obtain an improved learning algorithm by an application of Theorem 6.41:

Example 6.46 (Mistake-bounded on-line learning, continued). Continuing Example 6.45, suppose we know that there is an on-line learning algorithm in the class $\mathcal{U}$ that makes m mistakes in the worst case when learning the concept class $\mathcal{C}$. Then the natural sensing function is m-viable for $\mathcal{U}$ with $\mathcal{S}(\mathcal{C})$. Therefore, Theorem 6.41 applies to give a universal on-line learning algorithm that achieves a mistake bound of $O(m^2)$ for any class $\mathcal{C}$ efficiently learnable in m mistakes since the viability condition holds perfectly, and the bounding function for viability is $m \geq 1$. Actually, moreover, since the sensing is 1-strongly safe, the more careful accounting of the errors in Theorem 6.41 we sketched earlier (for separate safety and viability bounding functions) would give that the mistake bound is only $O(m)$.

6.2.5   On the non-triviality of strong sensing functions

Recall that the existence of an $\mathcal{S}$-universal strategy implies the existence of a sensing function that is safe with respect to $\mathcal{S}$ (see Proposition 6.26). However, this sensing function is trivial (i.e., it is identically 1), and its safety with respect to $\mathcal{S}$ just follows from the fact that the $\mathcal{S}$-universal strategy achieves the goal when coupled with any server in $\mathcal{S}$. Clearly, this safety property may no longer hold with respect to servers outside $\mathcal{S}$, and specifically with respect to servers that are not helpful at all.

We stress that these sensing functions were always unsafe with unhelpful servers, even if the class $\mathcal{S}$ was the class of all helpful servers, which, recall, we saw in Theorem 2.37 could not happen with sensing from finite executions. While on the one hand, we believe that sensing functions that are also safe with respect to a wider class of servers are desirable, on the other hand, in the case of finite executions, we saw that this strong safety property also limited the class of goals that could be achieved with sensing. This point was most clearly made in the context of computational goals in Section 3.3.

Now, turning to the cases in which we designed *strong* sensing functions – e.g., those in Example 6.31 – we observe that these sensing functions were actually safe with respect to any server, just as were our sensing functions for the analogous goals in finite executions. We note that it is desirable to have sensing functions that are strongly safe, because such functions offer bounds on the number of errors made by the universal strategy (see Theorems 6.36 and 6.41).

We show now that this is (unfortunately) no coincidence: it turns out that a strong sensing function with respect to a sufficiently rich class of helpful servers is actually safe with respect to any server. In other words, if V is strongly safe with respect to $\mathcal{S}$, which may contain only $\mathcal{U}$-helpful servers, then V is strongly safe with respect to any server (including servers that are not helpful to any user). Thus, *a strongly safe sensing function cannot be trivial.*

The proof is essentially a slightly more involved variant of the proof of Theorem 2.37. Considering a class of helpful servers that are each helpful when they communicate with users that send sufficiently long messages and may behave arbitrarily otherwise, we show that (strong) safety with respect to this class implies (strong) safety with respect to all servers. Specifically, for each user strategy U, we will consider the class $\mathsf{pad}(U)$ of all user strategies that prepend messages of U by a sufficiently long prefix, and show that (strong) safety with respect to the class of all $\mathsf{pad}(U)$-helpful servers implies (strong) safety with respect to all servers.

Theorem 6.47 (Strong safety w.r.t. helpful servers implies same w.r.t. all servers). *Let $G = (\mathcal{E}, R)$ be a compact goal which is achievable by the pair (U, S). Let $\mathsf{pad}_i(U)$ denote a user strategy that prepends $0^{i-1}1$ to each message sent by U, and suppose that V is (B, ϵ)-strongly safe with respect to U and each $\{\mathsf{pad}_i(U) : i \in \mathbb{N}\}$-helpful server (and G). Then, V is (B, ϵ)-strongly safe with respect to the user U and every server (and G).*

Proof Suppose, towards the contrary, that there exists an arbitrary server S^* such that V is not (B, ϵ)-strongly safe with respect to (U, S^*) and G. The strong safety property implies that the sensing failure of V is witnessed by finite prefixes of the relevant executions. Specifically, for some $E \in \mathcal{E}$ and some initial state σ_1, with probability (strictly) greater than ϵ, a random execution of (E, U, S^*) starting at σ_1 contains a finite prefix that witnesses the sensing failure. Recall that there are two cases depending on whether $R'(\sigma_1) = 0$ or $R'(\sigma_1) = \perp$.

Starting with the first case, we suppose that with probability at least $\epsilon(\mathsf{sz}(\sigma_1)) + \delta$ (for some $\delta > 0$), the random execution $\overline{\sigma}$ is such that $V(\sigma_i) = 1$ for all $i \leq B(\mathsf{sz}(\sigma_1))$ and $R_B(\sigma) = 0$. Note that the first event depends only on the B-long prefix of σ, denoted $\sigma_{[1,B]}$. Thus, with probability at least $\epsilon + \delta$, this prefix is such that (1) V is identically 1 on all its states, and (2) with positive probability this prefix is extended to a random execution that is unsuccessful (per R_B). Fixing any such prefix, we note that event (2) is also witnessed by a finite prefix; that is, with positive probability, a random extension of this prefix contains a (longer) prefix that witnesses the violation of R_B. Using the fact that the latter event refers to a countable union of fixed prefix events, we conclude that there exists $\ell \in \mathbb{N}$ such that with positive probability the said violation is seen in the ℓ-step prefix. Furthermore, by viewing the probability of the former event as a limit of the latter events, we can make the probability bound within an additive $\delta/3$ of its original value. The same process can be applied across the various B-long prefixes, and so we conclude that there exists an $\ell \in \mathbb{N}$ such that, with probability at least $\epsilon + \delta/3$, a violation is due to the ℓ-long prefix of a random execution. Similar considerations apply also to the second aforementioned case (where $R'(\sigma_1) = \perp$).

Next, we note that we can upper-bound the length of the messages that are sent by U in the first ℓ steps of most of these random executions. That is, there exists an $i \in \mathbb{N}$ such that, with probability greater than ϵ, the sensing function V fails in a random ℓ-step execution prefix during which U sends messages of length at most i. At this point we are ready to define a helpful server that also fails this sensing function.

Firstly, we consider the strategy $\tilde{U} = \mathsf{pad}_{i+1}(U)$, and define a hybrid strategy $\tilde{S}$ such that $\tilde{S}$ behaves like S^* on messages of length at most i and behaves more like S otherwise. Specifically, upon receiving a message of length greater than i, the strategy $\tilde{S}$ omits the first $i+1$ bits, feeds the result to S, and answers as S does. Clearly, $(\tilde{U}, \tilde{S})$ achieves the goal G, and so $\tilde{S}$ is $\mathsf{pad}(U)$-helpful. On the other hand, by the foregoing argument, it is the case that V fails with probability greater than ϵ in a random execution of $(E, U, \tilde{S})$. Thus, V is not (B, ϵ)-strongly safe with respect to U and $\tilde{S}$ (and G), which contradicts our hypothesis regarding safety with respect to all helpful servers (or rather all $\{\mathsf{pad}_j(U) : j \in \mathbb{N}\}$-helpful servers). The theorem follows. ∎

6.3 Extensions

In this section, we discuss various natural augmentations of our basic model, specifically the treatment of varying state sizes (see Section 6.3.1), a generalization of multi-session goals to concurrent session goals (see Section 6.3.2), and a relaxation of the notion of robustly achieving goals (in Section 6.3.3) to allow a nonzero probability of failure and to allow user strategies to start from a set of initial states. Further extensions will be motivated and introduced in Chapter 7.

6.3.1 Varying state sizes

Our basic treatment, provided in Sections 6.1 and 6.2, postulates that the size of the various states remains invariant throughout the execution. This postulate was made mainly for the sake of simplicity, and we waive it here both for the sake of generality and because the generalization seems essential to an appealing result that appears in Section 7.2.3.

Extending the definitional treatment

Recall that the size of the various states in the execution is used only as a basis for defining various bounds, which are stated as functions of the state's size. Given that the state's size may change, the question that we face is how to express these bounds in such a case.[24] Recall that we use bounds of two types.

1. *Bounds that determine the length of various intervals*, including the length of intervals in which the temporal decision is suspended (i.e., $R' = \perp$) or the delay of sensing (e.g., in the definition of safety). For

---

[24]While we believe that the definitional choices made here (i.e., in Section 6.3.1) are reasonable, we are far from being convinced that they are the best possible.

example, both types of delays appear in (Item 2 of) Definition 6.16 (which refers to strong sensing).

Since such bounds refer to some "transient" events (i.e., a state in which $R' = 0$ or the first state in a $\perp$-run under R'), it is natural to keep them expressed in terms of the size of the corresponding state (in which the event occurs).

2. *Bounds that determine the total number of various events*, including the number of allowed errors and/or detection failures (as in Definition 6.34 and Definition 6.40, respectively).

Since these bounds are "global" in nature, it makes no sense to associate them with any single event (or state or size). Instead, we may view each individual bad event (i.e., an error and/or detection failure) as contributing to a general pool, and weight its contribution with reference to the relevant size. (See Definition 6.48.)

In accordance with the foregoing discussion, the definitions of sensing functions (i.e., Definition 6.16 and, needless to say, Definition 6.14) remain intact (although the size of the various states in an execution may vary). We stress that, since our universal strategies refer to these bounds, it is important to maintain our postulation by which *the user knows the size of the current (global) state.*[25]

We now turn to the treatment of global bounds, like the bounds on the total number of errors (in Definition 6.34). Recall that Item 1 in Definition 6.34 states that the expected cardinality of $\{t \in \mathbb{N} : R'(\sigma_t) = 0\}$ is at most $B(\mathbf{sz}(\sigma_1))$, for every initial state σ_1. However, when the size of states may vary, it makes little sense to bound the number of errors with reference to the size of the initial state. Instead, we may consider an error at state σ_t as contributing an amount proportional to $1/B(\mathbf{sz}(\sigma_t))$ (towards the violation of the "error bound") and say that a violation occurs if the sum of all contributions exceeds 1.

Definition 6.48 (Varying size version of Definition 6.34). Let $G = (\mathcal{E}, R)$ be a compact goal and $R' : \Omega \to \{0, 1, \perp\}$ be as in Definition 6.6. For $B : \mathbb{N} \to \mathbb{N}$, we say that a pair of user-server strategies, (U, S), *achieves the goal G with B errors* if, for every $E \in \mathcal{E}$, a random execution $\overline{\sigma} = (\sigma_1, \sigma_2, \ldots)$ of the system (E, U, S) satisfies the following two conditions:

1. The expected value of the sum $\sum_{t \in \mathbb{N} : R'(\sigma_t) = 0} \frac{1}{B(\mathbf{sz}(\sigma_t))}$ is at most 1.

2. The expected value of the sum $\sum_{t \in \mathbb{N} : (\forall t' \in [t, t + B(\mathbf{sz}(\sigma_t))]) \, R'(\sigma_{t'}) = \perp} \frac{1}{B(\mathbf{sz}(\sigma_t))}$ is at most 1.

---

[25] Indeed, we relied on this postulation also in the fixed-size case, since it was used there in the same way. However, in the current context the state may change all the time, and the user should be aware of these changes (at least whenever it needs to determine the values of these bounds).

If $\bar{\sigma}$ is an execution in which the bounds corresponding to the foregoing conditions are both satisfied, then we write $R_B(\bar{\sigma}) = 1$. Finally, if $\bar{\sigma}$ is an execution such that $R'(\sigma_t) = 0$ or $(\forall t' \in [t, t + B(\mathbf{sz}(\sigma_t))]) \, R'(\sigma_{t'}) = \bot$, then we say that $\bar{\sigma}$ contains an *error in round t*.

Note that each individual bad event in Item 2 is defined with respect to the size at the corresponding time, and (like in Item 1) its contribution is defined with respect to the size at the corresponding time. However, in both items, the condition refers to the aggregate contribution, where each event may contribute a different amount to this sum. Observe that in the case that the state remains fixed throughout the execution, Definition 6.48 coincides with Definition 6.34.

A similar modification should be applied to the definition of robustly achieving a goal. Consequently, the refined definition of strong safety (i.e., Definition 6.35) is updated by merely postulating that R_B is as defined in Definition 6.48 (rather than as in Definition 6.34). Lastly, we generalized the definition of relaxed viability (i.e., Definition 6.40)[26] analogously to the foregoing modification (i.e., that yielded Definition 6.48).

Definition 6.49 (Varying size version of Definition 6.40). Let $G = (\mathcal{E}, R)$, S, U, and V be as in Definition 6.16. For $B : \mathbb{N} \to \mathbb{N}$ and $\epsilon \in [0, 1/3]$, we say that V is (B, ϵ)-*viable* with respect to (U, S) (and G) if, for every $E \in \mathcal{E}$ and every $\sigma_1 \in \Omega$, with probability at least $1 - \epsilon$, the value of the sum $\sum_{t \in \mathbb{N} : V(\sigma_t) = 0} \frac{1}{B(\mathbf{sz}(\sigma_t))}$ is no greater than 1. If $\epsilon = 0$, then we say that V is B-*viable*.

As commented in Section 6.2.4, the foregoing definitions are simplified versions of more general definitions that use different bounding functions for the various bounds that underly these definitions.

Extending the (fixed-size) universality results

The universality results stated in Section 6.2 can be generalized to the context of varying sizes, where we refer to the generalized definitions presented in Section 6.3.1. Actually, we can prove these generalized results only for goals in which the state size does not change dramatically from one round to the next one. For simplicity, we only consider one concrete case, in which the size can change at each round by at most one unit. (Note that goals that allow arbitrary changes in the state sizes can be emulated by the foregoing restricted goals by introducing an adequate number of dummy rounds.) Similarly, we consider only small bounding functions, while larger bounds can

---

[26]In order to avoid a possible controversy, we state Definition 6.49 only for constant values of ϵ, whereas Definition 6.40 allowed any $\epsilon : \mathbb{N} \to [0, 1/3]$. Note that $\epsilon = 0$ and $\epsilon = 1/3$ are indeed the most important cases (cf. Definition 6.16). Nevertheless, we mention that we believe that when allowing ϵ to vary, it is most natural to apply it to the initial state (indeed, as in Definition 6.40).

be handled by artificially increasing the size measure (which is an arbitrary function of the states).

Theorem 6.50 (Varying size version of Theorem 6.41). *Let* $G = (\mathcal{E}, R)$, $\mathcal{U}$, $\mathcal{S}$, V, ϵ, *and* $\mathcal{B}$ *be as in Theorem 6.41, except that here we refer to the varying-size generalization of the notions of achieving and sensing (and in particular to replacing Definition 6.40 by Definition 6.49). Suppose that* G *is such that in each execution* $\overline{\sigma} = (\sigma_1, \sigma_2, \ldots)$ *and at every time* t *it holds that* $|\mathsf{sz}(\sigma_{t+1}) - \mathsf{sz}(\sigma_t)| \leq 1$. *Further suppose that for every* $B \in \mathcal{B}$ *it holds that* $B(s + d) \leq B(s) + (d/2)$, *and that for every two functions in* $\mathcal{B}$ *it holds that one of them dominates the other (i.e., for every* $B_1, B_2 \in \mathcal{B}$ *and* $s, s' \in \mathbb{N}$, *if* $B_1(s) < B_2(s)$, *then* $B_1(s') \leq B_2(s'))$. *Then, there exists an* $\mathcal{S}$-*universal user strategy* U *such that for every* $S \in \mathcal{S}$ *there exists* $B \in \mathcal{B}$ *such that* (U, S) *robustly achieves the goal* G *with* $O(B^2)$ *errors, where the constant in the* O-*notation depends on* S. *Furthermore, if* B-*viability holds (i.e., the sensing function* V *is* $(B_i, 0)$-*viable with some* U_i) *and the composition of any* $U \in \mathcal{U}$ *with the sensing and enumeration strategies is also in* $\mathcal{U}$, *then, for every* $S \in \mathcal{S}$, *the complexity of* U *is upper-bounded by the complexity of some fixed strategy in* $\mathcal{U}$.

Recall that by saying that a "goal is achieved with a certain number of errors" we mean that the expected contribution of all errors is bounded by 1, where the contribution of each error is "normalized" with respect to the relevant size (as per Definition 6.48).

Sketch of proof We follow the outline of the proof of Theorem 6.41, while adapting the "accounting of failure indications." Recall that, in that proof (and while in the case of $\epsilon \equiv 0$), we introduced a universal user strategy U that switches from the user strategy U_i to the next strategy (i.e., U_{i+1}) after seeing sufficiently many failure indications, where "sufficiently many failures" meant a number that exceeds a predetermined bound that was expressed in terms of the fixed size (of states). Here, sufficiently many failures will mean an accumulated contribution that exceeds 1, where each contribution is normalized with respect to the relevant size (as per Definition 6.49). Specifically, suppose that U starts emulating U_i at round t_i, then *strategy* U *emulates* U_i *until a time* t_{i+1} *such that the sum* $\sum_{t \in (t_i, t_{i+1}]: V(\sigma_t) = 0} \frac{1}{B_i(\mathsf{sz}(\sigma_t))}$ *exceeds 1, and switches to* U_{i+1} *once the latter event occurs.*

We shall show tha Claims 6.42 and 6.43 remain essentially valid, when modified in accordance with the relevant new measures. Specifically, Claim 6.42 is modified as follows.

Claim 6.51. *Suppose that* V *is* B_i-*viable and* B_i-*strongly safe with respect to* (U_i, S), *and consider a random execution of* (E, U, S). *Then, if this execution ever emulates* U_i, *then it never switches to* U_{i+1}. *Furthermore, in this case, letting* Err *denote the set of rounds containing errors (as in Definition 6.48) it holds that* $\sum_{t \in \mathsf{Err}: t > t_i} \frac{1}{4B_i^2(\mathsf{sz}(\sigma_t))} \leq 1$, *where* t_i *is as above.*

Sketch of proof As in the case of Claims 6.37 and 6.42, the main part only relies on B_i-viability and follows from the construction of U. The furthermore part follows by observing that B_i-viability mandates an upper bound on the contribution of failure indications (w.r.t. V), whereas the B_i-strong safety condition translates the total contribution of errors (w.r.t. R') to a lower bound on the contribution of failure indications (w.r.t. V). Specifically, suppose for contradiction that $\sum_{t \in \mathsf{Err}: t > t_i} \frac{1}{B_i^2(\mathsf{sz}(\sigma_t))} > 4$. Consider $b > t_i$ such that both $\sum_{t \in \mathsf{Err} \cap (t_i, b]} \frac{1}{B_i^2(\mathsf{sz}(\sigma_t))} > 2$ and $\sum_{t \in \mathsf{Err}: t > b} \frac{1}{B_i^2(\mathsf{sz}(\sigma_t))} > 1$ hold, and let $\mathsf{Err}' = \{t \in \mathsf{Err} : t \in (t_i, b]\}$. Now, by the B_i-strong safety condition, for every $t' \in \mathsf{Err}'$ there exists $t'' \in [t', t' + B_i(\mathsf{sz}(\sigma_{t'}))]$ such that $V(\sigma_{t''}) = 0$ (because $R_{B_i}(\sigma_{t'})$ evaluates to 0). Let us denote the corresponding mapping by $\pi : \mathsf{Err}' \to (\mathbb{N} \setminus [t_i])$; that is, for every $t' \in \mathsf{Err}'$ it holds that $\pi(t') \in [t', t' + B_i(\mathsf{sz}(\sigma_{t'}))]$ and $V(\sigma_{\pi(t')}) = 0$. Then:

$$
\sum_{t > t_i : V(\sigma_t) = 0} \frac{1}{B_i(\mathsf{sz}(\sigma_t))} \geq \sum_{t \in \pi(\mathsf{Err}')} \frac{1}{B_i(\mathsf{sz}(\sigma_t))}
$$

$$
= \sum_{t' \in \mathsf{Err}'} \frac{1}{|\pi^{-1}(\pi(t'))|} \cdot \frac{1}{B_i(\mathsf{sz}(\sigma_{\pi(t')}))}
$$

$$
\geq \sum_{t' \in \mathsf{Err}'} \frac{1}{2B_i^2(\mathsf{sz}(\sigma_{\pi(t')}))}
$$

where the last inequality follows from the fact that $|\pi^{-1}(t'')| \leq 2B_i(\mathsf{sz}(\sigma_{t''}))$, which in turn follows by combining $\pi^{-1}(t'') \subseteq \{t' \in [t''] : t' + B_i(\mathsf{sz}(\sigma_{t'})) \geq t''\}$ with $|\{t' \in [t''] : t' + B_i(\mathsf{sz}(\sigma_{t'})) \geq t''\}| \leq 2B_i(\mathsf{sz}(\sigma_{t''}))$, where the last fact relies on two of the technical conditions of the theorem.[27] Using $\sum_{t' \in \mathsf{Err}'} \frac{1}{2B_i^2(\mathsf{sz}(\sigma_{t'}))} > 1$, we infer that $\sum_{t > t_i : V(\sigma_t) = 0} \frac{1}{B_i(\mathsf{sz}(\sigma_t))} > 1$, which causes the execution to switch to U_{i+1}, in contradiction to the main part. The furthermore part follows. ■

Regarding Claim 6.43, it is modified as follows.

Claim 6.52. *Let $i \geq 1$ and suppose that (U, S) does not robustly achieve the goal with $6i \max_{j \in [i]} B_j^2$ errors.[28] That is, letting Err be as in Claim 6.51, it holds that the expected value of $\sum_{t \in \mathsf{Err}} \frac{1}{\max_{j \in [i]} \{B_j^2(\mathsf{sz}(\sigma_t))\}}$ exceeds $6i$. Consider a random execution of (E, U, S), and let t_i, t_{i+1} be as above. Then, recalling that each V is B_j-strongly safe (w.r.t. (U_j, S)) it holds that the expected value of $\sum_{t \in \mathsf{Err}: t \in (t_i, t_{i+1}]} \frac{1}{B_i^2(\mathsf{sz}(\sigma_t))}$ is at most 6.*

---

[27] Specifically, using $|\mathsf{sz}(\sigma_{t'}) - \mathsf{sz}(\sigma_{t''})| \leq |t' - t''|$ and $B_i(s + d) \leq B_i(s) + (d/2)$, we upper-bound $|\{t' \in [t''] : t' + B_i(\mathsf{sz}(\sigma_{t'})) \geq t''\}|$ by $|\{t' \in [t''] : t' + B_i(\mathsf{sz}(\sigma_{t''})) + (t'' - t')/2 \geq t''\}|$.

[28] Here we use the technical hypothesis by which for every two functions in $\mathcal{B}$ it holds that one of them dominates the other. Hence, $\max_{j \in [i]} \{B_j^2\}$ is well defined, and if $B_1(s) < B_2(s)$ for some $s \in \mathbb{N}$ then $B_1(s') \leq B_2(s')$ holds for all $s' \in \mathbb{N}$.

Combining Claims 6.51 and 6.52 with the hypothesis that for our sensing strategy V for every $S \in \mathcal{S}$ there exists a user strategy $U_i \in \mathcal{U}$ such that V is B_i-viable and B_i-strongly safe with respect to (U_i, S), it follows that (U_i, S) robustly achieves the goal with B errors, where $B(s) = 6i \max_{j \in [i]} \{B_j^2(s)\}$.

Sketch of proof Following the proof of Claim 6.43, we proceed by induction on i. Let σ_1 be a state such that the expected value of $\sum_{t \in \mathsf{Err}} \frac{1}{\max_{j \in [i]} \{B_j^2(\mathsf{sz}(\sigma_t))\}}$ exceeds $6i$. By the induction hypothesis, the expected value of $\sum_{t \in \mathsf{Err}: t \leq t_i} \frac{1}{\max_{j \in [i-1]} \{B_j^2(\mathsf{sz}(\sigma_t))\}}$ is at most $6(i-1)$, and so the expected value of $\sum_{t \in \mathsf{Err}: t \in (t_i, t_{i+1}]} \frac{1}{B_i^2(\mathsf{sz}(\sigma_t))}$ is at least 6. By B_i-strong safety, for each of these $t \in \mathsf{Err} \cap (t_i, t_{i+1}]$ there exists $t' \in [t, t+B_i(\mathsf{sz}(\sigma_t))]$ such that $V(\sigma_{t'}) = 0$, and by an accounting similar to the one in the proof of Claim 6.51 it follows that $\sum_{t \in (t_i, t_{i+1}]: V(\sigma_t) = 0} \frac{1}{B_i(\mathsf{sz}(\sigma_t))} > 3$, which causes U to switch to emulating U_{i+1} before t_{i+1} (in contradiction to the definition of t_{i+1}). The claim follows. ■

As in the proof of Theorem 6.36, we need to extend the analysis to the general case in which $\epsilon \leq 1/3$ (rather than $\epsilon = 0$). The extension is analogous to the original one, where (as in the proof of Theorem 6.41) each repetition causes an overhead of $O(B^2)$ errors. ■

6.3.2 Concurrent session multi-session goals

In this section we consider a generalization of the notion of multi-session goals to concurrent session goals. In relation to the treatment of state sizes in Section 6.3.1, it is natural to comment on the state sizes in multi-session goals. It is natural to postulate that, in the basic formulation (i.e., Definition 6.7), the state size remains invariant during each session, and is thus determined by the start-session state of this session. In the case of concurrent sessions it is natural to define size as a function of the sizes associated with all active sessions.[29]

Our basic formulation of multi-session goals (see Definition 6.7) mandates that the current session ends before any new session can start. A more general formulation, which allows concurrent sessions, follows.

Definition 6.53 (Concurrent multi-session goals, sketch). A goal consisting of a non-deterministic strategy $\mathcal{E}$ and a referee R is called a *concurrent multi-session goal* if the following conditions hold.

---

[29]While the maximum size and the sum of sizes seem like natural choices, the *product* of the sizes may be better behaved: if we have a linear error bound, and sessions of size s_1 and s_2, then note that a strategy that successfully completes the two sessions in turn first incurs, e.g., up to $s_1 - 1$ errors of size $s_1 \cdot s_2$, and thus incurs total error less than $1/s_2$. Therefore, if the size returns to s_2 after the first session is terminated, the user can still afford to make up to $s_2 - 1$ errors of size s_2 while still incurring total failure less than one.

1. *The environment's states:* The local states of the environment consist of *(non-empty)* sequences of pairs, where each pair is called a *session state* and has a form as postulated in the first condition of Definition 6.7; that is, each session state is a pair consisting of an *index* and a *contents*, and belongs to one of three sets of session states called *start-session states*, *end-session states*, and *intermediate session states*. The initial local state corresponds to the single pair $(0, \lambda)$, and belongs to the set of end-session states.

2. *The referee verdict depends only on the end-session states:* The referee R is compact. Furthermore, the corresponding function R' evaluates to $\perp$ if and only if the current state contains no end-session state. Otherwise, the value of R' is a conjunction of the values of some Boolean predicate R'' that is applied to all the end-session states that appear in the current state.

3. *Starting new sessions:* At any round, the environment may start an arbitrary number of new sessions. This is done by moving non-deterministically to a state that contains a list of start-session states, each having an index that does not appear in the previous list of session states.[30] The contents of each of these new session states is determined by the environment based solely on the indices of the existing sessions (and is invariant of their contents; cf. Condition 3 of Definition 6.7).

4. *Execution of the current active sessions:* In addition to the above, the environment takes a move in each of the active sessions that are listed in the current state, where a session is called *active* if it is not in an end-session state. The environment's movement in each such session is probabilistic and is independent of the index as well as of the actual environment strategy (cf. Condition 4 of Definition 6.7). Furthermore, this movement maintains the index of the session.

Note that the state maintains the list of all non-active sessions (i.e., sessions that reached a end-session state). An alternative formulation may omit the non-active sessions from the state, and maintain instead an explicit counter that represents the number of sessions started so far.

We will develop an example of a concurrent-session goal modeling communication over an *unreliable* network in Chapter 9, where messages may be dropped and reordered in transit, as occurs with packets sent across the internet. Roughly, each session captures a message to be sent across the network; the reason we use a concurrent-session goal and not, e.g., a multi-session goal to capture this setting is that, in the interest of maintaining a high throughput, the user wishes to continue sending messages without needing to know whether or not an earlier message has been received. Thus, the

---

[30]Without loss of generality, this index may be the smallest integer that does not appear in that list.

natural way to capture this goal is to introduce sessions corresponding to *all* of the messages in the user's buffer, which is of course a concurrent session goal when the buffer may contain more than one message.

6.3.3 Partial robustness

As hinted in Section 6.1.3, the notion of robustly achieving a goal (see Definition 6.11) is too strong for the study of one-shot goals. Recall that this definition mandates that the goal is achieved no matter which global state the system is initiated in. In general, a more refined definition that quantifies over a subset of all possible global states is desirable, because it corresponds to natural settings and offers greater definitional flexibility. Most importantly, this refined definition allows us to consider the (natural case of the) set of all global states in which the user's local state is reset to some initial value. (Indeed, in contrast to resetting the environment, resetting the user seems feasible in many cases, and seems less demanding than resetting the server.)

We relax (and generalize) the notion of robustly achieving a goal by quantifying over a predetermined set of states (rather than over all states). We also allow an explicit specification of the success probability (rather than insisting that the success probability equals 1).

Definition 6.54 (Robustly achieving goals, revised). Let $\Theta \subseteq \Omega$ and $p : \mathbb{N} \rightarrow [0, 1]$. We say that a pair, (U, S), of user-server strategies (Θ, p)-*robustly achieves the goal* $G = (\mathcal{E}, R)$ if for every $E \in \mathcal{E}$ and every $\sigma_1 \in \Theta$ a random execution of the system (E, U, S) starting in state σ_1 is successful with probability at least $p(\mathbf{sz}(\sigma_1))$.

Definition 6.11 is obtained as a special case of Definition 6.54 by letting $\Theta = \Omega$ and $p \equiv 1$.

6.4 Embedding goals in finite executions into infinite executions

Our earlier study of goal-oriented communication in finite executions referred to the environment's state in the final round of an execution, and thus does not directly fit our main terminology for infinite executions (as presented in Section 6.1). Nevertheless, goals in finite executions can be viewed as a special case of general goals where this case is closely related to (but different from) a special case of multi-session goals. Thus, the framework of goals in infinite executions introduced in Section 6.1.1 is a strict generalization of the goals in finite executions we studied initially.

Definition 6.55 (Goals in finite executions as a special case of goals in infinite executions). A goal $G = (\mathcal{E}, R)$ is called a *one-shot goal* if the following conditions hold.

1. *The environment's states:* The local states of the environment are partitioned into two non-empty sets consisting of *non-terminating* states and *terminating* states. The initial local state belongs to the set of non-terminating states.

2. *The referee suspends its verdict until reaching a terminating state:* The referee R is compact. Furthermore, the corresponding function R' evaluates to $\perp$ if and only if the current state is a non-terminating state.

3. *Termination:* When in a terminating state, the environment just maintains its state; that is, for each actual strategy of the environment $E \in \mathcal{E}$, and each terminating state σ it holds that $E(\sigma) = \sigma$.

When in any non-terminating state, the environment follows its strategy as usual.

Thus, a typical execution of a system that refers to a one-shot goal consists of an actual finite execution that enters a terminating state, which is artificially propagated by an infinite sequence of repetitions of this state. It follows that *an execution is successful if and only if it enters a terminating state that evaluates to 1* (under R').

Robustly achieving one-shot goals. Recall that, as we noted in Section 6.3.3, the notion of robustly achieving a goal in infinite executions (see Definition 6.11) is too strong for the study of one-shot goals, because no execution that starts in a terminating state that evaluates to 0 (under R') can be successful.[31] Thus, we must relax the notion of robustly achieving a goal such that starting in such states is not considered. Hence, our starting point is Definition 6.54, which offers a general refined notion of robustly achieving a goal that is quantified over a predetermined set of states rather than over all states. Indeed, the flexibility provided by Definition 6.54 provides a good basis for defining robustly achievable one-shot goals. Specifically, we let Θ consist of all global states in which the current user's local state is empty and the environment's next local state is non-terminating. (That is, we wish to avoid not only states σ such that $\sigma^{(e)}$ is terminating, but also states σ that lead the environment to a terminating state in the next move, due to messages in transit.)

Definition 6.56 (Robustly achieving one-shot goals). For a one-shot goal $G = (\mathcal{E}, R)$, we say that a global state σ is *doomed* if for every $E \in \mathcal{E}$ it holds that $E(\sigma)^{(e)}$ is terminating, and we assume that G has states that are not doomed. Letting μ denote an unspecified negligible function, we say that a pair of user-server strategies, (U, S), *robustly achieves the one-shot goal*

---

[31]The same holds for any global state σ that causes the environment to immediately enter such a terminating state due to the messages currently in transit. We consider this case specifically since the environment usually terminates the session in response to a message that the user sends.

$G = (\mathcal{E}, R)$ if it $(\Theta, 1 - \mu)$-robustly achieves the goal $G = (\mathcal{E}, R)$ for Θ that contains all global states in which the user's local state is empty and the environment's local state is not doomed. If $\mu \equiv 0$, then we say that (U, S) robustly achieves the one-shot goal $G = (\mathcal{E}, R)$ *in a perfect manner*. We stress that if $\Theta = \emptyset$, then the goal G is not (robustly) achievable.

The foregoing adaptation of robust achievability to one-shot goals supports the following adaptation of Proposition 6.12 (and is therefore the analogue of Proposition 2.13 for this reformulated setting).

Proposition 6.57. *Let U, S and S_t be as in Proposition 6.12, and let U_t be a user strategy that plays the first t rounds using the user strategy U_0, then resets its local state to empty and plays all subsequent rounds using the user strategy U. Then, if (U, S) robustly achieves the one-shot goal $G = (\mathcal{E}, R)$, then so does (U_t, S_t).*

The proof proceeds as in the case of Proposition 6.12, while relying on the modified robust achievability hypothesis (which matches the modified construction of U_t).

Sensing in the context of one-shot goals. We are already quite familiar with the notion of sensing for finite executions, as first introduced in Section 2.3.1, and refined in Section 5.3. We now consider how to recover these notions within our infinite execution framework, as modifications of sensing in infinite executions

The notion of strongly *viable* sensing for infinite executions (cf. Definitions 6.15 and 6.16) is adapted to the current context in a way analogous to the adaptation applied to the notion of robustly achieving (cf. Definition 6.56 versus Definition 6.11). That is, a sensing function for a one-shot goal is considered *strongly viable* if the condition in Definition 6.15 holds for every $\sigma_1 \in \Theta$ (rather than for every $\sigma_1 \in \Omega$) and with probability $1 - \mu$ (rather than with probability $2/3$).

As for the *safety* condition, its formulation is greatly simplified by the special features of one-shot goals (i.e., the fact that the environment's state does not change once it enters a termination state). In particular, the difference between Definitions 6.16 and 6.15 disappears, and it suffices to refer to the value of R' at termination states. As a consequence of safety referring to the value of R' on terminating states though, the delay period for sensing must be eliminated, or else a "safe" sensing function could provide a failure indication *after* the session has terminated; actually, quite contrary to allowing any delays in sensing, recalling that the user often terminates a session by sending the environment a message, the sensing function must *predict* the value of R' *on the subsequent round* (e.g., from a doomed state), if it is to be of any use. This is of course, also in mild contrast to sensing in the finite execution framework, where sensing only needed to "guess" the referee's verdict in the current round, due to the technical difference in how termination of the execution is handled. Thus, the one-shot goal should correspondingly be formulated so that the referee's verdict is preserved to the next round when the environment receives the termination message from the user. Finally, for consistency with the foregoing adaptation, we also adapt the strong safety condition (cf. Definition 6.16) such that it holds with probability $1-\mu$ (rather than with probability $2/3$).

Deriving multi-session versions of one-shot goals. As we suggested when we defined multi-session goals in Section 6.1.1, for every one-shot goal, we can derive a natural multi-session version by letting the new environment initiate a new session each time the original (one-shot) environment enters a terminating state. Note that, in the derived multi-session goal, we may only expect to succeed in a $1 - \mu$ fraction of the sessions (where μ is the error probability allowed in Definition 6.56), whereas properly speaking, achieving a multi-session goal requires that we succeed in all but finitely many sessions. In order to overcome this difficulty, we extend the definition of one-shot goals by allowing the user to control the success probability as considered in Section 2.3.3. Formally, we consider a uniform family of user strategies, $\overline{U} = \{U_i\}_{i\in\mathbb{N}}$, along with a uniform family of negligible functions, $\overline{\mu} = \{\mu_i\}_{i\in\mathbb{N}}$ (e.g., $\mu_i(n) = \mu(n)/i^2$ for some negligible function μ), and require that (U_i, S) (Θ, μ_i)-robustly achieves the goal (for every $i \in \mathbb{N}$). An analogous adaptation will be applied to sensing functions so that they feature controllable safety, as introduced in Definition 2.32.

Chapter 7

The power of relaxed models

Recall that our main theorems for finite executions in Chapter 2 and Chapter 5 show that in order to construct an efficient, *reliable* protocol for achieving a goal, it must be possible to efficiently verify that the goal has been achieved. We know that this places limits on what kinds of goals we could hope to achieve—for example, as we saw in Section 3.3, any problem we can solve using such a communications protocol in polynomial time with the class of all helpful servers must lie in PSPACE. Some natural computational problems are outside PSPACE, though, and so it is very natural to wonder if some weaker benefit could be obtained for these problems via communication with helpful servers. Now, although we saw that strong sensing in the infinite execution model was also bound by similar limitations in Theorem 6.47, we *also* saw that it was possible to construct universal users from *weak* safety in Theorem 6.23, which was *not* bound by such limitations. We will see, in this chapter, that this gap can be exploited: when the *reliability* requirement of the protocols is relaxed in some natural ways, we can substantially extend the class of goals that we can achieve universally.

As a motivating first example, in Section 7.1.1, we will give a universal protocol for deciding any *computable* decision problem with all helpful servers in the infinite executions model of Chapter 6. We will then show in Section 7.1.2 how this protocol can be converted into a protocol for deciding the same problems in finite executions if we allow the protocol to err on a finite set of instances (which depends on the server and its initial state). In Section 7.2, we will return to the infinite execution setting, and consider what aspects of computational goals we used in the design of our protocols. We will introduce *exploration sessions* as an abstraction of the key property, and show how, together with the ability to *reset* the server, the protocol can be generalized to a universal protocol that only makes a finite number of

B. Juba, *Universal Semantic Communication*,
DOI 10.1007/978-3-642-23297-8_7,
© Springer-Verlag Berlin Heidelberg 2011

mistakes with each server *independent of the size parameter.*

7.1 Universal protocols for any computable decision problem

In this chapter, we're going to consider how, by either relaxing our expectations for the user, or by assuming more favorable conditions, we can obtain some stronger results. As usual in this work, computational goals will allow us to demonstrate quantitative improvements in what is achieved, and will point the way to more general results. In this section, we'll consider a couple of special scenarios in which a time-bounded user strategy can (almost) "go all the way," and obtain solutions to *any computable decision problem.* As both scenarios may properly be thought of as relaxations of a C-bounded universal setting, and Theorem 5.25 has established that C-bounded universal users only exist for problems that have C-competitive interactive proof systems – and so, e.g., Theorem 1.5 has established that universal users in the basic universal setting do not exist for problems outside PSPACE – this will be a dramatic demonstration of the expansion of the user's capabilities.

Briefly, the first scenario we consider is a cross between the basic universal setting in finite executions, and the multi-session infinite execution setting: we assume that the server is helpful in the *finite execution* sense, but we relax the requirements on the user, only requiring it to succeed in the *infinite execution* sense—thus, a stateful user strategy is invoked many times, and we will be happy if the user only fails in a bounded number of these sessions. In the second scenario, first considered in our paper [83], we restrict our attention to the finite execution setting, but relax our requirement on the user by allowing it to fail for *finitely many of the environment's non-deterministic choices.* In this case, if we then consider an exponential time user, we will find that it again can achieve the goal of computing any computable decision problem in this finite-error sense; since there's still an *enormous* gap between what exponential time competitive proof systems can handle and the class of all computable decision problems, this is again a meaningful demonstration.

Moreover, in the second setting, we'll notice that the construction delimits how badly a user strategy that isn't safe with all servers in the finite execution sense can fail with the class of all helpful servers. More specifically, in contrast to Theorem 2.37 and Theorem 5.13, which show that such a user must fail at least once with some helpful server, we find that the user need not fail more than a finite number of times, even if the user may fail infinitely many times with unhelpful servers. Thus, Theorem 2.37 and Theorem 5.13 do truly capture the extent of the "bad news" in the finite execution setting.

The two protocols are actually rather closely related, and in particular, the finite-error protocol can be thought of as a natural adaptation of the multi-session protocol to the finite execution setting. Thus, we will consider the protocol for the the multi-session setting first.

7.1.1   Efficient universal protocols for infinite executions

We already considered universal users for multi-session computational goals in Example 6.44 in Section 6.2.4: there, we applied the techniques we developed in the finite execution setting (to prove Theorem 3.12, for example) to find again that we could achieve the multi-session computational goal for any problem that had a competitive interactive proof system with any server that was helpful for the multi-session goal – i.e., in the infinite execution sense – with a quadratic blow-up in the number of errors by using Theorem 6.41 in the place of Theorem 2.35.

The reason we needed Theorem 6.41 (instead of, say, Theorem 6.36) was that helpfulness only guaranteed that the total number of errors incurred by a good user strategy was bounded, but errors could occur at any time. Earlier, in Example 6.31, we were able to obtain users from less sophisticated constructions whenever the desired problem had a *program checker*, but only when the server was assumed to be stateless. The technical reason that this eased matters was that a "good" user strategy would yield correct results immediately.

Another assumption on the server that provides a similar guarantee is the assumption that it is *helpful in the finite-execution sense*—then, if we simply run the finite-execution strategy on each session, no matter what state it is in at the end of a session, the helped user protocol obtains a correct answer from the server in the following session with probability p; in particular, for a computational problem Π and the finite-execution goal of solving Π G_Π, we could consider $\mathcal{S}_{G_\Pi,1}$, i.e., the class of servers that help some finite-execution user achieve G_Π with probability 1.

Now, the problem of achieving the *multi-session* goal of computing Π with the class $\mathcal{S}_{G_\Pi,1}$ can be viewed either as an alternative restriction of the basic universal setting in infinite executions (since $\mathcal{S}_{G_\Pi,1}$ is a subclass of the class of all helpful servers for the multi-session goal) or as a relaxation of the basic universal setting in finite executions, in which we invoke the same user strategy on many finite executions, but allow the user to "remember" what happened previously. In the latter case, we have also relaxed our requirements for correctness, allowing the user to make a few mistakes across the various finite executions. Either way, it is surely a natural setting to consider.

Now, returning to Example 6.31 for a moment, recall that every problem with the necessary competitive proof systems has a program checker (cf. Corollary 3.13), but the converse is generally considered unlikely to hold; therefore, this stronger assumption on the server allowed the user to accomplish a little more. Presently, we will develop a different technique that will allow us to push this further—the technique will resemble that used in the original "learning in the limit" [66] or "inductive inference" [29] constructions; in this case, though, rather than producing a hypothesis that *predicts*, e.g., the value of the function on values we haven't seen yet, we'll be able to use the server's help to *efficiently compute* a very hard function on any instance of our choice—under our still weaker assumption on the server (the stateless "solvers" of Example 6.31 are all contained in $\mathcal{S}_{G_\Pi,1}$), we'll be able to get users for all computable decision problems:

Theorem 7.1 (A time-efficient universal user for any computable decision problem). *Let Π be a computable decision problem, and let G be the multi-session goal of solving Π and G_Π be the finite-execution goal of solving Π. Let $\mathcal{S}_{G_\Pi,1}$ be the class of servers that are $(G_\Pi, 1)$-helpful in the finite execution sense. Then there is an $\mathcal{S}_{G_\Pi,1}$-universal user strategy for G. Moreover, in every execution, there exists a polynomial p such that the user strategy's running time in each session of size n is bounded by $p(n)$ in the RAM model.*

Proof We will first show, for any computable decision problem, how to construct a sensing function that is safe and viable with the class of all helpful servers (in the one-shot sense) for computing that function, and time-efficient on each round. At this point, it already follows from Theorem 6.23 that a universal user exists for this class of servers. We then argue that the universal user constructed in Theorem 6.23 is also time-efficient overall, completing the proof.

Construction of sensing.   Let $\Pi : \{0,1\}^* \to \{0,1\}$ be a computable decision problem. In particular, suppose that Π is computed by some algorithm A.

Our basic strategy in sensing will be to first produce a table of Π by simulating a constant number of steps of A on each round; we will then verify the answers produced by our current user strategy U against the table for Π as it is computed—if the verdict U would produce in a round does not match the value recorded in the table, sensing outputs 0. On the other hand, in each session (*after* the first time U terminates a session) where the environment provides an instance x such that the table does not yet contain the value of x, we will also record its verdict in a table of "unverified" answers provided by the current algorithm (each time sensing outputs 0, we skip to an empty table). Then, each time the simulation of A completes on some instance y, the sensing function will examine the table of unverified answers for the current user strategy for an earlier unverified guess for $\Pi(y)$ by this strategy; if one exists and this guess is incorrect, sensing will output 0 in that round. In all other cases, sensing will output 1.

Note that in the RAM model, this sensing function can be computed in a constant number of steps on each round—we store the unverified answers in a table starting from a "base" pointer and track the index of the lexicographically last unverified answer from the current strategy; when sensing outputs 0, "skipping to a new table" is achieved by replacing the base pointer with the index following the lexicographically last unverified answer. Lookup of an entry in one of our tables and simulation of a constant number of steps of A is trivially constant time.

Weak soundness of sensing. It is easy to see that the above construction satisfies weak soundness: when the user fails a session where the environment provided an instance x, there are three cases. In the first case, the user may still be executing during its first session, in which case either it only produces a single error, or else it must make an error during a later session, which we will argue next that we catch. The other two cases depend on whether or not the sensing function has computed $\Pi(x)$ yet. If it has, then we immediately see that the user's verdict is wrong, and output 0. If not, then the incorrect verdict is recorded in the table of unverified answers for the strategy. Then, once the sensing function completes its simulation of $A(x)$, either we will have already produced a 0 on some other round for some other reason, or else we will see that the verdict stored in the unverified answers table does not match $\Pi(x)$, and output 0. Thus, in any case, if there is an error after the end of the first session, the sensing function eventually outputs 0 with probability 1.

Strong viability of sensing. We note that by definition, for every $S \in \mathcal{S}_{G_\Pi,1}$, there is guaranteed to exist some user strategy U_S such that if it is run from its initial state, in each session of the execution with E and S in which E sends x to the user, U_S returns $\Pi(x)$ and terminates the session in some polynomial number of steps $p_S(\mathbf{sz}(\sigma))$. Thus, consider the infinite execution strategy U_S' that runs U_S from its initial state at the beginning of each session. Whenever we start running U_S', if we run it until U_S would terminate the current session (in at most $p_S(\mathbf{sz}(\sigma))$ rounds), then subsequently U_S' will run U_S from its initial state in each session. Thus, if we run U_S' with a grace period of p_S, it computes $\Pi(x)$ correctly on every round except for the first one. Note that our sensing function does not store the verdict produced by U_S' in its unverified answers table, so it only stores correct values for $\Pi(x)$ in the unverified answers table for U_S'. Since, by construction, the only ways sensing outputs 0 occur when the user either produces a verdict in a round that does not match an existing instance in our table for Π or when we complete the simulation of $A(x)$ for some instance x for which we an incorrect verdict is recorded in the unverified answers table, sensing does not output 0 with U_S' after the first session with probability 1. Therefore, our sensing function is strongly viable with every such S.

Time complexity of the universal user. Suppose we consider the class of polynomial time clocked user strategies in which each strategy is given by a pair (U, p) where U is a user strategy (in the general sense) and p is a polynomial, with the interpretation that, on each session, the strategy (U, p) runs U for at most $p(\mathbf{sz}(\sigma))$ steps (unless U terminates the session on its own), and then automatically terminates the session. This class is easy to enumerate; moreover, each strategy (U, p) is trivially time-bounded. In particular, we note that for the aforementioned strategy U_S' and polynomial p_S with the server S, the clocked strategy (U_S', p_S) behaves identically to U_S', and p_S is the desired bounding function for strong viability. We therefore can apply Theorem 6.23 to conclude that there is a $\mathcal{S}_{G_\Pi,1}$-universal user for the goal of computing Π in the infinite execution sense. Moreover, since strong viability holds perfectly, by the furthermore clause of the theorem and the fact that computation of the sensing function only requires $O(1)$ additional steps per round in the RAM model, the running time of the universal user in each session is indeed bounded by *some* fixed polynomial. ■

7.1.2 Universal protocols with bounded mistakes for finite executions

Theorem 7.1 exploited the fact that a user for an infinite execution goal could make mistakes to cope with the fact that *verifying* the server's answers was vastly more difficult than *communicating* with the server.[1] Thus, this construction suggests that perhaps by lowering our expectations for users in the finite execution setting and allowing them to make mistakes sometimes, we might be able to achieve a broader class of goals, perhaps even much more—in a sense, the construction we saw showed how the finite execution user could do more if we "ran it multiple times." We'll now consider a different relaxation in which the user is allowed to "make some mistakes," even though we have only one "session" to work with: namely, we'll ask that the user only err with the server for a bounded number of the non-deterministic choices that the environment could make, i.e., for a bounded number of the environment's actual strategies:

Definition 7.2 (Finite-error universal user). We say that a user strategy U is *finite-error $(\mathcal{S}, p)$-universal* for a class of servers $\mathcal{S}$ and a finite goal $G = (\mathcal{E}, R)$ if for every $S \in \mathcal{S}$, for all but finitely many $E \in \mathcal{E}$, in every execution in which the user is started from its initial state, the user achieves the goal in (E, U, S) with probability p.

Likewise, a user strategy is *weakly finite-error $(\mathcal{S}^*, p)$-universal* for a class of server-state pairs $\mathcal{S}^*$ and a finite goal $G = (\mathcal{E}, R)$ if for every pair $(S, \sigma^{(\mathrm{s})}) \in \mathcal{S}^*$, for all but finitely many $E \in \mathcal{E}$, the user achieves the goal in the execution (E, U, S) with probability p whenever U is started from its initial state and S is started from $\sigma^{(\mathrm{s})}$.

Strictly speaking, we will only work with finite-error *weakly* universal users in the following; note that the collection of environment strategies in

---

[1] Actually, in all fairness, this is a kind of abuse of the weakness of the conclusions of Theorem 6.23 and unquantified "achievement" in infinite executions more generally, to an extent *even more severe* than that employed in our use of enumerations, which we criticized for finite execution goals in Chapter 4 and will criticize again in the context of our infinite execution strategies in the next chapter. Our objective in the present chapter is more to understand where the real theoretical limits of the power of our universal users lie, and we can only ask for the reader's forbearance towards the fact that these limits are sometimes pretty far removed from any practical concerns.

which the user fails is *allowed to depend on the server and its initial state.*
We will also continue to restrict our attention to computational goals for the
rest of this section. Moreover, for the technique we will develop to work, *we
will need to presently restrict our attention to users that run in time* $2^{O(n)}$.
(Although at the end of this section, we'll briefly consider a variant of our
construction which has a polynomial time user strategy.)

Now, notice that in interactive proofs, if we utilize an exponential time
verifier, the arguments in IP = PSPACE "scale up" to give us proof systems
for precisely ESPACE (i.e., the class of decision problems solvable in space
$2^{O(n)}$); for the present purposes, the particularly relevant direction is the
containment that problems with proof systems with exponential time verifiers
must be contained in ESPACE—this follows from the technique sketched in
Proposition 3.11. Allowing the verifier to err on a finite set of instances
and run for a long time on instances where the proof fails does not change
the class of problems, since these "corrections" could be hard-coded into the
simulator for the proof system. Likewise, for the standard notion of universal
users running in time $2^{O(n)}$, an analogue of Theorem 3.12 holds – precisely,
Theorem 5.25 is the relevant direction – showing that any universal user
for such a problem Π yields an $2^{O(n)}$-time (competitive) interactive proof
system for Π, as discussed in Chapter 5. We can therefore conclude that
such universal users exist only for solving decision problems in ESPACE.

Thus, in this context, the following theorem is striking:

Theorem 7.3 (Weakly finite-error universal users for any computable problem). *Let Π be a computable decision problem, and let $\mathcal{C}$ be the class of agents
running in time $2^{O(n)}$. Then, for any $\epsilon \in [0, 1/3]$, for the class $\mathcal{S}^*$ of server-
state pairs $(S, \sigma^{(s)})$ such that S is $(G_\Pi, \mathcal{C}, 1 - \epsilon)$-helpful and $\sigma^{(s)}$ is any state
of S, there is a $(\mathcal{C}, 1-\epsilon)$-bounded weakly finite-error $(\mathcal{S}^*, 1-\epsilon)$-universal user
for G_Π.*

That is, by allowing the user to err on some set of instances, the class
of problems *provably* expands *dramatically*—as a consequence of the Space
Hierarchy Theorem, we know even EXPSPACE (problems solvable in space
$2^{\mathrm{poly}(n)}$) is not contained in ESPACE, which in turn, although it contains
many natural problems, does not begin to encompass nearly all computable
problems. Furthermore, although we do not see how to extend the technique
to handle, e.g., enumerable sets such as the halting set, we likewise don't
know of any formal obstacles preventing such an extension.

We will use the following enumeration in the construction

Lemma 7.4. *There is an enumeration of all triples $(\tilde{U}, y, k)$ where $\tilde{U}$ is
an interactive algorithm (probabilistic interactive Turing machine), $k \in \mathbb{N}$,
and $y \in \{0, 1\}^*$, such that if each $\tilde{U}$ is simulated in E_y for $2^{k|y|}$ steps in
enumeration order, the following properties are satisfied*

1. *Any fixed U^* and input x of length n is simulated for 2^{kn} steps within
$2^{O((|U^*|+k)n)}$ steps.*

2. For any fixed U^* and k^*, there is an integer $N(U^*, k^*)$ such that there are at most $N(U^*, k^*)$ pairs $(\tilde{U}, k')$ such that for any x, the triple $(\tilde{U}, x, k')$ is enumerated before (U^*, x, k^*).

3. For any fixed U^* and k^*, the triples (U^*, y, k^*) appear enumerated according to a standard length-increasing enumeration of binary strings.

Proof

Construction. The enumeration proceeds in phases, $i = 1, 2, \ldots$. In phase i, for each $j = 1, \ldots, i - 1$, we check if $j | i$. If so, we put $m = i/j$, and for each y of length m in standard order, we repeat the following. For each $\ell = 1, \ldots, j - 1$, we put $k = j - \ell$, and for each $\tilde{U}$ with a description of length ℓ (listed in some fixed order), the next triple is $(\tilde{U}, y, k)$.

Analysis. We verify the three claimed properties.

1. Notice first that when we are running the simulations for the tuples corresponding to a fixed ℓ, k, and y of length m, there are 2^ℓ such interactive algorithms and each is run for 2^{km} steps. Thus, for a fixed y, the simulations take

$$\sum_{k=1}^{j-1} 2^\ell 2^{km} = \sum_{k=1}^{j-1} 2^{km+j-k} = 2^j \sum_{k=1}^{j-1} 2^{k(m-1)} \le 2^{(j-1)m+2}$$

steps. There are 2^m y of length m, so the simulations for each m take at most $2^m 2^{(j-1)m+2} = 2^{jm+2}$ steps.

Now, notice that for a given phase i, there are at most i pairs (j, m) such that $j \cdot m = i$ so the total running time in a given phase i is at most

$$\sum_{(j,m):jm=i} 2^{jm+2} = \sum_{(j,m):jm=i} 2^{i+2} \le i2^{i+2} < 2^{2i+2}.$$

So in particular, up to the completion of the ith phase, the total running time is at most 2^{2i+3}. Since the triple (U^*, x, k) for x of length n is enumerated when $j = |U^*| + k$ and $i = j \cdot n = (|U^*| + k)n$, this triple is enumerated during the $(|U^*| + k)n$th phase, which thus completes within $2^{2(|U^*|+k)n+3}$ steps.

2. Notice that for any given y of length m, for a particular $|U^*|$ and k^*, we enumerate (U^*, y, k^*) whenever $j = j^* = |U^*| + k^*$. Prior to this triple, on the same index j^* we always enumerate the same set of pairs $(\tilde{U}, k)$ with $|\tilde{U}| + k = j^*$. Now, suppose we output (U^*, y, k^*) on index $i^* = j^* m$. Notice also that since i is strictly increasing, if we consider the triples output with different values of j, for a fixed length m, only pairs $(\tilde{U}, k)$ with $|\tilde{U}| + k = j < j^*$ can have been

enumerated since otherwise $j > j^*$ and we would have for some $i' \le i^*$ $i' = j \cdot m > j^* \cdot m = i^*$. Notice that there are at most j pairs $(|\tilde{U}|, k)$ satisfying $|\tilde{U}| + k = j$, and therefore at most $j2^j$ triples $(\tilde{U}, y, k)$ at any index $j \le j^*$, and hence $N(U^*, k^*) = 2^{2(|U^*|+k^*)+1}$ suffices.

3. For a fixed (U^*, k^*), for each y of some fixed length m, we output a triple containing (U^*, k^*) precisely once each time we consider $j^* = |U^*| + k^*$. Notice that, for a fixed m, we consider the strings y of length m in standard order. So, for each m, the triples (U^*, y, k^*) for y of length m are output in standard order. Again now, since i is strictly increasing, prior to m, we could only have considered j^* with $m' < m$ since otherwise we would have for $i' < i$ $i' = m' \cdot j^* > m \cdot j^* = i$. Thus, we output the triples (U^*, y, k^*) in the desired length-increasing standard order.

∎

Using Lemma 7.4, we are ready to adapt Theorem 7.1 to a finite execution setting.

Proof (of Theorem 7.3) We wish to construct a user U that, for all sufficiently long instances x, when interacting with a server S, computes $\Pi(x)$.

Our construction will be a finite-execution analogue of Theorem 7.1: the basic idea is to guarantee that in any execution (E_x, U, S), for the finite-execution goal G_Π, U simulates (a prefix of) an execution with the environment for the *infinite-execution* (multi-session) version of the goal. More precisely, we'll consider an infinite execution in which every instance x is non-deterministically chosen by the environment in some session, and output the user's verdict in that session. Then, since the user achieving the infinite-execution goal only errs in a finite number of sessions, we'll be able to conclude that our *finite execution* user only errs on a finite number of instances. Of course, this reasoning is only sound if the user really simulates the *same* non-deterministic environment strategy, independent of the instance x that the user is really interested in for the finite-execution goal. Since there are 2^n instances of length n, this requires our user to run in exponential time.

In slightly more detail then, instead of running the sensing function of Theorem 7.1 "in parallel" with the user's interaction with the server, we find it simpler to simply perform this computation up front. Thus, before starting to communicate with the server, the user computes $\Pi(y)$ on as many small instances y as he or she can within some growing time bound. Since we will run in exponential time, we will use a time bound of 2^n, but this is not essential.

Now, as in most of our constructions of universal users, we again enumerate user strategies, and for each guess $\tilde{U}$ for the user strategy helped by the server in our enumeration, we then check the answers $\tilde{U}$ obtains from the server on these small instances. We can then guarantee that if we would obtain an incorrect answer by following $\tilde{U}$ on y, for sufficiently long x, we will have already computed $\Pi(y)$ ourselves, and so we conclude that $\tilde{U}$ is not the user U^* who decides Π with the server's help, so we move on to the next guess $\tilde{U}$ in the enumeration. Thus, since U^* occurs at some finite index in the enumeration, there is some finite bound on the number of times we must change $\tilde{U}$, and hence some longest small instance y for which we need to compute $\Pi(y)$ to prompt a revision. As suggested earlier, we will embed all of our instances into the same fixed "infinite environment strategy" so that the server really misleads each incorrect ith $\tilde{U}$ on the same instances y_i.

Construction of U: Let $\{z_i \in \{0,1\}^*\}_{i=1}^{\infty}$ be the standard enumeration of binary strings. Since Π is decidable, let M be a decision procedure for Π, let $T(y)$ denote the running time of M on input y, and let $K_n = \max\left\{k : \sum_{i=1}^{k} T(z_i) < 2^n\right\}$. On input x, U first simulates M on inputs $z_1, z_2, \ldots$ for up to 2^n steps, and thus computes $\Pi(z_1), \ldots, \Pi(z_{K_n})$. U then enumerates triples $(\tilde{U}, y, k)$ according to the enumeration guaranteed to exist in Lemma 7.4.

For each $(\tilde{U}, y, k)$ with y of length m, U simulates $\tilde{U}$ to interact with S for up to 2^{km} steps in E_y, repeating the interaction up to $36(m + 1 + \log(1/\epsilon))$ times if it completes. If all $36(m + 1 + \log(1/\epsilon))$ interactions complete and $y \in \{z_1, \ldots, z_{K_n}\}$, U checks that the majority agrees with $\Pi(y)$; if not, U marks $(\tilde{U}, k)$ as FAULTY. Finally, if $y = x$, and $(\tilde{U}, k)$ is unmarked, U halts and outputs the majority answer for $(\tilde{U}, S)$ on x as its verdict.

Analysis: Observe first that only the user's stopping rule depends on x; otherwise, the user's interaction with the server is independent of x. Of course, in G_Π, the server is *also* oblivious to which strategy $E_x \in \mathcal{E}$ the environment has chosen. Since the server is $(G_\Pi, \mathcal{C}, 1 - \epsilon)$-helpful for the class $\mathcal{C}$ of users running in time $2^{O(n)}$, there is some U^* running in time $2^{k^* n}$ (in environments of size n) such that for all $E_y \in \mathcal{E}$, $\Pr[U^* \text{ returns } \Pi(y) \text{ in } (E_y, U^*, S)] \geq 1 - \epsilon$. For $k' = k^* + \log\log(1/\epsilon) + O(1)$, all $36(m + 1 + \log(1/\epsilon))$ interactions will complete within $2^{k'm}$ steps on inputs of length m. Observe that the enumeration guarantees that there are at most $N = N(U^*, k')$ pairs $(\tilde{U}, k)$ occurring prior to (U^*, k') on each input in the enumeration.

Claim 7.5. *There is a sequence of $r \leq \frac{2N^2}{\epsilon}$ instances $y_1, \ldots, y_r = z_\ell$ such that if $K_n \geq \ell$, then for each $(\tilde{U}, k)$ before (U^*, k') in the user's enumeration, either $(\tilde{U}, k)$ is marked as FAULTY, or else $(\tilde{U}, k)$ fools the user into outputting a wrong answer with probability at most $\frac{\epsilon}{2N}$*

Proof Consider the sequence of instances $y_1, y_2, \ldots$ where y_i is the first instance (in standard order) for which, on input y_i, the user computes $\Pi(y_{i-1})$ and for some $(\tilde{U}, k)$ before (U^*, k') in the enumeration, the user would output a wrong answer after concluding the simulations of $(\tilde{U}, S)$ on input y_i with probability at least $\epsilon/2N$. Let BADCOINS$((\tilde{U}, k), i)$ be the set of coin tosses that lead the user to this event.

Observe that, if $(\tilde{U}, k)$ would mislead the user into outputting an incorrect answer on some sequence of coin tosses on any $z_s \in \{y_1, \ldots, y_{i-1}\}$ and $K_n \geq s$, then after the simulations resulting from that sequence of coin tosses C_s, the user would notice that the answer obtained from $(\tilde{U}, S)$ on input z_s did not match the computed value $\Pi(z_s)$, and so by construction $(\tilde{U}, k)$ would be marked as FAULTY. Of course, by our choice of y_i, the user computes $\Pi(z_s)$ on input y_i. Therefore, since the user's behavior is deterministic on any fixed sequence of coin tosses, $(\tilde{U}, k)$ is marked as FAULTY on this input on any sequence of coin tosses having C_s as a prefix. In particular, by construction now, observe that since the user considers the instances in order and $(\tilde{U}, k)$ cannot mislead the user if it is marked FAULTY, the sets BADCOINS$((\tilde{U}, k), i)$ are prefix-free, and thus, for a fixed $(\tilde{U}, k)$, the events of picking a sequence of coin tosses that have a prefix in BADCOINS$((\tilde{U}, k), i)$ are disjoint, and so the probability of some such event occurring is the sum of the probabilities of the individual events.

Finally, observe that if there were more than $\frac{2N^2}{\epsilon}$ such instances, some $(\tilde{U}, k)$ must be fooling the user with probability at least $\epsilon/2N$ on more than $2N/\epsilon$ distinct instances. Since these are disjoint events, the probabilities would then sum to greater than one. ∎

Now, we observe that on any instance z, by our guarantee on the correctness of U^*, and since $\epsilon < 1/3$, (U^*, k') only has a majority of incorrect answers with probability at most $e^{-2m-2-\log(1/\epsilon)} < \frac{\epsilon}{4} 2^{-2m}$. Notice that each triple (U^*, y, k') is enumerated exactly once and thus, the probability that (U^*, k') is marked as FAULTY is less than $\sum_{m=1}^{\infty} 2^m \frac{\epsilon}{4} 2^{-2m} = \frac{\epsilon}{4}$.

Whenever (U^*, k') is not marked as FAULTY on some sequence of coin tosses, our choice of enumeration guarantees that for input x, there are at most N pairs $(\tilde{U}, k)$ prior to (U^*, k') such that $(\tilde{U}, x, k)$ appears in the enumeration. Notice that by our claim, if n is sufficiently large, either each such pair is marked as FAULTY or else causes the user to output an incorrect verdict with probability at most $\epsilon/2N$, and hence by a union bound, the user outputs an incorrect verdict before simulating (U^*, x, k') with probability at most $\epsilon/2$. Moreover, notice that when (U^*, k') is not marked as FAULTY, then the user outputs a correct verdict after completing the simulation for (U^*, x, k'), where our enumeration guarantees that this simulation will complete within $2^{O(n)}$ steps. Thus, the probability that the user does not output a correct verdict within $2^{O(n)}$ steps is at most $\epsilon/2 + \epsilon/4 < \epsilon$ as needed. ∎

The key point in Theorem 7.3 was that on every instance specified by the environment, the user simulated some prefix of a fixed execution with the server, and the only reason that the user needed to run in exponential time was so that all of the instances of length up to the length of the target instance could appear in a prefix within the user's time bound during the finite execution. Another way of accomplishing the same effect would be to consider problems in which the instances are encoded in unary—so that there are only n instances of length up to n. The reader can check that essentially the same construction suffices for such problems, and thus we also find:

Corollary 7.6 (Polynomial time weakly mistake-bounded universal users for computable unary problems). *Let Π be a computable unary decision problem. Then, for any $\epsilon \in [0, 1/3]$, for the class S^* of server-state pairs $(S, \sigma^{(s)})$ such that S is $(G_\Pi, 1 - \epsilon)$-helpful and $\sigma^{(s)}$ is any state of S, there is weakly finite-error $(S^*, 1 - \epsilon)$-universal user for G_Π that runs in polynomial time.*

Limits to the strength of sensing requirements in finite executions

Theorem 7.3 and Corollary 7.6 are not only demonstrations of the power of the ability to make errors: they also delimit the "bad news" presented by our theorems on the necessary strength of sensing in the basic and generic universal settings for finite executions, Theorems 2.37 and 5.13. Recall that those theorems showed that if a sensing function was not safe with the class of *all* server strategies, then the sensing function was also not safe with respect to their respective classes of all *helpful* user strategies; the proof, of course, proceeded by taking a server that fooled the sensing function and constructing a helpful server from it that still fooled sensing. In particular, since Propositions 2.26 and 5.12 showed that the sensing functions that indicated whether or not a universal user would halt were safe sensing functions, we had no hope of constructing universal users for the basic and generic universal settings unless the user strategies knew not to halt with an unhelpful server.

Now, if there was a server strategy that fooled sensing for infinitely many of the environment's non-deterministic choices, then the constructions of Theorems 2.37 and 5.13 could be used to construct helpful servers that could fool the sensing function with some user strategy on any *finite* subset of these environment strategies by simply embedding the helpful server with padding of some length given by the maximum of the finite padding lengths that Theorems 2.37 and 5.13 indicate for each environment strategy. So, if the user makes infinitely many mistakes with unhelpful servers, then in such a case we can construct "counterexample" helpful servers that force the user to make mistakes in any desired finite number of environment strategies from a fixed initial server state.

In this context, Theorem 7.3 and Corollary 7.6 now show examples of highly nontrivial goals (deciding arbitrary computable problems, and computable unary problems, respectively) for which unsafe user strategies cannot be forced to make infinitely many mistakes from any server state. That is, the fact that the user may make mistakes in infinitely many environments with an unhelpful server (as is surely the case here—both user strategies must make infinitely many mistakes with the trivial server if the problem is not in ESPACE) *does not* imply that the user must also make infinitely many mistakes with some helpful server. Indeed, moreover, Theorem 7.3 shows (along with Corollary 7.6) how to exploit this gap to construct nontrivial user strategies for which safe sensing is provably impossible.

7.2 Protocols for generic goals with exploration sessions and resettable servers

Perhaps the most remarkable aspect of Theorems 7.1 and 7.3 is that they show an example of a goal for which it is possible to construct universal users that are stunningly efficient relative to the complexity of sensing (as a function of the size parameter). In the interest of obtaining such efficiency more broadly, we now turn to developing a setting that abstracts the properties that the constructions of Theorem 7.1 and/or Theorem 7.3 relied on, to exhibit an analogous construction for a generic class of goals.

In a sense, the real key property exploited in Theorem 7.3 was that since the server was oblivious to the environment's actual choice of strategy, the environment implicitly allowed us to simulate communication with the server in any environment of our choosing. In the following section, we'll develop a notion of *exploration sessions* in which the environment is *explicitly* assumed to provide such an ability somehow (with, naturally, environments that don't communicate with the server as an example of environments providing this ability automatically). Effectively, this extension will allow us to evaluate candidate user strategies in "easy" environments, which will accomplish the desired decoupling of the complexity of sensing from the complexity of communication.

Now, the real weakness of Theorem 7.1 and Theorem 7.3 was that the number of errors that the user made, though it was always finite, could depend on the server's initial state, whereas in accordance with Definition 6.34, in our earlier constructions of universal users with bounded errors, specifically Theorem 6.36 and Theorem 6.41, we required that the number of failures should be bounded *independent* of the server's state. Now, the techniques we have available don't seem to allow us to obtain the usual standards, but in the second part of this section, we'll introduce the notion of *resettable* classes of servers that, on some standard indication, may each be reset to some respective fixed state. Thus, we finesse the weakness of the technique because we *do* obtain a fixed bound for the reset state, and in the final part of this section, we'll see how the technique developed in the first part of this chapter can yield universal users for which the number of errors is *independent of the environment's size*, provided that the server is resettable and that the environment supports exploration. This section is from joint work with Oded Goldreich and Madhu Sudan [70].

7.2.1   Multi-session goals with exploration sessions

Our basic formulation of multi-session goals (see Definition 6.7) mandates that the environment determines the initial state of new sessions obliviously of any previous actions of the (other) agents (i.e., actions of these agents in prior sessions). This is an artifact of the postulate that the environment's move at an end-session state only depends on the index of that state (i.e., the index of the last session), which means that whatever effects the user and server have had on the environment (during the last session) are dissolved at the beginning of a new session. This somewhat stringent postulate was made in order to develop a notion of sessions that are independent of one another (from the environment's point of view). In contrast, at the extreme, allowing the environment's actions (in each session) to depend on the entire history collapses such multi-session goals to general compact goals. An intermediate case, which seems very appealing, refers to multi-session executions in which the dependence of the environment's actions on the history of prior sessions is limited. Specifically, we restrict the dependence of the environment's actions on the history of prior sessions to the selection of the contents of the initial state in new sessions. Furthermore, we introduce a framework that allows us to consider cases where the selection of the initial state (of the new session) is further restricted.

In addition to the general appeal of the new framework, it facilitates the introduction of the notion of "exploration sessions:" these are sessions that are actually initialized by the user with the aim of assisting it to later perform better in "real" sessions that are invoked by the environment, as usual. Note that such sessions can be easily modeled (by the new framework) by having the user indicate at the end of the current session that it wishes to perform such an exploration and even have the environment behave as if it has selected a specific contents for the initial state of the next session.[2]

Definition 7.7 (History-dependent multi-session goals, sketch)**.** Let $\mathcal{H}$ be a family of functions, representing the allowed history-dependent actions of the environment when initiating a new session. A goal consisting of a non-deterministic strategy $\mathcal{E}$ and a referee R is called an $\mathcal{H}$-*dependent multi-session goal* if the following conditions hold.

1. *The environment's states:* As in Definition 6.7, the local states of the environment are partitioned into three non-empty sets consisting of *start-session* states, *end-session* states, and *(intermediate) session* states. Each of these states is a pair consisting of a *record (representing a digest of the history of prior sessions)* and a *contents (representing the actual state within the execution of the current session)*.[3] The ini-

---

[2]Indeed, such an effect can also be captured by the original formulation (i.e., of Definition 6.7) by an awkward modification of the environment's strategy. However, capturing such exploration sessions via Definition 7.7 seems more transparent.

[3]Indeed, the index of the current session (used in Definition 6.7) is a special case of the record (of prior sessions).

tial local state corresponds to the pair (λ, λ), and belongs to the set of end-session states.

2. *The referee behaves like in Definition 6.7;* that is, the corresponding temporal decision function R' evaluates to $\perp$ if and only if the current state is not an end-session state.

3. *Starting a new session:* When in an end-session state, the environment moves non-deterministically to a start-session state. Furthermore, like in Definition 6.7, this move is independent of the actual contents of the current end-session state. That is, for each actual strategy of the environment $E \in \mathcal{E}$, E is invariant over all possible end-session states that have the same record, and it fits some function in $\mathcal{H}$; that is, for each $E \in \mathcal{E}$ there exists $h \in \mathcal{H}$ such that for every end-session state $(r, \sigma') \in \{0, 1\}^* \times \Omega$, it holds that $E(r, \sigma') = h(r) \in \{0, 1\}^* \times \Omega$.[4]

Optional (as in Definition 6.7): The environment can also notify the user that a new session is starting, and even whether or not the previous session was completed successfully *(i.e., with R' evaluating to 1)*. Analogous notifications can also be sent to the server.

4. *Execution of the current session:* When in any other state, the environment moves probabilistically, while possibly updating the record, but its behavior is independent of the actual strategy. That is, for every $E_1, E_2 \in \mathcal{E}$ and every non-end-session state (r, σ'), the random variables $E_1(r, \sigma')$ and $E_2(r, \sigma')$ are identically distributed. Furthermore, the contents of that state changes obliviously of the record; that is, for every $E \in \mathcal{E}$ and pair of non-end-session states $((r_1, \sigma'), (r_2, \sigma'))$, the second element of $E(r_1, \sigma')$ is distributed identically to the second element of $E(r_2, \sigma')$ *(i.e., for every $\sigma'' \in \Omega$ it holds that $\sum_{r'} \Pr[E(r_1, \sigma') = (r', \sigma'')]$ equals $\sum_{r'} \Pr[E(r_2, \sigma') = (r', \sigma'')]$).*

Indeed, Definition 6.7 is a special case of Definition 7.7, obtained by requiring that for every $E \in \mathcal{E}$ and every state (r, σ') the first element of $E(r, \sigma')$ equals $r + 1$ if the state is an end-session state and equals r otherwise. Needless to say, here we are interested in other cases.

One natural type of history-dependence that is captured by Definition 7.7 is the dependence of (the initial contents) of the next session on the record of failures and successes of prior sessions. Another natural case, which refers to the aforementioned (multi-session goals with) exploration sessions, is defined next. In this case, the record maintains the number of sessions completed so far and possibly also an exploration request, denoted e, sent by the user (say, at the very end of the last session).

---

[4]Note that Condition 3 in Definition 6.7 can be stated in this manner, when r equals the current index i, and $\mathcal{H}$ is the set of all functions h over Ω such that $h(i) = (i + 1, h'(i))$ for some $h' : \mathbb{N} \to \Omega$. Alternatively, we can state the condition in Definition 6.7 by postulating that h only depends on the number of prior sessions recorded in r.

Definition 7.8 (exploration sessions, sketch). A *multi-session goal with exploration sessions* is an $\mathcal{H}$-dependent multi-session goal as in Definition 7.7 where for every $h \in \mathcal{H}$ it holds that $h(r) = (i + 1, e)$ if $r = (i, e)$, and otherwise the environment replaces the record $r = i$ by $i+1$ *(where $r = i$ and $i + 1$ are viewed as integers)*. Lastly, during the execution of a session, the record $r = i$ remains intact unless *(at the session's end)* the environment receives a special exploration request with contents e *(from the user)*, which sets the record to the value (i, e).

Indeed, $r = (i, e)$ encodes the event that session i ended with the user requesting exploration with contents e, and otherwise the record is viewed as merely encoding the number of sessions completed so far. In the latter case, the new session is initialized with a contents that only depends on the environment's non-deterministic choice (and on the number of sessions completed so far).

7.2.2 Resettable servers

A natural feature that many servers have is resettability: that is, a guarantee that these servers can be simply reset to a predetermined initial state. This resetting is performed in response to a simple predetermined user command (or message). Indeed, we distinguish the case in which the "resetting command" (or "resetting message") is known a priori from the case in which this command (or message) may not be known a priori. Needless to say, it is more advantageous to have servers of the first type, but we mention (see discussion below) that it is also beneficial to just have servers of the second type. Formally, we capture the difference by considering classes of resettable servers that respond to the same resetting command.

Definition 7.9 (User-resettable servers). A server strategy is called *user-resettable* (or just *resettable*) if upon receiving a special (*resetting*) message from the user, it moves to a predetermined state, which coincides with its initial local state. A class of resettable servers is called *uniformly resettable* if all servers in the class respond to the same resetting message.

Note that we do not assume that the servers in a uniformly resettable class have the same initial local state, nor do we assume any other common features (beyond resetting upon receiving the same message).

Uniformly vs non-uniformly resettable servers. In the rest of this section, we will refer to classes of uniformly resettable servers. As we shall see, uniform resettability can play a role in constructing universal user strategies, while it seems that non-uniformly resettable servers cannot play this role. Still, non-uniform resettability can be beneficial for achieving various goals, and this benefit may be inherited by universal strategies. Specifically, if a server tends to get stuck (or damaged by some effect of the environment), then being able to reset it (even by a server-specific message) is very beneficial.

One benefit of uniform resettability

The benefit of using uniformly resettable servers is demonstrated by considering the gap between Examples 6.31 and 6.44. Recall that both examples refer to solving computational problems posed by the environment, specifically, instances of a decision problem D_0. In Example 6.31, we showed that *solvers for arbitrary computationally equivalent problems* (i.e., equivalent to D_0) can be used for solving D_0, by relying on a program checker for D_0. In Example 6.44 we showed that we can do better if both D_0 and its complement have interactive proof systems (with relatively efficient provers); in such a case, we can solve D_0 by using *any server that is helpful for solving* D_0. That is, we can benefit from a considerably wider class of servers.

Recall that the interactive proof systems required in Example 6.44 yield program checkers (for the same decision problem), but the opposite direction is widely believed to be false (because it would imply $\mathrm{EXP} \subseteq \mathrm{PSPACE}$). This means that, in this context, benefiting from arbitrary helpful servers is harder than benefiting from all $\mathcal{D}$-solvers, where $\mathcal{D}$ is the class of problems that are computationally equivalent to D_0.

Here we note that the result of Example 6.31 can be extended to *any class of helpful servers that is uniformly resettable*. That is, we show that if D_0 has a program checker, then D_0 can be solved by using *any resettable server that is helpful for solving* D_0. Indeed, this extends the result in Example 6.31, because the class of all $\mathcal{D}$-solvers is a very restricted class of helpful servers that are uniformly resettable.

Proposition 7.10. *Suppose that the decision problem D_0 has a program checker. Let $\mathcal{U}$ denote the class of user strategies that run in probabilistic polynomial time, and $\mathcal{S}_0$ denote a class of uniformly resettable servers that are all $\mathcal{U}$-helpful (with a bounded number of errors)[5] for deciding D_0. Furthermore, suppose that the set of bounding functions $\mathcal{B}$ for the servers is enumerable. Then, there exists an $\mathcal{S}_0$-universal user strategy such that, for every $S \in \mathcal{S}_0$, when interacting with S, this universal strategy runs in probabilistic polynomial time.*

Indeed, the additionally required enumeration exists trivially in the case that $\mathcal{S}_0$ is a class of uniformly resettable servers that all have the same (known) helpfulness-error bound.

Proof The proof is a hybrid of the arguments used in Examples 6.31 and 6.44. As in both cases, we reduce the construction of a $\mathcal{S}_0$-universal strategy to the construction of an adequate user strategy for each server $S \in \mathcal{S}_0$. Furthermore, as in both cases, each such user strategy U is coupled with an adequate sensing function V that is viable with respect to S and safe with respect to $\mathcal{S}_0$. In our construction we use a program checker for D_0 (just as done in Example 6.31), but only provide a relaxed viability guarantee (as

---

[5] Here we refer to the notion of refined helpfulness, as defined at the end of Section 6.2.4.

in Example 6.44), because we use a wider class of helpful servers that (unlike in Example 6.31) includes servers that cause a bounded number of errors. Consequently, as in Example 6.44, we shall be using Theorem 6.41 (rather than Theorem 6.23, which was used in Example 6.31).

We mention that the enumeration of user strategies (required by Theorem 6.41) holds by definition of $\mathcal{U}$, whereas the mapping of users to the index of the corresponding error bound for the server can be obtained by replacing each possible user strategy U with the sequence $(U, B_1), (U, B_2), \ldots$. Thus, we focus on constructing an adequate user strategy U and an adequate sensing function V for every $S \in \mathcal{S}_0$, while assuming that we know the corresponding error bound (as well as the uniformly resetting message). This is done by following the approach of Example 6.31, which relies on using a program checker for D_0. In fact, following this approach, it suffices to show how to transform a resettable server into a memoryless strategy (i.e., a member of $\mathcal{F})^6$ such that S is transformed into a D_0-solver.

The transformation, which amounts to emulating a memoryless strategy by using a resettable strategy, proceed as follows. Let us assume first that this resettable strategy S is helpful without any errors, and consider the corresponding user strategy $u(S)$ that uses it. Recall that we are trying to emulate a memoryless strategy that is supposed to be a D_0-solver, while the messages that we attempt to answer come from the program checker (which the strategy U invokes on receiving a message from the environment). Upon receiving a new message (which is an instance of D_0), we reset the server, and start a new communication session using the said message as if it were received from the environment. (Note that we know the corresponding resetting message.) When we (or rather the corresponding user $u(S)$) detect that the communication session is completed (i.e., that $u(S)$ has determined its answer to the environment), we use the corresponding answer (i.e., the answer that $u(S)$ would have sent to the environment) as our response to the original message. We stress that all this activity is oblivious towards the environment; that is, we create sessions that do not exist with respect to the environment, while the server is unaware of their "unreal" nature (since by this goal's definition the environment only communicates with the user, whereas the environment neither sends messages to the server nor expects any messages from it).

Indeed, the foregoing transformation converts any resettable server strategy into a memoryless strategy, because in each emulation of the latter we invoke the former on the same initial local state (via resetting) and communicate with it using the same strategy $u(S)$. Furthermore, if $S \in \mathcal{S}_0$ makes no errors when communicating with $u(S)$, then S is transformed into a D_0-solver.

It still remains to deal with the case that $S \in \mathcal{S}_0$ makes a bounded number of errors when communicating with $u(S)$. The problem is that we only used

---

[6]As in Example 6.31, $\mathcal{F}$ denotes the class of all memoryless strategies (i.e., strategies that maintain no local state).

the first session in the interaction of S with $u(S)$, whereas this session may always produce a useless (e.g., random) answer. The solution is to let $u(S)$ engage in many sessions with S, all regarding the same instance, and rule by majority, where the number of such sessions is significantly larger than the (expected) error bound, denoted b. Specifically, in our ith emulation we reset the server $O(\log i)$ times, and after each resetting we run $3b$ ("unreal") sessions, all regarding the same instance that equals the ith original message of the environment (which we aim to answer). As our answer, we take the majority vote among these $O(\log i)$ trials, where each trial takes a majority vote among its $3b$ ("unreal") sessions. Thus, the probability that we err in our ith emulation is at most $1/(i+1)^2$, because each of the $O(\log i)$ trials errs with probability at most $1/3$. It follows that the *expected* total number of errors that the emulated D_0-solver commits is bounded by a constant (i.e., indeed, the constant 1 will do).

This completes the presentation of the transformation of every $S \in \mathcal{S}_0$ into a memoryless strategy, which is used by a corresponding user strategy, denoted U. Like in Example 6.31, we couple U with a sensing function V, which uses the checker's output in the corresponding invocation (which corresponds to a real session that is initiated with a D_0-instance, selected by the environment). This V is $O(1)$-viable with respect to (U, S), and is safe with respect to U and the class of all resettable servers (which contains $\mathcal{S}_0$). This suffices for a version of Theorem 6.41 that requires relaxed strong viability and weak safety (i.e., viability as in Theorem 6.41 and safety as in Theorem 6.23). The current proposition follows.[7] ∎

Digest. Proposition 7.10 demonstrates the benefit of (uniform) resetting. The effect of resetting occurs at two levels. Most conspicuously, resetting is used to emulate a memoryless server strategy, and the benefit is that a memoryless strategy may cause less harm than an arbitrary strategy. In particular, the damage caused by improper communication with a memoryless strategy is confined to the period of improper communication, and does not propagate to the future.

---

[7]Note that V is not quite strongly safe (with respect to the latter class), because the number of rounds used in each real session grows with its index (since we use increasingly more "unreal" sessions in our emulations), and for that reason we cannot apply Theorem 6.41 as is. The benefit in using Theorem 6.41 is that it provides an error bound for the universal strategy, a bound not stated in the current result. We mention that we could have obtained stronger results in a variety of natural cases. For example, if the size of the session's initial state (i.e., the length of the instance) grows such that the ith real session refers to size $\Omega(\log i)$ and if every bound B is polynomial, then we can obtain a polynomial safety bound.

7.2.3 A generic constant-error protocol for goals with exploration sessions and resettable servers

Recall that all prior (quantitative) universality results upper-bound the number of errors as a function of the state size (indeed, see Theorems 6.36, 6.41, and 6.50). The corresponding universal strategies switch away from a failing user strategy (which they emulate) as soon as they sense many errors, where these errors occur with respect to the actual goal that the user attempts to achieve. Instead, it would have been nice to cause fewer errors with respect to the actual goal, even at the expense of causing errors in some "side experiments" (indeed, explorations), while not slowing down progress on the actual goal by too much. We shall actually do even better with the strategy presented below.

The observation that underlies the following universal strategy is that the failure of a specific user strategy (with respect to a fixed server) can be accounted to some fixed state size (i.e., the minimal state size that causes failure). So if we can experiment with various state sizes, in parallel to doing our "real" activity, then we may be able to abandon a bad user strategy while causing a number of errors that is related to this fixed size (rather than being related to the potentially larger size with which we are actually concerned). These parallel attempts are performed in exploration sessions, and the formalism of Definition 7.8 guarantees that, from the environment's point of view, these explorations do not effect the "real" sessions and vice versa. Furthermore, resetting will be used so that all sessions (real or exploratory) look the same to the server, and so the server behaves in these explorations exactly as it would have behaved in real sessions.

Theorem 7.11 (Universality via exploration). *Let $G = (\mathcal{E}, R)$, $\mathcal{U}$, $\mathcal{S}$, V, ϵ, and $\mathcal{B}$ be as in Theorem 6.41, except that here we refer to the varying-size generalization as in Theorem 6.50. Suppose that G is a multi-session goal with exploration sessions, that $\mathcal{S}$ is a set of uniformly resettable servers, and that each strategy in $\mathcal{U}$ resets the server at the beginning of each new session. Further suppose that the number of rounds in a session of G is monotonically non-decreasing with the relevant size, and that the number of start-session states of any specific size is finite. Then, there exists an $\mathcal{S}$-universal user strategy U such that for every $S \in \mathcal{S}$ there exists a constant b such that (U, S) robustly achieves the goal G with b errors, where here we refer to error counts in the simple sense as in Definition 6.34 (and, e.g., in Theorem 6.36). Furthermore, the number of rounds spent in exploration sessions never exceeds a constant fraction of the total number of rounds.*

The constant b depends on the smallest size, denoted s, for which each of the prior user strategies tried for interacting with the server S fails. Specifically, b is proportional to the number of initial states (i.e., initial contents of start-session states) that have size at most s. We note that, while in many settings the said number of initial states is exponential in s, there are settings in which the number is polynomial in s (e.g., the environment may ask us to solve decision problems that relate to a sparse set, as in Corollary 7.6). We also note that the helpfulness of the servers in $\mathcal{S}$ holds with respect to a class of users that reset the server at the beginning of each session. While this class of user strategies is somewhat restricted, it seems natural to expect "helpful" severs to be helpful also with respect to that class.

Sketch of proof We focus on the special case in which the user strategies (in $\mathcal{U}$) carry no state across sessions and the environment never chooses the same initial state for two sessions. This case is quite natural, and allows us to present all the essential ideas.

Recall that the universal strategies used in all our proofs proceed by enumerating all strategies in $\mathcal{U}$ and emulating each U_i until encountering a sufficient number of failure indications. We do essentially the same, except that we try to maintain a balance between the number of rounds used in real sessions and the number of rounds used in exploration sessions. In a sense, our strategy can be described in terms of an imaginary environment strategy that introduces such exploration sessions. Furthermore, the exploration sessions are invoked such that all possible initial states (i.e., initial contents of start-session states) of a certain size are used before we use states of larger size. We stress that this activity is done in parallel to the execution of real sessions that are initiated by the real environment. Specifically, upon terminating the execution of a real session (initiated by the real environment), the imaginary environment (or rather our user) initiates new exploration sessions until the number of rounds used by all exploration sessions exceeds half the total number of rounds so far.

Noting that the foregoing execution necessarily refers to varying state sizes, we adopt the switching criterion used in the proof of Theorem 6.50. That is, we switch from emulating U_i to emulating U_{i+1} as soon as we reach a round t_{i+1} such that $\sum_{t \in (t_i, t_{i+1}]: V(\sigma_t)=0} \frac{1}{B_i(\mathbf{sz}(\sigma_t))}$ exceeds 1. We stress that this accounting (and corresponding switch) is done across all sessions, real sessions and exploration sessions alike.

A key observation regarding this interleaved execution of real sessions and exploration sessions is that each of these (partial) executions is oblivious of the other. This follows by the fact that (by hypothesis) each strategy $U_i \in \mathcal{U}$ starts each session by resetting the server. Thus, we can decouple the aforementioned interleaved execution into a real execution (containing no explorations) and an auxiliary execution that consists of all exploration sessions. Furthermore, the auxiliary execution is totally determined as a sequence of all possible explorations, ordered according to their initial states (where states of smaller size appear before states of larger size).

Another key observation is that if (U_i, S) does not achieve the goal G (or rather its real part), then there exists a constant s_i such that the contribution of exploration sessions having (initial state of) size at most s_i to the sum $\sum_{t \in \mathbb{N}: V(\sigma_t)=0} \frac{1}{B_i(\mathbf{sz}(\sigma_t))}$ exceeds 1. This follows from the fact that events that would occur in a real execution (of real sessions) will also occur in the auxiliary execution (of exploration sessions) whereas each of these executions consists of a sequence of mutually oblivious sessions, together with our assumption that the environment only uses each initial state at most once, so the corresponding (finite) set of initial states witnesses the failure of U_i with S.

We may now invoke Theorem 6.50, while considering only the exploration sessions. While these partial executions do not necessarily satisfy the additional technical requirements regarding $\mathcal{B}$, the reasoning underlying the proof of Theorem 6.50 applies, and so we may infer that the accumulated contribution of the rounds containing errors (in which exploration occurs) is upper-bounded by a constant that depends on $s = \max_{j \in [i-1]} \{s_j\}$, where (U_i, S) achieves the goal (and the s_js are as above). Specifically, the number of errors in these exploration sessions is bounded by i times the number of different initial states of size at most s, because errors occur only at the ends of sessions. We need to show that the number of errors that occur in real sessions can also be bounded in terms of s.

The last claim is shown by noting that the number of real sessions of size at least s that take place in the said period does not exceed the number of exploration sessions. This follows by the monotonicity hypothesis (which implies that the number of rounds taken by each session of size at least s is no less than the number of rounds taken by any session of size at most s). Thus, the total number of errors (both in exploration and real sessions) is bounded by twice the aforementioned upper bound (on the number of errors in exploration sessions). The theorem follows for this special case (i.e., where $\mathcal{U}$ consists of strategies that, unlike the universal strategy that we presented, carry no state across session).

When dealing with the general case, the failures at the various sessions are not fully determined by the initial state of each session (and the strategies employed) but can be affected by the history of the execution at the user's end. (Indeed, the environment's behavior is independent of the history and the same holds with respect to the server that is being reset by the user at the beginning of each session, but the user strategy may depend on previous sessions.) The solution to this problem is to enumerate finite sequences of sessions with start-session state having size that does not exceed a specific bound. We treat each such finite sequence as we treated a single session before; that is, our exploration sessions now consist of sequences of sessions taken from this enumeration. We stress that the emulated user strategy is reset at the beginning of each such sequence of exploration sessions, but the real execution maintains state across the real sessions. The enumeration guarantees that any finite sequence of sessions that causes too many failures with respect to strategy U will be encountered in finite time and cause the universal strategy to abandon U after a finite number of sessions. The theorem follows. ∎

Chapter 8

The error complexity of strategies in infinite executions

The basic theory of semantic communication in infinite executions introduced in Chapter 6 suffers from some of the same defects as the theory for finite executions from Chapter 2: namely, as discussed in Chapter 4, in that setting, the universal strategies we constructed suffered from an exponential overhead (in the length of the target strategy) in their running time, and we saw that such overhead was unavoidable in general. In the present chapter, we consider the analogous overhead in the *number of errors* incurred by a universal strategy in infinite executions. We will see that this overhead is also, in general, unavoidable by a similar argument, adapted from work with Oded Goldreich and Madhu Sudan [70].

It is natural to wonder if, similar to the development of the Bayesian setting of Chapter 4, we can lay down some natural conditions under which the overhead incurred by our generic constructions (such as Theorem 6.23 and Theorem 6.36) can be avoided. The specific constructions we introduced in Chapter 4 (i.e., Theorem 4.9 and its refinements) are easily seen to be unsuitable since they have a positive probability of error on each run, leading to infinitely many errors (in the same positive fraction of sessions) in the limit. Nevertheless, we will see that when the user strategies are assumed to come from some class of sufficiently simple strategies, universal strategies that only incur a polynomial number of errors in the length of the description of the relevant user strategy exist.

More specifically, in joint work with Santosh Vempala [86], we observe that for a restricted kind of goal – a multi-session goal in which each session consists of a single round – and sensing that provides feedback on the user's performance in a round on the following round and is viable with respect to

B. Juba, *Universal Semantic Communication*,
DOI 10.1007/978-3-642-23297-8_8,
© Springer-Verlag Berlin Heidelberg 2011

a class of simple user strategies, then the problem of constructing a universal user from the sensing function is *precisely* the problem of learning the class of concepts corresponding to the class of strategies in the on-line learning model introduced by Bārzdiņš and Freivalds [19] and investigated by Littlestone [101]. Thus, each solution to the on-line learning problem for a concept class yields a generic construction of a universal user from a sensing function that is viable with respect to the corresponding class of strategies – allowing us to translate the existing positive results – and vice-versa, allowing us to also translate the negative results.

We will further note that the lower bounds proved in Section 4.4 also suggest limits to the power of universal users based on the kind of sensing we have discussed thus far—between the lower bounds that we obtain from the on-line learning model and the lower bounds proved in Section 4.4, we will note that basic sensing seems to only be adequate for the construction of *efficient* universal users in very simple settings. We will observe that some natural kinds of richer feedback allow the construction of efficient universal users for correspondingly richer user strategies, and we will suggest the exploration of such richer feedback as a next step towards constructing universal users of suitable efficiency for real problems.

8.1 On the number of errors incurred with password-protected servers

Recall that the number of errors incurred by the universal user asserted in Theorem 6.36 (as well as in Theorem 6.23) is at least linear in the index of the server that it happens to use (with respect to a fixed ordering of all servers in the class). Thus, the number of errors is exponential in the length of the description of this server (i.e., the length of its index). We shall show that this overhead (w.r.t a user tailored for this server) is inherent whenever the universal user has to achieve any non-trivial goal with respect to a sufficiently rich class of servers. In particular, we will see how our observations concerning the *running time* overhead of a user in finite executions translate into overhead in terms of the number of errors.

Ultimately, we will parallel the development from Section 4.1. As our starting point, we adapt the definition of a nontrivial goal (originally given in Definition 3.2) to goals in infinite executions in the natural way, i.e., we restrict our attention to compact goals, and then subsequently refer to the referee's temporal decision function in place of the referee. For completeness, we give the amended definition below; recall that a *trivial server* sends empty messages to all other parties on every round.

Definition 8.1 (Nontrivial goals in infinite executions). Let T denote a trivial server. We say that a compact goal $G = (\mathcal{E}, R)$ is *nontrivial* w.r.t. a class of users $\mathcal{U}$ if for every user $U \in \mathcal{U}$ there is a $E \in \mathcal{E}$ such that the temporal decision function R' never outputs 1 in the execution (E, U, T).

Note that the notion of nontrivial is more restricted than the requirement that (U, T) does not achieve the goal. Nevertheless, the stronger requirement, which asserts that the temporal decision function R' never rules that the execution is tentatively successful, is very natural.

As for the "sufficiently rich" class of servers, just as in Section 4.1, we consider here one such possible class (or rather a type of class): specifically, we consider servers that become helpful (actually stop sending empty messages) only as soon as they receive a message from the user that fits their password. Such "password protected" servers are quite natural in a variety of settings. Actually, for the sake of robustness (both intuitive and technical)[1] for the case of infinite goals, we postulate that the password be checked at every round (rather than only in the first round, as considered in Definition 4.1 for finite executions). That is, in each round, the server will check that the message received is prepended with a string that matches its password. To distinguish these servers from our earlier notion of "password protected" servers, we will refer to this new class of servers as *password-prepending*.

Definition 8.2 (Password-prepending servers). For every server strategy S and string $x \in \{0, 1\}^*$, the *password-prepending version of S with password x (x-prepending version of S)*, denoted S^x, is the server strategy that upon receiving a message of the form xy, updates its state and sends messages as S would upon receiving y. Otherwise, S^x sends the empty messages to all parties, like the trivial server would, and does not update the state.

As in Chapter 4, for our demonstration (of overhead) to be meaningful, we should show that password-protected versions of helpful servers are essentially as helpful as their unprotected counterparts. Indeed, for starters, we establish the latter claim, where this holds with respect to classes of user strategies that are closed under a simple transformation (i.e., prepending of adequate passwords).

Proposition 8.3 (Password-prepending versions of helpful servers are helpful). *Let $\mathcal{U}$ be a class of user strategies such that, for any $U \in \mathcal{U}$ and any string $x \in \{0, 1\}^*$, there exists a strategy $U^x \in \mathcal{U}$ that acts as U except that it appends x to the beginning of each message that it sends to the server. Then, for every $\mathcal{U}$-helpful server S and every password $x \in \{0, 1\}^*$, the x-prepending version of S, denoted S^x, is $\mathcal{U}$-helpful. Furthermore, if (U, S) (robustly) achieves the goal, then (U^x, S^x) (robustly) achieves the goal with the same number of errors as (U, S).*

---

[1] In order for user strategies to robustly achieve goals with password-protected servers, the user must be ready to provide the password when started from any arbitrarily chosen state (as required by Definition 6.11). The most straightforward and natural way to ensure this is for the user to send the password on every message to the server. Thus, a natural type of password-protected servers that permits users to robustly achieve their goals consists of servers that expect all messages to be prepended by their password.

Proof Then, since S is $\mathcal{U}$-helpful, there exists $U \in \mathcal{U}$ such that (U, S) robustly achieves the goal. Since (U^x, S^x) send the same messages to the world as (U, S), it holds that (U^x, S^x) also robustly achieves the goal and incurs precisely the same number of errors as (U, S). Since $U^x \in \mathcal{U}$, it follows that S^x is $\mathcal{U}$-helpful. ∎

Having established the helpfulness of password-protected versions of helpful servers, we prove a lower bound on the number of errors incurred when achieving (nontrivial) goals by interacting with such servers.

Theorem 8.4 (On the overhead of achieving nontrivial goals with password-prepending servers). *Let $G = (\mathcal{E}, R)$ be a nontrivial compact goal and S be any server strategy. Then, for every user U and integer ℓ, there exists an ℓ-bit string x such that (U, S^x) does not achieve G in less than $2^{(\ell-3)/2}$ errors, where S^x denotes the x-prepending version of S.*

Note that the fact that the lower bound has the form $\Omega(2^{\ell/2})$ (rather than $\Omega(2^\ell)$) is due to the definition of errors (cf. Definition 6.34).[2]

Proof Let any user strategy U be given and let T be a trivial server. Since G is nontrivial, there exists $E \in \mathcal{E}$ such that the temporal decision function R' never evaluates to 1 in a random execution of (E, U, T). For starters, we assume (for simplicity) that in such random executions R' always evaluates to 0. Consider, a random execution of (E, U, S^x), when x is uniformly selected in $\{0,1\}^\ell$, Then, with probability at least $1 - m \cdot 2^{-\ell}$, the user U did not prepend the string x to any of the messages it sent in the first m rounds. In this case, the m-round execution prefix of (E, U, S^x) is distributed identically to the m-round execution prefix of (E, U, T), which means that it generates m errors. Using $m = 2^{\ell-1}$ it follows that, for a uniformly selected $x \in \{0,1\}^\ell$, the expected number of errors in a random execution of (E, U, S^x) is at least $2^{\ell-2}$. Hence, there exists a string $x \in \{0,1\}^\ell$ such that (U, S^x) does not achieve G in less than $2^{\ell-2}$ errors.

In the general case (i.e., when considering $\perp$-values for R'), we may infer that there exists a string $x \in \{0,1\}^\ell$ such that, with probability at least $1 - m \cdot 2^{-\ell}$, the temporal decision function R' does not evaluate to 1 in the first m rounds of a random execution of (E, U, S^x). In this case, this execution prefix contains at least $\sqrt{m}$ errors (see the two items of Definition 6.34), and the theorem follows (by setting $m = 2^{\ell-1}$). ∎

Combining Theorem 8.4 and Proposition 8.3, we demonstrate the necessity of the error overhead incurred by the universal strategy of Theorem 6.36.

---

[2]Indeed, the trivial server that prevents R' from ever evaluating to 1 may also be viewed by Definition 6.34 as making only $\sqrt{2^\ell}$ errors (for some adequate R'). In particular, we may consider the following behavior of R' for the case that the server never sends a message to the world. For every $i = 1, 2, \ldots$, and $j \in [2^{2i-2}, 2^{2i}]$, in round j the value of R' equals 0 if j is a multiple of 2^i and equals $\perp$ otherwise. Then, for every even ℓ, the first 2^ℓ rounds contain no $2^{\ell/2}$-long run of $\perp$, whereas the total number of zeros in these rounds is $\sum_{i=1}^{\ell/2} 2^i = O(2^{\ell/2})$.

Specifically, the latter strategy must work for server and user classes that are derived via Proposition 8.3. Now, Theorem 8.4 asserts that this class of 2^ℓ servers contains a server that causes an overhead that is exponential in ℓ, which in turn is closely related to the length of the description of most servers in this class.

8.2 On-line learning is equivalent to semantic communication with one-round goals

Now that we have established that an exponential number of errors in the description length of the desired user strategy is unavoidable in general, we would like to know *when* it can be avoided. Specifically, just as in Chapter 4, we would like to have some natural conditions under which we can develop efficient universal user strategies for goals in infinite executions. In this section, we investigate one possible class of conditions.

Specifically, we will restrict our attention to multi-session goals of communication in which each round corresponds to a distinct session, and furthermore assume that sensing with very good safety and viability is available to us, in which moreover, the sensing function is viable with respect to some simple class of user strategies. We will then see that a generic construction of universal users from such sensing functions is equivalent to the design of an on-line learning algorithm in the model introduced by Bārzdiņš and Frievalds [19] and used by Littlestone [101]. Thus, in this well-studied model, we will find that generic constructions of universal user strategies exist for a variety of classes of simple user strategies.

The direction explored in this section was motivated by conversations with Leslie Kaelbling and Leslie Valiant, and was developed in work with Santosh Vempala [86]. The current presentation owes its clarity to Oded Goldreich.

8.2.1 Fixed length multi-session goals

In Chapter 6, we introduced a series of definitions of goals for communication in infinite executions, starting from the most general basic notions given in Definition 6.1 to the most general *reasonable* definition of *compact goals* in Definition 6.6, to the natural special case of interest of multi-session goals in Definition 6.7. In the present section, we actually restrict our attention further still, to goals in which time is divided into sessions of a *fixed length*. Thus, we consider a special case of *multi-session goals* (that actually still captures Examples 6.3–6.5). We prefer to consider the special case here because the classes of user strategies we will consider are particularly simple, only generating messages for a fixed number of rounds (with emphasis on the case of just one round) and so the decision of "when to halt" is not at issue (cf. in particular the results of Chapters 2 and 5 concerning strategies in finite executions).

Definition 8.5 (Fixed length multi-session goals). A goal $G = (\mathcal{E}, R)$ is said to be a *k-round multi-session goal* if the following hold:

1. *(The environment's states.)* The environment's states are partitioned into k sets, $\Omega_1^{(e)}, \ldots, \Omega_k^{(e)}$. We refer to the elements of $\Omega_1^{(e)}$ as *start-session* states, and the elements of $\Omega_k^{(e)}$ as *end-session* states. In each case, the elements of $\Omega_i^{(e)}$ are a pair consisting of an integer *index* and a *contents*.

2. *(Starting a new session.)* When in an end-session state, the environment non-deterministically moves to a start-session state with an incremented index (i.e., $E(j, \sigma)^{(e)}$ is of the form $(j + 1, \sigma') \in \Omega_1^{(e)}$); furthermore, this non-deterministic choice is independent of the contents of the end-session state. That is, every $E \in \mathcal{E}$ satisfies the following: for every two end-session states with the same index, $(j, \sigma), (j, \sigma') \in \Omega_k^{(e)}$, $E(j, \sigma)^{(e)} = E(j, \sigma')^{(e)}$, and $E(j, \sigma)^{(e, \cdot)} = E(j, \sigma')^{(e, \cdot)}$.

3. *(Execution of a session.)* When the environment is in some state $(j, \sigma) \in \Omega_i^{(e)}$ for $i \neq k$, $E(j, \sigma)^{(e)}$ is a distribution over $\Omega_{i+1}^{(e)}$ such that every element in its support has index j. Furthermore, the distribution over contents and messages is independent of the index and the environment's actual strategy, i.e., for every $E_1, E_2 \in \mathcal{E}$ $(j, \sigma) \in E_1$ and $(j', \sigma) \in E_2$ the distribution over every component except the index in $E_1(j, \sigma)$ is the same as in $E_2(j', \sigma)$.

4. *(The referee suspends its verdict until reaching an end-session state.)* The referee R is compact, and the corresponding temporal decision function evaluates to $\perp$ iff the environment's state is not an end-session state.

Thus, in the setting of k-round multi-session goals, the referee provides a verdict once at the end of each k-round session, and we succeed at the goal if and only if we only fail in finitely many sessions.[3]

8.2.2 Generic users for goals implicitly specified by sensing

A variety of examples of sensing functions for natural goals for communication (at least in finite executions) were the subject of Chapter 3. By contrast, in this section, rather than directly or explicitly describing goals, we will assume

---

[3]In this context, we will also refer to the number of times the temporal decision function R' evaluates to 0 as *the number of errors*. As mentioned above, this is actually a simplification of the notion of errors used in Chapter 6 and Section 8.1 where the referee suspending a decision for too long was also considered to be an error. Of course, no such thing can happen in a k-round multi-session goal, so we may interchangeably use the terms "failure" and "error."

that we are given a sensing function for a goal—that is, the goal is *implicitly* described by the kind of feedback available to the user, and by the class of strategies that suffice to achieve good feedback as guaranteed by the viability condition. When we can construct a universal user strategy that achieves any goal given only this information, we say that the strategy is *generic*:

Definition 8.6 (Generic universal user). For a class of goals in infinite executions $\mathcal{G}$, a class of user strategies $\mathcal{U}$, and functions $B : \mathcal{U} \times \mathbb{N} \to \mathbb{N}$, $s : \mathbb{N} \to \mathbb{N}$ and $v : \mathbb{N} \to \mathbb{N}$, we say that an algorithm U is a *B-error $(\mathcal{U}, s, v)$-generic universal user for $\mathcal{G}$* if for any goal $G \in \mathcal{G}$, any server S, and any black-box sensing function V that is *s-strongly safe* with S for G and *v-viable* with S with respect to $\mathcal{U}$ for G, when U is provided the verdicts of V as auxiliary input, (U, S) robustly achieves G with

$$\min_{U_S \in \mathcal{U} : U_S \; v-\text{viable with } S} B(U_S, \cdot)$$

errors.

Where, in particular, we use the notion of robustly achieving goals with a bounded number of errors from Definition 6.34, the notion of strong safety from Definition 6.35, and the notion of viability from Definition 6.40. We note that these are the same notions as used in Theorem 6.41; the primary difference is two-fold: first, sensing for Definition 8.6 is assumed to be black-box, whereas Theorem 6.41 held even for grey-box sensing and, similarly, allowed for the bounding functions s and v for sensing to vary with the user strategy; and second, the number of errors incurred by Theorem 6.41 as stated was allowed to depend (arbitrarily) on the server S, whereas we demand a generic universal user in the present sense that obtains a bound that depends uniformly on the "best" user strategy in $\mathcal{U}$. That having been said, it may be verified that for any enumerable class of user strategies $\mathcal{U}$, and $B(U_i, n) = 3i \max\{s(n), v(n)\}^2$, the proof of Theorem 6.41 constructs a B-error $(\mathcal{U}, s, v)$-generic universal user for the class of compact goals. (Where U_i of course denotes the ith strategy in the given enumeration of $\mathcal{U}$.) As suggested, we would like user strategies that only make a number of errors that is *polynomial* in the length of the description of a target strategy in $\mathcal{U}$ (e.g., $\log i$ for U_i), i.e., B is a polynomial in $|U_S|$ and the size parameter of the execution.

Thus, we will consider what kind of feedback is necessary to construct a generic universal user that succeeds with a polynomial number of errors, given that it is viable with respect to a simple class of strategies. In particular, in Section 8.3, we show that if the class of user strategies $\mathcal{U}$ in the viability condition is sufficiently simple, then we can efficiently identify a good strategy for the class of one-round multi-session goals; in Section 8.4.1, on the other hand, we will see that even for one-round multi-session goals, we will need richer kinds of feedback to efficiently compute good strategies when $\mathcal{U}$ is not so simple. In both cases, the results will follow from an equivalence to an existing model of *on-line learning* that we describe in more detail next.

8.2.3   Model of mistake-bounded on-line learning

We have already introduced a multi-session goal of communication in Example 6.45 that captures the model of on-line learning we will discuss, but in the interest of establishing a tighter connection with the model, we turn to describing the original set-up in more detail. The mistake-bounded model of on-line learning that we consider was essentially introduced by Bārzdiņš and Frievalds [19] and we will follow the presentation of this model given by Littlestone [101]. In Littlestone's presentation, we assume that a *target concept* or *target function* f is drawn from some a priori fixed class of functions $\mathcal{C}$ and the learning algorithm is run across an infinite sequence of *trials* consisting of the following steps:

1. The algorithm is provided an *instance* $x \in X$ as input.

2. The algorithm produces a *prediction* from Y.

3. The algorithm receives *reinforcement* feedback, indicating whether its prediction was equal to $f(x)$.

In Littlestone's main setting of interest, $X = \{0,1\}^n$ and $Y = \{0,1\}$, and then n is a natural size parameter, and $\mathcal{C}$ is taken to be finite, but this is not essential for our purposes, so long as a suitable notion of size can be defined for X and members of $\mathcal{C}$. The main parameter of interest in evaluating these algorithms is the number of mistakes that they make in the worst case over sequences of trials and unknown target concepts:

Definition 8.7 (Mistake-bounded learning). For a given on-line learning algorithm A and a concept class $\mathcal{C}$ with *size parameter* $n : \mathcal{C} \to \mathbb{N}$, and any target concept $f : X \to Y$ for $f \in \mathcal{C}$, let $M_A(f)$ be the maximum, over all sequences of instances $\bar{x} = \{x_i \in X\}_{i=1}^{\infty}$, of the number of trials in which A outputs y such that $y \neq f(x_i)$. We then say that a learning algorithm A has *mistake bound* $m : \mathbb{N} \to \mathbb{N}$ if

$$\max_{f \in \mathcal{C}: n(f)=n'} M_A(f) \leq m(n')$$

for all $n' \in \mathbb{N}$. If the state of A does not change when the algorithm receives positive feedback, then we say A is a *conservative* algorithm.

Note that we can easily convert any $m(n)$-mistake-bounded learning algorithm A into a conservative algorithm A': A' simulates A, providing the instances to A, and repeating the predictions of A as its own. The only difference is that whenever A makes a correct prediction, A' resets the state of A to what it was at the beginning of the round. Now, whenever A' makes $m(n)$ mistakes, it has simulated A on a sequence of instances where A has also made $m(n)$ mistakes, so by the mistake bound of A, it does not make a mistake on the following round, no matter which input is provided; therefore, by repeatedly simulating A on this round with different instances as input, A' never makes another mistake, either.

Angluin's equivalence query model

Littlestone [101] also showed that the above model of on-line learning is essentially equivalent to the model of learning with *equivalence queries* (or *counterexamples*) given by Angluin [4], assuming a suitably general notion of representation of functions (e.g., circuits). Angluin's model is as follows: a target concept is again drawn from some fixed class $C \subseteq \{f : X \to Y\}$, and we fix some representation of functions $f : X \to Y$ (often, alternatively, a representation exclusively of functions in C). The algorithm is then given access to an *equivalence query oracle* for $f \in C$, which operates as follows: when the algorithm provides the oracle a representation of some function $g : X \to Y$, if $g = f$, the oracle responds "yes" and otherwise the oracle non-deterministically selects a member of the set $\{x \in X : g(x) \neq f(x)\}$ as its response.

Definition 8.8 (Learning with equivalence queries). For any class of target concepts $C \subseteq \{f : X \to Y\}$ with a size parameter $n : C \to \mathbb{N}$, and a given notion of representation of functions, an oracle algorithm $A^{(\cdot)}$ is said to *learn* C *with* $q(n)$ *equivalence queries* if, whenever A is provided an equivalence query oracle for some $f \in C$ of size n, A makes at most $q(n)$ queries to the oracle, outputs a representation of f, and halts.

For completeness, we will sketch Littlestone's argument showing the equivalence of mistake-bounded learning and learning with equivalence queries [101]:

From mistake-bounded learning to learning with equivalence queries. Given a learning algorithm A for a concept class $C \subseteq \{f : X \to Y\}$ with a given size parameter and mistake bound $m(n)$, we can obtain an algorithm $A^{(\cdot)}$ that learns C with $m(n) + 1$ equivalence queries (for an appropriate notion of representation) as follows. Suppose that we may represent functions by giving the state of A at the beginning of any trial (note that if A is deterministic, this implicitly defines a function taking instances from X to predictions in Y). Then $A^{(\cdot)}$ simulates A by first providing the oracle with the representation of the internal state of A at the beginning of each trial, halting and outputting this state if the oracle responds "yes;" otherwise, $A^{(\cdot)}$ feeds A the oracle's counterexample as the instance for the current trial and simulates it until the start of the next trial.

Since the sequence of counterexamples is a sequence of elements of X, it is the prefix of some sequence of trials—in particular, it is a sequence in which A makes a mistake on every step. Therefore since A is $m(n)$-mistake bounded, after A has been provided with at most $m(n)$ counterexamples, regardless of which element $x \in X$ it is provided next, it must output $y = f(x)$ as its prediction—thus, the algorithm's internal state at this point is a representation of f, as needed, and the equivalence query oracle will return "yes" by the $(m(n) + 1)$th query.

We also note that if, on concepts of size n, A runs in time $t(n)$ on each trial and never uses more than space $s(n)$, then there is a natural circuit representation of A on concepts of size n that has size $O(t(n)s(n))$. Broadly speaking, then, for algorithms that are time and space efficient per trial, circuits are a sufficient representation of functions for the equivalence with the equivalence query model to hold.

From learning with equivalence queries to mistake-bounded learning. Given an oracle algorithm $A^{(\cdot)}$ that learns a concept class $\mathcal{C}$ with given size parameter in $q(n)$ equivalence queries, we can construct a $q(n)$-mistake-bounded learning algorithm for $\mathcal{C}$ as follows. At the beginning of each trial, if $A^{(\cdot)}$ is not waiting on a query to its oracle to be answered, A simulates $A^{(\cdot)}$ until it either makes a query, or outputs a function g; in the latter case, A provides $g(x)$ as its prediction for the instance x given in every subsequent trial, and since $A^{(\cdot)}$ only outputs a representation of the target function f, we see that in this case A makes no more mistakes. In the former case, if $A^{(\cdot)}$ queries its oracle with function g, A provides $g(x)$ as its prediction in every subsequent trial until it makes a mistake; it then finds that $g(x) \neq f(x)$ for the most recent instance x, and provides this instance as the oracle's response to its last query. Since this is a valid response from an equivalence query oracle, we see that $A^{(\cdot)}$ will therefore output a representation of the target concept f in at most $q(n)$ queries; since we only make one mistake following each of the queries $A^{(\cdot)}$ makes during its simulated run, the learning algorithm A thus constructed makes at most $q(n)$ mistakes, as claimed.

8.2.4 Equivalence of on-line learning and generic universal users for one-round goals

Earlier, we noted that we could capture the mistake-bounded on-line learning model with a (one-round) multi-session goal of communication in Example 6.45; we then noted that Theorem 6.41 gave a universal on-line learning algorithm with an *asymptotically* optimal mistake bound. It turns out that, for the special case of the class of one-round multi-session goals (and servers with 1-strongly safe and 1-viable sensing), on-line learning actually captures universal strategies as well. Actually, for *generic* constructions of universal users from sensing that is viable with respect to a class of users $\mathcal{U}$, there is a connection to mistake-bounded on-line learning of $\mathcal{U}$ that runs even deeper: the algorithms are *identical*.

Theorem 8.9 (Mistake-bounded on-line learning algorithms are generic universal users for one-round goals). *Let $\mathcal{G}$ be a class of one-round multi-session goals in which the user's incoming messages on each round are drawn from a set $\Omega^{(\cdot,\mathrm{u})}$, and its outgoing messages are from the set $\Omega^{(\mathrm{u},\cdot)}$. Let $\mathcal{U}$ be a class of functions $\{U : \Omega^{(\cdot,\mathrm{u})} \rightarrow \Omega^{(\mathrm{u},\cdot)}\}$ with a size parameter $n : \mathcal{U} \rightarrow \mathbb{N}$. Then a conservative $m(n)$-mistake-bounded learning algorithm for $\mathcal{U}$ is an*

m'-error $(\mathcal{U}, 1, 1)$-generic universal user for $\mathcal{G}$ with error bound $m'(U, n') = m(n(U)) + 1$, and conversely, an m'-error $(\mathcal{U}, 1, 1)$-generic universal user for $\mathcal{G}$ with error bound $m'(U, n') = m(n(U))$ is a $m(n)$-mistake-bounded learning algorithm for $\mathcal{U}$.

Proof

($\Rightarrow$:) We suppose we are given a conservative $m(n)$-mistake bounded learning algorithm A for $\mathcal{U}$. We will show that A serves as a generic universal user as follows. Suppose we are given $G \in \mathcal{G}$, a server S, and a black-box sensing function V that is 1-strongly safe with S for G and 1-viable with S with respect to $\mathcal{U}$ for G.

The target concept. In this case, by the definition of 1-viability, there exists $U_S \in \mathcal{U}$ such that if the user sends the same messages as U_S, after one round V will provide a positive indication on every round. Thus, U_S will correspond to the target concept for the learning algorithm.

Instances, predictions, and reinforcement. Each round of the execution will correspond to a trial for the learning algorithm. Suppose we provide the incoming messages to A as the instance, take the predictions of A as the outgoing messages, and provide the verdict of V on the following round as the reinforcement. In particular, note that if A sends the same outgoing message as U_S, A will receive a positive indication from the sensing function, which we take as positive feedback. Conversely, if V produces a negative indication, then A must not have sent the same outgoing message as U_S would have sent on the incoming messages in that round. V may also produce positive indications when the outgoing message A sent differs from what U_S would have sent, but in this case since A is conservative, the state of A does not change.

Now, since A is an $m(n)$-mistake-bounded learning algorithm for $\mathcal{U}$, we are guaranteed that it only receives negative reinforcement $m(n)$ times in any execution.

A bound on the number of errors. Since V is 1-strongly safe for G with respect to S, our bound on the number of times V evaluates to 0 translates directly into a bound on the number of errors. Since G is a 1-round multi-session goal, R' evaluates to 0 or 1 on each round; whenever it evaluates to 0 (i.e., an error occurs), the 1-strong safety of V must guarantee that either that is the only error that will occur, or that V evaluates to 0 in the current round. V is therefore only allowed to evaluate to 1 when an error occurs once, so the number of errors is greater than the number of times V evaluates to 0 by at most 1, and we see that our strategy therefore makes at most $m(n) + 1$ errors, as promised.

($\Leftarrow$:) Let a target concept $U \in \mathcal{U}$ and any sequence of instances $\bar{x} = \{x_i \in \Omega^{(\mathrm{e,u})} \times \Omega^{(\mathrm{s,u})}\}_{i=1}^{\infty}$ be given. We will show how to embed the corresponding sequence of trials into a one-round multi-session goal with a 1-safe and 1-viable sensing function for some server S.

The goal and server. Consider the following one-round multi-session goal $G_U = (\mathcal{E}, R_U)$: the environment non-deterministically chooses $(\sigma_i^{(\mathrm{e,u})}, \sigma_{i+1}^{(\mathrm{s,u})}) \in \Omega^{(\mathrm{e,u})} \times \Omega^{(\mathrm{s,u})}$ for each round i, and sends $(\sigma_i^{(\mathrm{e,u})}, b)$ to the user and $\sigma_{i+1}^{(\mathrm{s,u})}$ to the server. The temporal decision function R_U' for the referee R_U then is satisfied in session i if the user returns $U(\sigma_i^{(\mathrm{e,u})}, \sigma_i^{(\mathrm{s,u})})$. Let S be the server that forwards the message it received from the environment in the previous round to the user in the current round.

The sensing function. Let V_U be the sensing function that returns 1 if the user's message on the ith round is $U(\sigma_i^{(\mathrm{e,u})}, \sigma_i^{(\mathrm{s,u})})$. Note that when the user executes with S, V_U computes R_U', so V_U is 1-strongly safe with S for G_U. Furthermore, whenever the user sends the same message as $U \in \mathcal{U}$, V_U is trivially satisfied on the following round, so V_U is also 1-viable with S with respect to $\mathcal{U}$ for G_U.

The execution. We can embed $\bar{x}$ in an execution in the following way: let the execution start from the state where $\sigma^{(\mathrm{e,u})} = x_1^{(\mathrm{e,u})}$, $\sigma^{(\mathrm{s,u})} = x_1^{(\mathrm{s,u})}$, and $\sigma^{(\mathrm{e,s})} = x_2^{(\mathrm{s,u})}$, and suppose that the environment's non-deterministic choice for the ith round is $(x_{i+1}^{(\mathrm{e,u})}, x_{i+2}^{(\mathrm{s,u})})$. Then, we can check that in each ith round of this execution, the user receives x_i.

A bound on the number of mistakes. Now, supposing that we are given an m'-error $(\mathcal{U}, 1, 1)$-generic universal user for $\mathcal{G}$ A, and for every target concept $U \in \mathcal{U}$, A robustly achieves G_U with $m'(U, n') = m(n(U))$ errors when given the feedback from V_U in an execution with S—in particular, in the execution we constructed for a given sequence of trials $\bar{x}$. By definition of G_U, now, A makes an error in the ith round iff it does not send the same messages as U in that round, so when A is provided the feedback from V_U, it makes at most $m(n(U))$ mistakes in the sequence of trials $\bar{x}$. We now note that V_U computes the same function as the learner's reinforcement, so when A is provided access to the reinforcement instead of A, it still only makes $m(n(U))$ mistakes, as needed. ∎

8.3 Consequences of the equivalence: universal user strategies from on-line learning algorithms

We now turn to exploiting Theorem 8.9 to obtain generic constructions of efficient universal users for one-round multi-session goals. We will describe a couple of examples of on-line learning algorithms – for parity functions and linear threshold functions – and then turn to surveying the literature for a number of additional examples. The examples we describe (notably the improved algorithm for linear threshold functions) are from joint work with Santosh Vempala [86].

8.3.1 Parity strategies

We start with an extremely simple example of a user strategy, for which the corresponding on-line learning algorithm is similarly simple: *parity strategies*. Consider an environment strategy E and server strategy S for which the incoming message to the user in each round is given by an n-bit Boolean vector for some n. A parity strategy for the user simply sends the parity of a fixed subset of those bits on each round to the other parties:

Definition 8.10 (Parity strategies). The *class of parity strategies, $\mathcal{U}_\oplus$*, is the following set of user strategies. We identify the user's incoming messages $\Omega^{(e,u)} \times \Omega^{(s,u)}$ with $\{0,1\}^n$. Then, for each subset $a \in \{0,1\}^n$, the strategy U_a that, on incoming messages $x \in \{0,1\}^n$, sends $\sum_{i=1}^n a_i x_i \pmod 2 \stackrel{\text{def}}{=} \langle a, x \rangle \in \{0,1\}$ to the server and environment is in $\mathcal{U}_\oplus$.

In particular, we will assume that we have a goal $G = (\mathcal{E}, R)$ and a class of servers $\mathcal{S}$ such that for each $E \in \mathcal{E}$ and $S \in \mathcal{S}$, the length of incoming messages to the user remains fixed throughout the execution, so that on each round the user receives an n-bit vector of incoming messages. In this case, the relevant members of $\mathcal{U}_\oplus$ are described by an n-bit string, $a \in \{0,1\}^n$, and we will likewise call the size of such an execution n.

It now turns out that there is a simple algorithm for learning $\mathcal{U}_\oplus$ in n mistakes, yielding an $n+1$-error $(\mathcal{U}_\oplus, 1, 1)$-generic universal user for the class of one-round multi-session goals.

Theorem 8.11 (On-line learning algorithm for parities). *There is an n-mistake-bounded on-line learning algorithm for $\mathcal{U}_\oplus$, that runs in time $O(n^3)$ on each trial.*

Proof We will maintain a set of *constraints* given as follows: each time, for an instance x, that we predicted b and made a mistake, we will introduce a constraint: $(x_i, b_i) = (x, b \oplus 1)$ corresponding to the condition $\langle a, x_i \rangle = b_i$. Now, given a list of constraints, we use Gaussian elimination to find a candidate a such that every constraint in our current list is satisfied. On each subsequent trial, for an instance x we then supply $\langle a, x \rangle$ as our prediction. It is well-known that this may be computed in time $O(n^3)$.

We now note that if, from a set of constraints $\{(x_i, b_i)\}_{i=1}^{\ell}$, on an instance x' we incorrectly predicted b', x' must be linearly independent of $\{x_1, \ldots, x_\ell\}$ since whenever $x' = \sum_{i=1}^{\ell} \alpha_i x_i$, letting U_{a^*} be the target function, we also have

$$\langle a^*, x' \rangle = \sum_{i=1}^{\ell} \alpha_i \langle a^*, x_i \rangle = \sum_{i=1}^{\ell} \alpha_i U_{a^*}(x_i) = \sum_{i=1}^{\ell} \alpha_i \langle a, x_i \rangle = \langle a, x' \rangle$$

and thus we would have had $\langle a, x' \rangle = U_{a^*}(x')$.

Now, we see that after we have made n mistakes, we have n linearly independent constraints, and a^* must be the uniquely specified candidate a; therefore, we subsequently supply $U_{a^*}(x)$ as our prediction for x, and make no more mistakes. ∎

8.3.2 Linear threshold strategies

We now turn to a class of well-studied functions in learning theory, linear threshold functions.

Definition 8.12 (Linear threshold strategies). The *class of linear threshold strategies* in n dimensions with b-bit weights, $\mathcal{U}_{\mathsf{LT}(n,b)}$, is the following set of user strategies. We identify the user's incoming messages with $\mathbb{Q}^n$. Then, for each *weight vector* $w \in \{-2^{b+1}+1, \ldots, -1, 0, 1, \ldots, 2^{b+1}-1\}^n$ and *threshold* $c \in \{-2^{b+1}+1, \ldots, -1, 0, 1, \ldots, 2^{b+1}-1\}$, the user strategy that on incoming message $x \in \mathbb{Q}^n$ sends

$$U_{w,c}(x) = \begin{cases} 1 & \sum_{i=1}^{n} w_i x_i \geq c \\ 0 & \text{otherwise} \end{cases}$$

to the server and environment is in $\mathcal{U}_{\mathsf{LT}(n,b)}$.

The first on-line algorithm for learning linear threshold functions is the classic *perceptron algorithm* [124, 117, 114], and its discovery and analysis predates our model of on-line learning. The perceptron algorithm is *not* efficient; one of the main contributions of Littlestone [101] was the introduction of an *efficient* on-line algorithm for learning linear threshold functions, when the weights are all positive.[4]

The first algorithm for efficiently learning linear threshold functions with general coefficients was proposed by Maass and Turán [104], based on the

---

[4]Littlestone's algorithm *also* has the special feature that it has only a logarithmic dependence on the "number of attributes," i.e., in $\{0, 1\}^n$, the number of mistakes only grows *logarithmically in n*. Because of this property, Littlestone's algorithm is still widely used as a starting point in more sophisticated constructions, even though we know that learning algorithms for more general linear threshold functions exist.

classic *Ellipsoid algorithm* [91, 76]. Subsequently, Maass and Turán generalized their algorithm to a reduction to the problem of *finding feasible points in convex programs given by a separation oracle* [107]:

Definition 8.13 (Convex feasibility with a separation oracle). Let a convex set $K \subset \mathbb{R}^n$ be given. For $r \in \mathbb{N}$, we say that K has *guarantee* r if the volume of $K \cap \mathsf{Ball}(0, r)$ is at least r^{-n}. A *separation oracle* for K answers queries of the form $x \in \mathbb{Q}^n$ with "yes" if $x \in K$ and otherwise non-deterministically returns a vector $v \in \mathbb{Q}^n$ and $c \in \mathbb{Q}$ such that $\langle x, v \rangle \geq c$, but that for every $y \in K$, $\langle y, v \rangle < c$. If the longest vector v returned by the separation oracle is ℓ bits, we will say that the oracle is ℓ-*bounded*.

Now, we say that an oracle algorithm $A^{(\cdot)}$ solves the search problem of *convex feasibility with an ℓ-bounded separation oracle* in time $t(n, \log r, \ell)$ and query complexity $q(n, \log r, \ell)$ if, for any ℓ-bounded separation oracle for a convex body K with guarantee r, $A^{(\cdot)}$ produces a point in K in time $t(n, \log r, \ell)$, and making at most $q(n, \log r, \ell)$ queries to the oracle.

Thus, as there are several different efficient algorithms for solving convex programs in this model – besides the Ellipsoid algorithm, there is an algorithm by Vaidya [151], and an algorithm based on random walks due to Bertsimas and Vempala [27] – we have several different efficient algorithms for mistake-bounded learning of linear threshold functions, which improve on the original in both the computation time and the number of mistakes. Both of these improved algorithms make at most $O(n \log r)$ queries.

Actually, the algorithms given by Maass and Turán [104, 107] were for a slightly different problem than the one we consider here: in their model, the instance space was assumed to be bounded integer points (as opposed to $\mathbb{Q}^n$), and the time and query complexity of their algorithm depended the size of these integers. Although it is rather clear that we cannot hope to eliminate the dependence of the computation time on the size of the instances (if we hope to perform arithmetic operations on them!), it turns out that the dependence on the size of instances in the mistake bound can be eliminated, using some techniques for solving convex programming problems when the convex set K is not of full dimension due to Grötschel, Lovász and Schrijver [75, 76]. The technique will require the following classical theorem due to Dirichlet [55]:

Theorem 8.14 (Simultaneous Diophantine Approximation). *For any $x \in \mathbb{R}^n$ and $\varepsilon \in (0, 1)$, there exist $p \in \mathbb{Z}^n$ and $q \in \mathbb{N}$ such that $q \leq \varepsilon^{-n}$ and $\max_i |qx_i - p_i| < \varepsilon$.*

In particular, we will need to *find* Diophantine approximations efficiently, which is enabled by applying the lattice basis reduction algorithm of Lenstra, Lenstra, and Lovász [96] to find short vectors (and indeed, this was one of the original applications of the algorithm):

Theorem 8.15 (LLL algorithm for finding short vectors). *There is a polynomial time algorithm that, given a basis $b_1, \ldots, b_n \in \mathbb{Q}^n$ for a lattice L, finds a nonzero vector v in the lattice such that $\|v\| \leq 2^{(n-1)/2} \min\{\|u\| : u \in L(b_1, \ldots, b_n) \setminus \{0\}\}$.*

The LLL algorithm may be applied to find Diophantine approximations like so:

Proposition 8.16 (Diophantine Approximation Algorithm). *There is a polynomial time algorithm that, on input $x \in \mathbb{Q}^n$ and a rational $\varepsilon \in (0,1)$, returns $p \in \mathbb{Z}^n$ and $q \in \mathbb{N}$ such that $q \leq \sqrt{n+1}\,2^{n/2}\varepsilon^{-n}$ and $\|qx - p\| < \sqrt{n+1}\,2^{n/2}\varepsilon$.*

Proof Consider the lattice in $\mathbb{R}^{n+1}$ given by the following basis:

$$
\begin{bmatrix}
1 & 0 & \cdots & 0 & -x_1 \\
0 & 1 & \cdots & 0 & -x_2 \\
\vdots & \vdots & \ddots & \vdots & \vdots \\
0 & 0 & \cdots & 1 & -x_n \\
0 & 0 & \cdots & 0 & \varepsilon^{n-1}
\end{bmatrix}
$$

Note that the coefficient vector $(p,q) \in \mathbb{Z}^{n+1}$ guaranteed to exist by Dirichlet's Simultaneous Diophantine Approximation Theorem gives a vector in this lattice of length less than $\sqrt{n+1}\varepsilon$, and thus the LLL algorithm applied to this basis gives us a coefficient vector (p', q') such that $\|p' - q'x\| < \sqrt{n+1}\,2^{n/2}\varepsilon$ and $q < \sqrt{n+1}\,2^{n/2}\varepsilon^{-n}$. ∎

We now present the improved learning algorithm for halfspaces using an algorithm for solving convex feasibility with a separation oracle:

Theorem 8.17 (On-line learning algorithm for linear threshold functions). *Suppose there is an algorithm that solves convex feasibility with an ℓ-bounded separation oracle in time $t(n, \log r, \ell)$ and query complexity $q(n, \log r)$ for polynomials t and q. Then there is an $m(n,b)$-mistake bounded on-line learning algorithm for $\mathcal{U}_{\mathsf{LT}(n,b)}$ running in time $t'(n, \log b, \ell)$ on each trial for some other polynomial t' where ℓ is the length in bits of the longest instance $x \in \mathbb{Q}^n$ we receive, and $m(n,b) = O(n \cdot q(n, b + \log n))$.*

Proof

Overview. The basic observation is that the weight vector and threshold of the function $U_{w,c}$ is an integer point in $[-2^{b+1}+1, 2^{b+1}-1]^{n+1}$, where the latter is a convex set, and a counterexample x to a proposed linear threshold (w', c') defines a hyperplane such that either $\langle (w',c'), (x,-1) \rangle \geq 0 > \langle (w,c), (x,-1) \rangle$ or $\langle (w,c), (x,-1) \rangle \geq 0 > \langle (w',c'), (x,-1) \rangle$, and either way $(x,-1)$ and 0 gives us a separating hyperplane.

Thus, we will be able to pass our counterexamples to the algorithm for finding feasible points, and the algorithm will terminate once it finds some point $(\tilde{w}, \tilde{c})$ such that any halfspace of the remaining feasible set not containing $(\tilde{w}, \tilde{c})$ has volume less than the guarantee, which normally implies that $(\tilde{w}, \tilde{c})$ is in the convex set (by convexity of the target set, a separating hyperplane for $(\tilde{w}, \tilde{c})$ exists iff it falls outside the target)—note that by correctness, the algorithm *must* output some such point, since it only knows the set of separating hyperplanes constraining the feasible set and a lower bound on the volume of the target convex set, and so otherwise, the target convex set may still lie in a halfspace not containing $(\tilde{w}, \tilde{c})$. Therefore, if we find a counterexample to $(\tilde{w}, \tilde{c})$, the set of hyperplanes given by our counterexamples must define a set containing (w, c) of volume less than the guarantee.

By choosing the guarantee sufficiently small, we will be able to ensure that there is a hyperplane such that all of the points with integer coordinates (including the target (w, c)) lie in this hyperplane; we will then be able to find this hyperplane, and reduce to the problem of finding a feasible point in a lower dimensional space by projecting onto it. After we repeat this process $n + 1$ times, we will uniquely determine (w, c).

The algorithm. For $d = 0, \ldots, n$, we will construct a sequence of translations and rotations (R_d, Δ_d) so that for the projection $\Pi_d : \mathbb{R}^{n+1-d} \to \mathbb{R}^{n-d}$ that drops the last coordinate and the transformation $T_d : \mathbb{R}^{n+1-d} \to \mathbb{R}^{n+1-d}$ given by $T_d(x) = R_d(x - \Delta_d)$, the linear threshold vector (w, c) of the target concept satisfies $T_d^{-1}((\Pi_d \circ T_d)(w, c), 0) = (w, c)$.

Finding a small set containing (w, c): Let $A^{(\cdot)}$ be the algorithm for finding feasible points. We run $A^{(\cdot)}$ in $\mathbb{R}^{n+1-d}$ with a guarantee of $r = \max\{2^{b+1}\sqrt{n+1-d}, n+1-d\}$; since $[-2^{b+1} + 1, 2^{b+1} - 1] \subset \text{Ball}(0, 2^{b+1})$, this guarantees that the final set will have $(n+1-d)$-dimensional volume at least $(n+1-d)^{-(n+1-d)} > \frac{1}{(n+1-d)!}$, so it cannot contain $(n-d+2)$ points that do not lie in the same plane, i.e., a simplex in dimension $n+1-d$. Each time $A^{(\cdot)}$ queries its oracle on some point $z \in \mathbb{R}^{n+1-d}$, we use $(w', c') = (T_0^{-1} \circ \cdots \circ T_{d-1}^{-1})(z)$ as our candidate linear threshold until we make a mistake on some instance $x_{d,i} \in \mathbb{Q}^n$. We then return $(T_{d-1} \circ \cdots \circ T_0)(\pm x_i, +1)$ to $A^{(\cdot)}$ as the separating hyperplane. Finally, $A^{(\cdot)}$ returns $\tilde{z}$, and we again use $\tilde{z}$ to obtain one more candidate linear threshold $(\tilde{w}, \tilde{c})$ such that once we obtain a counterexample $x_{d,k}$, the feasible region K determined by our counterexamples $x_{d,1}, \ldots, x_{d,k}$ has $(n+1-d)$-dimensional volume less than $\frac{1}{(n+1-d)!}$.

Finding a hyperplane near (w, c): We now find an $(n-d)$-dimensional hyperplane that is ε-close to (w, c) for a sufficiently small ε (to be chosen later). Consider the set of hyperplanes within ε of the entire feasible region K, $V = \{(v, a) : \forall y \in K, a \leq \langle v, y \rangle \leq a + \varepsilon\}$. Note that if (v_1, a_1) and (v_2, a_2) are both in V, then for all $y \in K$, $\lambda a_1 + (1 - \lambda)a_2 \leq \langle y, \lambda v_1 + (1 - \lambda)v_2 \rangle \leq \lambda a_1 + (1 - \lambda)a_2 + \varepsilon$, so V is a convex set.

We can provide a separation oracle for V as follows. Given a candidate (v, a), we note that K is defined by a set of linear constraints, the basic constraints $-2^{b+1} - 1 \leq y_i \leq 2^{b+1} - 1$, and one linear constraint for each $(T_{d-1} \circ \cdots \circ T_0)(x_{d,i}) = z_i$, either $\langle z_i, y \rangle \geq 0$ or $\langle z_i, y \rangle < 0$. Therefore, maximizing (resp. minimizing) the linear functional $\langle v, y \rangle$ over K is an instance of linear programming, which we can solve in polynomial time. If the minimum y^* has $\langle v, y^* \rangle < a$, then $(-y^*, 1)$ and $\delta = a - \langle v, y^* \rangle$ is a separating hyperplane; similarly, if the maximum y^* has $\langle v, y^* \rangle > a + \varepsilon$, then $(y^*, -1)$ and $\delta = \langle v, y^* \rangle - a$ is a separating hyperplane.

Thus, we can invoke our algorithm for convex feasibility using this separation oracle to find a point $(v, a) \in V$.

Rounding to a hyperplane containing (w, c)**:**   Now, we find an $(n-d)$-dimensional hyperplane containing (w, c) as follows: We now invoke our algorithm for finding simultaneous Diophantine approximations to find a rounding of (v, a) to $(v'/q, a'/q)$ such that $q < \sqrt{n+2}2^{(n+1)/2}\epsilon^{-n}$ and $\|q(v, a) - (v', a')\| < \sqrt{n+2}2^{(n+1)/2}\epsilon$. Then, for every integer point $y \in K$,

$$|\langle v', y \rangle - a'| \leq |\langle v' - qv, y \rangle| + |\langle qv, y \rangle - qa| + |qa - a'|$$
$$< \sqrt{n+1}2^{b+1}\|v' - qv\| + q|\langle v, y \rangle - a| + |a' - qa|$$
$$< 2(n+2)2^{(b+1)+(n+1)/2}\epsilon + \sqrt{n+2}2^{(n+1)/2}\epsilon^{-n}\varepsilon$$

so, for $\epsilon = \frac{1}{3(n+2)}2^{-((b+1)+(n+1)/2)}$ and

$$\varepsilon = 3^{-(n+1)}2^{-(n+1)((b+1)+(n+1)/2+\log(n+2))},$$

we find that $|\langle v', y \rangle - a'| < 1$. Since (v', a') and y are integer vectors, this implies that $\langle v', y \rangle = a'$, so v' and a' define the plane containing the integer points in K.

The desired Δ_d is now given by translating this hyperplane back to the origin, and R_d is given by rotating its normal to the $(n+1-d)$th standard basis vector, completing the dth iteration of the main loop.

Mistake bound.   Since it is clear that the algorithm runs in polynomial time on each iteration (i.e., on each trial) it only remains to show the claimed mistake bound. Note that we only make a mistake when the algorithm $A^{(\cdot)}$ for solving convex feasibility makes a query to its oracle or outputs a point at the end of an iteration. Since in the dth iteration $A^{(\cdot)}$ makes $q(n-d, \log r, \ell)$ queries, there are at most $O(q(n-d, b + \log(n-d)))$ mistakes in the dth iteration, and thus $O(n \cdot q(n, b + \log n))$ mistakes overall. ∎

On the optimal number of mistakes

Noting that the best known algorithms for solving convex feasibility make $O(n \log r)$ queries, this translates into on-line learning algorithms that make

$O(n^2(b + \log n))$ mistakes—and thus, $(\mathcal{U}_{\mathsf{LT}(n,b)}, 1, 1)$-generic universal users that also make $O(n^2(b + \log n))$ errors. Although this is similar to the performance achieved by Maass and Turán for their problem, (their algorithm found arbitrary halfspaces over $\{1, \ldots, n\}^d$ in time $O(d^2(\log n + \log d))$) it is *not* optimal for *this* problem.

It is possible to achieve a better bound by using the *halving algorithm* of Bārzdiņš and Frievalds [19]: on each trial t, the algorithm maintains the set $C_t = \{f \in C : \forall i = 1, \ldots, t-1 \; f(x_i) = f^*(x_i)\}$ of consistent hypotheses; on instance x_t, it predicts some y consistent with at least half of the remaining functions. Thus, each time it makes a mistake, the size of C_t is reduced by half, and we can make no more than $\log C$ mistakes before $|C_t| = 1$ and the target is uniquely identified. In the case of $\mathcal{U}_{\mathsf{LT}(n,b)}$, each hypothesis can be represented by $n + 1$ $(b + 1)$-bit numbers, so $|\mathcal{U}_{\mathsf{LT}(n,b)}| < 2^{(n+1)(b+1)}$, and therefore the halving algorithm is an $(n + 1)(b + 1)$-mistake bounded learning algorithm for $\mathcal{U}_{\mathsf{LT}(n,b)}$. Of course, unlike our algorithm based on convex programming, it does not run in polynomial time. The existence of an *efficient* mistake-optimal algorithm for this problem is an open question.

8.3.3 Demonstrating optimality via Littlestone's method

Littlestone [101] also introduced a useful technique for proving lower bounds on the number of mistakes needed to learn classes of Boolean functions in the on-line learning model, and the technique was subsequently generalized beyond Boolean functions by Auer et al. [13] (they also generalize the technique to other on-line learning settings). It turns out to be easy to use the technique to prove *optimal* lower bounds for a number of natural classes, as shown by Maass and Turán [105, 106, 107]. In particular, Maass and Turán [107] used Littlestone's method to show that $\Omega(d^2 \log n)$ mistakes are necessary to learn halfspaces over $\{1, \ldots, n\}^d$. We will review this technique, and likewise use it to show (essentially) optimal lower bounds for $\mathcal{U}_\oplus$ and $\mathcal{U}_{\mathsf{LT}(n,b)}$.

Definition 8.18 (*k*-mistake tree). A *mistake tree* for a class $C \subseteq \{f : X \to Y\}$ is a rooted, binary tree labeled as follows:

1. Each internal node is labeled with $x \in X$

2. The outgoing edges from any internal node labeled x are labeled with pairs, $(C_1, y_1), (C_2, y_2) \in 2^C \times Y$ such that $y_1 \neq y_2$, every $f \in C_i$ has $f(x) = y_i$, and if the edge from the node's parent is labeled with (C_0, y), then $C_1 \cup C_2 \subseteq C_0$.

3. Each leaf is labeled with $f \in C$ such that $f \in C_0$ for the set $C_0 \subseteq C$ in the label of the edge from the leaf's parent.

If the mistake tree is a complete binary tree of height k, we say it is a *k-mistake tree*.

In the following sense, k-mistake trees are all we need to prove lower bounds on the number of mistakes necessary to learn any class of functions:

Theorem 8.19 (Mistake trees give optimal lower bounds [101, 13]). *Suppose that $K(\mathcal{C})$ is the largest integer k for which $\mathcal{C}$ has a k-mistake tree. Then learning $\mathcal{C}$ requires exactly $K(\mathcal{C})$ mistakes.*

The proof of the relevant direction for our purposes, showing that a k-mistake tree suffices to give a lower bound of k mistakes is very intuitive, so we will sketch it here. We think of the adversary as *choosing a hard target function based on the algorithm's behavior*—that is, rather than the target having been fixed in advance, the adversary uses the tree to generate an execution with any given learning algorithm that is consistent with some target function, and such that the learner makes k mistakes. We then know that the learning algorithm makes k mistakes on the given target function. The adversary uses the tree to force the algorithm to find an execution in which it makes k mistakes like so: during the execution, the adversary traces a path in the k-mistake tree from the root to a leaf, such that at each internal node, the learner makes a mistake on the example used to label that node. This can be achieved since each time the learner makes a prediction y, we can take a branch of the tree *not* labeled by y, and we know that all of the leaves of the subtree under that branch are consistent with the learner having made a mistake at this point.

While Theorem 8.19 is striking on its own merits, it says nothing of whether or not an optimal k-mistake tree is easy to construct. Most remarkably of all, it turns out that they often are easily constructed.

Example 8.20 (A lower bound for parity strategies). We can construct a n-mistake tree for parity strategies as follows: at level $i = 1, \ldots, n$, the nodes are labeled with the ith standard basis vector, the outgoing edges from a node with incoming edge $(\mathcal{C}_0, b)$ are labeled $(\{U_a \in \mathcal{C}_0 : a_i = b\}, b)$ for $b \in \{0,1\}$, and each leaf is labeled with U_{a*} such that $a_i^* = b_i$ if the path to the leaf has labels $b_1, \ldots, b_n$. It is easy to see that the tree is an appropriately labeled complete binary tree of depth n, so this is a n-mistake tree. Theorem 8.19 then shows that at least n mistakes are necessary. As Theorem 8.11 showed how to learn a parity strategy in n mistakes, this is optimal.

To show a lower bound on the number of mistakes needed to learn their class of halfspaces, Maass and Turán adapted an argument for giving a lower bound on the number of threshold functions by Muroga [116] and generalized to non-Boolean inputs by Hampson and Volper [78]. A simplified argument can be given for our version of the question, showing that nb mistakes are necessary to learn $\mathcal{U}_{\mathsf{LT}(n,b)}$. Since the halving algorithm achieves $(n+1)(b+1)$ mistakes, this is almost optimal.

Example 8.21 (A lower bound for linear threshold strategies). We will construct an nb-mistake tree in n layers of b internal nodes each, such that in the ith layer, we only query multiples of the ith standard basis vector, e_i, and thus at the end of the ith layer, we will have nodes identified with $\{U_{(w,c)} \in \mathcal{U}_{\mathsf{LT}(n,b)} : (w_1, \ldots, w_i) = (w_1^*, \ldots, w_i^*)\}$ for some weights $(w_1^*, \ldots, w_i^*)$. In particular, the queries in layer i will only constrain w_i^*. Let $w_{i,j}^*$ denote the jth bit of w_i^*.

For simplicity, we will only use functions with threshold 1. In each ith layer, we will perform binary search along the ith coordinate axis to "find" $1/w_i^*$—the first query is at $1 \cdot e_i$ with edges labeled $y_{i,0} \in \{0, 1\}$ such that the set of linear threshold functions with label $y_{i,0} = 0$ have $w_i^* \geq 1$ and the set with label $y_{i,0} = 1$ have $w_i^* \leq 0$; on subsequent nodes in the ith level reached by a path with labels $y_{i,0}, y_{i,1}, \ldots, y_{i,j}$, we fix $y_{i,k} = w_{i,k}^*$, and the node is labeled by $x_{i,j} = \alpha_{i,j} \cdot e_i$ for

$$\alpha_{i,j} = (-1)^{y_{i,0}} \left(2^{b+j} + \sum_{k=1}^{j} y_{i,k} 2^{b+1-k} \right)^{-1}$$

Note that for the given choices of $w_{i,0}^*, \ldots, w_{i,j}^*$, $w_i^* \cdot \alpha_{i,j} \geq 1$ iff $w_{i,j+1}^* = 1$, and that up to $j = b - 1$, $(w_{i,1}^*, w_{i,0}^*)$ are still undetermined. (Though this may not hold for $j = b$ if $y_{i,0} = \cdots = y_{i,b-1} = 0$, since we still need $w_i^* \geq 1$, forcing $w_{i,0}^* = 1$.) Thus, as promised, at the end of the ith layer, the outgoing edges are labeled with sets $\{U_{(w,c)} \in \mathcal{U}_{\mathsf{LT}(n,b)} : (w_1, \ldots, w_i) = (w_1^*, \ldots, w_i^*)\}$ for some weights $(w_1^*, \ldots, w_i^*)$, and we see that we can therefore choose a label $U_{(w^*,1)}$ for each leaf, giving an nb-mistake tree. By Theorem 8.19, nb mistakes are therefore necessary to learn $\mathcal{U}_{\mathsf{LT}(n,b)}$.

8.3.4 Generic users for other classes of strategies: a survey

We now turn to surveying the literature for other classes of functions with efficient on-line learning algorithms. Most of the relevant work in this area has been towards algorithms for *Boolean* functions, but we will even see a few examples for richer (but still small) message spaces.

Boolean strategies

Maass and Turán [105] gave efficient mistake-bounded learning algorithms for a number of simple concept classes. Over a space of instances consisting of n integers, the indicator function of a half-interval requires precisely $\log n$ mistakes, and learning the indicator function of an arbitrary subset of n integers requires precisely n mistakes. More substantially, over the space of pairs of integers $(i, j) \in \{1, \ldots, n\}^2$, the indicator function of a linear order (i.e., evaluates to 1 on (i, j) if $i < j$) can be learned in $O(n \log n)$ mistakes, and the indicator function of a "matching" (i.e., evaluates to one on a set of pairs (i, j) such that each i appears in precisely one pair) can be learned in $O(n)$ mistakes. Maass and Turán [106] also showed how to learn the indicator functions for geometric sets such as boxes and balls over $\{1, \ldots, n\}^d$ in $O(\log n)$ mistakes for constant d. Subsequently, these results were improved by Maass and Warmuth [108] and later generalized further by Bshouty and Mazzawi [39] as discussed below.

The class of functions representable by k-sink width-two branching programs was shown to be learnable by Bergadano et al. [24]; note that *general* width-two branching programs can represent general DNF and CNF formulas (shown by Borodin et al. [34]) and two-sink *width-three* branching programs can represent general CNF and DNF formulas (shown by Ergün, Kumar, and Rubinfeld [58]), which are *not* known to be learnable. An early algorithm due to Angluin [4] (adapting the similar algorithm of Valiant in the PAC model [152]), however, learns functions expressible by k-CNF and k-DNF formulas (for *constant k*) in $O(n^k)$ mistakes. Littlestone [101] also proves a composition theorem that allows his algorithm to be used in this setting as well, and it learns a formula with ℓ terms in $O(k\ell \log n)$ mistakes.

Several other composition theorems have been proved, starting with Kearns, Li, and Valiant [88] and Pitt and Warmuth [120]; the most recent composition theorem is due to Bshouty and Mazzawi [39], giving mistake-efficient learning algorithms for any class of functions obtained by the composition of a class having a mistake-efficient algorithm with any class of functions having polynomial-size shatter coefficient (e.g., as given by Sauer's Lemma [131] for classes of constant VC-dimension). By applying this composition theorem with a learning algorithm for linear threshold functions, Bshouty and Mazzawi obtain a learning algorithm for the class of depth-two neural networks with constant fan-in at the hidden nodes that makes only a polynomial number of mistakes (improving an earlier result of Auer et al. [11]) and a learning algorithm for functions given by a weighted threshold of substring indicator functions. Also, by composing with the above algorithms for k-CNF, they can learn unions of a constant number of boxes in n-dimensional space and any number of unions of boxes in d-dimensional space for fixed d (improving the earlier results of Maass and Turán [106] and Maass and Warmuth [108]).

A striking result, due to Auer and Long [12], shows that whenever a class of functions can be learned with a polynomial number of mistakes and a logarithmic number of *membership queries* (as discussed by Angluin [4]), the function can still be learned in a polynomial number of mistakes without membership queries. This is actually just one special case of their technique, which provides essentially the only known method for learning functions with richer outputs, as we discuss next.

Strategies with larger message spaces

For a space of outgoing messages $Y = \Omega^{(\mathrm{u},\mathrm{s})} \times \Omega^{(\mathrm{u},te)}$, Auer and Long [12] show the following. Suppose that there is an $m'(n)$-mistake-bounded on-line learning algorithm for the class of functions $\mathcal{C} \subseteq \{f : X \to Y\}$ in a model where, after making a prediction on input instance $x \in X$, the learner is told the value of $f(x) \in Y$; then, there is an $m(n)$-mistake-bounded on-line learning algorithm for C in our model for mistake-bounded learning (as given in Definition 8.7) for $m(n) = O(|Y| \log |Y| m'(n))$. Thus, when the space of outgoing messages $|Y|$ is polynomially large, and a class is learnable in this stronger model, we obtain an algorithm with a good mistake bound in our model. For many classes of functions, it essentially follows from Corollary 4.21 that the dependence on $|Y|$ obtained by Auer and Long is already nearly the best possible, as we will see in the next section.

Their approach is roughly to simulate weighted copies of the algorithm from the strong model, and make predictions according to a weighted vote of the copies. When the winning prediction is correct, we know the value of $f(x)$, and we can provide appropriate feedback to all of the copies. Whenever this winning prediction is incorrect, however, we "split" each copy into more weighted copies of the algorithm (having the same total weight), with each copy simulating an execution in which the algorithm received a different value for $f(x)$. Whenever we discover that a copy's prediction is wrong, either because it was in the winning coalition on a wrong prediction, or in a losing coalition on a correct prediction, we decrease the weight of that copy by a multiplicative factor. The absolute mistake bound for the algorithm guarantees an absolute lower bound on the weight of the copy that receives the correct values, and the weights of the other copies decay exponentially, so that within the claimed bound, the algorithm that received correct responses has learned the function and is always in the winning coalition. We then predict correctly on every round and no longer need to create new copies.

Now, although the running time may be exponential in the mistake bound (since on each mistake we multiply the number of copies by roughly $|Y|$), it is still at least a fixed overhead for each fixed server, still computationally efficient for $|Y| = O(\log n)$ (corresponding to $\log \log n$-bit messages), and still gives an efficient mistake bound for several classes of strategies that we otherwise do not know how to learn—for example, mistake-bounded on-line learning algorithms for linear functions in the full-feedback model were given by Cesa-Bianchi, Long, and Warmuth [42] and by Littlestone, Warmuth, and Long [100]. Subsequently, algorithms for learning piecewise-linear convex functions and, more generally, for learning any function obtained by taking the maximum of a constant number of functions from classes such that any two members of the class cross at most a constant number of times (including low-degree polynomials, sparse polynomials, and weighted sigmoid activation functions) were also given for this model by Auer et al. [13]. It would be interesting to know whether or not more computationally efficient algorithms could be obtained for classes where Auer and Long's transformation has been applied, even with a worse (polynomial) dependence on $|Y|$ and in less generality, i.e., even only for a special case.

Strategies for k-round multi-session goals

Auer and Long's technique can also be applied to give generic universal users for k-round multi-session goals for $k > 1$ (it is efficient for size parameter n if $k = O(\log n)$)—analogous to Theorem 8.9, on-line learning algorithms for their *"k-trial delayed, ambiguous reinforcement"* model give generic universal users for k-round multi-session goals, given 1-safe and k-viable sensing for any class of stateless Boolean strategies that has an efficient mistake-bounded learning algorithm. Precisely, if there is an $m(n)$-error $(\mathcal{U}, 1, 1)$-generic universal user for the class of 1-round multi-session goals, then there is an $m'(n)$-error $(\mathcal{U}, 1, k)$-generic universal user for the class of k-round multi-session goals for $m'(n) = (2^{k+1} \ln 2k) m(n)$. Once again, the overhead of making predictions and updating the copies grows exponentially in k, but for k small, the technique still yields efficient universal users for goals that would not otherwise be known to have efficient universal strategies.

8.4 Overcoming the limitations of basic sensing with richer feedback

Not all of the news Theorem 8.9 presents is good—the strength of the equivalence between the models of on-line learning algorithms and generic universal user strategies can also be used to transfer results showing that classes cannot be learned efficiently in the on-line learning model to results showing that efficient generic universal users for those same classes do not exist. Unfortunately, as we will see, under standard assumptions, this includes most of the natural simple classes of strategies we might be interested in. Of course, these results only show that *generic* constructions of universal users from our *standard* notion of sensing is impossible—we will note some simple ways in which richer sensing feedback demonstrably broadens the class of strategies for which (generic) universal users can be constructed. The technical portions of this section are from joint work with Santosh Vempala [86].

8.4.1 Limitations of basic sensing

We will begin by taking stock of what we have already seen: at the outset of this chapter, Theorem 8.4 showed that when user strategies could prepend passwords to their messages, an exponential lower bound on the number of errors followed for *any nontrivial goal* with classes including password-protected servers. Now, for the case of one-round multi-session goals, we actually also know that a lower bound on the number of *rounds* before the referee's temporal decision function is satisfied translates into a lower bound on the number of errors. In this case, the lower bounds from Chapter 4 can give lower bounds for other classes of strategies. In particular, we can show the following:

Theorem 8.22 (Exponential lower bounds for large message spaces). *Let $\mathcal{U}$ be a class of stateless user strategies computing functions $U : X \to Y$ such that for every outgoing message y and incoming message x, some $U \in \mathcal{U}$ satisfies $U(x) = y$. Let $G = (\mathcal{E}, R)$ be the goal of mistake-bounded on-line learning given in Example 6.45 and let $S = S(\mathcal{U})$ be the class of servers corresponding to the class of user strategies $\mathcal{U}$. Then for any user strategy, there is some $S^* \in S(\mathcal{U})$ such that the user strategy makes at least $|Y|/3$ errors with probability at least $1/2$, and at least $|Y|/2$ errors in the worst case.*

Proof For any S_U in $S(\mathcal{U})$, we let $\Theta_{S_U,E}$ be the set of states where S_U received an incorrect prediction; note that since every server has the same behavior in these states, they are perfectly indistinguishable. Now, for any outgoing message $\sigma^{(u,s)}$ and incoming message vector $\sigma^{(e,u)}$, there is some $U \in \mathcal{U}$ that would produce the message $\sigma^{(u,s)}$, and hence some server $S_U \in S$ that does not exit $\Theta_{S_U,E}$ unless it receives $\sigma^{(u,s)}$; in particular, since there are $|Y|$ different messages, this implies that for any distribution on user strategies, some message is sent with probability at most $|Y|^{-1}$, and thus, whatever message the environment sends, some server does not exit $\Theta_{S_U,E}$ with probability at least $1 - |Y|^{-1}$ when the user's strategy is chosen according to that distribution. Corollary 4.21 then implies that there is some $S^* \in S(\mathcal{U})$ with which $\frac{|Y|}{(1+1/\delta)}$ rounds are necessary to exit $\Theta_{S_U,E}$ with probability δ. Since we made a mistake on every round in which the execution remained in states in $\Theta_{S_U,E}$, the claims now follow by taking $\delta = 1/2$, and by letting $\delta \to 1$. ∎

It is easy to construct *specific* examples for which learning functions on a message space Y requires an overhead of $|Y| - 1$—Auer and Long [12] describe one such example. Theorem 8.22, on the other hand, applies to many cases of interest, such as linear transformations:

Example 8.23 (Lower bound for learning linear transformations). Let $\mathcal{U}$ be the class of linear transformations $A : \mathbb{F}^n \to \mathbb{F}^n$ for some finite field $\mathbb{F}$. Suppose that the instance space is given by $\mathbb{F}^n \setminus \{0\}$. Now, for any nonzero $x, y \in \mathbb{F}^n$ we know that there is some $A_{x,y}$ such that $A(x) = y$. So, Theorem 8.22 shows that any on-line learning algorithm makes at least $(|\mathbb{F}|^n - 1)/2$ mistakes in the worst case.

We remark that it would be possible to learn the class of linear transformations if we had full feedback, much as we learned the class of parity strategies $\mathcal{U}_\oplus$ in Section 8.3.1; therefore, Auer and Long's [12] transformation gives an essentially optimal mistake bound for learning linear transformations for all dimensions and field sizes. In particular, when this mistake bound is superpolynomial, no algorithm can achieve a polynomially bounded number of mistakes.

Negative results for Boolean functions: a survey

We can exploit Theorem 8.9 more directly to recover some well-known impossibility results for learning even *Boolean* functions. In particular, Angluin [4] noted that an efficient mistake-bounded learning algorithm gives an efficient PAC-learning algorithm, since we can simulate the equivalence queries by taking a reasonable size sample, so that with probability $1 - \delta$, the proposed function will only pass if it agrees with the correct function on at least a $1 - \varepsilon$-fraction of the domain, as required by PAC-learning. So, negative results for efficient *PAC-learning* translate directly to negative results for efficient *mistake-bounded* learning, which translate to negative results for generic universal users.

Valiant [152] originally noted that pseudorandom functions could not be efficiently learned in the PAC model, which shows that if one-way functions exist, then the class of polynomial-size Boolean circuits cannot be learned efficiently (since pseudorandom functions were constructed from pseudorandom generators by Goldreich, Goldwasser, and Micali [69], and in turn, pseudorandom generators were constructed from one-way functions by Håstad et al.[79]). Pitt and Warmuth [120] subsequently gave a notion of reducibility and, in particular, a notion of prediction-completeness that showed hardness for learning other classes of functions; these results were further exploited by Kearns and Valiant [89] to show that under standard cryptographic assumptions – e.g., the hardness of factoring, deciding quadratic residuosity, and inverting the RSA function – DFAs, general Boolean formulae, and constant-depth threshold circuits cannot be learned efficiently. In particular, we note that the hardness of learning DFAs implies that even logspace decision strategies cannot be learned efficiently, and strategies that recognize strings generated by a context-free grammar cannot be learned efficiently. Kharitonov [92] showed that the class of AC_0 circuits cannot be learned unless the Blum-Blum-Shub pseudorandom generator [30] can be broken. Finally, a result by Klivans and Sherstov [93] shows that, under the assumption that the unique Shortest Vector Problem cannot be efficiently approximated to within a $\tilde{O}(n^{1.5})$-factor (cf., the LLL algorithm provides a $O(2^n)$ approximation), intersections of n^ϵ halfspaces cannot be learned efficiently. This implies that general polynomial-size depth-two neural networks and depth-three arithmetic circuits cannot be learned efficiently.

We remark that to the best of our knowledge, at this point, the only natural candidate Boolean function classes that have not been classified as learnable or unlearnable for this model are the class of *polynomial-size decision trees*, which were shown by Bshouty to be learnable in both the membership query PAC model [38] and in the membership and equivalence query learning model [37], and relatedly, the classes of *general polynomial-size CNF and DNF formulae* and *small width branching programs*. The nearest negative result, by Angluin [5] for learning decision rees, only holds for proper equivalence queries, i.e., only for functions represented by decision trees.

8.4.2 Richer feedback

Thus, the equivalence of generic universal users for one-round multi-session goals and mistake-bounded on-line learning algorithms gives a fairly clear picture of which classes of strategies we can efficiently learn generically from basic sensing – i.e., with success/fail feedback – and which classes we cannot learn efficiently from such feedback. Unfortunately, this boundary falls well short of where we would like—we can only learn strategies with very small message spaces, and under standard cryptographic assumptions, even then only for fairly simple classes of user strategies, even given that the user strategy is stateless.

Recall that our motivation for focusing on this notion of sensing was that we had results, such as Theorem 6.41, effectively saying that whenever sensing was possible, it was feasible to achieve a goal with any helpful server. In the finite execution setting, we had a variety of results in the same vein as Theorem 2.25, showing that this kind of feedback was moreover *necessary* for the construction of universal users. As we are primarily interested in user strategies that do not experience such severe overhead as that suffered by these constructions, though, we find that we are strongly motivated to leave this notion of sensing behind and investigate some notions of *stronger* feedback (that may not always be available).

Thus, again, we view negative results showing that $(\mathcal{U}, 1, 1)$-generic universal users cannot be mistake-efficient and/or implemented time-efficiently merely as limitations of *basic sensing*, and so we seek alternative notions of sensing that do not suffer these limitations. For example, recall that Auer and Long [12] showed how some useful, richer kinds of feedback can be simulated given only basic sensing, but only if the feedback is still limited in the sense that it can be simulated by a logarithmic number of queries; if we assume that these kinds of feedback are directly available, then since we don't need to simulate the feedback, we don't experience the overhead suffered by their technique.

Example 8.24 (Efficient universal linear transformation strategies from richer sensing). Concretely, consider the class of user strategies computing linear transformations $A : \mathbb{F}^n \to \mathbb{F}^n$ for some finite field $\mathbb{F}$, as considered in Example 8.23. There, we saw that given only basic sensing, any generic universal strategy experiences at least $(|\mathbb{F}|^n - 1)/2$ errors for one-round multi-session goals, where Auer and Long's technique yields a universal strategy making $\tilde{O}(|\mathbb{F}|^n)$ errors. Suppose now that we had richer sensing feedback, that not only provided positive or negative indications, but on a negative indication also provided some index $i \in \{1, \ldots, n\}$ such that if on the previous round we received an incoming message vector $x \in \mathbb{F}^n$ and responded with $y \in \mathbb{F}^n$, a viable linear transformation strategy A would not have responded with $(A(x))_i = y_i$. Then, e.g., for $\mathbb{F}_2$, we could use the algorithm from Theorem 8.11 to learn each ith row of a viable linear transformation on $\mathbb{F}_2^n$ in n mistakes, for n^2 mistakes (and time $O(n^3)$ per round) overall. Auer and

Long's technique can then also be used to simulate access to $(A(x))_i$ over $\mathbb{F}_q$ for $q > 2$ with an overhead of $\tilde{O}(q)$ mistakes, thus allowing us to use essentially the same learning algorithm over $\mathbb{F}_q$. As long as the field size is still small, this yields polynomial error and polynomial time bounded universal strategies, in contrast to the exponential lower bound of Example 8.23.

A similar kind of feedback would enable us to construct efficient universal users for k-round multi-session goals, given that there are stateless viable user strategies for which there exists a time and mistake efficient on-line learning algorithm for the user strategies when restricted to any single round. Namely, if the sensing function also told us that the user's messages in some ith round of the previous session was unsatisfactory, then this feedback could be used to learn the user strategy for each round separately, even if k is polynomially large.

Another kind of feedback that may be useful is "directional" feedback, as considered by Barland [18]. Precisely, assuming that the user's messages are identified with points in $\mathbb{R}$, we mean sensing that on negative indications additionally indicates whether, when the user responded y to an incoming message x, user strategies U that would have obtained positive indications would have sent messages satisfying $U(x) > y$ or $U(x) < y$, i.e., whether y was "too low" or "too high." Incidentally, Auer et al. [13] considered this kind of feedback, and showed that the natural notion of mistake tree for this kind of feedback yields optimal lower bounds on the number of mistakes required to learn from this feedback.

Relationship to the finite execution setting

We note that given the standard notion of sensing in finite executions (Definition 2.22), a result qualitatively similar to that achieved by Auer and Long [12] is trivial for one-round user strategies:

Proposition 8.25. *Let G be a goal for communication in finite executions, let $\mathcal{S}$ be any class of server strategies, and let V be a sensing function (in the sense of Definition 2.22) that for every $S \in \mathcal{S}$ is $(1-\epsilon)$-safe for G and $(1-\delta)$-viable for G with some one-round user strategy U_S^* with S. Then there is an $(\mathcal{S}, 1 - \epsilon/\delta)$-universal user strategy running in expected time $\delta^{-1}t(n)|\Omega^{(u,\cdot)}|$ where $t(n)$ is the expected running time of the sensing function.*

Proof Let U be the following user strategy: to compute the message we will send on the current round, we simply run through the space $\Omega^{(u,\cdot)}$ of outgoing messages, simulating the verdict of our sensing function on each message, and output the first message that obtains a positive indication if one exists. (If no such message is found, we send an arbitrary message.) If a one-round strategy is viable with the given server S, then some message in this space causes the sensing function to give a positive indication with probability $1 - \delta$ on each round. Thus, in δ^{-1} rounds in expectation, we output a message and halt and our expected running time is as promised. We now note that since sensing is $1 - \epsilon$-safe and run δ^{-1} times in expectation, the probability of it obtaining a false positive indication with the user (and failing to achieve G) is at most ϵ/δ, as needed. ∎

When the space of outgoing messages is small, this strategy is efficient, and thus *none* of the strategies we discussed in Section 8.3 are interesting in the context of finite executions. By contrast, if the space of outgoing messages is large or the strategies run for many rounds, then the techniques from on-line learning with richer feedback may provide nontrivial examples of efficient universal strategies for goals and servers, given an appropriate adaptation of this notion of feedback to finite executions. In particular, this gives a potential alternative to the Bayesian constructions based on sampleable "prior" distributions for communication in finite executions described in Chapter 4.

Chapter 9

Towards applications: communication with a changing network protocol

We finally return to our original technical motivations for studying semantic communication, outlined in Section 1.1. Specifically, we will present a first attempt at designing end-user network protocols that can adapt to "simple" modifications of the protocol used on the network without third-party intervention. In practice, the network protocols we wish to modify serve the purpose of forwarding messages from one user to another—in effect, realizing a *channel* across the network. Thus, our task seems like an insurmountable challenge *a priori*, since we stressed earlier (at the outset of Chapter 2) that this goal is not verifiable in general. Therefore, in service of the design of a protocol, we will need to first develop a *verifiable* goal of communication for the network's users, and then exhibit a user protocol that achieves our goal.

Perhaps surprisingly, a pair of users can arrange for a scheme that allows them to verify that they receive the correct messages after a bounded adversarial modification of the network protocol, under the assumption that the encoding of data under the protocol is computable in a single pass by a small-space program, and given that the modification is computed by a short program with similar restrictions. (We note that protocols such as IPv4 and IPv6 merely attach a header to the data, and thus satisfy these restrictions.) In particular, our scheme is ultimately capable of coping with networks that drop and reorder the packets.

Thus, the work in the present chapter represents the culmination of several previous chapters: a *complexity-theoretic* restriction on the protocols (e.g., as discussed in Chapter 5) permits the *verification* of a goal, which then leads to an *algorithm* for the desired task (as developed in Chapter 2). Actually, the goal we wish to solve is most naturally cast in the *infinite execution* setting (of

B. Juba, *Universal Semantic Communication*,
DOI 10.1007/978-3-642-23297-8_9,
© Springer-Verlag Berlin Heidelberg 2011

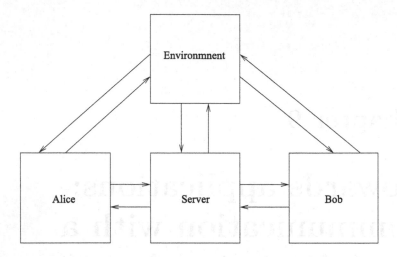

Figure 9.1: Our model network: Alice and Bob wish to communicate messages provided by the Environment via the Server.

Chapter 6), where we assume that the users wish to send an infinite sequence of messages correctly, and we argue that with high probability, *no* errors are *ever* encountered when a (sufficiently simple) modification of the network's protocol occurs.

9.1 Model of communication under a changing network protocol

Our model of the problem of communicating under a changing network protocol departs from our basic model in a variety of essential ways. Most notably, we assume that there are *two* users who, much as in Shannon's model [135], wish to agree on a scheme for communication in advance; communication, in this case, therefore means that they wish to realize the abstraction of a reliable channel. The difficulty is that their communication is mediated by the network, modeled by an adversarially chosen server. So, in order to get messages from one user to the other, the users need to conform to the protocol imposed by the server. Accomplishing communication under such conditions would be impossible in general, but we are able to achieve it by assuming that the network's protocol is some "simple" modification of an earlier protocol known to both the sender and receiver.

9.1.1 Setting and goal of communication

Precisely, as illustrated in Figure 9.1, we will consider a system with *four* entities: two *users* – Alice and Bob – a *server*, and an *environment*. We will

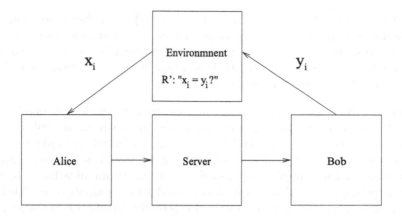

Figure 9.2: The streaming messages goal. On each session, the environment provides Alice with x_i, which she wishes to communicate to Bob; Bob returns a string y_i to the environment at the end of the session, and the goal is achieved if $y_i = x_i$.

assume that Alice and Bob can exchange messages with the server and the environment, and as before, the communication proceeds in rounds; just as described in Chapter 2, on each round, each of the entities computes new messages and a new state from its old state and the messages it received on the previous round, and at the end of the round, these messages are simultaneously passed across each of the channels, for use at the start of the next round.

We suppose that Alice wishes to send messages to Bob, but she cannot do so directly because Alice and Bob do not share a binary channel—rather, she must send the messages to the server, and if the messages conform to the server's protocol, then the server will forward the message to Bob on the next round. Formally, in our model, we suppose that the messages that Alice wishes to send to Bob are supplied to her by the environment, and that once Bob receives a message, he passes it back to the environment. Recalling that the users in our system correspond to, e.g., the drivers and libraries for sending messages across the network, saying that "the environment supplies Alice with a message" corresponds to an invocation of these lower-level systems to send messages across the network, and likewise, "returning the message to the environment" corresponds to this sub-system passing the received message back to some user-level application.

We will actually present two goals here. The first, cleaner and simpler goal, illustrated in Figure 9.2, is suitable for sending messages one way across a reliable network (e.g., across a LAN); we will initially work with this simpler goal.

Definition 9.1 (Goal for streaming messages). The *goal of streaming messages* is a multi-session goal for communication in which the environment non-deterministically chooses a string $x_i \in \{0,1\}^{\leq n}$ in the ith session and sends it to the first user on each round. The second user may elect to terminate the session at any time by sending the environment some $y \in \{0,1\}^*$. The temporal decision function R' is satisfied in an end-session state if the second user terminated the session by sending $y = x_i$.

The second, more demanding goal is intended to model communication over the internet. It considers the case where the users might wish to send messages in both directions and the network is allowed to randomly drop and adversarially reorder messages (note that we must assume *some* kind of restriction on the dropping of messages to allow communication). In this case, although we could attempt to only model the guarantees provided by the IP layer, and only ask that the users correctly decode the messages that they actually receive, it will turn out that we will necessarily achieve a more demanding goal, since we will need to verify that we used a working protocol to send messages. (We postpone an in-depth discussion of these issues until Section 9.3.) Thus, more akin to the guarantee provided by the TCP layer, our goal will be the reliable delivery of messages. Along these lines, we also impose a "polynomial" bound on the extent to which the delivery of messages may be delayed, for use in calculating the timeout (i.e., half the "maximum RTT").

Definition 9.2 (Goal for unreliable datagrams). The *goal of sending datagrams with max-delay $d(n)$ and failure probability $\delta(n)$* is a concurrent-session goal for communication in which the environment non-deterministically chooses a string $x_i \in \{0,1\}^{\leq n}$ for the ith session, non-deterministically chooses either Alice or Bob, and sends x_i to the selected user at the beginning of the ith session; the other user is considered the "addressee" of the message.

The environment will interpret messages from the server as indicating the contents of datagrams it receives and the source and destination of the datagrams. For each such datagram indicated by the server to the environment, independently with probability $\delta(n)$, the environment responds with a message indicating "drop" and otherwise, (with probability $1 - \delta(n)$) the environment non-deterministically responds with an integer in the range $[0, d(n) - 4]$ indicating how long the message should be delayed – note that a message takes four rounds to traverse our network under normal circumstances – respecting the restriction that it does not indicate that more than one message should be delivered to either user on any given round; in particular, if there are already messages scheduled to be delivered to the user on every round for the next $d(n) - 4$ rounds, then the environment also responds with a "drop" message.[1]

---

[1] Precisely, for every history of communication (including the indication of dropped messages) up to each current round and infinite choice of sessions, the environment's actual strategy has selected a valid delivery time for the server's next message; this schedule is then modified in the actual strategy by the random (independent) choice of whether or not to drop the message instead.

If a user sends a nonempty message y to the environment such that some ith active session with that user designated as the recipient has $x_i = y$ and i is the smallest index with that user designated as the recipient, then the ith session is considered terminated with success. Otherwise, if y is nonempty, then the temporal decision function is unsatisfied for that round.

9.1.2 Model of network protocols and bounded changes

We will adopt a rather simple, weak model for our network protocols: roughly, we assume that the protocols encode a single message into a single packet, and that this encoding can be computed by a small-space algorithm that only makes a single pass over the data. This choice of format is not arbitrary; rather, it is the strongest (most general) natural candidate class of algorithms for which our basic tasks, described in Section 9.2.1, are known to be achievable. In particular, we will rely on the construction of *deterministic extractors* for extracting random bits from the outputs of these functions when the function itself is unknown, and on the ability to efficiently decide whether or not these functions are *injective* and easily *invert* them. We remark that while the task of deterministic extraction seems plausible for stronger classes of algorithms – a *conditional* construction of a deterministic extractor for general polynomial time functions was given by Trevisan and Vadhan [147] – it is easy to construct families of logspace functions (with two-way access to their inputs) where efficiently inverting the function would imply that P = NP (e.g., the Boolean formula evaluation function). It is also similarly easy to construct examples where efficiently determining whether or not the pre-image of a function has size 1 or greater would imply P = NP (e.g., computing the identity on unsatisfying assignments to a CNF formula and mapping satisfying assignments to a canonical unsatisfying assignment). Thus, it seems unlikely that much stronger classes of algorithms can be used for a scheme resembling ours.

Fortunately, the class of algorithms we use is still strong enough to capture real network protocols—an overview of a variety of such protocols is given in the textbook by Peterson and Davie [119]. The protocols used at the IP layer, for example, do no more than attach a header to the data to form a packet, and Ethernet protocols similarly involve no more than headers and checksums (e.g., CRC involves computing the modular reduction over a finite field). The class of algorithms and changes we use can support such headers and simple checksums, as well as some counting operations across packets.

We will use the following "program-independent" definition of space complexity

Definition 9.3 (Bits of state). We say that a user algorithm U *maintains* $s(n)$ *bits of state* with respect to an environment strategy $\mathcal{E}$ with size parameter $n = n(E)$, a server strategy S, and an efficiently computable encoding map ψ taking the configurations of U to $\{0,1\}^*$ if in any execution (E, U, S), the image of ψ is a subset of $\{0,1\}^{s(n(E))}$. If the algorithm maintains $s(n)$ bits of state with respect to all server strategies, then we simply say that it maintains $s(n)$ bits of state.

The key point of this definition is that the encoding map bounds the size of the configuration graph needed to simulate the machine in an execution. Otherwise, we will follow the terminology introduced by Rabin and Scott [122] for relating finite state machines to Turing machines, notably using their notions of one-way tapes and end markers. The precise meaning of these terms is somewhat obvious, so we do not bother to recall the definition.

Precisely, the class of protocols we consider is the following:

Definition 9.4 (Streaming protocols). A *space-$s(n)$ streaming protocol with maximum stretch C and maximum message size N or $(s(n), C, N)$-streaming protocol* is given by a deterministic interactive Turing machine with Boolean input and output alphabets satisfying the following conditions:

1. *Bounded state:* Maintains $s(n)$ bits of state on inputs of length at most n

2. *One-way tape with end marker:* Computes its message in a single pass over a one-way input tape with end marker

3. *Bounded stretch:* Outputs a string of length at most CN on inputs of length at most N

4. *Injectivity:* For any two "wait for reply" states σ and σ' and inputs $x \neq x'$ of length at most N, the message output from state σ on input x differs from the message output from state σ' on input x'.

The fourth condition guarantees that a streaming protocol is injective with respect to messages, and therefore that a complementary decoding protocol exists; it actually turns out that the decoding can always be performed in time polynomial in $2^{s(n)}$, as we review in Section 9.2.1.

We will focus on $s(n) = O(\log n)$ in the sequel. Strictly speaking, we will work with some maximum message size N that is assumed to be known to both users and not much larger than the actual lengths of individual messages n that the users wish to send per round (e.g., $N \approx 4n$). N and n should be regarded as "comparable size" constants, and thus s is a "relatively small" constant. We will specify the actual quantitative relationships we need later, but the issue will be that our running time will only be a polynomial in 2^s.

The modifications to these protocols will be modeled by the following class of functions:

Definition 9.5 (Bounded modifications). A *space-$s'(n)$ bounded modification with stretch C' and program length $\ell(n)$ of a streaming protocol U or $(\ell(n), s'(n), C')$-bounded modification of U f* is a function of program length $\ell(n)$ computable by a deterministic Turing machine over Boolean input and output alphabets with a one-way input tape with end marker, satisfying the following constraints:

1. *Bounded state:* Maintains $s'(n)$ bits of state on inputs of length up to n

2. *Bounded stretch:* Outputs a string of length at most $C'N$ on inputs of length at most N

3. *Injectivity:* For any two "wait for reply" states σ and σ' of U and inputs $x \neq x'$ of length at most N (the maximum length for U), for the messages m output by U from state σ on input x and the message m' output by U from state σ' on input x', $f(m) \neq f(m')$.

Note, in particular, given an $(s(n), C, N)$-streaming protocol U and an $(\ell(n), s'(n), C')$-bounded modification f of U, the protocol $f(U)$ that applies f to the output of U is an $(s(n) + s'(Cn), C \cdot C', N)$-streaming protocol.

We are now ready to describe the class of servers we are prepared to work with. We begin by describing a class of "reliable" servers for our reliable communication goal, described in Definition 9.1:

Definition 9.6 (Reliable servers under bounded modifications). For a given streaming protocol U, the *class of reliable servers using $(\ell(n), s'(n), C')$-bounded modifications to U* is the following class of servers: for each streaming protocol $U' = f(U)$ for some $(\ell(n), s'(n), C')$-bounded modification f of U, there is a server $S(U')$ in the class that, whenever it receives a message from the first user that is an output of U', it forwards that message to the second user on the next round, and otherwise does nothing (i.e., drops the message).

Much as with $s(n)$ earlier, we will also focus on $s'(n), \ell(n) = O(\log n)$, where effectively this means that s' and ℓ should be taken to be "small" relative to n, and our running time will depend polynomially on $2^{s'}$ and 2^{ℓ}— observing that a bounded modification f could concatenate its input with a password of length $\ell(n) - O(1)$, $S(f(U))$ is a password-protected version of $S(U)$, so the class of servers using $(\ell(n), s'(n), C')$-bounded modifications to U includes all password-prepending versions of $S(U)$ with passwords of length $\ell(n) - O(1)$. Since, furthermore, the goal is $(t(n), 2^{-n}t(n))$-nontrivial, a variant of Theorem 4.4 shows that such an exponential dependence on ℓ is unavoidable.

Before moving on, we note that our approach can also capture networks employing completely unknown protocols, as long as the protocol is sufficiently simple:

Example 9.7 (Bounded modifications of the identity function). For the streaming protocol U_I that maintains no state across inputs, and simply computes the identity function, the class of protocols obtained by $(\ell(n), s'(n), C')$-bounded modifications of U_I is just the class of (stateless) protocols that compute injective encodings of their inputs that stretch n bits to at most

$C'n$ bits, and that can be computed in space $s'(n)$ with one-way access to their input by programs of length at most $\ell(n)$. In particular, the class of reliable servers using $(\ell(n), s'(n), C')$-bounded modifications to U_I is just the class of servers using such short and small-space single-pass encodings.

We now turn to give a definition of the class of servers we intend to work with as our model of unreliable networks in the unreliable communication goal of Definition 9.2. To this end, we need the servers to drop or delay even valid messages, as specified by the environment. This goal also introduced two-way communication over the goal of Definition 9.1; to reflect the fact that packets with different destinations have different headers, we will actually define our server with respect to two "protocols," one for sending messages to the first user, and one for sending messages to the second user. Of course, in generalizing to more users, we would like a single protocol that any ith user can use, which takes the jth user's address as a second input to compute a packet that will be delivered to the jth user. One would hope that this would result in greater efficiency, since a user only has to learn a single protocol to communicate with all other users in the network, and we will discuss approaches to generalizing our schemes later, in Section 9.4. In any case, for the time being, we only consider two users, and thus there is no harm in simply modeling the protocols as depending non-uniformly on the addressee.

Definition 9.8 (Unreliable servers under bounded modifications)**.** For a given pair of streaming protocols U_1 and U_2, the *class of unreliable servers using $(\ell(n), s'(n), C')$-bounded modifications to U_1 and U_2* is the following class of servers. For each pair of $(\ell(n), s'(n), C')$-bounded modifications to U_1 and U_2, f_1 and f_2, there is a server $S(f_1(U_1), f_2(U_2))$ with the following behavior.

Whenever it receives a message m from user i such that m is the output of $f_j(U_j)$ on some input x from some state σ, it records (m, x, i, j) and sends a message indicating that it received a message with contents x from user i addressed to user j to the environment; note that the server might indicate receipt of up to two such messages per round, one from the first user and one from the second. If the environment responds that this message should be delayed for k rounds for some integer k, then the server augments the record (m, x, i, j) with a counter (m, x, i, j, k), decrementing k on each round, and finally sending m to user j when k reaches 0. If, on the other hand, the environment responds that the message should be dropped, then the record (m, x, i, j) is deleted. If it receives a message that is neither an output of $f_1(U_1)$ nor an output of $f_2(U_2)$, then it is immediately dropped.

On the breadth of applicability of the model. Naïvely, it may seem like these modifications cannot change the functionality of the protocol— and indeed, from the perspective of the end-users, the basic functionality (of sending and receiving messages) remains unchanged. It does not follow that the functionality with respect to the rest of the network remains unchanged, however. For example, suppose the network's protocol is modified to include a checksum; although the end-users may simply ignore the functionality provided by the new checksum (and simply learn to conform to the syntax of the protocol, oblivious of its functionaility), other nodes on the network may inspect the checksum and use it to request retransmission of a corrupted packet. Our definition of modified networks only requires that packets of the old format can be converted to packets that conform to the new format by a simple transformation—preserving the old functionality without necessarily preserving the old syntax.[2]

9.2 An end-user algorithm for decoding messages sent under a modified network protocol

We now show how to address the key problem in adapting to changes to the network's protocol: *verifiably* decoding a message sent under a new protocol. In the exposition of our scheme, we assume for the moment that Alice knows the new protocol but Bob does not, and that the network is reliable; we will postpone these issues until Section 9.3. Thus, the only problem we face is how Bob can decode Alice's messages.

As usual, the crux of the problem is distinguishing a correct decoding from incorrect ones; given a method for verifying correctness, we can complete the scheme by enumerating encodings. Our scheme for verification is extremely simple. At a high level, Alice first sends a random message to Bob, which they use to agree on a member of a *pairwise-independent hash family*, by applying a *deterministic extractor* to the encoding. Subsequently, Alice tags each message with its hash value under the common function; Bob can then verify that he decodes the correct message by comparing the tag he decodes with the hash value of the message he decodes. As a consequence of pairwise independence, the hash function will only agree with the tag on an incorrect decoding of the message with exponentially small probability.

9.2.1 Algorithms for deterministic extractors and inverting transducers

Recall that our protocols are given by interactive Turing machines that maintain $s(n)$ bits of state and compute their messages by making a single pass over a one-way input tape with an end marker. For given input and output

---

[2]In fact, it turns out that our algorithms *can* learn to use some new functionality, provided that the implementation is sufficiently simple, and provided that it leads to a noticeable improvement in the probability that an acknowledgement is received. Improving other measures of performance is an open issue.

lengths n and m, or fixed maximum input length N, we can obtain two different corresponding non-uniform representations of the functions computed by our protocol.

Fixed maximum input length N: $2^{s(N)}$-state transducer representation. We recall that a *finite state transducer* is given by

1. An input alphabet A and an output alphabet B

2. A set of states Q, with initial state q_- and a set of accepting states Q_+

3. A transition relation $R \subseteq Q \times A \cup \{\varepsilon\} \times B \cup \{\varepsilon\} \times Q$ where ε denotes the empty word.

The natural interpretation of the transition relation is as a labeled directed graph on vertex set Q, where each edge has one *input label* from $A \cup \{\varepsilon\}$ and one *output label* from $B \cup \{\varepsilon\}$. Given an input word $x \in A^*$ (where the $*$ is, of course, the Kleene star, denoting any finite length string of symbols from A), the set of outputs associated with x by the transducer is precisely the set of words $y \in B^*$ that can be obtained by concatenating the output labels on any path in the transducer from q_- to Q_+ for which the input labels are the symbols of x in order, with any number of occurrences of ε input labels in between.

For a given algorithm and maximum input length N, the corresponding finite state transducer will have the $2^{s(N)}$ states our algorithm uses on inputs up to length N as its state set, and the transition relation will be given by our Turing machine's transition function in the natural way; we will also include the "end of input" marker transitions from each state as transitions with ε input labels. We will generally specify an initial state (it may be a predetermined initial configuration or one of the "wait for reply" states), and Q_+ will be the set of "wait for reply" states. It is easily verified that, on inputs of length up to N, the finite state transducer we have just described associates the output string produced by our protocol with each input, and can be constructed from the interactive Turing machine description of the protocol in time polynomial in $2^{s(N)}$ and N.

Since our interactive Turing machine is deterministic, actually, the finite state transducer has at most one successful path for each input label, so the finite state transducer is said to be *unambiguous*, which of course means that it computes a (partial) function. All of the background and results we will require on finite-state transducers are covered by Sakarovitch [130].

Given input length n and output length m: width-$2^{s(n)}$ branching program representation. For our purposes, a *width-w branching program* is a directed acyclic graph in which the vertices are arranged in *layers* of w vertices each, in which each edge has an input label from $A \cup \{\varepsilon\}$ and an output label from $B \cup \{\varepsilon\}$ for alphabets A and B, and each edge from a vertex in some ith layer with an output label in B points to a vertex in the $(i+1)$th layer, while vertices in any ith layer with an output label of ε point to another vertex in the ith layer.[3] There is a designated *starting state* in the first layer. On a given input word $x \in A^n$, an output $y \in B^m$ is produced by concatenating the output labels on a path in our graph for which the nonempty input labels correspond to the symbols of x in order.

The branching program associated with our protocol on input length n and output length m has $m+1$ layers, in which each layer has a copy of the $2^{s(n)}$ states of the algorithm required by inputs of length n; in accordance with our convention above, for each state in the ith layer and transition from that state with output label ε specified by the algorithm's transition function, the edge points to the corresponding next state in the same layer; otherwise, the transition points to the corresponding next state in the next layer. It is easy to see that, for any desired initial state of our algorithm (i.e., either its initial configuration or one of its "wait for reply" configurations) for which, on input $x \in \{0,1\}^n$, our protocol would produce output $y \in \{0,1\}^m$, the branching program also produces y. Again, it is easily seen that we can efficiently construct the branching program in time polynomial in $2^{s(n)}$, n, and m.

The roles of uniform representations of functions versus their non-uniform representations   Note that, although our algorithms will all operate on these non-uniform representations of our protocols, we still prefer to think of our protocols as being described by a "program," i.e., a uniform representation, since ultimately our scheme will resort to enumerating programs, rather than enumerating the non-uniform representations. We could do the latter at the cost of some blow-up (our running time will depend exponentially on the number of bits of state used by our algorithms anyway), but we still prefer to separate the dependence on the space complexity from the dependence on the program length in our enumeration.

Deterministic extractors for small-space sources

We first fix some terminology and notation. Recall that $\Delta(X, Y)$ denotes the statistical distance between two distributions X and Y, and that a distribution X is said to have *min-entropy* k if no element in its support occurs with probability greater than 2^{-k}. We now recall the definition of a deterministic extractor:

Definition 9.9 (Deterministic extractor). For a class of sources $\mathcal{X}$, a function $\mathsf{Ext} : \{0,1\}^n \to \{0,1\}^m$ is a ϵ-*deterministic extractor* if for every $X \in \mathcal{X}$, $\Delta(U_m, \mathsf{Ext}(X)) \le \epsilon$.

---

[3]The usual convention is that *all* edges originating in the ith layer are directed to vertices in the $(i+1)$th layer. We can obtain such a representation if we allow input labels from A^* and "collapse" paths of edges with ε outputs to the final edge that crosses to the $(i+1)$th layer—such an edge must exist by the assumption that the graph is acyclic.

Crucially for our application, Ext should work given only a sample from some $X \in \mathcal{X}$, without needing to know which source $X \in \mathcal{X}$ its inputs are drawn from. This will allow us to extract near-perfect randomness from a packet of random bits without knowing the encoding format, given that the protocol is an $(s(n), C, N)$-streaming protocol. This is because when such protocols are used to encode randomly chosen inputs, the resulting distribution is essentially a space-$s(n)$ source, as described in the work of Kamp et al. [87]:

Definition 9.10 (Space-$s(n)$ source). A *space-$s(n)$ source* on $\{0,1\}^m$ is given by a layered directed acyclic graph with $m + 1$ layers in which the layers are numbered $0, \ldots, m$, each layer has at most $2^{s(n)}$ vertices, each edge crosses from some layer i to a layer $i + 1$, and there is a designated start vertex in layer 0. The edges have labels (p, b) for $p \in [0,1]$ and $b \in \{0,1\}$, satisfying that the edges $e_1, \ldots, e_k$ leaving any vertex in the graph have labels $(p_1, b_1), \ldots, (p_k, b_k)$ respectively, satisfying $\sum_{i=1}^{k} p_i = 1$.

A space-$s(n)$ source on $\{0,1\}^m$ is sampled by taking a random walk starting from the designated start vertex in layer 0, and choosing independently at each step among the outgoing edges from a given vertex with labels $(p_1, b_1), \ldots, (p_k, b_k)$, choosing the jth edge with probability p_j, and concatenating the labels b_i on the chosen edges. The *distribution* of the source is the distribution on $\{0,1\}^m$ of outputs of this sampling procedure.

The only difference between the packets produced by our protocols on random inputs and the space-$s(n)$ sources of Kamp et al. is that our packets may be of variable length. This technicality is easily dealt with by the following lemma:

Lemma 9.11 $((s(n), C, N)$-streaming protocols on random inputs give space-$s(n)+1$ sources). *Let X be the output distribution of an $(s(n), C, N)$-streaming protocol run from its initial state on a random input of length $n \leq N$, and let* $\mathsf{pad} : \{0,1\}^{\leq Cn} \to \{0,1\}^{Cn+1}$ *be given by $x \mapsto x10^*$ for the unique member of $x10^*$ of length $Cn + 1$. Then $\mathsf{pad}(X)$ is the distribution of a space-$s(n) + 1$ source on $Cn + 1$ bits with total entropy n.*

Proof Consider the branching program representation of our protocol on inputs of length n and outputs of length up to Cn. We add an additional state to each layer that outputs 0 on input label ε and transitions to the next layer, and add an edge with input label ε and output label 1 transitioning from each "wait for reply" state to the new state in the next layer. It is easy to see that this branching program computes the result of applying f to the output of our protocol, and has at most $2^{s(n)} + 1$ states per layer.

We now obtain the space-$s(n) + 1$ source as follows: we map the labels on the edges with inputs from $\{0,1\}$ to edges with probability $1/2$, and map the labels on the edges with input label ε to edges with probability 1, and collapse paths on these edges within a layer to the final edge crossing to the next layer, so that all edges cross from one layer to the next. Now, since the protocol is computed by a deterministic machine and each bit of the protocol's input is 0 or 1 with probability $1/2$ independently, it is easily verified that a path through this space-$s(n) + 1$ source has the same probability as the corresponding path through the branching program representation of our protocol on a random input of length n; since the output labels are the same, they therefore also produce the same distribution on $Cn + 1$. In particular, since the protocol computes an injective map on inputs of length n and f is injective on the outputs of the protocol, the source also has entropy n. ∎

The work of Kamp et al. produced a variety of deterministic extractors for these small-space sources, and we will use their result for constant entropy rate, paraphrased slightly for convenience:

Theorem 9.12 (Deterministic extractor for small-space sources with constant entropy rate [87]). *There is a function $s(n) = O(n)$ such that if $\mathcal{X}$ is a class of space-$s(n)$ sources on $\{0,1\}^N$ with min-entropy n for $N \leq Cn$ for some constant C, then for any constant $\delta \in (0,1)$, there is a polynomial time computable ϵ-deterministic extractor* $\mathsf{Ext} : \{0,1\}^N \to \{0,1\}^m$ *for* $m = (1 - \delta)n$ *and* $\epsilon = 2^{-\Omega(n/\log^3 n)}$.

Inverses of single-pass logspace computable functions

Given a space-bounded interactive Turing machine and an input length bound, there are two operations our scheme requires. First, we must be able to decide whether or not the Turing machine computes a valid encoding of its inputs, i.e., whether or not it is injective in the appropriate sense. Second, given the interactive Turing machine representation of our protocol, we need to efficiently invert the function to decode the message. Both of these can be efficiently carried out on the finite-state transducer representation of our protocols, as we review next. For more background and details, the reader is encouraged to consult the book by Sakarovitch [130].

Computing inverses of an injective finite-state transducer. Recall that our finite-state transducer representation associates, in general, a *set* of outputs with each given input; more generally, for input alphabet A and output alphabet B, it defines a relation $T \subseteq A^* \times B^*$. Thus, it is easily seen that given a finite-state transducer computing a function f, a finite-state transducer with the same size computing the pre-image of that function is obtained by exchanging the input and output labels on each edge (and thus also swapping the input and output alphabets). Of course, the function f is injective if and only if its pre-image is a partial function. In this case, to obtain $f^{-1}(y)$ for some given $y \in B^*$, we need only find a valid path from the start state to some accept state where the "input" labels for the pre-image transducer are the symbols of y, and concatenate the "output" labels.

Proposition 9.13 (Computing inverses of an $(s(n), C, N)$-streaming protocol). *Given $y \in \{0, 1\}^m$ and an $(s(n), C, N)$-streaming protocol, there is an algorithm running in time $O(m^2 \cdot 2^{2s(N)})$ that computes the input x on which the protocol outputs y when one exists.*

Proof Implicitly, the algorithm is a dynamic programming algorithm on the branching program representation of the protocol. For $i = 0, \ldots, m$, we maintain a list of the possible configurations the algorithm could be in and the input word that brings the algorithm from one of its initial configurations to the current configuration, or mark it as "overloaded," meaning more than one input generates the i symbol prefix and reaches this configuration.

To compute the $(i + 1)$th list from the ith, for each state in the current list, we make two passes. On the first pass, we consider the transitions from configurations in the current list in which the output label matches y_{i+1}, and we mark configurations of the machine in the next list by concatenating the input word with the input label on that transition; if some word is already marked with another input word, we change the mark to "overloaded," and if the configuration in the ith list is marked with "overloaded," then we mark the configuration in the next list with "overloaded" as well. On the second pass, we consider the new list of configurations, and perform a breadth-first search on the transitions with output label ε from the configurations marked with an input word; again, we mark the new configurations with an input word obtained by concatenating the source node's input word with the input label of the transition connecting them, unless the source was marked "overloaded" or the configuration is already marked with a different input word, in which case we (again) mark it as "overloaded." Since the comparisons and marking can be done in $O(m)$ time, these two passes each take $O(m2^{2s(N)})$ time.

It is easily verified by induction that the input words in each ith list constructed in this way do take the algorithm from one of its initial states to the configurations in the list, producing output $y_1 \cdots y_i$. Thus, if $i = m$, then the input words marking each of the "wait for reply" configurations are the input words that could have produced y from one of the algorithm's initial configurations. By definition, therefore, there must be at most one such label x, which must have been the input. ∎

We also note that the algorithm we just presented can also be used to detect a violation of injectivity at a single output, by outputting "overloaded" if any "wait for reply" state has an "overloaded" mark. In the next section, we will recall an efficient algorithm that checks that a function is injective up to a given input length.

Deciding injectivity of a finite-state transducer. The key property possessed by our streaming protocols is that they are injective with respect to inputs of length up to N, and bounded modifications are not much more than functions that respect this property. Our scheme for adapting to bounded modifications will involve enumerating candidate functions, and it will be essential to only use functions that are at least injective on the inputs we actually see—in this regard, the modification to the algorithm presented in Proposition 9.13 which we noted above would actually suffice. It will simplify the analysis and reduce the number of faulty candidates we try, however, if we simply test that the algorithm is injective (up to the maximum input length).

Perhaps surprisingly, we can *efficiently* decide whether or not our algorithm is injective by considering the finite-state transducer for the pre-image, which we saw was itself easily obtained from the finite-state transducer representation of the function. The function is injective if and only if the pre-image finite-state transducer computes a partial function; Schützenberger [132] first noticed that this property was *decidable*, and the first polynomial time algorithm was given by Gurari and Ibarra [77].[4] The running time of Gurari and Ibarra's algorithm was still somewhat impractical, though; an improved algorithm has since been given by Béal et al. [20]:

Theorem 9.14 (Functionality of finite-state transducers is efficiently decidable [20]). *Given an n-state transducer with $m \geq n$ transitions and maximum transition label size K, there is an algorithm that decides in time $O(Km^4)$ whether or not the finite-state transducer computes a partial function.*

In summary, we obtain the following corollary:

Corollary 9.15 (Injectivity is efficiently decidable). *There is an algorithm to decide whether or not a space-$s(n)$ interactive Turing machine is injective from its "wait for reply" states on inputs of length up to N in time $O(2^{4s(N)})$.*

Proof We first obtain the finite-state transducer representation of our machine, and swap the input and output labels to obtain the "pre-image transducer." We then give the finite-state transducer a new start state with $(\varepsilon, \varepsilon)$ transitions to each of the states corresponding to a "wait for reply" configuration of our original machine. We can then apply the algorithm from Theorem 9.14 to this finite-state transducer. The running time is $O(2^{4s(N)})$ since each of the $2^{s(N)}$ old states had at most two outgoing transitions, and we added at most another $2^{s(N)}$ transitions. The result decides whether or not our interactive Turing machine satisfied the injectivity property since it was injective if and only if the pre-image was a partial function, where we note that this is precisely the relation computed by the pre-image transducer. ∎

---

[4]The background necessary for these older works is given by Berstel [26], which was in many cases re-worked and improved by Sakarovitch [130] who, again, presents all of these results.

9.2.2 The user decoding strategy and its implementation

Now that we have recalled the algorithms for achieving the basic tasks that the user will employ, we are nearly ready to describe the decoding strategy. The basic strategy is that the messages will be tagged with a hash value, permitting us to verify that we decoded the correct message, since the hash value of a different message cannot be constructed using a given message's hash value. Such information-theoretically secure signature schemes were first proposed by Gilbert, MacWilliams, and Sloane [63], and the explicit application of hashing as an "authentication" scheme was first proposed by Wegman and Carter [154].[5] The property of the hash function that will guarantee that the hash values are hard to construct is *pairwise independence*. Recall:

Definition 9.16 (Pairwise independent hash family [40]). A family of functions $\mathcal{H} = \{h : A \to B\}$ is said to be *pairwise independent* if for every distinct $x, x' \in A$ and every pair $y, y' \in B$,

$$\Pr_{h \in \mathcal{H}}[h(x) = y \text{ and } h(x') = y'] = \frac{1}{|B|^2}$$

where the probability is over a uniformly random choice of $h \in \mathcal{H}$.

In particular, it is easily verified that the following standard construction is a pairwise independent hash family with $2\lceil \log q \rceil$-bit descriptions:

Construction 9.17 (Finite field hash family). Let $\mathbb{F}_q$ be a finite field of size q. Let $\mathcal{H}$ be the family of functions $h_{a,b} : \mathbb{F}_q \to \mathbb{F}_q$ given by $h_{a,b}(x) = a \cdot x + b$ for $a, b \in \mathbb{F}_q$.

We will use $q = 2^m$; thus, there is a natural map between members of $\mathbb{F}_q$ and binary strings of length m, and the members of our hash family have $2m$-bit representations. Likewise, for strings of length $n \leq m$, we can easily embed the string of length n in, say, the first n bits of a string of length m, and use the previous map to obtain an element of $\mathbb{F}_q$.

The user decoding strategy

Now, the scheme is as follows, for $n < m$ and $2m < N$:

Algorithm 9.18 (User decoding strategy). Fix an $(s(n), C, N)$-streaming protocol U and a deterministic extractor Ext for space-$s(n) + s'(n) + 1$ sources

---

[5]Although the actual "improved" scheme they suggest does not provide the level of security we need for our purposes—they suggest a way to eliminate the dependence on $|A|$ in the specification of a hash family at the cost of a worse dependence on $|B|$, where we need $|B| > |A|$. Thus, for our purposes, their original scheme [40] seems to be the most efficient.

on $\{0,1\}^{C \cdot C' \cdot N + 1}$ with entropy N, extracting $\delta N = 2m$ bits for $\delta \in (0,1)$. Let $\mathsf{pad} : \{0,1\}^* \to \{0,1\}^{C \cdot C' \cdot N + 1}$ be the padding function described in Lemma 9.11. Fix an irreducible polynomial of degree m, and thus a representation of the hash functions over $\mathbb{F}_{2^m}$ described in Construction 9.17.

Let any $(\ell(n), s'(n), C')$-bounded modification f to U be given. Let $U' = f(U)$ be the modified protocol, and let $S(U')$ be the reliable server using protocol U' (cf. Definition 9.6). We assume that Alice knows U'.

At the beginning of the first session, Alice and Bob perform the following initialization sub-protocol:

1. Alice chooses $r \in \{0,1\}^N$ uniformly at random, and computes $(a,b) \in \{0,1\}^m \times \{0,1\}^m$ by $(a,b) = (\mathsf{Ext} \circ \mathsf{pad})(U'(r))$.

2. Alice sends $m_0 = U'(r)$ to the server.

3. Bob receives m_0 from the server, and computes $(a,b) = (\mathsf{Ext} \circ \mathsf{pad})(m_0)$.

Across the sessions, Bob uses an efficient enumeration (in terms of the program lengths) of the space-$s'(n)$ bounded Turing machines with one-way access to their input tape with end markers, and enumerates the programs of length up to $\ell(n)$. We will let g denote the "current" member in the enumeration. Before the first session, g is initialized to the first program such that $g(U)$ satisfies the streaming protocol injectivity property up to input length N (cf. Definition 9.4). We will let $h_{a,b}$ denote the member of the hash family described in Construction 9.17 corresponding to $a, b \in \{0,1\}^m$.

Now, each ith session, $i = 1, 2, \ldots$ proceeds as follows:

1. Alice receives $x_i \in \{0,1\}^n$ from the environment.

2. Alice sends $m_i = U'(x_i, h_{a,b}(x_i))$ to the server.

3. Bob receives m_i from the server.

4. While either $g(U)^{-1}(m_i)$ has no pre-image of length $n + m$ or $g(U)^{-1}(m_i) = (x,y) \in \{0,1\}^n \times \{0,1\}^m$ such that $y \neq h_{a,b}(x)$, Bob sets g to the next program such that $g(U)$ is injective up to length N.

5. Bob sends $x \in \{0,1\}^n$ such that $g(U)^{-1}(m_i) = (x,y)$ to the environment.

The user strategy's running time

Before we move on, we will note that the user strategy is efficient: that is, in each session, the user strategies have an implementation running in time polynomial in n, N, m, $2^{\ell(n)}$, $2^{s(N)}$, and $2^{s'(N)}$. (Thus, polynomial time in n when $\ell(n)$, $s(n)$, and $s'(n)$ are $O(\log n)$ and N and m are bounded by polynomials in n.) We will separately consider the time spent on the initialization sub-protocol, the time spent by Bob on the enumeration, and the time spent to encode and decode messages per session. A randomized algorithm can be used by Alice and Bob to find and agree on an irreducible polynomial of degree m in expected time $O(m^{2+o(1)} \log m)$ [22, 17, 140].

The running time of the initialization sub-protocol. The key computational step performed in the initialization sub-protocol is computing $\mathsf{Ext} \circ \mathsf{pad}$. The extractor we use, given in Theorem 9.12, was given to be computable in polynomial time (in N); likewise, it is easily verified that the padding function pad described in Lemma 9.11 can be computed in time $C \cdot C' \cdot N + 1 = O(N)$. The remaining tasks are easy: an $(s(n)+s'(n), C \cdot C', N)$-streaming protocol encodes N bits in at most $2^{s(N)+s'(N)}$ steps. Thus, the running time in this sub-protocol is polynomial in N, $2^{s(N)}$, and $2^{s'(N)}$.

The cost of encoding and decoding messages. As we noted previously, encoding is efficient: we encode $n + m \le N$ bits in time $2^{s(N)+s'(N)}$. Likewise, as a consequence of Proposition 9.13, Bob can find a length $m + n$ inverse of $g(U)$ in time $O(m^2 n^2 2^{2(s(N)+s'(N))})$. Since the multiplication and reduction of polynomials of degree m can be trivially done in time $O(m^2)$, our hash functions can be evaluated in time $O(m^2)$, and we find that the time spent computing an inverse dominates Bob's running time. Therefore, except for the time Bob spends searching for the next candidate modification g in his enumeration, his running time for each round is $O(m^2 n^2 2^{2s(N)} 2^{2s'(N)})$. Alice, on the other hand, runs for at most $2^{s(N)+s'(N)}$ steps on every round.

The cost of the enumeration. We first note that there are at most $2^{\ell(n)}$ programs of length $\ell(n)$, and we have assumed that the enumeration itself is efficient (in $\ell(n)$). Now, given the $(s(n), C, N)$-streaming protocol U, and some length $\ell(n)$ program g, Corollary 9.15 tells us that we can decide whether or not the composed program $g(U)$ satisfies the injectivity conditions of an $(s(n)+s'(n), C \cdot C', N)$-streaming protocol in time $O(2^{4(s(N)+s'(N))})$. We will also count the time spent by incorrect algorithms failing the hash check in the time for the enumeration—where we recall that our hash functions can be evaluated in time $O(m^2)$, and the composed programs $g(U)$ can be inverted in time $O(m^2 n^2 2^{2(s(N)+s'(N))})$, which dominates $O(m^2)$. Thus, the total running time spent on the enumeration over all phases is at most

$$O(2^{\ell(n)}(\mathrm{poly}(\ell(n)) + m^2 n^2 2^{2(s(N)+s'(N))} + 2^{4(s(N)+s'(N))}))$$

which is a polynomial in m, n, $2^{\ell}(n)$, $2^{s(N)}$, and $2^{s'(N)}$.

In particular, since the total running time Bob spends on the enumeration is bounded, in every execution, for sufficiently large i his running time per round is bounded by the cost to invert $g(U)$ and evaluate the hash function, which is $O(m^2 n^2 2^{2(s(N)+s'(N))})$.

9.2.3 Analysis of the user decoding strategy

We will now argue that when the users employ the strategy described in Algorithm 9.18, they are able to use the network as a channel with high probability, as per Definition 9.1, with the class of reliable servers described in Definition 9.6. Precisely, we prove the following theorem:

Theorem 9.19 (The user strategy achieves the goal of streaming messages with reliable servers). *Let $m < N/2$ and $m \geq n + s(N) + \ell(N) + \log \frac{4}{\epsilon}$ with $\epsilon \geq 2\epsilon_0(N)$ for some $\epsilon_0(N) = 2^{-\Omega(N/\log^3 N)}$, and let any $(s(n), C, N)$-streaming protocol U be given. Then the user decoding strategy described in Algorithm 9.18 robustly achieves the goal of streaming messages with zero errors with probability $1 - \epsilon$ from the user's initial states with the class of reliable servers using $(\ell(n), s'(n), C')$-bounded modification to U.*

Proof Given N, $s(N) + s'(N)$, C, and C', the function $\epsilon_0(N)$ is the error of the extractors claimed in Theorem 9.12.

Selecting a hash function: the initialization sub-protocol. Note that since $m_0 = U'(r)$ is in the range of the protocol U' user by the server, the server forwards m_0 to Bob; then, since the extractor is deterministic, Alice and Bob obtain the same pair of strings $(a, b) \in \{0,1\}^m \times \{0,1\}^m$ at the end of the initialization sub-protocol. Thus, since they have agreed on a representation of the elements of $\mathbb{F}_{2^m}$, after the initialization sub-protocol, they can both evaluate the same hash function $h_{a,b} : \{0,1\}^m \to \{0,1\}^m$.

We will ultimately argue that if Alice and Bob had a uniformly chosen hash function $h_{a,b}$ after the initialization sub-protocol, then the probability that Bob ever outputs a string that is not x_i in session i under the strategy described in Algorithm 9.18 is at most $\epsilon/2$. Since Lemma 9.11 guarantees that $\mathsf{pad}(m_0)$ is a sample from a space-$s(N) + s'(N) + 1$ source with entropy N, we can apply Theorem 9.12 to find that the output of the extractor used in the initialization sub-protocol is $\epsilon_0(N)$-close to uniform and $\epsilon_0(N) \leq \epsilon/2$, the probability of an error ever occurring is then at most ϵ, as needed.

We now proceed to the main claim.

Claim 9.20 (Pairwise independence implies first errors detected). *Fix an $(s(n), C, N)$-streaming protocol U, a bounded modification of U, U', and a deterministic function g such that $g(U)$ is injective with respect to the "wait for reply" states of U. Then, in any execution in which the users follow the strategy in Algorithm 9.18 while Bob uses g as his current function in the enumeration, the probability that in the first round where $g(U)^{-1}(m_i) = (x', y')$ such that $(x', y') \neq (x_i, h_{a,b}(x_i))$, (x', y') also satisfy $y' = h_{a,b}(x')$ is at most $\epsilon 2^{-\ell(n)-1}$.*

Proof We first note that given its current configuration, U' computes a deterministic function of its input; thus, m_i is uniquely determined by the $s(N)$-bit configuration of U', σ, and its input (x_i, y_i). Similarly, since $g(U)$ is injective with respect to inputs of length up to $N > m + n$, $g(U)^{-1}$ specifies at most one (x', y') on input m_i. Thus, (x', y') is uniquely specified by (x_i, y_i) and σ, where $y_i = h_{a,b}(x_i)$. Now, by pairwise independence of $h_{a,b}$,

$$\Pr_{(a,b) \in \{0,1\}^m \times \{0,1\}^m} [y' = h_{a,b}(x') | y_i = h_{a,b}(x_i), U' \text{ sent } x_i \text{ from state } \sigma] \leq \frac{1}{2^m}$$

where, by a union bound over the $2^{s(N)}$ possible configurations of U' and $2^{n+1} - 1$ possible messages x_i of length up to n, we find that $y' = h_{a,b}(x')$ with probability at most $2^{n+1+s(N)-m} \leq 2^{-(\ell(N)+\log(2/\epsilon))}$ ∎

The theorem will now follow easily. We note that since f is an $(\ell(n), s'(n), C')$-bounded modification of U, f appears in Bob's enumeration of the programs of length up to $\ell(n)$. Let j^* be the index of f in the enumeration. Now, let session i_j be the session in which Bob begins using the jth program for g. It is clear that if $i_{j^*} < \infty$, then since Alice sends m_i in the image of $(x_i, h_{a,b}(x_i))$ under U' and Bob computes $f(U)^{-1}(m_i) = U'^{-1}(m_i) = (x_i, h_{a,b}(x_i))$, Bob will make no errors after session i_{j^*} with probability 1. We turn to bounding the probability of errors in all earlier sessions:

Claim 9.21. *For every $j < j^*$, there are no errors in sessions $i_j, \ldots, i_{j+1} - 1$ with probability $1 - \epsilon 2^{-\ell(n)-1}$.*

Proof Note first that we may assume that the jth function is injective with respect to the outputs of U on messages of length up to N, since otherwise Bob will detect this using the algorithm described in Corollary 9.15 and immediately move on to the $(j+1)$th program, so $i_j = i_{j+1}$.

Now, given that the jth function is injective, if from the current configuration of U' and environment strategy $\{x_i \in \{0,1\}^{\leq n}\}_{i=i_j}^{\infty}$, it happens that $g(U)^{-1}(m_i) = (x_i, h_{a,b}(x_i))$ for every $i \geq i_j$, then there are no errors in sessions $i \geq i_j$, and again the claim holds. Thus, suppose that i^* is the first session in which Alice sends some m_{i^*} such that $g(U)^{-1}(m_{i^*}) \neq (x_i, h_{a,b}(x_i))$. Claim 9.20 then shows that with probability at least $1 - \epsilon 2^{-\ell(n)-1}$, for $(x', y') = g(U)^{-1}(m_{i^*})$, $y' \neq h_{a,b}(x')$, and thus Bob switches to the $(j+1)$th function in session i^*. Since i^* was the first such session, there were no errors in sessions $i_j, \ldots, i^* - 1$, and the claim follows. ∎

Therefore, by a union bound over all $j < j^* \leq 2^{\ell(n)}$, there are no errors in the sessions up to i_{j^*} with probability $1 - \epsilon 2^{\ell(n)-1} \cdot 2^{\ell(n)} = 1 - \frac{\epsilon}{2}$, and if $i_{j^*} < \infty$, likewise there are no errors in any later sessions with probability 1. Thus, when $h_{a,b}$ is uniformly chosen, the probability that the users ever make an error is at most $\epsilon/2$, which was all that we needed to show. ∎

On the error rate and bits per message

Before moving on, we will make a few remarks about the relationships among the parameters required to apply Theorem 9.19 to an efficient implementation of Algorithm 9.18. First, we note that the main constraints on the error achievable are the error introduced by the extractor (requiring $\epsilon > \epsilon_0(N) = 2^{-\Omega(N/\log^3 N)}$), and the requirement that $\epsilon > 2^{-(N/2-n-s(N)-\ell(N))+1}$ so that a suitable choice of m exists. For example, if $N = 4n$ as suggested earlier, then for $s(n), \ell(n) = O(\log n)$ (as mandated by time-efficiency concerns), the second constraint only specifies $\epsilon > 2^{-(n-s(n)-\ell(n))+O(1)}$, while the first constraint requires $\epsilon > 2^{-\Omega(n/\log^3 n)}$, so the first constraint is the limiting factor on the error probability bound we can achieve with this scheme. Thus, an improvement in the construction of deterministic extractors over that of Kamp et al. [87] would translate directly into an improvement in the achievable error probability.

Second, we note that the scheme effectively reduces the maximum message size per session from N to n. Thus, if $N = 4n$, we only get $N/4$ bits per message sent across the network; effectively, this means that our maximum bit-rate is reduced by a factor of four. Since our scheme demands $N > 2m > 2n$, our scheme cannot achieve a rate better than $N/2$. The limiting factors here are again two-fold: first, specifying a hash function takes $2m$ bits, which necessitates $2m \leq N$, and second, we must send the hash value together with a message, which then imposes the requirement that $m+n \leq N$. Although we cannot hope to do too much better with the kinds of "information-theoretic" techniques we use – the union bound over messages of length up to n requires $m > n$ – one could hope to circumvent both of these problems by exploiting the computational limitations of the protocols. That is, we only need a (one-time) signing function s for which we can bound

$$\Pr[\exists x \in \{0,1\}^{\leq n} : g(U)^{-1}(U'(x, s(x))) = (x', y') \text{ s.t. } x' \neq x \text{ and } y' = s(x')]$$

where $g(U)^{-1}$ and U' are both polynomial time functions, and furthermore only have $s(N)$ bits of information, e.g., about other pairs $(x'', s(x''))$. Thus, we could make do with either a signature scheme s that is secure against the usual polynomial time adversaries, or else one that is secure in the *bounded-storage model* introduced by Maurer [109]. In fact, a signature scheme with the level of security we desire for the bounded-storage model was proposed by Ding and Rabin [54], but unfortunately their signatures are likewise at least n bits for n bit messages. It turns out, though, that there are other reasons we may wish to introduce signature schemes using stronger assumptions, as we will discuss in Section 9.4, and in this case we may also achieve a better rate by using these more powerful signatures.

On the other hand, if the number of messages sent by the users is relatively small (subexponential in N) rather than an infinite stream as we have considered here, then we might also hope to do better by using a hash function with m logarithmic in the number of messages, which would then be sublinear in N, giving us a rate closer to 1. The correctness of the scheme would then follow from a union bound over the sequence of messages actually sent (note that a uniformly chosen hash function works equally well for any such sequence of messages) instead of a union bound over all possible messages. Such a scheme could even cope with a case where the number of messages sent exceeds our initial bound by periodically refreshing the hash function, incrementing m each time to keep the total failure probability bounded. We could repeat this until m reaches $N/3$ bits, at which point we would no longer be able to send a new hash function together with a signature under the old hash function. Of course, in this case, the rate would also degrade each time we chose a new hash function, and the resulting scheme would be somewhat more complicated since we would need to track the number of messages sent and introduce a mechanism for refreshing the hash function. We leave such details to an interested reader.

9.3 End-to-end scheme for communication across an unreliable network with a modified protocol

In Section 9.2, we saw how the goal of streaming messages (Definition 9.1) could be achieved, even though the recipient of the messages did not know the message format. Although the model considered there is a fair model of a LAN, we are much more interested in whether our approach could be adapted to cope with changes to the internet protocols. We have already noted that our model of single-pass logspace computable protocols reasonably captures the protocols used at the IP layer, and likewise, the IPv4 to IPv6 transformation can be performed by switching short headers (again, overviews of IP and other protocols are given by Peterson and Davie [119]), and is thus also captured by our model of "bounded changes." We now turn to adapting our algorithm for the goal of streaming messages in a reliable FIFO network to a algorithm accomplishing the same task as achieved by the IP layer, "sending datagrams across an unreliable network." Actually, for reasons explained below, we will go a little further out of necessity, and provide reliable transmission across an unreliable network, as modeled in Definition 9.2.

Unfortunately, we can't immediately plug in our work from the previous section for several reasons. The first reason is that the two users need to agree on a hash function in their first message, which could be reordered or dropped by the server in this setting. In a sense, overcoming this problem amounts to showing how the initial handshake in TCP can be accomplished without initially needing to know how to decode messages, and how this can provide our hash function as an output. The second problem is that since we now assume that neither user knows the network protocol, the recipient must send acknowledgements so that the sender can verify that its messages were received—thus, leading us inevitably to providing a reliable delivery guarantee similar to that provided by TCP. The third problem is that since the network is unreliable, a single failure to send a message should not "disqualify" a protocol—even good protocols can fail sometimes, so a plain enumeration of algorithms will not work; although we might be able to guarantee that we can always send messages eventually by using an enumeration in which the protocols appear infinitely often, we wouldn't expect the performance of such a scheme to be satisfactory. Instead, we will use the multiplicative weights scheme of Auer et al. [10] to learn the most effective algorithm, which will allow us to maintain a good rate of transmission, even in the face of failures.

Of course, since our *original* goal was merely to show how we can cope with changes to the protocol used at the IP layer, we only show how to modify the aspects of TCP that are relevant to this end. Thus, we don't address all of the features of TCP here, notably excluding the closing of connections, estimating the round-trip time, and congestion control, though there should be no problem incorporating such features into the algorithm we present.

9.3.1 A review of the key sub-protocols of TCP

We reiterate that our ability to construct a reliable universal user scheme hinges on our ability to verify that our goals have been achieved; therefore, the groundwork for our scheme lies in the existing protocols for reliable communication over an unreliable network, that is, TCP as introduced by Cerf and Kahn [41] and subsequently refined by Postel et al. [150] (the authoritative reference on TCP, and an alternative to our review, is given by Stevens [143]). As our scheme amounts to a reworking of parts of TCP to cope with a lack of knowledge of the protocol used at the IP layer, we first review the features of TCP that permit reliable transmission of data, and show how they permit achieving the goal described in Definition 9.2 when the network protocol is known to both users.

Reliable data transmission: sequence numbers, ACKs, and time-outs

The goal achieved by TCP is similar to that of Definition 9.2: ultimately, streams of bytes are exchanged between the two parties sharing a TCP connection. At a high level, the individual bytes in the stream are indexed by *sequence numbers*, and reliability is provided by the recipient of a byte stream sending back *acknowledgements* indicating that it has received all bytes up to the acknowledged sequence number—if the sender does not receive an acknowledgement of a byte that was sent before a *timeout*, then the sender attempts to send a second copy of the data.[6]

Our model of this exchange as a (partial) approach to achieving the goal described in Definition 9.2 with a known network protocol is thus as follows.[7] There are r-bit sequence and acknowledgement fields attached to the messages exchanged by the users; these will indicate the index of a message modulo 2^r—that is, the ith message that one user sends to the other will have a sequence number of $i \bmod 2^r$, while acknowledgement of the jth message is achieved by sending $j \bmod 2^r$ in the acknowledgement field. For these numbers to be meaningful, there must only be a limited "window" of sequence numbers that one user can send to the other—otherwise, supposing message i is dropped, the recipient may later mistake message $i + 2^r$ for message i. Although TCP supports variable window sizes, we will disregard this feature in our model and assume a fixed window size of 2^{r-1} messages, i.e., the window ranges from the index following the last message acknowledged, $i_0 + 1 \bmod 2^r$ to $i_0 + 2^{r-1} \bmod 2^r$. Thus, until the sender receives an acknowledgement of message $i_0 + 1$, the sender must not attempt to send a message with index beyond $i_0 + 2^{r-1}$.

Still, when a user receives messages out-of-order, those messages are buffered, and thus the sender can continue to send messages up to the allowed sequence number, or up until the lack of an acknowledgement triggers a timeout. In our model network, the timeout is equal to the maximum round-trip time of a message, $2d(n)$. For the sake of simplicity, we will reduce the number of parameters by only considering two window sizes. In one case, we combine these two conditions, and assume that $r = \log d(n) + 2$, i.e., so that $2^{r-1} = 2d(n)$, and we encounter a timeout if and when we reach the end of the allowed window. In the other case, we use a 1-bit sequence number, so after each message we immediately reach the end of the window and must wait for either an acknowledgement or for a timeout, which occurs $2d(n)$ steps later, before we try to send the next message—the *"stop and wait"* protocol. Thus, corresponding to these two settings for the sizes of the sequence number field, we have the following two protocols:

Protocol 9.22 (Stop and wait protocol). We use a window of size *one* (i.e., $r = 1$). The user maintains three message indices, i indicating the last

---

[6]In reality, unlike our model, the timeouts are computed based on estimates of the round-trip times, which leads to the possibility that multiple copies of the same data could arrive. The sequence numbers allow the receiver to reject such data so long as the finite set of sequence numbers has not already "wrapped around" in the interim. As the size of the sequence number field is generally set large enough so that this doesn't occur in practice, we disregard it in our model. We note again that these aspects of TCP and more are described in much more detail by Stevens [143].

[7]*Strictly* speaking, what we are presenting is a *message-stream* sliding window protocol inspired by TCP, which by contrast is a *byte-stream* protocol. That is, TCP acknowledges *bytes*, while we acknowledge *messages*—and so for example, in TCP, bytes may be repackaged in longer packets on retransmission, which we will expressly forbid. Looking ahead, the reason we change this aspect of the design is that we will care to know what happened to every packet we sent, and use this feedback to learn the packet format.

message sent by the environment, i_0 indicating the last message the user attempted to send across the network, and j indicating the low-order bit of the last message sent to the environment (initially, $i = i_0 = j = 0$). The user will also maintain a timeout counter, t, initialized to 0.

The user maintains a *send buffer*: each time the environment sends the user a new message, i is incremented, and that new message, together with the current value of i, is placed at the end of the send buffer. The send buffer contains all messages that have not yet been acknowledged by the recipient; thus, unless the buffer is empty, at the beginning of a round, i_0 equals the index attached to the first message in the buffer.

At the beginning of a round, the user first checks any messages received from the server; if there is an acknowledgement i' such that $i_0 \bmod 2 = i'$ and the buffer is not empty, then the user removes the message with index i_0 from the start of the buffer, increments i_0, and sets $t = 0$. If that message contains a sequence number $j' \neq j$, then we will return the attached message to the environment at the end of the round, and we set $j = j'$.

Next, if the user received a message from the environment to be sent, the user adds that message to the send buffer and increments i as described above.

Finally, if the timeout counter $t = 0$ and the send buffer is not empty, the user sends a message to the server containing the first message in the send buffer with sequence number $i_0 \bmod 2$ and acknowledging j, sets $t = 2d(n)$. Otherwise, the user decrements t and, if it received a message from the server at the beginning of the round, it sends a message acknowledging j to the server.

Protocol 9.23 (Delay-bound protocol). The user maintains five message indices, i indicating the last message sent by the environment, i_0 indicating the first unacknowledged index of a message to be sent across the network, j_0 indicating the index of the last message sent to the environment, j indicating the last index in the receive buffer such that every index in the range $(j_0, j]$ is contained in the receive buffer, and k indicating the index of the last message in the send buffer sent across the network. (See Figure 9.3.) Initially, $i_0 = i = j_0 = j = k = 0$.

The user maintains two buffers: a *send buffer* and a *receive buffer*. The send buffer functions the same as in the stop and wait protocol: each time the environment provides a new message to be sent by the user, the user appends that message together with its index to the end of the send buffer, and increments the index. The receive buffer contains all messages that need to be returned to the environment together with their indices. At the end of the round, if the first message in the receive buffer has index $j_0 + 1$, it is removed from the buffer and returned to the environment, and j_0 is incremented.

At the beginning of a round, the user first checks for any messages received from the server. If there is an acknowledgement i' such that i' is in the

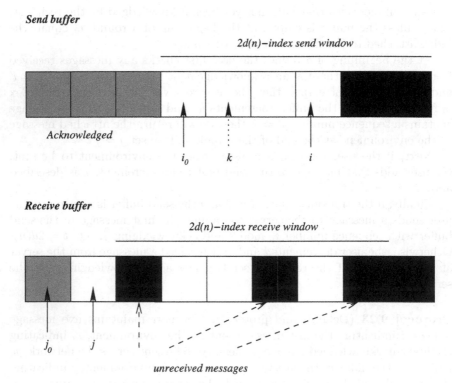

Figure 9.3: The buffers used by the delay-bound protocol. White entries contain a message, black entries indicate no message has been written for that index yet, and shaded entries indicate that the entry was written and removed. In the send buffer, k loops over the entries from i_0 to i. In the receive buffer, j_0 is necessarily the last shaded entry whereas the index following j is necessarily the first black entry.

window $[i_0 \bmod 4d(n), i_0 + 2d(n) \bmod 4d(n)]$, then the user sets i_0 to the representative of $i' + 1$ in the range $[i_0, i_0 + 2d(n)]$, and removes the messages in the send buffer with indices less than this new value of i_0; we then say that i_0 is updated on this round, and we set k to $i_0 - 1$.

Similarly, if the user receives a message with a sequence number j' in the window $[j + 1 \bmod 4d(n), j + 2d(n) \bmod 4d(n)]$ such that no other message in the receive buffer has the same sequence number modulo $4d(n)$, the user inserts the message into the receive buffer in the appropriate location, with an index $\tilde{j}$ corresponding to the representative of j' in the range $[j, j + 2d(n)]$. If $\tilde{j} = j + 1$, every message in the range $[j + 1, j^*]$ for some j^* is then contained in the buffer. We therefore set $j = j^*$ and we say that j is updated on this round.

Next, if the user received a message from the environment to be sent, that message is appended to the end of the send buffer and i is incremented as described previously.

Finally, if the send buffer is not empty and $k < i_0 + 2d(n)$, we set $k = k + 1$; otherwise, if the send buffer is not empty, a timeout has occurred for the message index i_0, and we set $k = i_0$. We then send a message to the server at the end of the round containing the message with index k along with $k \bmod 4d(n)$ as its sequence number, acknowledging $j \bmod 4d(n)$. If the send buffer was empty but j was updated, we send a message to the server simply acknowledging $j \bmod 4d(n)$. (We also send a message to the environment if a message with index $j_0 + 1$ is in the receive buffer, as described previously.)

Notes on the correctness. We include the stop and wait protocol primarily for the sake of exposition: its correctness is fairly easy to see. There is at most one message being sent in a given direction with a given sequence number at any point, and we do not move on until that sequence number is acknowledged. Since the drops occur independently with probability $\delta(n)$, the probability that neither the message nor the acknowledgement is dropped is $(1 - \delta(n))^2$; thus, after $\left\lceil \frac{2d(n)}{(1 - \delta(n))^2} \right\rceil$ rounds, the protocol has sent a message and seen an acknowledgement with probability greater than $1/3$, and it is clear that we see an acknowledgement in a "polynomial" number of rounds (in $d(n)$ and $1 - \delta(n)$) in expectation. In particular, the protocol eventually succeeds at sending every message with probability 1.

In moving to the delay-bound protocol, the analysis is similar, but we need to take more care to see that the sequence numbers won't be re-used too soon, so that they suffice to uniquely index the messages of current concern. We first argue that we won't mistake an acknowledgement for an old message for an acknowledgement for a current (unacknowledged) message. We note that i_0 can only increment by Δ after the messages $i_0, \ldots, i_0 + \Delta$ were sent where, since we send at most one message on a given round and the maximum round-trip time for an acknowledgement is $2d(n)$, the minimum index we could receive an acknowledgement for is

$i_0 - 2d(n) + \Delta$. Since only acknowledgements to sequence numbers in the window $[i_0 + \Delta + 1 \bmod 4d(n), i_0 + \Delta + 2d(n) \bmod 4d(n)]$ will be subsequently accepted, where we can verify that the range of indices for which old acknowledgements may still be delivered is $[i_0 + \Delta - 2d(n), i_0 + \Delta]$, and this range modulo $4d(n)$ falls entirely outside the range of acknowledgements we will accept (and indeed, this range of old numbers taken modulo $4d(n)$ is the complement of the range we accept), we will not skip sending messages due to these old acknowledgements.

The argument that we will not confuse old messages for new messages due to their sequence numbers is similar: we note that the sender never advances its index k of a message to send beyond $2d(n)$ indices from the last acknowledgement from the receiver (and only advances it by Δ after having sent Δ messages). Thus, when the receiver acknowledges some index j, the oldest messages the sender could be sending have index at least $j - 2d(n)$. The range of messages the receiver is willing to accept is $[j+1, j+2d(n)]$, and we can again note that $[j - 2d(n), j]$ and $[j+1, j+2d(n)]$ taken modulo $4d(n)$ partition $[0, 4d(n) - 1]$. Thus, the receiver never mistakes an old message for a new one.

The expected number of rounds after our first attempt that pass before a message is sent by the delay-bound protocol is the same number of rounds as in the stop and wait protocol, so we again find that it succeeds at sending every message eventually with probability 1. The delay-bound protocol is intuitively much more efficient, though. Rather than waiting for an acknowledgement, in the meantime we attempt to send many more messages—that is, the expected *latency* may be the same but the *throughput* is higher. Moreover, an acknowledgement is sent each time a message gets through, so the probability that a timeout occurs on a given message is lower. We won't analyze this protocol any further, however. The point is merely to illustrate how reliable communication is possible as groundwork for the schemes we will present in Sections 9.3.2 and 9.3.4.

Establishing the connection: the three-way handshake

The protocol of sequence numbers and acknowledgements described in the previous section describes the "steady-state" behavior of a TCP connection, capturing how TCP achieves reliable data transmission across an unreliable network. There are still other parts to TCP that we have not yet described, though. A TCP connection is only active for a finite amount of time—connections are *closed* at some point (by a protocol which we will not be concerned with here) which leads to the need for an explicit protocol to *open* the connection: the issue is that after a connection has been closed, stray packets from the connection may yet be moving through the network and delivered to their destination at some later point. Thus, if a new connection is later opened, and these stray packets have sequence numbers (or acknowledgements) in the active window of that new connection, the protocol may confuse the packets from the old connection for packets from the new connection. The guard against this danger (such as it is) is to establish a random starting sequence number when a connection is opened. The initialization protocol achieving this establishment of sequence numbers, which will be an important basis for our own initialization protocol, is known as a *three-way handshake.*

In the "typical" case, one end-user (unfortunately for us, usually known as the "server") is in the *passive open* state, meaning that some process is watching for incoming packets. The connection is then initiated by another end-user entering the *active open* state, and sending the first user a packet initiating the handshake. In an atypical situation, which we will address later, *both* users may enter the active open state before receiving each other's packets, and establish a connection by engaging in a "four-way handshake."

For the typical case, we will refer to the first user, in the passive open state, as Alice, and we refer to the second user, who attempts to initiate communication by entering the active open state, as Bob. The packets are marked with a pair of flags, indicating whether they contain an initial sequence number, an acknowledgement of a sequence number, or both. (Note that *all subsequent* messages containing acknowledgements will have the corresponding *ACK* flag set, but only messages exchanged containing *initial* sequence numbers, i.e., during the handshake, will have the first flag – the *SYN* flag – set.) Bob initiates the three-way handshake by sending Alice a packet with a random initial sequence number; Alice responds to this packet by sending an acknowledgement of Bob's sequence number *plus one*,[8] together with her own randomly chosen initial sequence number. Bob responds with an acknowledgement of Alice's sequence number – again, plus one – and the protocol is complete, and the users can exchange data using the protocol described in the earlier section, starting from the acknowledged initial sequence numbers (i.e., with a random offset to the indices).

Of course, any number of things may go wrong during the handshake, notably including loss of packets. The same timeout rules as before apply, though, and if Bob (or Alice) do not receive an acknowledgement of their sequence numbers before the timeout occurs, then the packet is re-sent. Similarly, Alice and Bob ignore packets with acknowledgements to sequence numbers other than their expected sequence number during the handshake— which, since this expected sequence number is uniformly distributed, avoids the issue mentioned earlier of them accepting an acknowledgement from an earlier connection during the handshake with all but negligible probability.

When both users attempt to initiate communication before receiving each other's packets, we have already described their first messages: they send a randomly chosen sequence number. Now, to handle this case, we must describe *how they respond to a packet containing no acknowledgements.* Note that every packet sent during normal execution of the protocol contains an

---

[8]The decision to add one is somewhat arbitrary, but it is taken to be the value of the sequence number field that Alice is anticipating on the first message from Bob.

acknowledgement of the last sequence number received—the *only* packets without acknowledgements are packets sent from the active open state when initiating a connection. Thus, when a user receives a packet without an acknowledgement, they know that they are instead engaging in a four-way handshake. The user responds to this message almost precisely as they would if they had been in the passive open state in the case of the three-way handshake: they respond by acknowledging the other user's sequence number plus one, together with their own sequence number, the *same* sequence number they sent in the original message. This way, even if the original packet is lost, the other user successfully completes the handshake and begins sending data, with packets containing an acknowledgement of our sequence number anyway. In any case, the user waits until an acknowledgement of that sequence number (plus one) is received before attempting to send data, and re-sends the acknowledgement packet if a timeout occurs.

In summary, the protocol in the language of Definition 9.2, using r-bit sequence numbers and our value $2d(n)$ as a timeout is as follows:

Protocol 9.24 (TCP handshake). *Passive open:*

1. Wait until a packet with the SYN flag set arrives (with r-bit sequence number i).

2. Choose a sequence number modulo 2^r, $j \in \{0,1\}^r$, uniformly at random.

3. Until receiving an acknowledgement of sequence number $j+1$ (mod 2^r), repeat the following:

    (a) Send a packet with the SYN flag set, with sequence number j and acknowledging $i + 1$ (mod 2^r).

    (b) *(Timeout)* Wait $2d(n)$ rounds.

Active open:

1. Choose a sequence number modulo 2^r, $i \in \{0,1\}^r$, uniformly at random.

2. Until receiving an acknowledgement of sequence number $i+1$ (mod 2^r) or receiving a packet with the SYN flag set but not the ACK flag, repeat the following:

    (a) Send a packet with the SYN flag set, with sequence number i (and no ACK flag set).

    (b) *(Timeout)* Wait $2d(n)$ rounds.

3. *(Four-way handshake)* If a packet with the SYN flag set (with sequence number j) but not the ACK flag was received, repeat the following until receiving an acknowledgement of sequence number $i + 1$ (mod 2^r):

(a) Send a packet with the SYN flag set, with sequence number i, acknowledging sequence number $j + 1$ (mod 2^r).

(b) *(Timeout)* Wait $2d(n)$ rounds.

Since the goal in Definition 9.2 doesn't need to terminate connections, we won't need to review the correctness of Protocol 9.24 in any detail. Rather, it will serve as a starting point for our own sub-protocol for exchanging *hash functions* (extending the initialization sub-protocol from Algorithm 9.18) in the next section.

9.3.2 A modified end-user scheme for reliable communication

We now possess the pieces to permit a user to verify that their messages are sent, received, and decoded properly, given that their partner at the other end of the network knows the network protocol: verification of sending and receiving is provided by TCP's acknowledgement and sequence numbering scheme, illustrated in Protocol 9.22 and Protocol 9.23, while verification of correct decoding was provided by Protocol 9.18 in Section 9.2.2. Unlike in Section 9.2.2, however, enumeration no longer suffices to complete the scheme when the protocol is unknown. The main difficulties stem from two sources of unreliability in the scheme. First, and most clearly, the server itself (as described in Definitions 9.2 and 9.8) may be unreliable by definition. Moreover, though, even if the server were assumed to be reliable, as a consequence of our partner at the other end of the network not knowing the protocol, our partner cannot be assumed to reliably send acknowledgements.

Of course, despite their distinct origins, these two issues amount to the same problem: even a good protocol for sending messages may fail the TCP verification scheme sometimes as a consequence of an acknowledgement failing to arrive. Thus, we will see how to dispose of both with a single new idea—instead of using an enumeration to search for a protocol to use for sending messages, we will use a more sophisticated *multiplicative weights* scheme for which the success rate at sending approaches the success rate of the "correct" protocol.

The unreliability of the network and our partner also hinders the initialization sub-protocol for agreeing on a hash function in Algorithm 9.18. Fortunately, this can be overcome by introducing acknowledgements to the initialization, much as in the TCP handshake protocol (described in Protocol 9.24). The key insight here is that even though we do not yet know the protocol, an encoded random message still specifies a hash function, and the associated hash function can be used to sign the acknowledgement, which thus simultaneously tells us whether our partner has received our hash function, tells us *which* hash function our partner has received (i.e., from which encoding it was derived), and allows us to decode the acknowledgement if so.

Ultimately, much as in Section 9.3.1, we will exhibit two schemes. The first will be an adaptation of the stop and wait protocol described in Protocol 9.22 which, much as was the case previously, has the virtue of a relatively tractable thorough analysis, while allowing us to exhibit all of the main ideas. The second scheme, which we delay presenting until Section 9.3.4, is of course a modification of the higher throughput delay-bound protocol described in Protocol 9.23, which will require exhibiting a modification of the multiplicative weights scheme that still functions when the feedback is delayed.

The bounded modification weighting scheme

We will use a result due to Auer et al. [10] that gives a strategy for repeatedly choosing "actions" from a set of size K, with the guarantee that the "reward" obtained by these choices is close to the reward that could have been obtained by repeatedly choosing a single fixed action, even though the strategy is not told which fixed action we are considering. The analogy to our setting should be clear: the K "actions" correspond to our (bounded-size) set of bounded modifications of our original protocol, and taking an action corresponds to sending a message under the corresponding encoding, with "reward" of 1 obtained if an acknowledgement of the message returns before the timeout (and zero reward is obtained otherwise). Thus, the strategy should be nearly as successful at sending messages as the (unknown) modified protocol used on the network.

The power of the guarantee provided by Auer et al. (stated below in Theorem 9.26) is such that it holds even when the rewards depend on the history of actions chosen previously. Such a guarantee turns out to be *crucial* when the rewards depend on the adaptive strategies of the two parties at opposite ends of the network, specifically in our setting where the reward depends on *whether or not a party manages to successfully send an acknowledgement*— after all, the aim of our adaptive strategy is to learn how to send messages across the network successfully in the first place.

The relevant algorithm for our purposes is the following:

Algorithm 9.25 (Exp3.P.1 [10]). On input $\delta \in (0,1)$, for each $r \geq 1$, put $T_r = 2^r$, $\delta_r = \frac{\delta}{(r+1)(r+2)}$, and set $r^* = \min\{r \in \mathbb{N} : \delta_r \geq Ke^{-KT_r}\}$.

For $r = r^*, r^* + 1, \ldots$, repeat the following:

1. Put $\alpha = 2\sqrt{\ln(K/\delta_r)/KT_r}$ and $\gamma = \min\left\{\frac{3}{5}, 2\sqrt{\frac{3K\ln K}{5T_r}}\right\}$.

2. For $i = 1, \ldots, K$, put $w_i(1) = \exp\left(\frac{\alpha\gamma}{3K}\right)$.

3. For $t = 1, 2, \ldots, T_r$, repeat the following:

   (a) For $i = 1, \ldots, K$, put $p_i(t) = (1 - \gamma)\frac{w_i(t)}{\sum_{j=1}^{K} w_j(t)} + \frac{\gamma}{K}$.

   (b) Choose $i_t \in [K]$ at random with distribution $p_1(t), \ldots, p_K(t)$.

(c) Use strategy i_t and receive reward $x_{i_t}(t) \in [0,1]$.

(d) For $j \in [K] \setminus \{i_t\}$ set

$$w_j(t+1) = w_j(t) \exp\left(\frac{\gamma \alpha}{3 p_j(t) K}\right)$$

and set

$$w_{i_t}(t+1) = w_{i_t}(t) \exp\left(\frac{\gamma}{3K}\left(\frac{x_{i_t}(t)}{p_{i_t}(t)} + \frac{\alpha}{p_{i_t}(t)}\right)\right).$$

Algorithm 9.25 provides the following guarantee (which differs slightly from those established by Auer et al. [10]):

Theorem 9.26 (The weighting scheme approaches the average reward of any fixed strategy [10]). *Let $\delta \in (0,1)$. For $T \geq 2^{r^*}$ for the value r^* specified in Algorithm 9.25, put $c(T) = 2\ln(2 + \log_2 T)$. Then, if $R(T) = \sum_{t=1}^T x_{i_t}(t)$ for the rewards $x_{i_t}(t)$ obtained by the strategy described in Construction 9.25 and R^* is the reward obtained by some fixed strategy in our set,*

$$R^*(T) - R(T) \leq \frac{10}{\sqrt{2}-1}\sqrt{2KT\left(\ln\frac{K}{\delta} + c(T)\right)}$$

with probability at least $1 - \delta$.

That is, the difference between the average reward obtained by the weighting scheme in Algorithm 9.25 and the average reward obtained by the fixed strategy goes to zero at a rate of $O(\sqrt{\ln\ln T / T})$. The full analysis (yielding this improved bound) is provided in Appendix C.

Since our variant of the stop and wait protocol will wait for feedback before attempting to send its next message, we will be able to apply Theorem 9.26 to the analysis of that protocol essentially as written. When we turn to the analysis of the modified delay-bound scheme, however, we will find that there are a few differences between the setting there and the setting of Auer et al., the foremost being that in the delay-bound scheme, the scheme will require sending the next messages before feedback is received—where the feedback may be delayed by up to $2d(n)$ rounds. In order to simultaneously connect the weights to both the performance of the best fixed strategy and to the performance of the algorithm, the analysis of Exp3 relies on the fact that the probabilities of each strategy are closely related to their current relative weighting; if the weighting changes (i.e., due to feedback from other rounds) between when we sample a strategy and when we update the weights according to the reward we obtained, then this close relationship may no longer hold. We can finesse this issue, though, by using $2d(n)$ independent sets of weights in a round-robin fashion, so that by the time we return to a set of weights, we know the reward obtained by its last strategy. Overall, it is not hard to see that such a strategy matches the reward obtained by the best strategy up to $\tilde{O}(\sqrt{d(n)KT})$. We will return to this point in the analysis of the algorithm in Section 9.3.4.

Establishing a connection

We now begin describing our strategy for reliable communication, using the stop and wait scheme for reliable transmission. We will first describe the modified handshake scheme, and in the following section we will describe the algorithm for sending and receiving messages, after the handshake has successfully completed. During the handshake, we will assume that every message from the environment (to be sent to the other user) is stored in order in a send buffer (cf. Protocol 9.22).

The parameters. Throughout, we will need to fix the same parameters as used by our decoding strategy in Algorithm 9.18. Thus, fix $(s(n), C, N)$-streaming protocols U_A and U_B for sending messages to Alice and Bob respectively, and suppose we wish to adapt to any $(\ell(n), s'(n), C')$-bounded modifications f_A and f_B, applied to U_A and U_B, respectively; let $U'_A = f_A(U_A)$, $U'_B = f_B(U_B)$, and $S(U'_A, U'_B)$ be the unreliable server using U'_A and U'_B.

Now, for the decoding strategy, fix a deterministic extractor Ext for space-$s(n) + s'(n) + 1$ sources on $\{0, 1\}^{C \cdot C' \cdot N + 1}$ with entropy N, extracting $2m$ bits (thus, as in Algorithm 9.18, we will need to assume that $N > 2m$), and let pad $: \{0, 1\}^{\leq C \cdot C' \cdot N} \to \{0, 1\}^{C \cdot C' \cdot N + 1}$ be the padding function described in Lemma 9.11. Fix a representation of hash functions over $\mathbb{F}_{2^m}$, as described in Construction 9.17.

We will parse our encoded messages into six fields: the contents (or message) field of length at most n, the sequence number and acknowledgement fields (which are each 1-bit in the stop and wait scheme, but $\log d(n) + 1$ bits in the scheme of Section 9.3.4), the 1-bit SYN flag field, a 1-bit LEAD flag field (generally indicating which user's hash function was selected, if only one), and an m-bit hash tag field. We therefore also need $m > n' = n + 4$ for the present section, and $m > n' = n + 2 \log d(n) + 4$ for the scheme in Section 9.3.4.

Algorithm 9.27 (Handshake under bounded modification). Returns a value for the LEAD flag (from $\{0, 1\}$) together with a pair of hash functions (specified by a pair of elements of $\mathbb{F}_{2^m}$), the first to be used to send messages, and the second to be used to decode received messages.

We assume that on each round that a message is received from the environment, it is stored in a buffer, and we maintain an index i indicating how many such messages we have stored.

Passive open:

1. Wait until a message m_0 arrives from the server.

2. Put $(a, b) = (\text{Ext} \circ \text{pad})(m_0)$.

3. For each $(\ell(n), s'(n), C')$-bounded modification g_2 in an infinitely repeating enumeration, repeat the following:

- Send a message with empty contents, sequence number 0, acknowledging 0, with the LEAD flag cleared and the SYN flag set, along with its hash under $h_{a,b}$ using $g_2(U)$.

- For $t = 2d(n), \dots, 1$, on each round, repeat the following:

  – If a message m_0' arrives from the server, for each $(\ell(n), s'(n), C')$-bounded modification g_1, repeat the following:

    * If $g_1(U)^{-1}(m_0') = (x, y)$ (y of length m) such that x contains a message part of length at most n, does not have the SYN flag set, and is a message acknowledging sequence number 0, and $y = h_{a,b}(x)$, return $(0, h_{a,b}, h_{a,b})$.

Active open: For each $(\ell(n), N, C')$-bounded modification g, initialize $m_g, m_g' = \perp$.

1. For each $(\ell(n), N, C')$-bounded modification g_2 in an infinitely repeating enumeration, repeat the following:

   (a) If $m_{g_2} = \perp$, choose $r_{g_2} \in \{0, 1\}^N$ uniformly at random, compute $m_{g_2} = g_2(U(r_{g_2}))$ (from the initial state of U) and compute $h_{g_2} = (\mathsf{Ext} \circ \mathsf{pad})(m_{g_2})$.

   (b) Send m_{g_2} to the server.

   (c) For $t = 2d(n), \dots, 1$, repeat the following on each round where a message m_0 is received:

      i. If $m_0 = m_{g_2}$, discard it and continue to the next round.

      ii. Otherwise, for each $(\ell(n), s'(n), C')$-bounded modification g_1 and g_2', repeat the following:

         • If $m_{g_2'} \neq \perp$ and $g_1(U)^{-1}(m_0) = (x, y)$ is such that x has sequence number 0 with the SYN flag set and $y = h_{g_2'}(x)$, return $(1, h_{g_2'}, h_{g_2'})$.

      iii. Go to step 2 (four-way handshake).

2. *(Four-way handshake)* Put $(a, b) = (\mathsf{Ext} \circ \mathsf{pad})(m_0)$.

3. Wait t rounds.

4. Resuming our enumeration of $(\ell(n), N, C')$-bounded modifications g_2, repeat the following:

   (a) If $m_{g_2}' = \perp$, for a message x with empty contents, sequence number 0, acknowledging 0, the LEAD flag cleared, and the SYN flag set, compute $m_{g_2}' = g_2(U(x, h_{a,b}(x)))$.

   (b) Send m_{g_2}'.

   (c) For $t' = 2d(n), \dots, 0$, repeat the following on each round in which a message m_0' was received:

  i. If $m_0' = m_{g_2}'$, discard it.
 ii. Otherwise, for each $(\ell(n), s'(n), C')$-bounded modification g_1, repeat the following:

   A. If $g_1(U)^{-1}(m_0') = (x, y)$ is such that x has a message part of length at most n, does not have the SYN flag set, and acknowledges sequence number 0 and $y = h_{a,b}(x)$, return $(0, h_{a,b}, h_{a,b})$.

   B. Otherwise, for each $(\ell(n), s'(n), C')$-bounded modification g_2' repeat the following:

   • If $m_{g_2'} \neq \perp$ and $g_1(U)^{-1}(m_0') = (x, y)$ is such that x has sequence number 0 with the SYN flag set and $y = h_{g_2'}(x)$, return $(b, h_{a,b}, h_{g_2'})$ where $b = 1$ if $h_{a,b} > h_{g_2'}$ in a natural ordering on hash functions, and $b = 0$ otherwise.

One aspect of the handshake that may be confusing at first is why we explicitly drop messages at a few points. The issue is that when we don't know the protocol, we may well accidentally send a packet back to ourselves— e.g., if a bounded modification swaps the "source" and "destination" fields of the packet (or simply offsets the bits in the packet so that the "source" field ends up in the "destination" field). We will need to argue that we are unlikely to drop packets from the other user in the analysis.

We postpone the analysis of our handshake scheme until Section 9.3.3, so we will only make a few remarks here about how our scheme can be understood with respect to the TCP handshake (described in Protocol 9.24). Intuitively, our packets encoding random bits correspond to packets with the SYN flag but not the ACK flag set, and in the analysis we need to argue that they will not be confused for packets which would have the ACK flag set—cf. Lemma 9.30. Likewise, the hash functions we extract from these random packets play essentially the same role as the random sequence number in the TCP handshake.[9] The difference between our protocol and the TCP handshake arises since we need a full packet of random bits to specify a hash function, whereas the TCP handshake could simply include the chosen sequence number in a reply to the first message. Thus, in a four-way handshake, our modified handshake needs to wait for a second message from the other user to see whether the hash function the other user is tagging its messages to us with was taken from one of our initial random packets, or whether that user decided to use the hash function we acknowledged receipt of in our acknowledgement of the first message we received (as if we had been in the passive open state).

---

[9] As such, the hash functions could be used to detect stray packets from old connections: supposing we retain the hash functions from recent connections, we can also check to see if the packets decode with valid hash tags using one of the hash functions from an old connection. We chose not to address this aspect of the scheme here, since we don't address termination of connections.

Reliable transmission scheme under an unknown modification

We now present the modification of the stop and wait protocol (Protocol 9.22) for reliably sending messages under an unknown bounded modification of the network. In a manner analogous to the scheme we presented for reliable networks (Algorithm 9.18), we will assume that we begin execution of our algorithm in the same round as the modified handshake scheme (Algorithm 9.27) returned, and we will provide the hash functions and setting of the LEAD flag from the handshake scheme as inputs to the transmission scheme, just as the initialization sub-protocol provided a hash function to the transmission scheme for reliable networks.

Recall that each end-user's goal can be considered as a pair of sub-goals: the user wishes to send messages to its partner, and wishes to receive the messages sent by its partner. The hash functions provided by the handshake scheme are the key to verifiably receiving messages properly, just as in Algorithm 9.18. On the other hand, the acknowledgement scheme of TCP (e.g., in the stop and wait protocol of Protocol 9.22) is the key to verifiably sending messages to our partner.

As alluded to in the introduction to this section, unlike in the scheme for reliable networks, it will not suffice to simply enumerate bounded modifications to learn how to send messages; rather, we will use the multiplicative weighting scheme Exp3.P.1 of Auer et al. described in Algorithm 9.25. Due to its relative complexity, we will not repeat the details of the scheme here. Instead, we will treat it as a black box: the scheme will suggest a bounded modification for us to use for sending a message, and before we request a new bounded modification from the scheme, we will provide it with a reward value—which will be 1 if we received an acknowledgement to the message we sent, and 0 otherwise. It should be evident that Theorem 9.26 will apply to this set-up to give us a bound on the fraction of messages that receive acknowledgements.

Algorithm 9.28 (Adaptive stop and wait scheme). We take as input a triple, (h_1, h_2, b) where h_1 and h_2 are hash functions (each specified as a pair of elements from $\mathbb{F}_{2^m}$) and $b \in \{0, 1\}$.

We also take as input the send buffer from the handshake scheme, and the index i of the number of messages in the buffer. We initialize $i_0 = 0$, indicating the index of the last message sent so far (i.e., the first message sent will have index 1) and $i' = 0$ indicating the number of messageless acknowledgements sent since the last message. We will also maintain a bit j indicating the low-order bit of the last index of a message sent to the environment (i.e., the 1-bit sequence number of the corresponding message), thus initialized to 0, and a count j' of the number of messageless acknowledgements we have received since the last message, also initialized to 0. We also have a buffer x_{old}, initialized to $\perp$, containing the contents of the last message we sent to the server, and a counter t indicating the number of rounds since we last sent a message, initialized to 0.

1. If $b = 1$, go to step 3; otherwise, until a message is received from the server, on each round that a message is received from the environment, add it to the send buffer and increment i.

2. For the message m' received from the server, try each $(\ell(n), s'(n), C')$-bounded modification g_1, until $g_1(U)^{-1}(m') = (x, y)$ such that x has length at most n' and $y = h_2(x)$. If some g_1 was not found, return to step 1, and otherwise do the following:

   (a) If the SYN flag was set in x, go back to step 1.

   (b) If the contents field of x is nonempty, send the contents field of x to the environment at the end of the round and set $j = j + 1$ (mod 2).

3. Query Exp3.P.1 for a bounded modification g_2.

4. *(Nonempty send buffer)* If $i > i_0$:

   (a) Set $i_0 = i_0 + 1$ and $i' = 0$.

   (b) For a message x with contents equal to the message in the send buffer at index i_0, the SYN flag cleared, the LEAD flag set to b, sequence number i_0 (mod 2), and acknowledging j, send $g_2(U(x, h_1(x)))$ to the server at the end of the round.

   (c) Set $x_{\text{old}} = x$.

5. *(Sending empty acknowledgement)* Otherwise:

   (a) Increment i'.

   (b) For the message x with contents equal to the empty message, the SYN flag cleared, the LEAD flag set to b, sequence number $i_0 + i'$ (mod 2), and acknowledging j, send $g_2(U(x, h_1(x)))$ to the server at the end of the round.

   (c) Set $x_{\text{old}} = x$.

6. Set $t = 0$.

7. While $t < 2d(n)$, wait until the next round and do the following:

   (a) Increment t.

   (b) If a message was received from the environment, add it to the end of the send buffer and increment i.

   (c) If a message m' was received from the server, try each $(\ell(n), s'(n), C')$-bounded modification g_1, until $g_1(U)^{-1}(m') = (x, y)$ such that x has length at most n' and $y = h_2(x)$ or $y = h_1(x)$ (in this latter case, if the LEAD field is set to b, drop the message and go to the next iteration of the loop).

(d) If some successful g_1 was found, do the following:

- *(Leftover message)* If the SYN flag in x is set, go to the next iteration of the loop.
- *(Duplicate message)* Or, if the contents field is empty and the sequence number is $j + j'$ (mod 2), or the contents field is nonempty and the sequence number is j (mod 2), go to the next iteration of the loop.
- Or, if the contents field is nonempty and the sequence number is not equal to j, set $j' = 0$, send the contents field of x to the environment at the end of the round and set $j = j + 1$ (mod 2); if the message acknowledges $i_0 + i'$ (mod 2), return reward 1 to Exp3.P.1 and go to step 12.
- Or, if the contents field is empty and the sequence number is $j + j' + 1$ (mod 2), increment j', return reward 1 to Exp3.P.1 and go to step 12.

8. *(Timeout)* Return reward 0 to Exp3.P.1.

9. Query Exp3.P.1 for a new bounded modification g_2.

10. Compute $g_2(U(x_{\mathsf{old}}, h_1(x_{\mathsf{old}})))$ and send it to the server at the end of the round.

11. Return to step 6.

12. *(Pause)* While $t < d(n)$, wait until the next round and increment t.

13. Go to step 3.

We remark that, in contrast to Algorithm 9.18, we no longer maintain the same "current guess" g for the protocol used by the sender across messages. This is necessary because the algorithm used by the sender is no longer fixed across messages—note that Exp3.P.1 (Algorithm 9.25), governing the sender's choice of encoding, samples from a changing distribution over the possible bounded modifications, and it is possible for two different bounded modifications to successfully send a packet across the network, but encode the packet's data differently. Intuitively, we would obtain a more efficient decoding algorithm if we replaced the fixed enumeration with an adaptive one, to match the changing relative frequencies of the sender's encodings. Unfortunately, the dynamics of Exp3.P.1 in our randomized network are complicated; we could replace our fixed enumeration order with, e.g., the well-known "move-to-front" order, which is known to never examine more than a factor of two more indices than the optimal ordering policy in hindsight [142], but we still have no idea what the cost of this optimal ordering policy is. Since we don't know how to obtain a tighter analysis than that yielded by the fixed enumeration, we opt to leave the simpler algorithm in place, and leave the choice of adaptive ordering to the practitioner.

Our schemes from the protocol-level perspective. Given that our objective was to show how a given task (reliable communication) can be achieved in the presence of a changing network protocol, we have presented our schemes as algorithms, and we will analyze the performance of these algorithms. In the field of networking, on the other hand, it is usually customary to describe a protocol decoupled from its implementation as an algorithm. Given that our algorithm is rather close to an algorithm implementing the specification of TCP, it may be somewhat instructive to point out how our scheme (i.e., at a protocol level) differs from the TCP/IP architecture.

We have effectively modified the (local) architecture by allowing the transport layer to provide feedback to the internet layer on its performance. When processing an incoming packet, this feedback constitutes a single bit indicating whether or not the internet layer successfully decided the message. When encoding an outgoing packet, the transport layer again provides a single bit to the internet layer per packet, indicating whether or not the packet was acknowledged; this bit may be delayed by up to $2d$ rounds (when a time-out is triggered). *The crucial point is that we can show that this feedback is sufficient to guarantee that the internet layer functions properly, and thus to adapt its behavior in response to external changes.* The main modification that we make at the transport layer is thus that in order to provide feedback to the internet layer on its performance at decoding, we assume that the sender signs their transport-layer packet.[10]

9.3.3   Analysis of the modified stop and wait scheme

We are now ready to present the analysis of our end-to-end scheme based on the stop and wait protocol. Our construction is divided into two parts, the handshake scheme (Algorithm 9.27) that permits the users to agree on hash functions, and the adaptive stop and wait scheme (Algorithm 9.28) that takes the hash functions as input and achieves the goal of sending datagrams in an unreliable network (Definition 9.2) with a bounded modification of a known server (Definition 9.8). We will analyze the two parts separately in the next section, when we present a more efficient scheme for sending messages, but we will still use Algorithm 9.27 to agree on hash functions, and so the analysis we provide here will still apply.

Both constructions rely on the following key lemma establishing that a uniformly chosen hash function from a pairwise independent hash family permits us to decode messages reliably. The present lemma is a variant of Claim 9.20 from the proof of Theorem 9.19, the analysis of the decoding strategy in reliable networks.

Lemma 9.29 (Pairwise independence implies decoding works with high probability). *Fix any $(s(n), C, N)$-streaming protocol U a family of pairwise-*

---

[10]This is very similar to an authentication functionality (optionally) provided under "Encapsulating Security Payload" as provided by IPsec [90].

independent hash functions $\{h : \{0,1\}^{\leq n} \to \{0,1\}^m\}$, *and a message* x *of length up to* n *(with* $n + m < N$*). Then, for any pair of* $(\ell(n), s'(n), C')$*-bounded modifications of* U, g_1 *and* g'_1, *for a uniformly chosen function* h, *the probability that,* $g'_1(U)^{-1}(g_1(U(x, h(x)))) = (x', y')$ *such that* $y' = h(x')$ *for some* x' *of length up to* n *but* $x \neq x'$ *is at most* $2^{s(N)+2\ell(n)-m}$.

Proof Given a configuration of U, $g_1(U)$ is uniquely determined by its input; since $g'_1(U)$ is injective with respect to these inputs of length up to N, we see that on any message, $g'_1(U)^{-1}$ specifies at most one pair (x', y') such that y' has length m and x' has length up to n. Therefore, given the configuration of U and (x, y), $g'_1(U)^{-1}(g_1(U(x, y)))$ specifies at most one such pair (x', y').

We know we are given that $y = h(x)$; but, since h was uniformly chosen from a pairwise independent hash family,

$$\Pr_h \left[y' = h(x') \; \middle| \; \begin{array}{l} y = h(x), \\ g_1(U(x, y)) \text{ outputs } m_0 \text{ from } \sigma, \\ g'_1(U)^{-1}(m_0) = (x', y') \end{array} \right] \leq \frac{1}{2^m}$$

We now take a union bound over the $2^{s(N)}$ configurations U could be in on inputs of length up to N, and over the $2^{2\ell(n)}$ pairs of bounded modifications (g_1, g'_1) that were used for encoding and decoding, respectively, to find that the probability that $g'_1(U)^{-1}$ ever produces a valid hash tag for some $x' \neq x$ is at most $2^{s(N)+2\ell(n)-m}$, as claimed. ∎

Analysis of the handshake

The correctness of our handshake scheme broadly relies on two things: first, that the different types of messages sent during the scheme are correctly distinguished by the users, and second, that the users can correctly identify which hash function their partner received based on the hash tag of an acknowledgement.

In particular, as described earlier, random messages in our handshake scheme play a role analogous to the messages with the ACK flag cleared sent in the TCP handshake (described in Protocol 9.24)—they establish a choice of random hash function, analogous to the choice of a random sequence number. As the users may send many such messages before receiving an acknowledgement, the correctness of our handshake scheme will rely on the users' ability to distinguish these random messages from messages acknowledging receipt of such messages. The following lemma establishes that this is possible, and is representative of the various cases establishing the first claim:

Lemma 9.30 (Random messages do not decode to valid signatures). *Fix a pairwise-independent hash function* $h : \{0,1\}^{n'} \to \{0,1\}^m$, *an* $(s(n), C, N)$*-streaming protocol* U, *a bounded modification of* U, U', *and a pair of deterministic functions,* g_1 *and* g_2 *such that each* $g_i(U)$ *is injective with respect* to the "wait for reply" states of U. Then, if $r \in \{0,1\}^N$ is chosen uniformly at random, the probability that $g_2(U(r))$ is in the range of U' and $g_1(U)^{-1}(g_2(U)(r)) = (x, y)$ is such that $y = h(x)$ is at most $2^{n'+s(N)-N}$.

Proof Since $g_1(U)$ is injective with respect to the wait for reply states of U, given a wait for reply configuration σ of U and a message m, the (x, y) such that $g_1(U(m)) = (x, y)$ is uniquely determined. There are thus at most $2^{n'+s(N)}$ messages m such that $g_1(U)^{-1}(m) = (x, h(x))$—at most $2^{s(N)}$ wait for reply configurations yielding at most $2^{s(N)}$ distinct encodings for the $2^{n'}$ possible strings for x.

Now, likewise, since $g_2(U)$ is injective, $g_2(U(r))$ is distributed uniformly over 2^N messages. Thus, the probability assigned to any set of at most $2^{n'+s(N)}$ messages under the distribution $g_2(U(r))$ is at most $2^{n'+s(N)-N}$; in particular, since the probability that $g_2(U(r))$ is $g_1(U)^{-1}(x, h(x))$ for some string x *and* is in the range of U' can only be less, it is at most $2^{n'+s(N)-N}$ as well. ∎

The second claim, that users can correctly identify which hash function their partner received based on the hash tag of the acknowledgement, will follow since Lemma 9.29 establishes that we can decode correctly, and then given the decoding, the tag produced by one of our hash functions will uniquely identify that hash function. As we will see, the arguments will all be similar to Lemmas 9.29 and 9.30.

Theorem 9.31 (Users agree on hash functions following the handshake). *Suppose $n' = n + 4$ (i.e., for the modified stop and wait scheme),*

$$2m \geq n' + 4\ell(n) + s(N) + \log\frac{1}{\epsilon} + 4$$

and a user returning from the handshake with a value 1 for the LEAD flag subsequently sends a message with the SYN flag cleared, acknowledging sequence number 0, and tagged with their hash function for sending messages.

Then the handshake terminates for both users and at the end of the handshake, the hash function that the first user will use to send message is the same as the hash function that the second user will use to decode messages, and likewise, the hash function that the first user will use to decode messages is the same as the hash function that the second user will use to encode messages, and furthermore,

1. *Both users will return from the handshake scheme in at most $\frac{4d(n)2^\ell}{(1-\delta(n))^2}$ rounds in expectation.*

2. *Either both users will have the same hash function that is uniformly chosen, or else the users will have hash functions that are independently and uniformly chosen.*

3. *One user will obtain $b = 0$ and the other will obtain $b = 1$.*

4. *Random messages remaining in the system after the users return from the handshake scheme that were not tagged with one of the hash functions that the users use for decoding do not decode to messages with a valid hash tag under any $(\ell(n), s'(n), N)$-bounded modification.*

with probability at least $1 - \epsilon - 2\epsilon_0(N)$ *(for the function ϵ_0 specified in Theorem 9.12).*

Proof

Overview. We will follow a strategy familiar from Theorem 9.19: we will argue that the handshake is correct if the hash functions used by the users were actually uniformly chosen; we then apply Theorem 9.12 to conclude that the handshake works correctly with slightly higher error probability due to the imperfect randomness yielded by the extractors. Since we will already count the statistical distance towards the error probability, we may subsequently assume (i.e., during the analysis of the transmission scheme) that the hash functions were sampled uniformly.

At least one user must be in the active open state to initiate a connection; let Alice be this user, and let Bob be the other user. There will be two cases, depending on whether Bob is in the passive open state or in the active open state, and then if both users are in the active open state, three sub-cases depending on which user's hash functions they commit to using (Alice's, Bob's or both). We will have to argue that the users agree on hash functions with high probability in each case separately.

First, however, to guarantee that the algorithm makes progress, we need to show that Alice does not accidentally drop Bob's messages with high probability; otherwise, if there is only one encoding that Bob can use to send messages to Alice, it may be that Alice drops those messages. Once we know that the users receive each others' messages, we next argue that the users successfully distinguish the two types of messages: messages containing N random bits and messages tagged with a hash value for some hash function. This is also important to making progress through the algorithm (and using the receipt of messages to confirm progress) because messages tagged with hash values are considered to be "acknowledgements" of receipt of a packet of random bits. Given these two claims, we know that the users progress through the algorithm and eventually return from the handshake and move on to transmitting data; the running time will also follow easily once the users make progress.

Now, the users come to agree on the hash functions returned by the scheme by using the hash value tagged to the acknowledgement to infer which hash function their partner received. For this to work, we need only argue that the tag of the first received hash function is unlikely to collide with the tag of any other hash function sent by the user. Fortunately, since the number of hash functions is relatively small, this will hold with high probability, and so we find that the scheme is correct.

The algorithm terminates. So, we begin with the claim that Alice does not drop Bob's messages with high probability. Unfortunately, the proof of this claim amounts to a somewhat tedious case analysis, showing that each type of message that Alice sends collides with a message that Bob would send with very low probability. The rest of the proof will have a similar flavor.

Claim 9.32. *If the hash functions were uniformly chosen, then with probability greater than* $1 - (5/16 + 1/256)\epsilon$*, no packet from Bob is ever dropped when Alice drops packets because they match packets she recently sent. In particular, for any hash function derived from one of Alice's random messages, none of Alice's random messages will not decode to a message with a valid tag under the hash function under any bounded modification.*

Proof Note that there are two points in the scheme where Alice may drop packets, one in the first loop, and one in the second loop, during a four-way handshake.

First loop. At the first point, Alice only drops packets when they are the encoding of a random string $r = r_{g'_2}$ under $g'_2(U)$ for some bounded modification g'_2. Since Alice has only been sending such packets to Bob up to this point, Bob either replies with an acknowledgement tagged with some hash function, encoded under some protocol g_2, or if he is also in the active open state, he may be sending his own random message encoded under some bounded modification of U, $g_2(U)$.

In the latter case, it is easy to see that the messages will differ: since the bounded modifications are still injective, the probability that $g_2(U)$ hits any particular $g'_2(U(r))$ is at most 2^{-N}. A union bound therefore gives that the probability that any of the $2^{\ell(n)}$ bounded modifications g_2 that Bob could be using map his random string to any of the encodings of Alice's random string under any of the $2^{\ell(n)}$ bounded modifications g'_2 is at most

$$2^{2\ell(n)-N} < 2^{2\ell(n)-2m} < \frac{\epsilon}{256}$$

since $N > 2m > 4\ell(n) + \log(1/\epsilon) + 8$.

The former case is slightly more involved. For each of the $2^{\ell(n)}$ encodings (one for each of the bounded modifications g_2), Alice sends a random string under that encoding, and likewise, Bob could be sending an acknowledgement tagged by any one of the $2^{\ell(n)}$ hash functions h_{g_2} specified by these bounded modifications. If Bob tags his message with a hash function $h \neq h_{g_2}$ where m_{g_2} is the last message sent by Alice, Lemma 9.30 guarantees that m_{g_2} is a valid encoding under h with probability at most $2^{n'+s(N)-N} < 2^{4\ell(n)}\frac{\epsilon}{16}$, so by a union bound over the $2^{\ell(n)}$ possibilities for m_{g_2}, the $2^{\ell(n)}$ possibilities for h, and the $2^{\ell(n)}$ possible encodings g_1 that Bob could be using to encode his acknowledgement, we have a total probability of error of less than $\epsilon/16$ in this case.

We still haven't handled the case when Bob tags his message with h_{g_2} and Alice's last message was m_{g_2}. Here, we find that since m_{g_2} is the encoding of a random N-bit message and the encodings are injective, m_{g_2} is uniformly distributed over a set of size 2^N. On the other hand, the n'-bit message part x of Bob's acknowledgement is fixed, and there are at most 2^m possible values for $y = h_{g_2}(x)$. Now, by a union bound over the $2^{\ell(n)}$ possible encodings $g_1(U)$ that Bob could be using, we see that the probability that m_{g_2} hits some valid encoding of $(x, h_{g_2}(x))$ is at most $2^{m+\ell(n)-N}$. A union bound over the $2^{\ell(n)}$ messages m_{g_2} that Alice sends gives a total probability of at most

$$2^{m+2\ell(n)-N} < 2^{2\ell(n)-m} < \frac{\epsilon}{16}$$

by our assumptions on N and m. Note that this establishes the second part of the claim.

Second loop. In the second loop, Alice has fixed a hash function $h_{a,b}$ to use to tag messages, extracted from some message m_0 send by Bob (who is necessarily in the active open state). In this case, if Bob's message is a packet of random bits (i.e., sent in his first loop) then by the same reasoning as in the first loop, we see that when Bob sends $m \neq m_0$, that the probability that one of Alice's tagged messages $m' = m$ is at most $\epsilon/16$, and likewise for $m = m_0$, the probability that $m' = m$ is at most $\epsilon/16$.

The only case remaining to consider is when Bob tags his message, too. In this case, we see that since Alice is still in the handshake, Bob must be using some h_{g_2} specified by one of Alice's messages from the first loop. In this case, we have that $h_{a,b}$ and h_{g_2} are independently chosen. In particular, if we assume $h_{a,b}$ is uniformly distributed, we see that for the fixed message x encoded in each m' send by Alice, $h_{a,b}(x)$ is uniformly distributed over $\{0, 1\}^m$. Therefore, for any pair of encodings y_1 used by Bob and y'_2 used by Alice to encode $(x, h_{g_2}(x))$ and $(x, h_{a,b}(x))$ respectively, the probability that some g'_2 has $g'_2(U(x, h_{a,b}(x)))$ matching $g_1(U(x, h_{g_2}(x)))$ for any g_1 is at most $2^{2\ell(n)-m} < \epsilon/16$. Totaling the bounds obtained gives the stated claim. ∎

We may therefore henceforth assume that every message Alice receives was sent by Bob, and that every message sent by Bob is received by Alice with probability $(1 - \delta(n))$, independently.

We next argue that Alice does not mistake one of Bob's random messages for an acknowledgement signed by one of her own hash functions:

Claim 9.33. *With probability greater than $1 - \epsilon/16$, none of the hash functions h generated by random packets sent by Alice will have a random message m_{g_1} (for a bounded modification g_1) sent by Bob that will decode to a message with a valid tag under h under any bounded modification $g_1(U)^{-1}$.*

Proof By a union bound over the $2^{\ell(n)}$ hash functions h_{g_2} Alice obtains under the $2^{\ell(n)}$ bounded modifications g_2 applied to random strings, and the

$2^{2\ell(n)}$ possible pairs of bounded modifications (g_1, g_1') such that Alice could be using $g_1'(U)^{-1}$ to decode a random message encoded using g_1 by Bob, it follows from Lemma 9.30 that the probability that any such message from Bob decodes to some $(x, h_{g_2}(x))$ is at most

$$2^{3\ell(n)} 2^{n' + s(N) - N} < 2^{n' + 3\ell(n) + s(N) - 2m} \leq \frac{\epsilon}{16}$$

by our initial hypothesis on m. ∎

Therefore, if Bob is in the active open state and Alice receives one of his random messages, she will detect this and jump to the four-way hand-shake portion of the scheme with probability greater than $1 - \epsilon/16$. It's clear, conversely, that if Bob sent Alice a message signed by one of her hash functions, then by the point in the inner loop where she reaches the bounded modification g_1 used by Bob and the hash function h_{g_2} used by Bob, she will compute $g_1(U)^{-1}(g_1(U(x, h_{g_2}(x)))) = (x, h_{g_2}(x))$, and so she will not mistake the tagged message for a random message (though we haven't yet argued that she gets the *same* hash function as Bob used). We therefore immediately find by inspection that (given that Alice correctly distinguishes random messages from tagged messages) the users progress through the algorithm, and eventually return.

The users agree on hash functions following termination.   Towards correctness, we first note that the following claim holds:

Claim 9.34. *If none of Bob's messages are dropped, then with probability at least $1 - \epsilon/16$, the hash function Alice uses for sending messages is obtained from the first message received from Bob; the hash function Alice uses for decoding received messages is obtained from the first message she received from Bob that he tagged with a hash function.*

We also note that similarly, with probability at least $1 - \epsilon/16$, Bob correctly distinguishes random messages from tagged messages, and so a similar claim holds for Bob, whether he is in the active open state or the passive open state.

The key is, now, to argue that the decoding of a tagged message specifies the message used to derive the hash function, and therefore also the hash function. By Lemma 9.29, if we assume that the hash function was uniformly chosen, then with probability at least $1 - 2^{s(N) + 2\ell(n) - m} \geq 1 - \epsilon/8$, Alice decodes the message (x, y) correctly; since $h_{g_2}(x)$ is uniformly distributed over $\{0, 1\}^m$ for any message x, and there are at most $2^{\ell(n)}$ other hash functions, and therefore at most $2^{\ell(n)}$ values that $h_{g_2}(x)$ might hit resulting in the potential for error, by a union bound, h_{g_2} only collides with one of the other hash functions at x with probability at most $2^{\ell(n) - m}$. Using our relationship between m and the other parameters (and using $s(N), \ell(n) \geq 1$) we find that the probability of such a collision is at most $\epsilon/64$. (Note that we only need to worry that the *first* tagged message is decoded correctly.) Thus, with probability at least $1 - \epsilon/64$, the hash function h_{g_2} used to tag the message is uniquely identified by $h_{g_2}(x)$. A similar argument, of course, holds for the first tagged message decoded by Bob.

We are essentially done with correctness: we consider four cases, and now note that since the hash functions are obtained from the extractor described in Theorem 9.12 applied to a packet from a space-$s(n)$ source, Lemma 9.11 shows that the hash functions obtained are indeed $\epsilon_0(N)$-close to uniformly chosen.

1. First, if Bob is in the passive open state, he waits until he receives a random packet from Alice. We see that he will use the hash function extracted from this packet for both sending and receiving messages; since he tags his messages with this hash function, we see that Alice identifies this hash function correctly with probability $1 - \epsilon/64$, and she uses it for both sending and receiving. We note that the use of the extractor only increases the probability of an error (in Alice identifying the hash function correctly) by $\epsilon_0(N)$. In this case, Bob obtains $b = 0$ and Alice obtains $b = 1$.

2. Now, the remaining three cases occur when Bob is in the active open state; we first consider the case where Bob and Alice receive each other's random packets first.

   We note that with probability at least $1-(5/8+1/128)\epsilon$, neither of them ever drops messages sent by the other. In this case, they both correctly identify the packets as being random with probability at least $1 - \epsilon/8$, and then subsequently use the specified hash function to tag their messages in the second loop. We now observe that they both correctly identify the hash functions used on their respective acknowledgements with probability at least $1-\epsilon/32$, which is decreased by at most $2\epsilon_0(N)$ by them each using hash functions obtained from the extractor. In this case, we note that (with probability at least $1 - 2^{-N} > 1 - \epsilon/256$, plus the overhead incurred by the extractors that is already accounted for) they return different hash functions for encoding and decoding, and indeed, the hash function Alice will use for encoding is the same as the one Bob uses for decoding, and vice-versa. Furthermore, in this case, since $h_1 \neq h_2$, one of them obtains $b = 1$ and the other obtains $b = 0$.

3. If Alice receives Bob's random packet first, but Bob receives Alice's acknowledgement first, then Bob correctly identifies the hash function used by Alice with probability at least $1 - \epsilon/64$, which is decreased by at most $\epsilon_0(N)$ by the extractor; note now that Bob will use this hash function for both sending and receiving. Subsequently, Alice will later receive a message from Bob tagged with this hash function; since she decodes it correctly (noting that the SYN flag is not set) and correctly identifies the hash function used with probability at least $1 - \epsilon/64$,

(again decreased by at most $\epsilon_0(N)$ by the extractor) she therefore uses the same hash function as Bob for both sending and receiving subsequently. Here, Alice obtains $b = 1$ and Bob obtains $b = 0$.

4. Finally, the case where Alice receives an acknowledgement of Bob having received a random packet is similar to the previous case.

We therefore see that with probability at least $1 - \epsilon - 2\epsilon_0(N)$, Alice and Bob do not drop each other's messages, and return a pair of hash functions so that the hash function used by Alice to encode is the same as the hash function Bob uses to decode and vice-versa, and the hash functions obtained may indeed be assumed to be uniformly chosen. Furthermore, since we already argued that none of the hash functions the users might select would decode the existing random messages to messages with valid tags under any bounded modification, the only part we have left to argue is the running time.

The algorithm's running time.   As for the running time in this case, we note that there is at least one valid protocol for sending in each direction, and we use it once every $2d(n)2^{\ell(n)}$ rounds; since each message is dropped independently with probability $1 - \delta(n)$, the message sends successfully after $\frac{1}{1-\delta(n)}$ attempts in expectation. Since in any case, we need to wait (at most) for the first successful acknowledgement of our first successfully sent message, this takes at most $\frac{4d(n)2^\ell}{(1-\delta(n))^2}$ rounds in expectation, as claimed. ∎

Analysis of the adaptive stop and wait scheme

We are now ready to establish the correctness of our scheme for sending messages. Roughly speaking, this will follow from our ability to decode messages given that the users agree on hash functions (i.e., Lemma 9.29) and the correctness of the acknowledgement scheme used by TCP. The (relative) efficiency of our adaptive scheme will follow from Exp3.P.1 achieving a rate of success that approaches the success rate of the unknown bounded modification of the network protocol.

Theorem 9.35 (The adaptive stop and wait scheme achieves the goal of sending messages in an unreliable network under bounded modifications). *Suppose $n' = n + 4$, $2m < N$, and*

$$m \geq n' + s(N) + 2\ell(n) + \log \frac{16}{\epsilon}$$

with $\epsilon > 5\epsilon_0(N)$ for the ϵ_0 specified by Theorem 9.12 applied to space-$s(N) + s'(N) + 1$ sources. Suppose further that we are given $(s(n), C, N)$-streaming protocols U_A and U_B and any $(\ell(n), s'(n), C')$-bounded modifications f_A and f_B, applied to U_A and U_B respectively, where $U'_A = f_A(U_A)$, $U'_B = f_B(U_B)$, and $S(U'_A, U'_B)$ is the unreliable server using U'_A and U'_B.

Then a pair of users following the handshake scheme described in Algorithm 9.27, and subsequently following the adaptive stop and wait scheme described in Algorithm 9.28 using the parameters returned by the handshake scheme successfully achieve the goal of sending datagrams with max-delay $d(n)$ and failure probability $\delta(n)$ with $S(U_A', U_B')$ with probability at least $1 - \epsilon$.

Furthermore, a message sent in round $R > 2d(n)(i^* + 2^{\ell(n)+1}/(1 - \delta(n))^2)$ where

$$i^* = \min\{i : \log_2(e)i2^{\ell(n)} > \ell(n) + \log(\log i + 1)(\log i + 2) + \log \frac{4}{\epsilon}\}$$

is expected to arrive by round

$$\frac{4d(n)2^{\ell(n)}}{(1 - \delta(n))^2} + \frac{2d(n)(1 + \delta(n))}{1 - \delta(n)} \left(R + O\left(\sqrt{R2^{\ell(n)}\left(\ell(n) + \log \frac{\log R}{\epsilon}\right)}\right)\right)$$

at the latest.

Proof

Overview. The analysis will, of course, initially resemble the analysis of our decoding scheme in reliable networks, given in the proof of Theorem 9.19: we have already considered the analysis of the handshake scheme (Algorithm 9.27) in Theorem 9.31, which serves a role analogous to the initialization sub-protocol for the original scheme; what remains is to show that the hash functions obtained from the handshake scheme suffice to decode messages properly under the present, slightly different conditions. This will follow easily from Lemma 9.29.

Establishing that the messages can be successfully decoded essentially reduces the analysis of the correctness of our modified scheme to the analysis of the stop and wait protocol when the network protocol is known to the users (Protocol 9.22), sketched in Section 9.3.1. This analysis shows that the messages are delivered by their designated recipient to the environment in order, and thus the goal (as described in Definition 9.2) is achieved.

To argue that the messages are sent somewhat efficiently, we will need to show that the multiplicative weighting scheme learns to send messages reliably. For the scheme to work, however, it needs feedback for *every* kind of message we send, including acknowledgements, which we must argue is provided. Given that we have such feedback, Theorem 9.26 can be applied twice to give a bound on how often the users choose a bad protocol when interacting with each other, i.e., first establishing that a user with our scheme does well with a partner who knows the protocol, and second establishing that the partner can actually use our scheme instead of knowing the protocol, without failing too many times.

All messages are decoded correctly.   We begin by noting that our condition on m implies that

$$2m \geq n' + 4\ell(n) + s(N) + \log \frac{32}{\epsilon}$$

so we can apply Theorem 9.31 to find that, as long as a user who obtains value 1 for the LEAD flag sends messages according to our scheme (cf. steps 1 and 3), the users agree on hash functions with probability at least $1 - \epsilon/64 - 2\epsilon_0(N) > 1 - (2/5 + 1/64)\epsilon$ (since we have assumed $\epsilon > 5\epsilon_0(N)$). So we will assume that one user begins the stop and wait scheme with b set to 1 and the other has b set to 0. Let Alice be the user with b set to 1, and let Bob be the other user.

Theorem 9.31 already guarantees that neither user mistakes a random message for a message with a valid tag using their hash function. We can also show that every other message decodes correctly with high probability: by a union bound over all $2^{n'+1}$ messages x of length at most n', Lemma 9.29 guarantees that the probability that any message x tagged with a uniformly chosen hash function h encoded with a bounded modification g_1 of U decodes under another bounded modification g_1' to a message $x' \neq x$ that has a valid tag under h is at most $2^{n'+1+s(N)+2\ell(n)-m} \leq \epsilon/8$ by our assumption on m; therefore, with probability at least $1 - \epsilon/4$, for any pair of bounded modifications of U used for encoding and decoding, neither user will ever decode a message tagged with their hash function to any message other than the intended message.

Messages are received in order.   Now, given that the users obtain the encoded messages from any packet correctly, note that in particular, when a user decodes a message, the algorithm discards any messages with the SYN flag set or with the LEAD field set to b. Since only Alice's messages have the LEAD field set to 1 and only Bob's messages have the LEAD field set to 0, Alice only continues to process messages sent by Bob and vice-versa. Likewise, since the only types of messages sent by the handshake scheme are either random or have the SYN flag set, (where we already know that random messages fail decoding, and are therefore dropped) the users also ignore any packets left in the system from the handshake scheme. We therefore limit our attention to packets sent by Alice during the stop and wait scheme that are delivered to Bob and vice-versa.

Moreover, it is easy to see that since the users wait at least $d(n)$ rounds before sending messages (i.e., they either wait until a timeout or hold at step 12 until $d(n)$ rounds have passed) and messages are delivered within $d(n)$ rounds if at all, there is at most one message that was sent by Alice during the stop and wait scheme in the system at any time, and at most one that was sent by Bob.

We now introduce the notion of an *active message at round r*: Alice's first message sent during the stop and wait scheme is an active message from the first round until it is first delivered to Bob, and inductively, a message sent on a round after a user receives an active message, acknowledging the sequence number of that active message is also an active message for each round until it is delivered to the other user. (Thus, Bob's acknowledgement of Alice's first message is an active message until Alice receives a copy of it, Alice's acknowledgement of Bob's acknowledgement is an active message until Bob receives it, and so on.) We will also refer to the sender of an active message as an *active user* in a round.

Note that it follows by induction on the number of rounds that there is always precisely one active message on every round. Thus, noting that there is at most one other message in the system that was sent during the stop and wait scheme, we can refer to this other message as the *inactive message at round r*, if it exists.

In particular, since we can see by induction that the messages sent by a user who executed the portion of the algorithm starting from step 3 (starting with Alice's first message) are always active messages, the only messages that can be inactive messages are sent after a timeout; in this case, since the message was active at some earlier round (before it was received) and the active user (its recipient) has not yet received an acknowledgement of the active message it sent in response (since then the message it sent would not be active), the inactive message must be stored in x_{old} for the active user, and is therefore dropped if it is received. Thus, the users only forward a message's contents to the environment and return to step 3 when they receive active messages.

On the other hand, since either the sequence number of subsequent active messages differ from the sequence number of a message stored in x_{old} or the contents differ, we see that a user will not drop the next active message it receives from its partner. Thus, given that the active message decodes correctly, it will be forwarded to the environment and an acknowledgement will be sent in response, so the message will cease to be active in following rounds.

Now, because the messages from Alice to Bob are sent in Alice's active messages in order, Bob forwards them to the environment while they are active, and the messages are only active until they are forwarded to the environment, the messages are delivered to the environment in order. The same holds for the messages sent from Bob to Alice by the same argument. We therefore see that we will achieve the goal, provided that we eventually send each message correctly, so we next turn to analyzing the performance of Exp3.P.1 in this context.

The multiplicative weights scheme learns to send most messages.
We note first that we provide Exp3.P.1 with one unit of reward each time we receive an acknowledgement. Therefore, *the reward we receive up to round r is the total number of acknowledgements we have received up to round r.* Since we return to step 3 and send the next active message precisely when we

receive an acknowledgement of our last message, as long as the total reward eventually tends to infinity, we will eventually send every message, and we will achieve the goal. In pursuit of this, we turn to calculating a lower bound on the reward obtained by Exp3.P.1.

First, suppose that both Alice and Bob knew the network's protocol, and used this instead of Exp3.P.1. In this case, each one of Alice's messages is still dropped with probability $1 - \delta(n)$, and if it is not dropped, then the Borel-Cantelli lemma guarantees that Bob acknowledges her message eventually with probability 1. Thus, if in a sequence of rounds, Alice is the active user in T of them, she receives reward $(1-\delta(n))T$. Since the same expression holds for Bob, and one of the users is active in any given round, the total reward accrued by the users in T attempts to send an active message is $(1 - \delta(n))T$.

We note that both users attempt to re-send their last message each time the active message is not received. This implies several things. First, when Bob is the active user, both users have made the same number of attempts at sending messages. Second, on a round when Alice's active message is received by Bob, the total number of attempts is the users' total reward plus twice the number of failed active attempts. Therefore, in expectation, there are T attempts to send active messages after the users individually send $(1 + \delta(n))T$ messages. In particular, in expectation, the users each receive reward $\frac{1}{2}(1 - \delta(n))T$ in $\frac{1}{2}(1 + \delta(n))T$ attempts, that is, reward $\frac{1-\delta(n)}{1+\delta(n)}T$ after sending T messages.

Now, suppose that Alice uses Exp3.P.1 with parameter $\delta_0 = \epsilon/4$ instead. Since Theorem 9.26 shows that, for a function

$$\Delta(T, \delta_0, \ell(n)) = \frac{10}{\sqrt{2} - 1}\sqrt{T2^{\ell(n)+1}\left(\ln\frac{2^{\ell(n)}}{\delta_0} + 2\ln(2 + \log_2 T)\right)}$$

the reward obtained by Exp3.P.1 after T attempts at sending messages (active or inactive) is not worse than that obtained by the correct protocol by more than $\Delta(T, \delta_0, \ell(n))$ with probability at least $1-\delta_0$; in particular, for any fixing of the environment's random choices of whether or not to drop messages, it does as well as the correct protocol with probability at least $1 - \delta_0$, so in expectation over the environment's choices, the total positive feedback received by the users together after T attempts at sending active messages by either user is at least $(1 - \delta(n))T - \Delta(T, \delta_0, \ell(n))$.

We now consider Bob's perspective: when he sends an active message, since he is using the correct protocol, it is delivered with probability $(1-\delta(n))$; actually, whenever the active message is delivered, we see that Bob eventually receives reward (of one of the two types) so Bob's expected reward after T attempts at sending as the active user is still $(1 - \delta(n))T$. We find now that when Bob uses Exp3.P.1 instead, the total positive feedback received by the users together out of T attempts decreases again by at most $\Delta(T, \delta_0, \ell(n))$ with probability at least $1 - \delta_0$.

Therefore, in total, after T attempts at sending active messages, in expectation over the environment, the users together receive reward at least $(1 - \delta(n))T - 2\Delta(T, \delta_0, \ell(n))$ with probability at least $1 - 2\delta_0$ over the algorithm's random choices. By a similar calculation as before, after the users send $(1+\delta(n))T+4\Delta(T, \delta_0, \ell(n))$ messages in total, the users attempt to send active messages at least T times in expectation between them. In particular, (noting that $T > \frac{1}{1+\delta(n)}(T - 4\Delta(T, \delta_0, \ell(n)))$ and Δ is a monotone increasing function of T) this implies that after the users send T messages, they receive total reward at least

$$\frac{1 - \delta(n)}{1 + \delta(n)}T - \left(2 + \frac{4}{1 + \delta(n)}\right)\Delta(T, \delta_0, \ell(n)).$$

That is, since the users make the same number of attempts and each receive the same reward after Bob sends as the active user, the users each receive reward at least

$$\frac{1 - \delta(n)}{1 + \delta(n)}T - \left(1 + \frac{2}{1 + \delta(n)}\right)\Delta(T, \delta_0, \ell(n))$$

in expectation over the environment's random choices, with probability at least $1 - 2\delta_0 = 1 - \epsilon/2$ over the user's random choices, after attempting to send messages T times for

$$T > \min\{i : log_2(e)i2^{\ell(n)} > \ell(n) + \log(\log i + 1)(\log i + 2) + \log\frac{4}{\epsilon}\}.$$

Now, recalling the connection between reward and acknowledgements, this means that with probability at least $1 - \epsilon/2$, each user successfully sends at least

$$\frac{1 - \delta(n)}{1 + \delta(n)}T - O\left(\sqrt{T2^{\ell(n)}\left(\ell(n) + \log\frac{\log T}{\epsilon}\right)}\right)$$

messages after T attempts; since the users wait at most $2d(n)$ rounds before making their next attempt at sending messages, and at most one new message is introduced per round – either from the environment, or an empty acknowledgement – a message introduced by the environment in round R is returned to the environment by the other user after at most

$$\frac{2d(n)(1 + \delta(n))}{1 - \delta(n)}\left(R + O\left(\sqrt{R2^{\ell(n)}\left(\ell(n) + \log\frac{\log R}{\epsilon}\right)}\right)\right)$$

rounds of the stop and wait scheme in expectation. So, in particular, every message is eventually sent with probability 1 in this case, and Algorithm 9.28 (together with the handshake scheme of Algorithm 9.27) achieves the goal with zero errors with probability $1 - \epsilon$ as claimed. ∎

9.3.4   An improved end-user scheme for reliable communication

Theorem 9.35 (together with Theorem 9.31) has established that we can successfully communicate across an unreliable network when the protocol is modified, using the adaptive stop and wait scheme described in Algorithm 9.28. Unfortunately, the rate of the scheme is rather poor: it maintains a send window of size one, forcing the users to wait for an acknowledgement between sending messages. Obviously, in order to obtain a more reasonable scheme, we will need to consider larger send windows.

The difficulty that arises when modifying the adaptive stop and wait scheme to use a larger send window is that our scheme for adapting to the modification, using Exp3, must incorporate any feedback from the current round before being used to obtain a protocol to use on the following round. This has two somewhat serious ramifications: first, we cannot reuse Exp3 to send the next message until we either receive an acknowledgement or experience a timeout; and second, we should not proactively retransmit all unacknowledged messages that have timed out, since many of these may have actually arrived. As suggested earlier, at the outset of Section 9.3.2, we will finesse the first issue by using a number of copies of the weights for Exp3 equal to the size of the send window, so that we can invoke them in a round-robin fashion to obtain a higher throughput, but the second issue remains in force. Thus, when we experience a timeout on some transmission, we will only retransmit the first unacknowledged message in the send buffer, and wait until some prefix of the send buffer is acknowledged before retransmitting any more messages. In other words, due to the limitations of our learning scheme, retransmissions will still follow a stop and wait scheme in our improved scheme. Fortunately, the scheme is still an improvement, since we can still freely fill the send window, and retransmissions will only need to be sent for a $\delta(n)$-fraction of messages. How much of an improvement we obtain, however, depends on the latency $d(n)$ relative to the fraction of dropped messages $\delta(n)$, and we will discuss the performance later.

Dealing with these different behaviors depending on whether messages need to be retransmitted or not leads to a substantially more complex algorithm, and in response we have adopted a more modular presentation of the algorithm. We will provide an overview first.

Broadly speaking, the algorithm has three *states*: Active, Timeout recovery, and Idle. The *Active state* merely fills the send window until either a timeout is experienced for the first message in the send window – which causes the algorithm to transition to the Timeout recovery state – or the algorithm exhausts the send buffer, which causes a transition to the Idle state. The *Timeout recovery state* retransmits the first message in the send buffer until it is acknowledged; if, after receiving an acknowledgement, all messages that have experienced a timeout are acknowledged, the algorithm returns to the Active state, and otherwise, the algorithm retransmits the next unacknowledged message in the send buffer. In the latter case, the send window is still not completely full, so while waiting for an acknowledgement of this retransmission, the algorithm continues to fill the send window. Finally, the *Idle state* adds an empty message to the send buffer so that it can continue to provide acknowledgements—the analysis of the adaptive stop and wait scheme shows that it is crucial for *every* message to be acknowledged, and since the acknowledgement must be sent using a protocol obtained from some set of weights, it effectively must occupy some position in the send window (this message needs an acknowledgement so that we can provide feedback to Exp3).

There are also two common subroutines across the states that process incoming messages from the server, and messages to be forwarded to the environment. The former subroutine essentially performs the user decoding strategy of Algorithm 9.18, together with some bookkeeping in the send and receive buffer—processing acknowledgements of our sent messages, in particular. The latter subroutine simply returns the received messages to the environment in order, respecting the fact that we can only send one message per round (so in particular, if we had been missing only the first message of a long block of messages, once we receive that message, we can only send the remaining messages one at a time).

We now present the improved scheme:

Algorithm 9.36 (Adaptive delay-bound scheme). We take as input a pair of hash functions h_1 and h_2 provided by the handshake scheme, a value $b \in \{0, 1\}$, and the initial send buffer containing i messages. We will assume that the entries in the send buffer have a field for storing the number of rounds that elapsed between when the previous entry in the send buffer was first sent and when the corresponding entry was sent (may be set to $\perp$ for the first entry).

We initialize the following parameters:

$i_0 = \min\{1, i\}$ The index of the first unacknowledged message in the send buffer.

$j_0 = 0$ The sequence number of the last message removed from the receive buffer.

$j = 0$ A sequence number where every member of the interval $(j_0, j]$ of sequence numbers is in the receive buffer such that this interval is as long as possible.

$j' = 0$ The last received sequence number.

$k_0 = 0$ A sequence number where every member of the interval $[i_0 \bmod 2d(n), k_0]$ in the send buffer has been sent, and such that this interval is as long as possible.

$k = \perp$ The index of the last retransmitted message.

$\ell = \bot$ The sequence number of the last message in the send buffer to time out. (Set to $\bot$ if no such message exists.)

$s = \infty$ The number of rounds until the next timeout (i.e., until ℓ advances to $\ell + 1 \mod 2d(n)$).

$t = 0$ The number of rounds since the last message was sent.

$t' = \bot$ Counts down from $2d(n)$ to 1, indicating the number of rounds until the next retransmission of the first unacknowledged message in the send buffer.

We also initialize $d(n)$ copies of weights for Exp3.P.1.

If the send buffer is empty ($i = 0$) then we enter the Idle state; otherwise, we enter the Active state.

Idle:

1. Set $s = \infty$, $\ell = \bot$.

2. Add an empty message to the end of the send buffer with t and increment i and k_0 (mod $2d(n)$).

3. Query the copy of Exp3.P.1 with index $i_0 \mod d(n)$ to obtain bounded modification g_2.

4. For a message x with empty contents, the SYN flag cleared, the LEAD flag set to b, sequence number $i_0 \mod 2d(n)$, and acknowledging j, send $g_2(U(x, h_1(x)))$ to the server, and set $t = 0$.

5. For $t' = 2d(n), \ldots, 1$, repeat the following:

   (a) Wait until the next round, process received messages, and increment t.

   (b) If a message m' was received from the server, process message(m').

   (c) If a message was received from the environment, add it to the end of the send buffer, increment i, set $t' = \bot$, and enter the Active state.

   (d) *(Empty message acknowledged)* If $i_0 > i$, go to step 2

6. *(Timeout)* Provide reward 0 to the copy of Exp3.P.1 with index $i_0 \mod d(n)$, set $k = i_0$, and go to step 3.

Active:

1. If $t \mod 2 = 1$, do the following:

   (a) If a message m' was received from the server, process message(m').

   (b) If a message was received from the environment, add it to the end of the send buffer and increment i.

    (c) If $s = 0$, enter the Timeout recovery state.

    (d) Wait until the next round, process received messages, increment t, and decrement s.

2. If a message m' was received from the server, process message(m').

3. If a message was received from the environment, add it to the end of the send buffer and increment i.

4. If $s = 0$, enter the Timeout recovery state.

5. If $i_0 > i$, enter the Idle state.

6. If $k_0 \neq i_0 + d(n) - 1 \bmod 2d(n)$, do the following:

    (a) Increment $k_0 \bmod 2d(n)$, set k' to the representative of k_0 in the interval $[i_0, i_0 + d(n)]$, and set the round count field associated with index k' in the send buffer to t; if $s = \infty$, set $s = 2d(n)$.

    (b) Query the copy of Exp3.P.1 with index $k_0 \bmod d(n)$ to obtain a bounded modification g_2.

    (c) For a message x with contents equal to the message stored at index k' in the send buffer, the SYN flag cleared, the LEAD flag set to b, sequence number k_0, and acknowledging j, send a message $g_2(U(x, h_1(x)))$ to the server and set $t = 0$.

7. Wait until the next round, process received messages, increment t and decrement s.

8. Go to step 1.

Timeout recovery:

1. Set $\ell = i_0 \bmod 2d(n)$.

2. If $k_0 \neq i_0 \bmod 2d(n)$, set s to the round count associated with index $i_0 + 1$ in the send buffer.

3. Return reward 0 to the copy of Exp3.P.1 with index $i_0 \bmod d(n)$, and query it for a new bounded modification g_2.

4. Set $k = i_0$.

5. For a message x with contents equal to the message stored at index k in the send buffer, the SYN flag cleared, the LEAD flag set to b, sequence number $i_0 \bmod 2d(n)$, and acknowledging j, send a message $g_2(U(x, h_1(x)))$ to the server.

6. For $t' = 2d(n), \ldots, 1$, do the following:

(a) Wait until the next round, process received messages, increment t, and decrement s.

(b) If $s = 0$, set $\ell = \ell + 1 \mod 2d(n)$, and if $\ell \neq k_0$, set s equal to the round count associated with the index of the send buffer that is the representative of $\ell + 1 \mod 2d(n)$ in the range $[i_0, i_0 + d(n)]$; otherwise, if $\ell = k_0$, set $s = \infty$.

(c) If a message was received from the environment, add it to the end of the send buffer and increment i.

(d) If a message m' was received from the server, process message(m').

(e) *(Retransmission acknowledged)* If $i_0 \neq k$, do the following:

    i. If ℓ is not in the range $[i_0 \mod 2d(n), k_0]$, set $\ell = \bot$, and enter the Active state.

    ii. Otherwise, go to step 3.

(f) Otherwise, if $t \neq 1 \mod 2$ and $k_0 \neq i_0 + d(n) - 1 \mod 2d(n)$, do the following:

    i. Increment $k_0 \mod 2d(n)$. Set the round count field associated with the representative of k_0 in the range $[i_0, i_0 + d(n)]$ in the send buffer to t; if $s = \infty$, set $s = 2d(n)$.

    ii. Query the copy of Exp3.P.1 with index $k_0 \mod d(n)$ for a new bounded modification g_2.

    iii. For a message x with contents equal to the message stored at the representative of k_0 in the range $[i_0, i_0 + d(n)]$ in the send buffer, the SYN flag cleared, the LEAD flag set to b, sequence number k_0, and acknowledging j, send a message $g_2(U(x, h_1(x)))$ to the server and set $t = 0$.

7. *(Retransmission timeout)* Go to step 3.

Process message(m')

1. Try each $(\ell(n), s'(n), C')$-bounded modification g_1 until $g_1(U)^{-1}(m') = (x, y)$ such that x has length at most n' and $y = h_2(x)$. If no such g_1 exists, return.

2. If x has the SYN flag set or the LEAD flag set to b, return.

3. If x acknowledges some sequence number $\tilde{i}$ in the interval $[i_0 \mod 2d(n), k_0]$, do the following:

    (a) For the representative i' of $\tilde{i}$ in the range $[i_0, i_0 + 2d(n)]$, provide reward 1 to the copies of Exp3.P.1 with indices in the range $[i_0 \mod d(n), i' \mod d(n)]$

    (b) Increment s by the sum of the associated round counts associated with entries $i_0 + 1, \ldots, i' + 1$ of the send buffer

(c) Set $i_0 = i' + 1$, and if $\tilde{i} = k_0$, also set $k_0 = \tilde{i} + 1 \bmod 2d(n)$.

4. If x has sequence number $\tilde{j}$ in the interval $[j+1 \bmod 2d(n), j+d(n) \bmod 2d(n)]$, add it to the receive buffer, and otherwise return.

5. If $j = \tilde{j} - 1 \bmod 2d(n)$, advance j to the index preceding the first empty position in the receive buffer in the window $[j+1 \bmod 2d(n), j + d(n) \bmod 2d(n)]$.

Process received messages
If $j \neq j_0$, do the following:

1. Set $j_0 = j_0 + 1 \bmod 2d(n)$.

2. At the end of the round, forward the message contents stored in the receive buffer at index j_0 to the server.

One aspect of the algorithm that may be confusing is that when we are filling the send window, we explicitly wait at least one round between messages (i.e., check that $t \neq 1 \bmod 2$). We enforce this because some bounded modifications may accidentally address a message intended for our partner back to us—a similar concern arose in the construction of the handshake scheme of Algorithm 9.27. In this case, we have the LEAD field to distinguish such misdirected messages from messages addressed to us by our partner, but we still need to guarantee that we do not flood the server with such messages, since the server is permitted to drop messages addressed to us (by, e.g., our partner) if too many messages arrive. Sending messages in alternating rounds guarantees that the total number of messages that could be addressed to us at any given time in this simple scenario does not exceed the server's capacity to deliver them.

Similar remarks to those following the description of the adaptive stop and wait scheme, concerning the time efficiency of decoding, also apply here, and we summarize them briefly. In short, when proceeding through the list of the various bounded modifications in decoding an incoming message, it would almost surely be beneficial to use an adaptive enumeration such as a move-to-front list. We have not done so because we do not know how to analyze the performance of the optimal ordering policy (relative to modifications obtained by Exp3.P.1) and in any case, the optimal running time is somewhat beside the point here.

Further modifications from a protocol-level perspective. Beyond the required modifications to the TCP/IP protocol architecture we discussed following the description of Algorithm 9.28, the adaptive delay-bound scheme crucially requires that the transport-layer protocol is *message-oriented* as opposed to *byte-oriented*.[11] The reason is that in order to provide the relevant

---

[11] Recall that, as we noted earlier in Footnote 7, we have presented all of our schemes as message-oriented for simplicity, but in reality TCP is a byte-oriented protocol, which may repackage additional bytes into its messages upon retransmission.

feedback to the internet layer, we need to know which *packets* arrived rather than which *bytes* arrived, and if retransmitted packets contained an arbitrary range of bytes, we wouldn't be able to allocate feedback correctly upon retransmission.

Analysis of the improved scheme

We now analyze our adaptive delay-bound scheme. The correctness of the scheme essentially follows arguments we have given previously—we know that, using the hash functions provided by the handshake scheme, decoding of messages proceeds without error by an argument essentially identical to the one given in the proof of Theorem 9.35. Likewise, we know that the given space of sequence numbers will uniquely identify messages within the users' send windows by essentially the same argument as given in the analysis of the "delay-bound" scheme presented in our review of TCP in Section 9.3.1 (and in fact, the size of the sequence number field was chosen to be as small as possible). Hence, our focus will be on the performance of the scheme, in terms of the number of rounds needed to send a given number of messages (assuming that the send buffer is full, and we don't need to enter the Idle state).

We will see that the performance of the adaptive delay-bound scheme is generally better than the performance of the adaptive stop and wait scheme, but how much better depends on the relative size of the latency $d(n)$ and the probability of a dropped message, $\delta(n)$. In particular, we will show that our use of multiple copies of Exp3 to obtain better throughput does not delay the "learning rate" of the overall algorithm appreciably beyond what was experienced in the stop and wait scheme. There are essentially three cases: if $d(n) << 1/\delta(n)$, then we spend most of our time in the Active state, and we get throughput close to $1/2$ (since we only send a message on every other round), whereas if $d(n) >> 1/\delta(n)$, then we spend most of our time in the Timeout recovery state, and get poor throughput, but at least we outperform the stop and wait scheme by roughly a $1/\delta(n)$ factor (for an overall throughput of roughly $\frac{1-\delta(n)}{2d(n)\delta(n)}$ messages per round), since approximately that many packets arrive successfully between failures. Finally, if $d(n) \sim 1/\delta(n)$, then the expected number of messages sent between dropped messages is roughly the size of the send window, and we oscillate between the two states and obtain "moderate" throughput.

Theorem 9.37 (The adaptive delay-bound scheme sends messages in an unreliable network more efficiently). *Suppose $n' = n + 2\log d(n) + 4$, $2m < N$, and*

$$m \geq n' + s(N) + 2\ell(n) + \log \frac{16}{\epsilon}$$

with $\epsilon > 5\epsilon_0(N)$ for the ϵ_0 specified by Theorem 9.12 applied to space-$s(N) + s'(N) + 1$ sources. Suppose further that we are given $(s(n), C, N)$-streaming *protocols U_A and U_B and any $(\ell(n), s'(n), C')$-bounded modifications f_A and f_B, applied to U_A and U_B respectively, where $U'_A = f_A(U_A)$, $U'_B = f_B(U_B)$, and $S(U'_A, U'_B)$ is the unreliable server using U'_A and U'_B.*

Then a pair of users following the handshake scheme described in Algorithm 9.27, and subsequently following the adaptive delay-bound scheme described in Algorithm 9.36 using the parameters returned by the handshake scheme successfully achieve the goal of sending datagrams with max-delay $d(n)$ and failure probability $\delta(n)$ with $S(U'_A, U'_B)$ with probability at least $1-\epsilon$.

Furthermore, assuming that we always have $i \geq i_0 + d(n)$, after $d(n) \cdot i^*$ messages are sent by the adaptive delay-bound scheme where

$$i^* = \min\{i : log_2(e)i2^{\ell(n)} > \ell(n) + \log(\log i + 1)(\log i + 2) + \log \frac{4}{\epsilon}\}$$

we have spent at most

$$2 + \frac{2\delta(n)}{1 - \delta(n)}(d(n) + 2\delta(n)) + o(1)$$

rounds per delivered message.

Proof We first note that as in the proof of Theorem 9.35, the conclusion of Theorem 9.31 implies that the users do not mistake messages sent during the handshake scheme for messages with contents that should be forwarded to the environment; likewise, by a nearly identical argument as in the proof of Theorem 9.35, Lemma 9.29 implies that decoding with the hash functions provided by the handshake proceeds without error with high probability. This also implies that the users ignore messages that were not sent by their partner during the adaptive delay-bound scheme. We therefore only need to show that the sequence number scheme is suitably chosen to guarantee that messages are correctly delivered to the environment by their designated recipient, and that the scheme provides the claimed rate of delivery.

Messages are delivered in order. We first argue that the sequence number scheme for the adaptive delay-bound scheme suffices to guarantee that every message is forwarded by its recipient to the environment exactly once, and in order. The argument is similar to that given for the (non-adaptive) delay-bound protocol in Section 9.3.1.

We first argue that a sender does not mistakenly take an acknowledgement for an old message using the same sequence number as an acknowledgement for a currently unacknowledged message, guaranteeing that we don't prematurely give up on sending a message. We note that the send window $[i_0 \bmod 2d(n), k_0]$ comprises a range of at most $d(n)$ indices since we only advance k_0 to $i_0 + d(n) \bmod 2d(n)$ in either the Active state or the Timeout recovery state (in the Idle state, the send window has size at most one). In particular, therefore, for a given value of k_0, the "smallest" sequence number we can send is $k_0 - d(n) \bmod 2d(n)$. Now, k_0 can only advance to

$k_0 + \Delta$ after the messages $k_0, k_0 + 1, \ldots, k_0 + \Delta$ have been sent, where we also guarantee that we only advance the upper end of the send window at most once every other round, so k_0 can only advance to $k_0 + \Delta$ after 2Δ rounds have passed; in particular, within $2d(n) - 1$ rounds, k_0 can only advance to $k_0 + d(n) - 1 = k_0 - d(n) - 1 \bmod 2d(n)$, i.e., one index short of the smallest sequence number we could have sent. Since we process incoming messages at the start of the round (before incrementing k_0) and the maximum round-trip time for a message is $2d(n)$ rounds, this means that k_0 will not reach the point where it could be confused for an old acknowledgement. In particular, every message in the send buffer up to index $i_0 - 1$ has therefore been acknowledged by our partner.

We now show that the receiver does not mistake an old message for a new message using the same sequence number, guaranteeing that we only send an acknowledgement once we receive the intended message. Assume by induction that we have received messages up to index j. (The base case, $j = 0$, holds trivially.) Again, it is crucial that the send window comprises a range of at most $d(n)$ indices. When the sender sends a message with sequence number $\tilde{j}$, therefore, the oldest message that could be in the send window has sequence number $\tilde{j} - d(n) + 1 \bmod 2d(n)$; likewise, as we argued above, once the sender sends a message with sequence number $\tilde{j}$, since the maximum delay is $d(n)$ and k_0 advances by at most one index per round, the old messages that could still be present in the network may only have sequence numbers in the range $[\tilde{j} - d(n) + 1 \bmod 2d(n), \tilde{j} \bmod 2d(n)]$. In particular, since the process message routine only stores a new message in the receive buffer when it receives a sequence number in the window $[j + 1 \bmod 2d(n), j + d(n) \bmod 2d(n)]$, where by the induction hypothesis we have received messages up to index j (so therefore the sender must have *sent* messages up to index j), we see that any old messages we might receive must have sequence numbers falling in the window $[j - d(n) + 1 \bmod 2d(n), j \bmod 2d(n)]$, where this is precisely the set of indices that the receiver ignores. Therefore, we only store the sender's message with index j' at index j' in the receive buffer, and hence only advance j to $j + \Delta$ after we have received all of the messages with indices in the range $[j + 1, j + \Delta]$, so the induction hypothesis holds, and we only ever acknowledge a sequence number j after receiving all messages up to index j.

Taken together, these arguments show that messages are delivered to the environment in the process received messages routine in order once they are received, and that messages remain in the send buffer until they are acknowledged (and hence received). Therefore, so long as every message is eventually sent correctly and acknowledged, the scheme will achieve the goal. It is easy to see that this happens—in the 2^r iterations of the next phase r, the designated copy of Exp3.P.1 for that sequence number independently chooses the "correct" bounded modification with probability at least $2\sqrt{\frac{3 \ln 2\ell(N)}{52^{r + \ell(N)}}}$, where across all states we attempt to send the first message in the send window at least once every $2d(n)$ rounds, and this message arrives with probability

$(1 - \delta(n))$. Therefore, the Borel-Cantelli Lemma guarantees that the first message in the send window is always *eventually* sent successfully with probability 1. Since there are only countably many messages, they are all sent successfully with probability 1, and thus the goal is achieved.

Analysis of delivery rate. We now show that the adaptive delay-bound scheme achieves the claimed rate of delivery, given that $i \geq i_0 + d(n)$—that is, given that there are always enough messages in the send buffer to fill the send window. (Note that otherwise the rate at which messages are added to the send buffer may be a bottleneck.) As in the proof of Theorem 9.35, we will identify the amount of reward received by (a copy of) Exp3.P.1 with the number of acknowledgements received and apply Theorem 9.26 twice, initially moving from the case where both parties use the modified protocol to the case where one party uses Exp3.P.1, then to the desired case where both parties use Exp3.P.1.

Thus, we begin by calculating the rate at which acknowledgements are received when both parties know the network protocol, that is, the rate at which i_0 advances. The key here is to consider how many times each message is dropped: each dropped message delays the advance of i_0 by up to $2d(n)$ steps, and the expected number of drops is $\frac{\delta(n)}{1-\delta(n)}$. Therefore, each message is delayed by $\frac{2d(n)\delta(n)}{1-\delta(n)}$ rounds in expectation due to dropped messages; otherwise, messages are sent at a rate of once every two rounds, so when a message is not dropped (with probability $1 - \delta(n)$) and an acknowledgement arrives, it "costs" two rounds, for a cost of $2(1 - \delta(n))$ rounds in expectation.

Finally, we need to consider the cost due to an acknowledgement failing to arrive within the next $2d(n)$ rounds. There are two ways in which this might occur: the first is that some message sent by our partner is dropped at least twice, and the second is that some number of consecutive messages in our partner's send window are all dropped consecutively, forcing us to wait in the Timeout recovery state. In the second case, each such dropped message may cost us an additional two rounds of waiting, for a total expected cost of at most $\frac{2\delta(n)}{1-\delta(n)}$. For the first case, there is an expected cost of $\frac{2d(n)}{1-\delta(n)}$ rounds due to (consecutive drops of) our partner's retransmissions. In the meantime, our send window fills, and so this cost is an additional delay shared by the $d(n)$ unacknowledged messages in our send window. Thus, the additional delay per message is

$$\frac{1}{d(n)}\delta(n)^2 \frac{2d(n)}{1 - \delta(n)} + \frac{2\delta(n)}{1 - \delta(n)}$$

and the total number of rounds per message we spend is therefore at most

$$2(1 - \delta(n)) + \frac{2\delta(n)}{1 - \delta(n)}(d(n) + 1 + \delta(n)) = 2 + \frac{2\delta(n)}{1 - \delta(n)}(d(n) + 2\delta(n))$$

rounds of delay in expectation per message.

Now, we note that each copy of Exp3.P.1 receives a $1/d(n)$-fraction of the messages, and hence since every message is acknowledged once, a $1/d(n)$-fraction of the total number of acknowledgements. By Theorem 9.26, we know that once the number of messages sent by each copy is greater than i^*, using Exp3.P.1 with $\delta_0 = \epsilon/4$ instead of the "correct" bounded modification incurs an additional $\tilde{O}(\sqrt{T/d(n)})$ failed attempts to send by each copy once T attempts have been made overall, yielding a total of $\tilde{O}(\sqrt{d(n)T})$ additional "dropped messages" out of T across all $d(n)$ copies, where each dropped message incurs an additional delay of at most $2d(n)$ rounds. Since this is bounded independent of T, as $T \to \infty$, the use of Exp3.P.1 therefore incurs $o(1)$ (really, $\tilde{O}(\sqrt{d(n)^3/T})$) additional rounds per message. Likewise, once both players use Exp3.P.1, each time either a player drops a message, both players experience an additional delay of at most $2d(n)$ rounds in waiting for that message to be retransmitted. Since this is at most twice the delay from the previous setting, which was $o(1)$, the overall cost is at most $o(1)$ additional rounds per message. ∎

9.4 On extending the schemes to networks connecting many users

In the previous section, we presented schemes that permitted two users to communicate across a packet network using an unknown modification of an earlier packet format known to both users. A problem with the model we used, however, is that we failed to account for the presence of the other users on the network. We considered the possibility that one of our two users might accidentally forward a message to themselves, but we had ignored the possibility that the user might accidentally send a packet to *some other, unrelated user*. In particular, we assumed that the only messages received by the two users had been sent by one of them, but if we accidentally initiate communication with a user other than the intended recipient, then we may not achieve our intended goal at all! Thus, the essential problem comes down to how the network manages identities (by which we primarily mean addresses for our purposes), and we will briefly discuss some approaches to dealing with these problems.

We are not aware of any way of coping with such problems without either relying on some additional infrastructure or else some knowledge about the address scheme used by the network protocol. So, although we will present some approaches to coping with these issues, all of our approaches will entail additional design decisions, and hence none will be entirely "universal." The aim will instead be to place relatively minimal restrictions on the space of protocols, so as to allow as large a design space as possible for future versions.

On the application to the update from IPv4 to IPv6

The situation is still bleak concerning even the *specific* example of a change in the network protocol we have in mind, that of transitioning from IPv4 to IPv6. At the outset, in motivating our definition of unreliable servers (Definition 9.8), we assumed that the modification of the network protocol for the two users consisted of *two independent* modifications of the existing protocol, one that Alice would use to send messages to Bob, and one that Bob would use to send messages to Alice. Since IPv4 and IPv6 merely attach different headers to a packet of data, this was sufficient to capture the transition from IPv4 to IPv6 with respect to two users. This approach does not scale for several reasons. The first undesirable aspect of this approach is that it requires learning a new "modification" for each new user we might want to communicate with, whereas the packet format in both IPv4 and IPv6 depends "uniformly" on the addressee's IP address, so we would hope that our protocol might preserve this aspect, and we would only need to learn one protocol for use in communicating with any user on the network. The more serious problem, as we noted above, is that we have no way of distinguishing users, and so our schemes do not guarantee that they establish communication with the right user (or even communicate correctly with *any* user) in the case where there are many users on the network.

In both cases, the ultimate problem is that IPv4 and IPv6 use completely different addressing schemes—and indeed, the major motivation for the change in the protocol was that the IPv4 address space was in danger of being exhausted. In particular, without some kind of outside assistance, the user does not have much hope of finding their addressee's new address in this larger address space. This strongly suggests that we will need to rely on the existence of some kind of "address translation," either by some simple embedding of the old address space in the new space (e.g., padding by 0s), or by some service on the network, where unfortunately neither has been provided for the transition from IPv4 to IPv6. We will discuss in more detail at the end of this section some such possible approaches that could have been taken to allow the transition to be handled automatically.

9.4.1 Approaches for protocols using the same addresses

We first consider the simpler case where both protocols identify users by the same fixed address strings. Our approaches here are tantamount to making some mild additional assumption(s) about the protocol.

Approach #1: partially fix the packet format.

The simplest approach in this vein, suggested by Eran Tromer [148], is to assume that the source and destination addresses are always, e.g., at the start of the packet. If the rest of the packet is independent of the addresses, then there is no more to be said. On the other hand, if there is any part of the packet that depends on the addresses – for example, a checksum – then we are left with the task of verifying that the bounded modification does not change the address.

A simple approach here that will always work is to check that the address fields are correct prior to sending the packet, and count it as "dropped" otherwise. It is immediate to see that this works, and reduces the problem to the one considered in this chapter. For the special case of logspace streaming protocols we considered here, it should also be possible to check that the protocol computes the identity map on n bit prefixes using dynamic programming—from a given state, we can check what bits may be output next, and so we can (one bit at a time) verify that the next output bit matches the "latest" input bit. The only complication is that the algorithm may read many input bits before producing output, but we can handle this by recording how many bits of output we have already accounted for from a given state. (Note that if we reach the same state on two different paths while "accounting for" two different lengths of prefixes of the output, then it is easily seen that the machine would not compute the identity function properly, so we would immediately reject.) That is, if b bits are accounted for, to check that the $(b + 1)$th bit matches, we first find the states where the algorithm outputs its next bit – i.e., skip that bit – and then recursively "skip" the next $b - 1$ bits in the same manner; finally, as in the original case, we have the set of states where b bits have been output, and we check that the $(b + 1)$th bit matches the input.

Approach #2: unforgeable addresses.

A slightly heavier approach is inspired by our solution to the problem of decoding correctly: namely, if we assume that "valid addresses" are in the form of (address, signature) pairs, then so long as the signatures cannot be forged by our bounded modifications, with high probability our bounded modifications will not produce any valid address besides the source or destination as output. Supposing we assume further that the network will not attempt to deliver a packet with a bad address (i.e., one without a valid signature), this reduces the problem to the one considered here. (This functionality is somewhat similar to that provided by the "Authentication Headers" included in IPsec [90].)

Again, in the special case of logspace streaming protocols that we considered here, even the simple signature scheme based on pairwise-independent hashing works with high probability since we only need to ensure that for any of the polynomially many states that the algorithm could be in when reading an input (address, signature) pair, it only subsequently outputs the (independently distributed) signature for another address with (exponentially) small probability. So for a sufficiently long signature (at least doubling the length of the address, unfortunately) we know that some hash function is secure for all addresses against all bounded modifications. To avoid such overhead in the lengths of the addresses in this case, it might be desirable to instead use a signature scheme based on a computational assumption (e.g., using a collision-resistant hash function, as introduced by Damgård [50] – in particular, a type of "stream computable" hash function especially suitable for the model of protocols considered here was also later introduced by Damgård [51] – or, surprisingly, using *any* one-way function [123][12]) rather than an information-theoretic scheme like we used. In such a case, since the users have already agreed on *some* key and we would only have a computational security guarantee anyway, it would also make sense to similarly use a computationally secure scheme at the end-user level as well (since the length of the signatures there had a serious impact on the transmission rate of the schemes).

9.4.2 Approaches for protocols using different addresses

We now turn to discussing some approaches for coping with the more challenging situation where the network does not manage identities in the same way across protocols. As we noted at the beginning of this section, precisely this issue arose in the transition from IPv4 to IPv6, and would arise any time that the protocol was changed in response to, e.g., the exhaustion of a finite address space.

Approach #1: a simple embedding of the old address space.

A very natural approach in the case where the address space has simply been enlarged is to reserve a block of the new address space for the old addresses; in the case of IP, for example, consider a scheme in which each old 32-bit IPv4 address corresponded to a 128-bit IPv6 address obtained by prepending 96 zeros to the old address. More generally, we could assume that the old address space *always* embeds into the new address space by padding with *some* appropriate number of zeros, and in this case end-users only need to guess the correct amount of padding.

Of course, this approach should be combined with one of our methods for ensuring that the packet is either delivered to the intended recipient (i.e., that we have computed a valid address) or that it is not delivered at all. Placing the addresses at the start of the packet does not seem to work, unfortunately, since if insufficient padding is used, but zeros appear in the high order bits of both addresses, then we might accidentally initiate communication with an old address in which the bits have been "shifted up," and similarly if excessive padding is used and zeros appear in the low order bits of the first address, then the network might mistake the addresses for ones with zeros in the *high order* bits instead. Either way, if we do not use exactly the right amount of padding, we may get into trouble with some addresses. We seem to require some other "check" that the sender "intended" to prepend the address with

---

[12] And of course, the textbook by Goldreich [68] contains a comprehensive overview of signature schemes.

a given number of 0s, and in this case the obvious approach is to assume that the addresses are signed by the same signature scheme under both protocols (i.e., using Approach #2 from the previous subsection). This in turn assumes the use of a signature scheme that allows for signing messages of arbitrary lengths, which rules out our information-theoretically secure schemes, and suggests that we should instead rely on computationally secure schemes as discussed above.

Approach #2: a verifiable (address translation) service.

Our final approach assumes the existence of some service on the network, reachable by some simple protocol taking as input a pair of source and destination addresses, that translates addresses from the old protocol to addresses under the new protocol, and forwards the response to the new address of, e.g., the source address. Of course, we would like to be able to reach this service without knowing precisely the (new) protocol for accessing it. In particular, we assume that the protocol for accessing the service is simple in the sense of being computed by a short program, and does not need an additional "address" as input to reach the service. The natural approach here is to assume that the service uses a public-key signature scheme to sign its messages (again, requiring a computationally secure scheme as discussed earlier), where the public key is known to all users on the network. In this way, supposing that the service responds to requests with messages consisting of signed (old address, new address) pairs, an end-user can be assured that it has obtained valid translations provided by the translation service. We can then use our verifiable decoding technique to recover the messages from the translation service, using the known public key instead of engaging any handshake or initialization sub-protocol.

Of course, once we have assumed the existence of such a powerful service, it would be somewhat underwhelming to only use it for address translation—note that we could even similarly assume that some such service existed that would, when contacted, send an updated program for sending and receiving packets under the new network protocol (this is similar to another suggestion by Eran Tromer [148]). Then, we would only need to learn how to communicate with the update service in order to obtain the new network protocol. As noted earlier, since we know how to verify that messages were sent by the update service (using the assumed key) in this case, we can at least ignore messages sent to us from other users that we might accidentally contact while attempting to obtain the update from the service. Thus, the techniques we considered here should suffice when such a service exists.

Chapter 10

Conclusions and directions for future work

Let us take a step back and reflect on what has been achieved. Our original motivation was to construct universal users for goals of practical interest, to free the designs of computer systems from the constraints imposed by our desire for backwards-compatibility, that is, by the need for these systems to strictly adhere to existing protocols. In order to address this issue, we first needed to understand clearly what it was we wanted to achieve: we therefore needed to consider precisely what purpose those protocols had served, so that we could attempt to design something to take their place. We were thus led to propose successively richer theories of semantic communication in Chapters 2, 5, and finally 6. In each case, we proposed that the systems achieved a *goal for communication* with a partner ("server") employing a fixed protocol, and so we wished to replace the systems using fixed protocols with a system using a *universal protocol*, which could adapt to a variety of different partner protocols. The degree of flexibility of our new systems is captured precisely by the size of the class of protocols with which they operate.

In each case, we have seen that some form of *sensing* with respect to the goal and the class of protocols is *necessary* for the design of a universal user, and that with few exceptions (in Chapter 5, e.g., when we compared our user to classes of protocols that couldn't be efficiently enumerated such as non-uniform classes), sensing for a class and a goal sufficed to construct universal users that could adapt to every fixed protocol in that class. Moreover, in Chapters 3, 5, 6, and 9, we saw that sensing could be achieved with many natural goals for communication and broad classes of protocols—indeed, often with the class of *all* protocols for which robust achievement of the goal was possible. In such cases, our universal protocols were as flexible as possible.

Unfortunately, this degree of flexibility was prohibitively expensive: protocols may, in general, involve hard-coded strings, and so the password lower

B. Juba, *Universal Semantic Communication,*
DOI 10.1007/978-3-642-23297-8_10,
© Springer-Verlag Berlin Heidelberg 2011

bounds we considered in Chapters 4 and 8 showed that these maximally flexible protocols needed to run in exponential time in the lengths of the protocols to which they were adapting, in the worst case. We were therefore led to consider protocols that could run more efficiently at the cost of some flexibility in Chapter 8, or that suffered a graceful decrease in performance as more flexibility was demanded of them in Chapter 4.

Ideally, we would have liked to find some "universal principles" capturing protocols that are easy to adapt to—perhaps some universal notion of "simplicity" or "learnability," as for example some would claim Kolmogorov complexity, computational depth, or some other such notion to provide (cf. for example, work by Adelman [3], Levin [98], and Antunes et al. [7] capturing NP search problems that have efficient algorithms). The problem with all of these notions for our purposes, as discussed in Chapter 4, is that there is always some "slack" in the notion of simplicity: Kolmogorov complexity is only invariant over the choice of programming language up to an additive "$O(1)$" term, and our overhead is exponential in this "$O(1)$" term, which may be quite large in practice (and indeed, may be *arbitrarily* large in general). The kinds of problems we encounter here are essentially similar to those captured by the "No Free Lunch" theorems [158, 159], which roughly say that *some* source of "bias" is necessary for learning and search to perform better than naïve random guessing. Thus, there does not appear to exist a single "silver bullet" restriction of the class of protocols under which we could safely assume our partner protocols will operate.

Consequently, it seems like although we can buy flexibility at the cost of some overhead in the running time, there's no way to guarantee that the protocols developed in isolation and employed by different communities will experience low overhead when brought into operation with one another. Said differently, it seems that even if we aren't strictly bound to follow a specific protocol or a specific class of protocols when developing a new component, there will always be some benefit to obeying such restrictions in the efficiency of operation of the overall system; conventions and agreement among members of a community will still provide tangible benefits. In this sense, the models and approaches developed in Chapters 4 and 8 are about as powerful as one could realistically hope for, and we believe that they will provide a solid starting point for the development of systems supporting such flexibility.

10.1   Directions for future work

We now outline what we believe to be the major avenues for future research that have been opened by the work presented here. Roughly, the ultimate goal is to construct flexible protocols under the refined models of Chapters 4 and 8. The starting point, however, is to develop our understanding of how to construct systems that support sensing for various concrete goals of interest. In short, we believe that the "scaffolding" of such concrete goals and protocols is essential to provide the context in which meaningful improvements in the protocols' efficiency can be developed.

Given such concrete examples, the respective models of Chapters 4 and 8 provide rather different directions of research. The main challenge raised by Chapter 8 is to obtain richer kinds of feedback that allow richer classes of protocols to be learned efficiently, whereas the main challenge of Chapter 4 lies in the design of servers that are "easy to use" with respect to some "natural" distribution on protocols. We will see that this latter question seems quite closely related to the problem of designing usable computer interfaces.

10.1.1 Concrete universal systems

So far, we have seen a few examples of "serious" applications for which we were able to construct protocols, specifically protocols for universal delegation of computation in Section 5.5.2, and the adaptive packet network protocols developed in Chapter 9. Our main motivation, as stated in Section 1.1, was the construction of such protocols, and we believe that there should be more opportunities for the development of such "universal," "flexible," or "adaptive" protocols, along similar lines. Specifically, we hope that the development of explicit "flexible" protocols for any of the numerous *real* applications pursued by work in distributed systems and algorithms will be a source of good problems for future research.

In particular, we suggest that the paradigm employed in the development of the adaptive packet network protocol of Chapter 9 may be instructive in the following sense: notice that, although it was *impossible* to make a *universal* protocol for the "general" goal of sending messages over a network (e.g., as essentially captured by Example 6.20), by assuming that the packets contained messages sent by the higher-level variant of TCP of our own design, we were able to obtain sufficiently informative feedback from the packets to learn how to use the network. To be more explicit, the general paradigm suggested by this example is that when a protocol architecture is divided into levels (as with TCP/IP), the higher-level protocol may be modified to afford the lower-level protocol more flexibility by providing it feedback.

Of course, even the *specific* problem we attempted to address with the protocol we developed in Chapter 9 is still, at best, only *partially* solved, and another somewhat more obvious (but perhaps no less ambitious!) research problem suggested by this work is to correct these deficiencies. A major problem, as described at some length in Section 9.4, is that the protocol does not currently handle networks of more than two end-users, as a consequence of difficult issues concerning *addresses*. We described a few preliminary suggestions about how one might attempt to handle these issues in Section 9.4, but we have no sense of which, if any, of the suggestions we considered would turn out to be effective solutions. A second problem, which we'll consider in more detail in the next section, is that the multiplicative weights scheme we used to learn the network protocol is really not as computationally efficient as we would need for a real system.

10.1.2   Reducing the overhead of concrete systems

The computational overhead suffered by our techniques for constructing universal protocols currently prohibit any of our example constructions from being useful in practice. This shortcoming of our basic techniques motivated us to develop approaches that experience less overhead at some cost in the degree of flexibility, in Chapters 4 and 8. While we feel that the techniques described in these chapters serve as a starting point, neither one is yet quite sufficient to reduce the overhead suffered by our examples to the point where they may actually be useful in practice.

Directions for work on using restricted classes of protocols

For the approach developed in Chapter 8, the most powerful classes of protocols (and richest kinds of goals) for which we could develop efficient universal protocols fell well short of anything of much practical interest: our overhead (using, e.g., Auer and Long's technique [12]) was exponential in the number of rounds or the size of the messages we wished to compute, and even then, we could at best use protocols that had no state and computed their next message by, e.g., composing a linear threshold function with some other simple function of the incoming messages. We suggested that perhaps these limitations could be overcome by considering richer kinds of feedback, but we could only propose a couple of "natural seeming" candidates for such feedback.

It seems like bad practice to attempt to propose "good candidates" for useful feedback out of context, since what is mathematically natural may turn out to be infeasible for our purposes in practice—for example, while the membership query model is a *very* natural learning model in many respects, it seems totally inappropriate here. In a sense, the *proper* way to approach this problem seems to be to first develop concrete protocols for a variety of examples of real goals (e.g., as suggested in the previous section) *and then* consider what kinds of feedback those systems could actually provide. While a general study of which kinds of feedback allow learning which kinds of models would also address our problem, the space of "free parameters" we just indicated seems to be too large and rich to yield interesting results any time soon, if ever—there's no reason to suspect that the space of "kinds of feedback" should be any less rich than the space of "learnable models," and likewise no reason to believe that their interaction should be easily understood. In any case, we believe that the study of some specific examples, apart from expediting the design of useful protocols, may also play some role in illuminating which considerations may be relevant to a more general study, just as our specific example of proof systems for computational goals (that we *originally* considered [83]) led to the more general notions of basic sensing considered in the present work.

So, to reiterate, we suggest taking concrete examples of protocols, e.g., as developed in Chapter 9, and considering how those protocols might be modified to provide additional feedback (and/or by further restricting the class of protocols considered) to allow the learning problem to be solved more efficiently. Of course, in the *specific* case of the adaptive packet network protocol developed in Chapter 9, we needed something stronger than the on-line learning algorithms we considered in Chapter 8—instead of enumerations, we needed to invoke the Exp3 algorithm of Auer et al. [10] for the "nonstochastic bandit problem." Improving the efficiency of such algorithms for *special cases* of strategies, even in the full-feedback "experts learning" setting (i.e., where the value obtained by *all* strategies is provided), is a well-known and challenging problem; work in this (easier) setting is summarized by Cesa-Bianchi and Lugosi [43].

Directions for work in the Bayesian setting

In the case of the Bayesian setting described in Section 4.2, although we have a technique for constructing universal users for sampleable distributions, we did not provide *any* examples of *servers* with low benchmark running times for "real" distributions or goals of interest;[1] instead, our work there simply assumed that such a server had been constructed by some benevolent "server designer" who had optimized the benchmark running time of his or her belief distribution over user strategies, and obtained some "reasonable" level of performance. This is troubling, of course, because a construction of a user is meaningless without the existence of complementary constructions of servers that actually do operate well with the user.

Our lack of nontrivial constructions of such servers was not an oversight: it is not clear how to construct them. Moreover, we didn't provide any useful-seeming techniques for the construction of good servers, or even any guidance as to how the server designer's problem might be solved. The best we can achieve formally at present is to design a server to work with a user protocol that is as short as possible, and then invoke the length-weighted uniform distribution as considered in Example 4.5, but this provides nothing better than the enumeration guarantee, and we don't expect the lengths of the user protocols to be short enough for this to be a suggestion of any practical merit. Thus, this problem is wide open at the moment, even for any *specific* nontrivial goal.

What we have found, though, is that this problem seems to be closely related to a problem considered in Human-Computer Interaction, the problem of designing usable interfaces. Roughly, the server designer's problem is to construct a server that exploits a given, sampleable prior distribution in the same way that the interface designer constructs an interface that exploits

---

[1]The reader may be interested to know that the protocol for packet networks presented in Chapter 9 developed out of attempts to design easy-to-use servers for the goal of printing.

the distribution of human behavior to guide the user to his or her desired outcome efficiently. We'll describe this connection in more detail next.

10.1.3   Connections to the usability of computer interfaces

Perhaps surprisingly, some of the most promising and interesting directions for future work involve communication with *human users*, which we touched on only briefly in Section 3.2.2 in the context of search engines. As pointed out by Gregory Abowd [2], the models used to study human-computer interaction are remarkably similar to the model we introduced for semantic communication. Although this is not so remarkable in hindsight – after all, most instances of human-computer interaction are properly viewed as goal-oriented behavior in which the human communicates with the computer via its interface – it is encouraging that the models turned out to be so similar. In particular, this connection suggests two possibilities: the first is that since the *practice* of interface design yields incontrovertibly real examples of the design of helpful servers in the model of Chapter 4 and we viewed this as a hard problem, it would be interesting to see what can be gleaned from the techniques used to design such interfaces towards the design of helpful servers in a more abstract setting. The second possibility is that the theory might help inform the practice of design. There are a variety of design principles that the designers of interfaces employ to guide the design of usable systems, and there is hope that we might be able to develop a mathematical theory of usability, in which these design principles appear as *theorems*. We hope that such a theory not only captures the existing design principles, but moreover allows us to apply abstract reasoning to devise new ones that may be less obvious but (hopefully) no less useful.

The server designer's problem and the design of usable interfaces

The basic model of interaction between humans and computers fits neatly into our basic framework: a human *user* wishes to accomplish a *goal* by communicating with a computer, i.e., a *server* in our basic terminology. In particular, we suppose that the interface has been designed to allow a family of possible tasks to be achieved, and we associate each such task with some non-deterministic choice of environment in the (formal) definition of a goal for communication. Our main theorem(s) about universal communicators – Theorem 2.25 and its variants – say that the existence of safe and viable sensing functions is necessary for users to achieve a given goal with the server. The converse direction of Theorem 2.25 says that once these criteria are in place, a user can engage in a laborious process of trial-and-error to accomplish any task, but this is of course not the end of the story—neither users nor good designers would be satisfied with such a system. The other half of the framework was laid out in Section 4.2 of Chapter 4, where we introduced a distribution capturing "natural user algorithms," and assumed that a server designer wished to both maximize the probability that natural algorithms would accomplish a task, and also minimize the average running time experienced by these algorithms.

Of course, at this point, the questions that concern the designers of user interfaces no longer concern algorithms for users (let alone the design of "universal users") but rather, the design of *servers* that are easily used by *most* users. This is essentially the problem faced by the benevolent "server designer," down to the success criterion: identifying user behavior with algorithms, and the designer's prior distribution with (empirically defined) "natural user behavior," the server designer's problem may be stated as that *natural user behavior should (almost) always achieve the user's goals*, and moreover, *should achieve the goals as quickly as possible* (i.e., with as little effort by the user as possible).

Now, Human-Computer Interaction is a thriving field in its own right, with its own variety of models proposed by researchers for various purposes at various times. Of course, as the actual models of interaction proposed by researchers vary, often refining one aspect or another, most models of interaction can be viewed as refinements of the model sketched above. For example, Abowd's framework for interaction [1] – which was intended to formally model relationships between the "result" (informally, the computer's state as it relates to progress towards the user's goal) and the input and output – while also described as a network of communicating agents, divides the computer into an agent representing the "system" or "core," and an "interface," which is itself divided into an agent handling "input," and an agent handling "output." In this case, the most natural correspondence with our model is obtained by taking the "system" or "core" to be part of the *environment* so that the user's goal refers to the state of the system, and taking the agents comprising the *interface* together as the *server*. Thus, Abowd's model is a natural refinement of ours, and we'll come back to the problems Abowd considered in the last section.

The design of helpful servers in practice

Now, the *design* of user interfaces (as opposed to the consideration of properties of proposed designs) by contrast demands a model that refines our conception of the *user*—a step that involves the models and methods of *cognitive science* or *psychology*, as opposed to *computer science*. Fortunately, in our model, we can as well consider an empirically defined "design distribution," so the only difficulty this step poses is the question of whether or not we are too far removed from the questions we were interested in answering. Given that the design of good user interfaces provides a positive example of something – easy-to-use server designs – that we'd like to capture and provide more broadly (analogous to the positive examples of intelligent behavior motivating AI), we believe that this analogy does not take us too far afield.[2]

Quite a bit is already known about how to design user interfaces, and in particular, the influential book by Norman [118] lays out a refined model of the user that permits Norman to consider what distinguishes good interfaces from bad interfaces in a variety of real examples. Roughly speaking, Norman's model may be interpreted as telling us about the distribution of natural user behavior—for example, human users have only a rather limited amount of working memory, but this working memory limitation can be overcome by giving structure to what must be remembered; or, as another example, human users tend to make mistakes, and when they discover that they have made a mistake, tend to try reworking the low-level aspects of what they have just done – i.e., "did I make a performance error?" – as opposed to the high-level aspects, e.g., "was it really a good idea to do that?" These observations motivate Norman to state a variety of *design principles*, which we will discuss in more detail in the next section. (A variety of design principles are also proposed by Thimbleby [144].) The point we wish to consider at present is how good designs use the design principles in order to accommodate a wide variety of natural user behavior.

As we will discuss in the next section, we are *already* implicitly familiar with several of these design principles—they are captured by our notion of safe and viable sensing, and we believe that we understand them pretty well. The relevant, new design principles for us will be those that concern how to exploit the distribution of natural behavior to solve the server designer's problem. Although it may seem fuzzy to the practicing computer scientist, models of the user are really crucial to solving this problem. Specifically, good designs take advantage of what Norman calls "natural mappings" and "affordances." In the case of natural mappings, this means that the proper use of the interface should satisfy some analogy with its effect and the task structure—as, e.g., when a rising level of light or sound represents "more" of something, or when the arrangement of controls is spatially similar to the objects those controls manipulate. In the case of affordances (which may be more culturally determined), this means that the control elements of the interface should be operated in accordance with a "folk" understanding of their properties: knobs should be turned, handles pulled, and buttons pressed. Thimbleby [144] similarly proposes the (perhaps clearer) principles, "match the user's task sequence," "be consistent, utilize symmetry," and "speak the user's language."

Just to be clear, we *aren't* advocating devising a distribution on user algorithms to mimic these kinds of folk understandings and analogies—at some level, that's essentially the problem research in AI has tried to solve,

---

[2]Also, unlike AI, the seemingly hard part of the problem is *already* being solved by computers via known techniques—we have *positive examples* of good *algorithms* for usable interfaces. The only mismatch here is that the *distribution of user behavior* is not known to be easily sampleable; or, said differently, it does not seem to be an "algorithmically natural" distribution (and this is the problem faced in AI).

and it would only reduce our "hard problem" to a harder one. Instead, we advocate an examination of how these properties of the distribution are used, and whether some more algorithmically natural distributions (e.g., a size-weighted uniform distribution over decision trees) feature similar properties that can be exploited. For example, one potentially useful principle proposed by Thimbleby is, "allow users to create shortcuts"—we might hope that such a perspective could aid the development of servers that can adapt to the user. Moreover, some of these properties refer to the "task structure." It would also be worthwhile to consider, on a case-by-case basis along the lines discussed in Section 10.1.2, whether or not any of the *specific* goals for which we wish to design universal users have some kind of appropriate structure that can be exploited in a manner similar to how real-world interfaces exploit such structure.

Towards a theory of the design of usable interfaces

One direction of research in Human-Computer Interaction took a formal-methods approach – e.g., as developed in Dix's book [56] – in which design principles similar to those described above as suggested by Norman [118] or WYSIWYG ("what you see is what you get") were expressed in full formality, so that proposed systems could be rigorously and automatically verified to satisfy the principles. The hope, of course, was to automatically uncover (subtle) design flaws that might not otherwise be discovered during testing. We earlier described Abowd's model [1] for interaction; Abowd developed this model in service of his *main* contribution, which was the proposal of a specification language for the system and user interface to support the verification of these design principles. What is relevant about this direction of research for our purposes was that it considered how these design principles could be captured formally (and therefore mathematically), which in turn raises the possibility that a clean mathematical framework could be established that captures these properties of good interfaces as *theorems*. Indeed, as we have alluded to previously, following a suggestion by Gregory Abowd [2], we find that the Bayesian framework developed in Section 4.2 to capture efficient semantic communication under "similar beliefs" seems that it may (unintentionally) serve such purposes.

Recall that our main theorems about universal communicators show that safe and viable sensing with a server (from a given class) must be feasible for users to achieve a given goal with that class of servers. Suppose we interpret this statement as concerning a requirement on a user interface— this is natural and sensible, since we are considering the case of a user who doesn't already know how to use the interface we are designing, and must be prepared to cope with a variety of different potential designs. We can then recover several of the usual design principles easily from the properties of our sensing functions. First of all, the fact that the sensing function must be *safe* implies that the user must be able to easily determine that his or her goal has been achieved—bridging the "gulf of evaluation," in Norman's words [118]; the fact that the function that tells the user behavior to halt must, in particular, be a safe sensing function corresponds *precisely* to a lack of "completion errors" as discussed by Thimbleby [144]. Second, the fact that the sensing function must be *viable* implies that there must be some "mental model" (or set of rules) that allow the user to easily use the interface to accomplish any of the various tasks he or she might have in mind, thus bridging Norman's "gulf of execution." Implicitly here, we also require that the interface should, from any state, provide enough information so that this set of rules determines what the user should do next, covering several other principles concerning "visibility" and feedback. Likewise, we've taken it as a given that the goal (and hence the system to be manipulated) is "forgiving," and therefore resistant to error; the viability condition also may be interpreted as saying that moreover, recovery from *any* error can be easily accomplished, given the proper mental model of how to use the interface, and this was yet another one the principles advocated by both Norman and Thimbleby.

As we noted earlier, the basic framework of Chapter 2 alone did not capture the interface design problem satisfactorily. The richer Bayesian framework of Section 4.2 seemed to be much more appropriate, and we noted in the previous section that optimizing the performance of the server with a distribution representing "natural user behavior" would imply taking advantage of the principles of exploiting natural mappings and using affordances properly. Actually, we'll see more than this: we'll see that this optimization (essentially) implies a variety of more explicit design properties proposed by Thimbleby.

To reiterate, we assume that a goal is fixed, and that the user will use some universal strategy for that goal using the distribution of natural user behaviors (e.g., for concreteness, a user constructed using Corollary 4.10). Then the server designer's problem is

(1) Maximize the probability that the user eventually achieves his or her goal

(2) Minimize the expected running time of the user, subject to condition (1)

and we believe that *these* principles are sufficient to capture usable interfaces. Of course, Condition (1) already suggests that the server should be safe and viable with the user's sensing function, and thus feedback should be provided and completion errors avoided as described above; the interesting additional principles for the Bayesian setting are consequences of Condition (2) that we describe next.

Note that the running time of our universal user is a function of the probability that a strategy drawn from the design distribution succeeds and the expected running time of a randomly drawn user, given that it succeeds. Suppose we interpret the weight assigned to a behavior in the distribution over user behaviors as a stand-in for the "complexity" of the behavior, cf. the "length-weighted" uniform distributions over programs of Example 4.5. Then, optimizing the *probability of success* of the typical behavior from this distribution amounts to keeping the required mental model simple (relative to the available natural mappings, affordances, etc.), or perhaps more explicitly, minimizing *the length of the user manual* (which might as well be taken to be an algorithm for the user), as well as ideally allowing multiple different simple models to accomplish the same tasks. Both minimizing the length of the user manual and permitting multiple mental models to accomplish the same task – which Thimbleby calls "permissivity" – were design principles explicitly suggested by Thimbleby. Optimizing the *performance* of a typical behavior from this distribution corresponds to keeping the average cognitive load (e.g., time complexity) required of a user who operates under one of these models (at random) as low as possible, and this would roughly correspond to Norman's principle of simplifying the structure of the task. (Thimbleby also considers this principle implicitly when he suggests minimizing the lengths of sequences of user actions as one aspect of design quality.)

Now, Thimbleby *also* advocates reducing the user's *memory* requirements, which would correspond to minimizing the expected *space complexity* of (successful) behaviors drawn from this distribution as well, perhaps suggesting a revision of Condition (2) above to:

(2′) Minimize the expected t such that a universal user for the natural user strategy distribution runs in at most t steps and uses at most $\log t$ space.

The use of t and $\log t$ is of course somewhat arbitrary, but it is suggestive of the mathematically natural (and well-behaved) case of a polynomial time and logspace user strategy.[3]

Finally, Condition (2) (or 2′) also suggests the "right thing" to do if the user's goal is unachievable (something we didn't consider at any length in this thesis, since our focus was almost exclusively on *achievable* goals): namely, we want the user to halt as soon as possible and/or use as little memory as possible in this case. This is another principle proposed by Thimbleby, who states it as, "don't be rude."

So, we see that a number of the design principles for user interfaces can be obtained from the server designer's problem, where the latter has the advantage of being precisely formulated (up to the specification of a distribution of "natural user strategies," which remains variable or empirically defined). The real question and direction for future work, though, is whether or not the mathematical formulation leads to the discovery of new, interesting, and nontrivial design principles, and furthermore, whether or not these new principles stand up in practice.

---

[3]Which, in turn, may of course equivalently be described as a polynomial size two-way finite state transducer with a short effective representation, if one is more comfortable with the language of finite state machines that Thimbleby employs.

Appendix A

Background on probability

For the reader's convenience, we collect here some of the basic notions and lemmas concerning probability that are used extensively in this book. This appendix is *not* intended to be a complete introduction to probability, though.

A.1 Fundamentals of discrete probability

Recall that a probability measure or *distribution* is formally defined as a real-valued function P on subsets of a *sample space* Ω satisfying three properties:

1. *(additivity)* For disjoint subsets of Ω A and B, $P(A \cup B) = P(A) + P(B)$.

2. *(non-negativity)* For all subsets A of Ω, $P(A) \geq 0$.

3. $P(\Omega) = 1$.

When Ω is countable or finite, this is generally all that needs to be said. In more general cases (such as the set of all executions), though, the probability measure is only defined on a collection of *measurable* sets, satisfying certain properties that we recall in Section A.3.

We generally refer to a subset of Ω as an *event*, and write, e.g., $P[\cdots]$ as shorthand for $P(\{\omega \in \Omega : \cdots\})$. A (finite or infinite) family of events $\{A_1, A_2, \ldots\}$ is said to be *mutually independent* (under P) if for all subsets S of the family,

$$P\left(\bigcap_{A_i \in S} A_i\right) = \prod_{A_i \in S} P(A_i)$$

A *random variable* is a function defined on the sample space. If a random variable X is real-valued (and Ω is countable), its *expectation* under distribution P is

$$\mathbb{E}_P[X] \stackrel{\text{def}}{=} \sum_{x \in \text{range}(X)} x \cdot P[X = x]$$

B. Juba, *Universal Semantic Communication*,
DOI 10.1007/978-3-642-23297-8,
© Springer-Verlag Berlin Heidelberg 2011

Note that expectation is linear: for random variables X and Y and constants $a, b \in \mathbb{R}$, $\mathbb{E}_P[aX + bY] = a\mathbb{E}_P[X] + b\mathbb{E}_P[Y]$.

A family of random variables is said to be (mutually) independent if all families of events in which each random variable takes a fixed value are mutually independent. Note that if $\{X_i\}_{i=1}^k$ are mutually independent random variables,

$$\mathbb{E}_P\left[\prod_{i=1}^k X_i\right] = \sum_{x_1 \in \mathrm{range}(X_1)} x_1 P[X_1 = x_1] \cdots \sum_{x_k \in \mathrm{range}(X_k)} x_k P[X_k = x_k]$$

$$= \prod_{i=1}^k \mathbb{E}_P[X_i]$$

The probability of an event A conditioned on an event B is defined to be

$$P[A|B] \overset{\mathrm{def}}{=} \frac{P(A \cap B)}{P(B)}$$

and the expected value of a random variable X conditioned on an event A is defined to be

$$\mathbb{E}_P[X|A] \overset{\mathrm{def}}{=} \sum_{x \in \mathrm{range}(X)} x \cdot P[X = x|A]$$

Or, for another random variable Y, we can consider the random variable $\mathbb{E}_P[X|Y]$, which obtains value $\mathbb{E}_P[X|Y = y]$ when $Y = y$. Note that we can write

$$\mathbb{E}_P[\mathbb{E}_P[X|Y]] = \sum_{y \in \mathrm{range}(Y)} \left(\sum_{x \in \mathrm{range}(X)} x \cdot P[X = x|Y = y] \right) P[Y = y] = \mathbb{E}_P[X]$$

A.2   Inequalities

We now review the main inequalities used to reason about probabilities in this book.

A.2.1   The basics: Union Bound and Markov's Inequality

The first two inequalities are quite intuitive. We review them more for the sake of recalling terminology.

Proposition A.1 (Union bound). *For any two events A and B, $P(A \cup B) \leq P(A) + P(B)$.*

Proof Put $C = A \cap B$, and note that $P(C) \geq 0$ by nonnegativity of P. Then $A \cup B = A \setminus C \cup B \setminus C \cup C$, and furthermore, these three sets are disjoint. Likewise, $A = A \setminus C \cup C$ and $B = B \setminus C \cup C$, and these pairs of sets are also disjoint. Therefore by additivity,

$$\begin{aligned} P(A \cup B) &= P(A \setminus C) + P(B \setminus C) + P(C) \\ &\leq P(A \setminus C) + P(B \setminus C) + 2P(C) \\ &= P(A) + P(B) \quad \blacksquare \end{aligned}$$

Proposition A.2 (Markov's inequality). *Let X be a nonnegative random variable with finite expected value. Then for all $c > 0$, $P[X \geq c\mathbb{E}_P[X]] \leq 1/c$.*

Proof For convenience, we put $\lambda = c\mathbb{E}_P[X]$. So what we need to show is

$$\lambda \cdot P[X \geq \lambda] \leq \mathbb{E}_P[X]$$

Note that since X is nonnegative, we can "estimate" $\mathbb{E}_P[X]$ as

$$\mathbb{E}_P[X] = \sum_{x \in \text{range}(X)} x \cdot P[X = x] \geq \sum_{x \in \text{range}(X): x \geq \lambda} \lambda \cdot P[X = x]$$

where since for $x \neq x'$, $\{\omega : X(\omega) = x\}$ and $\{\omega : X(\omega) = x'\}$ are disjoint events, by additivity we find

$$\sum_{x \in \text{range}(X): x \geq \lambda} \lambda \cdot P[X = x] = \lambda \cdot P[X \geq \lambda]$$

and the proposition follows. $\blacksquare$

A.2.2 Tail bounds: Hoeffding's Inequality

A familiar fact from statistics is that in a large sample of independent draws of a real-valued random variable from a fixed distribution, the average value of the sample is usually close to the expected value of the random variable. While Markov's inequality implicitly gives us a means to bound the probability of seeing a sample with an average that falls far from the mean, it fails to capture the effect of the sample size.

We will show here that for a Boolean-valued ("Bernoulli") random variable, the probability that an average falls further from the mean by a fixed amount decays *exponentially* as the sample size increases. The usual application of this theorem is to amplify the correctness of a probabilistic algorithm by means of majority vote: as long as correct (Boolean) answers are obtained with probability bounded away from $1/2$ (we usually fix $2/3$ arbitrarily) then a sample of size $O(\log 1/\delta)$ suffices to obtain an answer that is correct with probability $1 - \delta$. The particular form we present here is generally credited to Hoeffding, but the technique is much older, and appears to be due to Bernstein. (The bounds are also frequently credited broadly to Chernoff.) There are numerous generalizations of this result, e.g., to *bounded* random variables, random variables with different distributions, to martingales, etc. that, although all follow from similar arguments, we will not need and so will not discuss here.

Theorem A.3 (Hoeffding's inequality). *Let $X_1, \ldots, X_m$ be independent Bernoulli random variables with parameter p. Then $\Pr\left[\frac{1}{m}\sum_{i=1}^{m} X_i > p + \delta\right] \le \exp(-2m\delta^2)$.*

Proof The key idea is that instead of considering $\frac{1}{m}\sum_{i=1}^{m} X_i$ directly, we will consider the "*moment generating function*," $\exp(t\sum_{i=1}^{m} X_i)$, and noting that $\exp(x) \ge 0$ for all x, apply Markov's inequality:

$$\Pr\left[\frac{1}{m}\sum_{i=1}^{m} X_i > p + \delta\right] = \Pr\left[\exp(t\sum_{i=1}^{m} X_i) > \exp(t \cdot m(p + \delta))\right]$$

$$\le \mathbb{E}\left[\exp(t \cdot \sum_{i=1}^{m} X_i)\right] \exp(-tm(p + \delta))$$

We now exploit the independence of the random variables. Note that since $\{X_i\}_{i=1}^{m}$ are mutually independent, so are $\{e^{X_i}\}_{i=1}^{m}$, and therefore

$$\mathbb{E}\left[\exp(t \cdot \sum_{i=1}^{m} X_i)\right] = \prod_{i=1}^{m} \mathbb{E}[e^{tX_i}]$$

But now since each X_i is a Bernoulli random variable with parameter p,

$$\prod_{i=1}^{m} \mathbb{E}[e^{tX_i}] = (p \cdot e^t + (1 - p))^m$$

Now, we choose t to minimize the bound

$$\exp(-tm(p + \delta))(p \cdot e^t + (1 - p))^m$$

which, for $p + \delta < 1$ (otherwise there is nothing to show), turns out to occur at

$$e^t = \frac{(1 - p)(p + \delta)}{p(1 - (p + \delta))}$$

Substituting this choice of t in the expression above gives a bound of

$$\left(\frac{(1 - p)(p + \delta)}{p(1 - (p + \delta))}\right)^{-m(p+\delta)} \left(p\frac{(1 - p)(p + \delta)}{p(1 - (p + \delta))} + (1 - p)\right)^m$$

which we can rewrite as

$$\exp\left[-m\left((p + \delta)\ln\frac{p + \delta}{p} + (1 - (p + \delta))\ln\frac{1 - (p + \delta)}{1 - p}\right)\right]$$

We can bound this expression as follows: put $q = p + \delta$ and note that unless $q \in (\delta, 1)$, there is nothing to prove. We now consider for an arbitrary constant c,

$$f_c(x) = q \ln \frac{q}{q - x} + (1 - q) \ln \frac{1 - q}{1 - (q - x)} - 4cx^2$$

We will examine the minima of f_c: differentiating w.r.t. x, we find

$$f_c'(x) = \frac{q}{q - x} - \frac{1 - q}{1 - (q - x)} - 8cx = x \left(\frac{1}{(q - x)(1 - (q - x))} - 8c \right)$$

So for $x \in (0, q)$, $f_c(x)$ can only attain (local) minima for $c \geq \frac{1}{2}$ since $\frac{1}{(q-x)(1-(q-x))} \geq 4$. Therefore, for $c < \frac{1}{2}$, since $f_c(0) = 0$ (and $f_c(q) \nearrow \infty$), $0 \leq f_c(x)$, and hence at $x = \delta$,

$$4c\delta^2 \leq q \ln \frac{q}{q - \delta} + (1 - q) \ln \frac{1 - q}{1 - (q - \delta)}$$

Letting $c \to 1/2$ and using this estimate in the above bound completes the proof. ■

A.3 Probability for infinite executions

Recall that a probability measure is defined with respect to a sigma-algebra that contains the sets of interest, which in our case is the set of successful executions (as well as other related sets). A *sigma-algebra* is a pair (X, Σ), where X is a set and $\Sigma \subseteq 2^X$, such that $\Sigma \neq \emptyset$ is closed under complementation and countable unions (i.e., $S \in \Sigma$ implies $X \setminus S \in \Sigma$ and $S_1, S_2, \ldots \in \Sigma$ implies $\cup_{i \in \mathbb{N}} S_i \in \Sigma$).

A.3.1 On the measurability of various sets of executions

In general (i.e., for a general referee that is not compact), the set of successful executions may not be measurable (with respect to the natural probability measure that assigns each prefix of a random execution a measure that corresponds to the probability that they occur). This follows from the fact that an arbitrary referee gives rise to an arbitrary subset of the set of all executions, whereas the set of executions is isomorphic to the set of real numbers. The compactness condition imposes a structure on the set of successful executions, and thus guarantees that this set is measurable (with respect to the natural probability measure).

The natural probability measure arises from a sigma-algebra that corresponds to all execution prefixes.

Definition A.4 (The natural probability measure of executions). For a system (E, U, S), we consider the sigma-algebra (X, Σ) such that X is the set of all possible executions of the system (E, U, S) and Σ equals the closure of the family of sets $\{E_{(i,\sigma)} : i \in \mathbb{N}, \sigma \in \Omega\}$ under complementation and countable union, where $E_{(i,\sigma)}$ denotes the set of executions $\overline{\sigma} = (\sigma_1, \sigma_2 \ldots)$ such that $\sigma_i = \sigma$. The *natural probability measure of executions*, denoted μ, is obtained by assigning each prefix of a random execution a measure that corresponds to the probability that it occurs.

Note that the mapping μ is indeed a probability measure for the foregoing sigma-algebra Σ, because it is (1) non-negative, (2) satisfies sigma-additivity (i.e., for any countable collection of pairwise disjoint sets $S_1, S_2, \ldots \in \Sigma$ it holds that $\mu(\cup_{i \in \mathbb{N}} S_i) = \sum_{i \in \mathbb{N}} \mu(S_i)$), and (3) trivially assigns measure 1 to Ω. As we shall see, for compact referees, the set of successful executions can be expressed as a countable union of sets in Σ.

Proposition A.5. *For any compact referee R, the set of successful executions is measurable with respect to the natural probability measure of executions.*

Proof Let R' be the temporal decision function associated with R (by the compactness hypothesis), and assume for simplicity that R' never assumes the value $\perp$. In this case, the set of successful executions is a countable union of the sets S_t, where S_t is the set of executions in which no failures occur after time t (i.e., $\overline{\sigma} \in S_t$ if for every $i > t$ it holds that $R'(\sigma_i) = 1$). On the other hand, S_t equals $\cap_{i>t} S'_i$, where $S'_i = \{\overline{\sigma} : R'(\sigma_i) = 1\}$ is a countable union of $E_{(i,\sigma)}$ such that $R'(\sigma) = 1$.

To handle the case that R' may assume the value $\perp$, we show that the set of executions containing no infinite runs of $\perp$ is measurable. The latter set is the complement of a countable union of the sets F_t, where F_t is the set of executions such that R' always evaluates to $\perp$ after time t (i.e., $\overline{\sigma} \in F_t$ if for every $i > t$ it holds that $R'(\sigma_i) = \perp$). On the other hand, F_t equals $\cap_{i>t} F'_i$, where $F'_i = \{\overline{\sigma} : R'(\sigma_i) = \perp\}$ is a countable union of $E_{(i,\sigma)}$ such that $R'(\sigma) = \perp$. ∎

We also remark that given a system (E, U, S) and a sensing function V, the set of executions in which the sensing function gives finitely many negative indications is also measurable by essentially the same argument.

A.3.2   The Borel-Cantelli Lemma

Often, in the study of discrete-time stochastic processes, one is interested in whether some event occurs infinitely often or only finitely many times. In particular, for our purposes, our definition of compact goals specifies that the referee's temporal decision function should only indicate failure finitely many times, so a user fails at a compact goal precisely when there are infinitely many such indications. The following standard lemma provides a convenient criterion for deciding which is the case:

Lemma A.6 (Borel-Cantelli). *Let $\{A_i\}_{i=1}^{\infty}$ be a family of events in some probability space. If $\sum_{i=1}^{\infty} \Pr[A_i]$ is finite, then with probability 1, only finitely many A_i hold. Conversely, suppose $\{A_i\}_{i=1}^{\infty}$ are mutually independent and $\sum_{i=1}^{\infty} \Pr[A_i]$ diverges to ∞; then with probability 1, infinitely many A_i hold.*

Proof Let E be the event that infinitely many A_i hold. Then, since E implies $\bigcup_{i \geq n} A_i$ holds for any $n \in \mathbb{N}$,

$$\Pr[E] \leq \Pr\left[\bigcup_{i \geq n} A_i\right] \leq \sum_{i=n}^{\infty} \Pr[A_i] \xrightarrow[n \to \infty]{} 0$$

So $\Pr[E] = 0$.

Conversely, now, since A_i are mutually independent, so are their complements $\bar{A}_i$. We note that if E fails to hold, some $\bigcap_{i=n}^{\infty} \bar{A}_i$ must hold, and thus

$$\Pr[\bar{E}] \leq \sum_{n=1}^{\infty} \Pr\left[\bigcap_{i=n}^{\infty} \bar{A}_i\right] = \sum_{n=1}^{\infty} \prod_{i=n}^{\infty} \Pr[\bar{A}_i]$$

by mutual independence of $\{\bar{A}_i\}_{i=1}^{\infty}$. Now, note that since $\sum_{i=1}^{\infty} A_i$ diverges, for any index n, we can find $N > n$ such that $\sum_{i=n}^{N} A_i \geq 1$. Noting that given the constraint $\sum_{i=n}^{N}(1 - A_i) \leq (N - n) - 1$, $\prod_{i=n}^{N}(1 - A_i)$ is then maximized when each $(1 - A_i) = 1 - \frac{1}{N-n}$,

$$\prod_{i=n}^{N}(1 - A_i) \leq \left(1 - \frac{1}{N - n}\right)^{N-n} \leq 1/e$$

and thus, since $\prod_{i=n}^{\infty} \Pr[\bar{A}_i] \leq e^{-k}$ for all k, each term is zero, and $\Pr[\bar{E}] = 0$. ∎

Appendix B

Interactive proofs

We now provide a short introduction to the theory of interactive proofs, with emphasis on the topics that are relevant to the work in this book. Although we generally assume some basic familiarity with the theory of algorithms and/or computational complexity at an undergraduate level here and throughout the book, we will strive to provide an otherwise self-contained introduction. The material presented here is important to our work for two reasons: first, it is crucial to some of the most compelling and interesting examples of universal protocols that we develop in Section 3.3 of Chapter 3; and second, it turns out that one of these examples was the original example presented in the first paper on this topic [83], summarized in Section 1.4.2 of Chapter 1. Thus, more generally, the notions of interactive proofs played an important role in motivating and guiding the development of the theory presented here.

B.1 Introduction

The notions of proof and verification have been important to theoretical computer science since the very beginning of the field, with its roots in the work by logicians such as Gödel and Church. Over the years, though, the notions of what constitutes a "proof" have changed: in the first place, the aforementioned early works introduced notions of computable functions so as to define what counted as a reasonable set of axioms, replacing the earlier informal notion of a logic. Subsequently, the introduction of the constraints of computational complexity (and in particular polynomial time verifiability) roughly coincided with the definition of NP and the development of the theory of NP-completeness in the work of Cook, Karp, and Levin in the early 1970s. Finally, motivated by some problems in the then-new theory of cryptography in the early 1980s, Goldwasser, Micali, and Rackoff [74] introduced interactive proofs, which (as the name suggests) were a more liberal notion of

B. Juba, *Universal Semantic Communication*,
DOI 10.1007/978-3-642-23297-8,
© Springer-Verlag Berlin Heidelberg 2011

"proof," that allowed a verifier to engage in a back-and-forth interaction with a prover, and (importantly) allowed the verifier to use a randomized verification strategy.[1] Another closely related notion of *"Arthur-Merlin" games* was independently introduced around the same time by Babai (and subsequently jointly with Moran) [16] in an attempt to bound the complexity of some computational problems in group theory. We will review these definitions in the present section, and see some examples.

It was later discovered in the work of Lund et al. [103] – and much to the surprise of researchers in the late 1980s – that this extension allowed for substantially greater expressive power than that possessed by the traditional NP proof systems; their exact power was identified with PSPACE (decision problems with polynomial space algorithms) shortly afterwards in the work of Shamir [134]. We will review these developments later, in Section B.2.

B.1.1   Motivation and definitions

The key notions of interactive proof systems can be motivated as richer analogues of the older notions of NP proof systems. We begin with the following view of NP:

Definition B.1 (NP proof system). A set $S \subseteq \{0,1\}^*$ is said to be in *NP* if there is a polynomial time *verification algorithm* V and a polynomial p such that

- *Completeness:* For every $x \in S$ of length n, there is a *witness* $w \in \{0,1\}^*$ of length at most $p(n)$ such that $V(x,w) = 1$.

- *Soundness:* For every $x \notin S$ of length n, for every $w \in \{0,1\}^*$ of length up to $p(n)$, $V(x,w) = 0$.

In other words, we may think of S as a set of *theorems*, which possesses an NP proof system if there are proofs of all theorems in S ("completeness") and only theorems in S ("soundness"), where a string w is said to constitute a "proof" of a theorem x if and only if $V(x,w) = 1$.

The following problem will serve as a running example illustrating our notions:

Example B.2 (Graph Isomorphism). A (directed) *graph* is given by a pair, (V, E) where V is a set of *vertices* and $E \subseteq V \times V$ is a set of *edges*. Now, two graphs (V_1, E_1) and (V_2, E_2) are said to be *isomorphic* if there exists a bijection $\phi : V_1 \to V_2$ such that $(u,v) \in E_1$ if and only if $(\phi(u), \phi(v)) \in E_2$. Note that in this case, the vertex sets must have the same size, and we can consider them to be labeled by the integers $1, \ldots, n$. Under this simplification,

---

[1]Yet another notion of *probabilistically checkable proofs* that focused on the use of randomization to minimize the number of bits read in a static proof was subsequently introduced in the 1990s and revolutionized the study of approximation algorithms, but we will not review this work here.

the graphs are isomorphic if and only if there is a permutation π on $1, \ldots, n$ such that $(i, j) \in E_1$ if and only if $(\pi(i), \pi(j)) \in E_2$.

Now, the *graph isomorphism* problem is: given a pair of edge sets E_1 and E_2 on vertex set $\{1, \ldots, n\}$ (given as a pair of $n \times n$ matrices), are these graphs isomorphic?

Naturally this problem is in NP: we can write any permutation on $\{1, \ldots, n\}$ as a table using $O(n \log n)$ bits. Now, our verification algorithm on input (E_1, E_2) and a table for a candidate permutation π simply loops over each pair of vertices (u, v), looks up the corresponding values of $\pi(u)$ and $\pi(v)$, and checks that the (u, v)-entry of E_1 matches the $(\pi(u), \pi(v))$ entry of E_2. The algorithm accepts if and only if every entry matches. Of course, the graphs are isomorphic if and only if some such table exists, and so we see that the graph isomorphism problem is in NP.

Interaction is introduced in the following way: we think of x as a claim proposed by a "prover" to a skeptical "verifier." In support of this claim, the prover sends a string w of length at most $p(n)$ as a proof; the verifier then runs the algorithm V on x and w to decide whether or not to accept the prover's claim. Thus, the prover and verifier engage in a simple "one round interaction" (i.e., the prover only sends a single message to the verifier). We could consider the generalization of the notion of an NP proof system to *multiple* rounds of interaction as follows. A *deterministic strategy* is a function from a communication history $(m_1, m_2, \ldots, m_\ell)$ and a common input x to either a new message $m_{\ell+1}$ or an *accept/reject* verdict.

Definition B.3 (Multi-round NP proof system). A pair of deterministic strategies (P, V) are a *multi-round NP proof system* for a set S if there is a polynomial p such that for every x of length n, there is an algorithm for V that runs in at most $p(n)$ steps in total before reaching a verdict, and furthermore

- *Completeness:* For every $x \in S$, in the interaction between P and V on common input x in which P sends the odd-numbered messages and V sends the even-numbered messages, V accepts.

- *Soundness:* For every $x \notin S$ and every prover strategy $\tilde{P}$, in the interaction between $\tilde{P}$ and V on common input x in which $\tilde{P}$ sends the odd-numbered messages and V sends the even-numbered messages, V rejects.

Note that the lengths of the prover's messages are implicitly bounded by the verifier's running time: if the prover sends a very long message (longer than $p(n)$ bits), the verifier does not have time to read it all, so a shorter message produces an identical outcome.

Naturally, the one-round interactions we described above are captured as a special case of this definition, so such proof systems exist for all of NP. It turns out, though, that this definition yields *no* additional power: given a multi-round NP proof system (P, V) for a set S, consider a verification algorithm V' that on input $(x, m_1, m_2, \ldots, m_\ell)$ accepts if and only if

1. For each even-numbered message $i = 2, 4, 6, \ldots, \ell - 1$,
$m_i = V(x, m_1, \ldots, m_{i-1})$.

2. $V(x, m_1, \ldots, m_\ell)$ produces an *accept* verdict.

It is not hard to see that V' also runs in polynomial time, and furthermore, $x \in S$ if and only if there is some (polynomial length) message history $(m_1, m_2, \ldots, m_\ell)$ that causes V' to accept.

The only change from Definition B.3 that we need to make in order to arrive at our final definition is that we allow the verifier's strategy to be *randomized*. That is, we give the verifier an additional private, random input $r \in \{0, 1\}^{p(n)}$ (on inputs of length n for an appropriate polynomial p). Of course, in order for the randomization to be able to provide any advantage, we also allow the verifier some probability of error. In this context, it is surprising that it does turn out to yield a *substantial* advantage.

Definition B.4 (Interactive proof system). A pair (P, V) is a *interactive proof system* for a set S if there is a polynomial p such that V is a randomized strategy that, on private input x, runs in at most $p(n)$ steps in total before reaching a verdict, and furthermore,

- *Completeness:* For every $x \in S$, in the interaction between P and V on common input x in which P sends the odd-numbered messages and V sends the even-numbered messages, V accepts with probability at least $2/3$.

- *Soundness:* For every $x \notin S$ and every prover strategy $\tilde{P}$, in the interaction between $\tilde{P}$ and V on common input x in which $\tilde{P}$ sends the odd-numbered messages and V sends the even-numbered messages, V rejects with probability at least $2/3$.

The choice of $2/3$ is of course arbitrary, and using Hoeffding's inequality, it can be amplified to any $1 - \epsilon$ in time $\text{poly}(n, \log 1/\epsilon)$ by repeating the protocol $O(\log 1/\epsilon)$ times and taking a majority vote to determine the verifier's final verdict.

Public-coin versus private-coin

Note that the verifier is provided coin tosses as a private, auxiliary input. We could also think of the verifier as being described by a randomized algorithm that tosses coins as needed, in an on-line fashion. Now, a *public-coin* proof system is one in which the verifier's coin tosses during a round are provided to the prover on the following round. (When we want to make the distinction clear, we refer to the usual interactive proof systems as *private-coin*.) Note that in a public-coin proof system, there is no need for the verifier to compute a message: since the prover also knows all of the verifier's inputs, the prover can compute the verifier's state on its own, and in particular could reconstruct any messages that the verifier would compute from these inputs. This is essentially the definition of *Arthur-Merlin games* as introduced by Babai and Moran [16].

Although it intuitively seems like public coin interactive proof systems are much weaker than private coin proof systems, we will see in Section B.2 that – at least with respect to *time-bounded* verifiers as considered here[2] – they are no less powerful, and every problem with a private coin interactive proof system has a public coin interactive proof system.

B.1.2 Example: Interactive proofs for Graph Non-Isomorphism

We saw, in Example B.2, that the graph isomorphism problem is in NP. Whether or not the graph *non*-isomorphism problem is also in NP (i.e., whether or not the graph isomorphism problem is in "*co*-NP") is a longstanding open question in complexity theory. Although there are some simple cases in which one can give a short proof – e.g., if the graphs have vertices with different degrees – at present, no one knows a *general* strategy for giving a short proof that graphs are not isomorphic. But, it turns out that a short *interactive* proof is possible.

Example B.5 (Interactive proof system for graph non-isomorphism [71]). Consider the following protocol: on common input (E_1, E_2), the verifier chooses $i \in \{1, 2\}$ and a permutation π uniformly at random. Then:

1. The verifier sends $\pi(E_i)$ (i.e., a matrix with $(\pi(i), \pi(j))$th entry equal to the (i, j)th entry of E_i) to the prover.

2. The prover sends $j \in \{1, 2\}$ to the verifier.

3. The verifier accepts if $i = j$ and rejects otherwise.

Now, if the graphs are not isomorphic, for every pair of permutations (π, π') $\pi(E_1) \neq \pi'(E_2)$ (since otherwise we could obtain an isomorphism) and therefore the prover can identify i by searching for a permutation π such that $\pi(E_i)$ equals the graph sent by the verifier. Thus, the prover can make the verifier accept with probability 1.

On the other hand, if the graphs *are* isomorphic, then there is some permutation π' such that $\pi'(E_1) = E_2$. Moreover, for a uniformly random

---

[2]The distinction is important: we could consider proof systems with weaker verifiers, say polynomial time and logspace bounded. Then the work of Condon [48] shows that private-coin proof systems exist for the same class of languages having *polynomial time* (i.e., and unrestricted space) verifiers, whereas Condon and Ladner [49] show that public-coin interactive proof systems with polynomial time and logspace verifiers can only exist for sets that can be decided in polynomial time.

permutation π, the distribution of $\pi \circ \pi'$ and π is identical. Therefore, *when the graphs are isomorphic*, the distribution of the graphs sent by the verifier in the first round is independent of the random choice of i, and so the prover has at most a 50-50 chance of guessing i, so the verifier rejects with probability at least $1/2$.

Thus, if the verifier repeats the above protocol twice and rejects if the prover fails to identify i correctly either time, the verifier still accepts non-isomorphic graphs with probability 1, and rejects isomorphic graphs with probability at least $3/4$, as needed.

B.1.3 The complexity of the prover

In our definition of an interactive proof system, we explicitly did not restrict the complexity of the prover. Naturally, this is so because if the prover could be implemented in probabilistic polynomial time (say), then the entire interaction between the prover and verifier could be simulated in probabilistic polynomial time, i.e., the set would belong to BPP. More generally, if the prover strategy could be computed within some complexity class $\mathcal{C}$ closed under probabilistic polynomial time reductions, then the set S captured by the proof system must be computable in $\mathcal{C}$.

Still, it is natural to consider just how powerful the prover strategy needs to be. In particular, it is natural to consider whether the prover needs to be substantially more powerful than this minimal requirement of being able to compute membership in S. This latter question is closely related to a classic question about the relationship between the search and decision versions of NP.

In slightly more detail, recall that we defined NP in terms of a verification algorithm that took two inputs, a string x for which we wanted to prove membership in S, and a witness w that served as the proof of membership in x. For many problems in NP, one is really interested not just in deciding whether or not $x \in S$, but actually *finding* a witness. (Theorem-proving is just one natural example.) This is referred to as an *NP search problem* associated with S, whereas the usual notion is the *decision problem*. A natural question associated with problems in NP is whether or not one can use an algorithm for solving the decision problem to solve an associated search problem—a *"search-to-decision" reduction*. Consider:

Example B.6 (Search-to-decision reduction for graph isomorphism). We first note that given a subroutine for deciding graph isomorphism, we can solve the problem of deciding whether or not a partial mapping $\pi : \{1, \ldots, v\} \to \{1, \ldots, n\}$ can be extended to an isomorphism of graphs with edge sets E_1 and E_2. We can accomplish this by constructing new graphs E_1' and E_2' on $(v + 1)n + v(v + 1)/2$ vertices with the following structure: E_1' is constructed from E_1 by introducing $n + i - 1$ vertices all attached to vertex i for $i = 1, \ldots, v$, creating an $n + i$ clique containing i, and E_2' is similarly constructed from E_2 by introducing $n + i - 1$ vertices all attached to vertex $\pi(i)$. We then simply test whether or not E_1' and E_2' are isomorphic.

We claim that π can be extended to an isomorphism taking E_1 to E_2 if and only if E_1' and E_2' define isomorphic graphs. Of course, given an isomorphism taking E_1 to E_2 that extends π, we can easily construct an isomorphism taking E_1' to E_2' by pairing up vertices in the cliques appropriately; it thus only remains to show that we can extract an isomorphism extending π from an isomorphism ϕ taking E_1' to E_2'. Towards this end, first note that no $n + v$-clique can appear in either E_1 or E_2, and since the cliques attached to $1, \ldots, v-1$ and $\pi(1), \ldots, \pi(v-1)$ respectively are only attached to one vertex in the graph, there is only one $n + v$ clique in each of E_1' and E_2', so ϕ must take the vertices of one $n + v$ clique to the other. It now follows by induction that, given that the cliques of size $n + i + 1, \ldots, n + v$ must be matched up by ϕ, and since no $n + i$ cliques appear anywhere else in E_1' or E_2', the $n + i$ cliques containing vertex i and $\pi(i)$ respectively must be paired up in ϕ. We therefore see that if i and $\pi(i)$ are not isolated, $\phi(i) = \pi(i)$ (and if i and $\pi(i)$ are isolated, we can easily find ϕ' that does satisfy this condition). Thus, since ϕ defines an isomorphism on the original n vertices of E_1' and E_2' that takes i to $\pi(i)$, π can be extended to the restriction of ϕ taking E_1 to E_2. We finally note that these graphs are at most quadratically larger than the original input, so this is a polynomial time reduction.

Now that we have this subroutine, an algorithm for finding an isomorphism is easy: for each vertex $v = 1, \ldots, n$ of the first graph, the algorithm first checks that the graphs are isomorphic, and then searches for a vertex u_v in the second graph such that the mapping π that takes $\pi(1) = u_1, \ldots, \pi(v) = u_v$ can be extended to an isomorphism (using the above subroutine). The algorithm then returns the mapping that takes i to u_i as its isomorphism.

Correctness is now easy: since the empty mapping can be extended to an isomorphism given that the graphs are isomorphic, we have that in each vth vertex, there is some isomorphism π' such that for each $v' < v$, $\pi(v') = \pi'(v')$. Of course, now, for $u_v = \pi'(v)$, if we put $\pi(v) = u_v$, we still have that π can be extended to π', so some choice of u_v exists. Finally, we note that once $u_1, \ldots, u_n$ have all been fixed, the mapping that takes i to u_i can only be "extended to an isomorphism" if it is an isomorphism, so the algorithm indeed returns an isomorphism.

Recalling that the prover's messages are essentially analogous to the witness in an NP proof system (cf. the connection between an NP proof system and the multi-round NP proof system given in Definition B.3) the analogous question in this case is whether or not the prover's messages can be generated using a subroutine for the decision version of the problem. This is precisely the definition introduced by Bellare and Goldwasser [21]:

Definition B.7 (Competitive interactive proof system). A pair of strategies $(P^{(\cdot)}, V)$ is a *competitive interactive proof system* for a set S if

- *Competitive prover:* $P^{(\cdot)}$ is a probabilistic polynomial time strategy given an oracle for S.[3]

- (P^S, V) is an interactive proof system for S.

Naturally, NP proof systems with a search-to-decision reduction are a special case of competitive interactive proof systems—and hence, as a consequence of Example B.6, graph isomorphism has a competitive interactive proof system. But now, note that in our proof system for graph non-isomorphism as given in Example B.5, the prover's strategy only requires querying an oracle for graph (non-)isomorphism to compute each one-bit response. Therefore, the interactive proof system we described for graph non-isomorphism is also a competitive interactive proof system, and one for a problem which is not known to belong to NP (let alone possess a search-to-decision reduction in any sense). In Section 3.3 of Chapter 3, we see that competitive interactive proof systems play a key role in characterizing the kinds of computational problems for which we can construct universal user protocols. Moreover, in Section 5.5 of Chapter 5, we generalize the notion of competitive interactive proofs to other classes of algorithms (i.e., we consider prover strategies belonging to other classes of algorithms), and find that analogously, these generalized competitive interactive proofs give characterizations of the computational problems for which universal users satisfying various resource bounds can be constructed.

B.2   Interactive proofs for PSPACE

We now turn to reviewing the algebraic techniques that utilize the full power of interactive proofs, allowing us to construct proof systems for arbitrary polynomial space computations with a time-efficient verifier, which plays a key role in the results of Section 3.3 in Chapter 3 The present section will develop the polynomial encodings used by the proof system, culminating in a presentation of the proof system for polynomial space computations.

Prerequisites.   In addition to some basic comfort with algorithms, as indicated above, we need some (minimal) undergraduate knowledge of algebra. Recall that a *field* is a set closed under associative addition and multiplication operations that satisfy a distributive law, with the additional ability to subtract and divide (except by zero). The basic fact that underlies everything that follows is that a nonzero polynomial of degree d over any field has at most d roots (since $d + 1$ points uniquely determine the coefficients of a polynomial). The reader interested in a more detailed development and algorithms for performing basic arithmetic over (finite) fields is encouraged to consult the textbook by Shoup [140].

---

[3]Recall that "given oracle access to a function f" simply means that we allow the algorithm to call a "subroutine" for f at the cost of one computation step.

B.2.1 Polynomial encodings

Our main technique for constructing interactive proofs will be the use of a polynomial encoding to reduce the verification of many values to a single "interpolated point" that is highly likely to witness any discrepancy in the claimed values. More precisely, we consider a polynomial interpolated through a list of claimed values; now, because two polynomials of a bounded degree d cannot agree on more than d points without being identical, as long as the size of our domain is large enough relative to the degree, it will be enough to check the value of this polynomial at a single (randomly chosen) point.[4]

More precisely, a basic kind of polynomial encoding is the following:

Definition B.8 (Low-degree extensions). Let $\mathbb{F}_q$ be the finite field of size q, and let $H \subseteq \mathbb{F}_q$ For any function $f : H^m \to \mathbb{F}_q$, the *low-degree extension* of f, denoted $\tilde{f}$, is an m-variate polynomial $p : \mathbb{F}_q^m \to \mathbb{F}_q$ of degree $|H| - 1$ in each variable such that on $z \in H$, $p(z) = f(z)$.

Another kind of specialized polynomial encoding of a function, obtained by "arithmetizing" a formula, is postponed until the next section.

Before we get ahead of ourselves, we need to establish that the low-degree extensions exist. Naturally, they do, as we can construct them by familiar polynomial interpolation. Moreover, this observation allows us to (space-) efficiently *evaluate* the low-degree extension. We will assume that arithmetic over $\mathbb{F}_q$ can be carried out in time poly$(\log q)$ and space $O(\log q)$; for a suitable representation of $\mathbb{F}_q$, this is true (see, e.g., Shoup's book [140] for details).[5]

Proposition B.9 (Computing Low-Degree Extensions). *Low-degree extensions exist. Moreover, the low-degree extension of a function f can be computed deterministically in space $O(m \log |H| + \log q)$ and time* poly$(|H|^m, \log q)$ *given (oracle) access to f.*

Proof Let $H \subseteq \mathbb{F}_q$ be given. For any $z \in H$, consider the polynomials

$$\delta_z(x) = \prod_{y \in H \setminus \{z\}} (z - y)^{-1}(x - y)$$

---

[4]That is, in the language of error-correcting codes, the key property is that distinct encodings have "high distance," i.e., they are a good error-correcting code. It is therefore satisfying that Meir [112] has established that the use of polynomials is not essential here, and that any (linear) code can be used as the fundamental building block for the development of this section. We opted not to present the results in such terms for several reasons: first, the adaptation comes at the cost of complicating the protocol somewhat; second, this would have required that we introduce the less-familiar terminology of error-correcting codes at this point; and third, the simplest constructions of error-correcting codes for our purposes would be precisely the polynomial encodings we are presently introducing.

[5]Fields of the form $q = 2^k$ or q prime are particularly convenient to use. The former have a convenient representation as polynomials over the Boolean field $\mathbb{F}_2$ modulo any irreducible polynomial over $\mathbb{F}_2$ of degree k, with sums and products given by the usual sums and products of polynomials. The latter is essentially integer arithmetic modulo q.

Note that δ_z has degree $|H|-1$ and can be evaluated in space $O(\log q+\log |H|)$ and time $\mathrm{poly}(|H|,\log q)$. By construction, it satisfies $\delta_z(z) = 1$, and for each $y \in H$ such that $y \neq z$, $\delta_z(y) = 0$.

Now, for our target function $f(x_1,\ldots,x_m)$, consider the function

$$\tilde{f}(x_1,\ldots,x_m) = \sum_{(z_1,\ldots,z_m)\in H^m} f(z_1,\ldots,z_m) \cdot \prod_{i=1}^{m} \delta_{z_i}(x_i)$$

$\tilde{f}$ has degree $|H| - 1$ in each variable, and is easily verified to agree with f on H^m by construction. Thus, a low-degree extension of any function f that may be evaluated in space $O(\log q + m \log |H|)$ and time $\mathrm{poly}(|H|^m, \log q)$ (modulo the cost of computing f) exists. ∎

The basic property of polynomial encodings alluded to above is that, for fixed m or ℓ, they are not only unique, but moreover differ in many places (if q is sufficiently large).

Lemma B.10 (Schwartz-Zippel). *Let p be a nonzero m-variate polynomial over $\mathbb{F}_q$ of degree at most $d \leq q$. Then the probability that p evaluates to 0 at a uniformly chosen $z \in \mathbb{F}_q$ is at most md/q.*

Proof We proceed by induction on m. For $m = 0$, a nonzero polynomial is a nonzero constant, that evaluates to 0 with probability 0. Now, for $m \geq 1$, we can repeatedly divide x_m out of p to obtain

$$p(x_1,\ldots,x_m) = \sum_{i=0}^{d} x_m^i \cdot p_i(x_1,\ldots,x_{m-1})$$

Suppose $(z_1,\ldots,z_m)$ are chosen uniformly at random. Now, as p is a nonzero polynomial, some p_i must be a nonzero $m - 1$-variate polynomial, and so by the induction hypothesis, $p_i(z_1,\ldots,z_{m-1}) = 0$ with probability at most $(m - 1)d/q$. Thus, the polynomial

$$q(x_m) = p(z_1,\ldots,z_{m-1},x_m)$$

is a univariate nonzero degree-d polynomial in x_m. Since q has at most d roots, for a uniformly chosen $z_m \in \mathbb{F}_q$, $q(z_m) = 0$ with probability at most d/q. A union bound therefore gives that p evaluates to zero with probability at most $(m - 1)d/q + d/q = md/q$ as claimed. ∎

Precisely, given distinct degree-d polynomials p and q, the Schwartz-Zippel Lemma applied to the polynomial $(p - q)$ – which is also of degree at most d – demonstrates that p and q differ in "most" places.

B.2.2 Arithmetization

In the previous section, we introduced polynomial encodings, and in particular, the "low-degree extension" of a function. Our protocol for PSPACE will be built from a different kind of polynomial encoding of a function, one obtained from a formula—roughly, we re-interpret the Boolean operations as operations over a larger field that agree with the original interpretations on 0 and 1 as elements in the larger field.

More precisely now, suppose we are given a Boolean formula φ over variables $x_1, \ldots, x_m$, inductively built from the the operations $\{\neg, \wedge\}$ (recall that this is a complete basis; we can, e.g., express "OR" via de Morgan's laws). The arithmetization of φ, denoted $\tilde{\varphi}$, is defined by induction on the structure of φ:

$$x_i \mapsto x_i \in \mathbb{F}_q[x_1, \ldots, x_m] \text{ (i.e., as a polynomial over } \mathbb{F}_q)$$
$$\neg\psi \mapsto (1 - \tilde{\psi})$$
$$\phi \wedge \psi \mapsto \tilde{\phi} \cdot \tilde{\psi}$$

Note that it follows by induction on the construction of $\tilde{\varphi}$ that for any Boolean assignment $(z_1, \ldots, z_m) \in \{0, 1\}^m$ to $(x_1, \ldots, x_m)$ (abusing notation and identifying $0, 1 \in \mathbb{F}_q$ with the Boolean field elements),

$$\varphi(z_1, \ldots, z_m) = 1 \Rightarrow \tilde{\varphi}(z_1, \ldots, z_m) = 1$$
$$\varphi(z_1, \ldots, z_m) = 0 \Rightarrow \tilde{\varphi}(z_1, \ldots, z_m) = 0$$

so $\tilde{\varphi}$ is a "polynomial encoding" of the function represented by φ, though not necessarily the same as the "low-degree extension"—the difference between a polynomial that we obtain from arithmetization and the low-degree encoding of a function is that in general, we may obtain a polynomial of higher degree from arithmetization. The degree of $\tilde{\varphi}$ in each variable is easily seen to be equal to the number of occurrences of that variable in φ; the size of the formula gives a convenient upper bound on the degrees for our purposes.

The advantage of arithmetizing a formula over a low-degree extension for the present purposes is that we can evaluate the polynomial encoding obtained via arithmetization *much* more efficiently—any standard algorithm for formula evaluation can be adapted to an algorithm that evaluates the arithmetization of a formula at any desired point in time polynomial in the length of the formula and the size of the field elements (i.e., $\text{poly}(|\varphi|, \log q)$—compare this with the $\text{poly}(2^m, \log q)$ running time of our algorithm for computing the low-degree extension over $H = \{0, 1\}$).

B.2.3 The Sum-Check protocol

The basic Sum-Check protocol, developed in the work of Lund, Fortnow, Karloff, and Nisan [103], provides an efficient proof system for claims of the form

$$\sum_{(z_1,\ldots,z_m)\in H^m} p(z_1,\ldots,z_m) = r$$

for a polynomial p over $\mathbb{F}_q$, $H \subseteq \mathbb{F}_q$, and $r \in \mathbb{F}_q$. It is useful in situations where H^m is (exponentially) large, but the verifier can efficiently evaluate p at arbitrary points in $\mathbb{F}_q^m$ (e.g., when p is obtained by arithmetization). It is not hard to see how such a protocol provides a proof system for counting the number of solutions to a Boolean formula, and we will describe such a proof system at the end of this section—historically, this was significant since it showed that interactive proofs were *much* more expressive than the traditional paradigm.

The protocol itself is quite simple: the variables summed over are eliminated one at a time, and a claim about a sum over the elements of H^i (i.e., in a polynomial with i variables) is reduced to a claim about the sum over the elements of H^{i-1} in the remaining $i-1$ variables. The "magic step" is that the Prover provides a polynomial in the ith variable that is claimed to represent the sums over H^{i-1}; since the degree of this polynomial is bounded, it suffices for the Verifier to check this polynomial at a *single* random point for the ith variable, as opposed to needing to check it for each setting of the ith variable from H. Therefore, in a sense, the work needed to verify the claim in the straightforward way decreases exponentially in the number of rounds—after the final round, when all m variables are eliminated, the Verifier only needs to evaluate the polynomial at a single point, instead of at every point in H^m.

Protocol B.11 (Sum-Check). On common input polynomial $p(x_1,\ldots,x_m)$ (of degree at most d in each variable), $H \subseteq \mathbb{F}_q$, and $r = r_m \in \mathbb{F}_q$

1. For $i = m, m-1, \ldots, 1$, repeat the following:

    (a) Prover: Send degree-d polynomial

    $$q_i(x_i) = \sum_{(z_1,\ldots,z_{i-1})\in H^{i-1}} p(z_1,\ldots,z_{i-1},x_i,y_{i+1},\ldots,y_m)$$

    to Verifier.

    (b) Verifier: Check $\sum_{z\in H} q_i(z) = r_i$; *reject* if not.

    (c) Verifier: Choose $y_i \in \mathbb{F}_q$ uniformly at random, and send it to the Prover. Set $r_{i-1} = q_i(y_i)$.

2. Verifier: Check that $p(y_1,\ldots,y_m) = r_0$; *accept* if so and *reject* otherwise.

We won't comment on the running time of the verifier presently. It generally depends on the difficulty of evaluating p, and is otherwise seen to be $\mathrm{poly}(m,d,|H|,\log q)$.

The analysis of the basic Sum-Check protocol is likewise delightfully simple; it is not much more sophisticated than the proof of the Schwartz-Zippel Lemma.

Lemma B.12 (Analysis of basic Sum-Check). *The Sum-Check protocol is an interactive proof system for claims of the form*

$$\sum_{(z_1,\ldots,z_m)\in H^m} p(z_1,\ldots,z_m) = r$$

with perfect completeness and soundness $1 - md/q$.

Proof We first note that perfect completeness follows from the fact that if the Prover follows the protocol, then in each ith round,

$$\sum_{z\in H} q_i(z) = \sum_{z\in H}\sum_{(z_1,\ldots,z_{i-1})H^{i-1}} p(z_1,\ldots,z_{i-1},z,y_{i+1},\ldots,y_m) = r_i$$

and in particular, after the final round we likewise obtain $p(y_1,\ldots,y_m) = r_0$, so the Verifier accepts.

We analyze the soundness by induction on the round $j = 0,\ldots,m-1$ ($i = m - j$): we claim that if

$$\sum_{(z_1,\ldots,z_m)\in H^m} p(z_1,\ldots,z_m) \neq r$$

then after the first $j = m - i$ rounds, either the Verifier rejects or

$$\sum_{(z_1,\ldots,z_i)H^i} p(z_1,\ldots,z_i,y_{i+1},\ldots,y_m) \neq r_i$$

with probability at least $1 - jd/q$. Note that after all m rounds, this implies that the Verifier rejects with probability at least $1 - md/q$, establishing the soundness of the proof system.

For $j = 0$, the claim is trivial. Thus, supposing it holds for $j - 1$, at round j we find that either the Prover sends a degree-d polynomial q_i such that

$$\sum_{z\in H} q_i(z) \neq r_i$$

in which case, the Verifier rejects immediately, or else

$$\sum_{z\in H} q_i(z) = r_i \neq \sum_{(z_1,\ldots,z_i)H^i} p(z_1,\ldots,z_i,y_{i+1},\ldots,y_m)$$

where in the latter case, it must be that the degree-d polynomial $q_i(x_i)$ is distinct from

$$\sum_{(z_1,\ldots,z_{i-1})H^{i-1}} p(z_1,\ldots,z_{i-1},x_i,y_{i+1},\ldots,y_m)$$

as a (degree-d) polynomial in x_i over $\mathbb{F}_q$. Therefore, we know that q_i agrees
with the above polynomial in at most d locations, and so the probability over
a random y_i that they agree is at most d/q. A union bound therefore gives
that the probability that

$$\sum_{(z_1,\ldots,z_{i-1})H^{i-1}} p(z_1,\ldots,z_{i-1},y_i,\ldots,y_m) \neq r_{i-1}$$

is at least $1 - (j-1)d/q - d/q = 1 - jd/q$, as needed. ∎

Interactive proofs for counting solutions

As an application (and a warm-up to the protocol for PSPACE) we now show
how to apply the Sum-Check protocol to obtain a proof system for claims
concerning the number of satisfying assignments to a Boolean formula.[6] The
protocol is again simple: given a Boolean formula φ over m variables, we apply Sum-Check to $H = \{0,1\}$ and the arithmetization $\tilde{\varphi}$ (taking q sufficiently
large). It will follow immediately from our work in the previous sections that
the result is an efficient proof system. Moreover, it turns out that this is a
competitive interactive proof system – i.e., that the *Prover* likewise has an
efficient implementation, given the ability to count the number of solutions
to a Boolean formula – which is significant in the context of Section 3.3.4
in Chapter 3. (It then follows from Theorem 3.12 that there is a universal
user for counting the number of solutions to a formula in the basic universal
setting.)

Theorem B.13 (LFKN protocol for counting solutions). *There is a competitive interactive proof system for claims of the form "φ has r solutions"
for a Boolean formula φ and $r \in \mathbb{N}$, with perfect completeness and soundness
$1 - \epsilon$, with a verifier running in time* $\mathrm{poly}(|\varphi|, \log 1/\epsilon)$.

Sketch of proof On input φ over m variables, r, and ϵ, the Prover will pro-
vide a prime number q such that $q > \max\{2^m, m|\varphi|/\epsilon\}$ and $q \leq \max\{2^{m+1}, 2m|\varphi|/\epsilon\}$—such a prime exists by Bertrand's Postulate, and can be veri-
fied to be prime by the Verifier using any standard primality test, see e.g.,
Shoup [140] for details. If $r > 2^m$, the Verifier rejects immediately.

We now run the Sum-Check protocol on inputs $\tilde{\varphi}$ (over $\mathbb{F}_q$), $H = \{0,1\}$,
$d = |\varphi|$, and r (recall that $\mathbb{F}_q$ for q prime is arithmetic modulo q). Note that
since $\tilde{\varphi}$ agrees with φ on $\{0,1\}^m$,

$$\sum_{(z_1,\ldots,z_m)\in\{0,1\}^m} \varphi(z_1,\ldots,z_m) = \sum_{(z_1,\ldots,z_m)\in\{0,1\}^m} \tilde{\varphi}(z_1,\ldots,z_m)$$

---

[6]This is usually stated as a proof system for "#P," the class of functions $\{0,1\}^* \to \mathbb{N}$
definable as the number of accepting paths of a non-deterministic polynomial time Turing
machine on input $x \in \{0,1\}^*$—it is a corollary of Cook's proof of the NP-completeness
of SAT (the usual proof) that counting satisfying assignments is "#P-complete" under
polynomial time reductions.

and $\tilde{\varphi}$ has degree at most $|\varphi|$ in each variable, so Lemma B.12 establishes that (i) if φ has r solutions and the Prover follows the protocol, the Verifier accepts in the Sum-Check protocol with probability 1 and (ii) if φ does not have r solutions, then the Verifier rejects in the Sum-Check protocol with probability at least

$$1 - md/q \geq 1 - \frac{m|\varphi|}{m|\varphi|/\epsilon} = 1 - \epsilon$$

by our choice of q. So we indeed have a proof system with the desired soundness and completeness.

All that remains is to consider the efficiency of the protocols. We note that there exist primality tests running in time $\mathrm{poly}(\log q)$, and on each iteration of the protocol, the Verifier is only evaluating a degree-$|\varphi|$ polynomial at two points and computing the sum, which can be done in time $\mathrm{poly}(|\varphi|, \log q)$, and choosing a random point in $\mathbb{F}_q$, which can be done in $O(\log q)$ (expected) time. Finally, the Verifier only needs to evaluate $\tilde{\varphi}$ at the point $(y_1, \ldots, y_m)$, which as we noted, can be done using a simple modification of standard formula evaluation algorithms in time $\mathrm{poly}(|\varphi|, \log q)$. Since $\log q \leq \max\{m, \log m + \log |\varphi| + \log 1/\epsilon\}$ by our choice of q, the Verifier is as efficient as claimed.

The Prover, by contrast, needs to choose the prime q and compute the polynomial $q_i(x_i)$ in each ith round. For the first task, note that if the Prover can compute the number of solutions to arbitrary Boolean formulas, the Prover can (in particular) use the search-to-decision reduction for SAT to find satisfying assignments to Boolean formulas. Therefore, applying Cook's reduction to a primality testing algorithm, the Prover can easily obtain a prime number in the desired range.

For the second task, given φ and $y_{i+1}, \ldots, y_m$, consider a non-deterministic Turing machine that, on input $x \in \mathbb{F}_q$, guesses $z_1, \ldots, z_{i-1} \in \{0,1\}^{i-1}$, and evaluates $\tilde{\varphi}(z_1, \ldots, z_{i-1}, x, y_{i+1}, \ldots, y_m) = s \in \mathbb{F}_q$. The machine then non-deterministically guesses a $\log q$-bit integer, and accepts iff the number guessed is at least s. Note that, for a given setting of $z_1, \ldots, z_{i-1}$, the machine has s accepting paths in the last part, and so overall, on input x, the machine has

$$\sum_{(z_1, \ldots, z_{i-1}) \in \{0,1\}^{i-1}} \tilde{\varphi}(z_1, \ldots, z_{i-1}, x, y_{i+1}, \ldots, y_m) = q_i(x)$$

accepting paths and runs in time $\mathrm{poly}(|\varphi|, \log q)$. Thus, using Cook's reduction, we can obtain a formula from this machine that has precisely so many accepting paths in polynomial time (in $|\varphi|$ and $\log q$). The prover can therefore compute the polynomial needed for each iteration of the protocol by evaluating this reduction at $|\varphi|$ points and interpolating the results over $\mathbb{F}_q$. ∎

B.2.4   Interactive proofs for Quantified Boolean Formula validity

Given a polynomial time Verifier protocol, it is not too difficult to construct a polynomial space algorithm for computing an "optimal" Prover strategy (i.e., one with which the Verifier is maximally likely to accept)—such a construction is essentially reviewed in the proof of Proposition 3.11 in Chapter 3, since it establishes that an optimal prover strategy reduces to any PSPACE-complete problem, which is a key ingredient in the construction of a universal user. The significance of the above observation to computational complexity theory more broadly, though, is that it establishes that every set with an interactive proof system can be decided by a polynomial space algorithm.

The work of Lund, Fortnow, Karloff and Nisan [103], reviewed in the previous sections, presented the Sum-Check protocol, and demonstrated that interactive proofs were far more powerful than had been previously suspected—prior to their work, it had been assumed that interactive proofs only existed for sets "slightly beyond" NP. Shortly thereafter, Shamir [134] extended their work to obtain an interactive proof system for a PSPACE-complete problem – Quantified Boolean Formula validity – establishing a tight characterization of the power of interactive proofs in terms of space complexity:

Theorem B.14 (Shamir's Theorem). IP = PSPACE

Several proofs of this theorem appear in the literature; in addition to Shamir's original proof [134], a simpler proof due to Shen [137] appeared shortly afterwards, and another proof due to Meir [112] employs arbitrary (linear) error-correcting codes instead of polynomial encodings as its basic building block. In the interest of appealing to the broadest possible audience, we will review Shen's proof.

Degree reduction operation

The basic idea underlying both Shamir's protocol and Shen's protocol is that we would like to extend our definition of arithmetization to quantified formulas, e.g., by taking $\forall x \varphi(x, y) \mapsto \tilde{\varphi}(0, y) \cdot \tilde{\varphi}(1, y)$, and then proving that the arithmetized formula evaluates to 1 using a variant of the Sum-Check protocol. The problem with this naïve approach is, of course, that the degree in the free variables (y, in the case of $\tilde{\varphi}(0, y) \cdot \tilde{\varphi}(1, y)$) doubles with each quantifier, so the potential number of points of agreement between distinct polynomial encodings doubles with each quantifier, potentially growing exponentially in the size of the formula. Since we can't afford to work with an exponentially larger field (the representations of our field elements are already polynomially large) we need an alternative approach. Shamir's original approach was to convert the formula into a special form in which variables did not appear unquantified too many times (so the degrees remained bounded). Shen's approach, on the other hand, was to introduce a *degree reduction operation* on the arithmetized formula.

Recall that for our polynomial encodings, the only crucial point is that the polynomial over the larger field should agree with the original formula when evaluated on an assignment to the free variables from $\{0,1\}^m$. Bearing this in mind, observe that the transformation

$$\tilde{\varphi}(x, y, \ldots) \mapsto x \cdot \tilde{\varphi}(1, y, \ldots) + (1 - x) \cdot \tilde{\varphi}(0, y, \ldots)$$

yields a polynomial that agrees with $\tilde{\varphi}$ whenever x is evaluated at 0 or 1, but is linear in x. If we apply this operation to the free variables after each quantifier, the degrees remain low, so polynomial encodings over a moderately large field remain useful.

On the other hand, the Verifier cannot apply the degree reduction operation on its own (note that computing the result of m degree reduction operations in the straightforward way involves evaluating $\tilde{\varphi}$ in 2^m points). We can ask the Prover to provide the result of the degree reduction operation, but recall that the Prover could cheat. Still, as long as the degrees remain low, we can use another polynomial encoding trick to reduce the evaluation of the degree reduction operation to the verification of a claim about the value of the resulting polynomial at a new, random point—again, since the degrees are low, if the polynomials are distinct, they will not agree at a random point with high probability.

Shen's protocol for quantified Boolean formulas

For convenience, we will start by defining the sequence of polynomials that the (honest) Prover sends during the course of Shen's protocol. For a quantified Boolean formula φ given in prenex normal form, with m quantifiers and no free variables (i.e., of the form $Q_1 x_1 \cdots Q_m x_m \phi(x_1, \ldots, x_m)$ where each $Q_i \in \{\exists, \forall\}$ and ϕ is a quantifier-free Boolean formula) we will inductively define the following sequence of reduced arithmetizations as follows.

- *(Base)* $\tilde{\varphi}_{m,m}(x_1, \ldots, x_m)$ is the earlier arithmetization of the quantifier-free portion, $\phi(x_1, \ldots, x_m)$.

- *(Degree reduction)* Given $\tilde{\varphi}_{i,j+1}(x_1, \ldots, x_i)$, $\tilde{\varphi}_{i,j}(x_1, \ldots, x_i)$ is the result of the degree reduction operation applied to x_j in $\tilde{\varphi}_{i,j+1}$:

$$\tilde{\varphi}_{i,j}(x_1, \ldots, x_i) = x_j \cdot \tilde{\varphi}_{i,j+1}(x_1, \ldots, x_{j-1}, 1, x_{j+1}, \ldots, x_i) +$$
$$(1 - x_j) \cdot \tilde{\varphi}_{i,j+1}(x_1, \ldots, x_{j-1}, 0, x_{j+1}, \ldots, x_i)$$

- *(Quantifier binding)* Given $\tilde{\varphi}_{i+1,1}(x_1, \ldots, x_{i+1})$, if $Q_i = \forall$, then

$$\tilde{\varphi}_{i,i}(x_1, \ldots, x_i) = \tilde{\varphi}_{i+1,1}(x_1, \ldots, x_i, 0) \cdot \tilde{\varphi}_{i+1,1}(x_1, \ldots, x_i, 1)$$

and likewise if $Q_i = \exists$,

$$\tilde{\varphi}_{i,i}(x_1, \ldots, x_i) = 1 - (1 - \tilde{\varphi}_{i+1,1}(x_1, \ldots, x_i, 0)) \cdot (1 - \tilde{\varphi}_{i+1,1}(x_1, \ldots, x_i, 1))$$

Note that $\tilde{\varphi}_{0,0}$ is a constant; $\tilde{\varphi}_{0,0} = 1$ if φ evaluates to 1, and $\tilde{\varphi}_{0,0} = 0$ otherwise.

Note that we have numbered the indices in reverse. In Shen's protocol, a claim about each $\tilde{\varphi}_{i,j}$ will be considered in order, "undoing" one of these operations (quantifier binding or degree reduction) in each iteration, until we are left with a claim about the basic arithmetization of the quantifier-free formula ϕ, which the Verifier can evaluate on its own.

Protocol B.15 (Shen's QBF protocol). On common input ϵ, a quantified Boolean formula φ given in prenex normal form, with m quantifiers and no free variables and a claim $r_{0,0} \in \{0, 1\}$:

1. *(Choosing a prime)* Prover: send a prime q such that $q > 2|\varphi|^2/\epsilon$ and $q \leq 4|\varphi|^2/\epsilon$.

2. Verifier: *reject* if q is not prime or not in the desired range.

3. For $i = 1, \ldots, m$ repeat the following:

   (a) *(Remove ith quantifier)* Prover: send the linear function in x,
   $$p_{i,0}(x) = \tilde{\varphi}_{i,1}(y_{1,i-1}, \ldots, y_{i-1,i-1}, x).$$

   (b) Verifier: if $Q_i = \forall$, check that $p_{i,0}(0) \cdot p_{i,0}(1) = r_{i-1,i-1}$ or else (if $Q_i = \exists$), that $1 - (1 - p_{i,0}(0)) \cdot (1 - p_{i,0}(1)) = r_{i-1,i-1}$ and *reject* if not.

   (c) Verifier: Choose $y_{i,i-1} \in \mathbb{F}_q$ uniformly at random, and send it to the Prover. Set $r_{i,0} = p_{i,0}(y_{i,i-1})$.

   (d) *(Undo degree reduction)* For $j = 1, \ldots, i$ repeat the following:

      i. Prover: send the polynomial in x_j,
      $$p_{i,j}(x_j) = \tilde{\varphi}_{i,j}(y_{1,i}, \ldots, y_{j-1,i}, x_j, y_{j+1,i-1}, \ldots, y_{i,i-1})$$

      ii. Verifier: if $i < m$, check that $p_{i,j}$ has degree at most 2 in x_j, and otherwise, that $p_{i,j}$ has degree at most $|\varphi|$, and *reject* if not. Check that $y_{j,i-1} \cdot p_{i,j}(1) + (1 - y_{j,i-1}) \cdot p_{i,j}(0) = r_{i,j-1}$ and *reject* if not.

      iii. Verifier: choose $y_{j,i} \in \mathbb{F}_q$ uniformly at random, and send it to the Prover. Set $r_{i,j} = p_{i,j}(y_{j,i})$.

4. Verifier: check if $\tilde{\phi}(y_1, \ldots, y_m) = r_{m,m}$, and *reject* if not. Otherwise, *accept*.

Analysis

Shamir's Theorem essentially follows from an analysis of a protocol for evaluating quantified Boolean formulas. For our purposes, the relevant statement is the following:

Theorem B.16 (Analysis of Shen's proof system for QBF). *Shen's QBF protocol is a public-coin proof system for claims of the form "$\varphi = r$" where φ is a quantified Boolean formula in prenex normal form with no free variables and $r \in \{0, 1\}$ with perfect completeness and soundness $1 - \epsilon$. The running time of the verifier is* $\mathrm{poly}(|\varphi|, \log 1/\epsilon)$.

Proof The fact that Shen's protocol is public coin follows by inspection: the verifier only chooses random $y_{i,j}$, which are all sent to the Prover. Likewise, it is easily verified that the proof system has perfect completeness, since the sequence of polynomials $\tilde{\varphi}_{i,j}(x_1, \ldots, x_i)$ for $i = 0, \ldots, m$ and $j = 1, \ldots, i$ are defined to satisfy each of the verifier's checks.

In particular, note that $\tilde{\varphi}_{i,1}(x_1, \ldots, x_i)$, as the result of applying the degree reduction to each variable of $\tilde{\varphi}_{i,i}$, is linear in each variable, and for $i < m$, $j = 1, \ldots, i$, $\tilde{\varphi}_{i,j}(x_1, \ldots, x_i)$ has degree 2 in variables $x_1, \ldots, x_{j-1}$, and is linear in $x_j, \ldots, x_i$. For $i = m$, $\tilde{\varphi}_{m,j}(x_1, \ldots, x_m)$ is the result of applying degree reduction operations to $\tilde{\varphi}_{m,m}(x_1, \ldots, x_m) = \tilde{\phi}(x_1, \ldots, x_m)$, i.e., the standard arithmetization of the quantifier-free portion, $\phi(x_1, \ldots, x_m)$. As we noted earlier, ϕ has degree at most $|\varphi|$ in each variable, and so $\tilde{\varphi}_{m,j}$ has degree at most $|\varphi|$ in $x_1, \ldots, x_{j-1}$ and is linear in $x_j, \ldots, x_m$. Note that the Verifier explicitly checks that the polynomial $p_{i,j}$ sent by the prover is either linear in x_i if $j = 0$, quadratic in x_j (if $i < m$ and $j \geq 1$) or at most $|\varphi|$ (if $i = m$ and $j \geq 1$).

Bearing this in mind, we can now argue by induction on the round that if the proof system starts with a false claim, at each round, either the Verifier rejects, or a new false claim is passed to the next round.

Claim B.17. *Suppose $\tilde{\varphi} \neq r_{0,0}$. Then for $i < m$, with probability at least $1 - \left(\frac{i(i-1)}{2} + j + 1\right)\frac{1}{q}$, either the Verifier rejects or*

$$\tilde{\varphi}_{i,j}(y_{1,i}, \ldots, y_{j,i}, y_{j+1,i-1}, \ldots, y_{i,i-1}) \neq r_{i,j}$$

and similarly, for $i = m$, for all $j = 0, \ldots, m$, either the Verifier rejects or

$$\tilde{\varphi}_{m,j}(y_{1,m}, \ldots, y_{j,m}, y_{j+1,m-1}, \ldots, y_{m,m-1}) \neq r_{m,j}$$

with probability at least $1 - \left(\frac{m(m-1)}{2} + 1 + j|\varphi|\right)\frac{1}{q}$.

Proof By induction on the round; for $(i, j) = (0, 0)$, the claim is trivial. For the induction step, there are two main cases, depending on whether $j = 0$ (removing a quantifier) or $j \geq 1$ (degree reduction on index j).

We will argue the $j = 0$ case first. Thus, we suppose we have established that either the verifier has rejected or else with probability at least $1 - \frac{(i-1)i}{2q}$

$$\tilde{\varphi}_{i-1,i-1}(y_{1,i-1}, \ldots, y_{i-1,i-1}) \neq r_{i-1,i-1}.$$

Now, the prover sends a linear function $p_{i,0}$; notice that if

$$p_{i,0}(x) = \tilde{\varphi}_{i,0}(y_{1,i-1}, \ldots, y_{i-1,i-1}, x),$$

then the formula fails the Verifier's check since either $Q_i = \forall$ and

$$\tilde{\varphi}_{i,0}(y_{1,i-1}, \ldots, y_{i-1,i-1}, 0) \cdot$$
$$\tilde{\varphi}_{i,0}(y_{1,i-1}, \ldots, y_{i-1,i-1}, 1) = \tilde{\varphi}_{i-1,i-1}(y_{1,i-1}, \ldots, y_{i-1,i-1})$$
$$\neq r_{i-1,i-1}$$

or similarly $Q_i = \exists$ and

$$1 - (1 - \tilde{\varphi}_{i,0}(y_{1,i-1}, \ldots, y_{i-1,i-1}, 0)) \cdot$$
$$(1 - \tilde{\varphi}_{i,0}(y_{1,i-1}, \ldots, y_{i-1,i-1}, 1)) = \tilde{\varphi}_{i-1,i-1}(y_{1,i-1}, \ldots, y_{i-1,i-1})$$
$$\neq r_{i-1,i-1}$$

so regardless of Q_i, either the Verifier rejects immediately or

$$p_{i,0} \neq \tilde{\varphi}_{i,0}(y_{1,i-1}, \ldots, y_{i-1,i-1}, \cdot),$$

where these are both linear functions. Thus, for a random $y_{i,i-1} \in \mathbb{F}_q$, the probability that

$$p_{i,0}(y_{i,i-1}) = \tilde{\varphi}_{i,0}(y_{1,i-1}, \ldots, y_{i-1,i-1}, y_{i,i-1})$$

is at most $1/q$. Recalling that $r_{i,0}$ is fixed to be $p_{i,0}$, we therefore conclude by a union bound that

$$r_{i,0} \neq \tilde{\varphi}_{i,0}(y_{1,i-1}, \ldots, y_{i,i-1})$$

with probability at least $1 - \left(\frac{i(i-1)}{2} + 1\right)\frac{1}{q}$.

It thus remains to consider the $j \geq 1$ (degree reduction) case. Here, there are two nearly identical subcases depending on whether $i < m$ or $i = m$. In either case we have

$$\tilde{\varphi}_{i,j-1}(y_{1,i}, \ldots, y_{j-1,i}, y_{j,i-1}, \ldots, y_{i,i-1}) \neq r_{i,j-1}$$

with probability either at least $1 - \left(\frac{i(i-1)}{2} + (j-1) + 1\right)\frac{1}{q}$ (if $i < m$) or at least $1 - \left(\frac{m(m-1)}{2} + 1 + (j-1)|\varphi|\right)\frac{1}{q}$ (if $i = m$).

In either case the Prover sends a polynomial $p_{i,j}$ such that either

$$p_{i,j}(x) = \tilde{\varphi}_{i,j}(y_{1,i}, x, y_{j+1,i-1}, \ldots, y_{i,i-1})$$

in which case,

$$y_{j,i-1}p_{i,j}(1) + (1 - y_{j,i-1})p_{i,j}(0) = p_{i,j-1}(y_{1,i}, \ldots, y_{j-1,i}, y_{j,i-1}, \ldots, y_{i,i-1})$$
$$\neq r_{i,j-1}$$

so the Verifier rejects immediately, or else $p_{i,j}$ is not equal to

$$\tilde{\varphi}_{i,j}(y_{1,i}, x, y_{j+1,i-1}, \ldots, y_{i,i-1}).$$

If $i < m$, both polynomials are quadratic, and if $i = m$, both polynomials have degree at most $|\varphi|$. Thus, for a random choice of $y_{i,j} \in \mathbb{F}_q$, a union bound gives

$$\tilde{\varphi}_{i,j}(y_{1,i}, \ldots, y_{j,i}, y_{j+1,i-1}, \ldots, y_{i,i-1}) \neq r_{i,j}$$

with probabiltiy at least $1 - \left(\frac{i(i-1)}{2} + j + 1 \right) \frac{1}{q}$ in the former subcase and at least $1 - \left(\frac{m(m-1)}{2} + 1 + j|\varphi| \right) \frac{1}{q}$ in the latter, as needed. $\blacksquare$

After the final round, if $\tilde{\varphi}_{m,m}(y_{1,m}, \ldots, y_{m,m}) \neq r_{m,m}$, then the Verifier rejects in the final step after evaluating

$$\tilde{\phi}(y_{1,m}, \ldots, y_{m,m}) = \tilde{\varphi}_{m,m}(y_{1,m}, \ldots, y_{m,m})$$

since the final check fails. Thus, the Verifier rejects with probability at least $1 - \left(\frac{m(m-1)}{2} + m|\varphi| + 1 \right) \frac{1}{q}$. Now, since $m \leq |\varphi|$ and $q > 2|\varphi|^2/\epsilon$, this is at least $1 - \epsilon$, so the proof system is $1 - \epsilon$ sound.

All that remains is to examine the Verifier's running time; we recall that the arithmetization of ϕ can be evaluated at an arbitrary point in time $\mathrm{poly}(|\phi|, \log q) = \mathrm{poly}(|\varphi|, \log 1/\epsilon)$. Otherwise, in each of the $\mathrm{poly}(|\varphi|)$ rounds, the Verifier is merely evaluating a constant number of polynomials of degree at most $|\varphi|$ at a constant number of points, each of which can be done in time $\mathrm{poly}(|\varphi|, \log q) = \mathrm{poly}(|\varphi|, \log 1/\epsilon)$, as needed. Finally, we again note that the primality test can be performed in $\mathrm{poly}(\log q) = \mathrm{poly}(|\varphi|, \log 1/\epsilon)$ time, so the Verifier's overall complexity is indeed $\mathrm{poly}(|\varphi|, \log 1/\epsilon)$, as claimed. $\blacksquare$

Appendix C

Game theory

In this book, we occasionally invoke theorems that, although frequently invoked in general theoretical computer science, are properly understood as being "game-theoretic." The two main examples, which we state and prove in this appendix, are a corollary to von Neumann's Min-max Theorem due to Loomis [102] and an *algorithm* for playing repeated games due to Auer et al. [10] that allows us to obtain good performance in the setting of Chapter 9.

It turns out, however, that one can obtain a proof of the Min-max Theorem (and Loomis' corollary) using a simpler version of the algorithm of Auer et al. mentioned above (this proof is actually due to Freund and Schapire [61], in earlier work). Thus, in a sense, we obtain the Min-max Theorem as a corollary of our development of the algorithm, in Section C.1.3. So, the basic version of the algorithm of Freund and Schapire is presented and analyzed in Section C.1.2; we then show how to extend it to the more demanding setting considered by Auer et al. in Section C.2.

C.1 Zero-sum games and the Min-max Theorem

C.1.1 Definitions

A *zero-sum* game is given by a pair of *strategy* sets, R and C, and a *payoff* matrix (function) $\mathbb{R}^{R \times C}$. The interpretation is that there is a game between two players, a *row player* who chooses a strategy $r \in R$ and a *column player* who chooses a strategy $c \in C$. Then, if the game has payoff matrix M, the players simultaneously make a choice from their respective strategy sets, and the row player obtains reward $M(r, c)$ while the column player obtains reward $-M(r, c)$. Naturally, each player wishes to maximize his or her own reward. From this perspective, it does not change the game if all entries in M are shifted by a fixed constant since this changes the outcome of the game by a

B. Juba, *Universal Semantic Communication*,
DOI 10.1007/978-3-642-23297-8,
© Springer-Verlag Berlin Heidelberg 2011

fixed amount, independent of the player's choices, and likewise, it does not change the game if the entries in M are scaled by any positive constant. Thus, in the case of a bounded game, we can without loss of generality henceforth take the payoffs to lie in the interval $[0, 1]$.

In game theory, it is standard to consider *mixed strategies*, which are simply distributions over the respective strategy sets of the players. The interpretation is that each player simultaneously and independently samples a strategy from their respective strategy sets according to the distributions, and obtains a payoff as before. The payoff for a pair of mixed strategies (P, Q) is then the expected value of M under this (product) distribution given by P and Q on $R \times C$; we will denote this as $M(P, Q)$. We refer to the mixed strategies that have a single strategy in their support as *pure strategies*, and (slightly abusing notation) also denote them by the strategy that appears in their support. (Note that this agrees with the earlier notation.)

In the following sections, we will focus on *repeated games*. That is, we initially fix a payoff matrix M, and then hold an infinite sequence of rounds, $t = 1, 2, 3, \ldots$. In each round t,

1. Based on the mixed strategies selected in rounds $1, \ldots, t-1$, the row player chooses a mixed strategy P_t.

2. Based on P_t in addition to the outcomes of prior rounds, the column player responds with a mixed strategy Q_t.

3. The players receive payoff $M(P_t, Q_t)$ and $-M(P_t, Q_t)$, respectively.

As stated, it seems as though unlike in the previous set-up where the players must move independently and simultaneously, the column player is at an advantage in this repeated game setting. The Min-max Theorem (reviewed in Section C.1.3), however, will show that there is no such advantage to "going second." In fact, in the next section, we will see an explicit strategy for the row player that obtains payoffs that are arbitrarily close to those that could have been obtained by "going second," from which the Min-max Theorem will follow easily.

C.1.2 Basic multiplicative weights strategy

Freund and Schapire [61] considered the following simple algorithm for playing a repeated game.

Algorithm C.1 (Multiplicative weights). Let an input parameter $\eta > 0$ be given. Let P_1 be the uniform distribution over R. On round $t = 1, 2, 3, \ldots$:

1. Play P_t.

2. After learning Q_t, compute the normalizing factor

$$Z_t = \sum_{r \in R} P_t(r) \exp(\eta M(r, Q_t)),$$

and then choose P_{t+1} so that for each $r \in R$,

$$P_{t+1}(r) = P_t(r) \cdot \frac{\exp(\eta M(r, Q_t))}{Z_t}$$

η is a "learning rate" parameter, and (as we will see in Corollary C.4) controls the ultimate payoff achieved by the algorithm. This simple algorithm is surprisingly good:

Theorem C.2 (Basic multiplicative weights achieves good payoffs [61]). *Let M be a zero-sum game with payoffs in $[0,1]$ and R finite. Then, after T rounds of Algorithm C.1,*

$$\sum_{t=1}^{T} M(P_t, Q_t) \ge a_\eta \max_P \sum_{t=1}^{T} M(P, Q_t) - c_\eta \ln |R|$$

for constants $a_\eta = \frac{\eta}{e^\eta - 1}$ and $c_\eta = \frac{1}{e^\eta - 1}$.

Note that we don't even need to assume C is finite (as long as $M(r, Q_t)$ is given to us somehow)—the bound on the payoffs guarantees $M(r, Q_t)$ is also bounded.

Its analysis will depend on the *Kullback-Leibler divergence*, which for a pair of discrete distributions P and Q defined on a common sample space ω is given by

$$KL(P\|Q) \stackrel{\text{def}}{=} \sum_{\omega \in \Omega} P(\omega) \ln \left(\frac{P(\omega)}{Q(\omega)} \right)$$

In slightly more detail, we can analyze the algorithm by using the KL-divergence of the proposed distribution in round t, P_t, from the optimal distribution as a potential function. Precisely, we use the following lemma:

Lemma C.3. *For any distributions $\tilde{P}$ and $Q_1, \ldots, Q_t$, the distributions $P_1, \ldots, P_{t+1}$ computed by Algorithm C.1 satisfy the following:*

$$KL(\tilde{P}\|P_t) - KL(\tilde{P}\|P_{t+1}) \ge \eta M(\tilde{P}, Q_t) - (e^\eta - 1)M(P_t, Q_t)$$

Proof By definition of KL-divergence, we first find

$$KL(\tilde{P}\|P_t) - KL(\tilde{P}\|P_{t+1}) = \sum_{r \in R} \tilde{P}(r) \ln \frac{\tilde{P}(r)}{P_t(r)} - \sum_{r \in R} \tilde{P}(r) \ln \frac{\tilde{P}(r)}{P_{t+1}(r)}$$

$$= \sum_{r \in R} \tilde{P}(r) \ln \frac{P_{t+1}(r)}{P_t(r)}$$

which, by the update rule of Algorithm C.1, equals

$$\sum_{r \in R} \tilde{P}(r)(\eta M(r, Q_t) - \ln Z_t) = \eta \sum_{r \in R} \tilde{P}(r)M(r, Q_t) - \ln Z_t = \eta M(\tilde{P}, Q_t) - \ln Z_t$$

Now, note that since $e^{\eta x} \leq 1 - (1 - e^{\eta})x$ for all η and $x \in [0, 1]$,

$$
\begin{aligned}
Z_t &= \sum_{r \in R} P_t(r) \exp(\eta M(r, Q_t)) \\
&\leq \sum_{r \in R} P_t(r)(1 - (1 - e^{\eta})M(r, Q_t)) \\
&= 1 - (1 - e^{\eta})M(P_t, Q_t)
\end{aligned}
$$

and then, since $\ln(1 - x) \leq -x$ for $x < 1$, $\ln Z_t \leq -(1 - e^{\eta})M(P_t, Q_t)$. So, putting everything together, we find

$$
KL(\tilde{P}\|P_t) - KL(\tilde{P}\|P_{t+1}) \geq \eta M(\tilde{P}, Q_t) - (e^{\eta} - 1)M(P_t, Q_t) \ \blacksquare
$$

With Lemma C.3 in hand, the proof of Theorem C.2 is easy:
Proof (of Theorem C.2) First note that for any distribution $\tilde{P}$,

$$
\sum_{t=1}^{T} \left(KL(\tilde{P}\|P_t) - KL(\tilde{P}\|P_{t+1}) \right) = KL(\tilde{P}\|P_1) - KL(\tilde{P}\|P_{T+1}) \leq \ln|R| - 0
$$

since P_1 is uniform over R and the KL-divergence is always nonnegative.

But now, also, Lemma C.3 gives that the sum of $KL(\tilde{P}\|P_t) - KL(\tilde{P}\|P_{t+1})$ over $t = 1, \ldots, T$ is at least

$$
\sum_{t=1}^{T} \left(\eta M(\tilde{P}, Q_t) + (1 - e^{\eta})M(P_t, Q_t) \right)
$$

and so therefore

$$
(e^{\eta} - 1) \sum_{t=1}^{T} M(P_t, Q_t) \geq \eta \sum_{t=1}^{T} M(\tilde{P}, Q_t) - \ln|R|
$$

Since this inequality holds for *every* distribution $\tilde{P}$, the theorem follows. (Note the maximum is achieved since R is finite.) $\blacksquare$

We now observe that for a *fixed* time horizon T, by choosing an appropriate η, Algorithm C.1 can approach the payoff achieved by the best mixed strategy:

Corollary C.4. *Using Algorithm C.1 with* $\eta = \log\left(1 + \sqrt{\frac{\ln|R|}{T}}\right)$ *for T rounds gives average reward at least*

$$
\frac{1}{T} \max_{P} \sum_{t=1}^{T} M(P, Q_t) - 2\sqrt{\frac{\ln|R|}{T}}
$$

Proof Note that $\eta \geq \frac{e^\eta - 1}{e^\eta}$ for $\eta > 0$. Therefore, the average payoff obtained by Algorithm C.1 is at least

$$\frac{e^{-\eta}}{T} \max_P \sum_{t=1}^{T} M(P, Q_t) - \frac{1}{e^\eta - 1} \frac{\ln |R|}{T}$$

which for our choice of η, we see is equal to

$$\frac{1}{T} \max_P \sum_{t=1}^{T} M(P, Q_t) - \frac{\sqrt{\ln |R|/T}}{1 + \sqrt{\ln |R|/T}} \geq \frac{1}{T} \max_P \sum_{t=1}^{T} M(P, Q_t) - \sqrt{\frac{\ln |R|}{T}}$$

Noting that $M(P, Q_t) \leq 1$ for all t and $\sqrt{\ln |R|/T} \geq 0$ gives the claimed bound. ∎

C.1.3 The Min-max Theorem and Loomis' Corollary

Recall that informally, the Min-max Theorem says that in a zero-sum game, there is no harm in going first. Intuitively, we will be able to show this by demonstrating that Algorithm C.1 allows us to *compute* an arbitrarily good strategy. There are many proofs of the Min-max Theorem, and this one is due to Freund and Schapire [61].

Theorem C.5 (Min-max). *For any zero-sum game M with bounded payoffs and R finite,*

$$\inf_Q \max_P M(P, Q) = \max_P \inf_Q M(P, Q)$$

Proof $\inf_Q \max_P M(P, Q) \geq \max_P \inf_Q M(P, Q)$ follows by noting that for any fixed choice of mixed strategy Q^*, $\max_P M(P, Q^*) \geq \max_P \inf_Q M(P, Q)$, since whatever P^* one considers for the RHS, the choice of Q^* is still available.

We thus need to show $\inf_Q \max_P M(P, Q) \leq \max_P \inf_Q M(P, Q)$. WLOG, we begin by rescaling the payoffs to the range $[0, 1]$. Fix any $\delta, \epsilon > 0$; for T_ϵ specified below, suppose we use Algorithm C.1 with the choice of η given in Corollary C.4 against a δ-optimal opponent, i.e., one who plays Q_t such that

$$M(P_t, Q_t) \leq \inf_Q M(P_t, Q) + \delta$$

in round t. Put $\bar{P} = \frac{1}{T_\epsilon} \sum_{t=1}^{T} P_t$. Now,

$$\max_P \inf_Q M(P, Q) \geq \inf_Q M(\bar{P}, Q) = \frac{1}{T_\epsilon} \inf_Q \sum_{t=1}^{T_\epsilon} M(P_t, Q) \geq \frac{1}{T_\epsilon} \sum_{t=1}^{T_\epsilon} \inf_Q M(P_t, Q)$$

which, by choice of Q_t, is at least $\frac{1}{T_\epsilon}\sum_{t=1}^{T_\epsilon}(M(P_t,Q_t)-\delta)$, i.e., the average payoff achieved by Algorithm C.1 up to some δ additional loss. Corollary C.4 shows that for our choice of η, this is in turn at least

$$\frac{1}{T_\epsilon}\max_P \sum_{t=1}^{T_\epsilon} M(P,Q_t) - 2\sqrt{\frac{\ln|R|}{T_\epsilon}} - \delta$$

which, for $\bar{Q}=\frac{1}{T_\epsilon}\sum_{t=1}^{T_\epsilon} Q_t$, equals

$$\max_P M(P,\bar{Q}) - 2\sqrt{\frac{\ln|R|}{T_\epsilon}} - \delta \geq \inf_Q \max_P M(P,Q) - 2\sqrt{\frac{\ln|R|}{T_\epsilon}} - \delta$$

Picking $T_\epsilon = \frac{4\ln|R|}{\epsilon^2}$ thus shows

$$\max_P \inf_Q M(P,Q) \geq \inf_Q \max_P M(P,Q) - \epsilon - \delta$$

and letting $\epsilon, \delta \to 0$ finishes the proof. ■

What we actually need, in Chapter 4, is the following corollary due to Loomis [102] which essentially says that another equality holds when the second player is forced to play a pure strategy:

Corollary C.6 (Loomis [102]). *For a zero-sum game M with bounded payoffs and R finite,*

$$\max_P \inf_{c\in C} M(P,c) = \inf_Q \max_{r\in R} M(r,Q)$$

Proof We observe that, for any Q^*, in the support of *any* response P^* there is some r^* such that $M(r^*,Q^*) \geq M(P^*,Q^*)$. Of course, the pure strategies r^* are also available as choices for P, so $\max_P M(P,Q^*) = \max_{r\in R} M(r,Q^*)$ and then since this equality holds for all choices of Q^*,

$$\inf_Q \max_{r\in R} M(r,Q) = \inf_Q \max_P M(P,Q)$$

By a similar argument, we also find $\max_P \inf_{c\in C} M(P,c) = \max_P \inf_Q M(P,Q)$, and thus the claim follows directly from the Min-max theorem. ■

C.2   Nonstochastic bandits: games with exploration

In the previous section, we saw how a very simple multiplicative weights algorithm (Algorithm C.1) could learn how to play *any* zero-sum game with a finite number of strategies nearly optimally. Next, we'll see how a related algorithm can allow us to compute good strategies in a much harsher setting, in which *only the payoff for the chosen strategy is revealed*, known as the *"multi-armed bandit"* problem.[1]

We will still allow the opponent's strategy to depend arbitrarily on the history of actions (and our algorithm). We will not focus on zero-sum games, however, and so our measure of quality will not be the "value" of the game; rather, we will focus on matching the payoff achieved by the best (pure) strategy in hindsight.[2] More generally, we will describe an algorithm due to Auer et al. [10] with a good reward bound that holds with arbitrarily high probability after a sufficient amount of time. We use this algorithm to learn a good protocol from unreliable (or "noisy") feedback in Chapter 9.

We will present the algorithm in two stages. The first stage, presented in Section C.2.1, describes the crucial adaptation of the multiplicative weights algorithm to allow it to compute *optimistic estimates* of the rewards provided by the various strategies in the bandit setting, in a sense reducing the problem to the more tractable case considered in the previous section. Unfortunately, due to the complications introduced into the algorithm, the analysis will no longer be so clean.

Subsequently, we will present a standard trick – restarting the algorithm with successively longer time horizons – to obtain an algorithm that performs well without a time horizon (e.g., in contrast to Corollary C.4, which showed how to choose a parameter for the basic multiplicative weights algorithm for a fixed time horizon). This will yield the final algorithm.

C.2.1   Estimating the reward in the bandit setting

The main twist in the bandit setting is the lack of information available to the algorithm about the quality of its alternatives: the algorithm is only allowed to play one strategy on each round, and only learns the reward obtained by the chosen strategy. Nevertheless, it turns out that it is possible to compute sufficiently good estimates for the quality of the options available to the algorithm to be able to perform well over time. As before, the algorithm will play a mixed strategy on each round, choosing each strategy r with probability $p_r(t)$ in round t. Our estimates $\hat{x}_r(t)$ for the reward that strategy r would obtain in round t are given by $\hat{x}_r(t) = x_r(t)/p_r(t)$ where $x_r(t)$ is the reward obtained by strategy r in round t *if the algorithm actually played strategy r in round t* and $\hat{x}_r(t) = 0$ otherwise. Note that we can compute $\hat{x}_r(t)$ for all r and t, and that this is an *unbiased* estimate of the reward

---

[1] Colloquially, a slot machine is sometimes referred to as a "one-armed bandit." The name is meant to be evocative of the problem faced by a gambler in a casino featuring many slot machines.

[2] Incidentally, it is not hard to show that approaching this measure implies that we also match the value of the game when the game is zero-sum.

obtained by strategy r in round t, i.e.,

$$\mathbb{E}_P[\hat{x}_r(t)] = p_r(t) \cdot \frac{x_r(t)}{p_r(t)} + (1 - p_r(t)) \cdot 0 = x_r(t)$$

(since the choice of r from P in round t is independent of the opponent's choices yielding the payoffs $x_1(t), \ldots, x_R(t)$).

The only catch now is that the estimates may have (arbitrarily) high variance. We first need to ensure that P gives sufficiently high weight to each strategy r to obtain a good estimate, which is accomplished by letting P be a mixture of the distribution given by the weights (e.g., along the lines of the basic multiplicative weights algorithm, Algorithm C.1) and the uniform distribution. These estimates still have variance that is too high for a good "high probability" bound on the algorithm's performance to hold, though. So furthermore, instead of a precise estimate, the algorithm adds a slack term proportional to $1/p_r(t)$ and uses these overestimates of the reward on each round. These estimates have the property that (for an appropriate choice of constant) when summed over all rounds for a fixed strategy, they are (close to) an upper bound on the total reward that strategy would have obtained with high probability; in this sense, they give *"upper confidence bounds."* Precisely:

Lemma C.7 (Upper confidence bounds). *For any $\alpha \in [\sqrt{\log(R/\delta)/RT}, 1]$*

$$\Pr\left[\exists r : \sum_{t=1}^{T} (\hat{x}_r(t) + \alpha/p_r(t)) + \alpha RT < \sum_{t=1}^{T} x_r(t) \right] \le \delta$$

Our algorithm will achieve total reward close to the best of these bounds. The presentation here actually follows the more elegant derivation given by Cesa-Bianchi and Lugosi [43].

Proof Let any $r \in \{1, \ldots, R\}$ be given. The key to the proof is to introduce the following quantities

$$Z_t \stackrel{\text{def}}{=} \exp\left(\alpha \sum_{t'=1}^{t} (x_r(t') - \hat{x}_r(t') - \alpha/p_r(t')) \right)$$

which, if we put $Z_0 = 1$, for $t = 1, \ldots, T$, we can also write as

$$Z_t = Z_{t-1} \exp(\alpha(x_r(t) - \hat{x}_r(t) - \alpha/p_r(t)))$$

and, as we will see, form a submartingale.[3] Our desired upper confidence bounds will follow from a standard tail bound argument via Z_T: $\mathbb{E}[Z_T]$ gives an upper bound on the probability of our upper confidence bound failing to hold. In particular, since

$$\Pr\left[\sum_{t=1}^{T} (\hat{x}_r(t) + \alpha/p_r(t)) + \alpha RT < \sum_{t=1}^{T} x_r(t) \right] = \Pr[\exp(\alpha^2 RT) < Z_T]$$

---

[3]i.e., fixing $Z_1, \ldots, Z_{t-1}$, $\mathbb{E}[Z_t | Z_1, \ldots, Z_{t-1}] \le Z_{t-1}$

Markov's inequality gives

$$\Pr[\exp(\alpha^2 RT) < Z_T] \leq e^{-\alpha^2 RT}\mathbb{E}[Z_T]$$

We will show by induction on t that $\mathbb{E}[Z_t] \leq 1$. Then since $\alpha \geq \sqrt{\ln(R/\delta)/RT}$, $e^{-\alpha^2 RT}\mathbb{E}[Z_T] \leq \delta/R$, and the claim will follow by a union bound over the choice of r.

Toward this end, first note that by definition, $Z_0 = 1$. For $t \geq 1$, now, since in round t $x_r(t)$ is fixed and the choice of r is independent of $x_r(t)$, $\mathbb{E}[x_r(t) - \hat{x}_r(t)] = 0$ and then since $x_r(t) \in [0,1]$ and $\hat{x}_r(t) \geq 0$,

$$\mathbb{E}[(x_r(t) - \hat{x}_r(t))^2] = x_r(t)\mathbb{E}[x_r(t) - \hat{x}_r(t)] + \mathbb{E}[\hat{x}_r(t)^2] - x_r(t)\mathbb{E}[\hat{x}_r(t)] \leq 1/p_r(t)$$

Now, since furthermore $\alpha \in [0,1]$, $\alpha(x_r(t) - \hat{x}_r(t) - \alpha/p_r(t)) \leq 1$, and then since $e^z \leq 1 + z + z^2$ for $z \leq 1$,

$$\begin{aligned}
\mathbb{E}[Z_t | Z_1, \ldots, Z_{t-1}] &= Z_{t-1}\mathbb{E}[\exp(\alpha(x_r(t) - \hat{x}_r(t) - \alpha/p_r(t)))] \\
&\leq Z_{t-1}\mathbb{E}[1 + \alpha(x_r(t) - \hat{x}_r(t)) + \alpha^2(x_r(t) - \hat{x}_r(t))^2] \cdot \\
&\qquad\qquad\qquad\qquad\qquad\qquad\qquad\qquad e^{-\alpha^2/p_r(t)} \\
&\leq Z_{t-1}(1 + \alpha^2/p_r(t))e^{-\alpha^2/p_r(t)}
\end{aligned}$$

Thus, since $1 + z \leq e^z$ for all z, we can conclude $\mathbb{E}[Z_t | Z_1, \ldots, Z_{t-1}]] \leq Z_{t-1}$. So applying the nested expectation gives $\mathbb{E}[Z_t] \leq 1$ as needed. ∎

We now state the algorithm; again, it is a variant of the basic multiplicative weights algorithm (Algorithm C.1) that uses the upper confidence bounds as its estimates of the payoffs, and mixes the uniform distribution with the strategy given by the weights on each round.

Algorithm C.8 (Exp3.P [10]). Given parameters $\alpha, \eta > 0$ and $\gamma \in (0,1]$, and time horizon T, initialize the weights $w_1(1), \ldots, w_R(1)$ to $\exp(\eta\alpha)$. In round $t = 1, \ldots, T$, repeat the following:

1. For each $r = 1, \ldots, R$, set

$$p_r(t) = (1 - \gamma)\frac{w_r(t)}{\sum_{i=1}^{R} w_i(t)} + \frac{\gamma}{R}$$

2. Choose r_t at random, letting $r_t = r$ with probability $p_r(t)$ for each $r = 1, \ldots, R$.

3. Play r_t and receive reward $x_{r_t}(t) \in [0,1]$.

4. For $r = 1, \ldots, R$, put

$$w_r(t+1) = w_r(t)\exp\left(\eta\left(\hat{x}_r(t) + \alpha/p_r(t)\right)\right)$$

Although we will still use a potential function, in contrast to our analysis of Algorithm C.1, we will use the *sum of the weights* as a potential, and in place of Lemma C.3, we have the following bound relating the reward obtained by the algorithm to the rate of growth of the weights:

Lemma C.9. *Let* $W_t = \sum_{r=1}^{R} w_r(t)$. *Then for* $\eta = \gamma/3R$, *and* $\alpha \leq 1$, *in round* t *of Algorithm C.8,*

$$\ln \frac{W_{t+1}}{W_t} \leq \frac{\eta}{1-\gamma} \left(x_{r_t}(t) + \alpha R + 2\eta \sum_{r=1}^{R} (\hat{x}_r(t) + \alpha/p_r(t)) \right)$$

Proof

$$\frac{W_{t+1}}{W_t} = \sum_{r=1}^{R} \frac{w_r(t)}{W_t} \exp(\eta(\hat{x}_r(t) + \alpha/p_r(t)))$$

$$= \sum_{r=1}^{R} \frac{p_r(t) - \gamma/R}{1-\gamma} \exp(\eta(\hat{x}_r(t) + \alpha/p_r(t)))$$

$$\leq \sum_{r=1}^{R} \frac{p_r(t) - \gamma/R}{1-\gamma} (1 + \eta(\hat{x}_r(t) + \alpha/p_r(t)) + \eta^2(\hat{x}_r(t) + \alpha/p_r(t))^2)$$

since $p_r(t) \geq \gamma/R$, and so $\eta(\hat{x}_r(t) + \alpha/p_r(t)) \leq 1$ and thus we were able to apply $e^z \leq 1 + z + z^2$ (for $z < 1$).

We note that $\sum_{r=1}^{R} p_r(t) - \gamma/R = 1 - \gamma$, so we have

$$\frac{W_{t+1}}{W_t} \leq 1 + \frac{\eta}{1-\gamma} \left(x_{r_t}(t) + \alpha R + \sum_{r=1}^{R} \eta p_r(t)(\hat{x}_r(t) + \alpha/p_r(t))^2 \right)$$

and thus as $\ln(1 + z) \leq z$ for all z,

$$\ln \frac{W_{t+1}}{W_t} \leq \frac{\eta}{1-\gamma} \left(x_{r_t}(t) + \alpha R + \sum_{r=1}^{R} \eta p_r(t)(\hat{x}_r(t) + \alpha/p_r(t))^2 \right)$$

Now, also $(a + b)^2 \leq 2a^2 + 2b^2$, so we find

$$\ln \frac{W_{t+1}}{W_t} \leq \frac{\eta}{1-\gamma} \left(x_{r_t}(t) + \alpha R + 2\eta \sum_{r=1}^{R} \hat{x}_r(t)^2 p_r(t) + 2\eta\alpha^2 \sum_{r=1}^{R} 1/p_r(t) \right)$$

Noting again that $x_r(t) \leq 1$,

$$\sum_{r=1}^{R} \hat{x}_r(t)^2 p_r(t) = \frac{x_{r_t}(t)^2}{p_{r_t}(t)} \leq \sum_{r=1}^{R} \hat{x}_r(t)$$

Applying this estimate and $\alpha \leq 1$ to the above expression yields the claim.

∎

The analysis of Algorithm C.8 easily follows now from these lemmas: on the one hand, Lemma C.7 shows that with high probability, the logarithm of each weight is close to an estimate on the reward obtained by the corresponding strategy, and on the other hand, Lemma C.9 shows that the logarithm of the sum of the weights is a lower bound on the reward obtained by the algorithm. We thus obtain:

Theorem C.10 (Exp3.P is almost as good as the best strategy in hindsight). *For any $\alpha \in [\sqrt{\log(R/\delta)/RT}, 1]$ and $\eta = \gamma/3R$, after T steps Algorithm C.8 achieves reward at least*

$$\left(1 - \frac{5}{3}\gamma\right) \max_r \sum_{t=1}^{T} x_r(t) - 2\alpha RT - \frac{3}{\gamma} R \ln R$$

with probability at least $1 - \delta$.

Proof As sketched above, we set $W_t = \sum_{r=1}^{R} w_r(t)$, and consider $\ln \frac{W_{T+1}}{W_1}$. On the one hand, Lemma C.9 shows that

$$\ln \frac{W_{T+1}}{W_1} = \sum_{t=1}^{T} \ln \frac{W_{t+1}}{W_t}$$

$$\leq \frac{\eta}{1-\gamma} \left(\sum_{t=1}^{T} x_{r_t}(t) + \alpha RT + 2\eta \sum_{r=1}^{R} \sum_{t=1}^{T} (\hat{x}_r(t) + \frac{\alpha}{p_r(t)}) \right)$$

but on the other hand, for every r,

$$\ln W_{T+1} \geq \ln w_r(t+1) = \eta \left(\sum_{t=1}^{T} (\hat{x}_r(t) + \frac{\alpha}{p_r(t)}) \right) + \eta\alpha$$

where we also have

$$\ln W_1 = \ln \sum_{r=1}^{R} \exp(\alpha\eta) = \eta\alpha + \ln R$$

we find overall that

$$\eta \max_r \left(\sum_{t=1}^{T} \hat{x}_r(t) + \frac{\alpha}{p_r(t)} \right) - \ln R \leq \frac{\eta}{1-\gamma} \left(\sum_{t=1}^{T} x_{r_t}(t) + \alpha RT + \right.$$

$$\left. 2\eta R \max_r \sum_{t=1}^{T} (\hat{x}_r(t) + \frac{\alpha}{p_r(t)}) \right)$$

Now, Lemma C.7 gives that for every r,

$$\sum_{t=1}^{T} (\hat{x}_r(t) + \alpha/p_r(t)) \geq \sum_{t=1}^{T} x_r(t) - \alpha RT$$

with probability at least $1 - \delta$. So, rearranging, we find that with probability $1 - \delta$,

$$(1 - \gamma - 2\eta R)\max_r\left(\sum_{t=1}^{T} x_r(t) - \alpha RT\right) - \frac{1-\gamma}{\eta}\ln R \le \sum_{t=1}^{T} x_{r_t}(t) + \alpha RT$$

which, using $\eta = \gamma/3R$, we can rearrange to obtain the claim. ∎

Much as before, an appropriate choice of parameters shows that Algorithm C.8 obtains excellent average reward for fixed time horizons:

Corollary C.11. *For any time horizon T and $\delta > 0$, using Algorithm C.8 with $\alpha = \sqrt{\log(R/\delta)/RT}$, $\gamma = \min\left\{\frac{3}{5}, 2\sqrt{\frac{3}{5}\frac{R\ln R}{T}}\right\}$, and $\eta = \gamma/3R$ gives reward at least*

$$\sum_{t=1}^{T} x_r(t) - 2\sqrt{RT\ln(R/\delta)} - 4\sqrt{\frac{5}{3}RT\ln R}$$

for every $r \in \{1, \ldots, R\}$ with probability at least $1 - \delta$.

Proof Note that if $T \le (20/3)R\ln R$ or $\delta \le Re^{-RT}$, then the claim holds trivially. Now, in particular, at $T \ge (20/3)R\ln R$, $\gamma \le 3/5$, and at $\delta \ge Re^{-RT}$, our choice of $\alpha < 1$, so Theorem C.10 holds. We furthermore note that for all r, $\sum_{t=1}^{T} x_r(t) \le T$, so for our choice of γ,

$$\frac{5}{3}\gamma\sum_{t=1}^{T} x_r(t) \le 2\sqrt{\frac{5}{3}RT\ln R}$$

and

$$\frac{3}{\gamma}R\ln R \le \frac{3}{2}\sqrt{\frac{5}{3}RT\ln R}$$

which gives the claim. ∎

In particular, as $T \to \infty$, the average reward approaches the best average reward in hindsight. We will see in the next section that it is possible to obtain similar behavior uniformly over all time horizons.

C.2.2 Optimizing the reward in the limit

We now present a standard trick to convert an algorithm which performs well given a time horizon fixed in advance to one that performs well with respect to any unknown (sufficiently long) time horizon. The basic trick is to run the algorithm repeatedly with an appropriate schedule of parameters T and δ to obtain a claim similar to Corollary C.11 without an explicit time horizon. Specifically, our final algorithm is the following:

Algorithm C.12 (Exp3.P.1 [10]). Given input parameter $\delta \in [0, 1]$, we put

$$i^* = \min\left\{i \in \mathbb{N} : i > 0, \frac{\delta}{i(i+1)} \geq Re^{-R2^i}\right\}$$

Then, for each $i = i^*, i^* + 1, i^* + 2, \ldots$, set $T_i = 2^i$, $\delta_i = \frac{\delta}{i(i+1)}$, $\alpha_i = \sqrt{\log(R/\delta_i)/RT_i}$, $\gamma_i = \min\left\{\frac{3}{5}, 2\sqrt{\frac{3}{5}\frac{R\ln R}{T_i}}\right\}$, and $\eta_i = \gamma_i/3R$, and run Exp3.P (Algorithm C.8) for T_i rounds with parameters α_i, γ_i, δ_i, and η_i.

Note that this is essentially Algorithm 9.25 as quoted in Section 9.3.2 of Chapter 9.

Corollary C.13. *For i^* as chosen in Algorithm C.12, $\delta \in [0, 1]$ and $T \geq 2^{i^*}$, with probability at least $1 - \delta$, after T rounds, Algorithm C.12 achieves reward at least*

$$\sum_{t=1}^{T} x_r(t) - \frac{10}{\sqrt{2}-1}\sqrt{2RT\left(\ln\frac{R}{\delta} + c(T)\right)}$$

for any $r \in \{1, \ldots, R\}$ and $c(T) = 2\ln(2 + \log_2 T)$.

Proof Let any $T \geq 2^{i^*}$ be given. Note that the choice of i^* guarantees $\delta_i \geq Re^{-RT_i}$ for all $i \geq i^*$. Note also that there exists $j \geq 1$ such that $2^{i^*+j-1} \leq T < 2^{i^*+j}$; then $T \leq \sum_{i=i^*}^{i^*+j-1} T_i$.

We now consider the performance of Algorithm C.12 in each of its runs. Let any r be given; Corollary C.11 yields that Algorithm C.8 obtains reward at least

$$\sum_{t=1}^{T} x_r(t) - \sum_{i=i^*}^{i^*+j-1}\left[10\sqrt{RT_i\ln(R/\delta_i)}\right]$$

with probability at least $1 - \sum_{i=i^*}^{i^*+j-1}\delta_i \geq 1 - \sum_{i=1}^{\infty}\frac{\delta}{i(i+1)} = 1 - \delta$. Now, the latter expression is at most

$$10\sqrt{R\ln(R/\delta_{i^*+j-1})}\sum_{i=i^*}^{i^*+j-1}\sqrt{T_i} \leq 10\sqrt{R\ln(R/\delta_{i^*+j-1})}\frac{2^{(i^*+j)/2}}{\sqrt{2}-1}$$

where of course, $2^{(i^*+j)/2} \leq \sqrt{2T}$ and

$$\ln(1/\delta_{i^*+j-1}) \leq 2\ln(i^* + j) - \ln\delta \leq c(T) - \ln\delta$$

for $c(T) = 2\ln(2 + \log_2 T)$. ∎

Bibliography

[1] Gregory D. Abowd. *Formal aspects of human-computer interaction.* PhD thesis, University of Oxford, 1991.

[2] Gregory D. Abowd. Personal communication, 2010.

[3] Leonard M. Adelman. Time, space, and randomness. Technical Report MIT-LCS-TM-131, MIT LCS, 1979.

[4] Dana Angluin. Queries and concept learning. *Mach. Learn.*, 2(4):319–342, 1988.

[5] Dana Angluin. Negative results for equivalence queries. *Mach. Learn.*, 5(2):121–150, 1990.

[6] Dana Angluin and Carl II. Smith. Inductive inference: Theory and methods. *ACM Comput. Surveys*, 15(3):237–269, 1983.

[7] Luis Antunes, Lance Fortnow, Alexandre Pinto, and Andre Souto. Low depth witnesses are easy to find. In *Proc. 22nd Conf. Computational Complexity*, 2007.

[8] Luis Antunes, Lance Fortnow, Dieter van Melkebeek, and N. V. Vinodchandran. Computational depth: Concept and applications. *Theor. Comput. Sci.*, 354(3):391–404, 2006.

[9] The Staff at the National Astronomy and Ionosphere Center. The Arecibo message of November, 1974. *Icarus*, 26:462–466, 1975.

[10] Peter Auer, Nicolò Cesa-Bianchi, Yoav Freund, and Robert E. Schapire. The nonstochastic multiarmed bandit problem. *SIAM J. Comput.*, 32(1):48–77, 2003.

[11] Peter Auer, Stephen Kwek, Wolfgang Maass, and Manfred K. Warmuth. Learning of depth two neural networks with constant fan-in at the hidden nodes (extended abstract). In *Proc. 9th COLT*, pages 333–343, 1996.

B. Juba, *Universal Semantic Communication*,
DOI 10.1007/978-3-642-23297-8,
© Springer-Verlag Berlin Heidelberg 2011

[12] Peter Auer and Philip M. Long. Structural results about on-line learning models with and without queries. *Mach. Learn.*, 36(3):147–181, 1999.

[13] Peter Auer, Philip M. Long, Wolfgang Maass, and Gerhard J. Woeginger. On the complexity of function learning. *Mach. Learn.*, 18(2–3):187–230, 1995.

[14] László Babai, Lance Fortnow, and Carsten Lund. Non-deterministic exponential time has two-prover interactive protocols. *Computational Complexity*, 1(1):3–40, 1991.

[15] László Babai, Lance Fortnow, Noam Nisan, and Avi Wigderson. BPP has subexponential time simulations unless EXPTIME has publishable proofs. *Computational Complexity*, 3:307–318, 1993.

[16] Laszlo Babai and Shlomo Moran. A randomized proof system and a hierarchy of complexity classes. *JCSS*, 36:254–376, 1988.

[17] Eric Bach and Jeffrey Shallit. *Algorithmic Number Theory*, volume 1. MIT Press, Cambridge, 1996.

[18] Ian Barland. *Some ideas on learning with directional feedback*. Master's thesis, UC Santa Cruz, 1992.

[19] Jānis Bārzdiņš and Rūsiņš Freivalds. On the prediction of general recursive functions. *Soviet Math. Dokl.*, 13:1224–1228, 1972.

[20] Marie-Pierre Béal, Olivier Carton, Christophe Prieur, and Jacques Sakarovitch. Squaring transducers: An efficient procedure for deciding functionality and sequentiality. *Theor. Comp. Sci.*, 292(1):45–63, 2003. Preliminary version appeared in LATIN 2000.

[21] Mihir Bellare and Shafi Goldwasser. The complexity of decision versus search. *SIAM J. Comput.*, 23(1):91–119, 1994.

[22] Michael Ben-Or. Probabalistic algorithms in finite fields. In *Proc. 22nd FOCS*, pages 394–398, 1981.

[23] Charles H. Bennett. Logical depth and physical complexity. In Rolf Herken, editor, *The Universal Turing Machine: A Half-Century Survey*, pages 227–257. Oxford University Press, Oxford, 1988.

[24] Francesco Bergadano, Nader H. Bshouty, Christino Tamon, and Stefano Varricchio. On learning branching programs and small depth circuits. In *EuroCOLT '97*, volume 1208/1997 of *LNCS*, pages 150–161. Springer, Berlin, 1997.

[25] Tim Berners-Lee, James Hendler, and Ora Lassila. The semantic web. *Scientific American*, pages 34–43, May 2001.

[26] Jean Berstel. *Transductions and Context-Free Languages*. B. G. Teubner, Stuttgart, 1979.

[27] Dimitris Bertsimas and Santosh Vempala. Solving convex programs by random walks. *J. ACM*, 51(4):540–556, 2004.

[28] Ned Block. Psychologism and behaviorism. *Philosophical Review*, 90(1):5–43, 1981.

[29] Lenore Blum and Manuel Blum. Toward a mathematical theory of inductive inference. *Inf. Control*, 28:125–155, 1975.

[30] Lenore Blum, Manuel Blum, and Michael Shub. A simple unpredictable pseudo-random number generator. *SIAM J. Comput.*, 15(2):364–383, 1986.

[31] Manuel Blum. A machine-independent theory of the complexity of recursive functions. *J. ACM*, 14(2):322–336, 1967.

[32] Manuel Blum. Personal communication, 2009.

[33] Manuel Blum and Sampath Kannan. Designing programs that check their work. *J. ACM*, 42(1):269–291, 1995. Preliminary version appeared in Proc. 21st STOC, pages 86–97, 1989.

[34] Allan Borodin, Faith E. Fich, Danny Dolev, and Wolfgang Paul. Bounds for width two branching programs. *SIAM J. Comput.*, 15(2):549–560, 1986.

[35] Robert S. Boyer and J. Strother Moore. MJRTY – a fast majority vote algorithm. In Robert S. Boyer, editor, *Automated Reasoning: Essays in Honor of Woody Bledsoe*, pages 105–117. Kluwer, Dordrecht, 1991.

[36] R. Braden. Requirements for internet hosts – communication layers. RFC 1122 (Standard), October 1989. Updated by RFCs 1349, 4379.

[37] Nader H. Bshouty. Exact learning Boolean functions via the monotone theory. *Inf. Comp.*, 123(1):146–153, 1995.

[38] Nader H. Bshouty. The monotone theory for the PAC-model. *Inf. Comp.*, 186(1):20–35, 2003.

[39] Nader H. Bshouty and Hanna Mazzawi. Exact learning composed classes with a small number of mistakes. In *COLT 2006*, volume 4005/2006 of *LNCS*, pages 199–213. Springer, Berlin, 2006.

[40] J. Lawrence Carter and Mark N. Wegman. Universal classes of hash functions. *JCSS*, 18(2):143–154, 1979.

[41] Vinton G. Cerf and Robert E. Kahn. A protocol for packet network intercommunication. *IEEE Trans. Comms.*, Com-22(5):637–648, 1974.

[42] Nicolò Cesa-Bianchi, Philip M. Long, and Manfred K. Warmuth. Worst-case quadratic loss bounds for a generalization of the Widrow-Hoff rule. In *Proc. 6th COLT*, pages 429–438, 1993.

[43] Nicolò Cesa-Bianchi and Gábor Lugosi. *Prediction, Learning, and Games*. Cambridge University Press, New York, 2006.

[44] Noam Chomsky. Three models for the description of language. *IRE Trans. Inf. Theory*, 2:113–124, 1956.

[45] Noam Chomsky. *Aspects of the Theory of Syntax*. MIT Press, Cambridge, 1965.

[46] Alan Cobham. The intrinsic computational difficulty of functions. In *Proc. 1964 International Congress for Logic, Methodology, and Phil. of Sci.*, pages 24–30. North-Holland, Amsterdam, 1965.

[47] Giuseppe Cocconi and Philip Morrison. Searching for interstellar communications. *Nature*, 184(4690):844–846, September 1959.

[48] Anne Condon. Space-bounded probabilistic game automata. *J. ACM*, 38(2):472–494, 1991.

[49] Anne Condon and Richard Ladner. Probabilistic game automata. *JCSS*, 36(3):452–489, 1988.

[50] Ivan Damgård. Collision free hash functions and public key signature schemes. In *EuroCrypt87*, volume 304 of *LNCS*, pages 203–216. Springer, Berlin, 1988.

[51] Ivan Damgård. A design principle for hash functions. In *Crypto89*, volume 457 of *LNCS*, pages 416–427. Springer, Berlin, 1990.

[52] Nikhil R. Devanur and Lance Fortnow. A computational theory of awareness and decision making. In *Proc. 12th Conference on Theoretical Aspects of Rationality and Knowledge*, pages 99–107, 2009.

[53] John Dewey. *Experience and Nature*. Norton, New York, 1929. First edition published in 1925.

[54] Yan Zong Ding and Michael O. Rabin. Hyper-encryption and everlasting security. In *Proc. 19th STACS*, volume 2285 of *LNCS*, pages 1–26. Springer-Verlag, Berlin, 2002.

[55] G. L. Dirichlet. Verallgemeinerung eines Satzes aus der Lehre von den Kettenbrüchen nebst einigen Anwendungen auf die Theorie der Zahlen. *SB Preuss. Akad. Wiss.*, pages 93–95, 1842. Reprinted in L. Kronecker (ed.), G. L. Dirichlet's Werke volume I, pages 635–638, Chelsea, New York, 1969.

[56] Alan John Dix. *Formal Methods for Interactive Systems*. Academic, San Diego, 1991.

[57] Jack Edmonds. Paths, trees, and flowers. *Canad. J. Math.*, 17:449–467, 1965.

[58] Funda Ergün, S. Ravi Kumar, and Ronitt Rubinfeld. On learning bounded-width branching programs. In *Proc. 8th COLT*, pages 361–368, 1995.

[59] Paul Fitz. CosmicOS. Open source project. http://cosmicos. sourceforge.net.

[60] Hans Freudenthal. *LINCOS: Design of a Language for Cosmic Intercourse*. North-Holland, Amsterdam, 1960.

[61] Yoav Freund and Robert E. Schapire. Adaptive game playing using multiplicative weights. *Games and Economic Behavior*, 29:79–103, 1999.

[62] Christopher Gauker. *Words without Meaning*. MIT Press, Cambridge, 2003.

[63] Edgar N. Gilbert, F. Jessie MacWilliams, and Neil J. A. Sloane. Codes which detect deception. *Bell Sys. Tech. J.*, 53:405–424, 1974.

[64] E. Mark Gold. *Models of goal-seeking and learning*. PhD thesis, UCLA, 1965.

[65] E. Mark Gold. Usages of natural language. Technical report, Inst. for Math. Studies in the Social Sci., Stanford U., 1966. Defense Technical Info. Center Accession Number AD0644521.

[66] E. Mark Gold. Language identification in the limit. *Inf. Control*, 10:447–474, 1967.

[67] E. Mark Gold. Universal goal-seekers. *Inf. Control*, 18:395–403, 1971.

[68] Oded Goldreich. *Foundations of Cryptography*, volume II. Cambridge University Press, New York, 2004.

[69] Oded Goldreich, Shafi Goldwasser, and Silvio Micali. How to construct random functions. *J. ACM*, 33(4):792–807, 1986.

[70] Oded Goldreich, Brendan Juba, and Madhu Sudan. A theory of goal-oriented communication. Technical Report TR09-075, ECCC, 2009.

[71] Oded Goldreich, Silvio Micali, and Avi Wigderson. Proofs that yield nothing but their validity or all languages in NP have zero-knowledge proof systems. *J. ACM*, 38(3):690–728, 1991.

[72] Oded Goldreich and Dana Ron. On universal learning algorithms. *Information Processing Letters*, 63:131–136, 1997.

[73] Shafi Goldwasser, Yael Tauman Kalai, and Guy N. Rothblum. Delegating computation: Interactive proofs for muggles. In *Proc. 40th STOC*, 2008.

[74] Shafi Goldwasser, Silvio Micali, and Charles Rackoff. The knowledge complexity of interactive proof systems. *SIAM J. Comput.*, 18(1):186–208, 1989.

[75] Martin Grötschel, László Lovász, and Alexander Schrijver. Geometric methods in combinatorial optimization. In W. R. Pulleybank, editor, *Proc. Silver Jubilee Conf. on Combinatorics*, Progress in Combinatorial Optimization, pages 167–183. Academic, New York, 1984.

[76] Martin Grötschel, László Lovász, and Alexander Schrijver. *Geometric Algorithms and Combinatorial Optimization*. Springer, New York, second edition, 1993.

[77] Eitan M. Gurari and Oscar H. Ibarra. A note on finite-valued and finitely ambiguous transducers. *Math. Sys. Theory*, 16:61–66, 1983.

[78] Steven E. Hampson and Dennis J. Volper. Representing and learning Boolean functions of multivalued features. *IEEE Trans. Sys. Man Cybern.*, 20(1):67–80, 1990.

[79] Johan Håstad, Russell Imagliazzo, Leonid A. Levin, and Michael Luby. A pseudorandom generator from any one-way function. *SIAM J. Comput.*, 28(4):1364–1396, 1999.

[80] C. A. R. Hoare. *Communicating Sequential Processes*. Prentice-Hall International, Englewood Cliffs, 1985.

[81] Marcus Hutter. *Universal Artificial Intelligence*. Springer, Berlin, 2004.

[82] Russell Impagliazzo and Avi Wigderson. P=BPP if E requires exponential circuits: Derandomizing the XOR lemma. In *Proc. 29th STOC*, pages 220–229, 1997.

[83] Brendan Juba and Madhu Sudan. Universal semantic communication I. In *Proc. 40th STOC*, pages 123–132, 2008.

[84] Brendan Juba and Madhu Sudan. Universal semantic communication II: A theory of goal-oriented communication. Technical Report TR08-095, ECCC, 2008.

[85] Brendan Juba and Madhu Sudan. Efficient semantic communication via compatible beliefs. In *Proc. 2nd Symp. Innovations in Computer Science*, pages 22–31, 2011.

[86] Brendan Juba and Santosh Vempala. Semantic communication for simple goals is equivalent to on-line learning. In *ALT 2011*, volume 6925 of *LNAI*, pages 277–291. Springer, Berlin, 2011.

[87] Jesse Kamp, Anup Rao, Salil Vadhan, and David Zuckerman. Deterministic extractors for small-space sources. In *Proc. 38th STOC*, pages 691–700, 2006.

[88] Michael Kearns, Ming Li, and Leslie Valiant. Learning Boolean formulas. *J. ACM*, 41(6):1298–1328, 1994.

[89] Michael Kearns and Leslie Valiant. Cryptographic limitations on learning Boolean formulae and finite automata. *J. ACM*, 41:67–95, 1994.

[90] S. Kent and K. Seo. Security architecture for the internet protocol. RFC 4301 (Proposed Standard), December 2005.

[91] L. G. Khachiyan. A polynomial algorithm in linear programming. *Doklady Akad. Nauk SSSR*, 244:1093–1096, 1979. English translation: Soviet Math. Doklady, 20, 191–194, 1979.

[92] Michael Kharitonov. Cryptographic hardness of distribution-specific learning. In *Proc. 25th STOC*, pages 372–381, 1993.

[93] Adam R. Klivans and Alexander A. Sherstov. Cryptographic hardness for learning intersections of halfspaces. *JCSS*, 75(1):2–12, 2009.

[94] Jaron Lanier. The complexity ceiling. In John Brockman, editor, *The Next Fifty Years: Science in the First Half of the Twenty-First Century*, pages 216–229. Vintage, New York, 2002.

[95] Jaron Lanier. Why Gordian software has convinced me to believe in the reality of cats and apples. *Edge*, 128, November 2003. Available online: http://www.edge.org/3rd_culture/lanier03/lanier_index.html.

[96] A. K. Lenstra, H. W. Lenstra, and L. Lovász. Factoring polynomials with rational coefficients. *Math. Ann.*, 261(4):515–534, 1982.

[97] Leonid A. Levin. Universal search problems. *Probl. Inform. Transm.*, 9:265–266, 1973.

[98] Leonid A. Levin. Randomness conservation inequalities; information and independence in mathematical theories. *Inf. Control*, 61(1):15–37, 1984.

[99] Ming Li and Paul Vitányi. *An Introduction to Kolmogorov Complexity and its Applications*. Springer-Verlag, New York, second edition, 1997.

[100] Nicholas Littlestone, Manfred K. Warmuth, and Philip M. Long. On-line learning of linear functions. *Computational Complexity*, 5(1):1–23, 1995.

[101] Nick Littlestone. Learning quickly when irrelevant attributes abound:
       A new linear-threshold algorithm. *Mach. Learn.*, 2(4):285–318, 1988.

[102] L. H. Loomis. On a theorem of von Neumann. *Proc. Nat. Acad. Sci.*,
       32:213–215, 1946.

[103] Carsten Lund, Lance Fortnow, Howard J. Karloff, and Noam Nisan.
       Algebraic methods for interactive proof systems. *J. ACM*, 39(4):859–
       868, 1992.

[104] Wolfgang Maass and György Turán. On the complexity of learning
       from counterexamples. In *Proc. 30th FOCS*, pages 262–267, 1989.

[105] Wolfgang Maass and György Turán. Lower bound methods and sepa-
       ration results for on-line learning models. *Mach. Learn.*, 9(3):107–145,
       1992.

[106] Wolfgang Maass and György Turán. Algorithms and lower bounds for
       on-line learning of geometrical concepts. *Mach. Learn.*, 14(3):251–269,
       1994.

[107] Wolfgang Maass and György Turán. How fast can a threshold gate
       learn? In S. J. Hanson, G. A. Drastal, and R. L. Rivest, editors, *Com-
       putational Learning Theory and Natural Learning Systems: Constraints
       and Prospects*, volume 1, pages 381–414. MIT Press, Cambridge, 1994.

[108] Wolfgang Maass and Manfred K. Warmuth. Efficient learning with
       virtual threshold gates. *Inf. Comp.*, 141(1):66–83, 1998.

[109] Ueli Maurer. Conditionally-perfect secrecy and a provably-secure ran-
       domized cipher. *J. Cryptology*, 5(1):53–66, 1992.

[110] David A. McAllester. Some PAC-Bayesian theorems. *Mach. Learn.*,
       37(3):355–363, 1999.

[111] Brian McConnell. *Beyond Contact: A Guide to SETI and Communi-
       cating with Alien Civilizations*. O'Reilly, Cambridge, 2001.

[112] Or Meir. IP = PSPACE using error correcting codes. Technical Report
       TR10-137, ECCC, 2010.

[113] Marvin Minsky. Communication with alien intelligence. In Edward
       Regis, editor, *Extraterrestrials: Science and Alien Intelligence*, pages
       117–128. Cambridge University Press, New York, 1985.

[114] Marvin Minsky and Seymour L. Papert. *Perceptrons: An Introduction
       to Computational Geometry*. MIT Press, 1988. First edition published
       in 1969.

[115] Edward F. Moore. Gedanken-experiments on sequential machines. In C. E. Shannon and J. McCarthy, editors, *Automata Studies*, pages 129–153. Princeton Univ. Press, Princeton, 1956.

[116] Saburo Muroga. *Threshold Logic and its Applications*. Wiley, New York, 1971.

[117] Nils J. Nilsson. *Learning Machines*. McGraw-Hill, New York, 1965.

[118] Donald A. Norman. *The Design of Everyday Things*. Basic, New York, 2002. First edition published in 1988.

[119] Larry L. Peterson and Bruce S. Davie. *Computer Networks: A Systems Approach*. Morgan Kaufmann, San Diego, second edition, 2000.

[120] Leonard Pitt and Manfred K. Warmuth. Prediction-preserving reducibility. *JCSS*, 41:430–467, 1990.

[121] Willard Van Orman Quine. *Word and Object*. MIT Press, Cambridge, 1960.

[122] Michael O. Rabin and Dana Scott. Finite automata and their decision problems. *IBM J. Res. Develop.*, 3(2):114–125, 1959.

[123] John Rompel. One-way functions are necessary and sufficient for secure signatures. In *Proc. 22nd STOC*, pages 387–394, 1990.

[124] Frank Rosenblatt. *Principles of Neurodynamics*. Spartan, Washington, 1962.

[125] Dan Roy and David Sontag. Personal communication, 2009.

[126] Stuart Russell and Peter Norvig. *Artificial Intelligence: A Modern Approach*. Prentice Hall, Englewood Cliffs, 1995.

[127] Stuart Russell and Devika Subramanian. Provably bounded optimal agents. *JAIR*, 2:575–609, 1995. Preliminary version appeared in IJCAI'93.

[128] Stuart Russell and Eric Wefald. *Do the Right Thing*. MIT Press, Cambridge, 1991.

[129] Carl Sagan, editor. *Communication with Extraterrestrial Intelligence (CETI)*. MIT Press, Cambridge, 1973.

[130] Jacques Sakarovitch. *Elements of Automata Theory*. Cambridge University Press, Cambridge, 2009.

[131] N. Sauer. On the density of families of sets. *J. Combinatorial Theory*, 13(1):145–147, 1972.

[132] Marcel Paul Schützenberger. Sur les relations rationnelles. In *Proc. 2nd GI Conf. on Automata Theory and Formal Languages*, volume 33 of *LNCS*, pages 209–213. Springer, Berlin, 1975.

[133] Nigel Shadbolt, Tim Berners-Lee, and Wendy Hall. The semantic web revisited. *IEEE Intelligent Sys.*, 21(3):96–101, 2006.

[134] Adi Shamir. IP = PSPACE. *J. ACM*, 39(4):869–877, 1992.

[135] Claude E. Shannon. A mathematical theory of communication. *Bell System Technical Journal*, 27:379–423, 623–656, 1948.

[136] John Shawe-Taylor and Robert C. Williamson. A PAC analysis of a Bayesian estimator. In *Proc. 10th COLT*, pages 2–9, 1997.

[137] Alexander Shen. IP = PSPACE: Simplified proof. *J. ACM*, 39(4):878–880, 1992.

[138] Stuart M. Shieber. *The Turing Test: Verbal Behavior as the Hallmark of Intelligence*. MIT Press, Cambridge, 2004.

[139] Stuart M. Shieber. The Turing test as interactive proof. *Noûs*, 41(4):686–713, December 2007.

[140] Victor Shoup. *A Computational Introduction to Number Theory and Algebra*. Cambridge University Press, New York, 2005.

[141] Michael Sipser. *Introduction to the Theory of Computation*. Course Technology, second edition, 2006.

[142] Daniel D. Sleator and Robert E. Tarjan. Amortized efficiency of list update and paging rules. *Communications of the ACM*, 28(2):202–208, 1985.

[143] W. Richard Stevens. *TCP/IP Illustrated, Volume 1: The Protocols*. Addison-Wesley, Reading, 1994.

[144] Harold W. Thimbleby. *Press on: Principles of Interaction Programming*. MIT Press, Cambridge, 2007.

[145] G. M. Tovmasyan, editor. *Extraterrestrial civilizations*. 1964. Translation from Russian available as NASA Technical Report NASA-TT-F-438; TT-67-51373.

[146] Luca Trevisan. The program-enumeration bottleneck in average-case complexity theory. In *Proc. 25th Conf. Computational Complexity*, pages 88–95, 2010.

[147] Luca Trevisan and Salil Vadhan. Extracting randomness from samplable distributions. In *Proc. 41st FOCS*, pages 32–42, 2000.

[148] Eran Tromer. Personal communication, 2010.

[149] Alan M. Turing. Computing machinery and intelligence. *Mind*, 59(236):433–460, 1950.

[150] John Postel, editor, USC-ISI. Transmission Control Protocol. RFC 793 (Standard), September 1981. Updated by RFC 3168.

[151] Pravin M. Vaidya. A new algorithm for minimizing convex functions over convex sets. *Mathematical Programming*, 73(3):291–341, 1996.

[152] Leslie G. Valiant. A theory of the learnable. *Communications of the ACM*, 27(11):1134–1142, 1984.

[153] Luis von Ahn, Manuel Blum, Nicholas Hopper, and John Langford. CAPTCHA: Using hard AI problems for security. In *Advances in Cryptology*, Eurocrypt, pages 294–311, 2003.

[154] Mark N. Wegman and J. Lawrence Carter. New hash functions and their use in authentication and set equality. *JCSS*, 22:265–279, 1981.

[155] Joseph Weizenbaum. Eliza—a computer program for the study of natural language communication between man and machine. *Communications of the ACM*, 17(7):36–45, 1966.

[156] Ludwig Wittgenstein. *The Blue and Brown Books: Preliminary Studies for the 'Philosophical Investigations'*. Harper & Row, New York, 1958.

[157] Ludwig Wittgenstein. *Philosophical Investigations*. Basil Blackwell, 2001. First edition published in 1953.

[158] David H. Wolpert. The lack of a priori distinctions between learning algorithms. *Neural Comp.*, 8(7):1341–1390, 1996.

[159] David H. Wolpert and William G. Macready. No free lunch theorems for optimization. *IEEE Trans. Evolutionary Comp.*, 1(1):67–82, 1997.

[160] Michael Wooldridge. The computational complexity of agent design problems. In *Proc. Fourth International Conf. Multi-Agent Systems (ICMAS'00)*, pages 341–348, 2000.

[161] Andrew C.-C. Yao. Some complexity questions related to distributed computing. In *Proc. 11th STOC*, pages 209–213, 1979.